Quality

Fourth Edition

Donna C. S. Summers
University of Dayton

PEARSON

Prentice
Hall

Upper Saddle River, New Jersey
Columbus, Ohio

Library of Congress Cataloging-in-Publication Data

Summers, Donna C. S.
    Quality / Donna C. S. Summers.—4th ed.
        p. cm.
    Includes bibliographical references and index.
    ISBN 0-13-118931-X
        1. Quality assurance.   2. Process control—Statistical methods.   I. Title.

TS156.6.S86 2006
658.5'62—dc22   2004063100

Executive Editor: Debbie Yarnell
Editorial Assistant: ReeAnne Davies
Production Editor: Louise N. Sette
Copy Editor: Carol Mohr
Design Coordinator: Diane Ernsberger
Cover Designer: Ali Mohrman
Production Manager: Deidra M. Schwartz
Marketing Manager: Jimmy Stephens

This book was set in Goudy and Helvetica by The GTS Companies/York, PA Campus. It was printed
and bound by R.R. Donnelley & Sons Company. The cover was printed by Phoenix Color Corp.

Pearson Education Ltd.   Pearson Education Australia Pty. Limited
Pearson Education Singapore Pte. Ltd.   Pearson Education North Asia Ltd.
Pearson Education Canada, Ltd.   Pearson Educación de Mexico, S.A. de C.V.
Pearson Education—Japan   Pearson Education Malaysia Pte. Ltd.

10 9 8 7 6 5 4 3
ISBN: 0-13-118931-X

To my loving family,
Karl,
and all my boys
and girls

Preface

One of the best ways to learn is through application. The examples, cases, and problems found in this book have been carefully cultivated from real life experiences of people who apply quality tools and techniques in their day-to-day work activities. Contributors had a variety of responsibilities: manufacturing engineers, industrial engineers, mechanical engineers, business managers, quality assurance engineers and managers, program managers, project managers, distribution and warehousing managers, utility distribution managers, and safety professionals. The industries they represent are just as diverse: government, utilities, building trades, manufacturing, armed forces, hospitals, and even the ballet. These examples, cases, and problems reflect the calculations they needed to make and the charts and graphs they needed to create in order to solve the customer issues they faced. Although the names have been changed, only minor modifications have been made in order to make it possible to use their experiences as teaching examples.

HOW THIS BOOK DIFFERS FROM OTHERS ON THE MARKET

While no text can be all things to all readers, this text provides insightful case studies, clear explanations of popular quality tools and techniques, plentiful illustrations to support explanations, and subject matter relevant to the challenges faced by today's organizations. This text utilizes industry examples in each chapter to enhance readers' understanding of the mechanics of the tools. The text is structured to provide what might be termed Just-in-time-learning. Relevant statistical and probabilistic concepts are covered in the text just before they are applied. This is particularly true with Chapters 4, 5, 6, and 7, as well as Chapters 8, 9, and 10. Example problems detail when it is appropriate to use a particular technique as well as how to set up and solve problems.

New to this edition are example problems titled **Real Tools for Real Life.** Less mathematically detailed, yet more comprehensive, **Real Tools for Real Life** examples provide insight into how a combination of quality tools and techniques may be applied to resolve a customer issue. These examples complement the *learning through applications* theme of the text. Many of these examples use several techniques and provide a summary for the chapter. Some topics, such as designing for quality and failure modes and effects analysis, are mentioned in the course of discussion in order to encourage the reader to investigate areas beyond the boundaries of the text.

In order to ensure appropriate topic coverage, the material covered has been selected based on the Certified Quality Engineer certification available through the American Society for Quality. As an additional check, the material in this text has been reviewed by members of industry.

KEY FEATURES OF THE TEXT

The unique features of this text were designed to develop a greater understanding of the complexities of quality improvement efforts. The use of comprehensive examples and case studies continues to be the book's strongest feature. Taken from real-life situations, these examples and cases support learning by asking readers to consider the application and interpretation of the quality assurance techniques they have studied.

There are five key features of this text:

1. Emphasis is placed on the practical application of quality principles. Process improvement and reduction of variation serve as the underlying themes.
2. Emphasis is also placed on the interpretation, understanding, and use of quality principles and concepts throughout the problem-solving process.
3. Computer software is provided with the text to support the extensive example problems, end-of-chapter problems, and case studies.
4. Detailed examples and case studies from a wide variety of industries, based on real-life situations, provide the student with an understanding of the knowledge and effort necessary to solve quality problems.
5. Within each chapter, continuity in student learning is maintained through the use of certain elements—a list of learning opportunities, italicized key words and concepts, integrated examples, a summary of lessons learned, formula summaries, and finally case studies.

NEW TO THIS EDITION

Enhancements for the fourth edition include additional examples and problems, updated industry-appropriate software, improved explanations, more website references, and more detailed descriptions of important quality concepts. Coverage of quality systems such as Six Sigma and ISO/TS 16949 has been updated and expanded. Chapters 1 and 14 provide more detail about certifications and careers in quality. Improvements have been made to the instructor's manual including additions to the test bank, example syllabi, and lecture notes for selected chapters.

The most significant change is **Real Tools for Real Life.** These features provide students with insight into how real people use the tools and concepts presented in this text.

Chapter 1
Real Tools for Real Life: One Company's Journey to Continuous Improvement

Chapter 2
Real Tools for Real Life: Following Dr. Deming's Teachings
Real Tools for Real Life: Tampering with the Process

Chapter 3
Real Tools for Real Life: Improving Servo Motors Quality Using Pareto Diagrams
Real Tools for Real Life: PLC, Inc. Announces Improvements to Reduce Supplier Parts Shortages

Chapter 13
Real Tools for Real Life: Using Quality Assurance Concepts to Reduce Product
Liability Risk

Chapter 14
Real Tools for Real Life: Becoming a Black Belt

Chapter 15
Real Tools for Real Life: Benchmarking at Remodeling Designs Inc.

ORGANIZATION OF THE TEXT

The text is divided into four parts: Setting the Stage, Control Charts for Variables, Control Charts for Attributes, and Expanding the Scope of Quality. The first part, Setting the Stage, includes Chapters 1, 2, and 3. Chapter 1, Quality Basics, introduces quality definitions and concepts. Chapter 2, Quality Advocates, presents information about the individuals who shaped the quality movement in the United States and abroad. Chapter 3, Quality Improvement: Problem Solving, provides the student with a foundation in quality problem solving.

The second part, Control Charts for Variables, begins with Chapter 4, a review of statistics. This presentation prepares the reader for Chapters 5, 6, and 7 on control charts for variables, process capability, and other variable control charts.

The third part, Control Charts for Attributes, begins with Chapter 8, a review of probability. Chapter 9, Quality Control Charts for Attributes, presents p, c, and u charts.

Extending the discussion of basic quality concepts, the fourth part encourages the reader to examine other areas beyond traditional control charts. Expanding the Scope of Quality comprises Chapters 10 through 15. In these chapters, the concepts of reliability, design of experiments, quality function deployment, quality costs, product liability, quality systems (ISO 9000, QS 9000, ISO/TS 16949 Six Sigma, and the Malcolm Baldrige Award), benchmarking, and auditing are all introduced.

The book concludes with eight appendices—dealing with values for the area under the normal curve; factors for computing $\overline{X}$, s, and R charts; values of t distribution, binomial and Poisson probability distributions; PQ Systems software; and a list of helpful websites—a comprehensive glossary; and a bibliography.

SUPPLEMENTARY MATERIAL

Significantly updated, the **instructor's manual** is divided into three sections. The first includes solutions to selected end-of-chapter problems. The second section provides sample answers to the case studies. The third section provides sample test questions for each chapter as well as the answers to those questions.

PowerPoint transparencies of selected figures from the text are available for instructor use.

The online instructor's manual and PowerPoint transparencies are available to instructors through the Summers catalog page at **www.prenhall.com.** Instructors can search for a text by author, title, ISBN, or by selecting the appropriate discipline from the pull-down menu at the top of the catalog home page. To access supplementary materials online, instructors need to request an instructor access code. Go to **www.prenhall.com,** click the **Instructor Resource Center** link, and then click **Register Today** for an instructor access code. Within 48 hours after registering you will receive a confirming e-mail including an instructor access code. Once you have received your code, go the site and log on for full instructions on downloading the materials you wish to use. One-time registration allows unlimited access to all instructor resource materials.

A **Student Solutions Manual** containing worked solutions to selected end-of-chapter problems is also available and can be packaged FREE with *Quality*, 4e. Contact your local Prentice Hall representative for details or simply request ISBN 0-13-224563-9 to order the text and student solutions manual package.

SOFTWARE AND THE USE OF COMPUTERS

In Chapters 3, 4, 5, 6, 7, and 9, the creation of control charts and histograms is taught. In order to provide students with the opportunity to work realistic problems containing lots of data, this text is packaged with an Excel-based software program. The PQ Systems software, CHARTrunner, is provided for those wishing to use Excel databases when creating charts. The software package is discussed in Appendix 7. For Chapter 11, the disc contains design of experiment software. The package has excellent help functions as well as a Quality Advisor to answer questions the student may have. The software package does have a timeout feature, but it can be reactivated by contacting PQ Systems at the number provided in Appendix 7.

ACKNOWLEDGMENTS

Without the help and insight of my students and the people who hire them, this text would not have been possible. I would like to express my sincere appreciation to all. Their input has been invaluable. I would also like to give a very heartfelt thanks to the individuals who contributed to the examples, cases, and **Real Tools for Real Life** examples: Paul Cushwa, Erich Eggers, Holly Fabry, Kevin Hess, Chris Honious, Mike Monnier, Aaron Rourke, and Craig Seifring. I am grateful for the support of Karl Summers, Steve Helba, and Debbie Yarnell. Without you this text would not have been possible. I would also like to extend my thanks to the reviewers, Danny Lee Morton, East Carolina University; Radha Balamuralikrishna, Northern Illinois University; and Marilyn Helms, Dalton State College.

Contents

List of Case Studies

I

Setting the
Stage

1

Quality Basics

 ■ *Learning Opportunities:*

1. To develop a definition for quality
2. To understand the complexities of defining quality
3. To become familiar with differing definitions of quality from such sources as the American Society for Quality Control, Dr. W. Edwards Deming, Philip Crosby, and Armand Feigenbaum
4. To gain insight into the evolution of total quality management concepts
5. To become familiar with the definitions of specifications, tolerance limits, inspection, prevention, quality, quality control, statistical quality control, statistical process control, total quality management, and process improvement
6. To understand the differences between the philosophies of inspection, quality control, statistical quality control, statistical process control, total quality management, and continuous improvement
7. To understand the differences between actions necessary in inspection, quality control, statistical quality control, statistical process control, total quality management, and continuous improvement
8. To understand that a variety of different approaches to organizing for quality exist, including standards like ISO 9000 and methodologies like Six Sigma ■

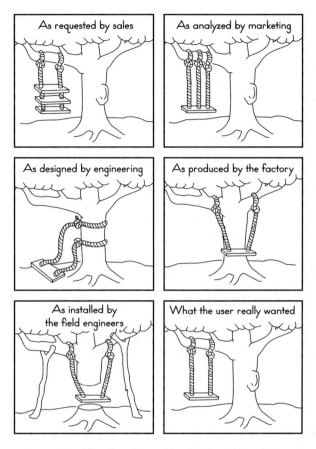

SOURCE: Don Kite, *Parts Pups,* Nov. 1971, and *Reader's Digest,* October 1973.

*T*he cartoon above is meant to make us chuckle a little about the difficulties consumers can experience in communicating what they want. But when you take a closer look, it isn't so funny. How can a company expect to stay in business if no connection is made between what the customer wants and what the company provides? This chapter begins the exploration of using process-improvement concepts to fulfill customers' needs, requirements, and expectations.

DEFINING QUALITY

For many companies, the reality of their situation is competition. They face competition on price, value, features, nearly everything related to the products and services they provide. Let's face it, customers have so many choices in today's marketplace, if they're not impressed, they'll go elsewhere. An organization's very survival is based on their ability to do what they said they would do faster, better, and cheaper than anyone else. Your success in your own job will be based upon your ability to find ways to design and implement processes that enable your organization to do what they do faster, better, and cheaper. A tall order for most of us, fortunately, the tools and techniques taught in this text will help. Effective employees in effective organizations everywhere in the world are already using them.

> From Wal-mart and cross-docking to Toyota and just-in-time, these companies know winning does not depend on a clever plan or a hot concept. It depends on how regular, mundane, basic work is carried out. If you can consistently do your work faster, cheaper, and better than the other guy, then you get to wipe the floor with him—without any accounting tricks. Relentless operational innovation is the only way to establish a lasting advantage. And new ideas are popping up all over.
>
> Operational innovation isn't glamorous. It doesn't make for amusing cocktail party conversation, and it's unlikely to turn up in the world of glam-business journalism. It's detailed and nerdy. This is old business, this is new business, this is real business. Get used to it.
>
> *Michael Hammer "Forward to Basics,"*
> *Fast Company, November, 2002.*

The topics in this text comprise a set of statistical tools that are equal to more than the sum of their parts. They provide users with the power to understand process behavior. With this knowledge, users can find ways to improve the way their organization provides its products and services. These tools can be applied to all sorts of processes including manufacturing, services, and government. Together, they provide a means of reducing process variation. The tools themselves are fundamental to good process management. Applying them is fundamental to good management, period.

The study of these tools begins with the definition of quality: The American Society for Quality Control defines **quality** as *a subjective term for which each person has his or her own definition. In technical usage, quality can have two meanings: (1) the characteristics of a product or service that bear on its ability to satisfy stated or implied needs and (2) a product or service free of deficiencies.*

Definitions have been developed by many prominent professionals in the field. Dr. W. Edwards Deming, well-known consultant and author on the subject of quality, describes quality as *nonfaulty systems*. To Dr. Deming, nonfaulty systems were error free systems that have the ability to provide the consumer with a product or service as specified. In *Out of the Crisis*, Dr. Deming stresses that quality efforts should be directed at the present and future needs of the consumer. Deming is careful to point out that future needs of the customer may not be identified *by* the customer but rather *for* the customer. The need for some of the products we use in our day-to-day lives (VCRs, microwaves, electronic mail, deodorants) was developed by the companies designing, manufacturing, and advertising these products. In other words, consumers do not necessarily know what they want until they have used the product or received the service. From there, consumers may refine the attributes they desire in a product or service.

Dr. Joseph M. Juran, in his book *Juran's Quality Control Handbook,* describes quality as *fitness for use.* In his text, *Quality Is Free,* Philip Crosby discusses quality as *conformance to requirements* and nonquality as *nonconformance.*

Quality can take many forms. The above definitions mention three types: quality of design, quality of conformance, and quality of performance. *Quality of design* means that the product has been designed to successfully fill a consumer need, real or perceived. *Quality of conformance*—conformance to requirements—refers to the manufacture of the product or the provision of the service that meets the specific requirements set by the consumer. *Quality of performance* means that the product or service performs its intended function as identified by the consumer. Clearly communicating the needs, requirements, and expectations of the consumer requires a more complete definition of quality.

Armand Feigenbaum, author of *Total Quality Control,* states that *quality is a customer determination which is based on the customer's actual experience with the product or service, measured against his or her requirements—stated or unstated, conscious or merely sensed, technically operational or entirely subjective—and always representing a moving target in a competitive market.* Several key words stand out in this definition:

- Customer determination: Only a customer can decide if and how well a product or service meets his or her needs, requirements, and expectations.
- Actual experience. The customer will judge the quality of a product or service not only at the time of purchase but throughout usage of the product or service.
- Requirements: Necessary aspects of a product or service called for or demanded by the customer may be stated or unstated, conscious or merely sensed.
- Technically operational: Aspects of a product or service may be clearly identified in words by the consumer.
- Entirely subjective: Aspects of a product or service may only be conjured in a consumer's personal feelings.

Feigenbaum's definition shows how difficult it is to define quality for a particular product or service. Quality definitions are as different as people. In many cases, no two customers will have exactly the same expectations for the same product or service. Notice that Feigenbaum's definition also recognizes that a consumer's needs, requirements, and expectations change over time and with different situations. Under some circumstances customer expectations will not remain the same from purchase to purchase or encounter to encounter. To produce or supply a quality product or service, a company must be able to define and meet the customer's reasonable needs, requirements, and expectations, even as they change over time. This is true whether the product is tangible (automobiles, stereos, or computers) or intangible (airplane schedules, hospital care, or repair service). Because of Feigenbaum's broad emphasis on customer requirements, this text will use his description of quality as its guide.

EXAMPLE 1.1   Tying It All Together*

This example, as well as the questions and case study at the end of the chapter, encourage you to think about quality from the viewpoints of customers and providers of products and services.

Scheduled air carriers handle about two million pieces of luggage each day. That's a lot of luggage to keep track of, and unfortunately sometimes the passenger and the bag don't end up going to the same place at the same time. Each day, approximately one-half of 1 percent (10,000) of the two million bags are mishandled. A mishandled bag either doesn't arrive with the passenger or it is damaged while en route. Each day, 100 unlucky travelers learn that their bags have been irretrievably lost or stolen. As late as 2001, on domestic flights airlines were liable for only $1,250 of the cost of lost, damaged, or delayed luggage. International travelers received $9.07 per pound of checked luggage. Passenger reports of lost, damaged, or delayed baggage on domestic flights steadily decreased throughout the 1990s only to rise by 2004 (Figure 1.1). What would be your definition of quality for this example? One hundred percent of the bags arriving with their passengers? Is one-half of 1 percent (99.5 percent good) an acceptable level of quality? What about the enormous amount of luggage being handled each day? Two million bags versus 10,000 bags mishandled? Seven hundred thirty million bags correctly handled annually versus 36,500 bags irretrievably lost or stolen? Do we hold other industries to such a high performance level? Do you turn in perfect term papers?

*K. Choquetter, "Claim Increase for Lost Baggage Still Up in the Air," *USA Today,* March 17, 1998.

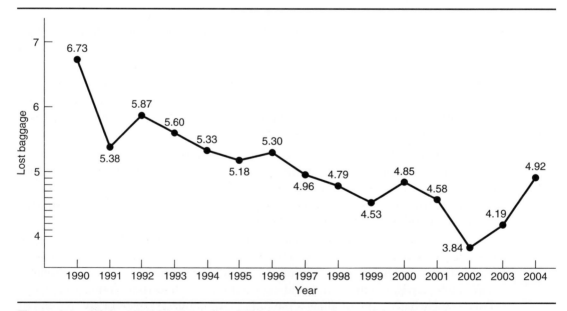

Figure 1.1   Mishandled Luggage (per 1000 passengers)
SOURCE: Based on information from K. Choquetter, "Claim Increase for Lost Baggage Still Up in the Air," *USA Today,* March 17, 1998 and www.dot.gov/airconsumer.

Can you identify the customers in this example? Are they the passengers or the airlines (as represented by the baggage handlers, the check-in clerks, and the lost-luggage finders)? What are their needs, requirements and expectations? In order to do a quality job in the eyes of passengers—i.e., in order to get the luggage to the right place at the right time—the airlines must label bags correctly, bar code them to ensure efficient handling, employ trained baggage handlers and clerks, and determine ways to reduce the number of mishandled bags. Passengers also play a role in the overall quality of the system. At a minimum, passengers must label bags clearly and correctly. Passengers must arrive in ample time before the flight and not overfill their suitcases so the suitcases do not unexpectedly open while being handled.

How will a customer recognize quality? Feigenbaum's definition of quality stresses that quality is a customer determination based on the customer's actual experience with the product or service and measured against his or her requirements. Different people will see this example differently. An individual about to make a very important presentation without needed clothing that was lost with a suitcase will be very angry. A traveler who receives his or her baggage on the next flight with only a small delay may be annoyed but minimally inconvenienced.

There are many aspects to quality. In this text, we explore techniques that enable us to improve the way we do business.

INGREDIENTS FOR SUCCESS

Corporate Culture

Companies seeking to remain competitive in today's global markets must integrate quality into all aspects of their organization. Successful companies *focus on customers* and their needs, requirements, and expectations. The *voice of the customer* serves as a significant source of information for making improvements to a company's products and services. A successful enterprise has a **vision** of how it sees itself in the future. This vision serves as a guide, enabling company leaders to create strategic plans supporting the organization's objectives. A clear vision helps create an atmosphere within an organization that is cohesive, with its members sharing a common culture and value system focused on the customer. Teamwork and a results-oriented, problem-solving approach are often mainstays in this type of environment.

Processes and Process Improvement

A **process** *takes inputs and performs value-added activities on those inputs to create an output* (Figure 1.2). Most of us do not realize how many processes we perform on a day-to-day basis. For instance, you go through a process when you select a movie to see. The input is the information about show times and places, whom you are going with, and what criteria you have for choosing a movie. The value-added activities are driving to the movie theater, buying a ticket, and watching the movie. And the output is the result, the entertainment value of the movie.

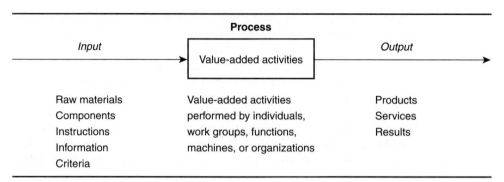

Figure 1.2   Processes

Industries have innumerable processes that enable them to provide products or services for customers. Think about the number of processes necessary to provide a shirt by mail order over the Internet. The company must have a catalog website preparation process, a website distribution process, a process for obtaining the goods it plans to sell, an ordering process, a credit-check process, a packaging process, a mailing process, and a billing process, to name a few. Other processes typically found in organizations include financial management; customer service; equipment maintenance and installation; production and inventory control; employee hiring, training, reviewing, firing, and payroll; software development; and product or service design, creation, inspection, packaging, delivery, and improvement.

Many processes develop over time, with little concern for whether or not it is the most effective manner in which to provide a product or service. To remain competitive in the world marketplace, companies must seek out wasteful processes and improve them. The processes providing the products and services will need to be quality-engineered, with the aim of preventing defects and increasing productivity by reducing process cycle times and eliminating waste. Many of the quality techniques discussed in this text support process improvement.

Variation

In any process that produces a product or provides a service, rarely are two products or service experiences exactly alike. Even identical twins have their differences. *Because **variation** is present in any natural process, no two products or occurrences are exactly alike*. In manufacturing, variation is often identified as the difference between the specified target dimension and the actual part dimension. In service industries, variation may be the difference between the type of service received and the type of service expected. Companies interested in providing a quality product or service use statistical process-control techniques to carefully study the variation present in their processes. Determining the reasons why differences exist between similar products or services and then removing the causes of these differences from the processes that produce them enable a company to more consistently provide a high-quality product or service. Think of it this way: If you are carpooling with an individual who is sometimes late, sometimes early, and sometimes on

Table 1.1   Specifications for Banking Transactions at Teller Windows Serving 10,000 Customers Monthly

Item	Specification
Customer Perception of Service/Quality	2 or Fewer Complaints per Month
Downtime of Teller Window Due to Teller Absence	Not to Exceed 5 Min per Day
Deposits Not Credited	1 or Fewer per Month
Accounts Not Debited	1 or Fewer per Month
Errors on Cash In and Out Tickets	1 or Fewer per Month
Missing and Illegible Entries	2 or Fewer per Month
Inadequate Cash Reserves	2 or Fewer Occurrences per Month

time, it is difficult to plan when you should be ready to leave. If, however, the person is always five minutes late, you may not like it, but you can plan around it. The first person exhibits a lot of variation; you never know when to expect him or her. The second person, although late, has very little variation in his or her process; hence you know that if you need to leave at exactly 5 P.M., you had better tell that person to be ready at 4:55. The best situation would be to be on time every time. It is this best situation at which companies are aiming when they seek to eliminate or reduce the variation present in a process. Methods of improving processes by removing variation are the focus of this text.

Product and service designers translate customer needs, requirements, and expectations into tangible requirements called *specifications*. **Specifications** *state product or service characteristics in terms of a desired target value or dimension.* In service industries, specifications may take the form of descriptions of the types of services that are expected to be performed (Table 1.1). In manufacturing, specifications may be given as nominal target dimensions (Table 1.2), or they may take the form of tolerance limits (Table 1.3). **Tolerance limits** *show the permissible changes in the dimension of a quality characteristic.* Parts manufactured between the tolerance, or specification, limits are considered acceptable. Designers should seek input from the customer, from engineering and manufacturing professionals, and from any others who can assist in determining the appropriate specifications and tolerances for a given item.

To manufacture products within specifications, the processes producing the parts need to be stable and predictable. A process is considered to be *under control* when the variability (variation) from one part to another or from one service to another is stable

Table 1.2   Specifications for Nominal Dimensions

Item	Nominal Dimension
Door Height	6 ft 6 inch
Theater Performance Start Time	8:00 P.M.
Wheelbase Length of a Car (in Catalog Shown to Customer)	110 inch
Frequency for a Radio Station	102.6 Hz
Calories in a Serving	100
Servings in a Package	8

Item	Specifications
Priority Overnight Delivery Time	Before 10:00 A.M.
Metal Hardness	R_c-44–48
Car Tire Pressure	30–35 psi
Heat-Treat Oven Temperature	1300–1400°C
Wheelbase Length of a Car	110 ± 0.10 in.
Household Water Pressure	550 ± 5 psi
Diameter of a Bolt	10.52–10.55 mm

Table 1.3   Specifications for Tolerance Limits

and predictable. Just as in the carpooling example, predictability enables those studying the process to make decisions concerning the product or service. When a process is predictable, very little variation is present. Statistical process-control practitioners use a variety of techniques to locate the sources of variation in a process. Once these sources are located, process improvements should be made to eliminate or reduce the amount of variation present.

EXAMPLE 1.2   Reducing Variation

Maps help us find the best route to get where we're going. At Transitplan Inc., map-making is serious business. Transitplan prints and distributes multicolor regional highway maps for locales all across the United States. Printing multicolored maps is tricky business. Rolls of white paper pass through printing presses containing plates etched with map designs. For multicolored maps, eight printing plates, each inked with a different color, are etched with only the items that will appear in that particular color. In many cases, the items are interrelated, as in the case of a yellow line inside two green lines to delineate an expressway. If the map printing plates are not aligned properly with each other and with the map paper, the colors may be offset, resulting in a blurry, unreadable map.

Transitplan's process engineers have worked diligently to reduce or eliminate variation from the map-printing process. Sources of variation include the printing plates, the inks, the paper, and the presses containing the plates. The engineers have improved the devices that hold the plates in place, eliminating plate movement during press cycles. They have developed an inventory-control system to monitor ink freshness in order to ensure a clean print. They have tested different papers to determine which ones hold the best impressions. These improvements have been instrumental in removing variation from the map-printing process.

With a stable printing process that exhibits little variation, process managers at Transitplan can predict future production rates and costs. They can respond knowledgeably to customer inquiries concerning map costs and delivery dates. If the map-production process were unstable, exhibiting unpredictable variation and producing both good and bad maps, then the process managers could only guess at what the future would bring (Figure 1.3).

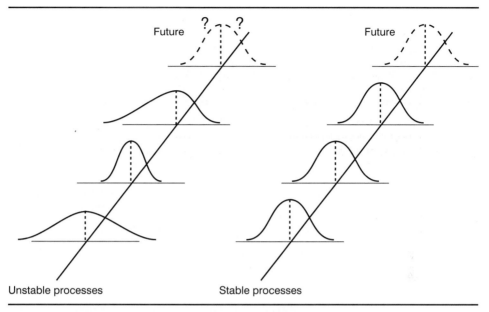

Figure 1.3   Predictions Based on Stable and Unstable Processes

Productivity

Some people believe that quality and productivity are the same or very similar. Actually, there is a difference between the two. To be productive, one must work efficiently and operate in a manner that best utilizes the available resources. Productivity's principal focus is on doing something more efficiently. Quality, on the other hand, focuses on being effective. Being effective means achieving the intended results or goals while meeting the customer's requirements. So quality concentrates not only on doing things right (being productive), but on doing the right things right (being effective). In manufacturing terms, if a company can produce 10,000 table lamps in 13 hours instead of in 23 hours, this is a dramatic increase in productivity. However, if customers are not purchasing these table lamps because they are ugly, then the company is not effective, and the increased productivity is meaningless. To remain competitive, companies must focus on effectively meeting the reasonable needs and expectations of their customers. Productivity and quality improvements come from managing work activities as processes. As process performance is measured and sources of variation are removed, the effectiveness of the process increases.

THE EVOLUTION OF QUALITY

Quality principles have evolved over time (Figure 1.4). Up until the advent of mass production, artisans completed individual products and inspected the quality of their own work or that of an apprentice before providing the product to the customer. If the customer experienced any dissatisfaction with the product, he or she dealt directly with the artisan.

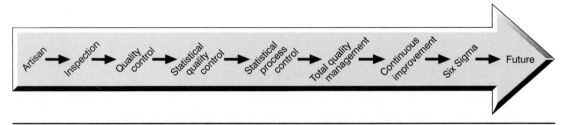

Figure 1.4   Evolution of Quality Principles

Firearms were originally created individually. The stock, barrel, firing mechanism, and other parts were fabricated for a specific musket. If part of the musket broke, a new part was painstakingly prepared for that particular firearm or the piece was discarded. In 1798, Eli Whitney began designing and manufacturing muskets with interchangeable parts. Firing mechanisms, barrels, or other parts could be used on any musket of the same design. By making parts interchangeable, Eli Whitney created the need for quality control.

In a mass production setting, the steps necessary to create a finished product are divided among many workstations which each perform a single repetitive operation. In order to be interchangeable, the parts must be nearly identical. This allows the assembler to randomly select a part from a group of parts and assemble it with a second randomly selected part. For this to occur without problems, the machines must be capable of producing parts with minimal variation, within the specifications set by the designer. If the parts are not made to specification, during assembly a randomly selected part may or may not fit together easily with its mating part. This situation defeats the idea of interchangeable parts.

Inspection

As the variety of items being mass-produced grew, so did the need for monitoring the quality of the parts produced by those processes. The customer no longer dealt directly with the individuals responsible for creating the product, and industries needed to ensure that the customer received a quality product. ***Inspection*** *refers to those activities designed to detect or find nonconformances existing in already completed products and services.* Inspection, the detection of defects, is a regulatory process.

Inspection involves the measuring, examining, testing, or gauging of one or more characteristics of a product or service. Inspection results are compared with established standards to determine whether or not the product or service conforms. In a detection environment, inspection, sorting, counting, and grading of products comprise the major aspects of a quality professional's position. This results in the general feeling that the responsibility for quality lies in the inspection department. Philosophically, this approach encourages the belief that good quality can be inspected into a product and bad quality can be inspected out of the product.

Inspection occurring only after the part or assembly has been completed can be costly. If a large number of defective products has been produced and the problem has gone unnoticed, then scrap or rework costs will be high. For instance, if a preliminary

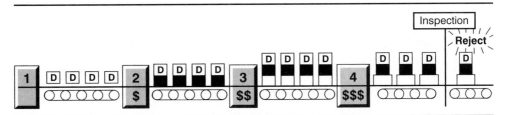

Figure 1.5   Consequences of Defects Compounded in Process

operation is making parts incorrectly, and inspection does not occur until the product has been through a number of other operations, a large number of defective items will have been fabricated before the defect is discovered by the inspectors. This type of mistake is very costly to the producer because it involves not only the defective aspect of the part but also the cost of performing work on that part by later workstations (Figure 1.5).

The same is true in a service environment. If the service has been incorrectly provided, the customer receiving the service must spend additional time in the system having the problem corrected. Even if the problems have been fixed, there is always the threat that the customer receiving the incorrect service may choose not to return.

Quality Control

Quality control (QC) *refers to the use of specifications and inspection of completed parts, subassemblies, and products to design, produce, review, sustain, and improve the quality of a product or service.* Quality control goes beyond inspection by

1. Establishing standards for the product or service, based on the customer needs, requirements, and expectations.
2. Ensuring conformance to these standards. Poor quality is evaluated to determine the reasons why the parts or services provided are incorrect.
3. Taking action if there is a lack of conformance to the standards. These actions may include sorting the product to find the defectives. In service industries, actions may involve contacting the customer and correcting the situation.
4. Implementing plans to prevent future nonconformance. These plans may include design or manufacturing changes; in a service industry they may include procedural changes.

These four activities work together to improve the production of a product or provision of a service.

Statistical Quality Control

Building on the four tenets of quality control, statistics were added to map the results of parts inspection. In the 1920s, statistical charts used to monitor and control product variables were developed by Walter A. Shewhart of Bell Telephone Laboratories. At the same time H. F. Dodge and H. G. Romig, also of Bell Telephone Laboratories, used statistics to develop acceptance sampling as a substitute for 100 percent inspection. The use of statistical methods for production monitoring and parts inspection became known as *statistical quality control (SQC), wherein statistical data are collected, analyzed, and interpreted to solve problems.* The primary concern of individuals involved in quality is the monitoring and control of variation in the product being produced or service being provided.

Statistical Process Control

Over time, companies came to realize that there was a need to be proactive when dealing with problems. Thus the emphasis shifted from utilizing statistical quality control methods for the inspection or detection of poor quality to their use in the prevention of poor quality. *Prevention of defects by applying statistical methods to control the process is known as statistical process control (SPC).*

Statistical process control emphasizes the prevention of defects. **Prevention** *refers to those activities designed to prevent defects, defectives, and nonconformance in products and services.* The most significant difference between prevention and inspection is that with prevention, the process—rather than solely the product—is monitored, controlled, and adjusted to ensure correct performance. By using key indicators of product performance and statistical methods, those monitoring the process are able to identify changes that affect the quality of the product and adjust the process accordingly. To do this, information gained about the process is fed back to those involved in the process. This information is then used to prevent defects from occurring. The emphasis shifts away from inspecting quality into a completed product or service toward making process improvements to design and manufacture quality into the product or service. The responsibility for quality moves from the inspectors to the design and manufacturing departments.

Statistical process control also seeks to limit the variation present in the item being produced or the service being provided. While it once was considered acceptable to produce parts that fell somewhere between the specification limits, statistical process control seeks to produce parts as close to the nominal dimension as possible and to provide services of consistent quality from customer to customer. To relate loss to only those costs incurred when a product or service fails to meet specifications is unrealistic. The losses may be due to reduced levels of performance, marginal customer service, a slightly shorter product life, lower product reliability, or a greater number of repairs. In short, losses occur when the customer has a less-than-optimal experience with the product or service. The larger the deviation from the desired value, the greater the loss. These losses occur regardless of whether or not the specifications have been met. Reducing process variation is important because any reduction in variation will lead to a corresponding reduction in loss.

Statistical process control can be used to help a company meet the following goals:

- To create products and services that will consistently meet customer expectations and product specifications
- To reduce the variability between products or services so that the results match the desired design quality
- To achieve process stability that allows predictions to be made about future products or services

Uniformity of Output
Reduced Rework
Fewer Defective Products
Increased Output
Increased Profit
Lower Average Cost
Fewer Errors
Predictable, Consistent Quality Output
Less Scrap
Less Machine Downtime
Less Waste in Production Labor Hours
Increased Job Satisfaction
Improved Competitive Position
More Jobs
Factual Information for Decision Making
Increased Customer Satisfaction
Increased Understanding of the Process
Future Design Improvements

Figure 1.6   Positive Results of Statistical Process Control

- To allow for experimentation to improve the process and to know the results of changes to the process quickly and reliably
- To minimize production costs by eliminating the costs associated with scrapping or reworking out-of-specification products
- To place the emphasis on problem solving and statistics
- To support decisions with statistical information concerning the process
- To give those closest to the process immediate feedback concerning current production
- To assist with the problem-solving process
- To increase profits
- To increase productivity

The positive results provided by statistical process control can be seen in Figure 1.6. Many of the techniques associated with SPC are covered in this text.

Total Quality Management

As the use of statistical process control grew in the 1980s, industry saw the need to monitor and improve the entire system of providing a quality product or service. Sensing that meeting customer needs, requirements, and expectations involved more than providing a product or service, industry began to integrate quality into all areas of operations, from the receptionist to the sales and billing departments to the manufacturing, shipping, and service departments. This integrated process improvement approach, involving all departments in a company in providing a quality product or service, became known as "total quality management" (Figure 1.7).

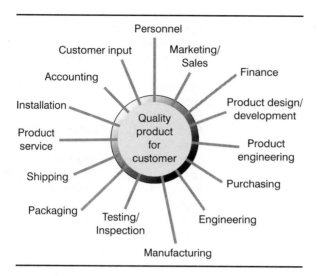

Figure 1.7   Department Involvement in Total Quality Management

Total quality management (TQM) is a management approach that places emphasis on continuous process and system improvement as a means of achieving customer satisfaction to ensure long-term company success. Total quality management focuses on process improvement and utilizes the strengths and expertise of all the employees of a company as well as the statistical problem-solving and charting methods of statistical process control. TQM relies on the participation of all members of an organization to continuously improve the processes, products, and services their company provides as well as the culture they work in.

Most important, quality management encourages a long-term, never-ending commitment to the improvement of the process, not a temporary program to be begun at one point in time and ended at another. The total quality process is a culture that top-level management develops within a company to replace the old management methods. Chapter 2 expands on the idea that the commitment to quality must come from upper management to guide corporate activities year after year toward specified goals. Given this long-term commitment to integrating quality into all aspects of the organization, companies pursuing quality management have an unwavering focus on meeting the customer's needs, requirements, and expectations. Since the customer's needs, requirements, and expectations are always changing, total quality management must be adaptable in order to pursue a moving target.

CONTINUOUS IMPROVEMENT

The **continuous improvement (CI)** philosophy focuses on improving processes to enable companies to give customers what they want the first time, every time. This customer-focused, process-improvement oriented approach to doing business results in increased satisfaction and delight for both customers and employees. Continuous improvement efforts are characterized by their emphasis on determining the best

Table 1.4   Continuous Improvement versus Traditional Orientation

Company Oriented Toward Continuous Improvement	Traditional Company
Customer Focus	Market-Share Focus
Cross-Functional Teams	Individuals
Focus on "What" and "How"	Focus on "Who" and "Why"
	Judgmental Attitudes
Attention to Detail	
Long-Term Focus	Short-Term Focus
Continuous Improvement Focus	Status Quo Focus
Process Improvement Focus	Product Focus
Incremental Improvements	Innovation
Problem Solving	Fire Fighting

method of operation for a process or system. The key words to note are *continuous* and *process*. Continuous improvement represents an ongoing, continuous commitment to improvement. Because the quest for continuous improvement has no end, only new directions in which to head, continuous improvement is a process, not a program.

One of the strengths of the CI process is that a company practicing these methods develops flexibility. A company focusing on continuous improvement places greater emphasis on customer service, teamwork, attention to details, and process improvement. Table 1.4 shows some other differences between a traditional company and one that practices continuous improvement.

The foundation of continuous improvement is a management philosophy that supports meeting customer requirements the first time, every time. Management must be actively involved with and committed to improving quality within the corporation. Merely stating that quality is important is not sufficient. Philosophies are easy to preach but difficult to implement. The strongest continuous improvement processes are the ones that begin with and have the genuine involvement of top-level management. This commitment is exemplified through the alignment of performance expectations and reward systems.

A variety of different approaches exist for integrating continuous improvement efforts into everyday business activities. The flowchart in Figure 1.8 illustrates a typical CI process. Note that many activities are ongoing and that several overlap. Most CI efforts begin with a vision. Visions, which are developed and supported by senior management, are statements describing how a company views itself now and in the future. A company's vision is the basis for all subsequent strategies, objectives, and decisions.

Top management often develops a mission statement to support the organization's vision. The mission sets the stage for improvement by making a strong statement about the corporation's goals. The mission statement should be short enough for its essence to be remembered by everyone, but it should also be complete. The mission statement should be timeless and adaptable to organizational changes. Examples of mission statements are shown in Figure 1.9.

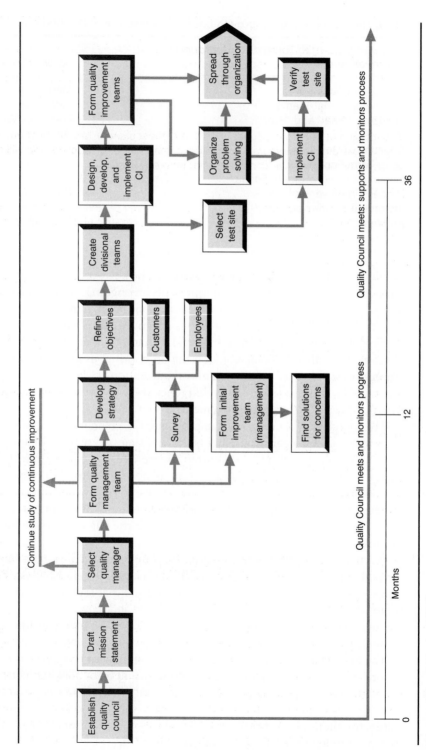

Figure 1.8   A Typical CI Process

Hospital

As a major teaching institution, we will continue to be a leader in providing a full range of health care services. Working together with our medical staff, we will meet and exceed our patients' needs for high-quality health care given in an efficient and effective manner.

Grocery Store

The mission of our store is to maintain the highest standards of honesty, trust, and integrity toward our customers, associates, community, and suppliers. We will strive to provide quality merchandise consistent with market values.

Student Project

Our mission is to provide an interesting and accurate depiction of our researched company. Our project will describe their quality processes as compared with the Malcolm Baldrige Award standards.

Pet Food Company

Our mission is to enhance the health and well-being of animals by providing quality pet foods.

Customer Service Center

Meet and exceed all our customers' needs and expectations through effective communication and inter-company cohesiveness.

Manufacturing

To produce a quality product and deliver it to the customer in a timely manner, while improving quality and maintaining a safe and competitive workplace.

Manufacturing

To be a reliable supplier of the most efficiently produced, highest quality automotive products. This will be done in a safe, clean work environment that promotes trust, involvement, and teamwork among our employees.

Figure 1.9   Examples of Mission Statements

 REAL TOOLS FOR REAL LIFE

One Company's Journey to Continuous Improvement

When PLC Inc. began operations three decades ago, their job shop specialized in machining large forgings into finished products. At that time, they utilized three separate inspections as their primary method of ensuring the quality of their products. The first inspection occurred following the initial machining operations, (grinding, milling, and boring) and before the part was sent to a subcontractor for heat-treating. After the part returned from heat treatment, key dimensions were checked at the second inspection. A final inspection was conducted before the finished part left the plant. With these three inspections, discrepancies between actual part dimensions and the specifications were found only after the part had completed several ma-chining operations. Though this method resulted in significant scrap and rework costs, PLC continued to use it with only one minor modification. They determined that occasional forgings were not up to standard so they added an incoming materi-als inspection to ensure the quality of the blank forgings.

Even with these four inspections, scrap and rework costs were still very high. If the forging passed incoming inspection and began to progress through the machin-ing operations, for a typical part, four to six operations would have been completed before any errors were caught during the in-process inspection that occurred before the part was shipped out to be heat-treated. The work done after the operation where the error occurred was wasted because each subsequent machining opera-tion was performed on a faulty part. Beyond a few minor measurements taken once they completed their work on the part, operators were not responsible for checking actual part dimensions against specifications. This type of inspection scheme was very costly to PLC because it involved not only the defective aspect of these large parts, but also the labor cost of performing work on a defective part by later work-stations.

In an attempt to correct this situation, PLC established a Quality Control Depart-ment. The members of this department developed a documented quality control pro-gram. The program was designed to ensure conformance to established standards for each product. They also initiated a corrective action plan that required a root cause analysis and corrective action for each nonconformance to standards. Fol-lowing this plan enabled them to implement corrective action plans that prevented future similar errors.

By the mid-1980s, the companies they did business with began requiring statisti-cal process control information. Statistical process control was a new concept for PLC. Fortunately they realized that the prevention of defects could make a signifi-cant impact on their profit performance. With this in mind, they set up control charts to monitor key characteristics over the long term and within a particular run.

Key characteristics like safety critical dimensions, working diameters, ID/OD for mating parts, radius, and any tight tolerances set by the designer were charted. Besides having each operator inspect his own work for each part production run, the first piece was inspected for all critical dimensions by the chief inspector on a coor-dinate measuring machine. Once the first part was approved, the operator had per-mission to run the rest of the parts in the lot. The "first part" designation applied to any part following a change to the process, such as a new operator, a new setup, a setup after broken tool, etc. By tracking the critical part dimensions, those monitoring the processes were able to identify changes that affected the quality of the product and adjust the process accordingly.

They sought additional ways to reduce the variation present in the process that prevented them from producing parts as close to the nominal dimension as possible. Thus, emphasis shifted away from inspecting quality into the parts and toward mak-ing process improvements by designing and machining quality into the product.

Realizing that in a job shop, the small lot sizes made significant use of statistical process control techniques difficult, PLC took a good hard look at the way they did business. In order to stay in this highly competitive business, PLC needed to determine what market need they were going to meet and how they were going to fill that need in an error-free, customer-service oriented manner. With this in mind, they began studying the ideas and concepts surrounding total quality management and continuous improvement. This lead them to consider all of their business operations from a process point of view instead of a part-by-part focus. Over the next few years, they applied continuous improvement concepts to how they managed their business.

Their continuous improvement efforts lead to an increase in their competitive position. In the 1990s, PLC began specializing in machining large complex parts for the aviation industry. Soon the shop was full of axles, pistons, steering collars, braces, and other parts for landing gear. The forgings brought in were made from many different kinds of materials including steel, a variety of alloys, and aluminum. Since the parts could cost anywhere from $6,500 to $65,000 each, not including material and heat treatment or coatings costs, PLC had to develop effective methods to run such a wide variety of material and part types on their machines. They realized they needed to shift their focus away from part inspection to controlling the processes that they used to make the parts.

When they asked themselves what really needed to improve in order to please their customers, they realized that reducing the number of tags on parts for out-of-specification conditions was critical. In order to do this effectively over the long term, PLC focused on processes, specifically designing processes, equipment, fixtures, and tooling to meet the needs of the product. This approach resulted in fewer setups, and reduced the number of times a part needed to be handled, which reduced the number of times a part could be damaged. Fewer setups also reduced the number of opportunities for mistakes in setups, incorrect or inaccurate setups. Better fixtures and tooling enabled the machining process to hold part dimensions throughout the part. Changes like these resulted in improved quality and throughput.

Their efforts paid off. As PLC improved their part uniformity, rework and defect rates fell and machine uptime increased as did labor productivity. These factors enabled them to increase output because less time was spent fixing problems and the focus shifted to where it belonged: making parts right the first time. Increased output enabled PLC to meet ship dates predictably. They were even able to reduce their prices while maintaining their profitability. As word got out to their customers about pricing, quality, and delivery, PLC was able to attract more and more business. Two plant expansions occurred as their competitive position improved with increasing customer satisfaction. Management at PLC felt that their increased understanding of the processes utilized in making parts enabled them to make better decisions and enhanced their focus on their customers.

Their continuous improvement changes included customer-focused changes, internal process changes, and human resources changes.

Customer-Focused Changes

Equipment   PLC acquired new machines of a better designs for machining long, relatively thin parts. For instance, they replaced a milling machine that used a cantilevered work-holding system with a horizontal milling machine. Having the part hang as a cantilever allowed vibration and tool movement to play a role in the machining of the part, affecting the ability to hold tolerance. This new machine significantly lowered rework due to the reduction in the variation inherent in the older process.

Machining   PLC made significant investments in their other machining operations. Their equipment now includes numerically controlled turning and three-axis contour machining centers, boring, honing, milling, grinding, and drilling machines. Most machines are able to perform multiple machining functions in one setup. The equipment is functionally grouped for efficient work flow and close tolerance control.

Job Tracking   PLC implemented a new system of job tracking. First, a manufacturing plan is created and reviewed with the customer. The manufacturing plan provides key information including part dimensions and the sequence of operations that the part will complete. Once approved, this information is converted to dimensional part drawings for each applicable workstation. Also included is a "traveler," a bill of material that moves through the operations with each part, that must be signed and dated by each operator as he or she completes the work. Inspections for the part are also noted on the traveler.

Internal Process Changes

Supplier Involvement   When quoting a job, sales engineers at PLC involve their tooling suppliers. The supplier is able to help select the best cutting tools for the type of job. Improved cutting tool technology enables the machining operations to run at higher speeds while holding part dimensions more accurately.

Gage Control System   A new gage verification system has resulted in fewer gage related errors. Each gage is now calibrated regularly and is part of a preventive maintenance program. These changes have significantly reduced the possibility of measurement error.

Inventory Control Systems   A new tooling inventory control system was recently installed. Using this system has resulted in fewer tooling selection errors which in the past had caused production delays. Inventory control is easier now that taking inventory is a visual task that has reduced the potential of not having the correct tool when it is needed. Cost savings are expected with this system because inventory can be monitored more easily, thus reducing the potential for lost or misplaced tools.

Smaller Lot Sizes   Recently, PLC has been moving toward single piece production runs rather than multiple part runs. This is possible with the new machining and cutting tool technology that allows the machine to run much faster. Now a single piece can be machined in less than one-third the time required previously. Not only is this a time savings, but if something goes wrong, only one part will be damaged. The single piece lot size also enables them to be very reactive to small customer orders.

Human Resources Changes

Cross-functional Involvement   PLC was quick to realize that an early understanding of what it would take to machine a part resulted in higher quality parts produced more efficiently. At PLC, sales engineers work with machine tool designers, as well as operators and tooling suppliers, when quoting jobs to establish the best machining practices for holding and cutting each particular part based on its material type.

> ***Communication***   Prior to their continuous improvement efforts, machine operators at PLC were not considered a valuable source of information. Now, management at PLC is working to increase operator involvement and enhance communication so that an operator will tell management when opportunities for improvement arise. Operators work together with engineers to conduct root cause analysis investigations and implement corrective actions. Operators are also involved in audits of proper use of procedures.
>
> Many of the improvements listed above came about because PLC had an understanding of the material presented in chapters in this text. As a result of their continuous improvement efforts, PLC have increased their efficiency and effectiveness. During the last three years, their growth rate has been 10–15% annually without adding any additional employees. For PLC, continuous improvement begins with the design of processes, tooling, machining centers, and fixtures that support producing quality parts. Well-designed processes and procedures combine to make quality parts and successful customers. **Q**

ORGANIZING FOR QUALITY

To make the journey from a company focused on inspection of completed products or services to a company that is proactive in meeting and exceeding the needs of their customers, many organizations follow particular methodologies or standards. ISO 9000 and QS 9000 are quality standards developed for the purpose of providing guidelines for improving a company's quality management system. Six Sigma is a methodology that also provides direction for a company seeking to improve its performance. Summarized below, a more complete discussion of these standards and methodologies may be found in Chapter 14.

Quality Standards

The most widely known of the quality standards are ISO 9000 and QS 9000. ISO 9000 was created to deal with the growing trend toward economic globalization. In order to facilitate doing business in a variety of countries, a series of quality standards was developed by the International Organization for Standardization. Applicable to nearly all organizations, the standards provide a baseline against which an organization's quality system can be judged. Eight key principles are integrated into the ISO 9000 standards: customer-focused organization, leadership, involvement of people, process approach, systems approach to management, continuous improvement, factual approach to decision-making, and mutually beneficial supplier relationships. Because of the similarities between these key principles and the continuous improvement philosophy, many organizations use ISO 9000 as the foundation of their continuous improvement efforts.

Prior to QS 9000, suppliers to the U.S. automotive companies were subjected to different, yet similar, quality system and documentation requirements from each automotive manufacturer. Recognizing the overlapping requirements, QS 9000 was developed by the major U.S. motor vehicle manufacturers and their suppliers to provide baseline quality system requirements. QS 9000 eliminates the redundant requirements while maintaining customer-specific, division-specific, and commodity-specific requirements. QS 9000 has two major components: ISO 9000 and customer specific requirements.

Six Sigma Methodology

The Six Sigma concept was developed at Motorola Corporation as a strategy to deal with product and system failures. The increasing complexity of systems and products used by consumers created higher than desired system failure rates. To increase system reliability and reduce failure rates, organizations following the Six Sigma methodology utilize a rigorous process-improvement methodology—define-measure-analyze-improve-control (DMAIC). This procedure encourages managing by fact with data and measurement tools, techniques, and systems. Many of the tools and techniques used by Six Sigma practioners are covered in this text (Figure 1.10). Six Sigma projects are chosen based on their ability to provide clearly defined and auditable financial results. Six Sigma encourages people at all levels in the company to listen to each other, to understand and utilize metrics, to know when and what kind of data to collect, and to build an atmosphere of trust. Six Sigma seeks to improve quality through reduced variation for every product, process, or transaction in a company, with the ultimate goal being to virtually eliminate all defectives. The Six Sigma methodology is covered in greater detail in Chapter 14.

Quality Philosophies	Chapters 1, 2
Performance Measures/Metrics	Chapter 3
Problem Solving Model	Chapter 3
Process Mapping	Chapter 3
Check Sheets	Chapter 3
Pareto Analysis	Chapter 3
Cause and Effect Diagram Analysis	Chapter 3
Scatter Diagrams	Chapter 3
Frequency Diagrams	Chapter 4
Histograms	Chapter 4
Statistics	Chapter 4
Data Collection:	
Data Types and Sampling Techniques	Chapters 4, 5
$\overline{X}$ and R Charts	Chapter 5
Process Capability Analysis	Chapter 6
P, u, c Charts	Chapter 9
Root Cause Analysis	Chapters 3, 4, 5, 6
Variation Reduction	Chapters 4, 5, 6, 7, 9
Six Sigma Philosophy	Chapter 14

Figure 1.10   Training Typically Required for Green Belt Certification and Related Chapters

BEYOND CONTINUOUS IMPROVEMENT

Over time, as consumers became more quality conscious, companies expanded their quality-management practices beyond the traditional manufacturing arena. Continuous improvement continues to evolve and embrace such concepts as optimization of processes, elimination of waste, and creation of a customer focus. Companies seeking to optimize business processes take a systems approach, emphasizing improving the systems and processes that enable a company to provide products or services for their customers. Examples of systems include ordering processes, billing processes, manufacturing processes, and shipping processes, among others. Improving processes means finding and eliminating sources of waste, such as idle time, rework time, excess variation, and underutilized resources. In today's world of global competition, companies must develop a customer-oriented approach to quality, studying how their product or service is used from the moment a customer first comes in contact with the product or service until the moment that the product is disposed of or the service is complete. Global competition has also encouraged companies to seek out and emulate *best practices*. The term "best practices" refers to choosing a method of work that has been found to be the most effective and efficient, i.e., with no waste in the process. As long as there is competition, companies will continue to seek ways in which to improve their competitive position. The quality concepts presented in this text provide a firm foundation for any company seeking to continually improve the way it does business. Case Study 1.1 lets you determine where companies are in there quality revolution.

WHO USES QUALITY TOOLS AND TECHNIQUES?

Nearly every organization that provides products and services to the public monitors its quality in some manner or another. A recent visit to the American Society for Quality's Career Center website (http://careers.asq.org/search) provided the job listings for over 120 jobs. These jobs were found at organizations worldwide and included pharmaceuticals, musical instruments, railways, hospitals, clinics, software, orthopedics, furniture, durable household goods, food production, glassware, technology, automotive, aerospace, shipping (train, plane, trucking, and boat), distribution, wireless technologies, toys, heavy machinery, education, entertainment, package delivery, and the list goes on. Job titles and descriptions included analysts, auditors, managers, inspectors, engineers, software developers, supervisors, and technicians. Figure 1.11 provides some sample job descriptions in the field of quality. Quality affects all organizations making training in quality tools and techniques valuable.

SUMMARY

A man purchased and installed a new answering machine in his home. After work each day, he checked his messages only to discover no messages on his answering machine. The next weekend, he returned the answering machine to the store, claiming it was defective because it didn't record messages. The helpful sales clerk asked him if

Analyst	Oversees and coordinates the organization's product and service data used for decision-making. Quantifies this data using statistical tools and techniques.
Auditor	Reviews and reports on internal and external processes critical for organizational quality.
Consultant	Offers advice and training on administrative and technical aspects of organizational quality. Assists in an organization's quality improvement efforts. This person has developed and maintains significant knowledge and expertise in one or several aspects of the quality field.
Coordinator/ Compliance Officer	Monitors and reviews organizational programs such as Six Sigma or ISO 9000. They are responsible for ensuring that appropriate data related to an organization's quality efforts is collected, organized, analyzed, reviewed, and utilized to further the organization's continuous improvement efforts.
Educator/ Instructor	Responsible for training and instructing others in quality tools and techniques.
Inspector	Inspects and reports on the quality of products, processes, services, and materials to ensure conformance to the specifications established by the customer.
Manager	Works through employees to ensure that the organization's processes provided products and services that meet the expectations set by their customers. Responsible for dealing with customers and their quality-related issues.
Quality Engineer	Responsible for the design, development, installation, testing, and use of the organization's quality assurance processes and procedures. When necessary, works with customers to develop specifications. Designs or selects and implements inspection and testing procedures and equipment. Works with management to develop quality assurance policies and procedures. Interfaces with other departments and suppliers to ensure customer quality.
Reliability Engineer	Uses reliability techniques to predict and evaluate product performance. Plans and conducts reliability tests, failure analyses, and performance tests. Analyzes field failures and customer complaints in order to improve product quality.
Software Quality Engineer	Applies quality tools and techniques to the design, development and implementation of software and software systems. Designs and conducts tests on software to verify and validate software performance capability.
Supervisor	Manages the activities of individuals who report directly. Concerned with the implementation of organizational policies and procedures related to quality.
Technician	Utilizes basic quality tools and techniques, including instrument/equipment calibration, to measure product, process, and material performance.

Figure 1.11   Job Title Definitions Related to Quality

he read the instructions. Yes, he had. Had he followed the instructions when installing the unit? Yes, he had. Had he attached cord A to plug B? Yes, he had. Well, since our products are of very high quality, the clerk said with a smile, the only explanation is that no one has called you.

Can we ever be that sure about the products and services that our company offers? Sure enough to say that the fault lies with the user, not the product or service? Probably not, but the quality tools and techniques taught in this text can help prevent the creation or provision of defective products and services.

In order to meet the challenges of a global economy, manufacturers and providers of services must balance the economic and profit aspects of their businesses with the goal of achieving total customer satisfaction. Quality must be designed into, built into, and maintained for each product or service provided by the company. Variation must be removed from the processes involved in providing products and services. Knowledge of consumer needs, requirements, and expectations will allow the company to succeed in the marketplace. Statistical process control, with its inherent emphasis on the creation of a quality product, is paramount in helping companies meet the challenges of global markets.

Dr. Joseph Juran once said that quality improvement ". . . requires the application of statistical methods which, up to the present time, have been for the most part, left undisturbed in the journals in which they appeared." The tools and techniques discussed in this text have formed the underpinnings of each of the major quality improvement initiatives including Total Quality Management and Six Sigma. These tools have affected the way people think, work, and act in relation to everyday work issues. Effective organizations recognize these powerful tools for what they are, the cornerstone to organizational success.

 ■ *Lessons Learned*

1. Quality is defined by a consumer's individual and reasonable needs, requirements, and expectations.
2. Processes perform value-added activities on inputs to create outputs.
3. Variation is present in any natural process. No two products or occurrences are exactly alike.
4. Specifications are used to help define a customer's needs, requirements, and expectations.
5. Productivity is doing something efficiently; quality focuses on effectiveness, doing the right things right.
6. The monitoring and control of quality has evolved over time. Inspection, quality control, statistical quality control, statistical process control, and total quality management are all aspects of the evolution of quality. ■

Chapter Problems

1. What is your definition of quality? How does your definition compare with Feigenbaum's?
2. Describe the differences among the definitions for quality given by the American Society for Quality, Dr. W. Edwards Deming, and Armand Feigenbaum.

3. Using Feigenbaum's definition, focus on the key aspects and discuss how a customer may define quality for having a muffler put on his or her car. Be sure to discuss the key terms identified in the definition of quality.

4. In your own words, describe the difference between productivity and quality.

5. Every day a dry cleaner receives a wide variety of clothes to clean. Some items may be silk, others may be wool, others rayon. Some fabrics may be delicate, other fabrics may be sturdier. Some clothing may contain stains. As a customer bringing your clothes in to be cleaned, what needs, requirements, and expectations can you identify? What must the dry cleaner do to do a quality job? How much would you be willing to pay for the service?

6. Describe the evolution of total quality management.

7. Define the following: specifications, tolerances, inspection, prevention.

8. Describe the philosophical differences between inspection, prevention, quality, quality control, statistical quality control, statistical process control, total quality management, and continuous improvement.

9. Describe the differences between the actions necessary in inspection, quality control, statistical quality control, statistical process control, and total quality management.

10. Choose and describe a quality (or nonquality) situation that you or someone close to you has experienced. What role did quality—and the customer's needs, requirements, and expectations—play in this situation? Describe how the creator of the product or the provider of the service could have dealt with the incident. What was your role in the situation? Could you have provided better quality inputs?

11. The following is a list of specifications for operating a hotel. Add four or five of your own customer specifications to this list.

Item	Specification
Customer Perception of Service/Quality:	2 or Fewer Complaints per Month
Downtime of Reservation/ Check-in Computer	Not to Exceed 15 Minutes per Month
Room Reservations Incorrect/ Overbooked	1 or Fewer Occurrences per Month
Credit Card Billing/ Transaction Errors	1 or Fewer per Month

12. Several department stores have coined famous mottos such as "the customer is always right" (John Wanamaker, Philadelphia department store magnate, 1865). Mr. Wanamaker went on to say: "It is our intention always to give

value for value in every sale we make and those who are not pleased with what they buy do us a positive favor to return the goods and get their money back." How does Mr. Wanamaker's philosophy relate to Feigenbaum's definition of quality?

13. Whenever you visit an organization (for instance, on a job interview or as your company's representative), you will need to recognize how that company views quality assurance. Describe how you would recognize the differences between a company practicing inspection functions versus one practicing statistical process control. Support your description with examples.

14. Whenever you visit an organization (for instance, on a job interview or as your company's representative), you will need to recognize how that company views quality assurance. Describe how you would recognize that the company is following a total quality management approach.

CASE STUDY 1.1
Quality Evolution: Where Are They Now?

Read the following scenarios and determine where these organizations are in the evolution of quality. What clues did you read that support your conclusions?

CLP INDUSTRIES

CLP Industries, an aircraft electrical systems and component supplier, designs and manufactures many components critical to the safe operation of commercial aircraft. Process improvement efforts emphasize the reduction of variation. Quality is an organization-wide approach to doing business. Quality is designed and manufactured into their products. Systems are in place that emphasize design control, process control, purchasing, inspection and testing, and control of non-conformances. Throughout the plant, processes have been mapped and investigated to remove non-value-added activities. Performance measures are used to monitor and control process performance. Workers in the plant are skilled in statistical process control tools and techniques. They participate in problem-solving teams on an as needed basis. CLP employees from all departments, including engineering, accounting, purchasing, sales, and manufacturing, participate in on- and off-site training opportunities in areas such as statistical process control basics, design of experiments, lean manufacturing, performance metrics, communicating with the customer, and others.

Representatives from the company participate actively in the International Aerospace Quality Group (IAQG). This organization works to establish commonality of quality standards and requirements, encourage continuous improvement processes at suppliers, determine effective methods to share results, and formulate responses to regulatory requirements. Plans are in place to upgrade their existing ISO 9000 Quality System to the AS9100 Quality Standard. Proposed for the aerospace industry worldwide, this quality standard seeks to standardize aerospace quality expectations on a global level. AS9100 adds 83 additional and specific requirements to the 20 elements of ISO 9001, including requirements for safety, reliability, and maintainability.

FIBERGLASS FORMULATIONS

Fiberglass Formulations manufactures fiberglass-based fittings for the automotive and boating industry. At Fiberglass Formulations firefighting is taken quite seriously. Recently, when one of their fiberglass curing ovens caught on fire, they reacted quickly to put out the fire. Encouraged by representatives from the Occupational Safety and Health Association (OSHA), they were determined to prevent future fires. Unfortunately, their approach to finding the root cause of the fire was less than organized. The responsibility for determining the cause of the fire was never assigned to a specific individual. None of the plant employees had been trained in root cause analysis or statistical methods.

Valiant efforts by the production supervisor yielded little insight into the cause. He was unable to obtain management support for a visit to the nearby equipment manufacturer to study the design of the machine in a search for possible causes. Members of the research lab took their own approach to determining the cause of the fiberglass fire. They analyzed the chemical makeup of the material in the oven at the time of the fire. They also sent some of the material away to a prominent testing lab to have its flammability studied. The process engineer also attacked the problem, calling in experts from the local university. With no responsible individual, no attempts were made to share information, limiting the usefulness of the efforts of the three individuals most closely involved.

In the meantime, production and part quality suffered, as did worker morale. Small fires were reported almost weekly, though workers became skilled at putting them out before they could cause any damage. Small, random fires soon became the status quo of doing business. Additional inspections were added at several workstations to make sure that parts damaged by the small fires did not reach the customers. Having satisfied OSHA with a report on the first fire, management soon lost interest in the fire, many of them unaware that the fires were continuing. Production losses, inspection costs, and quality problems related to the fires continue to mount.

TASTY MORSELS CHOCOLATES

Tasty Morsels Chocolates manufactures chocolate candy. Their main production line is fully automated, requiring little human intervention. Tasty Morsels uses charts to track production amounts, scrap rates, production times, order quantities, and delays in shipment. Every six weeks, these charts are collected and discussed by management. No statistical analysis takes place. Despite their efforts, they have production cost overruns. Cost overruns can be caused by excessive scrap rates, rework amounts, inspection costs, and overtime.

Two areas stand out as having problems. The first occurs following the cooling chamber. Chocolate is mixed until it reaches the right consistency, then it is poured into mold trays. As the chocolates leave the cooling chamber, two workers reorganize the chocolate mold trays on the conveyor belt. This non-value added, inspection-type activity essentially wastes the time of two workers. It also could result in damaged chocolates if the trays were to flip over or off of the conveyor.

Tasty Morsels Chocolates prides itself on their quality product. To maintain their high standards, before packaging, 4 workers inspect nearly every piece of chocolate as it emerges from the wrapping machine. A full 25% of the chocolate production is thrown out in a large garbage can. Though this type of inspection prevents poorly wrapped chocolates from reaching the consumer, this is a very high internal failure cost of quality. So far, though these two problems are apparent to nearly everyone in the plant, no efforts have been made to improve the process.

2

Quality Advocates

 ■ *Learning Opportunities:*

1. To become familiar with seven quality masters
2. To understand the philosophies of quality management and continuous improvement ■

Awesome Odds

Most individuals are motivated to do the best they can. Sometimes though, the goal seems too far away and too hard to reach. The problem appears too big to tackle. How does a company deal with these issues? How can managers enable their employees to do their best? This chapter discusses total management and the quality advocates who have encouraged its use. Through effective management, companies can significantly improve their levels of quality, productivity, effectiveness, and customer and employee satisfaction.

QUALITY ADVOCATES

Many individuals have proclaimed the importance of quality. The seven discussed in this chapter are among the most prominent advocates. You'll see that basic similarities exist among their ideas. Following a brief introduction to the seven men, we'll look at the concept of total quality management and explain some of the similarities found in the philosophies of these leading professionals.

Dr. Walter Shewhart

Like most of us, Dr. Walter Shewhart (1891–1967) believed that we could make great decisions if we had perfect knowledge of the situation. However, life rarely provides perfect knowledge and who has time to wait for it anyway? Since work needs to be done and decisions need to be made, Dr. Shewhart developed statistical methods that can be used to improve the quality of the processes that provide goods and services. While working at Bell Laboratories in the 1920s and 1930s, Dr. Shewhart was the first to encourage the use of statistics to identify, monitor, and eventually remove the sources of variation found in repetitive processes. His work combined two aspects of quality: the subjective aspect, what the customer wants; and the objective side, the physical properties of the goods or services, including the value received for the price paid. He recognized that when translating customer requirements to actual products and services, statistical measures of key characteristics are important to ensure quality.

Dr. Shewhart identified two sources of variation in a process. **Controlled variation,** *also termed* **common causes,** *is variation present in a process due to the very nature of the process.* This type of variation can be removed from the process only by changing the process. For example, consider a person who has driven the same route to work dozens of times and determined that it takes about 20 minutes to get from home to work, regardless of minor changes in weather or traffic conditions. If this is the case, then the only way the person can improve upon this time is to change the process by finding a new route. **Uncontrolled variation,** *also known as* **special or assignable causes,** *comes from sources external to the process.* This type of variation is not normally part of the process. It can be identified and isolated as the cause of a change in the behavior of the process. For instance, the commuter described in Chapter 1 would experience uncontrolled variation if a major traffic accident stopped traffic or a blizzard made traveling nearly impossible. Uncontrolled variation prevents the process from performing to the best of its ability.

It was Dr. Shewhart who put forth the fundamental principle that once a process is under control, exhibiting only controlled variation, future process performance can be predicted, within limits, on the basis of past performance. He wrote:

> A phenomenon will be said to be controlled when, through the use of past experience, we can predict, at least within limits, how the phenomenon may be expected to vary in the future. Here it is understood that prediction within limits means that we can state, at least approximately, the probability that the observed phenomenon will fall within the given limits.*

---

*Walter Shewhart, *Economic Control of Quality of Manufactured Product*. New York: Van Nostrand Reinhold, 1931, p. 6.

Though he was a physicist, Dr. Shewhart studied process control through the use of charting techniques. Based on his understanding of variation and the belief that assignable causes of variation could be found and eliminated, Dr. Shewhart developed the formulas and table of constants used to create the most widely used statistical control charts in quality: the $\overline{X}$ and R charts (Chapter 5 and Appendix 2). These charts (Figure 2.1) first appeared in a May 16, 1924 internal Bell Telephone Laboratories report. Later in his 1931 text, *Economic Control of Quality of Manufactured Product*, Dr. Shewhart presented the foundation principles upon which modern quality control is based.

In order to develop the charts, Dr. Shewhart first set about determining the relationship between the standard deviation of the mean and the standard deviation of the individual observations. He demonstrated the relationship by using numbered, metal lined, disk-shaped tags. From a bowl borrowed from his wife's kitchen, he drew these

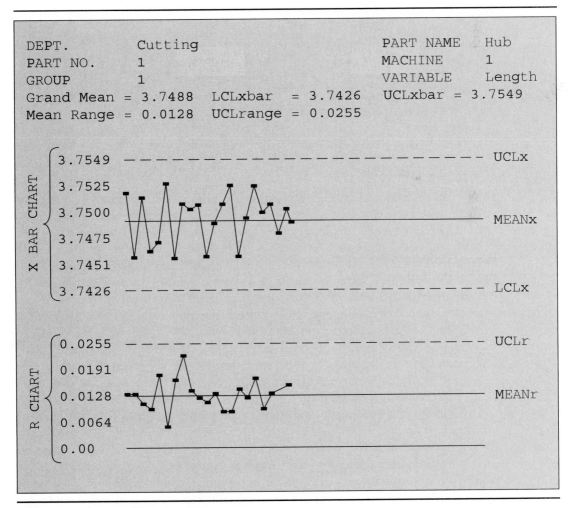

Figure 2.1   Typical $\overline{X}$ and R Charts

tags at random to confirm the standard deviation of subgroup sample means is the standard deviation of individual samples divided by the square root of the subgroup size.

$$s_x = \frac{s}{\sqrt{n}}$$

where

s_x is the standard deviation of the mean (standard error)
s is the standard deviation of individual observations
n is the number of observations in each subgroup mean.

The control charts, as designed by Dr. Shewhart, have three purposes: to define standards for the process, to aid in problem-solving efforts to attain the standards, and to serve to judge if the standards have been met. These charts are covered in detail in Chapters 5, 6, 7, and 9. Although Dr. Shewhart concentrated his efforts on manufacturing processes, his ideas and charts are applicable to any process found in non-manufacturing environments.

Statistical process control charts are more than a tool. They provide a framework for monitoring the behavior of a process and provide a feedback loop that enables organizations to achieve dramatic process improvements. Since their introduction in 1931, Dr. Shewhart's control charts have served to advance process improvement efforts in nearly every type of industry despite differing opinions about their appropriateness, applicability, limits derivations, sampling frequency, and use. It is a tribute to the ruggedness of Shewhart's invention that they remain the preeminent statistical process control tool.

Dr. W. Edwards Deming

Dr. W. Edwards Deming (1900–1993) made it his mission to teach optimal management strategies and practices for organizations focused on quality. Dr. Deming encouraged top-level management to get involved in the process of creating an environment that supports continuous improvement. A statistician by training, Dr. Deming graduated from Yale University in 1928. He first began spreading his quality message shortly after World War II. In the face of American prosperity following the war, his message was not accepted in the United States. His work with the Census Bureau and other government agencies led to his eventual contacts with Japan as that nation was beginning to rebuild. There he helped turn Japan into an industrial force to be reckoned with. His efforts resulted in his being awarded the Second Order of the Sacred Treasure from the Emperor of Japan. It was only after his early 1980s appearance on the TV program "If Japan Can, Why Can't We?" that Dr. Deming found an audience in the United States. Over time, he became one of the most influential experts on quality assurance.

Dr. Deming considered quality and process improvement activities as the catalyst necessary to start an economic chain reaction. Improving quality leads to decreased costs, fewer mistakes, fewer delays, and better use of resources, which in turn leads to improved productivity, which enables a company to capture more of the market, which enables the company to stay in business, which results in providing more jobs (Figure 2.2). He felt that without quality improvement efforts to light the fuse, this process would not begin.

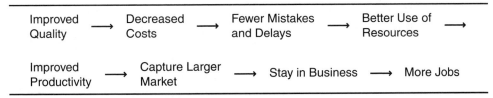

Figure 2.2   Deming's Economic Chain Reaction

Dr. Deming, who described his work as "management for quality," felt that the consumer is the most critical aspect in the production of a product or the provision of a service. Listening to the voice of the customer and utilizing the information learned to improve products and services is an integral part of his teachings. To Dr. Deming, quality must be defined in terms of customer satisfaction. Such a customer focus means that the quality of a product or service is multidimensional. It also means that there are different degrees of quality; a product which completely satisfies customer A, may not satisfy customer B.

Dr. Deming's philosophies focus heavily on management involvement, continuous improvement, statistical analysis, goal setting, and communication. His message, in the form of fourteen points, is aimed primarily at management (Figure 2.3). Dr. Deming's philosophy encourages company leaders to dedicate themselves and their companies to the long-term improvement of their products or services. Dr. Deming's first point—*Create a constancy of purpose toward improvement of product and service, with the aim to become competitive and to stay in business and to provide jobs*—encourages leadership to accept the obligation to constantly improve the product or service through

1. Create a constancy of purpose toward improvement of product and service, with the aim to become competitive and to stay in business and to provide jobs.
2. Adopt the new philosophy.
3. Cease dependence on inspection to achieve quality.
4. End the practice of awarding business on the basis of price tag alone. Instead minimize total cost.
5. Constantly and forever improve the system of production and service.
6. Institute training on the job.
7. Institute leadership.
8. Drive out fear.
9. Break down barriers between departments.
10. Eliminate slogans, exhortations, and targets for the work force.
11. Eliminate arbitrary work standards and numerical quotas. Substitute leadership.
12. Remove barriers that rob people of their right to pride of workmanship.
13. Institute a vigorous program of education and self-improvement.
14. Put everybody in the company to work to accomplish the transformation.

Figure 2.3   Deming's 14 Points
SOURCE: Reprinted from *Out of the Crisis* by W. Edwards Deming by permission of MIT and The W. Edwards Deming Institute. Published by MIT, Center for Advanced Educational Services, Cambridge, MA 02139. Copyright © 1986 by The W. Edwards Deming Institute.

innovation, research, education, and continual improvement in all facets of the organization. A company is like an Olympic athlete who must constantly train, practice, learn, and improve in order to attain a gold medal. Lack of constancy of purpose is one of the deadly diseases Dr. Deming warns about in his writings. Without dedication, the performance of any task can not reach its best. Dr. Deming's second point—*Adopt a new philosophy*—that rejects "acceptable" quality levels and poor service as a way of life, supports continuous improvement in all that we do. The 12 other points ask management to rethink past practices, such as awarding business on the basis of price tag alone, using mass inspection, setting arbitrary numerical goals and quotas, enforcing arbitrary work time standards, allowing incomplete training or education, and using outdated methods of supervision. Mass inspection has limited value because quality cannot be inspected into a product. Quality can be designed into a product and manufacturing processes can produce it correctly; however, after it has been made, quality cannot be inspected into it. Similarly, awarding business on the basis of price tag alone is shortsighted and fails to establish mutual confidence between the supplier and the purchaser. Low-cost choices may lead to losses in productivity elsewhere.

Leadership, along with the concepts of authority and responsibility, plays a significant role in all Dr. Deming's points. Without leadership, an organization and the people working within it are rudderless. Without effective leadership, the organization and its people cannot reach their full potential. Throughout his life, Dr. Deming encouraged leadership to create and manage systems that enable people to find joy in their work. Dr. Deming's point about driving out fear stresses the importance of communication between leadership and management. Effective leaders welcome the opportunity to listen to their employees and act on valid suggestions and resolve key issues. Dr. Deming also points out the need to remove barriers that rob individuals of the right of pride in workmanship. Barriers are any aspect of a job that prevent employees from doing their jobs well. By removing them, leadership creates an environment supportive of their employees and the continuous improvement of their day-to-day activities. Improved management-employee interaction, as well as increased communication between departments, will lead to more effective solutions to the challenges of creating a product or providing a service. Education and training also play an integral part in Dr. Deming's plan. Continual education creates an atmosphere that encourages the discovery of new ideas and methods. This translates to innovative solutions to problems. Training ensures that products and services are provided that meet standards established by customer requirements.

 REAL TOOLS FOR REAL LIFE

Following Dr. Deming's Teachings

KH Manufacturing makes components for the automotive industry. Unfortunately, several of the parts, due to design complexities, experienced numerous rejections from the customer. As a stopgap measure, KH instituted 100% inspection to minimize the chance of the customer receiving components that didn't meet specifications. Scrap rates were high. Due to the complexities of the components, rework, typically, was not an option.

When products don't live up to a customer's expectations, customers shop else-where. The automotive customer, recognizing that they faced a high probability of re-ceiving defective parts because 100% inspection is rarely 100% effective, began to "shop the work."

At KH Manufacturing, costs associated with 100% inspection and manufacturing replacement components mounted. The thought of losing a customer disturbed them. KH recognized that Dr. Deming's philosophy of "creating a constancy of pur-pose toward improvement of product and service" would enable them to keep the component job, become more competitive, stay in business, and provide jobs. Since 100% inspection is expensive and ineffective, KH wanted to enact process changes that would allow them to follow Dr. Deming's third point and "cease dependence on inspection to achieve quality."

Following Dr. Deming's fifth point, "constantly and forever improve the system of production and service," KH formed product improvement teams comprised of engi-neers and machine operators most closely associated with each component. Dr. Shewhart's $\overline{X}$ and R charts, recording process performance, formed the center of the improvement efforts.

The benefits of this approach to doing business were numerous. By "putting everyone in the company to work to accomplish the transformation," a change came over the production line. As operators learned to use and understand the $\overline{X}$ and R charts, they learned about their manufacturing processes. Process improvements, based on the knowledge gained from these charts, significantly improved compo-nent quality. Employee morale increased as they started to take an interest in their jobs. This was a big change for the union shop.

Changes happened on the individual level too. As management followed Dr. Deming's seventh, sixth, and eighth points "institute leadership" by "instituting training on the job," they were able to "drive out fear." One operator, who originally was very vocal about not wanting to be on the team, eventually ended up as a team leader.

Unbeknownst to his coworkers, this operator faced a significant barrier that "robbed him of his right to pride of workmanship" (Dr. Deming's 12th point). He had dropped out of school after sixth grade and had a very difficult time with math and reading. His understanding of math was so limited, he couldn't understand or calcu-late an average or a range. To hide his lack of math skills, he memorized which keys to use on the calculator. As he attended classes offered by the company, he learned how to plot and interpret data in order to make process adjustments based on trends and out of control points. The more involved he became in the improvement efforts, the more he realized how interesting his work had become. His involvement with the team inspired him to go back to school and get his High School Graduate Equiva-lency Degree at the age of 55. He followed Dr. Deming's 13th point, "institute a vig-orous program of education and self-improvement."

Rather than rely on "slogans, exhortations, and targets for the workforce," KH Manu-facturing followed Dr. Deming's advice and eliminated "arbitrary work standards and nu-merical quotas." KH was able to "cease dependence on inspection to achieve quality." They "substituted leadership," earning awards for being the most improved supplier. With their ability to manufacture complex components to customer specifications with nearly zero scrap, the plant has become the most profitable of the entire corporation.   Q

Dr. Deming defined quality as *"non-faulty systems."* At first glance this seems to be an incomplete definition, especially when compared to that of Dr. Feigenbaum. Consider, however, what is meant by a system. Systems enable organizations to provide their customers with products and services. Faulty systems cannot help but create faulty products and services, resulting in unhappy customers. By focusing attention on the systems that create products and services, Dr. Deming is getting at the heart of the matter.

Dr. Deming used the red bead experiment to help leaders understand how a process with problems can inhibit an individual's ability to perform at his or her best. Dr. Deming used this experiment to create an understanding of his point—*Remove barriers that rob people of their right to pride of workmanship.* To conduct his experiment, Dr. Deming filled a box with 1000 beads, 800 white and 200 red. Participants randomly scooped 100 beads from the box. The participants have no control over which beads the scoop picked up or the percentage of red beads in the box. Given these constraints, 20% of the beads selected were red. Since only white beads are acceptable, Dr. Deming chastised those who scooped red beads from the box even though they have no control over their performance. Similarly, employees in an organization may often be blamed for faulty performance when in actuality it is the system that is faulty. The red beads represent problems in the system or process that can be changed only through leadership involvement. To Dr. Deming, it is the job of leaders to create non-faulty systems by removing the "red beads."

Reducing the variation present in a system or process is one of the most critical messages Dr. Deming sent to leadership. To do this, he emphasized the use of the statistics and quality techniques espoused by Dr. Shewhart and covered in Chapters 3, 4, 5, 6, 7, and 9 in this text. According to Dr. Deming, process improvement is best carried out in three stages:

> Stage 1: Get the process under control by identifying and eliminating the sources of uncontrolled variation. Remove the special causes responsible for the variation.
>
> Stage 2: Once the special causes have been removed and the process is stable, improve the process. Investigate whether or not waste exists in the process. Tackle the common causes responsible for the controlled variation present in the process. Determine if process changes can remove them from the process.
>
> Stage 3: Monitor the improved process to determine if the changes made are working.

Dr. Deming used a second experiment, the funnel experiment, to describes how tampering with a process can actually make the performance of that process worse. For this experiment, beads are dropped from a funnel over a target. During the experiment, the funnel is moved in three different ways. The reason for moving the funnel is to try to get the beads to cluster around the target, thus exhibiting very little variation in where they land. At first, the funnel is held stationary above the target, resulting in the pattern shown in Figure 2.4 under Rule 1. Next, the funnel is moved each time to where the bead landed on the previous trial, creating the pattern shown in Figure 2.4 under Rule 2. The third method requires that the funnel be moved in the opposite direction from where the bead from the previous trial lands. This results in the pattern

Rule 1

No Compensation: Do not adjust the funnel position. Center the funnel over the target and leave it there for the duration of the experiment.

Rationale: Intuitively, we know that this is probably not the way to get the best results. However, this strategy will give us some baseline data. We can compare the results using one of the other rules with this baseline to measure our improvement. We could also be lucky enough to hit the target once in a while.

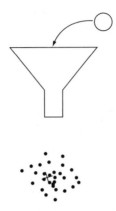

Rule 2

Exact Compensation: Measure the distance from the last drop to the target. Compensate for the error by moving the funnel the same distance, but in the opposite direction from its last position.

Rationale: This rule attempts to compensate for the inaccuracy of the funnel. If the funnel drops the bead off the target by a certain amount, it is reasonable to suppose that moving the funnel in the opposite direction by the same amount will improve the results. This rule requires us to remember the position of the funnel at the last drop.

(continued)

Figure 2.4 Deming's Funnel Experiment
SOURCE: Reprinted from *Quality Management,* © 2005, by permission of Prentice Hall/Pearson Education.

Rule 3

Overcompensation: Measure the distance from the last drop to the target, Center the funnel on the target; then move it the same distance from the target as the last drop, but in the opposite direction.

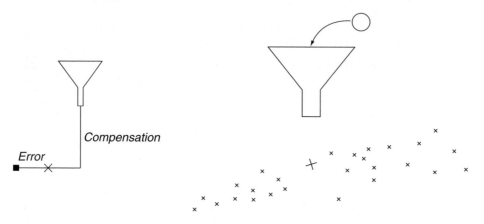

Rationale: In this case we use the target as a basis for our adjustment, rather than the last position of the funnel, as in Rule 2. This is probably our only recourse if we know only the position of the target and the last drop, and not the position of the funnel.

Rule 4

Consistency: Center the funnel over the last drop.

Rationale: The objective of Rule 4 is to maintain consistent results. Even if we miss the target, the results should be consistent, since we always aim for the position of the last drop. If we are off target, we can always take care of it later.

Figure 2.4   (*continued*)

shown in Figure 2.4 under Rule 3. Note that the smallest pattern, the one with the least amount of variation around the target, is the top one where the funnel is not moved. Using this experiment, Dr. Deming shows that tampering with a process, that is, moving the funnel actually increases the variation and results in poorer performance.

Tampering can be avoided by isolating and removing the root causes of process variation through the use of the Plan-Do-Study-Act (PDSA) problem-solving cycle.

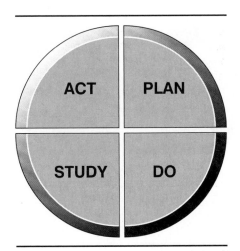

Figure 2.5   The Deming Cycle
SOURCE: Reprinted from *Out of the Crisis* by W. Edwards Deming by permission of MIT and The W. Edwards Deming Institute. Published by MIT, Center for Advanced Educational Services, Cambridge, MA 02139. Copyright © 1986 by The W. Edwards Deming Institute.

When tackling process improvement, it is important to find the root cause of the variation. Rather than apply a Band-Aid sort of fix, when seeking the causes of variation in the process, Dr. Deming encouraged the use of the PDSA cycle (Figure 2.5). Originally developed by Dr. Walter Shewhart, the PDSA cycle is a systematic approach to problem-solving. During the Plan phase, users of the cycle study a problem and plan a solution. This should be the portion of the cycle that receives the most attention, since good plans lead to well-thought-out solutions. The solution is implemented during the Do phase of the cycle. During the Study phase, the results of the change to the process are studied. Finally, during the Act phase, when the results of the Study phase reveal that the root cause of the problem has been isolated and removed from the process permanently, the changes are made permanent. If the problem has not been resolved, a return trip to the Plan portion of the cycle for further investigation is undertaken. The PDSA cycle of problem-solving will be covered in detail in Chapter 3.

   REAL TOOLS FOR REAL LIFE

Tampering with the Process

The Whisk Wheel Company has been notified by its largest customer, Rosewood Bicycle, Inc., that Whisk Wheel will need to dramatically improve the quality level associated with the hub operation. Currently the operation is unable to meet the specification limits set by the customer. Rosewood has been sorting the parts on the production line before assembly, but they want to end this practice. Figure 2.6 shows the product in question, a wheel hub. The hub shaft is made of chrome-moly steel. The dimension in question is the shaft length. The specification for the length is 3.750 $\pm$ 0.005 inch. The process involves taking 12 foot long chrome-moly steel shafts purchased from a supplier, straightening them, and cutting them to 3.750-inch length.

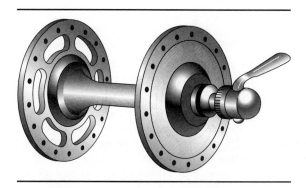

Figure 2.6   Hub Assembly
SOURCE: Reprinted from *Quality Management,* © 2005, by permission of Prentice Hall/Pearson Education.

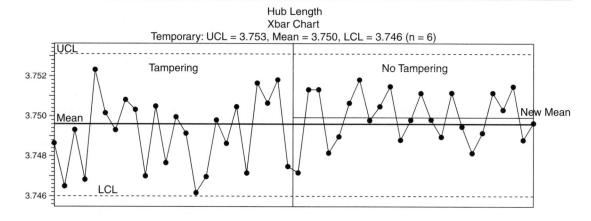

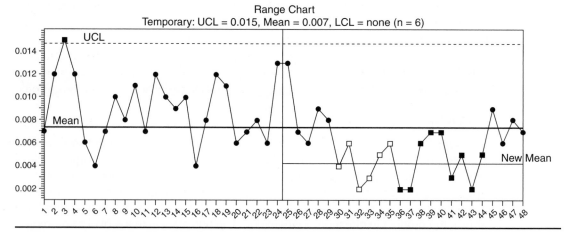

Figure 2.7   The Effects of Tampering on a System

In order to determine the root causes of variation in hub length, the engineers are studying the cutting operation and the operator. The operator performs the process in the following manner. Every 18 minutes, he measures the length of six hubs. The length values for the six consecutively produced hubs are averaged, and the average is plotted on $\overline{X}$ and R charts. Periodically, the operator reviews the evolving data and makes a decision as to whether or not the process mean (the hub length) needs to be adjusted. These adjustments can be accomplished by stopping the machine, loosening some clamps, and jogging the cutting device back or forth depending on the adjustment the operator feels is necessary. This process takes about five minutes and appears to occur fairly often.

Based on the engineers' knowledge of Dr. Deming's funnel experiment, they are quick to realize that the operator is adding variation to the process. He appears to be over-controlling (over-adjusting) the process because he cannot distinguish between common cause variation and special cause variation. The operator has been reacting to patterns in the data that may be inherent (common) to the process. The consequences of this mistake are devastating to a process. Each time an adjustment is made when it is not necessary, variation is introduced to the process that would not be there otherwise. Not only is quality essentially decreased (made more variable) with each adjustment, but production time is unnecessarily lost.

Use Figure 2.7 to compare the differences in the charts when an adjustment is made or no adjustment is made to the process. Note that the process has stabilized because no unnecessary adjustments have been made. The method of over-control has proved costly from a quality (inconsistent product) and a productivity (machine downtime, higher scrap) point of view.

Systems thinking was a critical aspect of Dr. Deming's work. He felt that all systems must have a specific goal to achieve. Clearly stating that goal will enable the people within the system to understand what they need to accomplish. By taking a systems approach, Dr. Deming hoped that people would understand that they are like an orchestra, seeking to blend their efforts together, to support each other, rather than play solos. Those taking the systems approach pay attention to the interactions between the parts. To be effective, an organization must manage the interactions between components in the system.

In his final book, *The New Economics*, Dr. Deming tied much of his life's work together when he introduced the concept of profound knowledge. There are four interrelated parts of a system of profound knowledge:

- An appreciation for a system
- Knowledge of variation
- Theory of knowledge
- Psychology

Effective leaders have an appreciation for the systems that work together to create their organization's products and services. They understand the interactions, interrelationships, and flow of a complex system. Those who have an appreciation for a system create alignment between their customers' needs, requirements, and expectations, the systems that produce products and services, and their organization's purpose. Their efforts focus on improving these systems by using the PDSA problem-solving method to remove the system faults that result in errors.

Knowledge of variation means being able to distinguish between controlled and uncontrolled variation. First defined by Dr. Walter Shewhart, common or controlled variation is the variation present in a process or system due to its very nature. This natural variation can only be removed by changing the process or system in some way. Special cause variation, also known as uncontrolled variation, is the variation present in a process due to some assignable cause. This source of variation in a process can be readily identified and removed from the system or process. Significant process improvement comes from obtaining statistical knowledge about a process through control charting, the study of variation and the gathering and analysis of factual data.

The theory of knowledge involves using data to understand situations by being able to comprehend how people learn. Dr. Deming encouraged the use of fact-based information when making decisions. Effective leaders gather and analyze information for trends, patterns, and anomalies before reaching conclusions.

An understanding of psychology enables us to understand each other better, whether as customers or employees. By understanding people, their interactions and their intrinsic motivations, leaders can make better decisions.

Knowledge of all these areas enables companies to expand beyond small process-improvement efforts and to optimize systems in their entirety rather than sub-optimize only their parts. This type of systems thinking both requires and allows organizations to focus on the long term.

Dr. Deming's influence continues today. Many of the concepts and ideas he espoused can be found in today's continuous improvement programs and international standards. For example, the year 2000 revision of the international quality standard, ISO 9000, places significant emphasis on management involvement and responsibility, including communicating customer requirements, developing an integrated overall plan to support meeting customer requirements, measuring key product and service characteristics, ongoing training, and demonstrating leadership.

Living the continuous improvement philosophy is not easy. The level of dedication required to become the best is phenomenal. Dr. Deming warned against the "hope for instant pudding." Improvement takes time and effort and does not happen instantly. The hope for instant pudding is one that afflicts us all. After all, how many of us wouldn't like all our problems to be taken care of just wishing them away? Dr. Deming's philosophies cover all aspects of the business, from customers to leadership to employees, and from products and services to processes. As evidenced by his 14th point—*Put everyone in the company to work to accomplish the transformation*—Dr. Deming's quality system is really an ongoing process of improvement. To him, quality must be an integral part of how a company does business. Organizations must continuously strive to improve; after all, the competition isn't going to wait for them to catch up!

Dr. Joseph M. Juran

Born December 24, 1904, Dr. Joseph M. Juran (1904–) immigrated from Romania to Minneapolis, Minnesota in 1912. In 1920, he enrolled in Electrical Engineering at the University of Minnesota. After earning his degree, he went to Western Electric as an engineer at the Hawthorne Manufacturing plant in Cicero, IL. There he served in one of the first inspection statistical departments in industry. During the Depression, he earned a law degree, just in case he needed an employment alternative. During World War II, he served in the Statistics, Requisitions, Accounts, and Control Section of the Lend-Lease administration. He was responsible for the procurement and leasing of arms, equipment, and supplies to WWII allies. Like Dr. Deming, Dr. Juran played a significant role in the rebuilding of Japan following WWII. Based on their work, both he and Deming were awarded the Second Order of the Sacred Treasure from the Emperor of Japan.

Dr. Juran's approach involves creating awareness of the need to improve, making quality improvement an integral part of each job, providing training in quality methods, establishing team problem solving, and recognizing results. Dr. Juran emphasizes the need to improve the entire system. To improve quality, individuals in a company need to develop techniques and skills and understand how to apply them. Dr. Juran's definition of quality goes beyond the immediate product or moment of service. To Dr. Juran, quality is a concept that needs to be found in all aspects of business. As shown in Figure 2.8, Dr. Juran contrasts big Q and little q to show the broad applicability of quality concepts.

During his career, Dr. Juran significantly influenced the movement of quality from a narrow statistical field to quality as a management focus. He attributes his change in emphasis to having read Margaret Mead's book *Cultural Patterns and Technical Change*

	Content of Little q	Content of Big Q
Products and services	Manufactured goods Point of Service	All products and services, whether for sale or not
Processes	Processes directly related to the manufacture of goods	All processes; manufacturing, support, business, etc.
Customer	Clients who buy the products	All who are affected, external and internal
Industries	Manufacturing	All industries; service, government, etc., whether for profit or not
Cost of Poor Quality	Costs associated with deficient manufactured goods	All costs that would disappear if everything were perfect

Figure 2.8   Big Q versus Little q

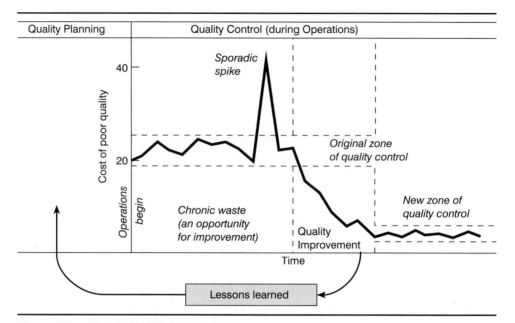

Figure 2.9   The Juran Trilogy Diagram
SOURCE: Reprinted with the permission of the Free Press, a division of Simon & Schuster, from *Juran on Leadership, for Quality: An Executive Handbook* by J. M. Juran. Copyright © 1989 by Juran Institute Inc.

(first edition, UNESCO, 1955). The book describes how a clash of cultures leads to resistance to change, as demonstrated by resistance in developing nations to the United Nations efforts to improve conditions. Dr. Juran felt this resistance to change could also be seen in clashes between management and employees. His book, *Managerial Breakthrough* (McGraw-Hill, 1964), discusses cultural resistance and how to deal with it. He felt that managing for quality is an offshoot of general management but is a science in its own right. He followed this book with a trilogy that outlines three key components of managing for quality.

The Juran trilogy makes use of three managerial processes: Quality Planning, Quality Control, and Quality Improvement (Figure 2.9 and Table 2.1). By following Dr. Juran's approach, companies can reduce the costs associated with poor quality and remove chronic waste from their organizations. *Quality Planning* encourages the development of methods to stay in tune with customers' needs and expectations. *Quality Control* involves comparing products produced with goals and specifications. *Quality Improvement* involves the ongoing process of improvement necessary for the company's continued success.

In his text *Juran on Leadership for Quality: An Executive Handbook*, Dr. Juran puts forth three fundamental tenets: upper management leadership, continuous education, and annual planning for quality improvement and cost reduction. Dr. Juran discusses the importance of achieving world-class quality by identifying the need for improvement, selecting appropriate projects, and creating an organizational structure that guides the diagnosis and analysis of the projects. Successful improvement efforts

Table 2.1   The Three Universal Processes of Managing for Quality

Quality Planning	Quality Control	Quality Improvement
Determine Who the Customers Are	Evaluate Actual Product Performance	Establish the Infrastructure
Determine the Needs of the Customers	Compare Actual Performance to Product Goals	Identify the Improvement Projects
Develop Product Features that Respond to Customers' Needs	Act on the Difference	Establish Project Teams
Develop Processes Able to Produce the Product Features		Provide the Teams with Resources, Training and Motivation to:
Transfer the Plans to the Operating Forces		Diagnose the Causes Stimulate Remedies Establish Controls to Hold the Gains

SOURCE: Reprinted with the permission of the Free Press, a division of Simon & Schuster, from *Juran on Leadership for Quality: An Executive Handbook* by J. M. Juran. Copyright © 1989 by Juran Institute Inc.

encourage breakthroughs in knowledge and attitudes. The commitment and personal leadership of top management must be assured in order to break through cultural resistance to change.

In the project-by-project implementation procedure (Table 2.2), project teams are set up to investigate and solve specific problems. To guide the project teams, the Juran program establishes a steering committee. The steering committee serves three purposes: to ensure emphasis on the company's goals, to grant authority to diagnose and investigate problems, and to protect departmental rights.

The project teams should be composed of individuals with diverse backgrounds. Diversity serves several purposes. It allows for a variety of viewpoints, thus avoiding preconceived answers to the problem. Having a diversified group also aids in implementing the solutions found. Group members are more willing to implement the solution because they have a stake in the project. The different backgrounds of the group members can also assist in breaking down the cultural resistance to change.

Juran's project teams are encouraged to use a systematic approach to problem solving. Group members use a variety of investigative tools to clarify the symptoms and locate the true cause(s) of the problem. When the cause is determined, finding a solution becomes a process of proposing remedies, testing them, and instituting the remedy that most effectively solves the problem. Controlling the process once changes have been made is important to ensure that the efforts have not been wasted. Improvements continue as the groups study and resolve other problems.

Still active at 100 years of age, in an interview with *Quality Progress* magazine May 2004, Dr. Juran had this advice for people: "become bilingual; learn to communicate

Table 2.2　Juran's Journey from Symptom to Cause: Quality Improvement in Action

Process	Activity	Steering Arm	Diagnostic Arm
	Assign Priority to Projects	X	
	Pareto Analysis of Symptoms		X
Journey from Symptom to Cause	Theorize on Causes of Symptoms	X	
	Test Theories: Collect, Analyze Data		X
	Narrow List of Theories	X	
	Design Experiment(s)		X
	Approve Design; Provide Authority	X	
	Conduct Experiment; Establish Proof of Cause		X
	Propose Remedies	X	
Journey from Cause to Remedy	Test Remedy		X
	Actions to Institute Remedy; Control at New Level	X	

SOURCE: Adapted with the permission of the Free Press, a division of Simon & Schuster, from *Juran on Leadership for Quality: An Executive Handbook* by J. M. Juran. Copyright © 1989 by Juran Institute Inc.

with senior managers by converting quality data into the language of business and finance." He is referring to the need to state quality goals in financial terms so that they can enhance the organization's overall business plan.

Dr. Armand Feigenbaum

Armand Feigenbaum (1920–) is considered to be the originator of the total quality movement. As stated in Chapter 1, Dr. Feigenbaum defined quality based on a customer's actual experience with the product or service. He wrote his landmark text, *Total Quality Control*, while he was still in graduate school at the Massachusetts Institute of Technology. Since its publication in 1951, it has been updated regularly and remains a significant influence on today's industrial practices. In his text, he predicted that quality would become a significant customer-satisfaction issue, even to the point of surpassing price in importance in the decision-making process. As he predicted, consumers have come to expect quality to be an essential dimension of the product or service they are purchasing.

To Dr. Feigenbaum, quality is more than a technical subject; it is an approach to doing business that makes an organization more effective. He has consistently encouraged treating quality as a fundamental element of a business strategy. In his article "Changing Concepts and Management of Quality Worldwide," from the December 1997 issue of *Quality Progress,* he asserts that quality is not a factor to be managed but a method of "managing, operating, and integrating the marketing, technology, production, information, and finance areas throughout a company's quality value chain with the subsequent favorable impact on manufacturing and service effectiveness." According to Dr. Feigenbaum, management is responsible for recognizing the evolution of the customer's definition of quality for their products and services. Quality systems are a method of managing an organization to achieve higher customer satisfaction, lower overall costs, higher profits, and greater employee effectiveness and satisfaction. Company leadership is responsible for creating an atmosphere that enables employees to provide the right product or service the first time, every time. Dr. Feigenbaum encourages companies to eliminate waste, which drains profitability, by determining the costs associated with failing to provide a quality product (see Chapter 12). Quality efforts should emphasize increasing the number of experiences that go well for a customer versus handling things when they go wrong. Statistical methods and problem-solving techniques should be utilized to effectively support business strategies aimed at achieving customer satisfaction. In its newest edition, his text serves as a how-to guide for establishing a quality system.

Philip Crosby

Philip Crosby's (1926–2001) message to management emphasizes four absolutes (Figure 2.10). The four absolutes of quality management set expectations for a continuous improvement process to meet. The first absolute defines quality as **conformance to requirements.** Crosby emphasizes the importance of determining customer requirements, defining those requirements as clearly as possible, and then producing products or providing services that conform to the requirements as established by the customer. Crosby felt it necessary to define quality in order to manage quality. Customer requirements must define the products or services in terms of measurable characteristics.

Prevention of defects, the second absolute, is the key to the system that needs to be in place in order to ensure that the products or services provided by a company

Figure 2.10   Crosby's Absolutes of Quality Management

Quality Definition: Conformance to Requirements
Quality System: Prevention of Defects
Quality Performance Standard: Zero Defects
Quality Measurement: Costs of Quality

meet the requirements of the customer. Prevention of quality problems in the first place is much more cost-effective in the long run. Determining the root causes of defects and preventing their recurrence are integral to the system.

According to Crosby, the performance standard against which any system must be judged is zero defects. This third absolute, **zero defects,** *refers to making products correctly the first time, with no imperfections.* Traditional quality control centered on final inspection and "acceptable" defect levels. Systems must be established or improved that allow the worker to do it right the first time.

His fourth absolute, **costs of quality,** *are the costs associated with providing customers with a product or service that conforms to their expectations.* Quality costs, to be discussed in more detail in Chapter 12, are found in prevention costs; detection costs; costs associated with dissatisfied customers; rework, scrap, downtime, and material costs; and costs involved anytime a resource has been wasted in the production of a quality product or the provision of a service. Once determined, costs of quality can be used to justify investments in equipment and processes that reduce the likelihood of defects.

In several of his books, Crosby discusses the concepts of a successful customer versus a satisfied customer. To him, a successful customer is one who receives a product or service which meets his or her expectations the first time. When a customer is merely satisfied, steps may have to have been taken to rework or redo the product or service until the customer is satisfied, for instance, a diner who receives an overcooked piece of meat and then insists that the meal be taken off his or her bill. In the action of satisfying a customer whose expectations were not met the first time, the company has incurred quality costs.

In some circumstances, quality may seem intangible. By discussing five erroneous assumptions about quality, Crosby attempts to make quality more understandable and tangible. The first erroneous assumption, quality means goodness, or luxury, or shininess, or weight, makes quality a relative term. Only when quality is defined in terms of customer requirements can quality be manageable. The second incorrect assumption about quality is that quality is intangible and therefore not measurable. If judged in terms of "goodness," then quality is intangible; however, quality is measurable by the cost of doing things wrong. More precisely, quality costs involve the cost of failures, rework, scrap, inspection, prevention, and loss of customer goodwill.

Closely related to the first two assumptions is the third, which states that there exists "an economics of quality." Here again, one errs in thinking that quality means building "luxuries" into a product or service; rather, quality means that it is more economical to do things right the first time.

Often workers are blamed for being the cause of quality problems. This is the fourth erroneous assumption about quality. Without the proper tools, equipment, and raw materials, workers cannot produce quality products or services. Management must ensure that the necessary items are available to allow workers to perform their jobs well.

The final erroneous assumption that Crosby discusses is that quality originates in the quality department. According to Crosby, the quality department's responsibilities revolve around educating and assisting *other* departments in monitoring and improving quality.

Crosby's quality management philosophy supports creating a greater understanding of the complexities of managing an organization. Much of his focus was on simplifying the concepts surrounding the definition of quality and the need to design systems that support the concept of producing products or supplying services containing zero defects.

Dr. Kaoru Ishikawa

One of the first individuals to encourage total quality control was Dr. Kaoru Ishikawa (1915–1989). Dr. Ishikawa, a contemporary of Dr. Deming and Dr. Juran, transformed their early teachings into the Japanese approach to quality. Because he developed and delivered the first basic quality control course for the Union of Japanese Scientists and Engineers (JUSE) in 1949 and initiated many of Japan's quality programs, he is considered the focus of the quality movement in Japan. Dr. Ishikawa is also credited with initiating quality circles in 1962. Like Dr. Deming and Dr. Juran, his devotion to the advancement of quality merited him the Second Order of the Sacred Treasure from the Emperor of Japan.

To Dr. Ishikawa, quality must be defined broadly. Attention must be focused on quality in every aspect of an organization, including the quality of information, processes, service, price, systems, and people. He played a prominent role in refining the application of different statistical tools to quality problems. Dr. Ishikawa felt that all individuals employed by a company should become involved in quality problem solving. He advocated the use of seven quality tools: histograms; check sheets; scatter diagrams; flowcharts; control charts; Pareto charts; and cause-and-effect, or fish-bone, diagrams. These tools, shown in Figure 2.11, are covered in detail in Chapter 3. Dr. Ishikawa developed the **cause-and-effect diagram** in the early 1950s. This diagram, used to find the root cause of problems, is also called the *Ishikawa diagram*, after its creator, or the *fish-bone diagram*, because of its shape.

Dr. Ishikawa promoted the use of **quality circles,** *teams that meet to solve quality problems related to their own work.* The quality circle concept has been adapted and modified over time to include problem-solving team activities. Membership in a quality circle is often voluntary. Participants receive training in the seven tools, determine appropriate problems to work on, develop solutions, and establish new procedures to lock in quality improvements.

In order to refine organizations' approach to quality, Dr. Ishikawa encouraged the use of a system of principles and major focus areas as a holistic way to achieve business performance improvement. Customers and the processes that fulfill their needs, wants, and expectations were critical to Dr. Ishikawa. He felt that a focus on customer-oriented quality would break down the functional barriers that prevent the creation of defect-free products. In order to do this, processes should be analyzed from the viewpoint of the customer. As quoted in *Quality Progress,* April 2004, like others in the field, he felt that "Quality should not be interpreted in the narrow

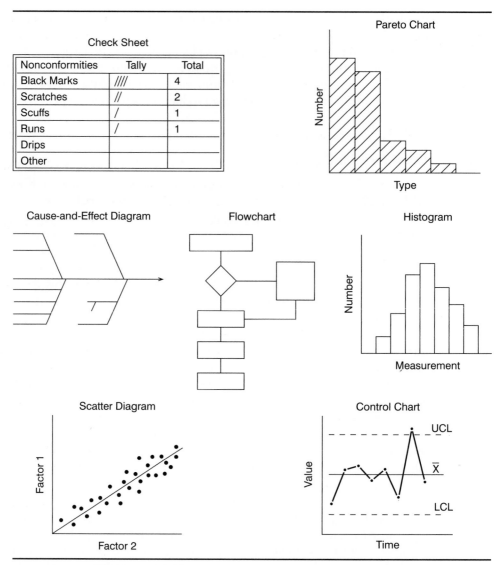

Figure 2.11   Seven Tools of Quality

sense but interpreted broadly, including price, delivery and safety, to satisfy consumer's needs."

As presented in *Quality Progress*, April 2004, his system includes six fundamentals which form the Japanese quality paradigm:

1. All employees should clearly understand the objectives and business reasons behind the introduction and promotion of company-wide quality control.

2. The features of the quality system should be clarified at all levels of the organization and communicated in such a way that the people have confidence in these features.
3. The continuous improvement cycle should be continuously applied throughout the whole company for at least three to five years to develop standardized work. Both statistical quality control and process analysis should be used, and upstream control for suppliers should be developed and effectively applied.
4. The company should define a long-term quality plan and carry it out systematically.
5. The walls between departments or functions should be broken down, and cross-functional management should be applied.
6. Everyone should act with confidence, believing his or her work will bear fruit.

The system also includes four major focus areas designed to influence quality through leadership:

1. **Market-in quality:** Leadership should encourage efforts that enable the organization to determine external customer needs, wants, requirements and expectations. By focusing on these elements and designing processes to deliver value to the market, an organization can increase its business competitiveness.

2. **Worker involvement:** Quality improvement through the use of cross-functional teams enhances an organization's ability to capture improvements to the work processes. Appropriate training in problem-solving tools and techniques is a must.

3. **Quality Begins and Ends with Education:** Education enhances an individual's ability to see the big picture. Education creates a deeper understanding of the activities that must take place in order for the organization to be successful.

4. **Selfless Personal Commitment:** Dr. Ishikawa lived his life as an example of selfless personal commitment. He encouraged others to do likewise, believing that improving the quality of the experience of working together helps improve the quality of life in the world.

Point 4 above summarizes Dr. Ishikawa's tireless, lifelong commitment to furthering the understanding and use of quality tools in order to better the processes that provide products and services for customers.

Dr. Genichi Taguchi

Dr. Genichi Taguchi (1924–) developed methods that seek to improve quality and consistency, reduce losses, and identify key product and process characteristics before production. Dr. Taguchi's methods emphasize consistency of performance and significantly reduced variation. Dr. Taguchi introduced the concept that the total loss to society generated by a product is an important dimension of the quality of a product. In his "loss function" concept, Dr. Taguchi expressed the costs of performance variation (Figure 2.12). Any deviation from target specifications causes loss, he said, even if the variation is within specifications. When the variation is within

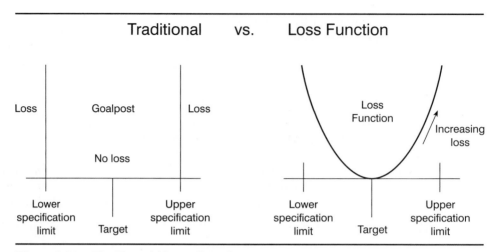

Figure 2.12   The Taguchi Loss Function

specifications, the loss may be in the form of poor fit, poor finish, undersize, over-size, or alignment problems. Scrap, rework, warranties, and loss of goodwill are all examples of losses when the variation extends beyond the specifications. Knowing the loss function helps designers to set product and manufacturing tolerances. Cap-ital expenditures are more easily justified by relating the cost of deviations from the target value to quality costs. Minimizing losses is done by improving the consistency of performance.

Dr. Taguchi is also known for his work in experiment design. Statistically planned experiments can identify the settings of product and process parameters that reduce performance variation. Dr. Taguchi's methods design the experiment to systematically weed out a product's or process's insignificant elements. The focus of experiment ef-forts is then placed on the significant elements. There are four basic steps:

1. Select the process/product to be studied.
2. Identify the important variables.
3. Reduce variation on the important variables through redesign, process improvement, and tolerancing.
4. Open up tolerances on unimportant variables.

The final quality and cost of a manufactured product are determined to a large extent by the engineering designs of the product and its manufacturing process.

SUMMARY

Many different definitions of quality exist, as do many different methods of achiev-ing quality. Similarities exist between each of the advocates presented in this chap-ter. Many of the quality improvement techniques presented in this text have their foundation in the teachings of one or more of these men. The two most prominent men in the field of quality, Dr. Deming and Dr. Juran, were contemporaries, both

Advocate	Definition of Quality	Known For
Shewhart	Two aspects to quality: Subjective: what the customer wants Objective: physical, measurable characteristics of goods or services	Statistical Process Control Charts

Deming	Quality is multidimensional and must be
	    defined in terms of customer satisfaction.
	Quality exists to differing degrees
	    depending on the customer.
		Fourteen Points

Juran	Fitness for use	Processes for Managing Quality

Feigenbaum	Quality must be defined in terms of
	    customer satisfaction. Due to the
	    changing needs of customers, quality
	    is multidimensional and dynamic.
		Total Quality Control Textbook

Crosby	Conformance to requirements. Quality must be defined in order to manage it.	Four Absolutes of Quality
Ishikawa	Quality must be defined comprehensively. Quality should be in every facet of the organization.	Cause and Effect Diagrams Quality Circles
Taguchi	Quality, or lack of it, is a loss to society.	Loss Function

Figure 2.13   Quality Advocates and Their Definitions of Quality

crusading for quality improvement. Both of them, as well as Dr. Crosby agree that problems originate in the system, not the worker. All recognize that problems can only be solved through top management leadership and problem-solving techniques, not colorful banners and slogans. Dr. Deming focused more on applying statistical methods as a remedy for quality problems, where Dr. Juran's experiences lead him to believe that managing for quality is vital. Figure 2.13 briefly summarizes each quality advocate's definition of quality as well as what he is best known for.

Lessons Learned

1. Dr. Shewhart developed statistical process control charts as well as the concepts of controlled and uncontrolled variation.
2. Dr. Deming is known for encouraging companies to manage for quality by defining quality in terms of customer satisfaction.
3. Dr. Deming created his fourteen points as a guide to management.
4. Dr. Juran's process for managing quality includes three phases: quality planning, quality control, and quality improvement.

5. Dr. Feigenbaum defined quality as "a customer determination which is based on the customer's actual experience with the product or service, measured against his or her requirements—stated or unstated, conscious or merely sensed, technically operational or entirely subjective—always representing a moving target in a competitive market."

6. Crosby describes four absolutes of quality and five erroneous assumptions about quality.

7. To Crosby, there is a difference between a successful customer and one who is merely satisfied.

8. Dr. Ishikawa encouraged the use of the seven tools of quality, including the one he developed: the cause and effect diagram.

9. Dr. Taguchi is known for his loss function describing quality and his work in the area of design of experiments. ■

Chapter Problems

1. Describe the three purposes of Dr. Shewhart's control charts.

2. How do Dr. Deming's 14 points interact with each other?

3. Which point from Dr. Deming's 14 points do you agree with the most strongly? Why?

4. Which of Dr. Deming's 14 points do you have a hard time understanding? Why do you think that is?

5. Describe a situation you have experienced where one of Dr. Deming's 14 points applies. Clearly state the point you are referring to. Clearly show how the point relates to your own experience.

6. Dr. Juran presented a concept he called Big Q, Little q. Describe the difference between Big Q and Little q.

7. Describe Dr. Juran's approach to quality improvement.

8. How do the steering/diagnostic arms of Dr. Juran's program work together?

9. a. What is Crosby's definition of quality?
   b. Explain Crosby's system of quality.
   c. What is Crosby's performance standard?
   d. Why do you believe this can or cannot be met?

10. What did Crosby mean when he discussed the difference between satisfied customers and successful customers?

11. People tend to make five erroneous assumptions about quality. What are two of these assumptions and how would you argue against them? Have you seen one of Crosby's erroneous assumptions at work in your own life? Describe the incident(s).

12. What follows is a short story about a worker who has requested additional education and training. Read the story and discuss which point or points

of Dr. Deming's, Dr. Juran's, and Crosby's philosophies are not being followed. Cite at least one point from each man's plan. How did you reach your conclusions? Back up your answers with statements from the story. Support your argument.

Inspector Simmons has been denied permission to attend an educational seminar. Although Simmons has attended only one training course for plumbing inspectors in his 15 years on the job, he will not be permitted to attend a two-week skills enhancement and retraining session scheduled for the coming month. The course devotes a significant amount of time to updating inspectors on the new plumbing regulations. While the regulations concerning plumbing have changed dramatically in the past five years, this is the third request for training in recent years that has been denied.

City commissioners have voted not to send Simmons for the $1,150 course, even though the plumbing guild has offered to pay $750 of the cost. The commissioners based their decision on a lack of funds and a backlog of work resulting from stricter plumbing standards enacted earlier this year. City commissioners do not believe that Simmons's two-week salary should be paid during the time that he is "off work." They also feel that the $400 cost to the city as well as travel expenses are too high. Although the city would benefit from Simmons's enhanced knowledge of the regulations, one city official was quoted as saying, "I don't think he really needs it anyway."

The one dissenting city commissioner argued that this is the first such course to be offered covering the new regulations. She has said, "Things change. Materials change. You can never stop learning, and you can't maintain a quality staff if you don't keep up on the latest information."

13. Briefly summarize the concept Dr. Taguchi is trying to get across with his loss function.

14. Describe Dr. Taguchi's loss function versus the traditional approach to quality.

15. Research Dr. Deming's "red bead" experiment. What does it show people?

16. Research Dr. Deming's funnel experiment. What is the experiment trying to show people?

17. Research Dr. Deming's profound knowledge system. What are its components? How do they work together? Describe each component's critical concept.

CASE STUDY 2.1
Quality and Ethics

In this chapter, the issues of commitment, involvement, motivation, responsibility, authority, training, education, and communication were discussed as they relate to quality in all aspects of a company. The following article presents a disastrous situation that could have been avoided had the principles of TQM been applied.

THE QUALITY-ETHICS CONNECTION*

There is a generalized and widespread perception that the United States is suffering from moral malaise—a breakdown in ethics that has pervaded every corner and stratum of society.

Signposts of this breakdown are everywhere. The current generation in power wrestles ineffectually with the problems it faces, such as hunger, poverty, environmental degradation, urban decay, the collapse of economic systems, and corruption in business and government.

This moral malaise is infecting U.S. institutions at the highest levels. Along with murderers, rapists, muggers, and thieves, there are religious leaders, political leaders, banking officials, and other business executives being carted off to jail.

A younger generation is questioning at a very early age whether it is realistic to expect morality in contemporary society. The answer to this question—and possibly a solution to this dilemma—can be found in the cross-application of quality management theory and the realm of ethics. There is a striking similarity between the issues Americans are facing in ethics and the issues that quality professionals are facing in U.S. businesses.

Ethical Base Not at Fault

In many ways, the apparent decline in individuals' and institutions' ethical behavior parallels the now well-understood decline in global competitiveness of the nation's industrial base. The United States became the world's role model in part because of a political system that recognized, for the first time in human history, the importance of individual rights and responsibilities in maintaining a free (and moral) society. Yet there is now a growing frustration among Americans because their ability to exercise those rights and responsibilities has been seriously impaired.

---

*This article by Marion W. Steeples, president of Resources for Quality, Denver, Colorado, appeared in the June 1994 issue of *Quality Progress*, the journal of the American Society for Quality, and is reproduced here with the permission of the Society.

Many people attribute the moral crisis problem to a breakdown in the ethical character of too many individuals within the society. They often cite the decline of the nuclear family, increased tolerance for alternative lifestyles, drug and alcohol abuse, disrespect for authority, or some other lapse of traditional values as the source of the malaise.

Yet, if the public were surveyed on their ethical beliefs, the results would likely show that, overall, Americans hold moral beliefs similar in most respects to those of their parents and grandparents. While some of the particulars of what constitutes moral behavior might have changed, Americans still hold to a personal ethic that emphasizes honesty, personal responsibility, tolerance, and good citizenship.

So the question becomes: If personal ethics have not substantially changed, what is the source of the ethical breakdown? The national rhetoric about ethics has overtones of despair in it; there is a belief that the individual has somehow lost the will to act ethically. Solutions tend to center on the need to indoctrinate students, from the earliest ages through college, in the finer points of their civic and ethical responsibilities.

This is a familiar tune to quality professionals. In U.S. factories, employees are repeatedly called to account for every sort of problem when, in fact, the source of the problem is not the employees or a department, but the system itself. A typical response to problems is exhorting employees to work harder, more diligently, and with greater care and attention to detail. The implication is that employees don't care about the outcome of their work.

To the contrary, employees typically come to work with the intention of doing the best job possible but are stymied and discouraged at every level in the system. Employees are consistently prevented from doing the right things by systems that discourage individual initiative, improved efficiency, and improved quality.

What if America's so-called "ethical crisis" were the result of similar structural deficiencies? What if the crisis were simply a matter of societal structures that do not support and sustain ethical behavior?

Societal and Corporate Structures

In my work as a quality practitioner and an examiner for the Malcolm Baldrige National Quality Award, I have seen a strong correlation between quality and ethics. Quality is the standard by which Americans measure the goods and services they value. Ethics is the standard by which Americans measure their own behavior and that of institutions.

In virtually every case, when a company improved quality, ethics also improved. This was evident not only in the employees' actions (e.g., decreased absenteeism, decreased internal thefts, and increased participation), but also in the company's actions (e.g., examining such conceptual problems as defining corporate purpose, introducing long-term thinking and integrated planning, and determining internal and external customers' needs and acting on those needs). These improvements occurred merely as a latent benefit of quality improvement. Improved ethics was rarely a stated goal of the quality improvement programs when they were initiated. Yet the benefit is real and universal.

The Great Chicago Flood

The Chicago flood of 1992 is a classic example of how a system breakdown resulted in what is typically attributed to individual moral lapses. In mid-April 1992, the Chicago River broke through a crack in a tunnel beneath the Chicago Loop's business district, and businesses in the nation's third largest city came to a halt. Water snaked through the 50-mile labyrinth of century-old freight tunnels, and 250 million gallons rushed into commercial-area basements. Electrical power was shut off to avert the possibility of explosions from transformers shorting out. More than 200,000 people were evacuated, and more than 120 buildings were dark for two days.

To stem the tide, crews labored around the clock drilling holes and plugging them with concrete. It took more than two weeks for the U.S. Army Corps of Engineers to drain the water.

This devastating underground flood took a heavy toll. The Chicago Board of Trade shut down, hampering worldwide trading, with crippling economic effects. City Hall, several office towers, and many retailers were closed. Fifteen buildings were unable to operate for at least a week. Estimates put the price tag of this snafu at $1.7 billion.

The irony is that, for an estimated $10,000, the disaster could have been prevented. On Jan. 14, 1992, two cable TV workers discovered a 20-foot-by-6-foot crack in the tunnel. Standing knee deep in water and mud, the crew videotaped the event, recording "This is a cave-in!"

The cable TV crew, however, had trouble finding the correct city government official to which they could report the incident—the local government was in the midst of a major reorganization to increase efficiency.

In late February, the cable TV workers were finally able to discuss the situation with the appropriate city official; they urged that the tunnel site be inspected. But when they talked to the city official again on March 2, they learned that little had been done. Finally, a city worker led an inspection, took photographs of the subterranean leak, and then waited a week for a drugstore to develop the prints.

On April 2, the city's bridge engineer sent a memo urging immediate action to his superior, the acting transportation commissioner. Two bids were obtained to repair the crack, but both were turned down in an attempt to get a lower price. It was business as usual.

On April 13, the tunnel burst. On April 14, the governor of Illinois declared Chicago a disaster area.

The city's response was predictable: Heads rolled in an effort to assign blame to individuals within the system. On April 15, Chicago's mayor fired the acting commissioner. Subsequently, an engineer was discharged and five others were disciplined. The city blamed individuals in the system without addressing the structural problems that made such a debacle possible in the first place. Yet, from a quality viewpoint, the system's inefficiencies are immediately apparent.

How Chicago Went Wrong

Like many traditional U.S. corporations, the city of Chicago suffered from structural problems generated by the specialization of functions and a horizontal management structure that made individual initiative to take positive action next to impossible. As quality slips through the functional cracks of these outmoded systems, ethics are not far behind. Any system that values efficiency over effectiveness also devalues ethical behavior.

Unfortunately, for the individual citizen or bureaucrat who still attempts to behave ethically, the fragmentation of the structures that make up an organization, such as a large city government, makes taking action difficult, if not impossible.

Before history has made its final judgment on the Chicago flood, it behooves those within the quality profession to point out that the emperor had no clothes on. Far from being assignable to the incompetence of one or more city employees, the disaster that overtook downtown Chicago was the obvious—and predictable—result of the fragmentation of the city's organizational structure.

Chicago was not acting as one organization but as many—each one with its own set of rules, agenda, and rewards for success. No individual within those separate departments has a stake in the final outcome, only a stake in his or her part.

The Chicago flood dramatizes what is the rule and not the exception in most U.S. organizations, public or private. Whenever there is a break in responsibilities and accountabilities, there is no structural way to ensure that responsible, ethical actions will result. To the contrary, the system in Chicago consistently frustrated every attempt by individuals to behave ethically.

What Could Have Made It Right?

For openers, the organization needed clearer direction and goals. The city government needed to build its structure based on these goals to ensure that connections within and between the departments and agencies were sound. These human connections work well only if an integrated organizational structure that aligns functions is in place.

When each department stands alone, the support needed to enable employees to do the right thing is nonexistent. Employees cannot be expected to continually and repeatedly go to heroic measures simply to perform their jobs. Some people can't do it; they simply don't know how to maneuver around the system. Others won't do it; it's simply too hard and asks too much, and the rewards of bucking the system are dubious. A faulty system can make employees powerless to make positive contributions. There are simply too many barriers.

It is important to reiterate that, at every stage in the flood fiasco, attempts were made to act ethically. The cable TV crew recognized the problem and attempted to notify the appropriate authorities, but the news was not quickly relayed or responded to. The various levels of engineers attempted to solve the problem, but they couldn't break through the layers of bureaucracy in time. Like the crumbling concrete in the tunnel, the decades-old policies and procedures became deadly impediments to the exercise of good judgment. The deluge of water that stopped downtown Chicago served only to mark the beginning of the challenging road that now lies before it and every city government. The old system is inadequate and, as thousands of Chicago residents can attest, the results have been disastrous.

The dollar cost for correcting things gone wrong, as in the Chicago flood, takes a heavy toll on the taxpayers. Moreover, there is the toll of disillusionment and a loss of trust, as was witnessed in the savings-and-loan debacle, in which the old system of checks and balances collapsed completely.

How Can Americans Make a Change?

Chicago's century-old tunnel system was once used to carry freight; now it carries electronic and communications gear. A system that once helped Chicago be productive is now a problem. Unfortunately, Chicago's situation represents business as usual in much of America. The organizational structures that Americans created during the industrial age don't always translate well in the information age. An earlier age of specialization has led to the current age of frustration.

Out of seemingly separate movements, quality and ethics have emerged as top issues in the national agenda. The issue of quality has been forced by economic reality: In a global economy, quality-leveraged companies are simply more competitive. Quality, in other words, provides a system for living up to the expectations and addressing the needs of customers.

In a strikingly similar fashion, the issue of ethics has emerged out of a sense that the United States' long-standing reputation as the model of democracy and as a moral force in the world has eroded. Americans consider themselves a moral people, dedicated to the high ideals laid out in such documents as the Constitution and Bill of Rights.

But citizens from Los Angeles, CA, to Washington, DC, are grappling with the apparent inability of U.S. systems to live up to their ethical expectations or to reasonably address their legitimate needs. They feel helpless when dealing with institutions that seem out of touch with reality and that don't have an innate sense of right and wrong. Such frustrations have grown beyond "big government" and "big industry." People encounter unresponsive, apparently amoral systems daily in such places as local public schools, grocery stores, doctors' offices, and banks.

The old systems make it difficult at best and impossible at worst for institutions to live up to their ethical expectations and to address Americans' legitimate needs. Thus, new systems need to be created—and that is where total quality management (TQM) comes in.

TQM provides a model for systematically creating responsive societal structures. It can build individual responsibility and initiative back into impervious and rigid systems. Reconfigured systems, based on a solid foundation of vision and purpose, ensure that rational, long-term thinking, rather than expediency, guides organizational decisions.

TQM offers a systematic way for organizations to link values and value. Experience shows that total quality companies are successful because they translate what customers value into quality requirements and practices. In that context, ethics can be viewed simply as a primary set of customer values. Creating ethical systems is a matter of building ethical expectations into systems and providing support to employees so that they can live up to those expectations.

By integrating the functions of an organization and by connecting quality and ethics, institutions can provide what is of value to customers and provide what is valuable to society. They must ensure the integrity of systems (quality) and the integrity of people (ethics). The absence of one affects the other.

TQM has proven itself as a way to rebuild infrastructure by integrating and aligning operations to provide value. But the paradox is that, inasmuch as quality systems can assist Americans' search for continued ethical improvement, quality itself is not possible without ethics. Quality theory provides a means for integrating systems to provide value. But only an ongoing discussion of ethics will provide a notion of what is meant by "value."

 Assignment

1. Discuss how the specific issues of communication, responsibility, authority, commitment, and motivation relate to quality in all aspects of a company's operation.
2. Discuss quality issues as they pertain to the Chicago incident. To organize your discussion, consider the following questions:

   - Who is management in this instance?
   - What was their level of commitment and involvement?
   - How were they at motivating employees?
   - Who had the responsibility?
   - Who had the authority?
   - Were the employees appropriately educated and trained?
   - Why did communication break down?

3

Quality Improvement: Problem Solving

 ■ *Learning Opportunities:*

1. To understand and utilize a systematic problem-solving process; to learn to ask the right questions, present information clearly and unambiguously, and make judgments based on the information
2. To understand and utilize a variety of techniques for effective problem diagnosis and problem solving
3. To learn to diagnose and analyze problems that cause variation in the manufacturing, process, and service industries ■

*H*ave you ever been lost? What is the first thing you need to do before proceeding? If you answered "find out where you are," then you realize that chance turnings may or may not get you to your desired destination.

When it came to problem solving, even Dr. Walter Shewhart realized that

All chance is but direction thou canst not see.

Problem solving is a bit like being lost. It isn't until you find out where you are that you can figure out where you need to go. Rather than take a chance, effective problem solvers figure out where they stand, what the problem really is, and what the cause of the problem is before proposing any solutions. This chapter seeks to teach problem-solving methods to help identify problems and their root causes.

PROBLEM SOLVING

Our plans miscarry because they have no aim. When a man does not know what harbor he is making for, no wind is the right wind.

Seneca, 4 B.C. – A.D. 65

In the day-to-day process of creating and providing products and services for customers, problems crop up. We all know it's true and often our workdays involve running from one problem to another, firefighting. We barely manage to tamp down the flames of one problem when another flares up elsewhere. To a certain extent, we're responsible for our own plight. Often, we attack problems with no plan and as the above quote points out, none of our efforts may be the right effort.

Problem solving, *the isolation and analysis of a problem and the development of a permanent solution*, is an integral part of the quality-improvement process. To solve problems effectively, people need to be trained in correct problem-solving procedures and techniques. Utilizing these procedures and techniques strengthens our ability to find permanent solutions to eliminate the problems. Rather than approach problems like lost drivers randomly turning on different streets in the hope of finding their destination, effective problem-solvers realize that the hit-or-miss approach to tackling problems may leave the real problem unsolved, the real root cause undiscovered, the real destination not reached.

STEPS IN PROCESS IMPROVEMENT

In order to locate and eliminate the root or real cause of a problem, problem solving should follow a logical, systematic method. Other, less systematic attempts at problem solving run the risk of attempting to eliminate the symptoms associated with the problem rather than eliminating the problem at its cause.

EXAMPLE 3.1   Root Cause Analysis

RQM Inc., an automobile manufacturer, purchases most of their parts from suppliers and assembles them at their final assembly plant. Over the past six months, they have been experiencing intermittent smoke/odor problems when the completed vehicles are started for the first time to drive off the assembly line. The problem does not occur with any pattern. Sometimes it reappears several times in a shift, sometimes it will not happen for days. The smoke is thick and white and the worse the smoke, the worse the odor. The odor carries a strong scent of ammonia and is causing the operators to complain of sudden violent headaches. Several operators have requested transfers to other positions.

Since this is a serious safety concern, a variety of Band-Aids were immediately proposed, such as starting all of the vehicles in a curtained area or inserting the tailpipe into a hose vented to the outside. Management recognized that these suggestions would merely cover up the problem rather than tackle its root cause. Instead, they formed a corrective-action problem-solving team to isolate the root cause of the problem and determine a solution. Cognizant that action must be taken for the short term, the operators in the area were required to wear respirators, and exhaust fans were temporarily added to the area.

While searching for a root cause of the problem, team members spoke with operators to see if they had any idea what the source of the white smoke might be. Several operators suggested that the team check the exhaust pipes. In some shipments, excess oil has been found in the exhaust pipes. If the pipes are soaked in oil, they are rejected, but perhaps some are getting through to assembly. Several of the people questioned didn't think the oil would cause a smell as bad as what was occurring.

At the same time that the team was discussing possible sources of the smoke with the operators, they also requested that air samples be taken during vehicle start-ups. Analysis of the air samples revealed that ammine was present in large amounts when the vehicles smoked during start-up. If the vehicles did not smoke on start-up, ammine was not present. The presence of ammine accounts for the ammonia smell.

Since the engine, manifolds, and catalytic converter parts come from several suppliers, the team set out to investigate the types of materials present, either in the finished parts, or during their assembly, that might release an ammonia type smell. At first, the team suspected that adhesives containing ammine were used during assembly. However, further investigation revealed that no adhesives containing ammine were used during vehicle or part assembly, thus ruling out adhesives as the root cause or source of the ammine.

While talking with suppliers, it came to light that the catalytic converter is coated with palladium in an ammine solution. Since this was the only source of ammine located, the team studied the process of manufacturing the converters. In the current process, the converters were coated with palladium in an ammine solution and then conveyed to an oven for drying. A gap was left on the conveyor between different lots of converters. When the converters were in the oven, hot air was forced up from the bottom to dry the converters. Team members determined that the gap between lots allowed an escape path for the heated air. Escaping hot air lowered the operating temperature to 250° Celsius, not the required 300°. The airflow and lower temperature dried the converters inconsistently, thus the reason for the intermittent nature of the problem. For those palladium coated converters that were not dried entirely, the heat created by the car engine during operation completed the drying, causing the white smoke and ammonia odor upon start-up. Once the converter dried, the smoke and smell disappeared. So this problem was never experienced by the customer, only during initial start-up.

Having determined the root cause of the problem, the team, working with the converter supplier, made the following changes. A jig is now placed between the different converter lots. This jig separates the lots but does not allow an escape path for hot air out of the oven. Other minor modifications were made to the oven to allow it to hold a temperature of 300° Celsius.

Having located the root cause of the problem, once the changes were made to the process, the smoke/odor problem disappeared. Though the team was disbanded, a representative from the team was assigned the duty of monitoring the situation to ensure that the problem does not reappear.

What is the best way for companies to make improvements? How do they prevent errors from occurring? How should they approach a situation like this? The problem-solving techniques presented in this chapter will help.

Problem-solving efforts should be objective and focused on finding the root cause of the problem. Proposed solutions, when implemented, should prevent a recurrence of the problem. Controls should be in place to monitor the solution to study its effectiveness. Teamwork, coordinated and directed problem solving, problem-solving techniques,

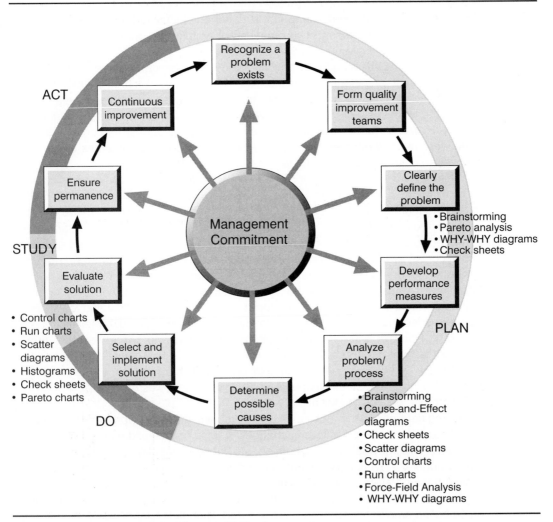

Figure 3.1   Problem-Solving Steps with Tools

and statistical training are all part of ensuring that problems are isolated, analyzed, and corrected. The concepts, tools and techniques taught in this chapter are integral to continuous improvement and Six Sigma methodologies.

Introduced in Chapter 2, Dr. Deming's Plan-Do-Study-Act (PDSA) cycle is the foundation for the systematic approach to problem solving that will followed in this chapter (Figure 3.1). As mentioned in Chapter 1, significant similarities exist between Six Sigma's Define, Measure, Analyze, Improve, Control (DMAIC) cycle and the PDSA cycle (Figure 3.2). These approaches to problem solving also share tools and techniques. Seven of these tools, flowcharts, Pareto charts, cause-and-effect

Define, Measure, and Analyze	Plan
1. Select appropriate metrics Key process output variables	1. Recognize a problem exists
2. Determine how these metrics will be tracked over time	2. Form a quality improvement team
3. Determine the current baseline performance of project/process	3. Clearly define the problem
4. Determine key process input variables that drive the key process output variables	4. Develop performance measures
	5. Analyze problem/process
5. Determine what changes need to be made to the key process input variables in order to positively affect the key process output variables	6. Determine possible causes
Improve	**Do**
6. Make the changes	7. Select and implement the solution
Control	**Study and Act**
7. Determine whether the changes have positively affected the key process output variables	8. Evaluate the solution
	9. Ensure permanence
8. If the changes made result in performance improvements, establish control of the key process input variables at the new levels.	10. Continuous improvement

Figure 3.2   Comparing PDSA with DMAIC

diagrams, check sheets, force-field diagrams, WHY-WHY diagrams, and scatter diagrams, will be discussed in this chapter. Other tools, such as control charts, histograms, and design of experiments, are topics covered in later chapters.

PLAN

In problem solving, both the PDSA cycle and Six Sigma's DMAIC steps place a strong emphasis on studying the current conditions and planning how to approach a problem. Well planned problem-solving efforts look at processes and products to determine how they are presently performing.

Step 1. Plan: Recognizing a Problem Exists and Establishing Priorities

Information concerning the problem(s) may have come from a number of different sources, departments, employees, or customers. Management involvement and commitment is crucial to the success of any major problem-solving process. Management should participate in the recognition and identification of problems, since they are ultimately responsible for seeing that problems are isolated and solved.

During the problem recognition stage, the problems will be outlined in very general terms. At this point in the problem-solving process, management has recognized or identified that a problem or problems exist. As yet, the specifics of the problem(s) have not been clearly defined.

An excellent way for management to get directly involved in the problem-solving process is for management to select problem-solving teams, give direction as to the problems to be tackled, and provide the personnel and financial resources as well as the knowledge to solve the problem.

Step 2. Plan: Forming a Quality Improvement Team

Once a problem situation has been recognized and before the problem is attacked, an ***interdisciplinary problem-solving or quality improvement team*** must be created. *This team will be given the task of investigating, analyzing, and finding a solution to the problem situation within a specified time frame. This problem-solving team consists of people who have knowledge of the process or problem under study.* Generally, this team is composed of those closest to the problem as well as a few individuals from middle management with enough power to effect change. The team may consist of people from engineering, manufacturing, purchasing, sales, and/or design departments, perhaps, even an outside vendor or a representative from the customer base. During the problem-solving process, the team can be supplemented on an as-needed basis with people who have expertise in the areas directly related to the problem solution. Upon the resolution of a project, the team will be disbanded or reorganized to deal with another problem.

Since a team is composed of a group of individuals who are united by a common goal, the best teamwork will occur when the individuals focus on the team's objectives rather than personal motives. While working together, team members must understand

and agree on the goals of the team. They must establish and adhere to team ground rules for behavior and performance expectations. To ensure harmony in the team, all members must participate and the responsibilities and duties must be fairly distributed. This means that each team member must understand what his/her role is in the completion of the project. Knowledge of how internal or external constraints affect the project is also helpful. Team members must possess a variety of skills, including problem-solving skills, planning skills, facilitation and communication skills, and feedback and conflict management skills.

For teams to work, management must set clear goals that are aligned with the mission and strategic direction of the firm. When management sets the direction, the team is much more focused and tends not to get bogged down in the problem-selection process. The team must know the scope and boundaries that it must work within. Management must communicate how the team's progress and performance will be measured. To be successful, teams need the appropriate skills in a supportive organizational culture and the authority to do the job that they have been asked to do. Management can do a lot to rid the team of the barriers that inhibit its performance. These barriers include: inadequate release time, territorial behavior from involved functional areas, lack of training, inadequate support systems, lack of guidance or direction, and lack of recognition. Upper management's sincere interest and support in the resolution of the problem is evidenced by their willingness to commit money and time for training in problem solving and facilitation. The teams will quickly become ineffective if the solutions they propose are consistently turned down or ignored. Management support will be obvious in management's visibility, diagnostic support, recognition, and limited interference.

Many different types of teams exist, including: management teams comprised of heads of departments to do strategic planning; cross-functional teams with representatives from a large variety of areas for the design or development of complex systems; self-directed work teams made up of employees grouped by complementary skills in order to carry out production processes; and project teams, which are often temporary groups of individuals from the appropriate functional areas with the necessary skills to work on a specific task.

EXAMPLE 3.2   Plastics and Dashes: Steps 1 and 2. Recognizing the Problem and Forming a Quality Improvement Team

Plastics and Dashes Inc. (P&D) supplies instrument panels and other plastic components for automobile manufacturers. Recently their largest customer informed them that there have been an excessive number of customer complaints and warranty claims concerning the P&D instrument panel. The warranty claims have amounted to over $200,000, including the cost of parts and labor. In response to this problem, Plastics and Dashes' management has initiated a corrective action request (Figure 3.3) and formed an improvement team to investigate. The steps they will take to solve this problem are detailed in the examples throughout this chapter. Q

CORRECTIVE/PREVENTIVE ACTION REQUEST

TO DEPARTMENT/VENDOR: | INSTRUMENT PANEL

DATE: | 8/31/2004 | ORIGINATOR: | R. SMITH

FINDING/NONCONFORMITY: | CUSTOMER WARRENTY CLAIMS FOR INSTRUMENT PANEL 360ID ARE
EXCESSIVE FOR THE TIME PERIOD 1/1/04–8/1/04

APPARENT CAUSE: | CLAIMS ARE HIGH IN NUMBER AND CITE ELECTRICAL PROBLEMS AND
NOISE/LOOSE COMPONENTS

ASSIGNED TO: | M. COOK | DATE RESPONSE DUE: | 10/1/04
ASSIGNED TO: | Q. SHEPHERD | DATE RESPONSE DUE: | 10/1/04

IMMEDIATE CORRECTIVE ACTION:
REPLACE COMPONENTS AS NEEDED; REPLACE ENTIRE DASH AT NO COST TO CUSTOMER
IF NECESSARY

ROOT CAUSE:

PREVENTIVE ACTION:

EFFECTIVE DATE:

ASSIGNEE | DATE | ASSIGNEE | DATE

QUALITY ASSURANCE | DATE | R. SMITH | 8/3/2004
| | ORIGINATOR | DATE

COMMENTS/AUDIT/REVIEW: | SATISFACTORY | UNSATISFACTORY

NAME | DATE

Figure 3.3 Plastics and Dashes: Corrective Action Request Form, Example 3.2

Step 3. Plan: Defining the Problem

Once established, the quality-improvement team sets out to clearly define the problem and its scope. A clear problem definition will help the team focus. Several techniques exist to help team members determine the true nature of their problem. The most basic of these is the check sheet.

Technique: Check Sheets

A check sheet is a data-recording device. A check sheet is essentially a list of categories. As events occur in these categories, a check or mark is placed on the check sheet in the appropriate category. Given a list of items or events, the user of a check sheet marks down the number of times a particular event or item occurs. In essence, the user checks off occurrences. Check sheets are often used in conjunction with other quality assurance techniques. Be careful not to confuse a check sheet with a checklist. The latter lists all of the important steps or actions that need to take place, or things that need to be remembered.

EXAMPLE 3.3   Plastics and Dashes: Check Sheets

The problem-solving team at Plastics and Dashes has a great deal of instrument panel warranty information to sort through. In order to gain a better understanding of the situation, they have decided to investigate each warranty claim from the preceding six months. A check sheet has been chosen to record the types of claims and to determine how many of each type exists.

To create a check sheet, they first brainstormed a list of potential warranty problems. The categories they came up with include: loose instrument panel components, noisy instrument panel components, electrical problems, improper installation of the instrument panel or its components, inoperative instrument panel components, and warped instrument panel. The check sheet created from this list will be used by the investigators to record the types of warranty problems. As the investigators make their determination, a mark is made in the appropriate category of the check sheet (Figure 3.4). Once all the warranty information has been reviewed, these sheets will be collected and turned over to the team to be tallied. The information from these sheets will help the team focus their problem-solving efforts. **Q**

Technique: Pareto Analysis

*The **Pareto chart** is a graphical tool for ranking causes of problems from the most significant to the least significant.* Dr. Juran popularized the Pareto principle for use in problem identification. First identified by Vilfredo Pareto, a 19th century engineer and economist, the Pareto principle, also known as the 80–20 rule, originally pointed out that the greatest portion of wealth in Italy was concentrated in a few families. Dr. Juran, stating 80% of problems come from 20% of causes, used Pareto's work to encourage management to focus their improvement efforts on the 20% "vital few."

Loose instrument panel components	///// ///// ///// ///// ///// ///// //
Noisy instrument panel components	///// ///// /////
Electrical problems	///// ///
Improper installation of the instrument panel or its components	///// ///// /////
Inoperative instrument panel components	///// ///// //
Warped instrument panel	/////
Other	

Figure 3.4   Plastics and Dashes: Warranty Panel Information Partially Completed Data Recording Check Sheet, Example 3.3

Pareto charts are a graphical display of the 80–20 rule. These charts are applicable to any problem that can be separated into categories of occurrences.

While the split is not always 80–20, the Pareto chart is a visual method of identifying which problems are most significant. Pareto charts allow users to separate the vital few problems from the trivial many. The use of Pareto charts also limits the tendency of people to focus on the most recent problems rather than on the most important problems.

A Pareto chart is constructed using the following steps:

1. Select the subject for the chart. This can be a particular product line exhibiting problems, or a department, or a process.
2. Determine what data need to be gathered. Determine if numbers, percentages, or costs are going to be tracked. Determine which nonconformities or defects will be tracked.
3. Gather data related to the quality problem. Be sure that the time period during which data will be gathered is established.
4. Use a check sheet to gather data. Record the total numbers in each category. Categories will be the types of defects or nonconformities.
5. Determine the total number of nonconformities and calculate the percent of the total in each category.
6. Determine the costs associated with the nonconformities or defects.
7. Select the scales for the chart. Y axis scales are typically the number of occurrences, number of defects, dollar loss per category, or percent. The x axis usually displays the categories of nonconformities, defects, or items of interest.
8. Draw a Pareto chart by organizing the data from the largest category to the smallest. Include all pertinent information on the chart.
9. Analyze the chart or charts. The largest bars represent the vital few problems. If there does not appear to be one or two major problems, recheck the categories to determine if another analysis is necessary.

EXAMPLE 3.4   Plastics and Dashes: Constructing a Pareto Chart

At Plastics and Dashes, the team members working on the instrument panel warranty issue first discussed in Example 3.2 have decided to begin their investigation by creating a Pareto chart.

Step 1. Select the Subject for the Chart.   The subject of the chart is instrument panel warranty claims.

Step 2. Determine What Data Need to Be Gathered.   The data to be used to create the chart are the different reasons customers have brought their cars in for instrument panel warranty work. Cost information on instrument panel warranty work is also available.

Step 3. Gather the Data Related to the Quality Problem.   The team has determined it is appropriate to use the warranty information for the preceding six months. Copies of warranty information have been distributed to the team.

Step 4. Make a Check Sheet of the Gathered Data and Record the Total Numbers in Each Category.   Based on the warranty information, the team has chosen the following categories for the x axis of the chart: loose instrument panel components, noisy instrument panel components, electrical problems, improper installation of the instrument panel or its components, inoperative instrument panel components, and warped instrument panels (Figure 3.4).

Step 5. Determine the Total Number of Nonconformities and Calculate the Percent of the Total in Each Category.   From the six months of warranty information, they also have the number of occurrences for each category:

1. Loose instrument panel components	355	41.5%
2. Noisy instrument panel components	200	23.4%
3. Electrical problems	110	12.9%
4. Improper installation of the instrument panel or its components	80	9.4%
5. Inoperative instrument panel components	65	7.6%
6. Warped instrument panel	45	5.2%

Warranty claims for instrument panels total 855.

Step 6. Determine the Costs Associated with the Nonconformities or Defects.   The warranty claims also provided cost information associated with each category.

1. Loose instrument panel components	$115,000
2. Noisy instrument panel components	$25,000
3. Electrical problems	$55,000
4. Improper installation of the instrument panel or its components	$10,000
5. Inoperative instrument panel components	$5,000
6. Warped instrument panel	$1,000

Step 7. Select the Scales for the Chart.   The team members have decided to create two Pareto charts, one for number of occurrences and the other for costs. On

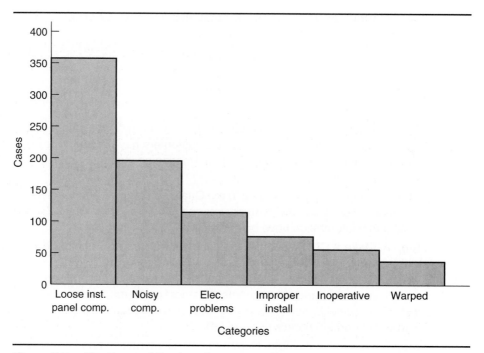

Figure 3.5   Plastics and Dashes: Instrument Panel Problems by Warranty Claim Type

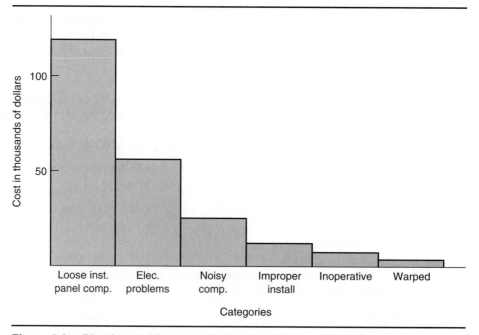

Figure 3.6   Plastics and Dashes: Costs of Instrument Panel Problems by Warranty Type

each chart, the x axis will display the warranty claim categories. The y axis will be scaled appropriately to show all the data.

Step 8. Draw a Pareto Chart by Organizing the Data from the Largest Category to the Smallest.   The Pareto charts are shown in Figures 3.5 and 3.6. A Pareto chart for percentages could also be created.

Step 9. Analyze the Charts.   When analyzing the charts, it is easy to see that the most prevalent warranty claim is loose instrument panel components. It makes sense that loose components might also be noisy and the Pareto chart (Figure 3.5) reflects this, noisy instrument panel components being the second most frequently occurring warranty claim. The second chart, in Figure 3.6, tells a slightly different story. The category "loose instrument panel components" has the highest costs; however, "electrical problems" has the second-highest costs.

   At this point, although all the warranty claims are important, the Pareto chart has shown that efforts should be concentrated on investigating the causes of loose instrument panel components. Solving this warranty claim would significantly affect warranty numbers and costs.

REAL TOOLS FOR REAL LIFE

Improving Servo Motors Quality Using Pareto Diagrams

Auto manufacturers often purchase assemblies, subassemblies, components, and parts for automobiles from suppliers and sub-suppliers. In this example, a sub-supplier makes servo motors for the HVAC system supplier. Servo motors activate each time you change the direction of airflow on the control panel of your car. Whenever you rotate the control to switch from floor to defrost or from vent to floor, etc., the servo motor kicks in to move the flaps inside the HVAC system so that the air comes out of the desired vent.

   In order to maintain the quality of the servo motors, critical-to-quality aspects of production line activities are monitored using Pareto diagrams. In this situation, the casing of the servo motor is checked for mounting bracket straightness, mounting hole size, and casing condition. Process engineers have created a Pareto diagram based on the following data:

Category	Occurrences
Bent Mounting Bracket	2
Casing	
Damaged	3
Cracked	3
Broken	10
Scratched	6
Hole size	
Too big	30
Too small	24

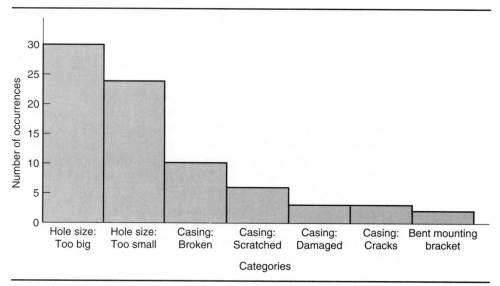

Figure 3.7   Real Tools for Real Life: Preliminary Pareto Diagram for Servo Motors

Figure 3.7 shows the Pareto diagram constructed by placing the categories on the x axis and arranging the categories according to the number of occurrences from highest to lowest.

Hole size has emerged with the greatest number of occurrences, 30 holes being too big and 24 holes too small. Based on this information, the process engineers know to focus their process improvement efforts on reducing hole size variation in

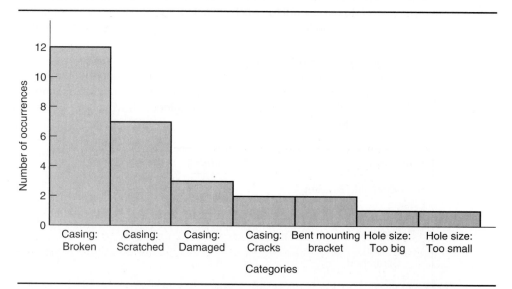

Figure 3.8   Real Tools for Real Life: Pareto Diagram Following Process Improvements

order to allow their improvements to have the greatest positive impact on the process. Determining the root cause of the problem will allow them to take more effective countermeasures to eliminate the source of variation in the hole-drilling process. Investigations revealed that loose drill bit and jig loading were the primary sources of variation in the hole-drilling process.

Steps were taken to replace the jigs in order to eliminate both problems. Operators received training in how to properly load a part into the jig. The new jig makes an audible click when the part is correctly seated in the jig. They also tested new drill designs to determine which style worked best and lasted the longest for the process. The test drills were run for 1000 cycles to determine how long the chucks stayed in place until the drill bit loosened. The drills have also been placed on a preventive maintenance program which will keep them in good operating condition until they have worked too many cycles and need to be replaced.

A second Pareto diagram (Figure 3.8), constructed following the installation of the new jigs and the use of the new drill shows that hole size variation has been significantly reduced. In keeping with Deming's philosophy of continuous improvement, the team has decided to study damage to the servo motor casing next.

REAL TOOLS FOR REAL LIFE

PLC, Inc. Announces Improvements to Reduce Supplier Parts Shortages

For several months, PLC, Inc. has been experiencing shortages of 250 parts per week on average. A team was formed to find ways to reduce these shortages. After much discussion and many meetings, the team proposed the following corrective actions to reduce shortages:

- Start contract negotiations with suppliers earlier
- Establish award fees and incentives
- Long term agreements with suppliers
- Allow supplier to ship parts 30 days early
- Add inventory buffer
- Dedicated personnel to process returns
- Add bank times to schedules
- Implement a "War Room" to monitor the status of parts delivery
- Add shop floor status meetings
- Additional expediting
- Dedicated resource teams

The team was congratulated for their outstanding effort and the recommendations were implemented immediately. Six months later a follow-up review of shortages revealed that the implemented actions did not reduce shortages, in fact, they actually increased to 300 parts per week.

One of the managers in the review meeting asked whether or not a root cause analysis had been conducted to determine reasons for shortages. None of the original

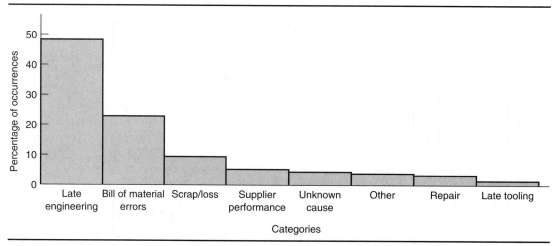

Figure 3.9   Real Tools for Real Life: Pareto Diagram for Late Parts

team members remembered conducting any formal analysis of the situation. A short while later, another team was formed to conduct the analysis.

The root cause analysis identified the following reason for late parts:

- Late Tooling   1.4%
- Other   3.9%
- Scrap/Loss   9.5%
- Repair   3.5%
- Unknown Cause   4.4%
- Supplier Performance   5.3%
- Late Engineering   48.4%
- Bill of Material errors   22.7%

This information was placed into a Pareto diagram (Figure 3.9) and presented to management. It was immediately obvious why the original recommendations failed to produce any improvements. They weren't dealing with the root cause of the problem: Late Engineering and Bill of Material errors. Another team, comprised of people associated with engineering and bill of material creation was formed to develop solutions for these causes.

Step 4. Plan: Developing Performance Measures

Measures of performance enable problem solvers to answer the question, How will we know the right changes have been made? Measures may be financial in nature, customer-oriented, or pertinent to the internal workings of the organization. Examples of financial measures are costs, return on investment, value added, and asset utilization.

Financial measures usually focus on determining whether or not the changes made will enhance an organization's financial performance. Companies use customer-oriented measures to determine whether or not their plans and strategies keep the existing customers satisfied, bring in new customers, and encourage customers to return. These measures may include response times, delivery times, product or service functionality, price, quality, or other intangible factors. Measures pertinent to the internal workings of an organization concentrate on the internal business processes that are critical for achieving customer satisfaction. These measures focus on process improvement and productivity; employee and information system capabilities; and employee satisfaction, retention, and productivity. They seek to provide the answers to questions such as these: Do our employees have the right equipment or information to do their jobs well? Do they receive recognition and support? What are their skills and competencies? What will be needed in the future? Key business measures include revenue dollars, labor rates, fixed and variable unit costs, gross margin rates, operating margin rates, inventory costs, general and administrative expenses, cash flow, warranty costs, product liability costs, and cost avoidance. Once developed, measures should be used to develop cost/benefit scenarios to help sell improvement recommendations to management. Figure 3.10 provides examples of typical measures of performance.

When creating measures it is important not to create measures for measurement's sake. Measures require gathering and analyzing data. Most organizations already have measures in place. Those measures need to be refined by asking questions: What does the organization need to know? What is important to our customers? What data are currently being gathered? How are the data being used? What measures currently exist? Are they useful? How does the organization use the information and measures already in existence? For any improvement project, care should be taken to avoid

---

Number of repeat customers
Service time
Number of sales
Number of returned product
Count of reasons for return
Number of deviations from product/service specifications
Number of incorrect procedures
Number of warranty claims
Number of deviations from organizational policies
Number of childhood immunizations
Number of children receiving preventive dental care
Number of patients developing infections while in ICU
Rework amounts
Scrap amounts
Profit
Number of missed opportunities

Figure 3.10   Examples of Measures of Performance

poorly defined measures. The following example provides some insight into process measures.

EXAMPLE 3.5   Plastics and Dashes: Instrument Panel Warranty Measures of Performance

The instrument panel warranty team has decided that they will need both customer and financial measures in order to know whether or not the changes being made are working.

> Financial measures
>> Warranty costs for each type of warranty claim
>
> Customer measures
>> Number of warranty claim types

By tracking these measures of performance, they will know whether or not the changes made to their processes are effective. If they are, then both warranty claims and their costs will decrease.   **Q**

EXAMPLE 3.6   Measures of Performance

A copy center is considering replacing a copy machine. Here is their proposed action and the measures they intend to use to answer the following question: How do we know we have made the correct change?

Proposed Action: Replace copy machine 815 with copy machine 1215.
Why?

A. Copy machine 1215 can run a larger number of impressions faster than copy machine 815.
B. The copy center has or could quickly develop a profitable customer base with the larger machine.

Measures of Performance: (How will we know A and B are true?)

1. Measure number of impressions made by existing 815 machine.
2. Measure average time it takes to complete a copying job with 815 machine.
3. Measure customer copy job delays caused by 815 performance (lead time).
4. Measure number of customers who must take job elsewhere to meet deadlines.

Compare these measures with the projected number of impressions and the average job time of the 1215 machine. If the comparison is favorable, install the 1215 machine.

After the installation of the 1215, how do we know whether or not it was a good idea?

Apply the four measures of performance to the 1215 and compare. What is the result of this comparison?   **Q**

Step 5. Plan: Analyzing the Problem/Process

In most organizations, very few people truly understand the myriad of activities in a process that it takes to create a product or service. Process maps are powerful communication tools that provide a clear understanding of how business is conducted within the organization. Identifying and writing down the process in pictorial form helps people understand just how they do the work that they do. Process maps have the ability to accurately portray current operations and can be used to evaluate these operations. A process map also identifies the activities that have been added to the process over time in order to adapt older processes to changes in the business. Once changes have been proposed, process maps are equally powerful for communicating the proposed changes to the process.

Technique: Process Maps

Process maps are known by many names including flowcharts, process flowcharts, and process flow diagrams. A *process map is a graphical representation of all the steps involved in an entire process or a particular segment of a process* (Figure 3.11). Diagramming the flow of a process or system aids in understanding it. Flowcharting is effectively used in the first stages of problem-solving because the charts enable those studying the process to quickly understand what is involved in a process from start to finish. Problem-solving team members can clearly see what is being done to a product or provided by a service at the various stages in a process. Process flowcharts clarify the routines used to serve customers. Problem or non-value-added activities nested within a process are easily identified by using a flowchart.

Process maps are fairly straightforward to construct. The steps to creating such charts are the following:

1. Define the process boundaries. For the purpose of the chart, determine where the process begins and ends.
2. Define the process steps. Use brainstorming to identify the steps for new processes. For existing processes actually observe the process in action.
3. Sort the steps into the order of their occurrence in the process.
4. Place the steps in appropriate flowchart symbols (Figure 3.12) and create the chart.
5. Evaluate the steps for completeness, efficiency, and possible problems such as non-value-added activities.

Because processes and systems are often complex, in the early stages of flowchart construction, removable 3-by-5-inch sticky notes placed on a large piece of paper or board allow creators greater flexibility when creating and refining a flowchart. When the chart is complete, a final copy can be made utilizing the correct symbols. The symbols can either be placed next to the description of the step or they can surround the information.

A variation on the traditional process flowchart is the deployment flowchart. When a deployment flowchart is created, job or department titles are written across the top of the page and the activities of the process that occur in that job or department are

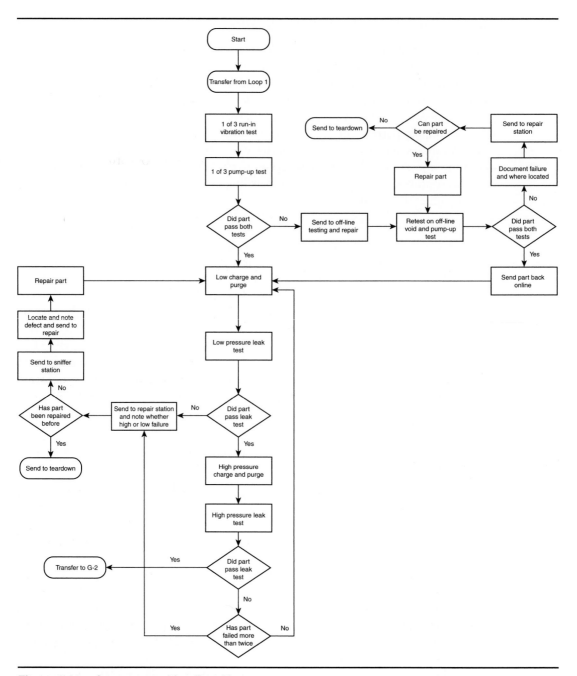

Figure 3.11 Compressor Line Part Flow

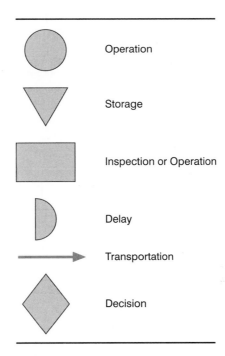

Figure 3.12   Flowchart Symbols

written underneath that heading (Figure 3.13). Flowcharts can also be constructed with pictures for easier understanding (Figure 3.15). When used as routing sheets, it is not unusual to see process flowcharts like Figure 3.16 which included additional details like process activities, operator self-inspection notes, and specifications.

EXAMPLE 3.7   Plastics and Dashes: Creating a Flowchart

The instrument panel warranty team has decided to create a flowchart of the instrument panel assembly process.

Step 1. Define the Process Steps. First, the team members brainstormed the steps in the assembly process. They double-checked their steps by observing the actual process. They wrote down each step on 3 × 5 sticky notes.

Step 2. Sort the Steps into the Order of their Occurrence in the Process. After reconciling their observations with their brainstorming efforts, the team sorted the steps into the order of their occurrence.

Step 3. Place the Steps in Appropriate Flowchart Symbols. With the steps in the correct order, it was a simple task to add the appropriate flowchart symbols and create the chart (Figure 3.14).

Step 4. Evaluate the Steps for Completeness, Efficiency, and Possible Problems. The team reviewed the finished chart for completeness. Several team members were unaware of the complete process. Because it creates a greater understanding of the process, this diagram will be helpful during later problem-solving efforts. **Q**

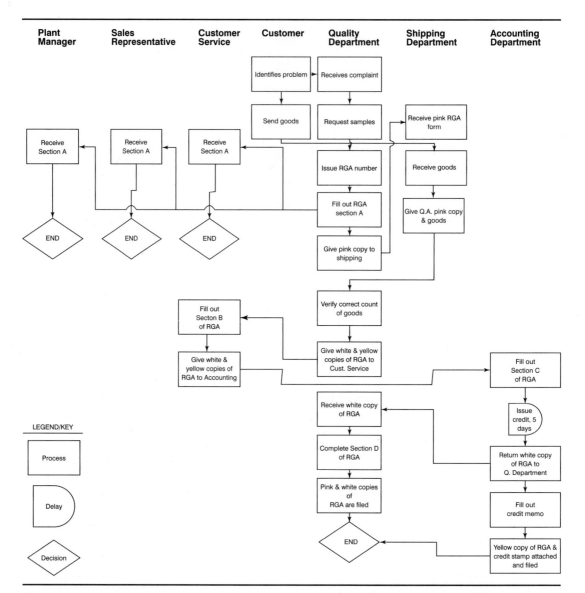

Figure 3.13   Deployment Process Flowchart for Return Goods Authorization (RGA) Forms

During the flowcharting process, members of the problem-solving team gain a greater understanding of their process. They will also begin to identify possible causes of problems within the process. It is now time to more clearly identify those possible causes and measure the process.

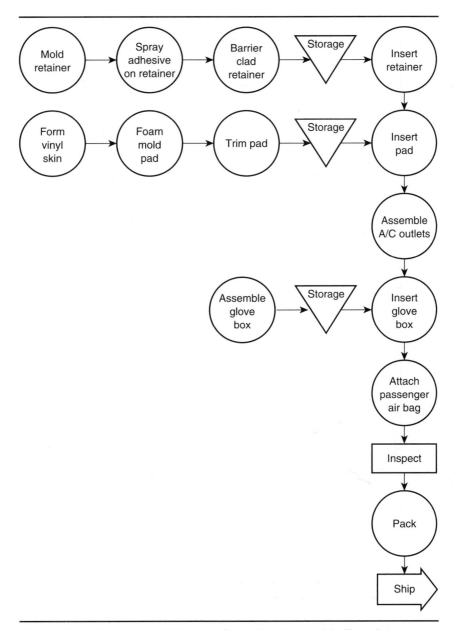

Figure 3.14   Plastics and Dashes: Glove Box Assembly Flowchart

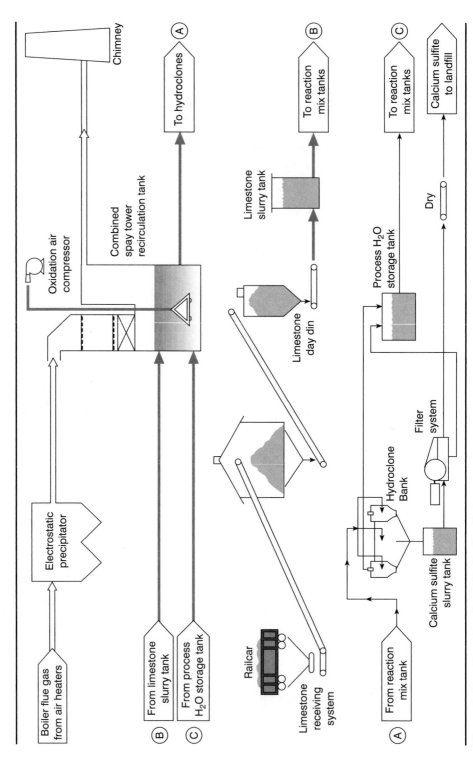

Figure 3.15   Flue Gas Desulfurization Process

90

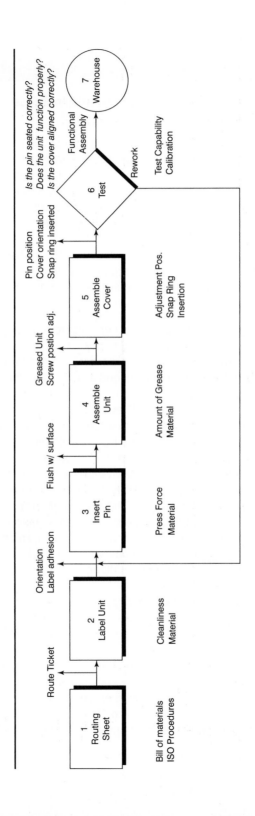

Figure 3.16   Process Flowchart with Instructions and Specifications

Variable	Target	Upper Spec	Lower Spec
Press Force	12 lbs	15 lbs	10 lbs
Amount of Grease	2 cc's	1.5 cc's	2.5 cc's

REAL TOOLS FOR REAL LIFE

Using a Process Map to Improve Work Flow and Increase Customer Satisfaction

Distribution centers pick, pack, and ship orders in one of two methods: wave (also called batch) and discrete. The newly appointed head of CH Distributors has been studying the flow of the pick, pack, and shipment of orders. In order to optimize this flow, Mr. H. considers the questions, How many times does a picker visit a particular location or area? How many items are picked? How much space is taken up? To better understand the flow, Mr. H. has created the process map shown in Figure 3.17.

After creating the process map based on observing the workers doing their jobs, Mr. H. studied it. He was able to identify where delays were occurring, where workers were idle, and where backlogs were created. Based on the process map and his observations, he made the following changes.

Workers now pick orders in order of receipt, regardless of customer, eliminating specialized pickers for each customer. This change eliminated picker idle time which occurred when no order for a particular customer existed. The change also balanced the workload among all of the pickers, eliminating bottlenecks.

Reorganized pack and ship areas. Previously spread throughout the entire distribution center, the pack and ship areas were combined into one layout. A 10-foot roller conveyor is used to move packages from the four packing stations to the two shipping stations. This change balanced the workload among packers and shippers. This change also allowed workers to interface more easily, enabling them to share process improvement ideas.

Reorganized the distribution center. The Pareto diagram provided information concerning the number of customer orders generated by a particular customer. The distribution center was reorganized to place high volume customers in close proximity with the pack and ship area. This change eliminated considerable walking and searching on the part of the pickers.

Cross-trained pickers, packers, and shippers. During peak times, all workers pick until queues have been generated at either the packing stations or the shipping stations. This change balanced the workload among all workers.

Moved the packaging of the order to the packing responsibility. This eliminated the bottleneck that occurred at the shipping station, while balancing the workload between the packers and shippers more effectively.

Allow packers to select optimum box size. Since shipping cost is based on the size of the box, this often results in shipping savings for the customer.

Figure 3.18 shows the new process flow map.

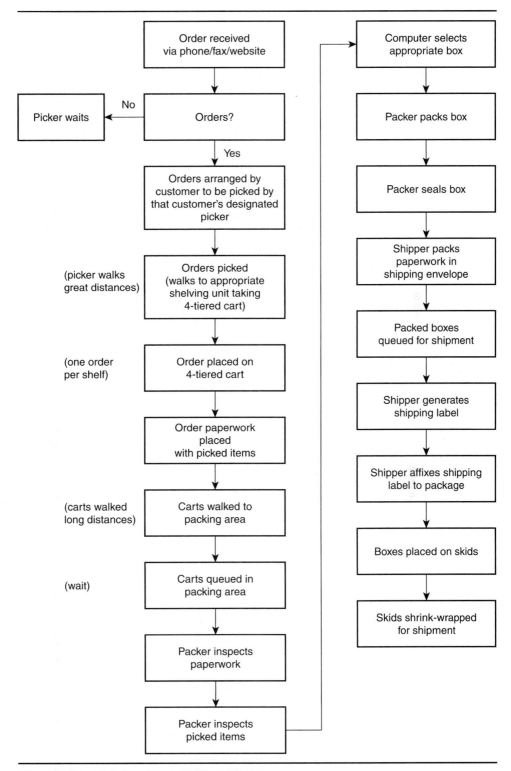

Figure 3.17 Existing Process Flow Diagram

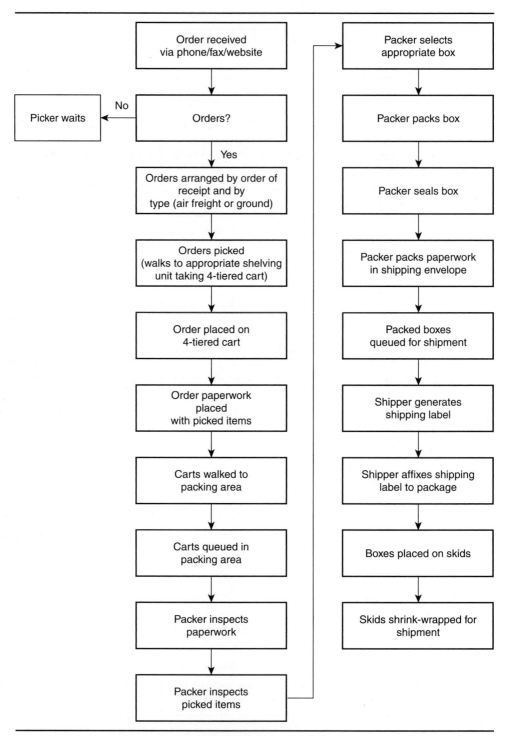

Figure 3.18   Revised Process Flow Diagram

REAL TOOLS FOR REAL LIFE

Using Process Maps Wisely

PLC, Inc. has been investigating the process of returning defective parts to suppliers. In the original process it took 175 hours, nearly four weeks, for a defective part to be returned to a supplier. There were 14 steps to complete, none of these steps ran in parallel.

A team comprised of engineers, purchasing agents, and shippers mapped the process and studied it in order to locate non-value-added activities. During four weeks of meetings, the team developed a new process. These improvements reduced the time from 175 hours to 69 hours. The new process included nine steps, two running in parallel (being completed at the same time).

When the team presented their proposed process changes to upper management, the managers asked the team to begin the exercise again, starting with a clean slate, keeping only what absolutely had to take place in order to get the job done. The team was given one hour to report their new process. The new process, developed in one hour, has four steps and takes one hour to complete. This process was achieved by eliminating the remaining non-value-added steps and empowering the workers to make key decisions.

Though they were able to develop a new, simplified process map for the defective part return process, while in their meeting it dawned on the team members that, in the big scheme of things, why were they allowing defective parts at all?

The team members learned two things from this experience: it doesn't pay to spend time fixing a badly broken process and sometimes the reason for the process needs to be eliminated.

Step 6. Plan: Determining Possible Causes

Determining the possible causes of a problem requires that the problem be clearly defined. The flowchart in Step 5 gave the problem solvers a greater understanding of the processes involved. Now the problem statement can be combined with knowledge of the process to isolate potential causes of the problem. An excellent technique to begin to determine causes is brainstorming.

Technique: Brainstorming

*The purpose of **brainstorming** is to generate a list of problems, opportunities, or ideas from a group of people.* Everyone present at the session should participate. The discussion leader must ensure that everyone is given an opportunity to comment and add ideas. Critical to brainstorming is that no arguing, no criticism, no negativism, and no evaluation of the ideas, problems, or opportunities take place during the session. It is a session devoted purely to the generation of ideas.

The length of time allotted to brainstorming varies; sessions may last from 10 to 45 minutes. Some team leaders deliberately keep the meetings short to limit opportunities to begin problem solving. A session ends when no more items are brought up. The result of the session will be a list of ideas, problems, or opportunities to be tackled. After being listed, the items are sorted and ranked by category, importance, priority, benefit, cost, impact, time, or other considerations.

EXAMPLE 3.8   Plastics and Dashes: Brainstorming

The team at Plastics and Dashes Inc. conducted a further study of the causes of loose instrument panel components. Their investigation revealed that the glove box in the instrument panel was the main problem area (Figure 3.19). They were led to this conclusion when further study of the warranty data allowed them to create the Pareto chart shown in Figure 3.20. This figure displays problems related specifically to the glove box.

In order to better understand why the glove box might be loose, the team assembled to brainstorm the variables associated with the glove box.

JERRY: I think you all know why we are here today. Did you all get the opportunity to review the glove box information? Good. Well, let's get started by concentrating on the relationship between the glove box and the instrument panel. I'll list the ideas on the board here, while you folks call them out. Remember, we are not here to evaluate ideas. We'll do that next.

SAM: How about the tightness of the latch?

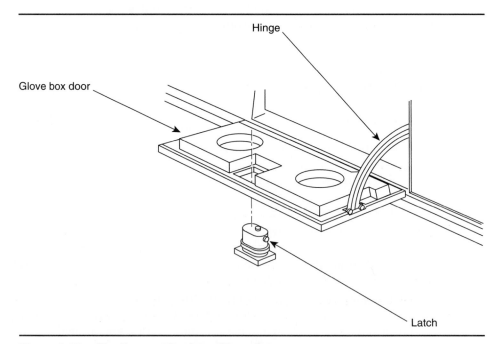

Figure 3.19   Plastics and Dashes: Glove Box

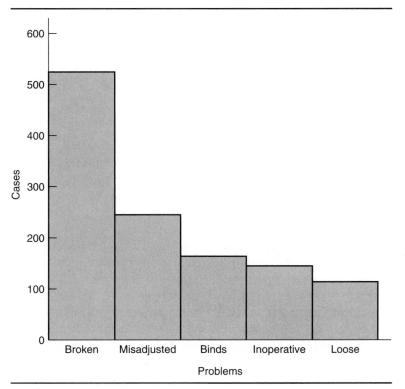

**Figure 3.20   Plastics and Dashes: Pareto Chart of Problems
Related to the Glove Box Latch**

FRANK: Of course the tightness of the latch will affect the fit between the glove box and the instrument panel! Tell us something we don't know.

JERRY: Frank, have you forgotten the rules of a brainstorming session? No criticizing. Sam, can you expand on your concept?

SAM: I was thinking that the positioning of the latch as well as the positioning of the hinge would affect the tightness of the latch.

JERRY: Okay. (Writes on board.) Tightness of Latch, Positioning of Latch, Positioning of Hinge. Any other ideas?

SUE: What about the strength of the hinge?

JERRY: (Writes on board.) Strength of Hinge.

SHARON: What about the glove box handle strength?

FRANK: And the glove box handle positioning?

JERRY: (Writes on board.) Glove Box Handle Strength. Glove Box Handle Positioning.

The session continues until a variety of ideas have been generated (Figure 3.21). After no more ideas surface or at subsequent meetings, discussion and clarification of the ideas can commence.

Positioning of the Glove Box
Strength of the Glove Box
Tightness of the Latch
Positioning of the Latch
Strength of the Latch
Positioning of the Hinge
Strength of the Hinge
Glove Box Handle Strength
Glove Box Handle Positioning
Glove Box Construction Materials

Figure 3.21   Variables Associated with the Glove Box

Technique: Cause-and-Effect Diagrams

Another excellent method of determining root causes is the cause-and-effect diagram. The **cause-and-effect diagram** is also called the Ishikawa diagram after Kaoru Ishikawa, who developed it, and the fish-bone diagram because the completed diagram resembles a fish skeleton (Figure 3.22). A chart of this type will help *identify causes for nonconforming or defective products or services*. Cause-and-effect diagrams can be used in conjunction with flowcharts and Pareto charts to identify the cause(s) of the problem.

This chart is useful in a brainstorming session because it organizes the ideas that are presented. Problem solvers benefit from using the chart by being able to separate a large problem into manageable parts. It serves as a visual display to aid the understanding of

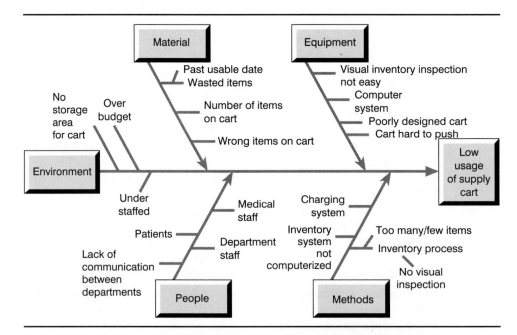

Figure 3.22   A Cause-and-Effect Diagram for Medical Supply Cart Usage

problems and their causes. The problem or effect is clearly identified on the right-hand side of the chart, and the potential causes of the problem are organized on the left-hand side. The cause-and-effect diagram also allows the session leader to logically organize the possible causes of the problem and to focus on one area at a time. Not only does the chart permit the display of causes of the problem, it also shows subcategories related to those causes.

To construct a cause-and-effect diagram:

1. Clearly identify the effect or the problem. The succinctly stated effect or problem statement is placed in a box at the end of a line.
2. Identify the causes. Discussion ensues concerning the potential causes of the problem. To guide the discussion, attack just one possible cause area at a time. General topic areas are usually methods, materials, machines, people, environment, and information, although other areas can be added as needed. Under each major area, subcauses related to the major cause should be identified. Brainstorming is the usual method for identifying these causes.
3. Build the diagram. Organize the causes and subcauses in diagram format.
4. Analyze the diagram. At this point, solutions will need to be identified. Decisions will also need to be made concerning the cost-effectiveness of the solution as well as its feasibility.

**EXAMPLE 3.9   Plastics and Dashes: Constructing a
                 Cause-and-Effect Diagram**

As the Plastics and Dashes Inc. instrument panel warranty team continued its investigation, it was determined that defective latches were causing most of the warranty claims associated with the categories of loose instrument panel components and noise.

Step 1. Identify the Effect or Problem.   The team identified the problem as defective latches.

Step 2. Identify the Causes.   Rather than use the traditional methods, materials, machines, people, environment, and information, this team felt that the potential areas to search for causes related directly to the latch. For that reason, they chose these potential causes: broken, misadjusted, binds, inoperative, loose.

Step 3. Build the Diagram.   The team brainstormed root causes for each category (Figure 3.23).

Step 4. Analyze the Diagram.   The team discussed and analyzed the diagram. After much discussion, they came to the following conclusions. Latches that were either broken, misadjusted, or inoperable or those that bind have two root causes in common: improper alignment and improper positioning. Latches that were loose or broken had a root cause of low material strength (those materials supporting the latch were low in strength). From their findings, the team determined that there were three root causes associated with defective latches: improper alignment, improper positioning, and low material strength.   **Q**

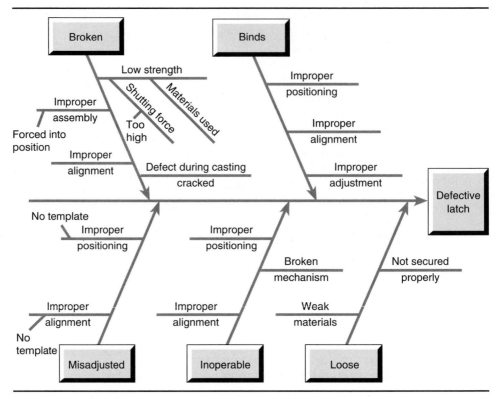

Figure 3.23   Plastics and Dashes: Cause-and-Effect Diagram

EXAMPLE 3.10   Constructing a Cause-and-Effect Diagram

At a furniture-manufacturing facility, the upholstery department is having trouble with pattern alignment. They have decided to use a cause-and-effect diagram to help them determine the root causes of pattern misalignment.

Step 1. Clearly Identify the Effect or Problem.   The upholstery department team identified the problem as an incorrectly aligned fabric pattern.

Step 2. Identify the Causes.   The team, representatives from all of the areas affected by pattern misalignment, brainstormed to identify the causes of pattern misalignment. To guide the discussion, they attacked just one possible cause at a time, starting with methods, materials, machines, people, and environment and ending with information. Under each major area, subcauses related to the major cause were identified.

Step 3. Build the Diagram.   During the brainstorming process, the diagram emerged (Figure 3.24).

Step 4. Analyze the Diagram.   At this point, solutions need to be identified to eliminate the causes of misalignment. Decisions also need to be made concerning the cost-effectiveness of the solutions as well as their feasibility.

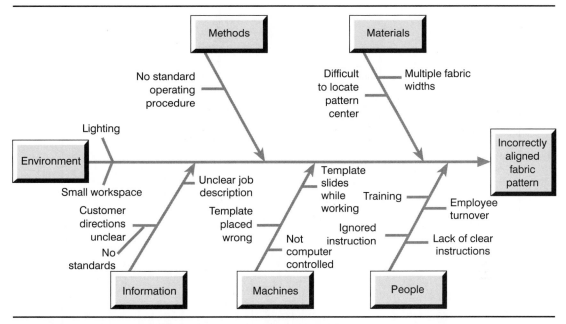

Figure 3.24   Cause-and-Effect Diagram for Example 3.10

An excellent technique for finding the root cause(s) of a problem is to ask "Why" five times. This is also an excellent method for determining what factors have to be in place in order to respond to an opportunity. **WHY-WHY *diagrams*** *organize the thinking of a problem-solving group and illustrate a chain of symptoms leading to the true cause of a problem.* By asking "why" five times, the problem solvers are stripping away the symptoms surrounding the problem and getting to the true cause of the problem. At the end of a session it should be possible to make a positively worded, straightforward statement defining the true problem to be investigated.

Technique: WHY-WHY Diagram

Developed by group consensus, the WHY-WHY diagram flows from left to right. The diagram starts on the left with a statement of the problem to be resolved. Then the group is asked why this problem might exist. The responses will be statements of causes that the group believes contribute to the problem under discussion. There may be only one cause or there may be several. Causes can be separate or interrelated. Regardless of the number of causes or their relationships, the causes should be written on the diagram in a single, clear statement. "Why" statements should be supported by facts as much as possible and not by hearsay or unfounded opinions. Figure 3.25 shows a WHY-WHY diagram the Plastics and Dashes problem-solving team completed for Instrument Panel Warranty Costs.

This investigation is continued through as many levels as needed until a root cause is found for each of the problem statements, original or developed during the discussions. Frequently five levels of "why" are needed to determine the root cause. In the end, this

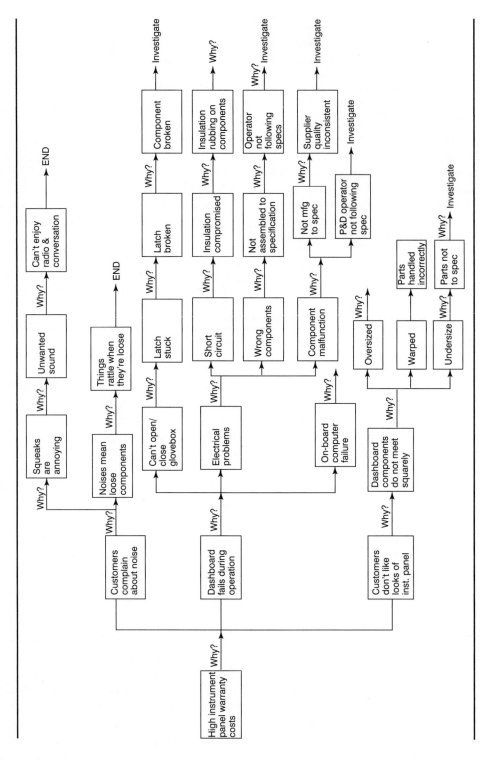

Figure 3.25   Plastics and Dashes: WHY-WHY Diagram for Instrument Panel, Work-in-Progress

process leads to a network of reasons the original problems occurred. The ending points indicate areas that need to be addressed to resolve the original problem. These become the actions the company must take to address the situation. WHY-WHY diagrams can be expanded to include notations concerning who will be responsible for action items and when the actions will be completed.

The WHY-WHY process is not meant to locate solutions; it is used primarily to identify the root causes of problems. Care should be taken not to propose solutions to the problem yet. Not enough is known about the problem to create a truly workable solution. Solutions enacted at this point may be shortsighted and might not include answers for the complexities involved in the problem. The problem analysis stage needs to come next, before any solutions are proposed.

Cause-and-effect and WHY-WHY diagrams allow us to isolate potential causes of problems. Once identified, these causes need to be investigated by measuring and organizing the data associated with the process. Measuring the process will help refine the investigators' understanding of the problem and help sort out relevant from non-relevant information. It will also help individuals involved with the problem maintain objectivity. Measuring can be done through the use of histograms, scatter diagrams, control charts, and run charts.

Technique: Histograms

A **histogram** is a graphical summary of the frequency distribution of the data. When measurements are taken from a process, they can be summarized by using a histogram. Data are organized in a histogram to allow those investigating the process to see any patterns in the data that would be difficult to see in a simple table of numbers. The data are separated into classes in the histogram. Each interval on a histogram shows the total number of observations made in each separate class. Histograms display the variation present in a set of data taken from a process (Figure 3.26). Histograms are covered in more detail in Chapter 4.

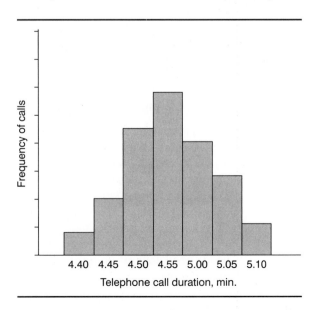

Figure 3.26   A Histogram

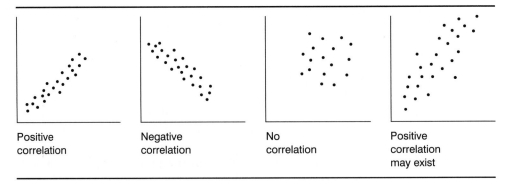

Positive correlation   Negative correlation   No correlation   Positive correlation may exist

Figure 3.27   Scatter Diagram Interpretations

Technique: Scatter Diagrams

*The **scatter diagram** is a graphical technique that is used to analyze the relationship between two different variables.* Two sets of data are plotted on a graph. The independent variable—i.e., the variable that can be manipulated—is recorded on the x axis. The dependent variable, the one being predicted, is displayed on the y axis. From this diagram, the user can determine if a connection or relationship exists between the two variables being compared. If a relationship exists, then steps can be taken to identify process changes that affect the relationship. Figure 3.27 shows different interpretations of scatter diagrams.

To construct a scatter diagram, use these steps:

1. Select the characteristic, the independent variable, you wish to study.
2. Select the characteristic, the dependent variable, that you suspect affects the independent variable.
3. Gather the data about the two characteristics.
4. Draw, scale, and label the horizontal and vertical axes.
5. Plot the points.
6. Interpret the scatter diagram to see if there is a relationship between the two characteristics.

EXAMPLE 3.11   Creating a Scatter Diagram

Shirley is the setup operator in the shrink-wrap area. In this area, 5-ft-by-5-ft cartons of parts are sealed with several layers of plastic wrap before being loaded on the trucks for shipment. Shirley's job is to load the plastic used in the shrink-wrapping operation onto the shrink-wrap machine, set the speed at which the unit will rotate, and set the tension level on the shrink-wrap feeder. To understand the relationship between the tension level on the feeder and the speed of the rotating mechanism, Shirley has created a scatter diagram.

The rotator speed is most easily controlled, so she has placed the most typically used speed settings (in rpm) on the x axis. On the y axis, she places the number of tears (Figure 3.28).

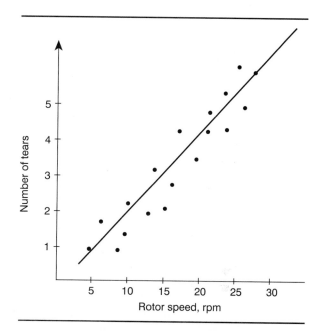

Figure 3.28   The Scatter Diagram for Example 3.11

The diagram reveals a positive correlation: As the speed increases, the number of tears increases. From this information, Shirley now knows that the tension has to be reduced in order to prevent the wrap from tearing. Using the diagram, Shirley is able to determine the optimal speed for the rotor and the best tension setting.

Technique: Control Charts

A **control chart** *is a chart with a centerline showing the average of the data produced.* It has upper and lower control limits that are based on statistical calculations (Figure 3.29). It is used to determine process centering and process variation and to locate any

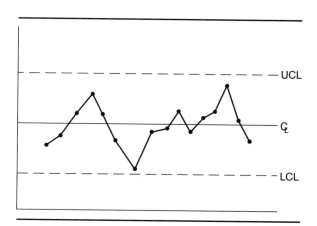

Figure 3.29   A Control Chart, Showing Centerline, Upper Control Limits, and Lower Control Limits

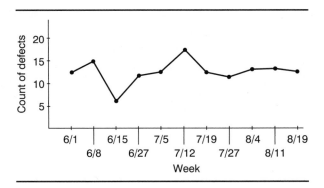

Figure 3.30   A Run Chart

unusual patterns or trends in the data. Control charts are covered in more detail in Chapters 5, 6, 7, and 9.

Technique: Run Charts

Run charts are similar to control charts. *They follow a process over time, reflected on the x axis.* The run chart is very good at reflecting trends in the measurements over time. Normally, one measurement is taken at a time and graphed on the chart. The y axis shows the magnitude of that measurement.

EXAMPLE 3.12   Plastics and Dashes Creates a Run Chart

Because of the recurring problems with dashboards, 100% inspection has been initiated temporarily at the dashboard assembly work area. A run chart is used to track the number of in-process failures found. Any and all types of instrument panel problems are recorded on this chart. Figure 3.30 shows the count of problems found on a weekly basis for the past 11 weeks. Cars experiencing instrument panel problems are taken off the line for repair. When process changes are made, this chart can be used to show how the changes affected the process. If the changes were effective, the count of problems will decrease.

DO

Step 7. Do: Selecting and Implementing the Solution

We have been applying problem-solving techniques to find the root cause of a problem. Once the cause has been identified, it is time to propose potential solutions. This begins the Do section of the PDSA cycle. This is the portion of the cycle that attracts everyone's attention. So great is the desire to do something that many problem-solvers are tempted to reduce the amount of time spent on planning to virtually nothing. The temptation to immediately propose solutions must be ignored. The best solutions are those that solve the true problem. They are found only after the root cause of that problem has been identified. The most significant portion of the problem-solving effort must be concentrated in the Plan phase.

At the other end of the spectrum are solutions that never get done. Implementation takes time and often people find innumerable reasons why the ideas won't work or shouldn't be implemented. Good management means good follow-through. Managers should make sure there is widespread active involvement in the implementation of solutions.

EXAMPLE 3.13   An Incomplete Picture

Tensions are high at PL Industries. Several departments have been reprimanded for low customer satisfaction ratings. The catalog department, in particular, has been under a lot of pressure to improve customer service on their toll-free service lines. Customers are complaining loudly about the amount of time they are kept waiting on hold for the next available operator. The catalog department's defense that they are doing the best they can has failed to impress upper management. In order to do something, management recently replaced the catalog department manager.

The new manager, who has training in statistics, offered no excuses for her new department's poor performance, asking only for time to study the situation. Within a few weeks time, she returned to upper management with information concerning toll-free-number users. Using a check sheet, she gathered data and created the Pareto chart in Figure 3.31. The chart shows that a significant number of the calls

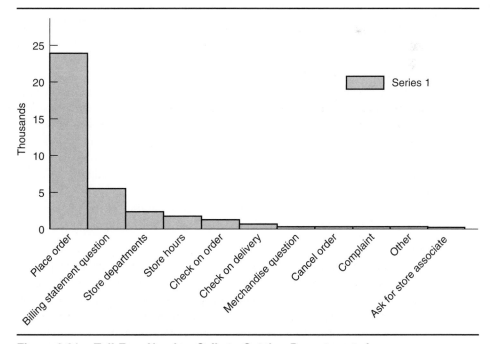

Figure 3.31   Toll-Free Number Calls to Catalog Department, June

	June	November
Total No. of Calls	36,633	58,801
Cost	$24,269	$25,823
Average Cost/Call	$0.66	$0.32
Average Wait (min)	3.86	0.32
Staff	15	15

Figure 3.32   Toll-Free Number: June Versus November

received on the toll-free line actually have nothing to do with the catalog department and must be transferred to other departments. An equally significant number of calls to the toll-free number are due to billing statement questions, which are not the responsibility of the catalog department.

By the conclusion of the meeting, statistical information has allowed PL Industries' upper management to develop a clearer understanding of the true nature of the problem. In the future, their focus will be on determining how to create a better billing statement as well as determining which departments should also have a toll-free number.

How will they know their efforts have been successful? Measures of performance allow investigators to close the loop and determine the effects of their changes. Look at Figure 3.32, which provides information about the toll-free number six months after the service had been expanded to include numbers for customer service, the stores, and the billing department. Notice the dramatic reduction in customer wait times with no additional catalog department staff. It is also important to notice that due to the significantly reduced wait time, the number of calls handled nearly doubled; however, the cost of operating all the toll-free numbers increased by only a little more than $1500.

It is important to recognize that applying these techniques does not mean that taking care of the immediate problem should be ignored. Immediate action should be taken to rectify any situation that does not meet the customer's reasonable needs, requirements, and expectations. These quick fixes are just that, a quick fix of a problem for the short term; they simply allow time for a long-term solution to be found. In no situation should a quick fix be considered the end of a problem. Problems are solved only when recurrences do not happen.

Selecting and implementing the solution is a matter of the project team's choosing the best solution for the problem under examination. The solution should be judged against four general criteria:

1. The solution should be chosen on the basis of its potential to prevent a recurrence of the problem. A quick or short-term fix to a problem will only mean that time will be wasted in solving this problem again when it recurs in the future.
2. The solution should address the root cause of the problem. A quick or short-term fix that focuses on correcting the symptoms of a problem will waste time because the problem will recur in the future.

3. The solution should be cost-effective. The most expensive solution is not necessarily the best solution for the company's interests. Solutions may necessitate determining the company's future plans for a particular process or product. Major changes to the process, system, or equipment may not be an appropriate solution for a process or product that will be discontinued in the near future. Technological advances will need to be investigated to determine if they are the most cost-effective solutions.

4. The solution should be capable of being implemented within a reasonable amount of time. A timely solution to the problem is necessary to relieve the company of the burden of monitoring the current problem and its associated quick fixes.

EXAMPLE 3.14   Plastics and Dashes: Glove Box Solutions

Because the team was able to identify the root causes of the glove box latch problem as improper alignment, improper positioning, and low material strength, they decided to make the following changes part of their solution:

1. Redesign the glove box latch. This solution was chosen to counteract low material strength.
2. Reposition the glove box door, striker, and hinge. This solution was chosen to counteract improper positioning and alignment. They also hoped this change would eliminate potential squeaks and rattles.
3. Reinforce the glove box latch. This solution was chosen to counteract breakage. By increasing the material at the latch position on the glove box door, they hoped to eliminate breakage. They also decided to use a stronger adhesive to reinforce the rivets securing the latch to the door.   **Q**

Implementing the solution is often done by members of the problem-solving team. Critical to ensuring the success of the solution implementation is assigning responsibilities to specific individuals and holding them accountable for accomplishing the task. Knowing who will be doing what and when will help ensure that the project stays on track.

Sometimes implementing solutions is complicated by a variety of factors, including conflicting departmental needs, costs, or priorities. Using a force-field analysis can help identify the issues affecting the implementation of a solution.

Technique: Force-Field Analysis

A *force-field analysis is a chart that helps teams separate the driving forces and the restraining forces associated with a complex situation.* These easy-to-develop charts help a team determine the positive or driving forces that are encouraging improvement of the process as well as the forces that restrain improvement. Teams may also choose to use force-field analysis as a source of discussion issues surrounding a particular problem or opportunity. Once the driving and restraining forces have been identified, the team can discuss how to enhance the driving forces and remove the restraining forces. This sort of brainstorming leads to potential solutions to be investigated.

EXAMPLE 3.15   Using Force-Field Analysis

At a local bank, a team has gathered to discuss meeting the customers' demands for improved teller window service. One of the major customer desires, as revealed by a survey, is to have more teller windows open at 9 A.M. So far the meeting has been a less-than-organized discussion of why more tellers are not at their windows at 9. To remove some of the finger-pointing and blame-laying, the leader has decided to use force-field analysis to focus the discussion.

By brainstorming, the team members identified the following as driving forces:

1. Improving customer service by having more windows open
2. Creating shorter lines for customers by serving more customers at one time
3. Relieving the stress of morning teller activities

Notice that the team has identified both internal (less stress) and external (happier customers) factors as the driving forces behind wanting to solve this problem.

The discussion of restraining forces is much more heated. Management has been unaware of the number of activities that need to be completed before opening the teller windows at 9 A.M. Slowly, over time, the amount of paperwork and number of extra duties have increased. Since this change has been gradual, it has gone unnoticed by all but the tellers. They accept it as part of their job but are under considerable stress to complete the necessary work by 9 A.M., given that their workday starts at 8:30 A.M. The restraining forces identified by the tellers are the following:

1. Money must be ready for Brinks pickup by 9 A.M.
2. Audit department needs balance sheet by 9 A.M.
3. Balance sheet is complicated, cumbersome, and inadequate.
4. Comptroller needs petty cash sheets, payroll, and other general ledger information.
5. Day begins at 8:30.

Table 3.1 presents the completed force-field diagram. A variety of suggestions are given to remove the restraining forces, including changing the starting and ending times of the day, adding more people, and telling the audit and comptroller departments to wait until later in the day.

Since it isn't economically feasible to add more people or increase the work hours, emphasis is now placed on asking the audit and comptroller departments what their needs are. Interestingly enough, while the bank has surveyed their external customers, they have not investigated the needs of the people working within

Table 3.1   Force-Field Analysis

Driving Forces	*Restraining Forces*
1. Improving Customer Service by Having More Windows Open 2. Creating Shorter Lines for Customers by Serving More Customers at One Time 3. Relieving the Stress of Morning Teller Activities	1. Money Must Be Ready for Brinks Pickup. 2. Audit Department Needs Balance Sheet by 9 A.M. 3. Balance Sheet Is Complicated, Cumbersome, and Inadequate. 4. Comptroller Needs Petty Cash Sheets, Payroll, and Other General Ledger Information. 5. Day Begins at 8:30 A.M.

Actions
1. Change the Starting and Ending Times of the Day.
2. Add More Tellers.
3. Tell the Audit and Comptroller Departments to Wait until Later in the Day.

---

the bank. In the discussions that followed with the audit's and comptroller's offices, it was determined that only the balance sheet has to be completed by 9 A.M. The other paperwork can be received as late as 11 A.M. and not affect the performance of the other departments. This two-hour time space will allow the tellers to open their windows at 9 for the morning rush and still complete the paperwork for the comptroller's office before 11. Having achieved a successful conclusion to the project, the team decided to work on reducing the complexity of the balance sheet as its next problem-solving activity. Perhaps a simpler balance sheet could reduce stress even more!   **Q**

STUDY

Step 8. Study: Evaluating the Solution, the Follow-up

Once implemented and given time to operate, problem-solving actions are checked to see if the problem has truly been solved. During the Study stage we study the results and ask: Is the solution we've chosen working? What did we learn? To determine if the solution has worked, the measures of performance created in Step 4 should be applied. Prior data collected during the analysis phase of the project should be compared with present data taken from the process. Control charts, histograms, and run charts can be used to monitor the process, both before and after. If these formats were used in the original problem analysis, a direct comparison can be made to determine how well the solution is performing. If the solution is not correcting the problem, then the PDSA process should begin again to determine a better solution.

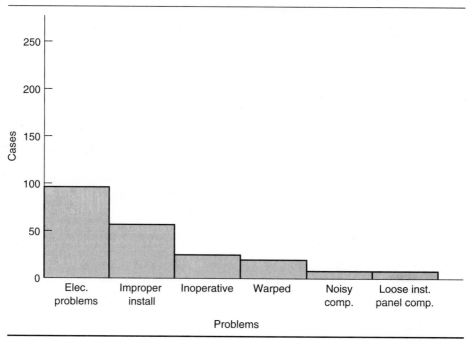

Figure 3.33   Plastics and Dashes: Pareto Chart of Instrument Panel Problems by Warranty Claim Type

EXAMPLE 3.16   Plastics and Dashes: Evaluating the Solution

The instrument panel warranty team implemented their solutions and used the measures of performance developed in Example 3.5 to study the solutions in order to determine whether or not the changes were working. Their original measures of performance were warranty costs and number and type of warranty claims. The Pareto chart in Figure 3.33 provides information about warranty claims made following the changes. When this figure is compared to Figure 3.5, showing warranty claims before the problem-solving team went into action, the improvement is obvious. Warranty costs declined in proportion to the decreased number of claims, to just under $25,000. A process measure also tracked the length of time to implement the changes, a very speedy five days.

ACT

Step 9. Act: Ensuring Permanence

The final stage, Action, involves making the decision to adopt the change, abandon it, or repeat the problem-solving cycle. If the change is adopted, then efforts must be made to ensure that new methods have been established so that the new level of quality performance can be maintained. Now that a follow-up investigation has revealed that the problem has been solved, it is important that improved performance continue. From Figure 3.1 it can be seen that "ensuring permanence" is part of the action phase. This phase of the quality-improvement process exists to ensure that the new controls and procedures stay in place. It is easy to believe that the "new and better" method should be utilized without fail; however, in any situation where a change has taken place, there is a tendency to return to old methods, controls, and procedures when stress is increased. It is a bit like switching to an automatic shift after having driven a manual shift car for a number of years. Under normal driving conditions, drivers will not utilize their left legs to operate a clutch pedal that does not exist in an automatic gear shift car. But place those same individuals in an emergency stop situation, and chances are they will attempt to activate a nonexistent clutch pedal at the same time as they brake. Under stress, people have a tendency to revert to their original training.

To avoid a lapse into old routines and methods, controls must be in place to remind people of the new method. It is helpful if people see how the new methods were designed and developed. Widespread active involvement in improvement projects helps ensure successful implementation. Extensive training and short follow-up training are very helpful in ingraining the new method. Methods must be instituted and follow-up checks must be put in place to prevent problem recurrences from lapses to old routines and methods. Solution implementation is a key step toward success.

**EXAMPLE 3.17   Plastics and Dashes: Ensuring Permanence
                  by Standardizing Improvements**

Plastics and Dashes asks each team to write up a brief but formal discussion of the problem-solving steps their team took to eliminate the root causes of problems. These discussions are shared with others involved in problem-solving to serve as a guide for future problem-solving efforts.

Step 10. Act: Continuous Improvement

Improvement projects are easy to identify. A review of operations will reveal many opportunities for improvement. Any sources of waste, such as warranty claims, overtime, scrap, or rework, as well as production backlogs or areas in need of more capacity, are potential projects. Even small improvements can lead to a significant impact on the organization's financial statement. Having completed one project, others wait for the same problem-solving process.

Upon completion of their project, teams often present their findings in the form of a final report or storyboard. The following Real Tools for Real Life feature describes one team's complete project from beginning to end. They used a variety of techniques from this chapter to support their problem-solving effort. Note that their process closely follows the problem-solving method laid out in Figure 3.1 at the beginning of this chapter. By sharing their success stories, these teams motivate others to tackle problems in their own areas.

REAL TOOLS FOR REAL LIFE

Root Cause Analysis of Out-of-Round Condition in an Aircraft Landing Gear Strut Support

The Team
Process Engineer
   Responsibility: Research operations and determine areas of concern.
Quality Engineer
   Responsibility: Develop and monitor part measurement system.
Industrial Engineer
   Responsibility: Implement process changes.

Team Mission   As a problem-solving team, we will concentrate on the causes of abnormal bowing of part J-8 (Figure 3.34). We will investigate in-house processes as well as possible supplier material inadequacies.

Customers   Our customers, both internal and external, and their needs and expectations are detailed in Figure 3.35.

Problem Statement   During the final boring operation, parts are being scrapped or reworked because of a concentricity problem with the inner member.

Measures of Performance   Key measures of performance were selected to monitor the effectiveness of future improvements. The measures of performance were identified as:

   Concentricity meets customer requirements
   Less variation present in process and parts
   Lower scrap levels
   Lower rework levels
   Lower tooling costs
   Improved throughput

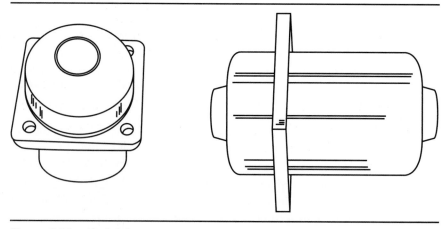

Figure 3.34   Part J-8

Customer Focus

Internal Customers	Needs and Expectations
Receiving	On-time delivery Order accuracy Operation to move to next
Inspection	Order accuracy On-time delivery Dimensional accuracy Lot size inspection requirements Calibrated inspection tools Dimensional requirements
Machining	Order accuracy On-time delivery Dimensional accuracy (previous op.) Reliable equipment Production requirements Training for operation of equipment
Product Testing	Conformance to FAA regulations Standardized testing equipment Current FAA regulations
Shipping	Achieve shipment goals Directions where, when, & how
Inventory	No buildup of excess inventory Parts available on demand
Sales	Quality parts Quality reputation
Product Development	Low cost Improved processes Market demand information
Employees (General)	Safe working conditions Incentives Fair wages Training Opportunity for $ advancement
Purchasing	Orders from customers Raw material requirements Funding to purchase materials

External Customers	Needs and Expectations
RQM Precision Machining	Material requirements
ABC Aerospace Corporation	Quality Parts
FAA Inspector	On-time delivery Meet FAA standards Current FAA regulations
Pilot	Durable parts Reliable parts Safe operation

Figure 3.35   Customer Expectations Related to Part J-8

PROBLEM ANALYSIS

Process Flowchart   We charted the process flow of Part J-8 through our plant, beginning with the customer order and ending when the customer receives the part (Figure 3.36). We charted the process in order to gain insight into possible problem areas created by our current process.

Process Information Diagrams   Histograms, $\overline{X}$ and R charts, and Pareto charts (Figures 3.37 through 3.39) were used to find out exactly where in the process the bowing of the inner member of Part J-8 was occurring. We determined that bowing was occurring at the press operation where the inner member is pressed into the outer casing.

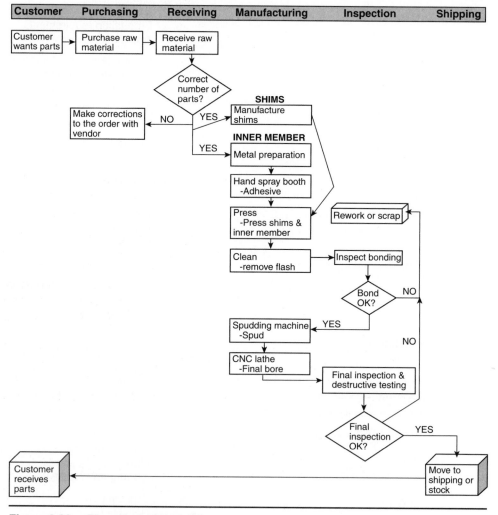

Figure 3.36   Flowchart of Part J-8

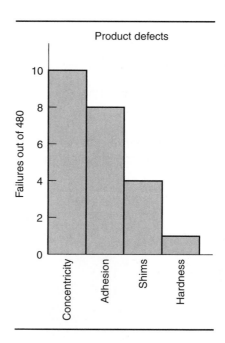

Product defects

Figure 3.37   Pareto Diagram of J-8 Product Defects

Cause and Effect Diagram   To clearly define the root causes of the problem at the press operation, a cause and effect diagram was created (Figure 3.40).

ROOT CAUSE DETERMINATION

By studying the process information gathered during the problem analysis phase, we were able to determine that the root cause of the bowing problem was occurring at the press operation. We investigated the operation and determined that only one fixture was used to press together all the parts in this part family. The problem was that on Part J-8 the press only made it halfway through the inner core. This resulted in an incorrect pressure being applied to the part, causing the part to bow.

A study of the detailed process setup instructions revealed a second, more critical problem. Though proper setup procedures have been defined for this part, over time, it has become standard practice to use the same fixture for all parts in the family, even though the appropriate fixture for each part exists. This tells us that the documented processes are not being followed.

PROBLEM SOLUTION

Before actions were taken to resolve the problem, a force-field analysis (Figure 3.41) was developed to understand the feasibility of implementing the changes needed to correct the situation. With the root cause of our problem defined, restraining and driving forces were taken into consideration to determine the appropriate actions to take.

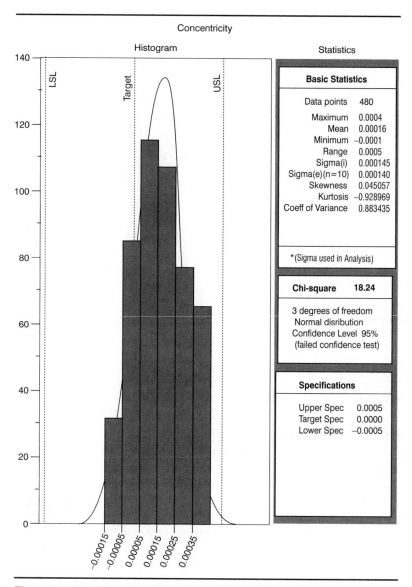

Figure 3.38   Histogram Showing J-8 Inner/Outer Diameter Concentricity

PLAN OF ACTION

Operator Training   Starting with the next batch of parts, the correct fixtures will be used. During the training session, we discussed the importance of following the appropriate procedures.

Fixture Tray   To ensure that the appropriate fixtures are used on each part, a new fixture tray has been created. Fixtures in this tray are clearly marked as to which part

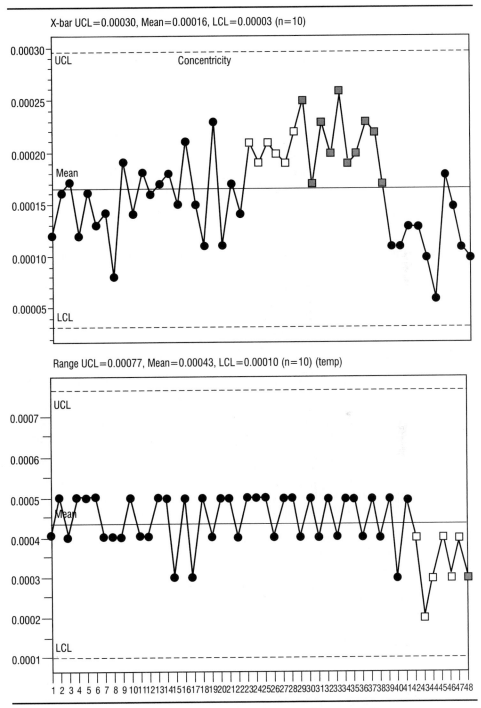

Figure 3.39   Control Chart of Inner/Outer Diameter Concentricity

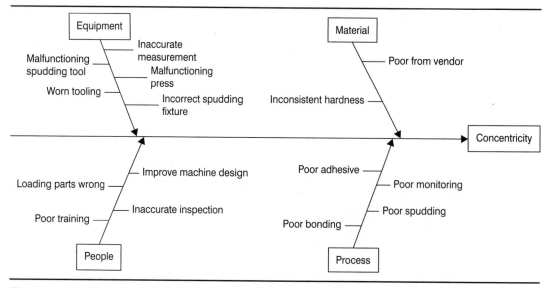

Figure 3.40   Cause-and-Effect Diagram for Concentricity Problems for Part J-8

Force-Field Analysis

Desired Change: Effectively meet customer needs by manufacturing concentric parts throughout the entire process.

Driving

(2)-Less rework
(0)-Less cost (rework, insp., etc.)
(1)-Quicker throughput
(2)-Improved customer satisfaction
(1)-Less inspection
(1)-Less scrap
(2)-Less non-value added activities
(0)-Management support
(0)-Enhance reputation
(0)-Increased contracts ($)
(2)-Required to meet FAA specification
(2)-Will be dropped from contracts
(0)-Incentives for employees
(0)-Motivated workforce

Restraining

(2)-Time/cost of problem solving
(3)-Not cost effective
(2)-Not important to customer
(1)-May increase cost of part
(0)-No employees w/ proper skills
(2)-Unavailable technology
(0)-Low employee satisfaction/motivation
(0)-Poor understanding of goal

Action Plans

1.) Perform cost/benefit analysis on rework, scrap, and customer dissatisfaction costs vs. costs required to solve the problem.
2.) Assign employees to investigate process to determine operation where parts fall out of concentricity.
3.) Implement recommendations to resolve concentricity problem.
4.) Use measures of performance to determine whether or not the implementation is effectively meeting our desired change.

Figure 3.41   Force-Field Analysis for J-8 Concentricity Improvements

they are to be used for. We feel this fixture tray will reduce operator fixture selection error. It also enables us to do a quick visual inspection of the tools for inventory and preventive maintenance purposes.

Additional Inspection   For the short term, additional inspection operations have been added to the process (Figure 3.42). These will be used to gather information

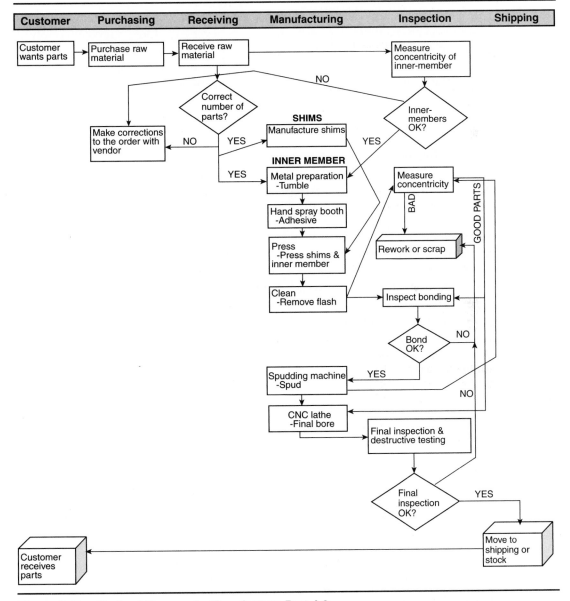

Figure 3.42   Revised Process to Manufacture Part J-8

about part concentricity and to track our measures of performance. These operations will be disbanded once we are sure that we have fixed the problem.

FOLLOW-UP

Each week, for the next six weeks, we will track the measures of performance in order to determine if the problem has been correctly detected and solved.   **Q.**

A project team's tasks don't end with the solution of one particular problem. The quality- and productivity-improvement process never ends. Once a problem is solved, teams are reformed to "do it all over again," this time with a new problem, opportunity, or project. Only through continual improvement can a company hope to move toward the future, improve its customer base, and ensure future profits.

SUMMARY

Teaching the tools of quality improvement and problem solving is actually the easiest part of the quality-improvement process. Helping individuals and groups apply those techniques in a problem-solving format is critical and difficult. Upper-management involvement in selecting issues to be investigated is important to the success of a quality-improvement program. Brainstorming and Pareto analyses also help identify where problem-solving efforts should be concentrated. Teach people the techniques and then use brainstorming to encourage them to uncover problems in their own area and begin to solve them. Figure 3.43 lists the problem-solving tools by type: problem/opportunity development tools, quantitative tools, control or tracking tools, and appraisal tools. Upper management should be involved in the entire process, from education to implementation. They should be the ones providing their people with a push in the right direction.

Problem/Opportunity Development Tools
    Brainstorming
    WHY-WHY Diagrams
    Flowcharts
    Force-Field Analysis
Quantitative Tools
    Histograms and Statistics
    Cause-and-Effect Diagrams
    Pareto Analysis
Control or Tracking Tools
    Control Charts
    Run Charts
    Scatter Diagrams
Appraisal Tools
    Check Sheets

Figure 3.43   Problem-Solving Tools

■ *Lessons Learned*

1. Problem solving is the isolation and analysis of a problem and the development of a permanent solution. Problem solving should be logical and systematic.
2. The following steps should be taken during the problem-solving process:

   Step 1. Recognize the problem; establish the priorities.
   Step 2. Form quality-improvement teams.
   Step 3. Define the problem.
   Step 4. Develop performance measures.
   Step 5. Analyze the problem/process.
   Step 6. Determine possible causes.
   Step 7. Select and implement the solution.
   Step 8. Evaluate the solution and institute the follow-up.
   Step 9. Ensure permanence.
   Step 10. Continuous improvement.

3. The following are techniques used in problem solving: brainstorming, Pareto analysis, WHY-WHY diagrams, flowcharts, force-field analysis, cause-and-effect diagrams, check sheets, histograms, scatter diagrams, control charts, and run charts.
4. Problem-solvers are tempted to propose solutions before identifying the root cause of the problem and performing an in-depth study of the situation. Adhering to a problem-solving method avoids this tendency.
5. Brainstorming is designed for idea generation. Ideas should not be discussed or criticized during a brainstorming session.
6. Flowcharts are powerful tools that allow problem-solvers to gain in-depth knowledge of the process.
7. Cause-and-effect diagrams enable problem solvers to identify the root causes of succinctly stated problems.
8. Steps must be taken to ensure that the new methods or changes to the process are permanent.
9. Don't be afraid to apply the techniques you know. ■

Chapter Problems

Problem Solving

1. Good root cause identification and problem-solving efforts begin with a clear problem statement. Why is a well-written problem statement necessary?
2. Describe the 10 steps of problem solving.
3. An orange juice producer has found that the fill weights (weight of product per container) of several of its orange juice products do not meet specifications. If the problem continues, unhappy customers will stop buying their

product. Outline the steps that they should take to solve this problem. Provide as much detail as you can.

4. Bicycles are being stolen at a local campus. Campus security is considering changes in bike rack design, bike parking restrictions, and bike registration to try to reduce thefts. Thieves have been using hacksaws and bolt cutters to remove locks from the bikes. Create a problem statement for this situation. How will an improvement team use the problem statement?

5. Read Example 3.17 on page 113. As if you were the project manager responsible for solving this problem, describe the steps you would take to plan this problem investigation.

6. A pizza company with stores located citywide uses one order call-in phone number for the entire city. Callers, regardless of their address, can phone XXX-1111 to place an order. Based on the caller's phone number, an automated switching service directs the call to the appropriate store.

   On a recent Friday evening, the pizza company lost as many as 15,000 orders when a malfunctioning mechanical device made calls to their phone number impossible. From about 5:30 to 8 p.m., when callers hoping to place an order phoned, they were met with either silence or a busy signal. This is not the first time this malfunction has occurred. Just two weeks earlier, the same problem surfaced. The pizza company and the company that installed the system are working to ensure the situation doesn't repeat itself. They believe a defective call switch is to blame.

   Based on what you have learned in this chapter, why is a structured problem-solving process critical to the success of finding and eliminating a problem? What steps do you recommend they follow?

7. When creating a problem statement, what are three guides to use?

Pareto Charts

8. During the past month, a customer-satisfaction survey was given to 200 customers at a local fast-food restaurant. The following complaints were lodged:

Complaint	Number of Complaints
Cold Food	105
Flimsy Utensils	20
Food Tastes Bad	10
Salad Not Fresh	94
Poor Service	15
Food Greasy	9
Lack of Courtesy	5
Lack of Cleanliness	25

Create a Pareto chart with this information.

9. A local bank is keeping track of the different reasons people phone the bank. Those answering the phones place a mark on their check sheet in the rows most representative of the customers' questions. Given the following check sheet, make a Pareto diagram:

Credit Card Payment Questions	245
Transfer Call to Another Department	145
Balance Questions	377
Payment Receipt Questions	57
Finance Charges Questions	30
Other	341

Comment on what you would do about the high number of calls in the "Other" column.

10. Once a Pareto chart has been created, what steps would you take to deal with the situation given in Problem 9 in your quality-improvement team?

11. Two partners in an upholstery business are interested in decreasing the number of complaints from customers who have had furniture reupholstered by their staff. For the past six months, they have been keeping detailed records of the complaints and what had to be done to correct the situations. To help their analysis of which problems to attack first, they decide to create several Pareto charts. Use the following table to create Pareto charts for the number of complaints, the percentage of complaints, and the dollar loss associated with the complaints. Discuss the charts.

Category	Number of Complaints	Percent of Complaints	Dollar Loss
Loose Threads	14	28	294.00
Incorrect Hemming	8	16	216.00
Material Flaws	2	4	120.00
Stitching Flaws	6	12	126.00
Pattern Alignment Errors	4	8	240.00
Color Mismatch	2	4	180.00
Trim Errors	6	12	144.00
Button Problems	3	6	36.00
Miscellaneous	5	10	60.00
	50	100	

12. Create a Pareto chart for the following safety statistics from the security office of a major apartment building. What does the chart tell you about their safety record and their efforts to combat crime? Where should they concentrate their efforts? In this example, does a low number of occurrences

necessarily mean those areas should be ignored? Does the magnitude of the injury done mean anything in your interpretation?

	1989	1990	1991	1992	1993	1994	1995	1996	1997	1998	1999
Homicide	0	0	0	0	0	0	0	0	0	1	0
Aggravated Assault	2	1	0	1	3	4	5	5	6	4	3
Burglary	80	19	18	25	40	26	23	29	30	21	20
Grand Theft Auto	2	2	6	15	3	0	2	10	5	2	3
Theft	67	110	86	125	142	91	120	79	83	78	63
Petty Theft	37	42	115	140	136	112	110	98	76	52	80
Grand Theft	31	19	16	5	4	8	4	6	2	4	3
Alcohol Violations	20	17	16	16	11	8	27	15	10	12	9
Drug Violations	3	4	2	0	0	0	0	2	3	2	1
Firearms Violations	0	0	0	0	0	1	0	0	1	0	0

13. Max's Barbeque Tools manufactures top-of-the-line barbeque tools. These tools are sold in sets that include knives, long-handled forks, and spatulas. During the past year, nearly 240,000 tools have passed through final inspection. Create a Pareto chart with the information provided in Figure P3.1 Comment on whether or not any of the categories may be combined. What problems should Max's tackle first?

14. PT Tool Inc. manufactures aircraft landing gear. The completed gear must perform to rigid specifications. Due to the expensive nature of the product, the landing gear must also meet customer expectations for fit and finish. To gather information about nonconformities that are occurring in their shop, a problem-solving team has utilized check sheets to record the nonconformities that they find on the parts during final inspection. When they encounter a problem, the inspectors check the appropriate category on the check sheet. Create a Pareto diagram from the check sheet. Based on the diagrams, where should PT Tool be concentrating their improvement efforts?

Check Sheet of Finish Flaws and Operational Flaws

Finish Flaws

Scratches	///// ///
Dents	//
Surface finish disfigurations in paint	////
Damage to casing	/
Wrong color	/

Final Inspection
Department 8
February

Defect	Totals	Defect	Totals
Bad handle rivets	1753	Buff concave	33
Grind in blade	995	Bent	32
Etch	807	Hit handle	27
Hit blades	477	Burn	16
Bad tines	346	Wrap	15
Bad steel	328	Burned handles	11
Rebend	295	Re-color concave	10
Cracked handle	264	Rivet	9
Rehone	237	Handle color	6
Cracked steel	220	Hafting marks handles	5
Nicked and scratched	207	Raw fronts	4
Haft at rivets	194	Pitted blades	4
High handle rivets	170	Scratched blades	4
Dented	158	Raw backs	3
Pitted bolsters	130	Water lines	3
Vendor rejects	79	Open handles	3
Holder marks	78	Seconds	3
Heat induct	70	Reruns	2
Open at rivet	68	DD edge	2
Finish	56	Bad/bent points	1
Edge	54	Stained rivets	1
Honing	53	Seams/holes	1
Cloud on blades	46	Open steel	1
Hafting marks steel	43	Narrow blades	1
Scratched rivets	41		
Burrs	41	Total inspected	238,385
High-speed buff	41	Total accepted	230,868
Stained blades	35	Total rejected	7,517
Crooked blades	34		

Figure P3.1   Problem 13

Operational Flaws

Mounting plate location off center	///// ///// /
Nonfunctional electrical system	//
Activation switch malfunction	/
Motor failure	////

15. Create a Pareto diagram using the check sheet provided in Problem 14 and the following information about the individual costs associated with correcting each type of nonconformity. Based on your Pareto diagram showing

the total costs associated with each type of nonconformity, where should PT Tool be concentrating their improvement efforts? How is this focus different from that in Problem 14?

Scratches	$ 145
Dents	$ 200
Surface finish disfigurations in paint	$ 954
Damage to casing	$ 6500
Wrong color	$ 200
Mounting plate location off center	$ 75
Nonfunctional electrical system	$ 5000
Activation switch malfunction	$ 300
Motor failure	$ 420

Measures of Performance

16. Describe a process. Based on the process you described, what are two measures that can be used to determine if the process you described is performing well?

17. Review problem 6. What are two measures of performance that can be used to determine if the changes they make are effective?

18. Review problem 8. What are two measures of performance that can be used to determine if the changes they make are effective?

19. Review problem 11. What are two measures of performance that can be used to determine if the changes they make are effective?

20. Review problem 14. What are two measures of performance that can be used to determine if the changes they make are effective?

Brainstorming

21. Brainstorm 10 reasons why a dinner order might arrive late to the guests' table.

22. Brainstorm 10 reasons why the university computer might malfunction.

23. Brainstorm 10 reasons why a customer may not feel the service was adequate at a department store.

24. How are brainstorming techniques used to discover potential corrective actions?

WHY-WHY Diagrams

25. Create a WHY-WHY diagram for how you ended up taking this particular class.

26. A mail order company has a goal of reducing the amount of time a customer has to wait in order to place an order. Create a WHY-WHY diagram about waiting on the telephone. Once you have created the diagram, how would you use it?

27. Apply a WHY-WHY diagram to a project you face at work or in school.

28. Create a WHY-WHY diagram for this problem statement: Customers leave the store without making a purchase.

Process Mapping

29. Create a flowchart for registering for a class at your school.

30. Create a flowchart for solving a financial aid problem at your school.

31. WP Uniforms provides a selection of lab coats, shirts, trousers, uniforms, and outfits for area businesses. For a fee, WP Uniforms will collect soiled garments once a week, wash and repair these garments, and return them the following week while picking up a new batch of soiled garments.

   At WP Uniforms, shirts are laundered in large batches. From the laundry, these shirts are inspected, repaired, and sorted. To determine if the process can be done more effectively, the employees want to create a flowchart of the process. They have brainstormed the following steps and placed them in order. Create a flowchart with their information. Remember to use symbols appropriately.

Shirts arrive from laundry.	Ask: Is shirt beyond cost-effective
Pull shirts from racks.	repair?
Remove shirts from hangers.	Discard shirt if badly damaged.
Inspect.	Sort according to size.
Ask: Does shirt have holes or	Fold shirt.
other damage?	Place in proper storage area.
Make note of repair needs.	Make hourly count.

32. Coating chocolate with a hard shell began with M&Ms during World War II. Coated candies were easier to transport because the coating prevented them from melting. Making coated candies is an interesting process. First the chocolate centers are formed in little molds. These chocolate centers are then placed in a large rotating drum that looks a bit like a cement mixer. Temperature controls on the drum maintain a low enough temperature to prevent the chocolate from softening. While rolling around in the drum, the chocolates are sprayed with sugary liquid that hardens into the white candy shell. Since the chocolates are constantly rotating, they do not clump together while wet with the sugary liquid. Once the white candy shell has hardened, a second, colored, sugar liquid is sprayed into the drum. Once the color coating dries, the colored candies are removed from the drum by pouring them onto a conveyor belt where each candy fits into one of thousands of candy shaped depressions. The belt vibrates gently to seat the candies into the depressions. Once they are organized on the belt, they proceed through a machine which gently imprints a maker's mark onto each candy with edible ink. Map this process.

33. Create a flowchart using symbols for the information provided in the table below.

Materials	Process	Controls
	Buy Filter	
	Buy Oil	
Wrench to Unscrew Oil Plug		
Oil Filter Wrench		
Oil Drain Pan		
	Start Car and Warm It Up (5 min)	
	Shut Off Car When Warm	
	Utilize Pan for Oil	
	Remove Plug	
	Drain Oil into Pan	
	Remove Old Filter with Wrench When Oil Is Completely Drained	
	Take Small Amount of Oil and Rub It Around Ring on New Filter	
	Screw New Filter On by Hand	
	Tighten New Filter by Hand	
	Add Recommended Number of New Quarts of Oil	
	Start Engine and Run for 5 min to Circulate Oil	
		Look for Leaks While Engine Is Running
	Wipe Dipstick Off	
		Check Oil Level Add More if Low
	Place Used Oil in Recycling Container	
	Take Used Oil to Recycling Center	
	Dispose of Filter Properly	

Cause-and-Effect Diagrams

34. What role does a cause-and-effect diagram play in finding a root cause of a problem?

35. A customer placed a call to a mail order catalog firm. Several times the customer dialed the phone and received a busy signal. Finally, the phone was answered electronically, and the customer was told to wait for the next available operator. Although it was a 1-800 number, he found it annoying to wait on the phone until his ear hurt. Yet he did not want to hang up for fear he would not be able to get through to the firm again. Using the problem statement "What makes a customer wait?" as your base, brainstorm to create a cause-and-effect diagram. Once you have created the diagram, how would you use it?

36. Create cause-and-effect diagrams for (*a*) a car that won't start, (*b*) an upset stomach, and (*c*) a long line at the supermarket.

37. The newly appointed warehouse manager of CH Distribution has been studying the flow of the pick, pack, and shipment of orders. To understand the process of picking orders in a warehouse, his team followed part pickers around on the job. Pickers received a computer printout of the order. The printout contains limited information, only the items required and who they were to be shipped to. The team noticed that some orders were large and some were small. All pickers have the same size carts meaning that sometimes there was empty space on the carts and sometimes the carts couldn't hold it all. They also noticed that light levels were low in the warehouse. Create a cause-and-effect diagram for the problem: Multiple trips to the same stocking area.

Force-Field Diagrams

38. For problem 37, create a force-field diagram for the issue: Reduce order picking time.

39. Create a force-field diagram for Problem 4, concerning bike thefts.

40. Create a force-field diagram for a restaurant where customers are waiting more than 10 minutes for their food.

The Big Picture

41. Revisit problem 6 concerning the pizza company. What techniques do you suggest they use to fully investigate their problem? In what way would the techniques you suggested be useful?

42. One hot summer evening, a woman returned home from work and was surprised when a harried man dashed from the side of the house and gasped:

> "Are you Mrs. G.?"
> "Yes."

With this admission, the man launched into his tale of his truly horrible day. It seems that he was employed by an air conditioning company and had been sent out to disconnect and remove an air conditioner at 10 Potter Lane. He had been informed that no one would be at home and that the cellar door would be left unlocked. When he arrived at 10 Potter Lane, everything was as he expected, so he got to work. He had just finished disconnecting the air conditioner when his office paged him. The office had given him the wrong address. What should he do? Reconnect it, the office replied. It wasn't as simple as that, because he damaged the air conditioner while removing it. After all, since the air conditioner was being replaced, he did not consider it necessary to be careful.

"How could this have happened?" asked Mrs. G.

We often read about or experience life's little errors. Sometimes they are minor disturbances to our routines and sometimes they are even funny, but occasionally mistakes cost significant time and money. How do companies avoid errors? How do they find the answer to the question: how could this have happened? What problem-solving techniques would you apply from this chapter to investigate the root cause of this problem?

43. Apply the 10 problem-solving steps described in this chapter to a problem you face(d) at work or in school.

CASE STUDY 3.1
Problem Solving

PART 1

WP Inc. is a manufacturer of small metal parts. Using a customer's designs, WP creates the tools, stamps, bends, forms the metal parts, deburrs, washes, and ships the parts to the customer. WP has been having a recurring problem with the automatic parts washer, used to wash small particles of dirt and oil from the parts. The parts washer (Figure C3.1.1) resembles a dishwasher. The recurrent problem involves the spray nozzles, which frequently clog with particles, causing the parts washer to be shut down.

Although the parts washer is not the most time-consuming or the most important operation at WP, it has been one of the most troublesome. The nozzle-clogging problem causes serious time delays, especially since almost every part manufactured goes through the parts washer. The parts-washing operation is a critical aspect of WP's quality process. It is also the only alternative for cleaning parts since EPA regulations

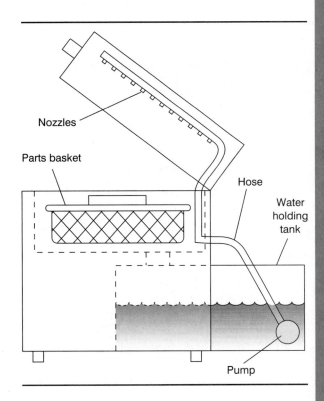

Figure C3.1.1   Automatic Parts Washer

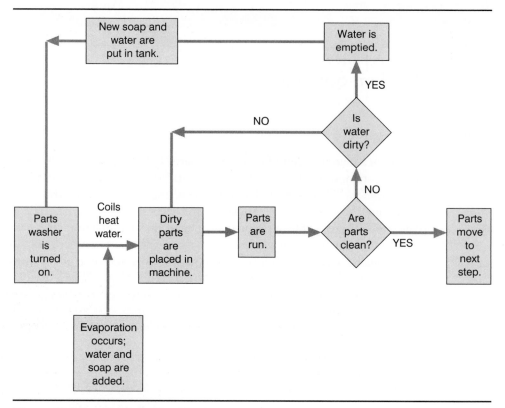

Figure C3.1.2   Process Flowchart

no longer allow the use of a vapor degreaser using trichloroethane 1,1,1. To better understand the process, study the process flowchart seen in Figure C3.1.2.

 Assignment

Create a problem-solving group and design a problem statement. Follow the problem-solving steps from Figure 3.2 on page 71 throughout this case.

PART 2

Intensive questioning of the operator monitoring the process yields the following information:

For about a month, the operator has been observing the parts washer and recording the behavior of the nozzles. A significant portion of the time, the nozzles do not spray as freely as they should. On seven occasions, the nozzles clogged completely. Two of these clogs happened midday; the remainder occurred at the end of the day. During the month, the nozzles did not clog in the morning. Each time the nozzles clogged, the operator took the opportunity to remove and inspect them. It appears that small particles become clogged in the tiny orifices of the nozzles. This restricts the flow of the soap-and-water solution through the nozzles, in turn causing the nozzles to clog further and eventually shutting the parts washer down. When dry, the small particles are white and flakelike in appearance.

 Assignment

Return to your problem-solving group and brainstorm possible identities for the particles. Revise your problem-solving statement on the basis of what you learned above. Detail the problem-solving steps that you would follow to discover the cause of the clogged nozzles. Given the information in the case, be as specific as possible.

PART 3

It is possible that the particles could be one or several of the following: (1) hard-water buildup, (2) calcium, (3) chips from the parts, (4) paint chips, (5) soap flakes, (6) something caused by a chemical reaction, (7) some type of gravel or dirt. Add your group's ideas to this list.

Further questioning of the operator discloses that the problem occurs most often after the old cleansing solution has been drained from the tank and new solution put in. This doesn't seem to make sense because if the cleansing solution has just been recently changed, the liquid in the tank should be free of particles.

Although this doesn't seem to make sense, tests are conducted in which new cleansing solution is put in the tank. After running the parts washer only two minutes, the nozzles are removed and inspected. To everyone's surprise, many particles have been collected by the nozzles. A study of the particles establishes that these particles are soap! Now it must be determined where these soap particles are coming from.

At the suggestion of one of the problem-solving team members, the tank is drained. The bottom of the tank is found to be coated with a layer of hard soap. Your team has decided to return to the conference room and use a cause-and-effect diagram to guide a brainstorming session to establish why there is a buildup of soap on the bottom of the tank.

While constructing a cause-and-effect diagram, note the following:

1. The water in the tank is heated, causing evaporation to occur. This in turn increases the concentration of the soap content in the solution. Following the written procedures, when the operator notes a decrease in the fluid level in the tank, he or she adds more of the soap-and-water solution. This activity increases the soap concentration even more. Once the soap reaches a certain concentration level, it can no longer be held in solution. The soap particles then precipitate to the bottom of the tank. In the cleaning process, the tank is drained and new solution is put in. This causes a disturbance to the film of

soap particles at the bottom of the tank, and the particles become free-floating in the tank.

2. The soap dissolves in the water best at an elevated temperature. A chart of the daily temperatures in the parts washer shows that the tank has not been held at the appropriate temperature. It has been too low.

3. No filtering system exists between the tank and the nozzles.

Assignment

Using the above information, create a cause-and-effect diagram for the problem of soap buildup on the bottom of the tank.

Assignment

Create a force-field analysis listing potential driving and restraining forces involved in correcting this problem. Brainstorm potential corrective actions.

Assignment

Combine the information from the case and your solutions to the assignments to create a management summary detailing the problem-solving steps taken in this case. Relate your summary to Figure C3.1.2.

CASE STUDY 3.2
Process Improvement

This case is the beginning of a four-part series of cases involving process improvement. The other cases are found at the end of Chapters 4, 5, and 6. Data and calculations for this case establish the foundation for the future cases; however, it is not necessary to complete this case in order to complete and understand the cases in Chapters 4, 5, and 6. Completing this case will provide insight into the use of problem-solving techniques in process improvement. The case can be worked by hand or with the software provided.

PART 1

Figure C3.2.1 provides the details of a simplified version of a bracket used to hold a strut in place on an automobile. Welded to the auto body frame, the bracket cups the strut and secures it to the frame with a single bolt and a lock washer. Proper alignment is necessary for both smooth installation during assembly and future performance. For mounting purposes the left-side hole, A, must be aligned on center with the right-side hole, B. If the holes are centered directly opposite each other, in perfect alignment, then the angle between hole centers will measure 0° . The bracket is created by passing

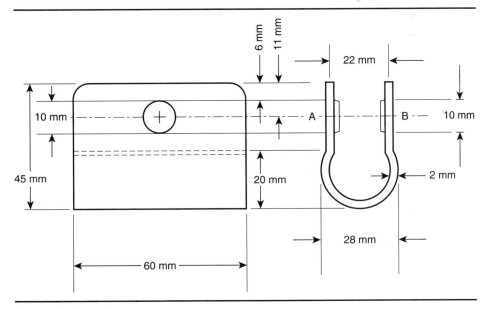

Figure C3.2.1   Bracket

coils of flat steel through a series of progressive dies. As the steel moves through the press, the bracket is stamped, pierced, and finally bent into appropriate shape.

Recently customers have been complaining about having difficulty securing the bracket closed with the bolt and lock washer. The bolts have been difficult to slide through the holes and then tighten. Assemblers complain of stripped bolts and snug fittings. The problem-solving cycle begins with "Recognizing the Problem and Establishing Priorities." Bracket customers have made management at WP Inc. well aware of the problem. Because management is unsure of the root cause of the problem, they proceed with the second step of problem solving and assemble a team. The team consists of representatives from process engineering, materials engineering, product design, and manufacturing. Beginning with Step 3. Plan: Defining the Problem, the team has decided to brainstorm the reasons why this problem has occurred.

 Assignment

Form a team and use the WHY-WHY diagram technique to determine why the bracket may be hard to assemble.

PART 2

In conjunction with the WHY-WHY diagram for why the bracket is not easily assembled, the team has decided to develop performance measures to answer the following question: How do we know that the changes we made to the process actually improved the process?

 Assignment

What performance measures does your team feel are necessary to answer this question: How do we know that the changes we made to the process actually improved the process?

PART 3

Continuing in the problem-solving cycle, the team proceeds with Step 5. In order to analyze the current process, the team visited the customer's assembly plant to determine where the brackets were used in the process and how the assembly was actually performed. There they watched as the operator randomly selected a strut, a bracket, a bolt, and a locknut from different bins. The operator positioned the strut in place, wrapped the bracket around it, and secured it to the frame by finger-tightening the bolt and locknut. The operator then used a torque wrench to secure the assembly. While they watched, the operator had difficulty securing the assembly several times. Back at their plant, the team also created a flowchart for WP's process of fabricating the bracket (Figure C3.2.2).

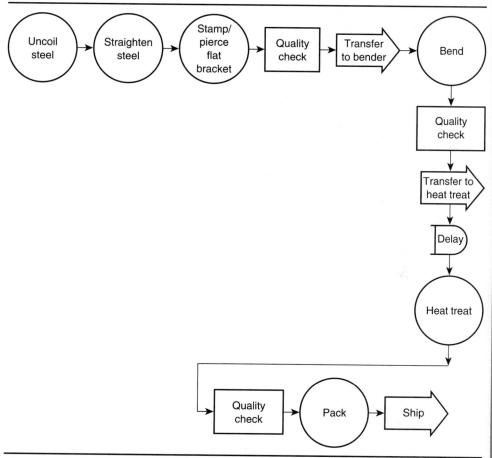

Figure C3.2.2   Flowchart of Bracket-Fabrication Process

After completing the flow diagram and verifying that it was correct, the team moved on to Step 6. Plan: Determining Possible Causes. They decided to use a cause-and-effect diagram to guide their efforts in brainstorming potential root causes for the problem: difficulty securing brackets closed with bolt and locknut.

 Assignment

Create a cause-and-effect diagram and brainstorm potential root causes for the problem: difficulty securing brackets closed with bolt and locknut.

PART 4

Through the use of a cause-and-effect diagram, the engineers determine that the most likely cause of the problems experienced by the customer is the alignment of the holes. At some stage in the formation process, the holes end up off center. Combining this information with the WHY-WHY diagram conclusion that hole alignment was critical for smooth installation during assembly narrows the search for a root cause. Unfortunately, the team still doesn't know why the holes are not properly aligned. They decide to create another cause-and-effect diagram that focuses on causes of improper hole alignment.

 Assignment

Create a second cause-and-effect diagram that focuses on the root causes of improper hole alignment.

PART 5

At this point in the problem-solving process, it would be appropriate to use statistical information to determine whether the holes are truly not properly aligned. The team would confirm their suspicions during the next production run by having the press operator take samples and measure the angle between the centers of the holes for each sample. This data would then be utilized to create a histogram and compare the process performance with the specification for the angle between insert hole A and insert hole B of 0.00° with a tolerance of ±0.30°. Hole alignment problems are confirmed through the use of histograms in Case Study 4.2, should you choose to use it. Histograms are one of the problem-solving techniques discussed in Step 6.

Determining Possible Causes

Assuming that hole alignment problems exist and are measurable, the team continues with their investigation. By studying the process, they determined that the fixture that holds the flat bracket in place during the bending operation does not securely hold the bracket in place. Changing the bracket fixture will be a relatively expensive undertaking. Although the engineers feel this change would eliminate the root cause of a problem as part of Step 7. Do: Selecting and Implementing the Solution, the team has decided to create a force-field analysis before going to management to request funding to make the change.

 Assignment

Create a force-field diagram that describes the forces driving the change to the fixture as well as the forces preventing the change from happening. Use your imagination; problem-solving is never as simple as "spend money."

 Assignment

Describe the remaining steps that the team would take to finish the problem-solving process and ensure that the problem does not return.

II

Control Charts for Variables

4

Statistics

Learning Opportunities:

1. To review basic statistical concepts
2. To understand how to graphically and analytically study a process by using statistics
3. To know how to create and intercept a frequency diagram and a histogram
4. To know how to calculate the mean, median, mode, range, and standard deviation for a given set of numbers
5. To understand the importance of the normal curve and the central limit theorem in quality assurance
6. To know how to find the area under a curve using the standard normal probability distribution (Z tables)
7. To understand how to interpret the information analyzed ■

If things were done right just 99.9 percent of the time, then we'd have to accept

■ One hour of unsafe drinking water per month
■ Two unsafe plane landings per day at O'Hare International Airport in Chicago
■ 16,000 pieces of mail lost by the U.S. Postal Service every hour
■ 20,000 incorrect drug prescriptions per year
■ 500 incorrect surgical operations each week
■ 22,000 checks deducted from the wrong bank accounts per hour
■ 32,000 missed heartbeats per person per year

Original source unknown.

Statistics

*E*ach *of the above statistics deals with the quality of life as we know it. We use statistics every day to define our expectations of life around us. Statistics, when used in quality assurance, define the expectations that the consumer and the designer have for the process. Processes and products are studied using statistics. This chapter provides a basic review of the statistical values most applicable to quality assurance.*

STATISTICS

Statistics help us understand everything from the weather to the census. **Statistics,** *the collection, tabulation, analysis, interpretation, and presentation of numerical data,* provide a viable method of supporting or clarifying a topic under discussion. Statistics are so commonplace that sometimes we accept statistics on their face value, without really determining whether or not they are correct. Misuses of statistics have lead people to distrust them completely as these two quotations show:

> *Figures often beguile me, particularly when I have the arranging of them myself; in which case the remark attributed to Disraeli would often apply with justice and force: "there are three kinds of lies: lies, damned lies, and statistics."**

Mark Twain

> *He uses statistics as a drunk uses a street lamp, for support rather than illumination.*

Andrew Lang

Correctly applied, statistics are the key that unlocks an understanding of process and system performance. In this chapter, we learn how to use statistics to illuminate our understanding of a situation, process, or product.

EXAMPLE 4.1   Statistical Difficulties

National and state monthly unemployment rates are used nationwide to gauge the performance of the U.S. economy. Calculating unemployment rates is complex. States calculate their own unemployment rates by utilizing data provided by the U.S. Labor Department. The dominant source of information is the Current Population Survey. This survey investigates employment status in 60,000 households across the U.S. Divided among the 50 states, this survey reaches 0.06 percent of the households nationwide, or one in every 1,600. States modify the jobless rate calculated from this survey with information about their own state's unemployment compensation claims as well as their own surveys of the business climate within their state.

In April 2001, the State of Ohio Department of Job and Family Services published an unemployment rate of 3.9 percent. This low unemployment rate contradicted the other physical evidence available at the time: a nationwide slowing of the economy, layoffs in the Ohio manufacturing sector, and an increasing number of unemployment compensation claims in the state. In fact, when the unemployment rate of 3.9 percent for April 2001 is compared with a rate of 4.1 percent for April 2000, the economy in Ohio appears to be improving. But the number of people filing for unemployment compensation in April 2001 was 68.8 percent higher than the filing rate in April 2000. These figures contradict each other. How can a greater number of people filing

---

*Ayres, A., editor. *The Wit and Wisdom of Mark Twain.* New York: Harper and Row, 1987, p. 221.

for unemployment result in a lower unemployment rate? Is there something wrong with these contradictory statistics? Is there something more to these statistics that we need to understand? Read on.

Source: *Wall Street Journal,* June 4, 2001.

This first example encourages us to look beyond the face value of the statistics and ask questions. Asking questions to fully understand information is critical to correctly interpreting it. In the following example, statistical data are used to verify that the course of action taken in the example resulted in benefits that outweighed the costs. Here, statistics have been correctly collected, tabulated, analyzed, interpreted, presented, and used to clarify the benefits of using seat belts.

EXAMPLE 4.2   How Do We Know We're Doing the Right Thing?

Seat belts, like air bags, are known to save lives in accidents. According to A. Nomani's *Wall Street Journal* article entitled "How Aggressive Tactics Are Getting Drivers to Buckle Up" (December 11, 1997), highway safety research estimates that if 85 percent of Americans utilized seat belts, each year 4,200 lives would be saved and 100,000 injuries would be prevented. The resulting annual savings in medical costs would be about $6.7 billion. Given that nationally, only 68 percent of the population uses seat belts, some states have put efforts in place to educate drivers and encourage seat-belt use. These efforts cost money. How do the states implementing such programs know whether or not the programs are effective? One way to determine this is to monitor changes in statistical data before and after the program has begun. North Carolina, beginning in 1994, implemented its "Click It or Ticket" program. The results are impressive. Seat-belt use, just 64 percent in 1993, jumped to 83 percent. There has been a 14 percent reduction in serious injuries and deaths, resulting in an estimated $114 million in health-care–related costs. Even with program costs exceeding $4.5 million, these statistics verify that investment in seat-belt educational and enforcement programs have had a positive effect. Based on these results many other states have enacted the same sorts of programs.

USE OF STATISTICS IN QUALITY ASSURANCE

In industry, quality improvement efforts have statistics as their foundation. Correctly collected and analyzed, statistical information can be used to understand and predict process behavior. The five aspects of statistics—collection, tabulation, analysis, interpretation, and presentation—are equally important when analyzing a process. Once gathered and analyzed, statistical data can be used to aid in decisions about making process changes or pursuing a particular course of action. Assumptions based on incomplete information can lead to incorrect decisions, unwise investments, and uncomfortable working environments.

POPULATIONS VERSUS SAMPLES

Statistics can be gathered by studying either the entire collection of values associated with a process or only a portion of the values. A **population** *is a collection of all possible elements, values, or items associated with a situation.* A population can contain a finite number of things or it may be nearly infinite. The insurance forms a doctor's office must process in a day or the number of cars a person owns in a lifetime are examples of finite populations. All the tubes of popular toothpaste ever made by a manufacturer over the product's lifetime represent a nearly infinite population. Limitations may be placed on a collection of items to define the population.

As the size of a population increases, studying that population becomes unwieldy unless sampling can be used. A **sample** *is a subset of elements or measurements taken from a population.* The doctor's office may wish to sample 10 insurance claim forms per week to check the forms for completeness. The manufacturer of toothpaste may check the weight of a dozen tubes per hour to ensure that the tubes are filled correctly. This smaller group of data is easier to collect, analyze, and interpret.

EXAMPLE 4.3   Taking a Sample

An outlet store has just received a shipment of 1,000 shirts sealed in cardboard boxes. The store had ordered 800 white shirts and 200 blue. The store manager wishes to check that there actually are 20 percent blue shirts and 80 percent white shirts. He doesn't want to open all of the boxes and count all of the shirts, so he has decided to sample the population. Table 4.1 shows the results of 10 random samples of 10 shirts each.

A greater number of blue shirts is found in some samples than in others. However, when the results are compiled, the blue shirts comprise 19 percent, very close to the desired value of 20 percent. The manager of the outlet store is pleased to learn that the samples have shown that there are approximately 20 percent blue shirts and 80 percent white.

Table 4.1   A Sampling of Shirts

Sample Number	Sample Size	Number of White Shirts	Number of Blue Shirts	Percentage of Blue Shirts
1	10	8	2	20
2	10	7	3	30
3	10	8	2	20
4	10	9	1	10
5	10	10	0	0
6	10	7	3	30
7	10	8	2	20
8	10	9	1	10
9	10	8	2	20
10	10	7	3	20
Total	100	81	19	19

Figure 4.1   The *Chicago Tribune,* Eager to Get the Scoop, Ran a Headline about Harry Truman that Proved False.

A sample will represent the population as long as the sample is random and unbiased. In a *random sample,* each item in the population has the same opportunity to be selected. A classic example of a *non*random sample was a newspaper poll conducted in the 1940s. The poll was conducted by telephone, in an era where only the wealthy had phones, and this caused the paper to incorrectly predict the results of a national presidential election (Figure 4.1). Statistical data quoted on TV and radio, in magazines and newspapers, and on the Internet may present an incomplete picture of the situation. When someone tells you that 9 out of 10 experts agree with their findings, in order to interpret and use this information it is critical to know how many were sampled, the size of the whole group, and the conditions under which the survey was made. As previously discussed, in statistics, knowledge of the source of the data, the manner in which the data were collected, the amount sampled, and how the analysis was performed is necessary to determine the validity of the information presented. To put statistical values in perspective, you must find answers to such questions as

> How was the situation defined?
> Who was surveyed?
> How many people were contacted?
> How was the sample taken?
> How were the questions worded?
> Is there any ambiguity?

EXAMPLE 4.4   Statistical Difficulties, Continued

In Example 4.1, we learned that the value for the state of Ohio unemployment rate contradicted the performance of the economy of that state. This example discusses what might be wrong with these contradictory statistics.

When the Ohio Department of Job and Family Services noted the anomaly, the department statisticians checked and rechecked their figures. They looked for errors in the calculations, incomplete survey information, or other sources of inconsistencies. When they didn't find any errors in the calculations at the federal or state level, they looked at the data itself. They asked questions like:

How were the terms *employment* and *unemployment* defined?
How many households were contacted?
Who was surveyed?
How was the sample taken?
Was there any ambiguity?

What they discovered was that the answers to each of these questions affected the calculations for their state's unemployment rate.

The definitions for employment versus unemployment complicated the calculations. The national survey reflects the employment status of people during the week of the 12th day of the month. Job loss after that date were not reflected in the survey. Also, anyone who worked a partial week, three or more days of work, was considered employed for that period.

Bias in the sample also exists due to the very small sample size. When calculating unemployment figures, the Ohio Department of Job and Family Services relies on information from the 2,000 Ohio households that are interviewed as part of the national Current Population Survey. The 2,000 surveyed account for only 0.04 percent of the total number of households. A further bias exists because the survey focuses primarily on households in Ohio's three major cities: Columbus, Cincinnati, and Cleveland. Ideally, the survey participants should represent all of Ohio's 88 counties. Virtually no samples are taken in approximately 25 percent of the counties.

Ambiguity is a factor because Ohio has such a mixture of employment opportunities. Industries in Ohio include automotive, manufacturing, mining, lumber, machine tooling, health services, insurance, banking and finance, public utilities, real estate, and the service industries like restaurants, hotels, and stores. In April, some of these sectors, particularly real estate and health services, were performing well. Manufacturing, however, lost 124,000 jobs.

All of these factors make calculating unemployment rates for the state of Ohio an imperfect process. As this example shows, statistical information must be carefully gathered in order to provide valuable information to the user.

Source: *Wall Street Journal,* June 4, 2001.

Another example of biased sampling could occur on the manufacturing floor. If, when an inspector receives a skid of goods, that inspector always samples from the top layer and takes a part from each of the four corners of the skid, the sample is biased. The parts in the rest of the skid have not been considered. Furthermore, operators observing this behavior may choose to place only the best-quality product in those corners. The inspector has biased the sample because it is not random and does not represent all of the parts of the skid. The inspector is receiving an incorrect impression about the quality in the entire skid.

Unbiased samples depend on other features besides randomness. Conditions surrounding the population should not be altered in any way from sample to sample. The sampling method can also undermine the validity of a sample. Ensure the validity of a sample by asking such questions as

How was the problem defined?
What was studied?
How many items were sampled?
How was the sample taken?
How often?
Have conditions changed?

Analyzed correctly, a sample can tell the investigator a great deal about the population.

DATA COLLECTION

Two types of statistics exist: deductive and inductive. Also known as *descriptive statistics,* **deductive statistics** *describe a population or complete group of data.* When describing a population using deductive statistics, the investigator must study each entity within the population. This provides a great deal of information about the population, product, or process, but gathering the information is time-consuming. Imagine contacting each man, woman, and child in the United States, all 250 million of them, to conduct the national census!

When the quantity of the information to be studied is too great, inductive statistics are used. **Inductive statistics** *deal with a limited amount of data or a representative sample of the population.* Once samples are analyzed and interpreted, predictions can be made concerning the larger population of data. Quality assurance (and the U.S. census) relies primarily on inductive statistics. Properly gathered and analyzed, sample data provides a wealth of information.

In quality control, two types of numerical data can be collected. **Variables data,** *those quality characteristics that can be measured,* are treated differently from **attribute data,** *those quality characteristics that are observed to be either present or absent, conforming or nonconforming.* While both variables and attribute data can be described by numbers, attribute data are countable, not measurable.

Variables data tend to be continuous in nature. When data are **continuous,** *the measured value can take on any value within a range.* The range of values that the measurements can take on will be set by the expectations of the users or the circumstances surrounding the situation. For example, a manufacturer might wish to monitor the thickness of a part. During the course of the day, the samples may have values of 0.399, 0.402, 0.401, 0.400, 0.401, 0.403, and 0.398 inch.

Discrete data consist of distinct parts. In other words, when measured, **discrete data** *will be countable using whole numbers.* For example, the number of frozen vegetable packages found on the shelf during an inventory count—ten packages of frozen peas, eight packages of frozen corn, 22 packages of frozen Brussels sprouts—is discrete, countable data. Since vegetable packages can only be sold to customers when the packages are whole and unopened, only whole-numbered measurements will exist; continuous measurements would not be applicable in this case. Attribute data, since the data are seen as being either conforming or not conforming to specifications, are primarily discrete data.

A statistical analysis begins with the gathering of data about a process or product. Sometimes raw data gathered from a process take the form of ungrouped data. *Ungrouped data are easily recognized because when viewed, it appears that the data are without any order.* **Grouped data,** on the other hand, *are grouped together on the basis of when the values were taken or observed.* Consider the following example.

EXAMPLE 4.5   Grouping Data

A company manufactures various parts for automobile transmissions. One part, a clutch plate, resembles a flat round plate with four keyways stamped into it (Figure 4.2). Recently, the customer brought to the manufacturer's attention the fact that not all of the keyways are being cut out to the correct depth. The manufacturer asked the operator to measure each keyway in five parts every 15 minutes and record the measurements. Table 4.2 shows the results. When management started to analyze and interpret the data they were unable to do so. Why?

An investigation of this raw, ungrouped data reveals that there is no way to determine which measurements belong with which keyway. Which keyway is too deep? Too shallow? It is not possible to determine the answer.

To rectify this situation, during the stamping process, the manufacturer placed a small mark below one of the keyways (Figure 4.3). The mark labels that keyway as number 1. Clockwise around the part, the other keyways are designated 2, 3, and 4. The mark does not affect the use of the part. The operator was asked to measure the keyway depths again, five parts every 15 minutes (Table 4.3).

By organizing the data according to keyway, it could then be determined that keyway number 2 is too deep, and keyway number 4 is too shallow.   **Q**

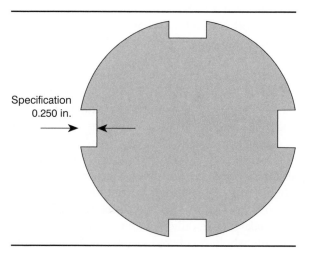

Specification
0.250 in.

Figure 4.2   Clutch Plate

Table 4.2   Clutch Plate Ungrouped Data (in inches)

0.247	0.245	0.271
0.254	0.260	0.276
0.268	0.278	0.268
0.261	0.260	0.230
0.231	0.224	0.243
0.241	0.224	0.225
0.252	0.222	0.232
0.258	0.242	0.254
0.266	0.244	0.242
0.226	0.277	0.248
0.263	0.222	0.236
0.242	0.260	0.262
0.242	0.249	0.223
0.264	0.250	0.240
0.218	0.251	0.222
0.216	0.255	0.261
0.266	0.247	0.244
0.266	0.250	0.249
0.218	0.235	0.226
0.269	0.258	0.232
0.260	0.251	0.250
0.241	0.245	0.248
0.250	0.239	0.252
0.246	0.248	0.251

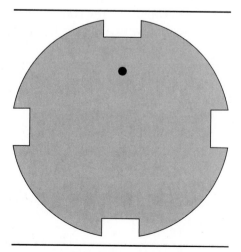

Figure 4.3   Clutch Plate with Mark

Table 4.3   Clutch Plate Grouped Data (in inches)

	Keyway 1	*Keyway 2*	*Keyway 3*	*Keyway 4*
Subgroup 1	0.250	0.261	0.250	0.240
Subgroup 2	0.251	0.259	0.249	0.242
Subgroup 3	0.250	0.258	0.251	0.245
Subgroup 4	0.249	0.257	0.250	0.243
Subgroup 5	0.250	0.262	0.250	0.244
Subgroup 6	0.251	0.260	0.249	0.245
Subgroup 7	0.251	0.258	0.250	0.241
Subgroup 8	0.250	0.259	0.249	0.247
Subgroup 9	0.250	0.257	0.250	0.245
Subgroup 10	0.249	0.256	0.251	0.244
Subgroup 11	0.250	0.260	0.250	0.243
Subgroup 12	0.251	0.258	0.251	0.244
Subgroup 13	0.250	0.257	0.250	0.245
Subgroup 14	0.250	0.256	0.249	0.246
Subgroup 15	0.250	0.257	0.250	0.246

MEASUREMENTS: ACCURACY, PRECISION, AND MEASUREMENT ERROR

The validity of a measurement comes not only from the selection of a sample size and an understanding of the group of data being measured, it also depends on the measurements themselves and how they were taken. Measurement error occurs while the measurements are being taken and recorded. *Measurement error is considered to be the difference between a value measured and the true value.* The error that occurs is one either of accuracy or of precision. *Accuracy refers to how far from the actual or real value the measurement is. Precision is the ability to repeat a series of measurements and get the same value each time.* Precision is sometimes referred to as *repeatability.*

Figure 4.4*a* pictures the concept of accuracy. The marks average to the center target. Figure 4.4*b*, with all of the marks clustered together, shows precision. Figure 4.4*c*

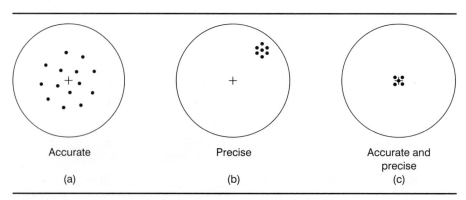

| Accurate | Precise | Accurate and precise |
| (a) | (b) | (c) |

Figure 4.4   Accuracy and Precision

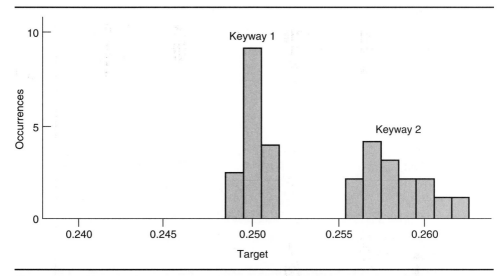

Figure 4.5   Data for Keyways 1 and 2 Comparing Accuracy and Precision

describes a situation in which both accuracy and precision exist. Example 4.6 and Figures 4.5, 4.6, and 4.7 illustrate the concepts of accuracy and precision.

EXAMPLE 4.6   Accuracy and Precision

Accuracy and precision describe the location and the spread of the data. Look at Figures 4.5, 4.6, and 4.7 showing the data from the Clutch Plate example. When compared, the difference in the keyways' accuracy and precision becomes apparent.

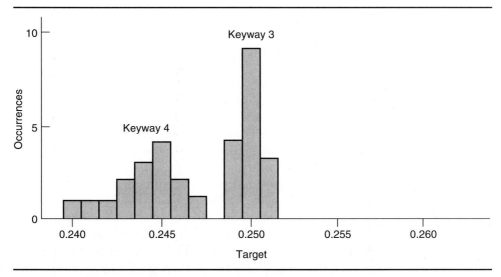

Figure 4.6   Data for Keyways 3 and 4 Comparing Accuracy and Precision

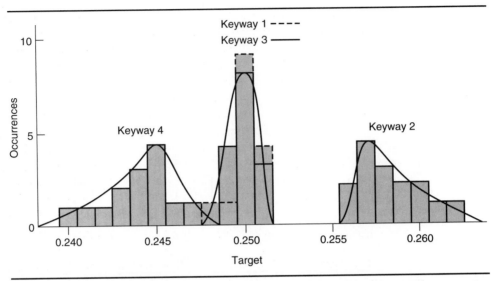

Figure 4.7   Data for Keyways 1 and 3 Are Both Accurate and Precise While Data for Keyways 2 and 4 Are Not.

The data for keyways 1 and 3 exhibit greater accuracy than that for keyways 2 and 4. Note how the data for keyways 1 and 3 are concentrated around the target specification of 0.250 inch. The data values for keyway 2 are greater than the desired target specification and those for keyway 4 are smaller. Notice, too, the difference in precision. Data for keyways 1 and 3 are precise, tightly grouped around the target. Data values for keyways 2 and 4 are not only far away from the target, they are also more spread out, less precise. Changes to this stamping process must be twofold, improving both the accuracy and the precision.

If accuracy and precision are missing from the data, the validity of the information and conclusions will be questioned. Accuracy and precision play an important role in ensuring that the data collected are valuable to those interpreting and presenting it.

Measurement errors may contribute to the lack of accuracy and precision. Measurement errors are not always the fault of the individual performing the measuring. In any situation, several sources of error exist, including environment, people, and machine error. Environmental problems, such as with dust, dirt, temperature, and water, cause measurement errors by disturbing either the products or the measuring tools. A soiled measuring tool will produce a faulty reading as will a layer of dust or oil on a part. Temperature may change the dimensions of products.

The choice and care of measuring devices is critical. The measuring instruments utilized must be able to measure at an accuracy level needed to monitor the process. For example, a meat thermometer would not be appropriate for monitoring the temperature in a hospital sterilizer. Proper care of measuring instruments includes correct handling and storage as well as calibration checks. A systematic calibration program verifies that the device is taking accurate readings of the items being measured. Calibration involves checking the gauge measurement against a known dimension. Recalibration should be done periodically to ensure that no measuring error exists. Recalibration should also be done after any improper handling occurs, such as dropping.

Significant figures and associated rounding errors affect the viability of a measurement. *Significant figures* *are the numerals or digits in a number, excluding any leading* *zeros used to place the decimal point.* Zeros following a digit—for example, 9.700—are significant if they have truly been measured. When working a statistical problem, you should use only the number of digits that the measuring devices are able to provide. If a micrometer reads to three decimal places, then all mathematical calculations should be worked to no more than three decimal places. With today's computers and calculators, there is a temptation to use all the numbers that appear on the screen. Since the measuring device may not have originally measured to that many decimal places, the number should be rounded to the original number of significant figures. Calculations are performed and then rounded to the number of significant figures present in the value with the smallest number of significant figures. When rounding, round to the next highest number if the figure is a 5 or greater. If the figure is 4 or below, round down. Consider the following examples:

$$23.6 \div 3.8 = 6.2 \qquad \text{(3.8 has fewest significant figures)}$$
$$3,456 \div 12.3 = 281 \qquad \text{(12.3 has three significant figures)}$$
$$3.2 \times 10^2 + 6,930 = 7.3 \times 10^3 \qquad \text{(3.2×10^2 has two significant figures)}$$
$$6,983 \div 16.4 = 425.79268 = 426 \text{ when rounded}$$

Human errors associated with measurement errors can be either unintentional or intentional. Unintentional errors result from poor training, inadequate procedures, or incomplete or ambiguous instructions. These types of errors can be minimized by good planning, training, and supervision. Intentional errors are rare and are usually related to poor attitudes; they will require improving employee relations and individual guidance to solve.

Proper measuring is critical to monitoring and controlling any process. A measurement is only as good as the person's reading of the measuring device, combined with the accuracy and precision of the measuring device itself. Those utilizing the measuring equipment must have the appropriate training and have been taught proper handling procedures. Proper care of measuring instruments and correct training of those using them will ensure that the raw data obtained with measuring instruments will be reliable. If this is an incorrect assumption, then any conclusions based on the data and subsequent analysis are useless.

DATA ANALYSIS: GRAPHICAL

A thorough statistical analysis of the data that has been gathered involves three aspects: graphical, analytical, and interpretive. A variety of different graphical methods exist, including the frequency diagram and the histogram.

Frequency Diagrams

A *frequency diagram* *shows the number of times each of the measured values occurred when the data were collected*. This diagram can be created either from measurements taken from a process or from data taken from the occurrences of events. When compared with the raw, ungrouped data, this diagram shows at a glance which values occur the most frequently as well as the spread of the data. To create a frequency diagram, the following steps are necessary:

1. Collect the data. Record the measurements or counts of the characteristics of interest.
2. Count the number of times each measurement or count occurs.
3. Construct the diagram by placing the counts or measured values on the x axis and the frequency or number of occurrences on the y axis. The x axis must contain each possible measurement value from the lowest to the highest, even if a particular value does not have any corresponding measurements. A bar is drawn on the diagram to depict each of the values and the number of times the value occurred in the data collected.
4. Interpret the frequency diagram. Study the diagrams you create and think about the diagram's shape, size, and location in terms of the desired target specification. We learn more about interpreting frequency diagrams later in the chapter.

EXAMPLE 4.7   Clutch Plate: Constructing a Frequency Diagram

To respond to customer issues, the engineers involved in the clutch plate problem are studying the thickness of the part. To gain a clearer understanding of incoming material thickness, they plan to create a frequency diagram for the grouped data shown in Table 4.4.

Step 1. Collect the Data.   The first step is performed by the operator, who randomly selects five parts each hour, measures the thickness of each part, and records the values (Table 4.4).

Table 4.4   Clutch Plate Grouped Data for Thickness (in inches)

Subgroup 1	0.0625	0.0626	0.0624	0.0625	0.0627
Subgroup 2	0.0624	0.0623	0.0624	0.0626	0.0625
Subgroup 3	0.0622	0.0625	0.0623	0.0625	0.0626
Subgroup 4	0.0624	0.0623	0.0620	0.0623	0.0624
Subgroup 5	0.0621	0.0621	0.0622	0.0625	0.0624
Subgroup 6	0.0628	0.0626	0.0625	0.0626	0.0627
Subgroup 7	0.0624	0.0627	0.0625	0.0624	0.0626
Subgroup 8	0.0624	0.0625	0.0625	0.0626	0.0626
Subgroup 9	0.0627	0.0628	0.0626	0.0625	0.0627
Subgroup 10	0.0625	0.0626	0.0628	0.0626	0.0627

Subgroup 11	0.0625	0.0624	0.0626	0.0626	0.0626
Subgroup 12	0.0630	0.0628	0.0627	0.0625	0.0627
Subgroup 13	0.0627	0.0626	0.0628	0.0627	0.0626
Subgroup 14	0.0626	0.0626	0.0625	0.0626	0.0627
Subgroup 15	0.0628	0.0627	0.0626	0.0625	0.0626
Subgroup 16	0.0625	0.0626	0.0625	0.0628	0.0627
Subgroup 17	0.0624	0.0626	0.0624	0.0625	0.0627
Subgroup 18	0.0628	0.0627	0.0628	0.0626	0.0630
Subgroup 19	0.0627	0.0626	0.0628	0.0625	0.0627
Subgroup 20	0.0626	0.0625	0.0626	0.0625	0.0627
Subgroup 21	0.0627	0.0626	0.0628	0.0625	0.0627
Subgroup 22	0.0625	0.0626	0.0628	0.0625	0.0627
Subgroup 23	0.0628	0.0626	0.0627	0.0630	0.0627
Subgroup 24	0.0625	0.0631	0.0630	0.0628	0.0627
Subgroup 25	0.0627	0.0630	0.0631	0.0628	0.0627
Subgroup 26	0.0630	0.0628	0.0629	0.0628	0.0627
Subgroup 27	0.0630	0.0628	0.0631	0.0628	0.0627
Subgroup 28	0.0632	0.0632	0.0628	0.0631	0.0630
Subgroup 29	0.0630	0.0628	0.0631	0.0632	0.0631
Subgroup 30	0.0632	0.0631	0.0630	0.0628	0.0628

Step 2. Count the Number of Times Each Measurement Occurs.   A check sheet, or tally sheet (as described in Chapter 3) is used to make this step easier (Figure 4.8).

Step 3. Construct the Diagram.   The count of the number of times each measurement occurred is placed on the y axis. The values, between 0.0620 and 0.0632,

0.0620	/
0.0621	//
0.0622	//
0.0623	////
0.0624	//// //// //
0.0625	//// //// //// //// //// /
0.0626	//// //// //// //// //// ////
0.0627	//// //// //// //// //// //
0.0628	//// //// //// //// ///
0.0629	/
0.0630	//// //// /
0.0631	//// //
0.0632	////

Figure 4.8   Clutch Plate Thickness Tally Sheet

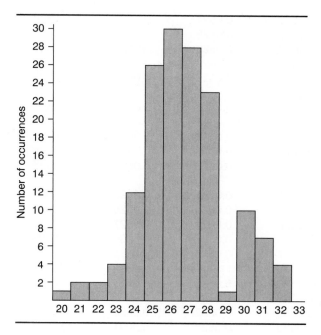

Figure 4.9   Clutch Plate Thickness Frequency Distribution (Coded 0.06)

are each marked on the x axis. The completed frequency diagram is shown in Figure 4.9.

Step 4. Interpret the Frequency Diagram. This frequency distribution is nearly symmetrical, but there is only one occurrence of the value 0.0629. The engineers should definitely investigate why this is so.

Histograms

Histograms and frequency diagrams are very similar. The most notable difference between the two is that on a histogram the data are grouped into cells. Each cell contains a range of values. This grouping of data results in fewer cells on the graph than with a frequency diagram. The x-axis scale on a histogram will indicate the cell midpoints rather than individual values.

Construction of Histograms

Histograms are begun in the same manner as are frequency diagrams. The data are collected and grouped, then a check sheet is used to tally the number of times each measurement occurs. At this point, the process becomes more complex because of the need to create the cells. The following example details the construction of a histogram.

EXAMPLE 4.8   Clutch Plate: Constructing a Histogram

The engineers working with the thickness of the clutch plate have decided to create a histogram to aid in their analysis of the process. They are following these steps:

Step 1. Collect the Data and Construct a Tally Sheet.   The engineers will use the data previously collected (Table 4.4) as well as the tally sheet created during the construction of the frequency diagram (Figure 4.8).

Step 2. Calculate the Range.   The *range, represented by the letter R, is calculated by subtracting the lowest observed value from the highest observed value.* In this case, 0.0620 is the lowest value and 0.0632 is the highest:

$$\text{Range} = R = X_h - X_l$$

where

$$R = \text{range}$$
$$X_h = \text{highest number}$$
$$X_l = \text{lowest number}$$
$$R = 0.0632 - 0.0620 = 0.0012$$

Step 3. Create the Cells.   In a histogram, data are combined into cells. Cells are composed of three components: cell intervals, cell midpoints, and cell boundaries (Figure 4.10). *Cell midpoints identify the centers of cells. A **cell interval** is the distance between the cell midpoints. The **cell boundary** defines the limits of the cell.*

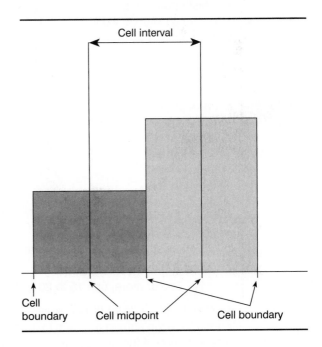

Figure 4.10   Histogram Cell Description

Cell Intervals   Odd-numbered cell intervals are often chosen for ease of calculation. For example, if the data were measured to one decimal place, then the cell intervals could be 0.3, 0.5, 0.7, or 0.9. If the gathered data were measured to three decimal places, then the cell intervals to choose from would be 0.003, 0.005, 0.007 and 0.009. (The values of 1, 0.1, and 0.001 are not chosen for a histogram because they result in the creation of a frequency diagram.) For this example, because the data were measured to four decimal places, the cell interval could be 0.0003, 0.0005, 0.0007, or 0.0009.

Cell interval choice plays a large part in the size of the histogram created. To determine the number of cells, the following formula is used:

$$h = \frac{R}{i} + 1$$

where

h = number of cells
i = cell interval
R = range

Since both i, the cell interval, and h, the number of cells, are unknown, creators of histograms must choose values for one of them and then solve for the other. For our example, if we choose a cell interval of 0.0003,

$$h = \frac{0.0012}{0.0003} + 1$$

$$h = 5$$

The histogram created will contain 5 cells.

For a cell interval value of 0.0005:

$$h = \frac{0.0012}{0.0005} + 1$$

$$h = 3$$

For a cell interval value of 0.0007:

$$h = \frac{0.0012}{0.0007} + 1$$

$$h = 3$$

As the cell interval gets larger, the number of cells necessary to hold all the data and make a histogram decreases. When deciding the number of cells to use, it is sometimes helpful to follow this rule of thumb:

For fewer than 100 pieces of data, use 4 to 9 cells.
For 100 to 500 pieces of data, use 8 to 17 cells.
For 500 or more, use 15 to 20 cells.

Another helpful rule of thumb exists for determining the number of cells in a histogram. Use the square root of n ($\sqrt{n}$), where n is the number of data points, as an approximation of the number of cells needed.

For this example, we will use a cell interval of 0.0003. This will create a histogram that provides enough spread to analyze the data.

Cell Midpoints   When constructing a histogram, it is important to remember two things: (1) Histograms must contain all of the data; (2) one particular value cannot fit into two different cells. Cell midpoints are selected to ensure that these problems are avoided. To determine the midpoint values that anchor the histogram, use either one of the following two techniques.

The simplest technique is to choose the lowest value measured. In this example, the lowest measured value is 0.0620. Other midpoint values are determined by adding the cell interval of 0.0003 to 0.0620 first and then adding it to each successive new midpoint. If we begin at 0.0620, we find the other midpoints at 0.0623, 0.0626, 0.0629, and 0.0632.

If the number of values in the cell is high and the distance between the cell boundaries is not large, the midpoint is the most representative value in the cell.

A second method of determining the midpoint of the lowest cell in the histogram is the following formula:

$$MP_l = X_l + \frac{i}{2}$$

In this formula, MP_l is the midpoint of the lowest cell. The lowest value in the distribution (X_l) becomes the first value in the lowest cell.

Using this formula for this example, the first midpoint would be

$$MP_l = 0.0620 + \frac{0.0003}{2} = 0.06215$$

The remaining midpoint values are determined in the same manner as before. Beginning with the lowest midpoint, 0.06215, add the cell interval of 0.0003, and then add 0.0003 to each successive new midpoint. Starting with a midpoint of 0.06215, we find the other midpoints at 0.06245, 0.06275, 0.06305, and 0.06335.

Cell Boundaries   The cell size, set by the boundaries of the cell, is determined by the cell midpoints and the cell interval. Locating the cell boundaries, or the limits of the cell, allows the user to place values in a particular cell. To determine the lower cell boundary, divide the cell interval by 2 and subtract that value from the cell midpoint. To calculate the lower cell boundary for a cell with a midpoint of 0.0620, the cell interval is divided by 2:

$$0.0003 \div 2 = 0.00015$$

Then, subtract 0.00015 from the cell midpoint,

$$0.0620 - 0.00015 = 0.06185, \text{ the first lower boundary}$$

To determine the upper cell boundary for a midpoint of 0.0620, add the cell interval to the lower cell boundary:

$$0.06185 + 0.0003 = 0.06215$$

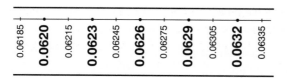

Figure 4.11   Cell Boundaries and Midpoints

The lower cell boundary of one cell is the upper cell boundary of another. Continue adding the cell interval to each new lower cell boundary calculated until all the lower cell boundaries have been determined.

   Note that the cell boundaries are a half decimal value greater in accuracy than the measured values. This is to help ensure that values can be placed in only one cell of a histogram. In our example, the first cell will have boundaries of 0.06185 and 0.06215. The second cell will have boundaries of 0.06215 and 0.06245. Where would a data value of 0.0621 be placed? Obviously in the first cell. Cell intervals, with their midpoint values starting at 0.0620, are shown in Figure 4.11.

Step 4. Label the Axes.   Scale and label the horizontal axis according to the cell midpoints determined in Step 3. Label the vertical axis to reflect the amount of data collected, in counting numbers.

Step 5. Post the Values.   The final step in the creation of a histogram is to post the values from the check sheet to the histogram. The x axis is marked with the cell midpoints and, if space permits, the cell boundaries. The cell boundaries are used to guide the creator when posting the values to the histogram. On the y axis, the frequency of those values within a particular cell is shown. All the data must be included in the cells (Figure 4.12).

Step 6. Interpret the Histogram.   As we can see in Figure 4.12, the data are grouped around 0.0626 and are somewhat symmetrical. In the following sections, we will study histogram shapes, sizes, and locations when compared to a desired

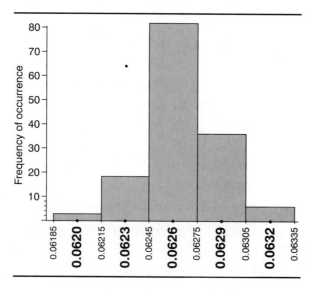

Figure 4.12   Clutch Plate Thickness Histogram

target specification. We will also utilize measures such as means, modes, and medians to create a clear picture of where the data are grouped (the central tendency of the data). Standard deviations and ranges will be used to measure how the data are dispersed around the mean. These statistical values will be used to fully describe the data comprising a histogram.

Analysis of Histograms

Shape, location, and spread are the characteristics used to describe a distribution (Figure 4.13).

Shape: Symmetry, Skewness, Kurtosis *Shape refers to the form that the values of the measurable characteristics take on when plotted or graphed.* Tracing a smooth curve over the tops of the rectangular areas used when graphing a histogram clarifies the shape of a histogram for the viewer (Figure 4.14). Identifiable characteristics include **symmetry,** or, in the case of lack of symmetry, **skewness** of the data; **kurtosis,** or *peakedness of the data;* and **modes,** *the number of peaks in the data.*

When a distribution is **symmetrical,** *the two halves are mirror images of each other.* The two halves correspond in size, shape, and arrangement (Figure 4.14). When a

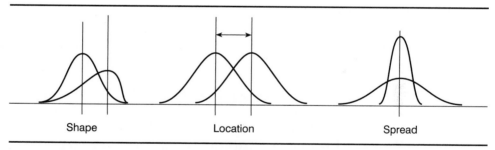

| Shape | Location | Spread |

Figure 4.13   Shape, Location, and Spread

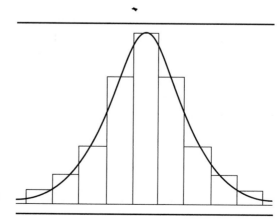

Figure 4.14   Symmetrical Histogram with Smooth Curve Overlay

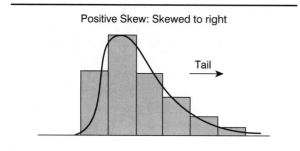

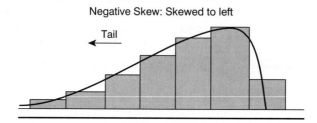

Figure 4.15   Skewness

distribution is not symmetrical, it is considered to be skewed (Figure 4.15). With a *skewed distribution, the majority of the data are grouped either to the left or the right of a center value, and on the opposite side a few values trail away from the center. When a distribution is skewed to the right, the majority of the data are found on the left side of the figure, with the tail of the distribution going to the right.* The opposite is true for a distribution that is *skewed to the left.*

Kurtosis describes the peakedness of the distribution. A *distribution with a high peak is referred to as leptokurtic; a flatter curve is called platykurtic* (Figure 4.16). Typically, the kurtosis of a histogram is discussed by comparing it with another distribution. As we will see later in the chapter, skewness and kurtosis can be calculated numerically. Occasionally distributions will display unusual patterns. *If the distribution displays more than one peak,* it is considered *multimodal. Distributions with two distinct peaks are called bimodal* (Figure 4.17).

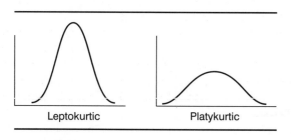

Figure 4.16   Leptokurtic and Platykurtic

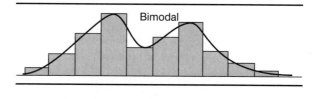

Figure 4.17   Bimodal Distribution

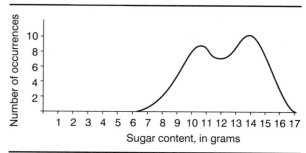

Figure 4.18   Cereal Sugar Content

EXAMPLE 4.9   Analyzing the Distribution

Sue's cereal manufacturing department has been monitoring the sugar content in a production run of cereal. Measurements have been taken every 15 minutes and plotted in a histogram. At the end of each day, Sue and Elizabeth, the company's nutritionist, discuss the distribution over the phone. Figure 4.18 shows the distribution that Sue now wants to describe to Elizabeth, who does not have the graph. Before she phones, what words should Sue jot down to clearly describe the distribution to Elizabeth?

In this case, the graph clearly shows two peaks in the data, one at 10.5 grams and the second at 14 grams. This bimodal distribution tells Sue and Elizabeth that the sugar concentration in the cereal produced this day peaked at two different points. The graph also shows a wide spread to the data, from 6 to 17 grams, as well as being skewed to the left. Sugar concentration in this particular cereal has not been consistent during the day's production run.

EXAMPLE 4.10   Clutch Plate Analyzing the Histogram

Analyzing Figure 4.12 based on the three characteristics of shape, location, and spread reveals that the clutch plate thickness data are fairly consistent. The **shape** of the distribution is relatively symmetrical, though skewed slightly to the right. The data are unimodal, centering on 0.0626 inch. Since we have no other distributions of the same type of product, we cannot make any comparisons or comments on the kurtosis of the data. **Location,** or where the data are located or gathered, is around 0.0626. If the engineers have specifications of 0.0625 $\pm$ 0.0003, then the center of the distribution is higher than the desired value. Given the specifications, the **spread** of the data is broader than the desired 0.0622 to 0.0628 at 0.0620 to 0.0632. Further mathematical analysis with techniques covered later in this chapter will give us an even clearer picture of the data.

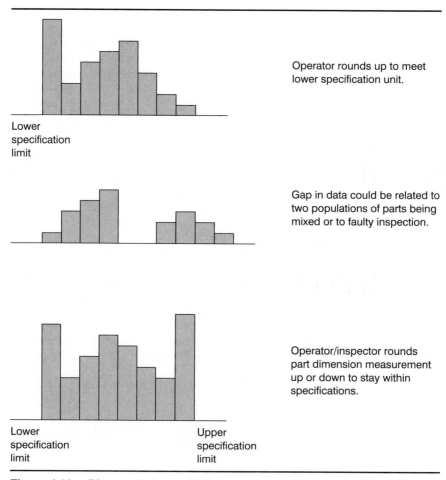

Operator rounds up to meet lower specification unit.

Gap in data could be related to two populations of parts being mixed or to faulty inspection.

Operator/inspector rounds part dimension measurement up or down to stay within specifications.

Figure 4.19   Discrepancies in Histograms

Histograms provide a visual description of the information under study. Discrepancies in the data, such as gaps or unusual occurrences, can be seen at a glance (Figure 4.19).

 REAL TOOLS FOR REAL LIFE

Reading Histograms

Automobile manufacturers and their suppliers are constantly looking for new plastic and composite materials that will be resistant to cracking, chipping, and discoloration, Engineers in W.T. Plastics' labs are measuring the size of cracks in a group of dashboards that has completed a rigorous series of tests designed to mimic stressful environmental conditions. The dashboards have come from two different lots of plastic. Figure 4.20 shows a histogram of the crack sizes.

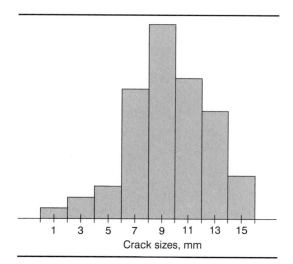

**Figure 4.20   Histogram for
Crack Sizes in Dashboards**

Upon learning that two different lots of dashboards have been combined, the head of the lab asks that the data be separated according to lot and two histograms be created (Figure 4.21). Data from two different populations should not be mixed into one statistical analysis. Now it is clear to all who view the chart that type A dashboards have a histogram that is slightly skewed to the left, while type B dashboards have a histogram that is skewed to the right. Type B's histogram is more leptokurtic than type A's. This means that type A's cracks vary more widely in size compared with type B's cracks.

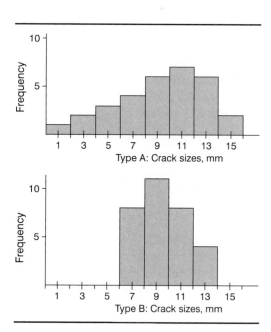

**Figure 4.21   Histogram for
Crack Sizes by Dashboard
Type**

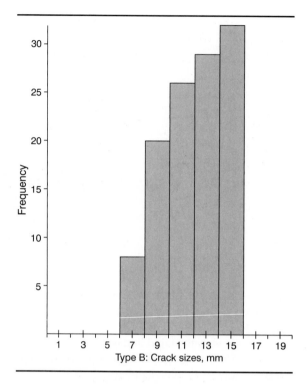

Figure 4.22   Cumulative
Frequency Distribution

Cumulative Frequency Distribution

A *cumulative frequency distribution* *shows the cumulative occurrences of all the values; the values from each preceding cell are added to the next cell until the uppermost cell boundary is reached.* Unlike a histogram, the cumulative frequency distribution adds the previous cell's number of occurrences to the next cell. Figure 4.22 shows a cumulative frequency distribution made from the information from Figure 4.21, type B dashboards.

DATA ANALYSIS: ANALYTICAL

More analytical methods of describing histograms exist. Though shape was easily seen from a picture, the location and spread can be more clearly identified mathematically. Location is described by measures of central tendency: the mean, mode, and median. Spread is defined by measures of dispersion: the range and standard deviation.

Location: Measures of Central Tendency

Averages, medians, and modes are the statistical values that define the center of a distribution. *Since they reveal the place where the data tend to be gathered, these values are commonly called the* **measures of central tendency.**

Mean

The **mean** *of a series of measurements is determined by adding the values together and then dividing this sum by the total number of values.* When this value is calculated for a population, it is referred to as the mean and is signified by μ. When this value is calculated for a sample, it is called the *average* and is signified by $\overline{X}$ (X bar). Means and averages can be used to judge whether or not a group of values is accurate. To calculate the mean of a population, use the following formula:

$$\mu = \frac{X_1 + X_2 + X_3 + \cdots + X_n}{n} = \frac{\sum\limits_{i=1}^{n} X_i}{n}$$

where

$$\mu = \text{mean value of the series of measurements}$$
$$X_1, X_2, \ldots, X_n = \text{values of successive measurements}$$
$$n = \text{number of readings}$$

The same formula can be used to calculate the average associated with a sample. To calculate the average of a sample, use the following formula:

$$\overline{X} = \frac{X_{s1} + X_{s2} + X_{s3} + \cdots + X_{sn}}{n} = \frac{\sum\limits_{i=1}^{n} X_i}{n}$$

where

$$\overline{X} = \text{average value of the sample measurements}$$
$$X_{s1}, X_{s2}, \ldots, X_{sn} = \text{values of sample measurements}$$
$$n = \text{number of readings}$$

EXAMPLE 4.11   Clutch Plate: Determining the Mean

Averages for each of the subgroups for the thicknesses of the clutch plate can be calculated.

1. Calculate the sum of each set of subgroup values:

Subgroup 1:

$$\Sigma X_1 = 0.0625 + 0.0626 + 0.0624 + 0.0625 + 0.0627$$
$$= 0.3127$$

2. Calculate the subgroup average by dividing the sum by the number of samples in the subgroup (n = 5):

Subgroup 1:

$$\overline{X} = \frac{0.0625 + 0.0626 + 0.0624 + 0.0625 + 0.0627}{5}$$
$$= \frac{0.3127}{5}$$
$$= 0.0625$$

Table 4.5 gives a list of the sums and averages calculated for this example. Once the averages for each subgroup have been calculated, a grand average for all of the subgroups

Table 4.5 Clutch Plate Thickness: Sums and Averages

						ΣX_i	X
Subgroup 1	0.0625	0.0626	0.0624	0.0625	0.0627	0.3127	0.0625
Subgroup 2	0.0624	0.0623	0.0624	0.0626	0.0625	0.3122	0.0624
Subgroup 3	0.0622	0.0625	0.0623	0.0625	0.0626	0.3121	0.0624
Subgroup 4	0.0624	0.0623	0.0620	0.0623	0.0624	0.3114	0.0623
Subgroup 5	0.0621	0.0621	0.0622	0.0625	0.0624	0.3113	0.0623
Subgroup 6	0.0628	0.0626	0.0625	0.0626	0.0627	0.3132	0.0626
Subgroup 7	0.0624	0.0627	0.0625	0.0624	0.0626	0.3126	0.0625
Subgroup 8	0.0624	0.0625	0.0625	0.0626	0.0626	0.3126	0.0625
Subgroup 9	0.0627	0.0628	0.0626	0.0625	0.0627	0.3133	0.0627
Subgroup 10	0.0625	0.0626	0.0628	0.0626	0.0627	0.3132	0.0626
Subgroup 11	0.0625	0.0624	0.0626	0.0626	0.0626	0.3127	0.0625
Subgroup 12	0.0630	0.0628	0.0627	0.0625	0.0627	0.3134	0.0627
Subgroup 13	0.0627	0.0626	0.0628	0.0627	0.0626	0.3137	0.0627
Subgroup 14	0.0626	0.0626	0.0625	0.0626	0.0627	0.3130	0.0626
Subgroup 15	0.0628	0.0627	0.0626	0.0625	0.0626	0.3132	0.0626
Subgroup 16	0.0625	0.0626	0.0625	0.0628	0.0627	0.3131	0.0626
Subgroup 17	0.0624	0.0626	0.0624	0.0625	0.0627	0.3126	0.0625
Subgroup 18	0.0628	0.0627	0.0628	0.0626	0.0630	0.3139	0.0627
Subgroup 19	0.0627	0.0626	0.0628	0.0625	0.0627	0.3133	0.0627
Subgroup 20	0.0626	0.0625	0.0626	0.0625	0.0627	0.3129	0.0626
Subgroup 21	0.0627	0.0626	0.0628	0.0625	0.0627	0.3133	0.0627
Subgroup 22	0.0625	0.0626	0.0628	0.0625	0.0627	0.3131	0.0626
Subgroup 23	0.0628	0.0626	0.0627	0.0630	0.0627	0.3138	0.0628
Subgroup 24	0.0625	0.0631	0.0630	0.0628	0.0627	0.3141	0.0628
Subgroup 25	0.0627	0.0630	0.0631	0.0628	0.0627	0.3143	0.0629
Subgroup 26	0.0630	0.0628	0.0620	0.0628	0.0627	0.3142	0.0628
Subgroup 27	0.0630	0.0628	0.0631	0.0628	0.0627	0.3144	0.0629
Subgroup 28	0.0632	0.0632	0.0628	0.0631	0.0630	0.3153	0.0631
Subgroup 29	0.0630	0.0628	0.0631	0.0632	0.0631	0.3152	0.0630
Subgroup 30	0.0632	0.0631	0.0630	0.0628	0.0628	0.3149	0.0630
						9.3981	

can be found by dividing the sum of the subgroup sums by the total number of items taken in all of the subgroups (150). A grand average is designated as $\overline{\overline{X}}$ (X double bar):

$$\overline{\overline{X}} = \frac{0.3127 + 0.3122 + 0.3121 + 0.3114 + \cdots + 0.3149}{150}$$

$$= \frac{9.3990}{150}$$

$$= 0.0627$$

Notice that an average of the averages is not taken. Taking an average of the averages will work only when the sample sizes are constant. Use the sums of each of the subgroups to perform the calculation.

Median

The *median is the value that divides an ordered series of numbers so that there is an equal number of values on either side of the center, or median, value.* An ordered series of data has been arranged according to their magnitude. Once the values are placed in order, the median is the value of the number that has an equal number of values to its left and right. In the case of finding a median for an even number of values, the two center values of the ordered set of numbers are added together and the result is divided by 2. Figure 4.23 shows the calculation of several medians.

EXAMPLE 4.12   Clutch Plate: Determining the Median

From the check sheet (Figure 4.9) the median of the clutch plate thickness data can be found. When the data are placed in an ordered series, the center or median number is found to be 0.0626. Each measurement must be taken into account when calculating a median. Do not use solely the cell midpoints of a frequency diagram or a histogram.

Mode

The *mode is the most frequently occurring number in a group of values.* In a set of numbers, a mode may or may not occur (Figure 4.24). A set of numbers may also have

---

23   25   26   27   28   29   25   22   24   24   25   26   25
Unordered set of numbers

22   23   24   24   25   25   25   25   26   26   27   28   29
Ordered set of numbers

Median = 25

---

1   2   4   1   5   2   6   7
Unordered set of numbers

1   1   2   2   4   5   6   7
Ordered set of numbers

Median = (2 + 4) ÷ 2 = 3

Figure 4.23   Calculating Medians

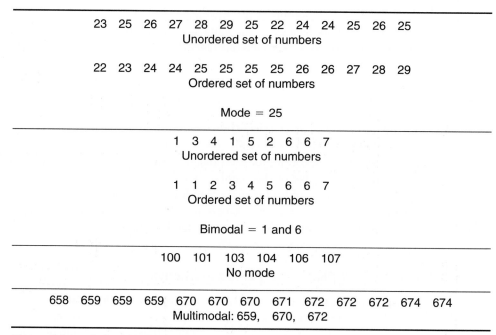

Figure 4.24   Calculating Modes

two or more modes. If a set of numbers or measurements has one mode, it is said to be unimodal. If it has two numbers appearing with the same frequency, it is called bimodal. Distributions with more than two modes are referred to as multimodal. In a frequency distribution or a histogram, the cell with the highest frequency is the mode.

EXAMPLE 4.13   Clutch Plate: Determining the Mode

The mode can be found for the clutch plate thickness data. The check sheet (Figure 4.9) clearly shows that 0.0626 is the most frequently occurring number. It is tallied 30 times.

The Relationship Among the Mean, Median, and Mode

As measures of central tendency, the mean, median, and mode can be compared with each other to determine where the data are located. Measures of central tendency describe the center position of the data. They show how the data tend to build up around a center value. When a distribution is symmetrical, the mean, mode, and median values are equal. For a skewed distribution, the values will be different (Figure 4.25). Comparing the mean (average), mode, and median determines whether or not a distribution is skewed and, if it is, in which direction.

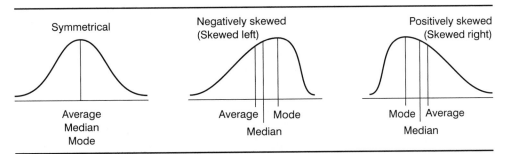

Figure 4.25   Comparison of Mean, Mode, and Median

EXAMPLE 4.14   Clutch Plate: Seeing the Relationship

Knowing the average, median, and mode of the clutch plate data provides information about the symmetry of the data. If the distribution is symmetrical, the average, mode, and median values will be equal. A skewed distribution will have different values. From previous examples, the values for the clutch plate are

$$Average = 0.0627 \text{ inch}$$
$$Median = 0.0626 \text{ inch}$$
$$Mode = 0.0626 \text{ inch}$$

As seen in the frequency diagram (Figure 4.26), the mode marks the peak of the distribution. The average, slightly to the right of the mode and median, pulls the distribution to the right. This slight positive skew is due to the high values for clutch plate thickness that occur in later samples.

Spread: Measures of Dispersion

The range and standard deviation are two measurements that enable the investigator to determine the spread of the data, that is, where the values fall in relation to each other and to the mean. Because these two describe where the data are dispersed on either side of a central value, they are often referred to as measures of dispersion. Used in conjunction with the mean, mode, and median, these values create a more complete picture of a distribution.

Range

As was pointed out in the discussion of the histogram earlier in this chapter, the *range is the difference between the highest value in a series of values or sample and the lowest value in that same series.* A range value describes how far the data spread. All of the other values in a population or sample will fall between the highest and lowest values:

$$R = X_h - X_l$$

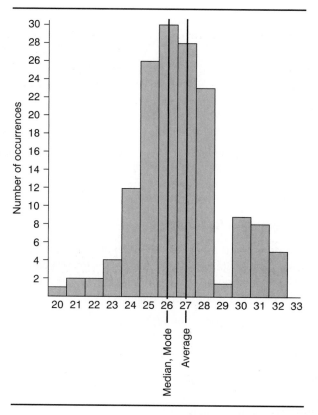

Figure 4.26   Comparison of Mean, Mode, and Median for the Clutch Plate

where

$$R = \text{range}$$
$$X_h = \text{highest value in the series}$$
$$X_l = \text{lowest value in the series}$$

EXAMPLE 4.15   Clutch Plate: Calculating Range Values

The flat round plate data comprises subgroups of sample size five (Table 4.5). For each sample, a range value can be calculated. For example:

Subgroup 1   0.0625   0.0626   0.0624   0.0625   0.0627

$$\text{Range} = X_h - X_l = 0.0627 - 0.0624 = 0.0003$$

Subgroup 2   0.0624   0.0623   0.0624   0.0626   0.0625

$$\text{Range} = X_h - X_l = 0.0626 - 0.0623 = 0.0003$$

The other ranges are calculated in the same manner. These range values are used in the next chapter to study the variation present in the process over time.

Standard Deviation

The range shows where each end of the distribution is located, but it doesn't tell how the data are grouped within the distribution. In Figure 4.27, the three distributions have the same average and range, but all three are different. *The **standard deviation** shows the dispersion of the data within the distribution.* It describes how the individual values fall in relation to their means, the actual amount of variation present in a set of data. The standard deviation, because it uses all of the measurements

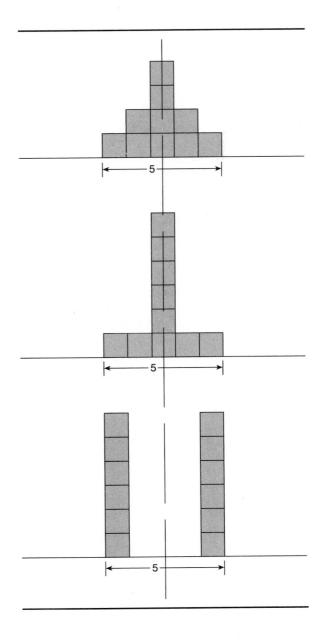

Figure 4.27   Different Distributions with Same Averages and Ranges

taken, provides more reliable information about the dispersion of the data. The range considers only the two extreme values in its calculation, giving no information concerning where the values may be grouped. Since it only considers the highest and lowest values, the range has the disadvantage of becoming a less accurate description of the data as the number of readings or sample values increases. The range is best used with small populations or small sample sizes of less than 10 values. However, since the range is easy to calculate, it is the most frequently used measure of dispersion.

When the measurements have been taken from each and every item in the total population, the standard deviation is calculated through the use of the following formula:

$$\sigma = \sqrt{\frac{\sum_{i=1}^{n}(X_i - \mu)^2}{n}}$$

where

σ = standard deviation of the population
μ = mean value of the series of measurements
X_i = $X_1, X_2, \ldots, X_n$ = values of each reading
n = number of readings

The standard deviation of the population is sometimes known as the *root mean square deviation*. When populations increase in size it becomes difficult to calculate without help from a computer.

A smaller standard deviation is desirable because it indicates greater similarity between data values—that is, the data are more precisely grouped. In the case of products, a small standard deviation indicates that the products are nearly alike. As discussed with the Taguchi loss function in Chapter 2, creating products or providing services that are similar to each other is optimal.

When the measurements are taken from items sampled from the entire population, the previous formula is modified to reflect the fact that not every item in the population has been measured. This change is reflected in the denominator. The standard deviation of a sample is represented by the letter s:

$$s = \sqrt{\frac{\sum_{i=1}^{n}(X_i - \overline{X})^2}{n - 1}}$$

where

s = standard deviation of the sample
$\overline{X}$ = average value of the series of measurements
X_i = $X_1, X_2, \ldots, X_n$ = values of each reading
n = number of readings

EXAMPLE 4.16   Clutch Plate: Determining the Standard Deviation of a Sample

In the case of subgroups comprising the clutch plate data, it is possible to calculate the sample standard deviation for each of the subgroups. For subgroup 1:

$$s_1 = \sqrt{\frac{\Sigma(X_i - X)^2}{n - 1}}$$

$$= \sqrt{\frac{(0.0624 - 0.0625)^2 + 2(0.0625 - 0.0625)^2 + (0.0626 - 0.0625)^2 + (0.0627 - 0.0625)^2}{5 - 1}}$$

$$= 0.0001$$

Standard deviations for the remaining subgroups can be calculated in the same manner.

EXAMPLE 4.17   Gas Mileage: Determining the Standard Deviation of a Sample

At an automobile-testing ground, a new type of automobile was tested for gas mileage. Seven cars, a sample of a much larger production run, were driven under typical conditions to determine the number of miles per gallon the cars got. The following miles-per-gallon readings were obtained:

36   35   39   40   35   38   41

Calculate the sample standard deviation.
First calculate the average:

$$X = \frac{36 + 35 + 39 + 40 + 35 + 38 + 41}{7}$$

$$= 37.7$$

which is rounded to 38. Then

$$s = \sqrt{\frac{(36 - 38)^2 + (35 - 38)^2 + (39 - 38)^2 + (40 - 38)^2 + (35 - 38)^2 + (38 - 38)^2 + (41 - 38)^2}{7 - 1}}$$

$$= 2.45$$

which is rounded to 3.

Using the Mean, Mode, Median, Standard Deviation, and Range Together

Measures of central tendency and measures of dispersion are critical when describing statistical data. As the following example shows, one without the other creates an incomplete picture of the values measured.

EXAMPLE 4.18   Seeing the Whole Picture

Two engineers were keeping track of the rate of water pipe being laid by three different crews. Over the past 36 days, the amount of pipe laid per day was recorded and the frequency diagrams shown in Figure 4.28 were created. When they studied the data originally, the two engineers calculated only the mean, mode, and median for each crew.

$$\text{Mean}_1 = 20 \quad \text{Median}_1 = 20 \quad \text{Mode}_1 = 20$$
$$\text{Mean}_2 = 20 \quad \text{Median}_2 = 20 \quad \text{Mode}_2 = 20$$
$$\text{Mean}_3 = 20 \quad \text{Median}_3 = 20 \quad \text{Mode}_3 = 20$$

On the surface, these distributions appear the same. It was not until the range and standard deviation for each of the three pipe-laying crews' work were calculated that the differences became apparent:

$$\text{Range}_1 = 4$$

$$\text{Standard deviation}_1 = 1.03, \text{rounded to } 1.0$$

$$\sigma = \sqrt{\frac{\begin{array}{c}3(18 - 20)^2 + 7(19 - 20)^2 + 16(20 - 20)^2 \\ + 7(21 - 20)^2 + 3(22 - 20)^2\end{array}}{36}}$$

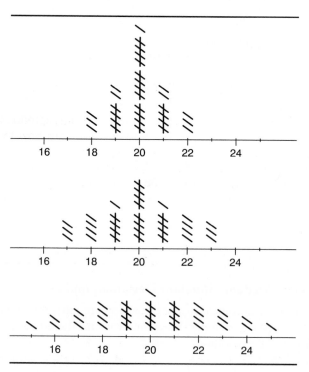

Figure 4.28   Frequency Diagrams of the Amount of Pipe Laid per Day in Feet

Range$_2$ = 6

Standard deviation$_2$ = 1.65, rounded to 1.7

$$\sigma = \sqrt{\frac{\begin{array}{c}3(17-20)^2 + 4(18-20)^2 + 6(19-20)^2 \\ + 10(20-20)^2 + 6(21-20)^2 + 4(22-20)^2 \\ + 3(23-20)^2\end{array}}{36}}$$

Range$_3$ = 10

Standard deviation$_3$ = 2.42, rounded to 2.4

$$\sigma = \sqrt{\frac{\begin{array}{c}1(15-20)^2 + 2(16-20)^2 + 3(17-20)^2 \\ + 4(18-20)^2 + 5(19-20)^2 + 6(20-20)^2 \\ + 5(21-20)^2 + 4(22-20)^2 + 3(23-20)^2 \\ + 2(24-20)^2 + 1(25-20)^2\end{array}}{36}}$$

Once calculated, the ranges and standard deviations revealed that significant differences exist in the performance of the three crews. The first crew was much more consistent in the amount of pipe they laid per day.

EXAMPLE 4.19   Clutch Plate: Seeing the Whole Picture

When we combine the analytical calculations with the graphical information from the previous examples, we see a more complete picture of the clutch plate data we are studying. The grand average, $\overline{\overline{X}}$ = 0.0627 inches, median (0.0626), and mode (0.0626) confirm that the histogram is skewed slightly to the right. Because we know the grand average of the data, we also know that the distribution is not centered on the desired target value of 0.0625 inches. The frequency diagram gives us the critical information that there are no plates with a thickness of 0.0629 inches. The range of our data is fairly broad; the frequency diagram shows an overall spread of the distribution of 0.0012 inches. In the next two chapters we will learn how to use the ranges and standard deviation values for the individual subgroups. In general, through their calculations and diagrams, the engineers have learned that they are making the plates too thick. They have also learned that the machining process is not producing plates of consistent thickness.

 REAL TOOLS FOR REAL LIFE

Monogramming and Embroidery Machine Arm Analysis

R&M Industries manufactures automated embroidery and monogramming machines. These machines are used to embroider or monogram designs on specialty items such as baseball caps, shirts, jackets, and other products. In order to create

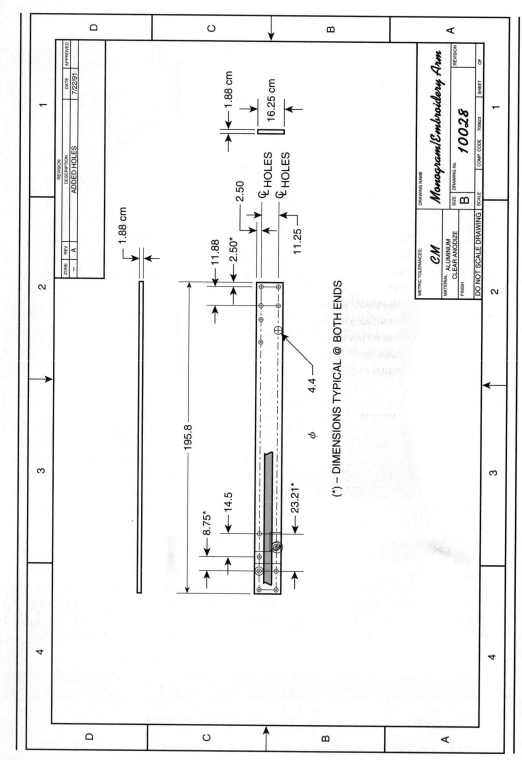

Figure 4.29 Monogram and Embroidery Arm

180

11.16	11.19	11.22	11.25	11.18
11.23	11.29	11.25	11.24	11.23
11.23	11.21	11.21	11.22	11.22
11.17	11.28	11.26	11.25	11.22
11.24	11.22	11.27	11.23	11.19

Figure 4.30   Data for Distance Between Hole Centers for the Monogramming and Embroidery Arm (in cm)

the embroidery work, the pantograph arm moves in the x and y directions through the use of servo motors. The arm has numerous through-holes for mounting, depending on the type of embroidery being created. R&M's engineers are testing the performance capabilities of a machine that produces a newly designed pantograph arm. This involves producing a limited number of parts, known as a runoff. The dimension being analyzed involves the mounting holes that hold a bearing and a mating part. The engineers are interested in the distance between the centers of the two holes (Figure 4.29), which has been specified as 11.25 cm. The measurements taken are shown in Figure 4.30.

The engineers created a frequency diagram with data collected from the 25 arms machined during the runoff (Figure 4.31). The measurements are spread between 11.16 and 11.29, with a majority of them grouped between 11.21 and 11.25. There is little precision or accuracy associated with the data.

Having completed a frequency diagram, R&M's engineers created a histogram. They chose a cell interval of 0.03, resulting in five cells, presenting a clear picture of the data. They chose the lowest value measured for their first midpoint. The cell boundaries were created by dividing the cell interval by two and subtracting that value from the midpoint to find the lower boundary.

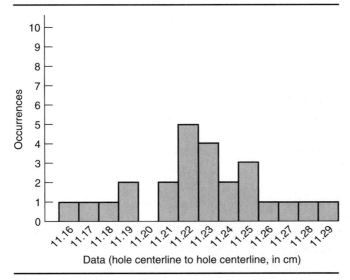

Data (hole centerline to hole centerline, in cm)

Figure 4.31   Frequency Diagram for Monogramming and Embroidery Arm Data

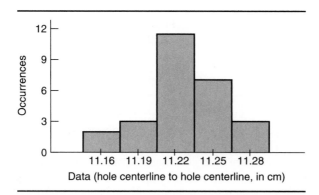

Figure 4.32   Histogram for Monogramming and Embroidery Arm Data

The histogram (Figure 4.32) has one peak and is nearly symmetrical. The data is grouped around 11.22 rather than the target specification of 11.25 cm. The average value is 11.23 cm, meaning that the distance between the centers of the holes is smaller than the desired target. The median of the data is also 11.23 cm. The mode is 11.22 cm. Though these values are nearly equal, they show that the distribution is skewed slightly to the right. The central tendency of the data is lower than the target specification of 11.25.

The spread of the data is rather large, from 11.16 to 11.29, a range of 0.13 cm. The standard deviation equals 0.03. Both the range and the standard deviation describe how the data is spread around the mean. In this case, the magnitude of the range and standard deviation indicate that the data are not tightly grouped; that is, the distance between the centers of the holes varies significantly from one pantograph arm to another. The variation present in the process will make assembly and use of the arm more difficult.

From the frequency diagram, histogram, and calculations, the engineers involved in the pantograph arm runoff have learned that the machine they are considering for purchase is unable to produce arms with consistent distances between the mounting hole centers. By collecting, tabulating, analyzing, and interpreting the data from the runoff, they have avoided purchasing a piece of equipment that is not able to produce parts to their specifications.

Other Measures of Dispersion

Skewness

When a distribution lacks symmetry, it is considered **skewed.** A picture of the distribution is not necessary to determine skewness. Skewness can be measured by calculating the following value:

$$a_3 = \frac{\sum_{i=1}^{h} f_i (X_i - \overline{X})^3 / n}{s^3}$$

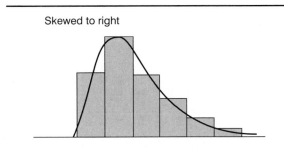

Skewed to right

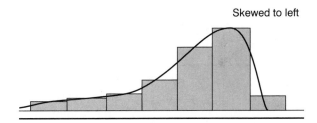

Skewed to left

Figure 4.33   Skewness

where

$$a_3 = \text{skewness}$$
$$X_i = \text{individual data values under study}$$
$$\overline{X} = \text{average of individual values}$$
$$n = \text{sample size}$$
$$s = \text{standard deviation of sample}$$
$$f_i = \text{frequency of occurrence}$$

Once determined, the skewness figure is compared with zero. A skewness value of zero means that the distribution is symmetrical. A value greater than zero means that the data are skewed to the right; the tail of the distribution goes to the right. If the value is negative (less than zero), then the distribution is skewed to the left, with a tail of the distribution going to the left (Figure 4.33). The higher the value, the stronger the skewness.

EXAMPLE 4.20   Gas Mileage: Determining the Skew

The investigators in Example 4.16 want to determine if the data gathered in their sample of 36, 35, 39, 40, 35, 38, 41 are skewed. They apply the following formulas:

$$\overline{X} = 38$$
$$s = 2$$

$$a_3 = \frac{\begin{array}{c}[(36 - 38)^3 + 2(35 - 38)^3 + (39 - 38)^3 + (40 - 38)^3 \\ + (38 - 38)^3 + (41 - 38)^3]/7\end{array}}{8}$$

$$= -0.46$$

The negative value for a_3 means that the data are skewed to the left.

Kurtosis

Kurtosis, the peakedness of the data, is another value that can be calculated:

$$a_4 = \frac{\sum_{i=1}^{h} f_i(X_i - \overline{X})^4/n}{s^4}$$

where

a_4 = kurtosis
X_i = individual data values under study
$\overline{X}$ = average of individual values
n = sample size
s = standard deviation of sample

Once calculated, the kurtosis value must be compared with another distribution or with a standard in order to be interpreted. In Figure 4.34, the distribution on the left side is more peaked than that on the right. Its kurtosis value would be larger.

EXAMPLE 4.21   Gas Mileage: Determining the Kurtosis

The investigators of Example 4.16 wanted to calculate the kurtosis:

$$a_4 = \frac{\begin{array}{c}[(36 - 38)^4 + 2(35 - 38)^4 + (39 - 38)^4 + (40 - 38)^4 \\ + (38 - 38)^4 + (41 - 38)^4]/7\end{array}}{16}$$

$$= 2.46$$

The engineers compared these data with the previous day's test, where the kurtosis was 1.42. Those data spread more broadly (were less peaked) than these. The distribution is getting narrower, a sign that the miles-per-gallon data are becoming more uniform.

CENTRAL LIMIT THEOREM

Much of statistical process control is based on the use of samples taken from a population of items. The central limit theorem enables conclusions to be drawn from

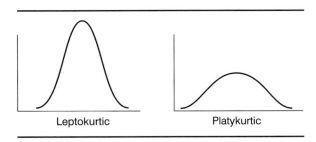

Figure 4.34   Kurtosis

the sample data and applied to a population. The **central limit theorem** *states that a group of sample averages tends to be normally distributed; as the sample size n increases, this tendency toward normality improves.* The population from which the samples are taken does not need to be normally distributed for the sample averages to tend to be normally distributed (Figure 4.35). In the field of quality, the central limit theorem supports the use of sampling to analyze the population. The mean of the sample averages will approximate the mean of the population. The variation associated with the sample averages will be less than that of the population. It is important to remember that it is the sample *averages* that tend toward normality, as the following example shows.

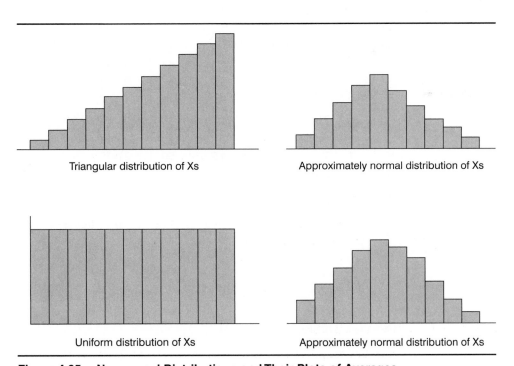

Figure 4.35   Nonnormal Distributions and Their Plots of Averages

EXAMPLE 4.22   Using the Central Limit Theorem

Roger and Bill are trying to settle an argument. Roger says that averages from a deck of cards will form a normal curve when plotted. Bill says they won't. They decide to try the following exercise involving averages. They are going to follow these rules:

1. They will randomly select five cards from a well-shuffled deck and write down the values (Figure 4.36). (An ace is worth 1 point, a jack 11, a queen 12, and a king 13.)

1	11	13	10	12	7	10.6	26	8	10	1	9	10	7.6
2	1	7	12	9	3	6.4	27	9	13	2	2	2	5.6
3	9	5	12	1	11	7.6	28	12	4	12	3	13	8.8
4	11	5	7	9	12	8.8	29	12	4	7	6	9	7.6
5	7	12	13	7	4	8.6	30	1	12	3	12	11	7.8
6	11	9	5	1	13	7.8	31	12	3	10	11	6	8.4
7	1	4	13	12	13	8.6	32	3	5	10	2	7	5.4
8	13	3	2	6	12	7.2	33	9	1	2	3	11	5.2
9	2	4	1	10	13	6.0	34	6	8	6	13	9	8.4
10	4	5	12	1	9	6.2	35	2	12	5	10	4	6.6
11	2	5	7	7	11	6.4	36	6	4	8	9	12	7.8
12	6	9	8	2	12	7.4	37	9	13	3	10	1	7.2
13	2	3	6	11	11	6.6	38	2	1	13	7	5	5.6
14	2	6	9	11	13	8.2	39	10	11	5	12	13	10.2
15	6	8	8	9	1	6.4	40	13	2	8	2	11	7.2
16	3	4	12	1	6	5.2	41	2	10	5	4	11	6.4
17	8	1	8	6	10	6.6	42	10	4	12	7	11	8.8
18	5	7	6	8	8	6.8	43	13	13	7	1	10	8.8
19	2	5	4	10	1	4.4	44	9	10	7	11	11	9.6
20	5	7	12	7	8	7.8	45	6	7	8	7	4	6.4
21	9	1	3	6	12	6.2	46	1	4	12	11	13	8.2
22	1	13	9	3	6	6.4	47	9	11	8	1	11	8.0
23	4	5	13	5	7	6.8	48	8	13	10	13	4	9.6
24	3	7	9	8	10	7.4	49	12	11	11	2	3	7.8
25	1	7	6	6	1	4.2	50	2	12	5	11	9	7.8

```
 1    LHT LHT LHT LHT  II
 2   LHT LHT LHT  IIII
 3   LHT LHT  IIII
 4   LHT LHT LHT  I
 5   LHT LHT LHT  I
 6   LHT LHT LHT  III
 7   LHT LHT LHT LHT  I
 8   LHT LHT LHT  I
 9   LHT LHT LHT LHT  I
10   LHT LHT LHT  II
11   LHT LHT LHT LHT  III
12   LHT LHT LHT LHT LHT
13   LHT LHT LHT LHT  II
```

Figure 4.36   Numerical Values of Cards and Frequency Distribution

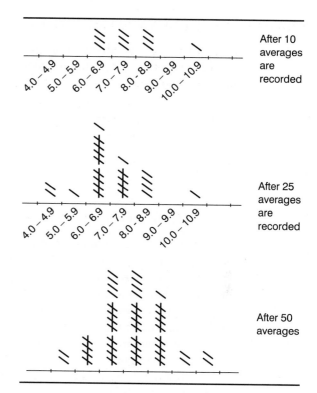

Figure 4.37   Distribution of Sample Averages

2. They will record the numerical values on a graph (Figure 4.36).
3. They will calculate the average for the five cards.
4. They will graph the results of step 3 on a graph separate from that used in step 2 (Figure 4.37).
5. They will then replace the five cards in the deck.
6. They will shuffle the deck.
7. They will repeat this process 50 times.

Figure 4.36 displays the results of steps 1 and 2. Since the deck was well shuffled and the selection of cards from the deck was random, each card had the same chance of being selected—1/52. The fairly uniform distribution of values in the frequency diagram in Figure 4.36 shows that each type of card was selected approximately the same number of times. The distribution would be even more uniform if a greater number of cards had been drawn.

Figure 4.37 graphs the results of step 4. Notice that as the number of averages recorded increases, the results look more and more like a normal curve. As predicted by the central limit theorem, the distribution of the sample averages in the final diagram in Figure 4.37 is approximately normal. This has occurred even though the original distribution was not normal.

NORMAL FREQUENCY DISTRIBUTION

The normal frequency distribution, the familiar bell-shaped curve (Figure 4.38), is commonly called a *normal curve*. A **normal frequency distribution** *is described by the normal density function*:

$$f(x) = \frac{1}{\sigma\sqrt{2\pi}}e^{-(x-\mu)^2/2\sigma^2} \qquad -\infty < x < \infty$$

where

$$\pi = 3.14159$$
$$e = 2.71828$$

The normal frequency distribution has six distinct features:

1. A normal curve is symmetrical about μ, the central value.
2. The mean, mode, and median are all equal.
3. The curve is unimodal and bell-shaped.
4. Data values concentrate around the mean value of the distribution and decrease in frequency as the values get further away from the mean.
5. The area under the normal curve equals 1. One hundred percent of the data are found under the normal curve, 50 percent on the left-hand side, 50 percent on the right.
6. The normal distribution can be described in terms of its mean and standard deviation by observing that 99.73 percent of the measured values fall within

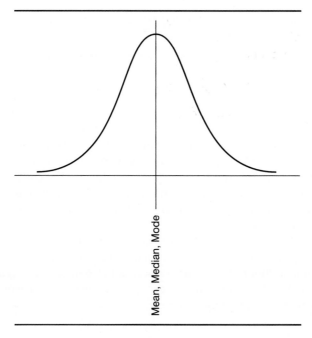

Figure 4.38   The Normal Curve

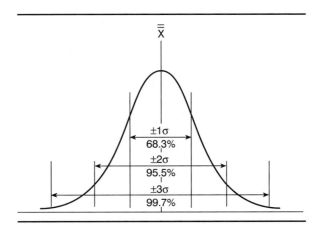

Figure 4.39 Percentage of Measurements Falling Within Each Standard Deviation

±3 standard deviations of the mean ($\mu \pm 3\sigma$), that 95.5 percent of the data fall within ±2 standard deviations of the mean ($\mu \pm 2\sigma$), and that 68.3 percent of the data fall within ±1 standard deviation ($\mu \pm 1\sigma$). Figure 4.39 demonstrates the percentage of measurements falling within each standard deviation.

These six features combine to create a peak in the center of the distribution, with the number of values decreasing as the measurements get farther away from the mean. As the data fall away toward the horizontal axis, the curve flattens. The tails of the normal distribution approach the horizontal axis and extend indefinitely, never reaching or crossing it.

While not all symmetrical distributions are normal distributions, these six features are general indicators of a normal distribution. (There is a chi square test for normality. Refer to a statistics text for a complete description of the chi square test.)

Standard Normal Probability Distribution: Z Tables

The area under the normal curve can be determined if the mean and the standard deviation are known. The mean, or in the case of samples, the average, locates the center of the normal distribution. The standard deviation defines the spread of the data about the center of the distribution.

The relationships discussed in features 5 and 6 of the normal frequency distribution make it possible to calculate the percentage of values that fall between any two readings. If 100 percent of the data are under the normal curve, then the amount of product above or below a particular value can be determined. These values may be dimensions like the upper and lower specification limits set by the designer or they can be any value of interest. The formula for finding the area under the normal curve is

$$f(x) = \frac{1}{\sigma\sqrt{2\pi}} e^{-(x-\mu)^2/2\sigma^2} \qquad -\infty < x < \infty$$

where

$$\pi = 3.14159$$
$$e = 2.71828$$

This formula can be simplified through the use of the standard normal probability distribution table (Appendix 1). This table uses the formula

$$f(Z) = \frac{1}{\sqrt{2\pi}} e^{-Z^2/2}$$

where

$$Z = \frac{X_i - \overline{X}}{s} = \text{standard normal value}$$
$$X_i = \text{individual X value of interest}$$
$$\overline{X} = \text{average}$$
$$s = \text{standard deviation}$$

This formula also works with population means and population standard deviations:

$$Z = \frac{X_i - \mu}{\sigma_{\overline{x}}} = \text{standard normal value}$$

where

$$X_i = \text{individual X value of interest}$$
$$\mu = \text{population mean}$$

$$\sigma_{\overline{x}} = \text{population standard deviation} = \frac{\sigma}{\sqrt{n}}$$

Z is used with the table in Appendix 1 to find the value of the area under the curve, which represents a percentage or proportion of the product or measurements produced. If Z has a positive value, then it is to the right of the center of the distribution and is X_i larger than $\overline{X}$. If the Z value is negative, then it is on the left side of the center and is X_i smaller than $\overline{X}$.

To find the area under the normal curve associated with a particular X_i, use the following procedure:

1. Use the information on normal curves to verify that the measurements are normally distributed.
2. Use the mean, standard deviation, and value of interest in the formula to calculate Z.
3. Find the Z value in the table in Appendix 1.
4. Use the table to convert the Z values to the area of interest.
5. Convert the area of interest value from the table to a percentage by multiplying by 100.

The table in Appendix 1 is a left-reading table, meaning that it will provide the area under the curve from negative infinity up to the value of interest (Figure 4.40). These

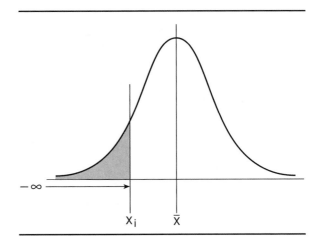

Figure 4.40   Normal Curve for Left-Reading Z Table

values will have to be manipulated to find the area greater than the value of interest or between two values. Drawing a picture of the situation in question and shading the area of interest often helps clarify the Z calculations. Values of Z should be rounded to two decimal places for use in the table. Interpolation between values can also be performed.

EXAMPLE 4.23   Clutch Plate: Using Standard Normal Probability Distribution

The engineers working with the clutch plate thickness data have determined that their data approximates a normal curve. They would like to determine what percentage of parts from the samples taken are below 0.0624 inch and above 0.0629 inch.

1. From the data in Table 4.5, they calculated an average of 0.0627 and a standard deviation of 0.00023. They used the Z tables to determine the percentage of parts under 0.0624 inch thick. In Figure 4.41 the area of interest is shaded.

$$Z = \frac{0.0624 - 0.0627}{0.00023} = -1.30$$

From Appendix 1: Area = 0.0968

or 9.68 percent of the parts are thinner than 0.0624 inch.

2. When determining the percentage of the parts that are 0.0629 inch thick or thicker, it is important to note that the table in Appendix 1 is a left-reading table. Since the engineers want to determine the percentage of parts thicker than 0.0629 (the area shaded in Figure 4.42), they will have to subtract the area up to 0.0629 from 1.00.

$$Z = \frac{0.0629 - 0.0627}{0.00023} = 0.87$$

Area = 0.8079

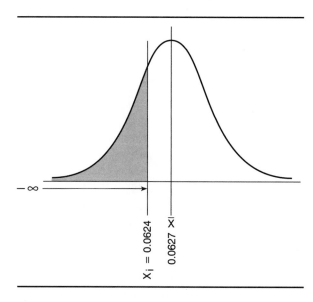

**Figure 4.41   Example 4.23:
Area Under the Curve,
$X_i = 0.0624$**

or 80.79 percent of the parts are *thinner* than 0.0629 inch. However, they want the percentage of parts that are *thicker* than 0.0629 inch. To find this area they must subtract the area from 1.0 (remember: 100 percent of the parts fall under the normal curve):

$$1.00 - 0.8079 = 0.1921$$

or 19.21 percent of the parts are thicker than 0.0629 inch.
3. The engineers also want to find the percentage of the parts between 0.0623 and 0.0626 inch thick: The area of interest is shaded in Figure 4.43. In this problem

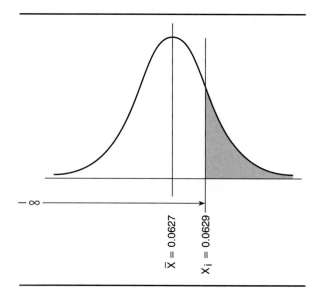

**Figure 4.42   Example 4.23:
Area Under the Curve,
$X_i = 0.0629$**

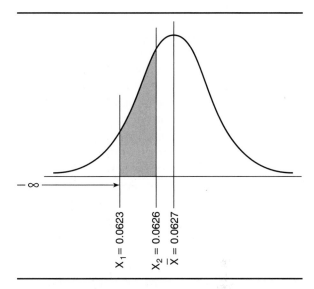

**Figure 4.43   Example 4.23:
Area Under the Curve
Between 0.0623 and 0.0626**

the engineers must calculate two areas of interest, one for those parts 0.0623 inches thick or thinner and the other for those parts 0.0626 inch thick or thinner. The area of interest for those parts 0.0623 inch and thinner will be subtracted from the area of interest for 0.0626 inch. and thinner.

First solve for parts 0.0623 inch or thinner:

$$Z_1 = \frac{0.0623 - 0.0627}{0.00023} = -1.74$$

$$Area_1 = 0.0409$$

or 4.09 percent of the parts are 0.0623 inches or thinner.

Then solve for parts 0.0626 inches or thinner:

$$Z_2 = \frac{0.0626 - 0.0627}{0.00023} = -0.44$$

$$Area_2 = 0.3300$$

or 33 percent of the parts are 0.0626 inches or thinner. Subtracting these two areas will determine the area in between:

$$0.3300 - 0.0409 = 0.2891$$

or 28.91 percent of the parts fall between 0.0623 and 0.0626 inches.

CONFIDENCE INTERVALS

When samples in a subgroup are averaged and the standard deviation calculated, these values are called point estimates. As a result of the central limit theorem, as long as they are random and unbiased samples, these subgroup sample averages can serve as estimators of the population mean. Determining whether or not the sample average is a good approximation of the population mean depends upon the spread of the sample data, the standard deviation of the distribution of the subgroup. The standard deviation, or standard error (SE), indicates the amount of error that will exist when the subgroup average is used to estimate the population mean.

Confidence interval testing is a technique that enables us to determine how well the subgroup average approximates the population mean. This straightforward calculation will enable us to make statements like: "there is a 95% probability that the sample average is a good estimator of the population mean" or "there is a 90% probability that the population mean is between X_1 and X_2." To determine X_1 and X_2, the end points for the confidence interval, use the formula:

$$\overline{X} \pm \frac{Z_{(\alpha/2)}\,(\sigma)}{\sqrt{n}}$$

where

$\overline{X}$ = sample average
n = number of samples
σ = population standard deviation
s = standard deviation (also $\sigma_{(n-1)}$)
α = probability that the population mean is not in the interval (alpha risk)
$1 - \alpha$ = probability the population mean is in the interval
$Z_{(\alpha/2)}$ = value from the Z table in Appendix 1 with an area of $\alpha/2$ to its right.

EXAMPLE 4.24   Confidence Interval Calculation Using α

Manufacturing medical devices requires the ability to meet close tolerances. For a particularly critical machine set-up, the manufacturing engineer conducted two run-offs for an injection molding machine. The first run-off, in which all of the molded parts were measured, the population mean was 0.800 mm with a population standard deviation, σ, of 0.007. From the second run-off, only 50 parts were sampled and their measurements taken. These randomly selected samples of parts have an average length of 0.822 mm and a standard deviation of 0.010. The manufacturing engineer would like to know, with 95% confidence, the interval values for the population mean for the second run-off.

$$0.822 \pm \frac{1.96\,(0.007)}{\sqrt{50}}$$

$$0.822 \pm 0.002$$

where

$$\overline{X} = 0.822$$
$$n = 50$$
$$\sigma = 0.007$$

$$\alpha = 0.05$$
$$1 - 0.05 = 0.95$$

$Z_{(\alpha/2)}$ = value from the Z table in Appendix 1 with an area of 0.025 to its right.

The interval is (0.820, 0.824). The engineer can be 95% confident that the population mean is between these two values.

The above formula, using the Z table, is considered a reasonable approximation if n ≥ 30. For smaller sample sizes there is not an easy method to determine if the population is normal. Under these circumstances, the t-distribution is used.

$$\overline{X} \pm \frac{t_{(\alpha/2)}\,(s)}{\sqrt{n}}$$

where

$\overline{X}$ = sample average
n = number of samples
s = standard deviation (also $\sigma_{(n-1)}$)
α = probability that the population mean is not in the interval (alpha risk)
$1 - \alpha$ = probability the population mean is in the interval
$t_{(\alpha/2)}$ = value from the t table
df = degrees of freedom (n − 1), the amount of data used by the measure of dispersion

The t value compensates for our lack of information about σ. The smaller the sample size, the more doubt exists, and the larger t must be. This t value is selected based on the degrees of freedom in the system, n − 1. Values for the t distribution appear in Appendix 3.

REAL TOOLS FOR REAL LIFE

Confidence Interval Calculation Using the t Distribution

Two machines have recently been installed at a manufacturing plant. In order to determine if additional noise dampening devices are needed, an industrial hygienist has taken several noise exposure measurements at a water jet cutting work center and a conventional stamping machine. He would like to determine with 90% confidence that these samples represent the mean noise exposure expected to be experienced by workers. The values represent the percentage of allowable daily dose. A value of 50% during an 8 hour shift represents 85 dB.

For the water jet cutting work center, the ratios recorded were $X_1 = 0.45$, $X_2 = 0.47$, and $X_3 = 0.44$, resulting in an $\overline{X} = 0.45$ and s = 0.015. The water jet noise value is calculated below.

$$0.45 \pm \frac{2.920\,(0.015)}{\sqrt{3}}$$

where

$$\overline{X} = 0.45$$
$$n = 3$$
$$s = 0.015$$
$$\alpha = 0.10$$
$$1 - \alpha = 0.90$$
$$t_{(\alpha/2)} = 2.920$$
$$df = 3 - 1 = 2$$

The interval is (0.425, 0.475). The hygienist can be 90% confident that the population mean is between these two values for the water jet cutting work center. Since these values are below the legal permissible decibel levels, no additional noise dampening is required.

For the conventional stamping machine, the ratios recorded were $X_1 = 0.55$, $X_2 = 0.75$, and $X_3 = 0.57$, resulting in an $\overline{X} = 0.62$ and $s = 0.11$.

$$0.62 \pm \frac{2.920\,(0.11)}{\sqrt{3}}$$

where

$$\overline{X} = 0.62$$
$$n = 3$$
$$s = 0.11$$
$$\alpha = 0.10$$
$$1 - \alpha = 0.90$$
$$t_{(\alpha/2)} = 2.920$$
$$df = 2$$

The interval is (0.43, 0.81). The hygienist can be 90% confident that the population mean is between these two values. Note that due to its large standard deviation, this is a much broader spread than the other interval. This broad interval includes values that are above the legal permissible decibel levels, and therefore, additional noise dampening is required.   **Q**

SUMMARY

Frequency diagrams and histograms graphically depict the processes or occurrences under study. Means, modes, medians, standard deviations, and ranges are powerful tools used to describe processes and occurrences statistically. Because of the central limit theorem, users of statistical information can form conclusions about populations of items based on the sample statistics. Since the behavior of the $\overline{X}$ values is predictable, when the values are different from an expected normal curve, there must be a reason why the process is not behaving normally. Knowing this, those working with a process can determine whether or not there is something wrong with the process that must be dealt with.

■ Lessons Learned

1. Quality assurance relies primarily on inductive statistics in analyzing samples.
2. Accuracy and precision are of paramount importance in quality assurance. Measurements should be both precise and accurate.
3. Histograms and frequency diagrams are similar. Unlike a frequency diagram, a histogram will group the data into cells.
4. Histograms are constructed using cell intervals, cell midpoints, and cell boundaries.
5. The analysis of histograms and frequency diagrams is based on shape, location, and spread.
6. Shape refers to symmetry, skewness, and kurtosis.
7. The location or central tendency refers to the relationship between the mean (average), mode, and median.
8. The spread or dispersion of data is described by the range and standard deviation.
9. Skewness describes the tendency of data to be gathered either to the left or right side of a distribution. When a distribution is symmetrical, skewness equals zero.
10. Kurtosis describes the peakedness of data. Leptokurtic distributions are more peaked than platykurtic ones.
11. A normal curve can be identified by the following five features: It is symmetrical about a central value. The mean, mode, and median are all equal. It is unimodal and bell-shaped. Data cluster around the mean value of the distribution and then fall away toward the horizontal axis. The area under the normal curve equals 1; 100 percent of the data is found under the normal curve.
12. In a normal distribution 99.73 percent of the measured values fall within ± 3 standard deviations of the mean ($\mu \pm 3\sigma$); 95.5 percent of the data fall within ± 2 standard deviations of the mean ($\mu \pm 2\sigma$); and 68.3 percent of the data fall within ± 1 standard deviation ($\mu \pm 1\sigma$).
13. The area under a normal curve can be calculated using the Z table and its associated formula.
14. The central limit theorem proves that the averages of nonnormal distributions have a normal distribution. ■

■ Formulas

$$R = X_h - X_l$$

$$\mu \text{ or } \overline{X} = \frac{X_1 + X_2 + X_3 + \cdots + X_n}{n} = \frac{\Sigma X_i}{n}$$

$$\sigma = \sqrt{\frac{\Sigma(X_i - \mu)^2}{n}}$$

$$s = \sqrt{\frac{\Sigma(X_i - \overline{X})^2}{n - 1}}$$

$$a_3 = \frac{\Sigma f_i(X_i - \overline{X})^3/n}{s^3}$$

$$a_4 = \frac{\Sigma f_i(X_i - \overline{X})^4/n}{s^4}$$

$$f(x) = \frac{1}{\sigma\sqrt{2\pi}}e^{-\frac{(x-\mu)^2}{2\sigma^2}} \qquad -\infty < x < \infty$$

where

$$\pi = 3.14159$$
$$e = 2.71828$$
$$f(Z) = \frac{1}{\sqrt{2\pi}}e^{-\frac{Z^2}{2}}$$
$$Z = \frac{X_i - \overline{X}}{s}$$
$$Z = \frac{X_i - \mu}{\sigma}$$

Chapter Problems

1. Describe the concepts of a sample and a population.

2. Give three examples each for continuous data and discrete data.

3. Describe one situation that is accurate, one that is precise, and one that is both. A picture may help you with your description.

4. Misunderstood, misused, or incomplete statistics can lead to incorrect decisions. Read the following information about air bag performance and discuss how the statistics could be misused in this situation. What type of questions will you ask to ensure that the statistics you are being told won't mislead you?

   Automotive manufacturers continue to seek ways to protect vehicle passengers in the event of an accident. Some of those changes, such as air bags, can be controversial. Air bags, designed to inflate automatically in accidents involving speeds of greater than 15 mph, have saved many lives. An air bag is a pretty impressive piece of equipment when you consider the protection it supplies. Even a collision at speeds as slow as 30 mph produces an impact on the body equivalent to falling off a three-story building.

Essentially an air bag inflates and stops your fall. Air bags first began to be offered on a wide variety of automobiles in the late 1980s. By 2001, 80 million vehicles on the road had air bags. Since their inception, records have been kept on accident statistics involving the deployment of air bags. As more and more air bags were installed in automobiles, it became obvious, unfortunately, that in some situations, air bags may kill. By 2001, 191 people, 116 of them children, had died from deployment of air bags. Alone, this statistic tells only part of the story. Missing are the statistics concerning how many lives have been saved by air bags (7,224 by 2001), how many of the children were unrestrained or improperly restrained in the front seat (the most recent statistic available is 61 people by 1998, 34 of the 38 children by 1998, nine infants in rear-facing restraints, 25 older children unrestrained), how many of the adults were not wearing seat belts at the time the air bag deployed (nearly all of the 23 by 1998). During the year 2000, one child died for every 8.9 million passenger airbags; in 1996 that number was one child fatality for every 870,000 passenger air bags. Although any death is a sad occurrence, statistical evidence points to a need to use seat belts in conjunction with air bags and to properly restrain children in the rear seat. Statistics also show that air-bag deployment in an accident is more likely to save lives than shorten them (7,224 lives saved versus 191 lost).

Allen, K., and Brehm, M. "Air Bag Switches Aren't the Answer; Seating Kids in the Back Protects Them." *USA Today*, March 7, 1997.

Freeman, S. "Child Deaths from Air Bags Decrease; Actions by Manufacturers, Parents Cited." *Wall Street Journal*, August 30, 2001.

Ledford, J. "The Lane Ranger: Measure Risk Before Deciding to Switch Air Bag." *The Atlanta Journal and Constitution*, November 22, 1997.

Nauss, D. "Less Powerful Air Bags OK'd for Cars, Trucks." *Los Angeles Times*, March 15, 1997.

Frequency Diagrams and Histograms

5. Make a frequency distribution of the following data. Is this distribution bimodal? Multimodal? Skewed to the left? Skewed to the right? Normal?

   225, 226, 227, 226, 227, 228, 228, 229, 222, 223, 224, 226, 227, 228, 225, 221, 227, 229, 230

6. NB Plastics uses injection molds to produce plastic parts that range in size from a marble to a book. Parts are pulled off the press by one operator and passed on to another member of the team to be finished or cleaned up. This often involves trimming loose material, drilling holes, and painting. After a batch of parts has completed its cycle through the finishing process, a sample of five parts is chosen at random and certain dimensions are measured to ensure that each part is within certain tolerances. This information (in mm) is recorded for each of the five pieces and evaluated. Create a frequency diagram. Are the two operators trimming off the same amount of material? How do you know?

Part Name: Mount
Critical Dimension: 0.654 ± 0.005
Tolerance: ±0.005
Method of Checking: Caliper

Date	Time	Press	Oper	Samp 1	Samp 2	Samp 3	Samp 4	Samp 5
9/20/92	0100	#1	Jack	0.6550	0.6545	0.6540	0.6540	0.6545
9/20/92	0300	#1	Jack	0.6540	0.6540	0.6545	0.6545	0.6545
9/20/92	0500	#1	Jack	0.6540	0.6540	0.6540	0.6540	0.6535
9/20/92	0700	#1	Jack	0.6540	0.6540	0.6540	0.6540	0.6540
9/21/92	1100	#1	Mary	0.6595	0.6580	0.6580	0.6595	0.6595
9/21/92	1300	#1	Mary	0.6580	0.6580	0.6585	0.6590	0.6575
9/21/92	1500	#1	Mary	0.6580	0.6580	0.6580	0.6585	0.6590
9/22/92	0900	#1	Mary	0.6575	0.6570	0.6580	0.6585	0.6580

7. Manufacturers of refrigeration systems for restaurant food storage are very concerned that their units are able to maintain precise temperature control. At AB's testing lab, a refrigeration unit has been equipped with newly designed seals. The temperature inside the unit has been monitored and measured every 30 minutes. Use the data from this test to construct and interpret a frequency diagram.

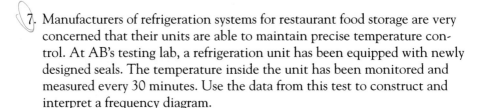

Temperature C									
4	8	6	7	7	10	8	11	9	13
8	5	9	6	9	10	7	8	7	
6	7	8	11	9	8	12	8	10	

8. PL Industries machines shafts for rocker arm assemblies. One particularly complex shaft is shown in Figure P4.1. The existing machining cell is currently unable to meet the specified tolerances consistently. PL Industries has decided to replace the existing machines with CNC turning centers. The following data are from a runoff held at the CNC vendor's facility. The indicated portion of the shaft was chosen for inspection. The diameter specifications for the round shaft are 7.650 + 0.02 mm. In order to prevent scrap for this particular operation, there is no lower specification. The data are scaled from 7.650, meaning that a value of 0.021 is actually 7.671 mm. Create a frequency diagram with the data.

0.011	0.013	0.018	0.007	0.002	0.020	0.014	0.006	0.002
0.006	0.004	0.003	0.010	0.015	0.011	0.020	0.020	0.012
0.015	0.004	0.009	0.020	0.012	0.011	0.012	0.004	0.017
0.010	0.011	0.018	0.015	0.010				

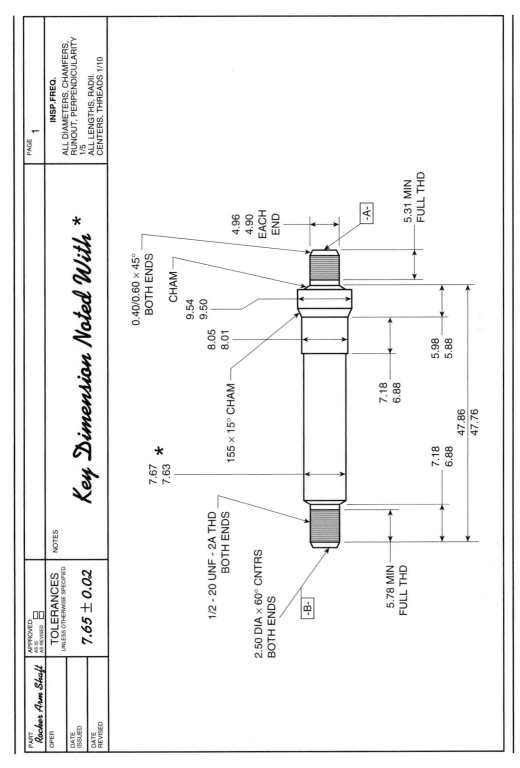

Figure P4.1   Problem 8

9. Create a histogram with the shaft data in Problem 8. Describe the distribution's shape, spread, and location.

10. Create and interpret a histogram using the data in problem 7.

11. Gold, measured in grams, is used to create circuit boards at MPL Industries. The following measurements of gold usage per batch of circuit boards have been recorded in a tally sheet. Create a histogram with the following information. Describe the shape, location, and spread of the histogram. The target value is 145 grams.

125	/	139	
126	/	140	ЖН
127		141	ЖН /
128	///	142	ЖН /
129	////	143	ЖН /
130		144	ЖН
131		145	ЖН ///
132	ЖН	146	ЖН ЖН
133		147	ЖН //
134	////	148	ЖН /
135	ЖН /	149	////
136	////	150	ЖН
137	////		
138	ЖН /		

12. At a local bank, the time a customer spends waiting to transact business varies between 1 and 10 minutes. Create and interpret a histogram with the following data:

Wait Time	Frequency
1 min	5
2 min	10
3 min	16
4 min	25
5 min	18
6 min	9
7 min	6
8 min	4
9 min	2
10 min	1

13. A manufacturer of CDs has a design specification for the width of the CD of 120 ± 0.3 mm. Create a histogram using the following data. Describe the distribution's shape, spread, and location.

Measurement	Tally
119.4	///
119.5	////
119.6	⫰⫰⫰ /
119.7	⫰⫰⫰ //
119.8	⫰⫰⫰ ⫰⫰⫰
119.9	⫰⫰⫰ ///
120.0	⫰⫰⫰ //
120.1	⫰⫰⫰
120.2	////

14. Use the concepts of symmetry and skewness to describe the histogram in Problem 7.

15. Why is it important to use both statistical measures and descriptive concepts when describing a histogram?

16. Create a histogram with the information from Problem 6. Is this histogram bimodal?

Measures of Central Tendency and Dispersion

17. What is meant by the following expression: the central tendency of the data?

18. What is meant by the following expression: measures of dispersion?

19. Why does the salary information for engineers provide more information than the salary information shown for inspectors?

	Min	Max	Std. Dev.	Sample Size	Average	Median
Engineer	$25,000	$80,000	$11,054	28	$48,298	$45,750
Inspector				5	$28,136	$27,000

20. Find the mean, mode, and median for the data given in problem 7.

21. Using the following sample data, calculate the mean, mode, and median:

1.116	1.122	1.125
1.123	1.122	1.123
1.133	1.125	1.118
1.117	1.121	1.123
1.124	1.136	1.122
1.119	1.127	1.122
1.129	1.125	1.119
1.121	1.124	
1.128	1.122	

22. Determine the mean, mode, and median of the information in Problem 6.

23. Determine the mean, mode, and median of the following numbers. What is the standard deviation? Mark 1, 2, and 3 standard deviations (plus and minus) on the diagram.

    225, 226, 227, 226, 227, 228, 228, 229, 222, 223, 224, 226, 227, 228, 225, 221, 227, 229, 230

    (These are all the data; that is, the set comprises a population.)

24. For the shaft data from Problem 8, determine the mean, mode, median, standard deviation, and range. Use these values to describe the distribution. Compare this mathematical description with the description you created for the histogram problem.

25. For Problem 11, concerning the amount of gold used to create circuit boards, determine the mean, mode, median, standard deviation, and range. Use these values to describe the distribution. Compare this mathematical description with the description you created in Problem 11.

26. For the CD data of Problem 13, determine the mean, mode, median, standard deviation, and range. Use these values to describe the distribution. Compare this mathematical description with the description you created in Problem 13.

27. Determine the standard deviation and the range of the numbers in Problem 7.

28. Determine the standard deviation and the range of the numbers in Problem 6.

29. Describe the histogram created in Problem 16 using the standard deviation, range, mean, median, and mode. Discuss symmetry and skewness.

30. Four readings of the thickness of the paper in this textbook are 0.076, 0.082, 0.073, and 0.077 mm. Determine the mean and the standard deviation.

31. WT Corporation noticed a quality problem with their stainless steel product. Corrosion pits were forming after the product was already in the hands of the consumer. After several brainstorming sessions by the engineering and quality departments, the problem was traced to improper heat-treating. Work progressed to determine specifically what the problem was and to give a recommendation for what could be done to eliminate it. It was determined that the small fluctuations in heating temperature and quenching time could be depriving the product of its full corrosion resistance. A simple and quick test was developed that allowed a heat treatment operator to roughly determine the product's ability to resist corrosion. The amount of retained austenite in a heat treated stainless steel product is related to the product's ability to resist corrosion. The smaller the amount of retained austenite, the better the product will resist corrosion. What

follows is one day's worth of test readings. Determine the range, standard deviation, mean, mode, and median for these data.

Time	Reading
7:00	12
	17
8:00	25
	23
9:00	21
	19
10:00	28
	25
11:00	31
	27
12:00	20
	28
1:00	23
	25
2:00	26
	29

32. How do the range, mean, standard deviation, median, and mode work together to describe a distribution?

33. Given the histogram shown in Figure P4.2, describe it over the phone to someone who has never seen it before. Refer to kurtosis, skewness, mean, standard deviation, median, mode, and range. Be descriptive.

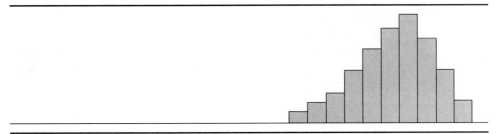

Figure P4.2   Problem 33

34. Pictured in Figure P4.3 are three normal curves. Assume the one on the left is the expected or acceptable curve for the process. How did the numerical magnitude of the standard deviation change for the middle curve? For the curve on the right?

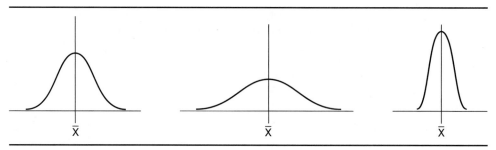

Figure P4.3   Problem 34

Normal Curve

35. If the average wait time is 12 minutes with a standard deviation of 3 minutes, determine the percentage of patrons who wait less than 15 minutes for their main course to be brought to their tables.

36. The thickness of a part is to have an upper specification of 0.925 and a lower specification of 0.870 mm. The average of the process is currently 0.917 with a standard deviation of 0.005. Determine the percentage of product above 0.90 mm.

37. The Rockwell hardness of specimens of an alloy shipped by your supplier varies according to a normal distribution with mean 70 and standard deviation 3. Specimens are acceptable for machining only if their hardness is greater than 65. What percentage of specimens will be acceptable? Draw the normal curve diagram associated with this problem.

38. Given the specifications of 7.650 ± 0.02 mm diameter for the shaft, use the information from Problem 8 to determine the percentage of shafts able to meet the specification limits.

39. If the mean value of the weight of a particular brand of dog food is 20.6 lb and the standard deviation is 1.3, assume a normal distribution and calculate the amount of product produced that falls below the lower specification value of 19.7 lb.

40. To create the rocker arm for a car seat recliner, the steel must meet a minimum hardness standard. The histogram of data in Figure P4.4 on page 207 provides the Rockwell hardness test results from a year's worth of steel coil production. Given an average of 44.795 and a standard deviation of 0.402, calculate the percentage of coils whose hardness is less than the minimum requirement of 44.000.

41. Global warming is a concern for this and future generations. Measurements of the earth's atmospheric temperature have been taken over the past 100 years. If the average temperature has been 50°F with a standard deviation of 18°F, what percentage of the temperatures have been between 0 and 90°F?

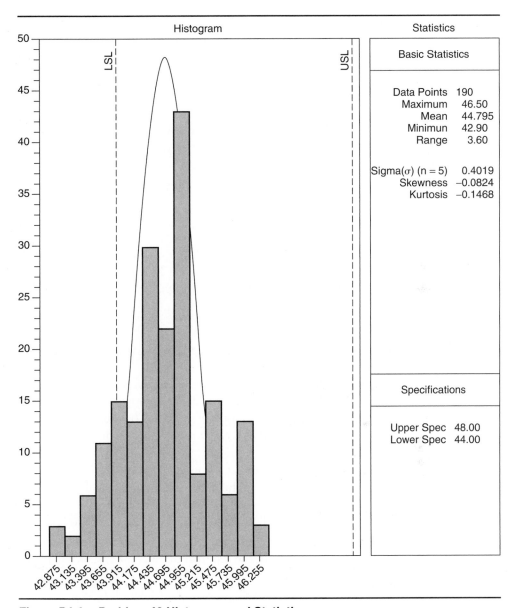

Figure P4.4   Problem 40 Histogram and Statistics

42. For the CD data from Problem 13, determine what percentage of the CDs produced are above and below the specifications of 120 ± 0.3 mm.

43. Joe and Sally run a custom car wash. All the washes and waxes are done by hand and the interiors are vacuumed. Joe and Sally need to do some planning in order to schedule cars for appointments. If the mean time for a cleanup is 45 minutes and the standard deviation is 10 minutes, what

percentage of the cleanups will take less than 65 and more than 35 minutes to complete? The data the couple has taken are normally distributed.

44. A lightbulb has a normally distributed light output with a mean of 3,000 foot-candles and standard deviation of 50 foot-candles. Find a lower specification limit such that only 0.5 percent of the bulbs will not exceed this limit.

45. The life of an automotive battery is normally distributed with a mean of 900 days and a standard deviation of 50 days. What fraction of these batteries would be expected to survive beyond 1,000 days?

46. Clearly describe the central limit theorem to someone who is unfamiliar with it.

47. A sample distribution (closely approximating a normal distribution) of a critical part dimension has an average of 11.85 inches and a sample standard deviation of 1.33 inches. The lower specification limit is 11.41 inches. The upper specification limit is 12.83 inches. What percentage of parts will be produced below the lower specification limit of 11.41 inches?

Confidence Interval Testing

48. NB Manufacturing has ordered the construction of a new machine to replace an older machine in a machining cell. Now that the machine has been built, a runoff is to be performed. The diameter on the test pieces were checked for runout. From the 32 parts sampled, the average was 0.0015 with a standard deviation of 0.0008. The engineers would like to know, with 90% confidence, the interval values for the population mean.

49. A manufacturer of lightbulbs has sampled 40 bulbs in order to determine the population mean life of the bulbs. The sample mean was 1200 hours with a standard deviation of 100. The manufacturer would like to know, with 95% confidence, the interval values for the population mean.

50. An automotive manufacturer has selected ten car seats in order to study the Rockwell hardness of the seat recliner mechanism. A sample of 8 has an average of 44.795 and a standard deviation of 0.402. At a 95% confidence level, what is the interval for the population mean?

CASE STUDY 4.1
Statistics

PART 1

Angie's company has recently told her that her pension money can now be invested in several different funds. They have informed all of their employees that it is the employee's decision which of the six risk categories to invest in. The six risk categories include conservative, secure, moderate, balanced, ambitious, and aggressive. Within each risk category, there are two fund choices. This gives each employee twelve funds in which to invest capital.

As the names suggest, each fund category attempts to invest the person's capital in a particular style. A conservative fund will find investments that will not expose the investor's money to risk. This category is the "safest." Money invested here is not exposed to great potential losses but it is not exposed to great gains either. The aggressive fund is for investors who believe that when nothing is ventured, nothing is gained. It takes the greatest risks. With this fund, investors have the potential to make great gains with their capital. Of course, this is also the fund that exposes the investor to the potential for great losses. In between, the other four categories mix the amount of risk an investor is subject to.

Angie is rather at a loss. In the packet from the investment company she has received over 150 pages of information about each of the accounts. For the past three nights, she has been trying to read it all. Now all of the information is running together in her head, and she has to make up her mind soon.

Just as she is about to give up and throw a dart at the dartboard, she discovers an investment performance update (Table C4.1.1) among the many pages of data. Remembering her statistical training, she decides to study the performance of the different funds over the past 11 years. To fully understand the values she calculates, she decides to compare those values with the market performance of three market indicators: treasury bills, the Capital Markets Index, and the Standard & Poor's 500 Index. These indicators are used by investors to compare the performance of their investments against the market.

 Assignment

From Table C4.1.1 calculate the average of each of the funds and market performance indicators.

Table C4.1.1   Funds and Market Indices, 1993–2003

	'93	'94	'95	'96	'97	'98	'99	'00	'01	'02	'03
Conservative											
C1	10.4	12.8	18.4	15.0	3.0	8.2	11.3	8.0	13.2	7.3	10.7
C2	10.9	14.0	24.2	15.9	2.5	8.7	13.7	10.2	17.9	8.0	11.6
Secure											
S1	18.2	10.2	23.7	18.9	7.8	12.0	23.0	4.4	21.2	8.0	8.2
S2	16.3	9.3	27.8	19.1	0.5	12.8	15.3	1.4	27.9	2.7	13.1
Moderate											
M1	14.5	10.0	29.7	23.2	11.6	16.0	19.7	0.8	29.5	7.6	7.5
M2	21.9	14.4	27.2	17.6	6.4	15.7	28.2	4.5	27.6	6.6	4.5
Balanced											
B1	29.2	9.2	24.7	17.3	2.3	21.8	22.8	1.4	20.8	7.7	7.5
B2	21.5	8.9	23.2	13.2	7.8	12.7	24.8	2.3	25.6	9.2	11.9
Ambitious											
A1	36.2	6.3	32.4	11.8	2.9	14.7	22.9	3.5	38.6	10.8	15.8
A2	27.3	2.6	33.5	14.7	3.4	15.1	32.8	−6.1	24.1	13.8	25.2
Aggressive											
G1	23.7	7.6	33.4	25.8	5.5	13.3	28.6	6.9	51.5	4.0	−4.1
G2	22.3	0.3	38.3	19.7	6.0	14.1	37.0	−2.1	57.6	6.4	−1.2
Treasury Bills											
	9.2	10.3	8.0	6.3	6.1	7.1	8.7	8.0	5.7	3.6	6.7
Capital Markets Index											
	17.7	8.3	28.6	16.5	3.4	13.2	21.6	1.0	25.0	8.4	13.4
Standard & Poor's 500											
	22.6	6.3	31.7	18.6	5.3	16.6	31.6	−3.1	30.4	7.6	10.1

PART 2

As her next step, Angie is going to interpret the results of her calculations. To make sure that she has a comfortable retirement, she has decided that she would like to have her money grow at an average of 15 percent or greater each year.

 Assignment

Use the average values you calculated to determine which funds will average greater than 15 percent return on investment per year.

PART 3

Angie has narrowed her list to those funds averaging a 15 percent or greater return on investment per year. That still leaves her with several to choose from. Remembering that some of the funds are riskier than others, Angie is quick to realize that in some years she may not make 15 percent or more. She may add 25 percent or higher to her total amount of pension, or she may lose 5 percent of her pension. An average value doesn't guarantee that she will make exactly 15 percent a year. An average reflects how well she will do when all of the good years (gains) and bad years (losses) are combined.

Angie has 20 years to work before she retires. While this gives her some time to increase her wealth, she is concerned that a few bad years could significantly lower the amount of money that she will retire with. To find the funds that have high gains or high losses, she turns her attention to the study of the range and standard deviation.

 Assignment

Calculate the range and standard deviation associated with each of the funds and market indicators with an average of 15 percent or greater return on investment.

PART 4

For all of the funds that she is interested in, Angie has noticed that the spread of the data differs dramatically. One of the ranges is almost 60 points! She has also noticed that the riskier the fund, the greater the range of values.

Since the ranges may have been caused by an isolated year that was particularly good or particularly bad, Angie turns her attention to the standard deviations, which also increase as the riskiness of the fund increases.

Decision time! Comparing the average return on investment yielded by the stock market (Standard & Poor's 500, Capital Markets Index) during this 11-year period, Angie notices that several of the investment funds have brought in returns that were less than the Standard & Poor's 500 market indicator. She decides to take them off her potential funds list. This removes M2 and B1 from consideration. She also removes from consideration any fund that has a large range and standard deviation. Because she is willing to take some risk, but not a dramatic one, she decides not to invest in the aggressive fund. This removes G1 and G2 from consideration. Now she can concentrate on a smaller group of funds: M1, A1, A2. So now, instead of having to devour hundreds of pages of information, Angie can look at the pages detailing the performance of these three funds and make her decision about which one to invest in.

To help make the choice between these funds, Angie has decided to use the Z tables to calculate the percentage of time that each fund's return on investment fell below the 12 percent that she feels that she absolutely has to make each year.

 Assignment

Assume a normal distribution and use the Z tables to calculate the percentage of each of the remaining funds' return on investments that fell below 12 percent in the past 11 years. Do not perform this calculation for the fund indicators.

CASE STUDY 4.2
Process Improvement

This case is the second in a four-part series of cases involving process improvement. The other cases are found at the end of Chapters 3, 5, and 6. Data and calculations for this case establish the foundation for the future cases; however, it is not necessary to complete this case or the case in Chapter 3 in order to complete and understand the cases in Chapters 5 and 6. Completing this case will provide insight into the use of statistical calculations and histograms in process improvement. The case can be worked by hand or with the software provided.

PART 1

Figure C4.2.1 provides the details of a bracket assembly to hold a strut on an automobile in place. Welded to the auto body frame, the bracket cups the strut and secures it to the frame via a single bolt with a lock washer. Proper alignment is necessary for both smooth installation during assembly and for future performance. For mounting purposes the left-side hole, A, must be aligned on center with the right-side hole, B. If the holes are centered directly opposite each other, in perfect alignment, then the angle between hole centers will measure 0°. As the flowchart in Figure C4.2.2 shows, the bracket is created by passing coils of flat steel through a series of progressive dies.

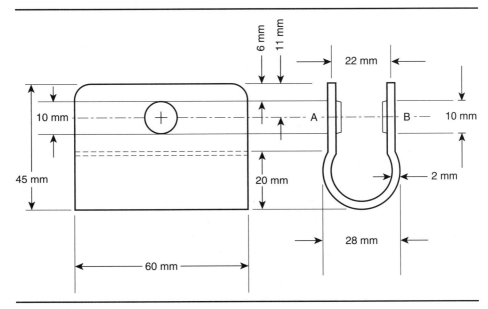

Figure C4.2.1   Bracket

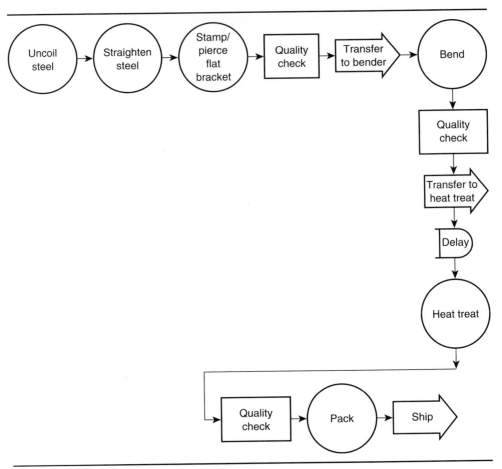

Figure C4.2.2   Flowchart of Bracket Fabrication Process

As the steel moves through the press, the bracket is stamped, pierced, and finally bent into the appropriate shape.

Recently customers have been complaining about having difficulty securing the bracket closed with the bolt and lock washer. The bolts have been difficult to slide through the holes and then tighten. Assemblers complain of stripped bolts and snug fittings. Unsure of where the problem is, WP Inc.'s management assembles a team consisting of representatives from process engineering, materials engineering, product design, and manufacturing.

Through the use of several cause-and-effect diagrams, the team determines that the most likely cause of the problems experienced by the customer is the alignment of the holes. At some stage in the formation process, the holes end up off-center. To confirm their suspicions, during the next production run, the bending press operator takes 20 sub-groups of size 5 and measures the angle between the centers of the holes for each sample (Figure C4.2.3). The specification of the angle between insert hole A and insert hole B

Subgroup															
Sample	1	2	3	4	5	6	7	8	9	10	11	12	13	14	15
1	0.31	0.27	0.30	0.30	0.25	0.18	0.26	0.15	0.30	0.31	0.18	0.22	0.19	0.14	0.29
2	0.29	0.23	0.30	0.20	0.20	0.26	0.27	0.21	0.24	0.25	0.16	0.30	0.28	0.27	0.23
3	0.30	0.31	0.28	0.21	0.19	0.18	0.12	0.24	0.26	0.25	0.21	0.21	0.26	0.25	0.27
4	0.28	0.23	0.24	0.23	0.26	0.24	0.20	0.27	0.27	0.28	0.29	0.24	0.29	0.28	0.24
5	0.23	0.29	0.32	0.25	0.25	0.17	0.23	0.30	0.26	0.25	0.27	0.26	0.24	0.16	0.23

Subgroup					
Sample	16	17	18	19	20
1	0.22	0.32	0.33	0.20	0.24
2	0.24	0.27	0.30	0.17	0.28
3	0.22	0.28	0.22	0.26	0.15
4	0.30	0.19	0.26	0.31	0.27
5	0.30	0.31	0.26	0.24	0.19

Figure C4.2.3   Hole A, B Alignment; Angle Above (+) or Below (−) Nominal

is 0.00° with a tolerance of ±0.30°. The values recorded in Figure C4.2.3 represent the distance above (or when a minus sign is present, below) the nominal value of 0.00°.

 Assignment

Utilize the data to create a histogram. Calculate the mean, median, mode, standard deviation, and range for all the data.

PART 2

Having a histogram and the accompanying statistical information tells the team a lot about the hole-alignment characteristics. Even more can be learned if these process data are compared with the specifications as set by the customers.

 Assignment

Use the calculations for the area under the normal curve to determine the percentage of brackets created with misaligned holes. Remember the specifications for the angle between insert hole A and insert hole B are 0.00° with a tolerance of ±0.30°. You will need to determine the percentage of brackets outside each side of the tolerance. How are they doing?

PART 3

Using the problem-solving method described in Chapter 3 (and followed in Case Study 3.2), the team has determined that the fixture that holds the flat bracket in place during the bending operation needs to be replaced. One of the measures of performance that they created during step 4 of their problem-solving process is the percentage of the parts that are out of specification. We calculated this value in part 2 of this case. Now that the fixture has been replaced with a better one, the team would like to determine whether or not changing the fixture improved the process by removing a root cause of hole misalignment.

 Assignment

Utilize the data in Figure C4.2.4 to create a histogram. Calculate the mean, median, mode, standard deviation, and range for all new data. Use the calculations for the area under the normal curve to determine the new percentage of brackets created with misaligned holes. Remember: the specifications for the angle between insert hole A and insert hole B are 0.00° with a tolerance of ±0.30°. You will need to determine the percentage of brackets outside each side of the tolerance. How are they doing when you compare their measure of performance, that is, the percentage of the parts out of specification both before and after the fixture has changed?

Subgroup Sample	1	2	3	4	5	6	7	8	9	10	11	12	13	14	15
1	0.03	0.06	0.06	0.03	−0.04	−0.02	−0.05	0.06	0.00	−0.02	−0.02	0.06	0.07	0.10	0.02
2	0.08	0.08	0.08	0.00	−0.07	0.06	−0.07	0.03	0.06	−0.01	0.06	0.02	−0.04	0.05	−0.05
3	−0.03	−0.01	0.05	0.05	0.00	0.02	0.11	0.04	0.02	0.00	−0.02	−0.01	0.08	0.03	0.04
4	0.07	0.08	−0.03	−0.01	−0.01	0.12	−0.03	0.03	−0.02	−0.10	0.02	−0.02	0.01	0.04	0.05
5	−0.02	0.02	0.03	0.07	−0.01	−0.07	0.03	0.01	0.00	−0.04	0.09	0.03	−0.04	0.06	−0.05

Subgroup Sample	16	17	18	19	20
1	−0.05	−0.06	−0.04	−0.06	−0.01
2	0.00	−0.02	−0.02	0.00	0.02
3	0.06	0.04	−0.01	0.00	0.05
4	−0.02	0.07	0.03	0.03	0.04
5	−0.01	−0.04	−0.02	0.04	0.03

Figure C4.2.4   Hole A, B Alignment Following Process Improvement; Angle Above (+) or Below (−) Nominal

5

Variable Control Charts

Control Chart Functions
Variation
Control Charts for Variables
$\overline{X}$ and R Charts
Summary
Lessons Learned
Formulas
Chapter Problems
Case Study 5.1   Quality Control for Variables
Case Study 5.2   Process Improvement
Case Study 5.3   Sample-Size Considerations

 ■ *Learning Opportunities:*

1. To understand the concept of variation
2. To understand the difference between assignable causes and chance causes
3. To learn how to construct control charts for variables, either $\overline{X}$ and R charts or $\overline{X}$ and s charts
4. To recognize when a process is under control and when it is not
5. To understand the importance of the R and s charts when interpreting variable control charts
6. To know how to revise a control chart in which assignable causes have been identified and corrected ■

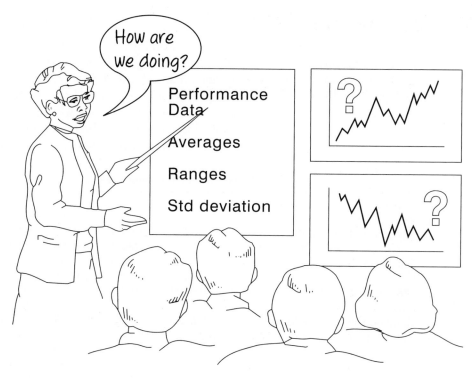

Profit Meeting

*I*s it possible for the people attending the meeting in the figure to answer the
question? How would they do it? Can the performance data, average, range, and
standard deviation be combined into a clear statement of their company's
performance? The study of a process over time can be enhanced by the use of control
charts in addition to the averages, ranges, and standard deviations calculated in the
previous chapter. Process variation is recorded on **control charts,** which are
powerful aids to understanding the performance of a process over time.

CONTROL CHART FUNCTIONS

In Chapter 4, a group of engineers started working on a process that produces clutch plates. So far their analysis of the process has included constructing a histogram and calculating ranges, averages, and standard deviations. The only shortcoming in their analysis is its failure to show process performance over time. Let's take a closer look at the data in Table 4.5, reproduced here in Table 5.1, and see why that may be important. When these averages are graphed in a histogram, the result closely resembles a normal curve (Figure 5.1a). Graphing the averages by subgroup number, according to

Table 5.1   Clutch Plate Thickness: Sums and Averages

						ΣX_i	$\bar{X}$
Subgroup 1	0.0625	0.0626	0.0624	0.0625	0.0627	0.3127	0.0625
Subgroup 2	0.0624	0.0623	0.0624	0.0626	0.0625	0.3122	0.0624
Subgroup 3	0.0622	0.0625	0.0623	0.0625	0.0626	0.3121	0.0624
Subgroup 4	0.0624	0.0623	0.0620	0.0623	0.0624	0.3114	0.0623
Subgroup 5	0.0621	0.0621	0.0622	0.0625	0.0624	0.3113	0.0623
Subgroup 6	0.0628	0.0626	0.0625	0.0626	0.0627	0.3132	0.0626
Subgroup 7	0.0624	0.0627	0.0625	0.0624	0.0626	0.3126	0.0625
Subgroup 8	0.0624	0.0625	0.0625	0.0626	0.0626	0.3126	0.0625
Subgroup 9	0.0627	0.0628	0.0626	0.0625	0.0627	0.3133	0.0627
Subgroup 10	0.0625	0.0626	0.0628	0.0626	0.0627	0.3132	0.0626
Subgroup 11	0.0625	0.0624	0.0626	0.0626	0.0626	0.3127	0.0625
Subgroup 12	0.0630	0.0628	0.0627	0.0625	0.0627	0.3134	0.0627
Subgroup 13	0.0627	0.0626	0.0628	0.0627	0.0626	0.3137	0.0627
Subgroup 14	0.0626	0.0626	0.0625	0.0626	0.0627	0.3130	0.0626
Subgroup 15	0.0628	0.0627	0.0626	0.0625	0.0626	0.3132	0.0626
Subgroup 16	0.0625	0.0626	0.0625	0.0628	0.0627	0.3131	0.0626
Subgroup 17	0.0624	0.0626	0.0624	0.0625	0.0627	0.3126	0.0625
Subgroup 18	0.0628	0.0627	0.0628	0.0626	0.0630	0.3139	0.0627
Subgroup 19	0.0627	0.0626	0.0628	0.0625	0.0627	0.3133	0.0627
Subgroup 20	0.0626	0.0625	0.0626	0.0625	0.0627	0.3129	0.0626
Subgroup 21	0.0627	0.0626	0.0628	0.0625	0.0627	0.3133	0.0627
Subgroup 22	0.0625	0.0626	0.0628	0.0625	0.0627	0.3131	0.0626
Subgroup 23	0.0628	0.0626	0.0627	0.0630	0.0627	0.3138	0.0628
Subgroup 24	0.0625	0.0631	0.0630	0.0628	0.0627	0.3141	0.0628
Subgroup 25	0.0627	0.0630	0.0631	0.0628	0.0627	0.3143	0.0629
Subgroup 26	0.0630	0.0628	0.0620	0.0628	0.0627	0.3142	0.0628
Subgroup 27	0.0630	0.0628	0.0631	0.0628	0.0627	0.3144	0.0629
Subgroup 28	0.0632	0.0632	0.0628	0.0631	0.0630	0.3153	0.0631
Subgroup 29	0.0630	0.0628	0.0631	0.0632	0.0631	0.3152	0.0630
Subgroup 30	0.0632	0.0631	0.0630	0.0628	0.0628	0.3149	0.0630
						9.3981	

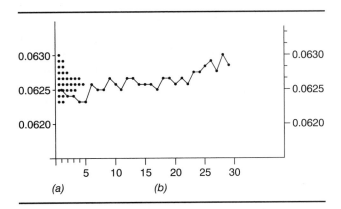

Figure 5.1   Chart with Histogram

when they were produced, gives a different impression of the data (Figure 5.1*b*). From the chart, it appears that the thickness of the clutch plate is increasing as production continues. This was not evident during the creation of the histogram or the analysis of the average, range, and standard deviation. A control chart enhances the analysis of the process by showing how that process is performing over time.

Control charts serve two basic functions:

1. Control charts are decision-making tools. They provide an economic basis for making a decision as to whether to investigate for potential problems, to adjust the process, or to leave the process alone.
   a. First and most important, control charts provide information for timely decisions concerning recently produced items. If an out-of-control condition is shown by the control chart, then a decision can be made about sorting or reworking the most recent production.
   b. Control chart information is used to determine the process capability, or the level of quality the process is capable of producing. Samples of completed product can be statistically compared with the process specifications. This comparison provides information concerning the process's ability to meet the specifications set by the product designer. Continual improvement in the production process can take place only if there is an understanding of what the process is currently capable of producing.
2. Control charts are problem-solving tools. They point out where improvement is needed. They help to provide a statistical basis on which to formulate improvement actions.
   a. Control chart information can be used to help locate and investigate the causes of the unacceptable or marginal quality. By observing the patterns on the chart the investigator can determine what adjustments need to be made. This type of coordinated problem solving utilizing statistical data leads to improved process quality.
   b. During daily production runs, the operator can monitor machine production and determine when to make the necessary adjustments to the process or when to leave the process alone to ensure quality production.

By combining control charts with an appropriate statistical summary, those study-ing a process can gain an understanding of what the process is capable of producing. This will enable them to make decisions concerning future production. The axiom applicable to being lost—you can't know which way to go if you don't know where you are—also applies to producing a quality product: you can't produce quality prod-uct in the future if you don't know what you're producing now. Control charts de-scribe where the process is in terms of current performance. Using statistical control charting creates a feedback loop enabling the organization to improve their processes, products, and services.

VARIATION

In manufacturing and service industries, the goal of most processes is to produce products or provide services that exhibit little or no variation. **Variation,** *where no two items or services are exactly the same*, exists in all processes. Although it may take a very precise measuring instrument or a very astute consumer to notice the varia-tion, any process in nature will exhibit variation. Understanding variation and its causes results in better decisions.

EXAMPLE 5.1   Variation in a Process

An industrial engineering department is seeking to decrease the amount of time it takes to perform a printer assembly operation. An analysis of the methods used by the operators performing the assembly has revealed that one of the operators com-pletes the assembly in 75 percent of the time it takes another operator performing the same assembly operation. Further investigation determines that the two operators use parts produced on different machines. The histograms in Figure 5.2 are based on measurements of the parts from the two different processes. In Figure 5.2*b* the spread of the process is considerably smaller, enabling the faster operator to assem-ble the parts much more quickly and with less effort. The slower operator must try a part in the assembly, discard the part if it doesn't fit, and try another part. Repeating the operation when the parts do not fit has made the operator much less efficient.

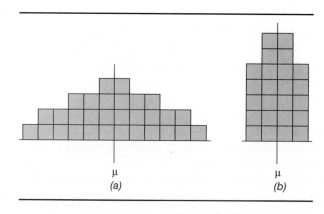

μ   μ
(a)   (b)

Figure 5.2   Histograms of Part Measurements from Two Machines

> This operator's apparent lack of speed is actually caused by the process and is not the fault of the operator. Had management not investigated variation in the process, they might have made incorrect judgments about the operator's performance. Instead, they realize that management intervention will be necessary to improve production at the previous operation and produce parts with less variation. $Q_{\succ}$

Several types of variation are tracked with statistical methods. These include:

1. Within-piece variation, or the variation within a single item or surface. For example, a single square yard of fabric may be examined to see if the color varies from one location to another.
2. Piece-to-piece variation, or the variation that occurs among pieces produced at approximately the same time. For example, in a production run filling gallon jugs with milk, when each of the milk jugs is checked after the filling station, the fill level from jug to jug will be slightly different.
3. Time-to-time variation, or the variation in the product produced at different times of the day—for example, the comparison of a part that has been stamped at the beginning of a production run with the part stamped at the end of a production run.

The variation in a process is studied by sampling the process. Samples are grouped into subgroups depending on whether or not the variation under study is piece-to-piece variation, within-piece variation, or time-to-time variation. The groupings of samples for piece-to-piece variation depend on the number of products analyzed during a particular time period. Within-piece variation samples are arranged in subgroups according to where in the process they are taken from. Samples for time-to-time variation are grouped according to the time of day that they were taken from the process.

Chance and Assignable Causes

Even in the most precise process no two parts are exactly alike. Whether these differences are due to chance causes in the process or to assignable causes needs to be determined. On the one hand, **chance,** or **common causes** *are small random changes in the process that cannot be avoided.* These small differences are due to the inherent variation present in all processes. They consistently affect the process and its performance day after day, every day. Variation of this type is only removable by making a change in the existing process. Removing chance causes from a system usually involves management intervention.

Assignable causes, on the other hand, *are variations in the process that can be identified as having a specific cause.* Assignable causes are causes that are not part of the process on a regular basis. This type of variation arises because of specific circumstances. It is these circumstances that the quality-assurance analyst seeks to find. Examples of assignable causes include a size change in a part that occurs when chips build up around a work-holding device in a machining operation, changes in the thickness of incoming raw material, or a broken tool. Sources of variation can be found in the process itself, the materials used, the operator's actions, or the environment. Examples of factors that can contribute to process variation include tool wear, machine vibration, and work-holding devices. Changes in material thickness, composition, or hardness are sources of variation. Operator actions affecting variation include overadjusting the machine, making an error during the inspection activity, changing the machine settings, or failing to properly align the part before machining. Environmental factors affecting variation include heat, light, radiation, and humidity.

To illustrate chance and assignable causes consider the following example.

EXAMPLE 5.2   Chance Causes and Assignable Causes

To create the flooring of an automobile, a flexible fiberglass form is affixed to carpet. This operation takes place in an oven and requires intense heat. In order to achieve a firm bond between the two materials, the temperature in the oven must remain between a very narrow range. RYMAX, a manufacturer of automobile flooring, operates several of these ovens in one area. The common causes, those causes affecting all of the ovens, are the temperature and humidity levels in the building. Special causes affect only certain ovens. Special causes would include leaving the oven door open to free a trapped form or a door that doesn't seal tightly. Can you think of other common or special causes for these ovens?

CONTROL CHARTS FOR VARIABLES

To create a control chart, samples, arranged into subgroups, are taken during the process. The averages of the subgroup values are plotted on the control chart. The **centerline** (ℂ) *of this chart shows where the process average is centered, the central tendency of the data.* The **upper control limit (UCL)** and **lower control limit (LCL),** *calculated based on* $\pm 3\sigma$, *describe the spread of the process* (Figure 5.3). Once the chart is constructed, it presents the user with a picture of what the process is currently capable of producing. In other words, we can expect future production to fall between these $\pm 3\sigma$ limits 99.73 percent of the time, providing the process does not change and is under control.

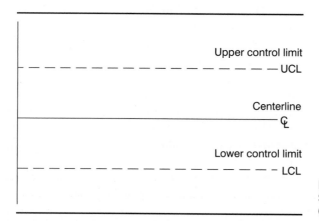

Figure 5.3   Control Chart Showing Centerline and Control Limits

Since control charts show changes in the process measurements, they allow for early detection of process changes. Instead of waiting until an entire production run is complete or until the product reaches the end of the assembly line, management can have critical part dimensions checked and charted throughout the process. If a part or group of parts has been made incorrectly, production can be stopped, adjusted, or otherwise modified to produce parts correctly. This approach permits corrections to be made to the process before a large number of parts is produced or, in some cases, before the product exceeds the specifications. Early detection can avoid scrap, rework, unnecessary adjustments to the process, and/or production delays.

Variables are the measurable characteristics of a product or service. Examples of variables include the height, weight, or length of a part. One of the most commonly used variable chart combinations in statistical process control is the $\overline{X}$ and R charts. Typical $\overline{X}$ and R charts are shown in Figure 5.4. $\overline{X}$ and R charts are used together to determine

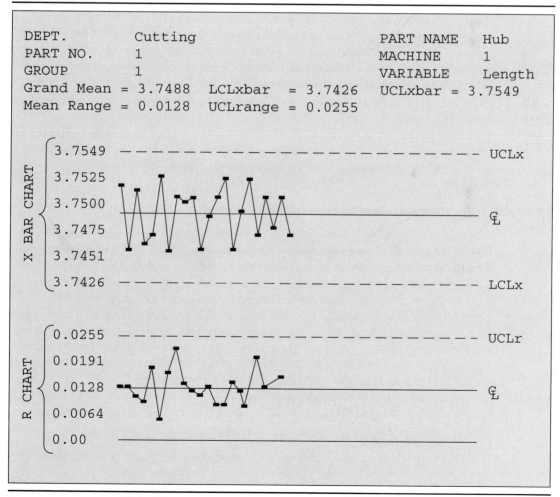

Figure 5.4   Typical $\overline{X}$ and R Chart

the distribution of the subgroup averages of sample measurements taken from a process. The importance of using these two charts in conjunction with each other will become apparent shortly.

$\overline{X}$ AND R CHARTS

The $\overline{X}$ chart is used to monitor the variation of the subgroup averages that are calculated from the individual sampled data. Averages rather than individual observations are used on control charts because average values will indicate a change in the amount of variation much faster than will individual values. Control limits on this chart are used to evaluate the variation from one subgroup to another.

The following steps and examples explain the construction of an $\overline{X}$ chart.

1. Define the Problem

In any situation it is necessary to determine what the goal of monitoring a particular quality characteristic or group of characteristics is. To merely say, "Improve quality," is not enough. Nor is it sufficient to say, "We would like to see fewer parts out of specification." Out of which specification? Is it total product performance that is being affected or just one particular dimension? Sometimes several aspects of a part are critical for part performance; occasionally only one is. It is more appropriate to say, "The length of these parts appears to be consistently below the lower specification limit. This causes the parts to mate incorrectly. Why are these parts below specification and how far below are they?" In the second statement we have isolated the length of the part as a critical dimension. From here, control charts can be placed on the process to help determine where the true source of the problem is located.

EXAMPLE 5.3   Printer Assembly: Defining the Problem

An assembly area has been experiencing serious delays in the construction of computer printers. As quality assurance manager, you have been asked to determine the cause of these delays and fix the problems as soon as possible. To best utilize the limited time available, you convene a meeting involving those closest to the assembly problems. Representatives from production, supervision, manufacturing engineering, industrial engineering, quality assurance, and maintenance have been able to generate a variety of possible problems. During this meeting, a cause-and-effect diagram was created, showing the potential causes for the assembly difficulties (Figure 5.5). Discussions during the meeting revealed that the shaft which holds the roller in place could be the major cause of assembly problems.

2. Select the Quality Characteristic to Be Measured

Variable control charts are based on measurements. The characteristics selected for measurement should be ones that affect product or service performance. Choice of a characteristic to be measured depends on what is being investigated. Characteristic

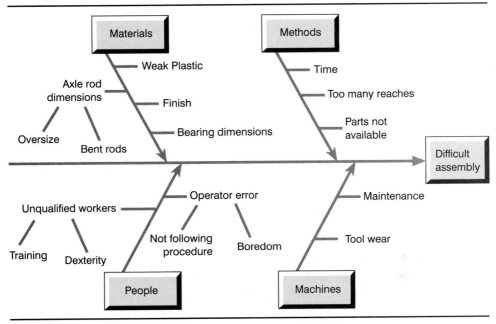

Figure 5.5   Printer Assembly: Cause-and-Effect Diagram

choice also depends on whether or not the process is being monitored for within-piece variation, piece-to-piece variation, or variation over time. Product or service characteristics such as length, height, viscosity, color, temperature, and velocity are typically used in manufacturing settings. Characteristics affecting performance are found in many aspects of a product, including raw materials, components, subassemblies, and finished products. Delivery times, checkout times, and service times are examples of characteristics chosen in a service industry. It is crucial to identify important characteristics; avoid the tendency to try to establish control charts for all measurements.

EXAMPLE 5.4   Printer Assembly: Identifying the Quality Characteristic

As the troubleshooting meeting described in Example 5.3 continues, further investigation reveals that the length of the shaft is hindering assembly operations. The characteristic to measure has been identified as piece-to-piece variation in the length of the shafts. To begin to study the situation, measurements of the lengths of the shafts will be sampled.

3. Choose a Rational Subgroup Size to Be Sampled

Subgroups, and the samples composing them, must be homogeneous. A *homogeneous subgroup will have been produced under the same conditions, by the same machine, the same operator, the same mold, and so on.* Homogeneous lots can also be designated by equal time intervals. Samples should be taken in an unbiased, random fashion. They should be representative of the entire population. Subgroup formation should reflect the type of variation under study. Subgroups used in investigating piece-to-piece variation will not necessarily be constructed in the same manner as subgroups formed to study time-to-time variation. The letter n is used to designate the number of samples taken within a subgroup. When constructing $\overline{X}$ and R charts, keep the subgroup sample size constant for each subgroup taken.

Decisions concerning the specific size of the subgroup—n, or the number of samples—require judgment. Sampling should occur frequently enough to detect changes in the process. Ask how often is the system expected to change. Examine the process and identify the factors causing change in the process. To be effective, sampling must occur as often as the system's most frequently changing factor. Once the number and frequency of sampling have been selected, they should not be changed unless the system itself has changed.

Realistically, sampling frequency must balance the value of the data obtained with the costs of taking the samples. Sampling is usually more frequent when control charts are first used to monitor the process. As process improvements are made and the process stabilizes, the frequency of sampling and subgroup size can be decreased.

When gathering sample data, it is important to have the following information in order to properly analyze the data:

1. *Who* will be collecting the data?
2. *What* aspect of the process is to be measured?
3. *Where* or at what point in the process will the sample be taken?
4. *When* or how frequently will the process be sampled?
5. *Why* is this particular sample being taken?
6. *How* will the data be collected?
7. *How many* samples will be taken (subgroup size)?

Some other guidelines to be followed include:

- The larger the subgroup size, the more sensitive the chart becomes to small variations in the process average. This will provide a better picture of the process since it allows the investigator to detect changes in the process quickly.
- While a larger subgroup size makes for a more sensitive chart, it also increases inspection costs.
- Destructive testing may make large subgroup sizes unfeasible. For example, it would not make sense for a fireworks manufacturer to test each and every one of its products.
- Subgroup sizes smaller than four do not create a representative distribution of subgroup averages. Subgroup averages are nearly normal for subgroups of four or more even when sampled from a nonnormal population.
- When the subgroup size exceeds 10, the standard deviation (s) chart, rather than the range (R) chart, should be used. For large subgroup sizes, the s chart gives a better representation of the true dispersion or true differences between the individuals sampled than does the R chart.

EXAMPLE 5.5   Printer Assembly: Selecting Subgroup Sample Size

The production from the machine making the shafts first looked at in Example 5.3 is consistent at 150 per hour. Since the process is currently exhibiting problems, your team has decided to take a sample of five measurements every 10 minutes from the production. The values for the day's production run are shown in Figure 5.6. **Q.**

DEPT.	Roller		PART NAME	Shaft
PART NO.	1		MACHINE	1
GROUP	1		VARIABLE	length

Subgroup	1	2	3	4	5
Time	07:30	07:40	07:50	08:00	08:10
Date	07/02/95	07/02/95	07/02/95	07/02/95	07/02/95
1	11.95	12.03	12.01	11.97	12.00
2	12.00	12.02	12.00	11.98	12.01
3	12.03 ①	11.96	11.97	12.00	12.02
4	11.98	12.00	11.98	12.03	12.03
5	12.01	11.98	12.00	11.99	12.02
X̄	11.99 ②	12.00	11.99	11.99	12.02
Range	0.08 ③	0.07	0.04	0.06	0.03

Subgroup	6	7	8	9	10
Time	08:20	08:30	08:40	08:50	09:00
Date	07/02/95	07/02/95	07/02/95	07/02/95	07/02/95
1	11.98	12.00	12.00	12.00	12.02
2	11.98	12.01	12.01	12.02	12.00
3	12.00	12.03	12.04	11.96	11.97
4	12.01	12.00	12.00	12.00	12.05
5	11.99	11.98	12.02	11.98	12.00
X̄	11.99	12.00	12.01	11.99	12.01
Range	0.03	0.05	0.04	0.06	0.08

Subgroup	11	12	13	14	15
Time	09:10	09:20	09:30	09:40	09:50
Date	07/02/95	07/02/95	07/02/95	07/02/95	07/02/95
1	11.98	11.92	11.93	11.99	12.00
2	11.97	11.95	11.95	11.93	11.98
3	11.96	11.92	11.98	11.94	11.99
4	11.95	11.94	11.94	11.95	11.95
5	12.00	11.96	11.96	11.96	11.93
X̄	11.97	11.94	11.95	11.95	11.97
Range	0.05	0.04	0.05	0.06	0.07

Figure 5.6   Values for a Day's Production   (*continued*)

Subgroup	16	17	18	19	20
Time	10:00	10:10	10:20	10:30	10:40
Date	07/02/95	07/02/95	07/02/95	07/02/95	07/02/95
1	12.00	12.02	12.00	11.97	11.99
2	11.98	11.98	12.01	12.03	12.01
3	11.99	11.97	12.02	12.00	12.02
4	11.96	11.98	12.01	12.01	12.00
5	11.97	11.99	11.99	11.99	12.01
$\overline{X}$	11.98	11.99	12.01	12.00	12.01
Range	0.04	0.05	0.03	0.06	0.03

$R = 0.05 = 12.02 - 11.97$

$$\frac{12.00 + 11.98 + 11.99 + 11.96 + 11.97}{5} = 11.98$$

Subgroup	21
Time	10:50
Date	07/02/95
1	12.00
2	11.98
3	11.99
4	11.99
5	12.02
$\overline{X}$	12.00
Range	0.04

Figure 5.6   (*continued*)

4. Collect the Data

To create a control chart, an amount of data sufficient to accurately reflect the statistical control of the process must be gathered. A minimum of 20 subgroups of sample size n = 4 is suggested. Each time a subgroup of sample size n is taken, an average is calculated for the subgroup. To do this, the individual values are recorded, summed, and then divided by the number of samples in the subgroup. This average, $\overline{X}_i$, is then plotted on the control chart.

EXAMPLE 5.6   Printer Assembly: Collecting Data

A sample of size n = 5 is taken at 10-minute intervals from the process making shafts. As shown in Figure 5.6, a total of 21 subgroups of sample size n = 5 have been taken. Each time a subgroup sample is taken, the individual values are recorded [Figure 5.6, (1)], summed, and then divided by the number of samples taken to get the average for the subgroup [Figure 5.6, (2)]. This subgroup average is then plotted on the control chart [Figure 5.7, (1)].

5. Determine the Trial Centerline for the $\overline{X}$ Chart

The centerline of the control chart is the process average. It would be the mean, μ, if the average of the population measurements for the entire process were known.

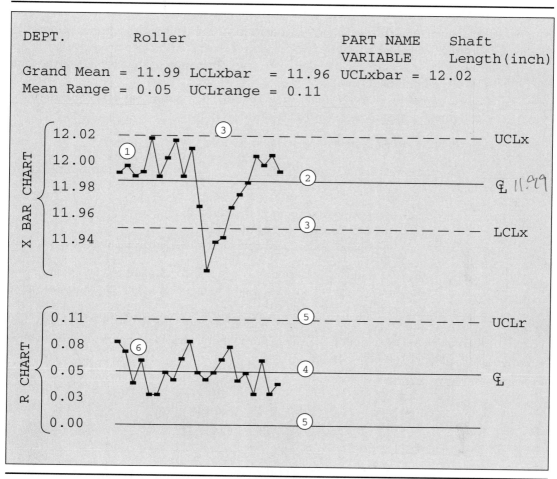

DEPT.   Roller   PART NAME   Shaft
                                               VARIABLE   Length(inch)
Grand Mean = 11.99 LCLxbar = 11.96 UCLxbar = 12.02
Mean Range = 0.05   UCLrange = 0.11

Figure 5.7   X̄ and R Control Charts for Roller Shaft Length

Since the value of the population mean μ cannot be determined unless all of the parts being produced are measured, in its place the grand average of the subgroup averages, $\overline{\overline{X}}$ (X double bar), is used. The grand average, or $\overline{\overline{X}}$, is calculated by summing all the subgroup averages and then dividing by the number of subgroups. This value is plotted as the centerline of the $\overline{X}$ chart:

$$\overline{\overline{X}} = \frac{\sum_{i=1}^{m} \overline{X}_i}{m}$$

where

$\overline{\overline{X}}$ = average of the subgroup averages
$\overline{X}_i$ = average of the ith subgroup
m = number of subgroups

6. Determine the Trial Control Limits for the $\overline{X}$ Chart

In Chapter 4 we learned that 99.73 percent of the data under a normal curve falls within $\pm 3\sigma$. Figure 5.1 showed how a control chart is a time-dependent pictorial representation of a normal curve displaying the distribution of the averages of the samples taken from the process.

Because of this, control limits are established at ± 3 standard deviations from the centerline for the process using the following formulas:

$$UCL_{\overline{X}} = \overline{\overline{X}} + 3\sigma_{\overline{x}}$$
$$LCL_{\overline{X}} = \overline{\overline{X}} - 3\sigma_{\overline{x}}$$

where

$$UCL = \text{upper control limit of the } \overline{X} \text{ chart}$$
$$LCL = \text{lower control limit of the } \overline{X} \text{ chart}$$
$$\sigma_{\overline{x}} = \text{population standard deviation of the subgroup averages}$$

The population standard deviation σ is needed to calculate the upper and lower control limits. Since control charts are based on sample data, Dr. Shewhart developed a good approximation of $3\sigma_{\overline{x}}$ using the product of an A_2 factor multiplied by $\overline{R}$, the average of the ranges. The $A_2\overline{R}$ combination uses the sample data for its calculation. $\overline{R}$ is calculated by summing the values of the individual subgroup ranges and dividing by the number of subgroups m:

$$\overline{R} = \frac{\displaystyle\sum_{i=1}^{m} R_i}{m}$$

where

$$\overline{R} = \text{average of the ranges}$$
$$R_i = \text{individual range values for the sample}$$
$$m = \text{number of subgroups}$$

A_2, the factor that allows the approximation $A_2\overline{R} \approx 3\sigma_{\overline{x}}$ to be true, is selected based on the subgroup sample size n. See Appendix 2 for the A_2 factors.

Upon replacement, the formulas for the upper and lower control limits become

$$UCL_{\overline{X}} = \overline{\overline{X}} + A_2\overline{R}$$
$$LCL_{\overline{X}} = \overline{\overline{X}} - A_2\overline{R}$$

After calculating the control limits, we place the centerline ($\overline{\overline{X}}$) and the upper and lower control limits (UCL and LCL, respectively) on the chart. The upper and lower control limits are shown by dashed lines. The grand average, or $\overline{\overline{X}}$, is shown by a solid line. The control limits on the $\overline{X}$ chart will be symmetrical about the central line. These control limits are used to evaluate the variation in quality from subgroup to subgroup.

**EXAMPLE 5.7   Printer Assembly: Calculating the $\overline{X}$ Chart
               Centerline and Control Limits**

Construction of an $\overline{X}$ chart begins with the calculation of the centerline, $\overline{\overline{X}}$. Using the 21 subgroups of sample size n = 5 provided in Figure 5.6, we calculate $\overline{\overline{X}}$ by summing all the subgroup averages based on the individual samples taken and then dividing by the number of subgroups, m:

$$\overline{\overline{X}} = \frac{11.99 + 12.00 + 11.99 + \cdots + 12.00}{21}$$

$$= \frac{251.77}{21} = 11.99$$

This value is plotted as the centerline of the $\overline{X}$ chart [Figure 5.7, (2)].

$\overline{R}$ is calculated by summing the values of the individual subgroup ranges (Figure 5.6) and dividing by the number of subgroups, m:

$$\overline{R} = \frac{0.08 + 0.07 + 0.04 + \cdots + 0.04}{21}$$

$$= \frac{1.06}{21} = 0.05$$

The A_2 factor for a sample size of five is selected from the table in Appendix 2. The values for the upper and lower control limits of the $\overline{X}$ chart are calculated as follows:

$$UCL_{\overline{X}} = \overline{\overline{X}} + A_2\overline{R}$$
$$= 11.99 + 0.577(0.05) = 12.02$$
$$LCL_{\overline{X}} = \overline{\overline{X}} - A_2\overline{R}$$
$$= 11.99 - 0.577(0.05) = 11.96$$

Once calculated, the upper and lower control limits (UCL and LCL, respectively) are placed on the chart [Figure 5.7, (3)].

7. Determine the Trial Control Limits for the R Chart

When an $\overline{X}$ chart is used to evaluate the variation in quality from subgroup to subgroup, the range chart is a method of determining the amount of variation in the individual samples. The importance of the range chart is often overlooked. Without the range chart, or the standard deviation chart to be discussed later, it would not be possible to fully understand process capability. Where the $\overline{X}$ chart shows the average of the individual subgroups, giving the viewer an understanding of where the process is centered, the range chart shows the spread or dispersion of the individual samples within the subgroup. The calculation of the spread of the measurements is necessary to determine whether the parts being produced are similar to one another or not. If the product displays a wide spread or a large range, then the individuals being produced are not similar to each other. Figure 5.8 shows that each of the subgroups has the same average; however, their samples spread differently. The optimal situation

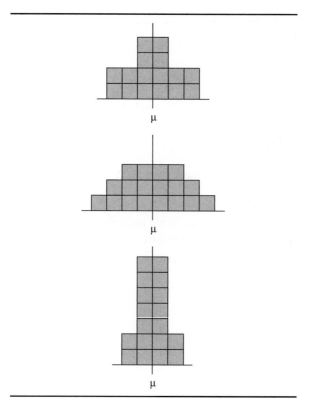

Figure 5.8   Histograms with Same Averages, Different Ranges

from a quality perspective is when the parts are grouped closely around the process average. This situation will yield a small value for both the range and the standard deviation, meaning that the measurements are very similar to each other.

Individual ranges are calculated for each of the subgroups by subtracting the highest value in the subgroup from the lowest value. These individual ranges are then summed and divided by the total number of subgroups to calculate $\overline{R}$, the centerline of the R chart. The range chart upper and lower control limits are calculated in a manner similar to the $\overline{X}$ chart limits.

$$\overline{R} = \frac{\sum_{i=1}^{m} R_i}{m}$$
$$UCL_R = \overline{R} + 3\sigma_R$$
$$LCL_R = \overline{R} - 3\sigma_R$$

where

UCL_R = upper control limit of the R chart
LCL_R = lower control limit of the R chart
σ_R = population standard deviation of the subgroup ranges

To estimate the standard deviation of the range σ_R for the R chart, the average of the subgroup ranges $(\overline{R})$ multiplied by the D_3 and D_4 factors is used:

$$UCL_R = D_4\overline{R}$$
$$LCL_R = D_3\overline{R}$$

Along with the value of A_2, the values of D_3 and D_4 are found in the table in Appendix 2. These values are selected on the basis of the subgroup sample size n.

The control limits, when displayed on the R chart, should theoretically be symmetrical about the centerline $(\overline{R})$. However, because range values cannot be negative, a value of zero is given for the lower control limit with sample sizes of six or less. This results in an R chart that is asymmetrical. As with the $\overline{X}$ chart, control limits for the R chart are shown with a dashed line. The centerline is shown with a solid line.

Even with subgroup values larger than six, frequently the LCL of the range chart is kept at zero. This is in keeping with the desire to achieve zero variation between the parts being produced. However, this approach is not recommended because points below the calculated lower control limit would be identified as special variation. The values below the lower control limit indicate that reduced variation is present in the process. If the cause of this decrease in variation could be found and replicated, then the variation present in the process would be diminished.

EXAMPLE 5.8   Printer Assembly: Calculating the R-Chart Centerline and Control Limits

Constructing an R chart is similar to creating an $\overline{X}$ chart. To begin the process, individual range values are calculated for each of the subgroups by subtracting the highest value in the subgroup from the lowest value [Figure 5.6, (3)]. Once calculated, these individual range values (R_i) are plotted on the R chart [Figure 5.7, (6)].

To determine the centerline of the R chart, individual range (R_i) values are summed and divided by the total number of subgroups to give $\overline{R}$ [Figure 5.7, (4)].

$$\overline{R} = \frac{0.08 + 0.07 + 0.04 + \cdots + 0.04}{21}$$

$$= \frac{1.06}{21} = 0.05$$

With n = 5, the values of D_3 and D_4 are found in the table in Appendix 2. The control limits for the R chart are calculated as follows:

$$UCL_R = D_4\overline{R}$$
$$= 2.114(0.05) = 0.11$$
$$LCL_R = D_3\overline{R}$$
$$= 0(0.05) = 0$$

The control limits are placed on the R chart [Figure 5.7, (5)].

8. Examine the Process: Control Chart Interpretation

Correct interpretation of control charts is essential to managing a process. Understanding the sources and potential causes of variation is critical to good management decisions. Managers must be able to determine if the variation present in a process is indicating a trend that must be dealt with or is merely random variation natural to the process. Misinterpretation can lead to a variety of losses, including

- Blaming people for problems that they cannot control
- Spending time and money looking for problems that do not exist
- Spending time and money on process adjustments or new equipment that are not necessary
- Taking action where no action is warranted
- Asking for worker-related improvements where process or equipment improvements need to be made first

If a process is understood and adjustments have been made to stabilize the process, then the benefits are many. Once the performance of a process is predictable, there is a sound basis for making plans and decisions concerning the process, the system, and its output. Costs to manufacture the product or provide the service become predictable. Quality levels and how quality compares with expectations can be determined. The effects of changes made to the process can be measured and evaluated with greater accuracy and reliability.

 REAL TOOLS FOR REAL LIFE

Monitoring Silicon Wafer Thickness

Data is a key aspect of computer integrated manufacturing at Whisks Electronics Corporation. Automated data acquisition systems generate timely data about the product produced and the process producing it. Whisks believes that decision-making processes can be enhanced by using valid data that have been organized in an effective manner. For this reason, Whisks uses an integrated system of automated statistical process-control programming, data collection devices, and programmable logic controllers (PLCs) to collect statistical information about its silicon wafer production. Utilizing the system relieves the process engineers from the burden of number crunching, freeing time for critical analysis of the data.

Customers purchase blank silicon wafers from Whisks and etch their own integrated circuits onto them. The silicon wafers must be made to a target value of 0.2500 mm. Whisks uses $\overline{X}$ to monitor wafer thickness and R charts to monitor the consistency of wafer thickness.

Using micrometers linked to PLCs, every 15 minutes, four wafers are randomly selected and measured in the order they are produced. These values (Figure 5.9) are stored in a database that is accessed by the company's statistical process control software. This subgroup size and sampling frequency were chosen based on the number of silicon wafers produced per hour.

					$\overline{X}$	R
Subgroup 1	0.2500	0.2510	0.2490	0.2500	0.2500	0.002
Subgroup 2	0.2510	0.2490	0.2490	0.2520	0.2503	0.003
Subgroup 3	0.2510	0.2490	0.2510	0.2480	0.2498	0.003
Subgroup 4	0.2490	0.2470	0.2520	0.2480	0.2490	0.005
Subgroup 5	0.2500	0.2470	0.2500	0.2520	0.2498	0.005
Subgroup 6	0.2510	0.2520	0.2490	0.2510	0.2508	0.003
Subgroup 7	0.2510	0.2480	0.2500	0.2500	0.2498	0.003
Subgroup 8	0.2500	0.2490	0.2490	0.2520	0.2500	0.003
Subgroup 9	0.2500	0.2470	0.2500	0.2510	0.2495	0.004
Subgroup 10	0.2480	0.2480	0.2510	0.2530	0.2500	0.005
Subgroup 11	0.2500	0.2500	0.2500	0.2530	0.2508	0.003
Subgroup 12	0.2510	0.2490	0.2510	0.2540	0.2513	0.005
Subgroup 13	0.2500	0.2470	0.2500	0.2510	0.2495	0.004
Subgroup 14	0.2500	0.2500	0.2490	0.2520	0.2503	0.003
Subgroup 15	0.2500	0.2470	0.2500	0.2510	0.2495	0.004

Figure 5.9   Silicon Wafer Thickness

The centerline and control limits of the X chart were calculated.

$$\overline{\overline{X}} = \frac{(0.2500 + 0.2503 + 0.2498 + \cdots + 0.2495)}{15}$$

$$\overline{\overline{X}} = 0.2500 \text{ mm}$$

where

$\overline{\overline{X}}$ = the centerline of the $\overline{X}$ chart
$\overline{X}$ = the individual subgroup averages
m = the number of subgroups

$$\overline{R} = \frac{(0.002 + 0.003 + 0.003 + \cdots + 0.004)}{15}$$

$$\overline{R} = 0.0037 \text{ mm}$$

Upper control limit, $\overline{X}$

$$UCL_{\overline{x}} = \overline{\overline{X}} + A_2\overline{R}$$
$$UCL_{\overline{x}} = 0.2500 + 0.729(0.0037)$$
$$UCL_{\overline{x}} = 0.2527 \text{ mm}$$

Lower control limit, $\overline{X}$

$$LCL_{\overline{x}} = \overline{\overline{X}} - A_2\overline{R}$$
$$LCL_{\overline{x}} = 0.2500 - 0.729(0.0037)$$
$$LCL_{\overline{x}} = 0.2473 \text{ mm}$$

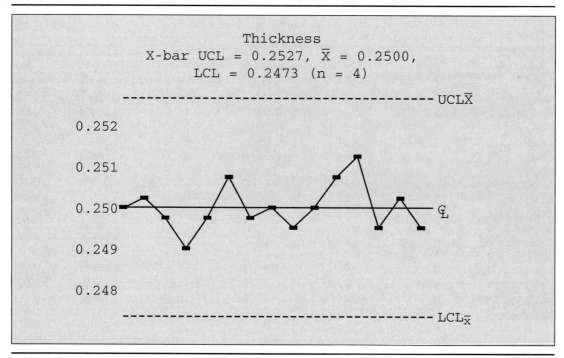

Figure 5.10 $\overline{X}$ Chart for Silicon Wafer Thickness

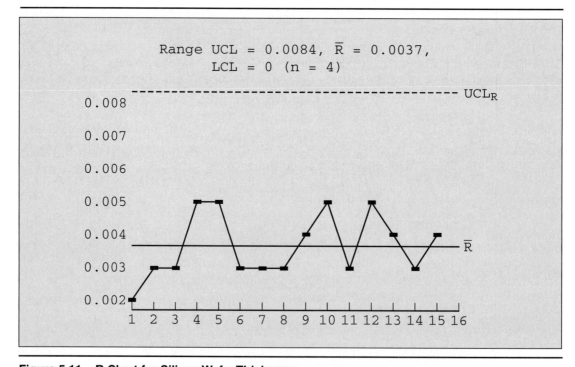

Figure 5.11 R Chart for Silicon Wafer Thickness

Upper control limit, R

$$UCL_R = D_4\overline{R}$$
$$UCL_R = 2.282(0.0037)$$
$$UCL_R = 0.0084 \text{ mm}$$

Lower control limit, R

$$LCL_R = D_3\overline{R}$$
$$LCL_R = 0(0.0037)$$
$$LCL_R = 0.0$$

$\overline{X}$ and R charts provide information about process centering and process variation. If we study the $\overline{X}$ chart (Figure 5.10), it shows that the wafer thickness is centered around the target value of 0.2500 mm. Studying the R chart and noting the magnitute of the values (Figure 5.11) reveals that variation is present in the process. Not all the wafers are uniform in their thickness. The customer's target value is 0.2500, while the process values have the potential to vary as much as 0.0084 (UCL). Whisks will have to determine the best method of removing variation from their silicon wafer production process. $\mathbf{Q_{\!\!\!\!\!\sim}}$

Process Variation Because variation is present in all aspects of our lives, we already have developed an understanding of what is usual or unusual variation. For instance, on the basis of a six-month history of commuting, we may expect our commute to work to take 25 minutes, give or take a minute or two. We would be surprised if the commute took only 15 minutes. We would look for an assignable cause: Perhaps traffic was lighter because we left earlier. By the same token, we would be upset if the commute took 40 minutes and we would want to know why. A traffic accident could be the assignable cause that meant such an increase in commuting time. We continually make decisions on the basis of an interpretation of the amount of variation from the expected value we encounter. Included in these decisions are whether or not we think this is random (chance) variation or unusual (assignable) variation.

The patterns or variation on a control chart are not too different from the variation that exists in everyday life. Whether we are following weight gain or loss, household expenses from month to month, or the gas mileage of our cars, variation exists. These values are never exactly the same from measurement to measurement. For example, in the corporate environment, sales, profits, and costs are never exactly the same from month to month.

State of Process Control *A process is considered to be in a state of control, or **under control,** when the performance of the process falls within the statistically calculated control limits and exhibits only chance, or common, causes.* When a process is under control it is considered stable and the amount of future variation is predictable. A stable process does not necessarily meet the specifications set by the designer nor exhibit minimal variation; a stable process merely has a predictable amount of variation.

There are several benefits to a stable process with predictable variation. When the process performance is predictable there is a rational basis for planning. It is fairly straightforward to determine costs associated with a stable process. Quality levels from time period to time period are predictable. When changes, additions, or improvements are made to a stable process, the effects of the change can be determined quickly and reliably.

When an assignable cause is present, the process is considered unstable, out of control, or beyond the expected normal variation. In an unstable process the variation is unpredictable, meaning that the magnitude of the variation could change from one time period to another. Quality-assurance analysts need to determine whether the variation that exists in a process is common or assignable. To treat an assignable cause as a chance cause could result in a disruption to a system or a process that is operating correctly except for the assignable cause. To treat chance causes as assignable causes is an ineffective use of resources because the variation is inherent in the process.

When a system is subject to only chance causes of variation, 99.73 percent of the parts produced will fall within $\pm 3\sigma$. This means that if 1,000 subgroups are sampled, 997 of the subgroups will have values within the upper and lower control limits. Based on the normal curve, a control chart can be divided into three zones (Figure 5.12). Zone A is ± 1 standard deviation from the centerline and should contain approximately 68.3 percent of the calculated sample averages or ranges. Zone B is ± 2 standard deviations from the centerline and should contain 27.2 percent (95.5 percent $-$ 68.3 percent) of the points. Zone C is ± 3 standard deviations from the centerline and should contain only approximately 4.2 percent of the points (99.7 percent $-$ 95.5 percent). With these zones as a guide, a control chart exhibits a state of control when:

1. Two-thirds of the points are near the center value.
2. A few of the points are on or near the center value.
3. The points appear to float back and forth across the centerline.

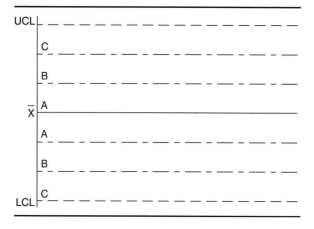

Figure 5.12   Zones on a Control Chart

4. The points are balanced (in roughly equal numbers) on both sides of the centerline.
5. There are no points beyond the control limits.
6. There are no patterns or trends on the chart.

While analyzing $\overline{X}$ and R charts, take a moment to study the scale of the range chart. The spread of the upper and lower control limits will reveal whether or not a significant amount of variation is present in the process. This clue to the amount of variation present may be overlooked if the R chart is checked only for patterns or out-of-control points. A sample $\overline{X}$ and R chart with all points within control limits can be found in Figure 5.13.

The importance of having a process under control cannot be overemphasized. When a process is under control, a number of advantages can be found. The process

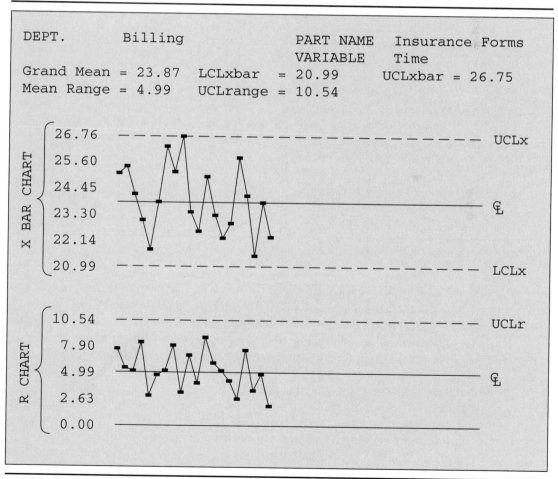

Figure 5.13   Control Chart with Grand Mean = 23.875

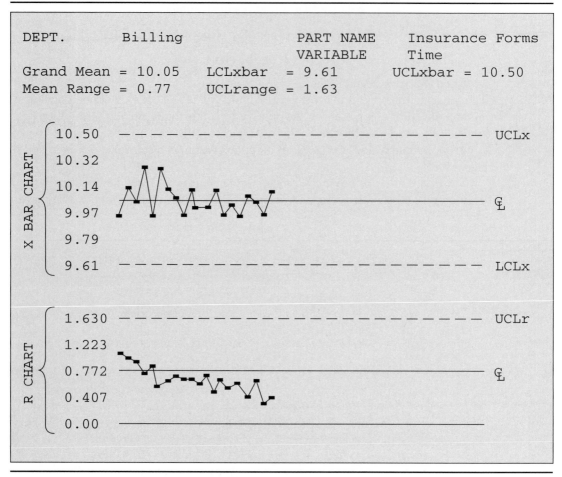

Figure 5.14   Control Chart with Grand Mean = 10.059

capability, which tells how the current production compares with the specification limits, can be calculated. Once known, the process capability can be used in making decisions concerning the appropriateness of product or service specifications, of the amount of rework or scrap being created by the process, and of whether the parts should be used or shipped. This topic will be covered in detail in Chapter 6.

Identifying Patterns A process that is not under control or is unstable displays patterns of variation. Patterns signal the need to investigate the process and determine if an assignable cause can be found for the variation. Figures 5.14 through 5.22 display a variety of out-of-control conditions and give some reasons why those conditions may exist.

Trends or steady changes in level A trend is a steady, progressive change in the location where the data are centered on the chart. In the Real Tools for Real Life feature, Figure 5.14 displays a downward trend on the R chart. Note that the points were found primarily in the upper half of the control chart at the beginning of the process and on the lower half of the chart at the end. The key to identifying a trend or steady change in level is to recognize that the points are slowly and steadily working their way from one level of the chart to another.

A trend may appear on the $\overline{X}$ chart because of tool or die wear, a gradual deterioration of the equipment, a buildup of chips, a slowly loosening work-holding device, a breakdown of the chemicals used in the process, or some other gradual change.

R-chart trends could be due to changes in worker skills, shifting work-holding devices, or wearout. Improvements would lead to less variation; increases in variation would reflect a decrease in skill or a change in the quality of the incoming material.

 REAL TOOLS FOR REAL LIFE

Common Cause Variation in a Process

Consider the following information concerning work performed at a local doctor's office. The office management wanted to see a serious improvement in the amount of time it took to process the insurance forms. Without giving any specific instructions, the management encouraged the staff to work harder and smarter.

Process improvements were needed since a decrease in the time required to process and file insurance claim forms would help alleviate a backlog of work. Errors being made on the forms also needed to be reduced. The individuals handling the insurance-form processing were a well-trained and experienced group who felt that they were all performing to the best of their ability, that this was a stable process. If it was a stable process, improvements would only come about with a change in the methods utilized to process and file the forms. To support this statement, the staff monitored their own performance, using control charts, for the next month.

This control charting, using an $\overline{X}$ and R chart combination, showed that completing and processing each insurance form required an average of 23.875 minutes (Figure 5.13). The R chart was examined first in order to gain an understanding of the precision or lack of variation present in the process. As shown by the R chart, there was a slight variation in the time required to process the forms. Overall, the performance appeared to be very stable; no points went beyond the control limits and there were no unusual patterns. The process exhibited only chance causes of variation.

When presented with these data, management realized they had to do more than encourage the staff to work harder or work smarter. Beginning with the control chart, further investigation into the situation occurred. As a result of their investigations, management decided to change the insurance form and implement a new computerized billing/insurance processing system. Upon completion of operator training, this system was monitored through control charts, and as can be seen in Figure 5.14, the processing time was reduced to an average of 10.05 minutes. Note the decreasing trend on the R chart showing that the work time continues to become more precise over time. An increase in performance of this magnitude was possible only through intervention by management and a major change to the existing system.

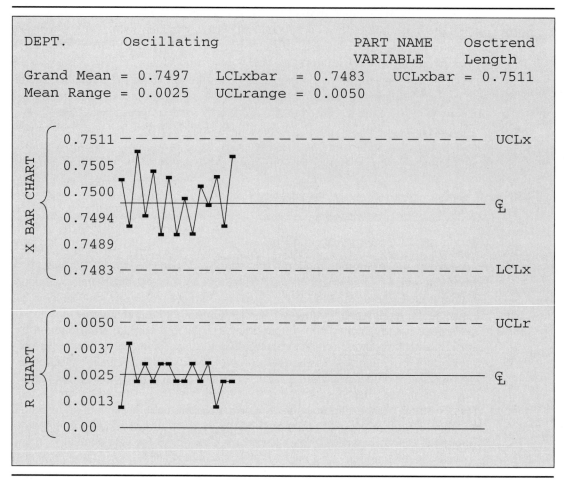

DEPT.   Oscillating   PART NAME   Osctrend
                                              VARIABLE   Length
Grand Mean = 0.7497   LCLxbar = 0.7483   UCLxbar = 0.7511
Mean Range = 0.0025   UCLrange = 0.0050

Figure 5.15   An Oscillating Trend

An oscillating trend would also need to be investigated (Figure 5.15). In this type of trend the points oscillate up and down for approximately 14 points or more. This could be due to a lack of homogeneity, perhaps a mixing of the output from two machines making the same product.

Change, Jump, or Shift in Level Figure 5.16 displays what is meant by a change, jump, or shift in level. Note that the process begins at one level (Figure 5.16a) and jumps quickly to another level (Figure 5.16b) as the process continues to operate. This change, jump, or shift in level is fairly abrupt, unlike a trend described above. A change, jump, or shift can occur either on the $\overline{X}$ or R chart or on both charts. Causes for sudden shifts in level tend to reflect some new and fairly significant difference in the process. When investigating a sudden shift or jump in level, look for significant changes that can be pinpointed to a specific moment in time. For the $\overline{X}$ chart, causes

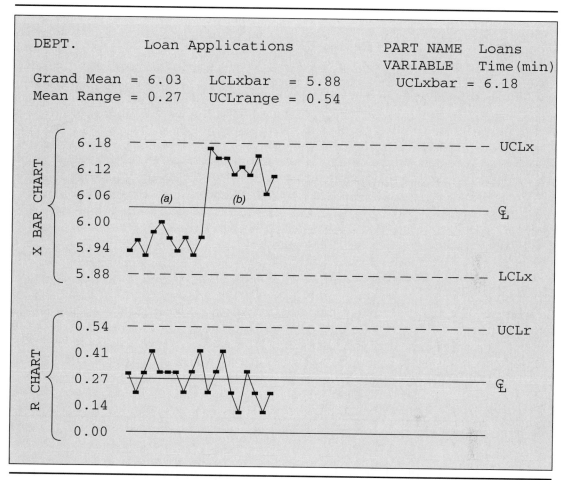

Figure 5.16   Change in Level

include new machines, dies, or tooling; the minor failure of a machine part; new or inexperienced workers; new batches of raw material; new production methods; or changes to the process settings. For the R chart, potential sources of jumps or shifts in level causing a change in the process variability or spread include a new or inexperienced operator, a sudden increase in the play associated with gears or work-holding devices, or greater variation in incoming material.

Runs   A process can be considered out of control when there are unnatural runs present in the process. Imagine tossing a coin. If two heads occur in a row, the onlooker would probably agree that this occurred by chance. Even though the probability of the coin landing with heads showing is 50-50, no one expects coin tosses to alternate between heads and tails. If, however, an onlooker saw someone toss six heads in a row, that onlooker would probably be suspicious that this set of events is not due to chance. The same principle applies to control charts. While the points on a control chart do

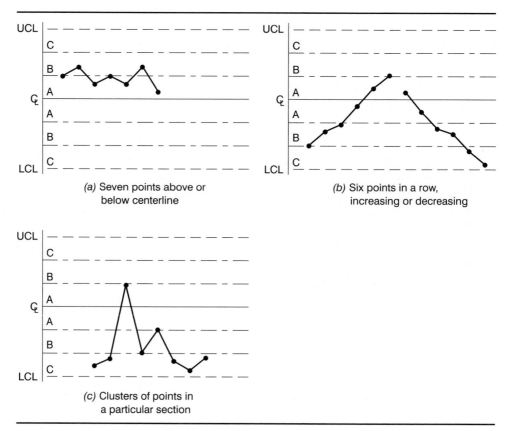

(a) Seven points above or
below centerline

(b) Six points in a row,
increasing or decreasing

(c) Clusters of points in
a particular section

Figure 5.17   Runs

not necessarily alternate above and below the centerline in a chart that is under control, the points are normally balanced above and below the centerline. A cluster of seven points in a row above or below the centerline would be improbable and would likely have an assignable cause. The same could be said for situations where 10 out of 11 points or 12 out of 14 points are located on one side or the other of the centerline (Figure 5.17a,b,c). A run may also be considered a trend if it displays increasing or decreasing values.

Runs on the $\overline{X}$ chart can be caused by temperature changes; tool or die wear; gradual deterioration of the process; or deterioration of the chemicals, oils, or cooling fluids used in the process. Runs on the R chart (Figure 5.18) signal a change in the process variation. Causes for these R-chart runs could be a change in operator skill, either an improvement or a decrement, or a gradual improvement in the homogeneity of the process because of changes in the incoming material or changes to the process itself.

Recurring Cycles   Recurring cycles are caused by systematic changes related to the process. When investigating what appears to be cycles (Figure 5.19) on the chart, it is

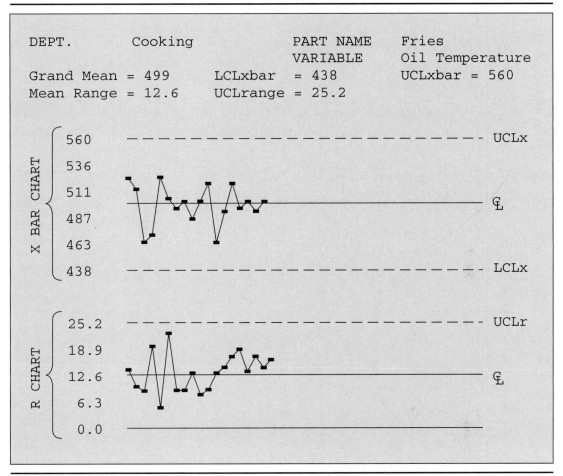

DEPT.   Cooking   PART NAME   Fries
                                VARIABLE   Oil Temperature
Grand Mean = 499   LCLxbar = 438   UCLxbar = 560
Mean Range = 12.6   UCLrange = 25.2

Figure 5.18   Run of Points

important to look for causes that will change, vary, or cycle over time. For the $\overline{X}$ chart, potential causes are tool or machine wear conditions, an accumulation and then removal of chips or other waste material around the tooling, maintenance schedules, periodic rotation of operators, worker fatigue, periodic replacement of cooling fluid or cutting oil, or changes in the process environment such as temperature or humidity. Cycles on an R chart are not as common; an R chart displays the variation or spread of the process, which usually does not cycle. Potential causes are related to lubrication cycles and operator fatigue.

Cycles can be difficult to locate because the entire cycle may not be present on a single chart. The frequency of inspection could potentially cause a cycle to be overlooked. For example, if the cycle occurs every 15 minutes and samples are taken only every 30 minutes, then it is possible for the cycle to be overlooked.

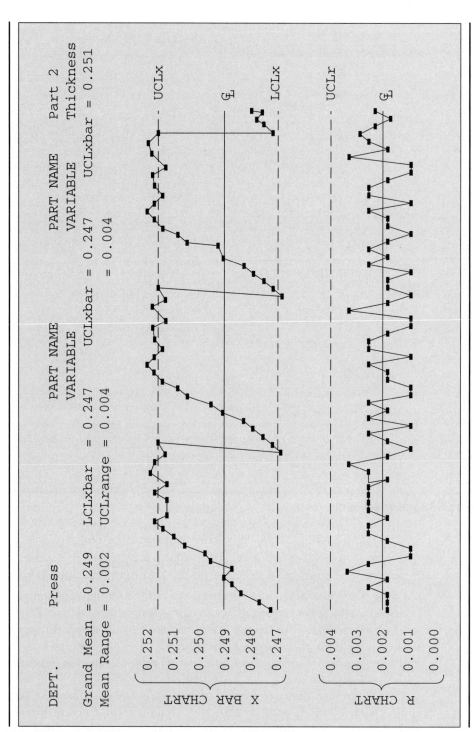

Figure 5.19   Cycle in Part Thickness

REAL TOOLS FOR REAL LIFE

Recurring Cycles

During the winter, a particular stamping operation at Company A experiences an unusual amount of machine downtime. Because of increasing material thickness, the operator has to make too many fine adjustments to the machine settings during daily operation. As can be seen in Figure 5.19, the parts increase in thickness as the morning progresses and then level out in the midafternoon. Investigation into the daily production and talks with the supplier of the steel do not reveal a cause for this trend. The charts from the supplier's production reflect that the material thickness throughout the roll conforms to specifications.

   A closer inspection of several days' worth of production laid side by side reveals the existence of a cycle. Further investigation shows that this cycle is related to the temperature of the material during the day. Under the current method, the coils of steel are left on the loading dock until needed. Because of the winter weather, the material is quite cold when brought into the building for use each morning. As the coil warms up in the heated plant during the day, it expands, making it thicker. This increase in thickness is evident on the control chart. Since only one coil is used each day, the cycle was not apparent until the charts from day-to-day production were compared.

Two Populations When a control chart is under control, approximately 68 percent of the sample averages will fall within $\pm 1\sigma$ of the centerline. When a large number of the sample averages appear near or outside the control limits, two populations of samples might exist. "Two populations" refers to the existence of two (or more) sources of data.

   On an $\overline{X}$ chart, the different sources of production might be due to the output of two or more machines being combined before sampling takes place. It might also occur because the work of two different operators is combined or two different sources of raw materials are brought together in the process. A two-population situation means that the items being sampled are not homogeneous (Figure 5.20). Maintaining the homogeneity of the items being sampled is critical for creating and using control charts.

   This type of pattern on an R chart signals that different workers are using the same chart or that the variation is due to the fact that raw materials are coming from different suppliers.

Mistakes The "mistakes" category combines all the other out-of-control patterns that can exist on a control chart (Figure 5.21). Mistakes can arise from calculation errors, calibration errors, and testing-equipment errors. They generally show up on a control chart as a lone point or a small group of points above or below the control limits. Finding these problems takes effort but is necessary if the process is going to operate to the best of its ability.

9. Revise the Charts

There are two circumstances under which the control chart is revised and new limits calculated. Existing calculations can be revised if a chart exhibits good control and

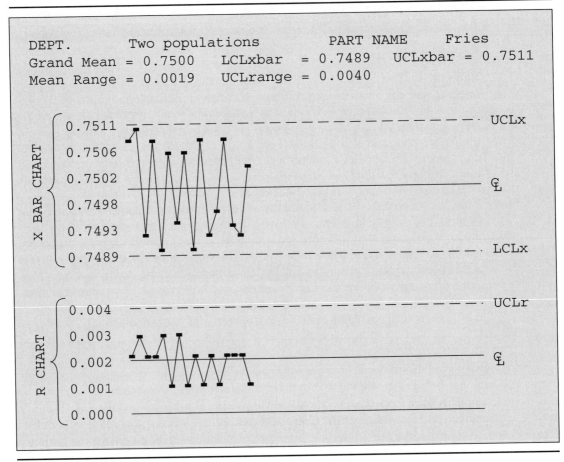

Figure 5.20   Two Populations

any changes made to improve the process are permanent. When the new operating conditions become routine and no out-of-control signals have been seen, the chart may be revised. The revisions provide a better estimate of the population standard deviation, representing the spread of all of the individual parts in the process. With this value, a better understanding of the entire process can be gained.

Control limits are also revised if patterns exist, provided that the patterns have been identified and eliminated. Once the causes have been determined, investigated, and corrected in such a way that they will not affect the process in the future, the control chart can be revised. The new limits will reflect the changes and improvements made to the process. In both cases the new limits are used to judge the process behavior in the future.

The following four steps are taken to revise the charts.

A. Interpret the Original Charts   The R chart reflects the stability of the process and should be analyzed first. A lack of control on the R chart shows that the process is not producing parts that are very similar to each other. The process is not precise. If the

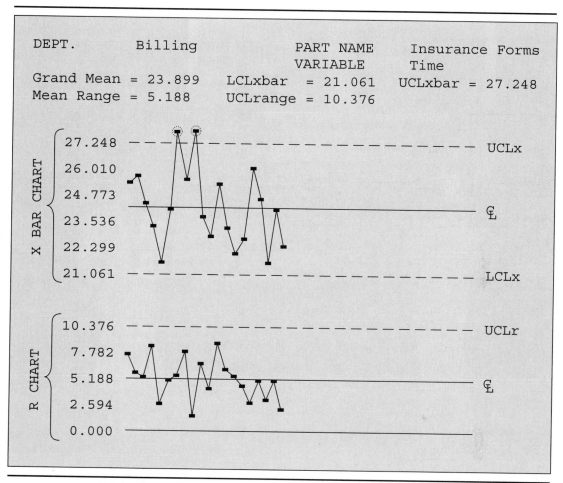

DEPT.   Billing   PART NAME   Insurance Forms
                                     VARIABLE   Time
Grand Mean = 23.899   LCLxbar = 21.061   UCLxbar = 27.248
Mean Range = 5.188   UCLrange = 10.376

Figure 5.21   Mistakes

R chart exhibits process control, study the $\overline{X}$ chart. Determine if cycles, trends, runs, two populations, mistakes, or other examples of lack of control exist. If both the $\overline{X}$ and R charts are exhibiting good control, proceed to step D. If the charts display out-of-control conditions, then continue to step B.

EXAMPLE 5.9   Printer Assembly: Examining the Control Charts

Returning to the computer printer roller shaft example, an examination of the $\overline{X}$ and R charts begins by investigating the R chart, which displays the variation present in the process. Evidence of excessive variation would indicate that the process is not producing consistent product. The R chart (Figure 5.22) exhibits good control. The points are evenly spaced on both sides of the centerline and there are no points beyond the control limits. There are no unusual patterns or trends in the data. Given these observations, it can be said that the process is producing parts of similar dimensions.

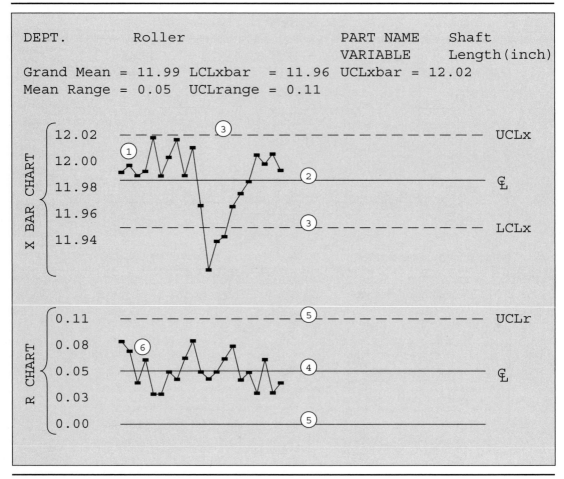

```
DEPT.          Roller                    PART NAME    Shaft
                                         VARIABLE     Length(inch)
Grand Mean = 11.99 LCLxbar  = 11.96 UCLxbar = 12.02
Mean Range = 0.05   UCLrange = 0.11
```

Figure 5.22   X̄ and R Control Charts for Roller Shaft Length

Next the X̄ chart is examined. An inspection of the X̄ chart reveals an unusual pattern occurring at points 12, 13, and 14. These measurements are all below the lower control limit. When compared with other samples throughout the day's production, the parts produced during the time when samples 12, 13, and 14 were taken were much shorter than parts produced during other times in the production run. A glance at the R chart reveals that the range of the individual measurements taken in the samples is small, meaning that the parts produced during samples 12, 13, and 14 are all similar in size. An investigation into the cause of the production of undersized parts needs to take place.

B. Isolate the Cause If either the X̄ or R chart is not exhibiting good statistical control, find the cause of the problem. Problems shown on the control chart may be removed only if the causes of those problems have been isolated and steps have been taken to eliminate them.

C. Take Corrective Action Take the necessary steps to correct the causes associated with the problems exhibited on the chart. Once the causes of variation have been removed from the process, these points may be removed from the control chart and the calculations revised.

EXAMPLE 5.10   Printer Assembly: A Further Examination of the Control Charts

An investigation into the differences in shaft lengths has been conducted. The $\overline{X}$ and R charts aid the investigators by allowing them to isolate when the differences were first noticed. Since the R chart (Figure 5.22) exhibits good control, the investigators are able to concentrate their attention on possible causes for a consistent change in shaft length for those three subgroups. Their investigation reveals that the machine settings had been bumped during the loading of the machine. For the time being, operators are being asked to check the control panel settings after loading the machine. To take care of the problem for the long term, manufacturing engineers are looking into possible design changes to protect the controls against accidental manipulation. $Q_{\!\rightarrow}$

D. Revise the Chart To determine the new limits against which the process will be judged in the future, it is necessary to remove any undesirable points, the causes of which have been determined and corrected, from the charts. The criteria for removing points are based on finding the cause behind the out-of-control condition. If no cause can be found and corrected, then the points *cannot* be removed from the chart. Groups of points, runs, trends, and other patterns can be removed in the same manner as removing individual points. In the case of charts that are exhibiting good statistical control, the points removed will equal zero and the calculations will continue from there.

Two methods can be used to discard the data. When it is necessary to remove a subgroup from the calculations, it can be removed from only the out-of-control chart or it can be removed from both charts. In the first case, when an $\overline{X}$ value must be removed from the $\overline{X}$ control chart, its corresponding R value is *not* removed from the R chart, and vice versa. In this text, the points are removed from *both* charts. This second approach has been chosen because the values on both charts are interrelated. The R-chart values describe the spread of the data on the $\overline{X}$ chart. Removing data from one chart or the other negates this relationship.

The formulas for revising both the $\overline{X}$ and R charts are as follows:

$$\overline{\overline{X}}_{new} = \frac{\Sigma \overline{X} - \overline{X}_d}{m - m_d}$$

$$\overline{R}_{new} = \frac{\Sigma R - R_d}{m - m_d}$$

where

$\overline{X}_d$ = discarded subgroup averages
m_d = number of discarded subgroups
R_d = discarded subgroup ranges

The newly calculated values of $\overline{\overline{X}}$ and $\overline{R}$ are used to establish updated values for the centerline and control limits on the chart. These new limits reflect that improvements have been made to the process and future production should be capable of meeting these new limits. The formulas for the revised limits are:

$$\overline{\overline{X}}_{new} = \overline{\overline{X}}_0 \qquad \overline{R}_{new} = R_0$$
$$\sigma_0 = R_0/d_2$$
$$UCL_{\overline{X}} = \overline{\overline{X}}_0 + A\sigma_0$$
$$LCL_{\overline{X}} = \overline{\overline{X}}_0 - A\sigma_0$$
$$UCL_R = D_2\sigma_0$$
$$LCL_R = D_1\sigma_0$$

where d_2, A, D_1, and D_2 are factors from the table in Appendix 2.

EXAMPLE 5.11   Printer Assembly: Revising the Control Limits

Since a cause for the undersized parts has been determined for the machine of Example 5.9 the values for 12, 13, and 14 can be removed from the calculations for the $\overline{X}$ and R chart. The points removed from calculations remain on the chart; they are crossed out. The new or revised limits will be used to monitor future production. The new limits will extend from the old limits, as shown in Figure 5.23.

Revising the calculations is performed as follows:

$$\overline{\overline{X}}_{new} = \overline{\overline{X}}_0 = \frac{\sum\limits_{i=1}^{m}\overline{X} - \overline{X}_d}{m - m_d}$$

$$= \frac{251.77 - 11.94 - 11.95 - 11.95}{21 - 3}$$

$$= 12.00$$

$$\overline{R}_{new} = R_0 = \frac{\sum\limits_{i=1}^{m}R - R_d}{m - m_d}$$

$$= \frac{1.06 - 0.04 - 0.05 - 0.06}{21 - 3}$$

$$= 0.05$$

Calculating the σ_0 for the process, when n = 5,

$$\sigma_0 = \frac{R_0}{d_2} = \frac{0.05}{2.326} = 0.02$$

$$UCL_{\overline{X}} = 12.00 + 1.342(0.02) = 12.03$$
$$LCL_{\overline{X}} = 12.00 - 1.342(0.02) = 11.97$$
$$UCL_R = 4.918(0.02) = 0.10$$
$$LCL_R = 0(0.02) = 0$$

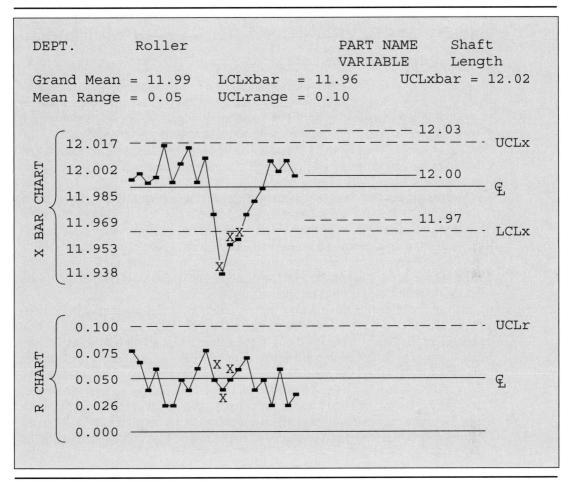

Figure 5.23   Extension of Limits on a Chart

10. Achieve the Purpose

Users of control charts are endeavoring to decrease the variation inherent in a process over time. Once established, control charts enable the user to understand where the process is currently centered and what the distribution of that process is. To know this information and not utilize it to improve the process defeats the purpose of creating control charts. As shown in the Real Tools for Real Life feature "Common Cause Variation in a Process" with Figures 5.13 and 5.14, as improvements are made to the process, the process becomes more centered, with a significant decrease in the amount of time needed to process the insurance forms. An investigation of the R chart reveals that the variation associated with the process also has decreased.

As the process improves, the average should come closer to the center of the specifications. The spread of the data, as shown by the range or the standard deviation, should decrease. As the spread decreases, the parts produced or services provided become more similar in dimension to each other.

REAL TOOLS FOR REAL LIFE

Surgical Stapler Fork Height Study

KjK, Inc. fineblanks precision metal parts for automotive, computer, and medical devices. While similar to conventional stamping, which has two forces at work: a clamping force and a stamping force; the fineblanking process has an additional force a work; a counter force. This counter force opposes the stamping force, causing the part to be extruded rather than sheared. The triple pressure fineblanking press and tooling construction combine to create an accurate production process with excellent repeatability.

KjK fineblanks the center shaft for a surgical suture (Figure 5.24). Used like a scissor, this tool closes small blood vessels during a surgical procedure. With one hand, the surgeon holds the scissors, with the other, pushes the plastic cylinder over the end of the forks. Doing so drops a small stainless steel clip into place between the forks. Sliding the cylinder back causes the forks to come together, closing the small stainless steel clip snuggly on the blood vessel. Releasing the grip allows the forks to return to their original position, ready for use again.

Smooth operation of the device depends on many factors, including the loading of the clip, how the forks hold the clip, and how the forks close the clip. Critical dimensions for appropriate operation of the suture include fork height, angle, and parallelism of the shaft. During the fineblanking process, one stroke of the press creates the shaft, angled forks, indentations and holes in the 302 gage, 0.048–0.052 in. thick steel. The thinness, angles, and length of the part make it a tricky, pliable part to fineblank. As many as 30% of the parts have been scrapped during a run; however the problems are intermittent. KjK has decided that a concentrated effort, using control charts and the Plan-Do-Study-Act cycle, needs to be made to improve the process.

During the planning stage, KjK assigned responsibilities, identified the variables in the process (Figure 5.25), and mapped the process (Figure 5.26). They also determined how many samples should be taken for each variable and what measuring tools should be used to gather the data. In order to clearly define the problem, control charts were created for each of the critical variables in the process (Figures 5.27 to 5.32).

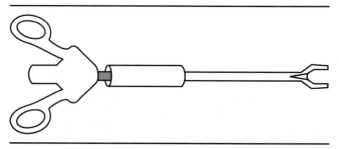

Figure 5.24   Surgical Suture

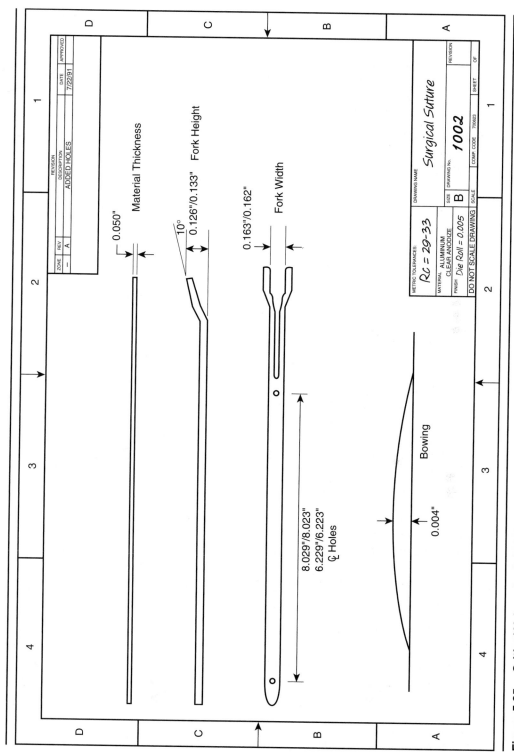

Figure 5.25   Critical Values for Surgical Suture

257

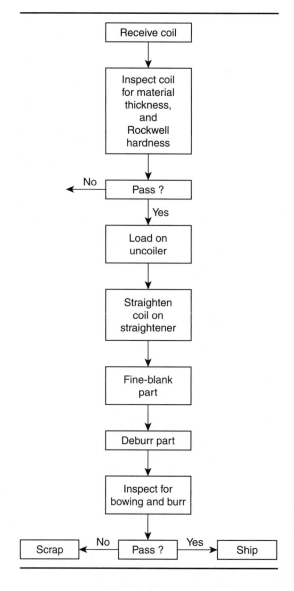

Figure 5.26   Process Map for Suture Component

It is immediately obvious when reviewing these control charts that only a few of the variables exhibit any variation. Bowing and camber in the part are negligible. Fork width, die roll, and Rockwell hardness are stable and within specification. Only material thickness and fork height exhibit variation. This knowledge enabled the problem solvers to focus on just two variables: fork height and material thickness.

Process engineers and tooling designers met to discuss the question: why are both fork height and material thickness exhibiting variation? Their cause-and-effect diagram pointed out a relationship between these two variables (Figure 5.33). For the next several runs, material thickness prior to blanking and fork height after

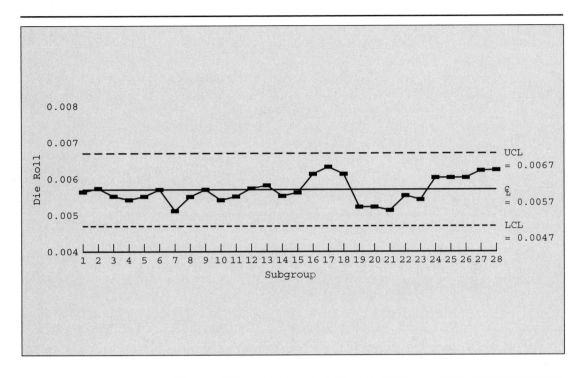

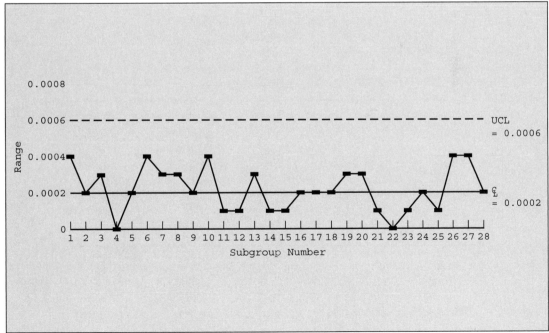

Figure 5.27   Die Roll at Fork Ends

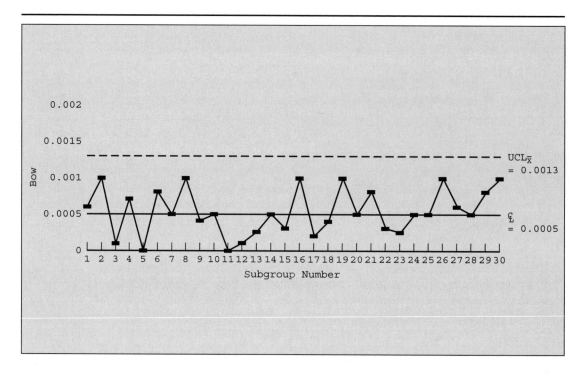

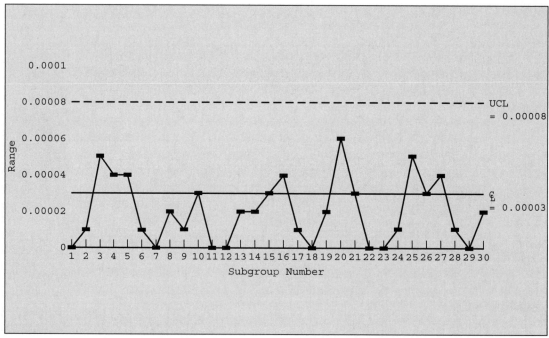

Figure 5.28   Flatness (Bowing)

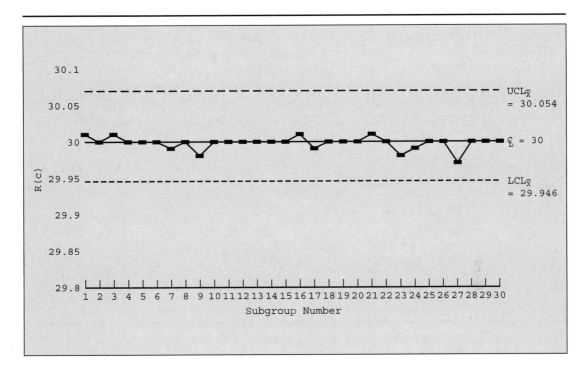

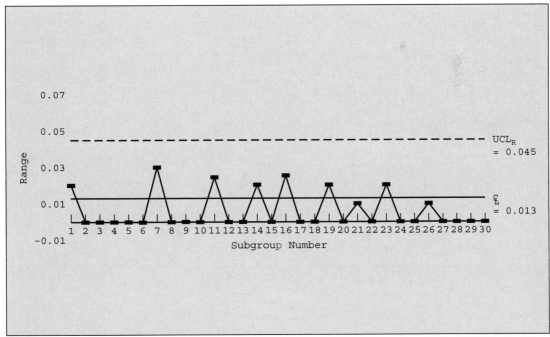

Figure 5.29   Rockwell Hardness (Rc)

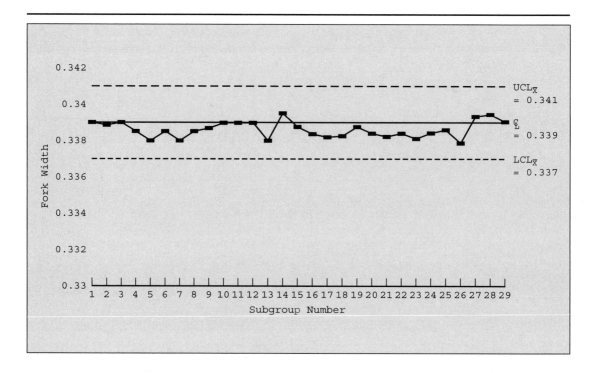

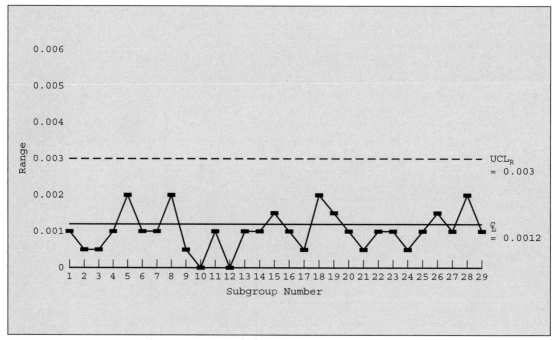

Figure 5.30 Fork Width

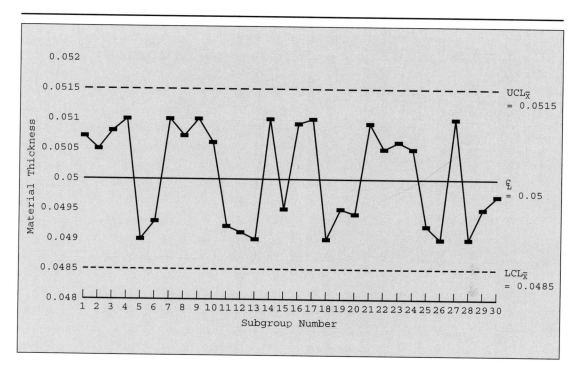

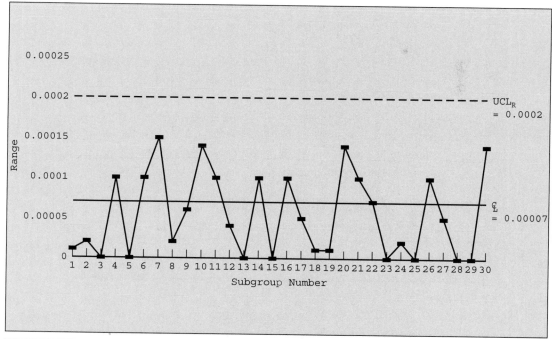

Figure 5.31   Material Thickness 0.049–0.051 in.

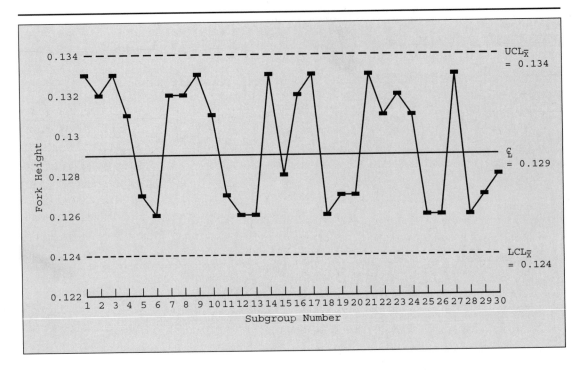

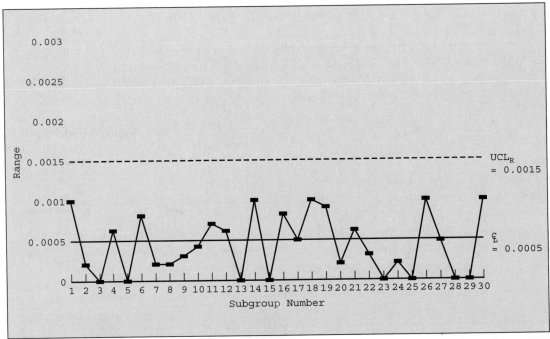

Figure 5.32   Fork Height 0.126–0.133 in. at 10˚

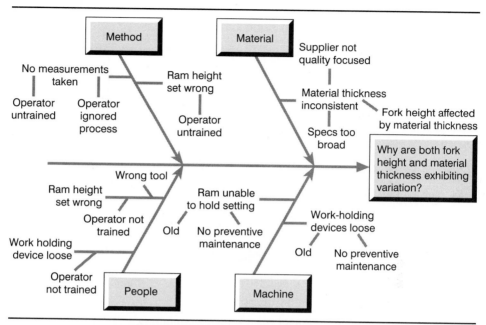

Figure 5.33   Real Tools for Real Life Cause and Effect Diagram for Fork Height and Material Thickness

blanking were monitored closely, sampled every 30 minutes in subgroups of a sample size of five.

A close comparison of these two variables revealed the source of the problem. Though the steel thickness was within specification, it tended toward two populations (Figure 5.34). Fork height also exhibited a tendency toward two populations. Thick material will make contact with the fine-blanking ram sooner, causing a larger fork angle and a greater fork height. Thin material will have less contact with the ram, causing a smaller fork angle and a shorter fork height (Figure 5.35). Making parts from steel of inconsistent thickness resulted in significant loss for KjK and their customer, reaffirming the Taguchi Loss Function and the necessity of producing product to a target specification.

KjK is working with the steel supplier to ensure that they provide steel at the target specification of 0.050 in. In the meantime, before each coil is run, the material thickness is checked and the ram height adjusted to ensure more consistent fork height.

$\overline{\text{X}}$ and s Charts

The $\overline{\text{X}}$ and range charts are used together in order to show both the center of the process measurements (accuracy) and the spread of the data (precision). An alternative combination of charts to show both the central tendency and the dispersion of the data is the $\overline{\text{X}}$ and ***standard deviation,*** or ***s, chart.*** When an R chart is compared with an s chart, the R chart stands out as being easier to compute. However, the s chart is more

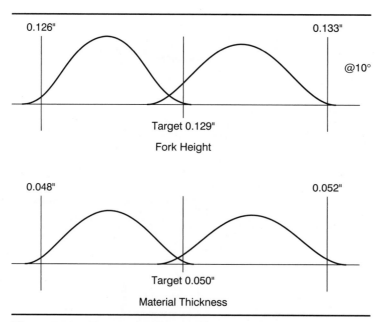

Figure 5.34   Tendencies Toward Two Populations

accurate than the R chart. This greater accuracy is a result of the manner in which the standard deviation is calculated. The subgroup sample standard deviation, or s value, is calculated using all of the data rather than just the high and low values in the sample like the R chart. So while the range chart is simple to construct, it is most effective when the sample size is less than 10. When the sample size exceeds 10, the range does not truly represent the variation present in the process. Under these circumstances, the s chart is used with the $\overline{X}$ chart.

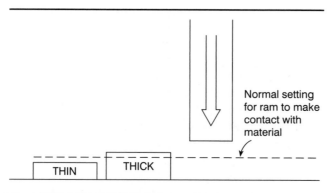

Thick material will make contact with the ram sooner, causing a larger fork angle and a greater fork height.

Thin material will have less contact with the ram, causing a smaller fork angle and a shorter fork height.

Figure 5.35   Relationship Between Ram Setting and Material Thickness

The combination of $\overline{X}$ and s charts is created by the same methods as the $\overline{X}$ and R charts. The formulas are modified to reflect the use of s instead of R for the calculations. For the $\overline{X}$ chart,

$$\overline{\overline{X}} = \frac{\sum\limits_{i=1}^{m} \overline{X}_i}{m}$$

$$UCL_{\overline{X}} = \overline{\overline{X}} + A_3\overline{s}$$

$$LCL_{\overline{X}} = \overline{\overline{X}} - A_3\overline{s}$$

For the s chart,

$$\overline{s} = \frac{\sum\limits_{i=1}^{m} s_i}{m}$$

$$UCL_s = B_4\overline{s}$$

$$LCL_s = B_3\overline{s}$$

where

s_i = standard deviation of the subgroup values
$\overline{s}_i$ = average of the subgroup sample standard deviations
A_3, B_3, B_4 = factors used for calculating 3σ control limits for $\overline{X}$ and s charts using the average sample standard deviation and Appendix 2

As in the $\overline{X}$ and R chart, the revised control limits can be calculated using the following formulas:

$$\overline{X}_0 = \overline{\overline{X}}_{new} = \frac{\sum\overline{X} - \overline{X}_d}{m - m_d}$$

$$s_0 = \overline{s}_{new} = \frac{\sum s - s_d}{m - m_d}$$

and

$$\sigma = s_0/c_4$$

$$UCL_{\overline{X}} = \overline{X}_0 + A\sigma_0$$

$$LCL_{\overline{X}} = \overline{X}_0 - A\sigma_0$$

$$UCL_s = B_6\sigma_0$$

$$LCL_s = B_5\sigma_0$$

where

s_d = sample standard deviation of the discarded subgroup
c_4 = factor found in Appendix 2 for computing σ_0 from $\overline{s}$
A, B_5, B_6 = factors found in Appendix 2 for computing the 3σ process control limits for $\overline{X}$ and s charts

EXAMPLE 5.12   X̄ and s Charts

This example uses the same roller shaft data as Example 5.5 except the range has been replaced by s, the sample standard deviation. A sample of size n = 5 is taken at intervals from the process making shafts (Figure 5.36). A total of 21 subgroups of measurements is taken. Each time a sample is taken, the individual values are

DEPT.	Roller		PART NAME	Shaft	
PART NO.	1		MACHINE	1	
GROUP	1		VARIABLE	length	

Subgroup	1	2	3	4	5
Time	07:30	07:40	07:50	08:00	08:10
Date	07/02/95	07/02/95	07/02/95	07/02/95	07/02/95
1	11.95	12.03	12.01	11.97	12.00
2	12.00	12.02	12.00	11.98	12.01
3	12.03 ①	11.96	11.97	12.00	12.02
4	11.98	12.00	11.98	12.03	12.03
5	12.01	11.98	12.00	11.99	12.02
X̄	11.99 ②	12.00	11.99	11.99	12.02
s	0.031 ③	0.029	0.016	0.023	0.011

Subgroup	6	7	8	9	10
Time	08:20	08:30	08:40	08:50	09:00
Date	07/02/95	07/02/95	07/02/95	07/02/95	07/02/95
1	11.98	12.00	12.00	12.00	12.02
2	11.98	12.01	12.01	12.02	12.00
3	12.00	12.03	12.04	11.96	11.97
4	12.01	12.00	12.00	12.00	12.05
5	11.99	11.98	12.02	11.98	12.00
X̄	11.99	12.00	12.01	11.99	12.01
s	0.013	0.018	0.017	0.023	0.030

Subgroup	11	12	13	14	15
Time	09:10	09:20	09:30	09:40	09:50
Date	07/02/95	07/02/95	07/02/95	07/02/95	07/02/95
1	11.98	11.92	11.93	11.99	12.00
2	11.97	11.95	11.95	11.93	11.98
3	11.96	11.92	11.98	11.94	11.99
4	11.95	11.94	11.94	11.95	11.95
5	12.00	11.96	11.96	11.96	11.93
X̄	11.97	11.94	11.95	11.95	11.97
s	0.019	0.018	0.019	0.023	0.029

Figure 5.36   Shafts, Averages, and Standard Deviations   (*continued*)

Subgroup	16	17	18	19	20
Time	10:00	10:10	10:20	10:30	10:40
Date	07/02/95	07/02/95	07/02/95	07/02/95	07/02/95
1	12.00	12.02	12.00	11.97	11.99
2	11.98	11.98	12.01	12.03	12.01
3	11.99	11.97	12.02	12.00	12.02
4	11.96	11.98	12.01	12.01	12.00
5	11.97	11.99	11.99	11.99	12.01
$\overline{X}$	11.98	11.999	12.01	12.00	12.01
s	0.016	0.019	0.011	0.022	0.011

Subgroup	21
Time	10:50
Date	07/02/95
1	12.00
2	11.98
3	11.99
4	11.99
5	12.02
$\overline{X}$	12.00
s	0.015

$$\frac{12.00 + 11.98 + 11.99 + 11.96 + 11.97}{5} = 11.98$$

$$\sqrt{\frac{(12 - 11.98)^2 + (11.98 - 11.98)^2 + (11.99 - 11.98)^2 + (11.96 - 11.98)^2 + (11.97 - 11.98)^2}{5 - 1}} = 0.016$$

Figure 5.36   *(continued)*

recorded [Figure 5.36, (1)], summed, and then divided by the number of samples taken to get the average [Figure 5.36, (2)]. This average is then plotted on the control chart [Figure 5.37, (1)]. Note that in this example, the values for $\overline{X}$ and s have been calculated to three decimal places for clarity.

Using the 21 samples provided in Figure 5.36, we can calculate $\overline{\overline{X}}$ by summing all the averages from the individual samples taken and then dividing by the number of subgroups:

$$\overline{\overline{X}} = \frac{251.76}{21} = 11.99$$

This value is plotted as the centerline of the $\overline{X}$ chart [Figure 5.37, (2)]. This is the centerline of the s chart [Figure 5.37, (4)].

Individual standard deviations are calculated for each of the subgroups by utilizing the formula for calculating standard deviations, as presented in Chapter 4 [Figure 5.36, (3)]. Once calculated, these values are plotted on the s chart [Figure 5.37, (6)].

The value, the grand standard deviation average, is calculated by summing the values of the sample standard deviations [Figure 5.36, (3)] and dividing by the number of subgroups m:

$$\overline{s} = \frac{0.031 + 0.029 + 0.016 + \cdots + 0.015}{21} = \frac{0.414}{21} = 0.02$$

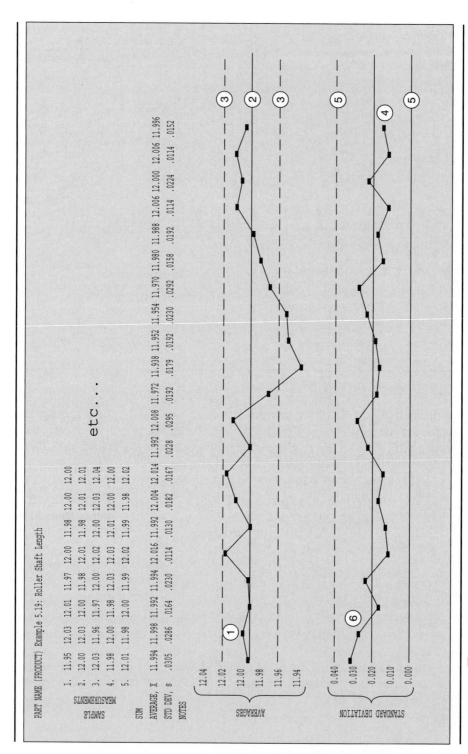

Figure 5.37 $\bar{X}$ and s Control Charts for Roller Shaft Length

The A_3 factor for a sample size of five is selected from the table in Appendix 2. The values for the upper and lower control limits of the $\overline{X}$ chart are calculated as follows:

$$UCL_{\overline{X}} = \overline{\overline{X}} + A_3\overline{s}$$
$$= 11.99 + 1.427(0.02) = 12.02$$

$$LCL_{\overline{X}} = \overline{\overline{X}} - A_3\overline{s}$$
$$= 11.99 - 1.427(0.02) = 11.96$$

Once calculated, the upper and lower control limits (UCL and LCL, respectively) are placed on the chart [Figure 5.37, (3)].

With n = 5, the values of B_3 and B_4 are found in the table in Appendix 2. The control limits for the s chart are calculated as follows:

$$UCL_s = B_4\overline{s}$$
$$= 2.089(0.02) = 0.04$$
$$LCL_s = B_3\overline{s}$$
$$= 0(0.02) = 0$$

The control limits are placed on the s chart [Figure 5.37, (5)].

The s chart (Figure 5.37) exhibits good control. The points are evenly spaced on both sides of the centerline and there are no points beyond the control limits. There are no unusual patterns or trends in the data. Given these observations, it can be said that the process is producing parts of similar dimensions.

Next the $\overline{X}$ chart is examined. Once again, an inspection of the $\overline{X}$ chart reveals the unusual pattern occurring at points 12, 13, and 14. These measurements are all below the lower control limit. When compared with other samples throughout the day's production, the parts produced during the time that samples 12, 13, and 14 were taken were much smaller than parts produced during other times in the production run. As before, this signals that an investigation into the cause of the production of undersized parts needs to take place.

Since a cause for the undersized parts was determined in the previous example, these values can be removed from the calculations for the $\overline{X}$ chart and s chart. The revised limits will be used to monitor future production. The new limits will extend from the old limits.

Revising the calculations is performed as follows:

$$\overline{\overline{X}}_{new} = \overline{X}_0 = \frac{\sum \overline{X} - \overline{X}_d}{m - m_d}$$
$$= \frac{251.76 - 11.94 - 11.95 - 11.95}{21 - 3}$$
$$= 12.00$$

$$\bar{s}_{new} = s_0 = \frac{\Sigma s - s_d}{m - m_d}$$

$$= \frac{0.414 - 0.0179 - 0.0192 - 0.0230}{21 - 3}$$

$$= 0.02$$

Calculating σ_0,

$$\sigma_0 = \frac{s_0}{c_4} = \frac{0.02}{0.9400} = 0.02$$

$$UCL_{\bar{x}} = 12.00 + 1.342(0.02) = 12.03$$

$$LCL_{\bar{x}} = 12.00 - 1.342(0.02) = 11.97$$

$$UCL_s = 1.964(0.02) = 0.04$$

$$LCL_s = 0(0.02) = 0$$

SUMMARY

Control charts are easy to construct and use in studying a process, whether that process is in a manufacturing or service environment. Control charts indicate areas for improvement. Once the root cause has been identified, changes can be proposed and tested, and improvements can be monitored through the use of control charts. Consider the situation described in the Real Tools for Real Life feature, "Common Cause Variation in a Process." The doctors and office manager were encouraging the people working in billing and insurance to work harder. When control charts revealed that this was the best the process was going to perform, major changes were made to the process. Changes that would not have otherwise been made resulted in increased productivity. Faster completion times and reduced errors mean a decrease in cost and an improvement in worker satisfaction and worker-management relations. The cost of refiling the claims was significantly reduced and payments are reaching the office faster.

Through the use of control charts, similar gains can be realized in the manufacturing sector. Users of control charts report savings in scrap, including material and labor; lower rework costs; reduced inspection; higher product quality; more consistent part characteristics; greater operator confidence; lower troubleshooting costs; reduced completion times; faster deliveries; and others.

■ *Lessons Learned*

1. Control charts enhance the analysis of a process by showing how that process performs over time. Control charts allow for early detection of process changes.
2. Control charts serve two basic functions: They provide an economic basis for making a decision as to whether to investigate for potential problems, adjust the process, or leave the process alone; and they assist in the identification of problems in the process.
3. Variation, differences between items, exists in all processes. Variation can be within-piece, piece-to-piece, and time-to-time.
4. The $\overline{X}$ chart is used to monitor the variation in the average values of the measurements of groups of samples. Averages rather than individual observations are used on control charts because average values will indicate a change in the amount of variation much faster than individual values will.
5. The $\overline{X}$ chart, showing the central tendency of the data, is always used in conjunction with either a range or a standard deviation chart.
6. The R and s charts show the spread or dispersion of the data.
7. The centerline of a control chart shows where the process is centered. The upper and lower control limits describe the spread of the process.
8. A homogeneous subgroup is essential to the proper study of a process. Certain guidelines can be applied in choosing a rational subgroup.
9. Common, or chance, causes are small random changes in the process that cannot be avoided. Assignable causes are large variations in the process that can be identified as having a specific cause.
10. A process is considered to be in a state of control, or under control, when the performance of the process falls within the statistically calculated control limits and exhibits only common, or chance, causes. Certain guidelines can be applied for determining by control chart when a process is under control.
11. Patterns on a control chart indicate a lack of statistical control. Patterns may take the form of changes or jumps in level, runs, trends, or cycles or may reflect the existence of two populations or mistakes.
12. The steps for revising a control chart are (a) examine the chart for out-of-control conditions; (b) isolate the causes of the out-of-control condition; (c) eliminate the cause of the out-of-control condition; and (d) revise the chart, using the formulas presented in the chapter. Revisions to the control chart can take place only when the assignable causes have been determined and eliminated. ■

■ *Formulas*

Average and Range Charts

$\overline{X}$ chart:

$$\overline{\overline{X}} = \frac{\sum\limits_{i=1}^{m} \overline{X}_i}{m}$$

$$UCL_{\overline{X}} = \overline{\overline{X}} + A_2\overline{R}$$

$$LCL_{\overline{X}} = \overline{\overline{X}} - A_2\overline{R}$$

R chart:

$$\overline{R} = \frac{\sum\limits_{i=1}^{m} R_i}{m}$$

$$UCL_R = D_4\overline{R}$$

$$LCL_R = D_3\overline{R}$$

Revising the charts:

$$\overline{X} = \overline{\overline{X}}_{new} = \frac{\sum\limits_{i=1}^{m} \overline{X} - \overline{X}_d}{m - m_d}$$

$$UCL_{\overline{X}} = \overline{X}_0 + A\sigma_0$$

$$LCL_{\overline{X}} = \overline{X}_0 - A\sigma_0$$

$$\sigma_0 = R_0/d_2$$

$$\overline{R}_{new} = \frac{\sum\limits_{i=1}^{m} R - R_d}{m - m_d}$$

$$UCL_R = D_2\sigma_0$$

$$LCL_R = D_1\sigma_0$$

Average and Standard Deviation Charts

$\overline{X}$ chart:

$$\overline{\overline{X}} = \frac{\sum\limits_{i=1}^{m} X_i}{m}$$

$$UCL_{\overline{X}} = \overline{\overline{X}} + A_3\overline{s}$$

$$LCL_{\overline{X}} = \overline{\overline{X}} - A_3\overline{s}$$

s chart:

$$\bar{s} = \frac{\sum_{i=1}^{m} s_i}{m}$$

$$UCL_s = B_4\bar{s}$$
$$LCL_s = B_3\bar{s}$$

Revising the charts:

$$X_0 = \overline{\overline{X}}_{new} = \frac{\sum_{i=1}^{m} \overline{X} - \overline{X}_d}{m - m_d}$$

$$s_0 = \bar{s}_{new} = \frac{\sum_{i=1}^{m} s - s_d}{m - m_d}$$

and

$$\sigma_0 = s_0/c_4$$
$$UCL_{\overline{X}} = X_0 + A\sigma_0$$
$$LCL_{\overline{X}} = X_0 - A\sigma_0$$

$$UCL_s = B_6\sigma_0$$
$$LCL_s = B_5\sigma_0$$

Chapter Problems

1. Describe the difference between chance and assignable causes.
2. How would you use variation to manage a group of people? Why should a manager be aware of assignable and chance causes?

$\overline{X}$ and R Charts

3. A large bank establishes $\overline{X}$ and R charts for the time required to process applications for its charge cards. A sample of five applications is taken each day. The first four weeks (20 days) of data give

$$\overline{\overline{X}} = 16 \text{ min} \qquad \bar{s} = 3 \text{ min} \qquad \overline{R} = 7 \text{ min}$$

Based on the values given, calculate the centerline and control limits for the $\overline{X}$ and R charts.

4. The data below are $\overline{X}$ and R values for 25 samples of size n = 4 taken from a process filling bags of fertilizer. The measurements are made on the fill weight of the bags in pounds.

Subgroup Number	$\overline{X}$	Range
1	50.3	0.73
2	49.6	0.75
3	50.8	0.79
4	50.9	0.74
5	49.8	0.72
6	50.5	0.73
7	50.2	0.71
8	49.9	0.70
9	50.0	0.65
10	50.1	0.67
11	50.2	0.65
12	50.5	0.67
13	50.4	0.68
14	50.8	0.70
15	50.0	0.65
16	49.9	0.66
17	50.4	0.67
18	50.5	0.68
19	50.7	0.70
20	50.2	0.65
21	49.9	0.60
22	50.1	0.64
23	49.5	0.60
24	50.0	0.62
25	50.3	0.60

Set up an $\overline{X}$ and R chart on this process. Interpret the chart. Does the process seem to be in control? If necessary, assume assignable causes and revise the trial control limits. If the average fill of the bags is to be 50.0 pounds, how does this process compare?

5. The data below are $\overline{X}$ and R values for 12 samples of size n = 5. They were taken from a process producing bearings. The measurements are made on the inside diameter of the bearing. The data have been coded from 0.50; in other words, a measurement of 0.50345 has been recorded as 345. Range values are coded from 0.000; that is, 0.00013 is recorded as 13.

Subgroup Number	$\overline{X}$	Range
1	345	13
2	347	14
3	350	12
4	346	11
5	350	15
6	345	16
7	349	14
8	348	13
9	348	12
10	354	15
11	352	13
12	355	16

Set up the $\overline{X}$ and R charts on this process. Does the process seem to be in control? Why or why not? If necessary, assume assignable causes and revise the trial control limits.

6. What is meant by the statement, "The process is in a state of statistical control"?

7. Describe how both an $\overline{X}$ and R or s chart would look if they were under normal statistical control.

8. $\overline{X}$ charts describe the accuracy of a process, and R and s charts describe the precision. How would accuracy be recognized on an $\overline{X}$ chart? How would precision be recognized on either an R or s chart?

9. Why is the use and interpretation of an R or s chart so critical when examining an $\overline{X}$ chart?

10. Create an $\overline{X}$ and R chart for the clutch plate information in Table 5.1 on page 220. You will need to calculate the range values for each subgroup. Calculate the control limits and centerline for each chart. Graph the data with the calculated values. Beginning with the R chart, how does the process look?

11. RM Manufacturing makes thermometers for use in the medical field. These thermometers, which read in degrees Celsius, are able to measure temperatures to a level of precision of two decimal places. Each hour, RM Manufacturing tests eight randomly selected thermometers in a solution that is known to be at a temperature of 3°C. Use the following data to create and interpret an $\overline{X}$ and R chart. Based on the desired thermometer reading of 3°, interpret the results of your plotted averages and ranges.

Subgroup	Average Temperature	Range
1	3.06	0.10
2	3.03	0.09
3	3.10	0.12
4	3.05	0.07
5	2.98	0.08
6	3.00	0.10
7	3.01	0.15
8	3.04	0.09
9	3.00	0.09
10	3.03	0.14
11	2.96	0.07
12	2.99	0.11
13	3.01	0.09
14	2.98	0.13
15	3.02	0.08

12. Interpret the $\overline{X}$ and R charts in Figure P5.1.

13. Interpret the $\overline{X}$ and R charts in Figure P5.2.

14. The variables control chart seen in Figure P5.3 is monitoring the main score residual for a peanut canister pull top. The data are coded from 0.00 (in other words, a value of 26 in the chart is actually 0.0026). Finish the calculations for the sum, averages, and range. Create an $\overline{X}$ and R chart, calculate the limits, plot the points, and interpret the chart.

$\overline{X}$ and s Charts

15. Create an $\overline{X}$ and s chart for the clutch plate information in Table 5.1 on page 220. You will need to calculate the standard deviation values for each subgroup. Calculate the control limits and centerline for each chart. Graph the data. Beginning with the s chart, how does the process look?

16. Create an $\overline{X}$ and s chart for the information given in Problem 14.

17. Precision Machines manufactures medical devices. One of their products, a stent, can be inserted in a blood vessel to repair it and maintain blood flow. The specifications for this tubing is a very precise 3.50 ± 0.01. Create and interpret an $\overline{X}$ and s chart with the data in Figure P5.4 on page 282.

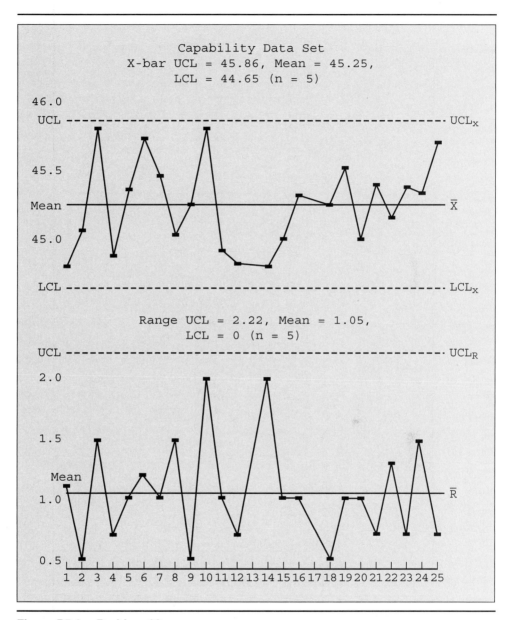

Figure P5.1   Problem 12

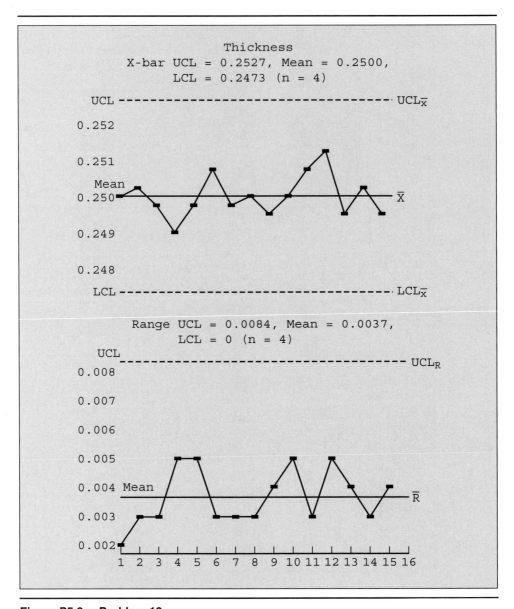

Figure P5.2   Problem 13

VARIABLES CONTROL CHART

PART NAME (PRODUCT) Pull Up Tab OPERATION (PROCESS) Main Score Residual PART NUMBER SPECIFICATION LIMITS .0028 +/- 0.0005

OPERATOR You MACHINE Press #34 GAGE 1 UNIT OF MEASURE 0.0001* ZERO EQUALS

DATE 9/21

	1:00	2:00	2:30	3:00	3:30
1.	28	27	28	26	25
2.	36	35	35	33	33
3.	32	33	33	31	31
4.	28	27	27	27	26
SUM	124	122	122	117	115
AVERAGE, X	31	31	31	29	29
RANGE, R	8	8	8	7	8

DATE 9/22

	1:00	2:00	2:30	3:00	3:30
1.	28	26	30	27	27
2.	34	27	35	29	31
3.	28	31	36	33	29
4.	30	33	33	33	26
SUM	120	117	134	122	113
AVERAGE, X	30	29	34	31	28
RANGE, R	6	7	6	6	5

DATE 9/23

	1:00	1:30	2:00	2:30	3:00	3:30
1.	25	25	23	24	24	25
2.	30	28	27	23	23	30
3.	28	25	26	27	27	29
4.	24	22	22	24	24	24
SUM	107	100	98	102	98	108
AVERAGE, X	27	25	25	26	25	27
RANGE, R	6	6	5	5	4	6

DATE 9/24

	1:00	1:30	2:00	2:30	3:00	3:30
1.	24	25	26	25	25	23
2.	29	27	28	26	26	27
3.	27	25	26	28	28	25
4.	24	24	24	27	28	24
SUM						
AVERAGE, X						
RANGE, R						

SAMPLE MEASUREMENTS

Figure P5.3 Problem 14

DEPT.	Machine		PART NAME	Whisk Wheel
PART NO.	92-01		MACHINE	Cutoff
GROUP	Quality Control		VARIABLE	

Subgroup	1	2	3	4	5
Time	07:00:00	07:18:00	07:36:00	07:54:00	08:12:00
Date	02/20/96	02/20/96	02/20/96	02/20/96	02/20/96
1	3.51	3.49	3.51	3.51	3.50
2	3.51	3.51	3.51	3.52	3.51
3	3.50	3.50	3.51	3.50	3.51
4	3.51	3.51	3.51	3.51	3.50
5	3.50	3.50	3.50	3.50	3.51
6	3.50	3.50	3.50	3.50	3.50

Subgroup	6	7	8	9	10
Time	08:30:00	08:48:00	09:06:00	09:24:00	09:42:00
Date	02/20/96	02/20/96	02/20/96	02/20/96	02/20/96
1	3.51	3.50	3.50	3.50	3.51
2	3.51	3.51	3.51	3.50	3.51
3	3.50	3.50	3.50	3.51	3.51
4	3.50	3.49	3.50	3.52	3.51
5	3.50	3.50	3.51	3.51	3.50
6	3.50	3.50	3.50	3.51	3.50

Subgroup	11	12	13	14	15
Time	10:00:00	10:18:00	10:36:00	10:54:00	11:12:00
Date	02/20/96	02/20/96	02/20/96	02/20/96	02/20/96
1	3.51	3.50	3.50	3.51	3.50
2	3.51	3.51	3.51	3.50	3.51
3	3.50	3.51	3.51	3.50	3.50
4	3.50	3.51	3.52	3.50	3.51
5	3.50	3.51	3.50	3.50	3.51
6	3.50	3.51	3.52	3.50	3.51

Subgroup	16	17	18	19	20
Time	11:30:00	11:48:00	01:10:00	01:28:00	01:46:00
Date	02/20/96	02/20/96	02/20/96	02/20/96	02/20/96
1	3.50	3.51	3.51	3.50	3.52
2	3.51	3.50	3.52	3.50	3.51
3	3.51	3.50	3.52	3.50	3.50
4	3.52	3.52	3.51	3.50	3.50
5	3.51	3.50	3.50	3.51	3.50
6	3.51	3.50	3.51	3.51	3.50

Subgroup	21	22	23	24	
Time	02:04:00	02:22:00	02:40:00	02:58:00	
Date	02/20/96	02/20/96	02/20/96	02/20/96	
1	3.51	3.51	3.52	3.51	
2	3.50	3.50	3.50	3.51	
3	3.50	3.50	3.51	3.50	
4	3.50	3.49	3.51	3.50	
5	3.50	3.51	3.50	3.50	
6	3.50	3.51	3.50	3.50	

Figure P5.4   Data for Problem 17

18. The environmental safety engineer at a local firm is keeping track of the air particulate readings for four separate areas within the plant. Create an $\overline{X}$ and s chart for the average amount of particulates found at the time of each sample (read down the columns for each particular time, n = 4). Interpret the chart. What is the drawback of constructing the chart based on the times the samples were taken versus the location in the plant that the samples were taken?

INITIAL PARTICULATES READINGS

DATE	4/15			4/16			4/17		
TIME	8:00 AM	4:00 PM	12:00 AM	8:00 AM	4:00 PM	12:00 AM	8:00 AM	4:00 PM	12:00 AM
NORTH PIT	300	350	480	365	400	470	410	375	500
SOUTH PIT	440	470	495	405	505	560	445	440	575
EAST PIT	275	300	360	300	300	325	260	295	355
WEST PIT	350	360	400	360	360	390	325	360	405

DATE	4/18			4/19			4/20		
TIME	8:00 AM	4:00 PM	12:00 AM	8:00 AM	4:00 PM	12:00 AM	8:00 AM	4:00 PM	12:00 AM
NORTH PIT	320	350	475	335	410	490	420	385	485
SOUTH PIT	485	505	545	415	520	575	430	440	520
EAST PIT	330	320	370	270	320	345	280	315	375
WEST PIT	225	370	410	350	370	400	335	370	415

DATE	4/21			4/22			4/23		
TIME	8:00 AM	4:00 PM	12:00 AM	8:00 AM	4:00 PM	12:00 AM	8:00 AM	4:00 PM	12:00 AM
NORTH PIT	290	330	450	310	390	390	325	400	495
SOUTH PIT	430	520	510	435	440	560	485	540	450
EAST PIT	285	315	350	295	305	330	250	265	360
WEST PIT	350	360	400	360	360	390	340	325	400

19. Using the information in Problem 18, create an $\overline{X}$ and s chart based on the daily average for each location in the plant (read across the columns for each pit, n = 3). Interpret the chart. What is the drawback of constructing the chart based on the location from which the samples were taken versus constructing a chart based on the times at which the samples were taken?

CASE STUDY 5.1
Quality Control for Variables

PART 1

This case study provides some details about the activities of the Whisk Wheel Company, which is currently in the process of applying statistical quality control and problem-solving techniques to their wheel hub operation. Whisk Wheel supplies hubs and wheels to a variety of bicycle manufacturers. The wheel hubs under discussion in this case fit on an all-terrain model bicycle.

Background

The Whisk Wheel Company has just been notified by its largest customer, Rosewood Bicycle Inc., that Whisk Wheel will need to dramatically improve the quality level associated with the hub operation. Currently the operation is unable to meet the specification limits set by the customer. Rosewood has been sorting the parts on the production line before assembly, but they want to end this procedure. Beginning immediately, Whisk Wheel will be required to provide detailed statistical information about each lot of products they produce. (A lot is considered one day's worth of production.) At the end of each day, the lot produced is shipped to Rosewood just-in-time for their production run.

The Product

Figure C5.1.1 diagrams the product in question, a wheel hub. The hub shaft is made of chrome-moly steel and is 0.750 inch in diameter and 3.750 inches long. The dimension in question is the length. The specification for the length is 3.750 $\pm$ 0.005 inches.

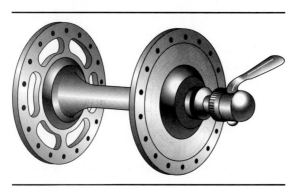

Figure C5.1.1   Hub Assembly

The Process

Twelve-foot-long chrome-moly steel shafts are purchased from a supplier. The shafts are straightened and then cut to the 3.750-inch length. Several different machines perform the cutting operation. The data presented here are for the production off one machine only.

Management Strategy

On the basis of new customer requirements, until greater control can be placed on the process, management has decided to intensify product inspection. This will allow the staff engineers to complete their study of the problem and recommend an action plan. Each piece produced will be inserted in a go/no-go gauge to determine if it meets specifications. This will work fairly well by preventing improperly sized shafts from going to the customer. Several managers want to make this a permanent arrangement, but some of the more forward-thinking managers feel that this will not get at the root cause of the problem. There is also the concern that 100 percent inspection is costly and not effective in the long term.

In the meantime, the staff engineers (including you) are continuing to study the problem more carefully. The following information is from today's production run. From the finished parts, an operator samples six hubs 24 times during the day.

  Assignment

On the computer, create a histogram from today's data (Figure C5.1.2). Write a summary of the results. Use the value of estimated sigma and the Z tables to calculate the percentage of parts produced above and below the specification limits.

DEPT.	Machine		PART NAME	Whisk Wheel	
PART NO.	01-92		MACHINE	Cutoff	
GROUP	Quality Control		VARIABLE		
Subgroup	1	2	3	4	5
Time	07:00:00	07:18:00	07:36:00	07:54:00	08:12:00
Date	01/30/96	01/30/96	01/30/96	01/30/96	01/30/96
1	3.757	3.753	3.744	3.755	3.757
2	3.749	3.739	3.745	3.753	3.760
3	3.751	3.747	3.740	3.753	3.751
4	3.755	3.751	3.741	3.749	3.754
5	3.749	3.751	3.742	3.739	3.750
6	3.759	3.744	3.743	3.747	3.753

Figure C5.1.2   Data for Day 1   (*continued*)

Subgroup	6	7	8	9	10
Time	08:30:00	08:48:00	09:06:00	09:24:00	09:42:00
Date	01/30/96	01/30/96	01/30/96	01/30/96	01/30/96
1	3.741	3.746	3.746	3.760	3.741
2	3.749	3.743	3.753	3.755	3.745
3	3.745	3.753	3.747	3.757	3.751
4	3.742	3.751	3.755	3.757	3.741
5	3.743	3.747	3.758	3.749	3.740
6	3.742	3.751	3.756	3.741	3.741

Subgroup	11	12	13	14	15
Time	10:00:00	10:18:00	10:36:00	10:54:00	11:12:00
Date	01/30/96	01/30/96	01/30/96	01/30/96	01/30/96
1	3.749	3.746	3.743	3.755	3.745
2	3.751	3.749	3.751	3.744	3.751
3	3.757	3.744	3.745	3.753	3.747
4	3.754	3.757	3.739	3.755	3.751
5	3.755	3.737	3.750	3.754	3.744
6	3.753	3.749	3.747	3.766	3.745

Subgroup	16	17	18	19	20
Time	11:30:00	11:48:00	12:06:00	01:06:00	01:24:00
Date	01/30/96	01/30/96	01/30/96	01/30/96	01/30/96
1	3.748	3.757	3.740	3.756	3.742
2	3.746	3.747	3.739	3.757	3.753
3	3.755	3.756	3.752	3.749	3.754
4	3.755	3.759	3.744	3.755	3.743
5	3.749	3.751	3.745	3.744	3.741
6	3.749	3.756	3.757	3.741	3.748

Subgroup	21	22	23	24	
Time	01:42:00	02:00:00	02:18:00	02:36:00	
Date	01/30/96	01/30/96	01/30/96	01/30/96	
1	3.752	3.746	3.745	3.752	
2	3.751	3.753	3.762	3.755	
3	3.749	3.741	3.753	3.753	
4	3.753	3.746	3.750	3.749	
5	3.755	3.743	3.744	3.754	
6	3.750	3.744	3.750	3.756	

Figure C5.1.2   **(continued)**

PART 2

Although process capability calculations have not been made, on the basis of the histogram, the process does not appear to be capable. It is apparent from the histogram that a large proportion of the process does not meet the individual length specification. The data appear to be a reasonable approximation of a normal distribution.

During a rare quiet moment in your day, you telephone a good friend from your quality-control class to reflect on the events so far. You also remember some of the comments made by your SQC professor about appropriate sampling and measuring techniques. After listening to your story, your friend brings up several key concerns.

1. Product Control   Basically, management has devised a stopgap procedure to prevent poor quality products from reaching the customer. This work—screening, sorting, and selectively shipping parts—is a strategy consistent with the "detect and sort" approach to quality control. Management has not really attempted to determine the root cause of the problem.

2. The Engineering Approach   While a little more on track, the focus of engineering on the process capability was purely from the "conformance to specifications" point of view. Appropriate process capability calculations should be based on a process that is under statistical control. No information has yet been gathered on this particular process to determine if the process is under statistical control. In this situation, process capability was calculated without determining if the process was in a state of statistical control—something you now remember your quality professor cautioning against.

Another consideration deals with the statistical significance of the sample using the "best operator and the best machine." Few or no details have been given about the sampling techniques used or the training level of the operator.

A Different Approach

After much discussion, you and your friend come up with a different approach to solving this problem. You gather together your fellow team members and plan a course of action. The goal of the group is to determine the source of variation in the process of producing wheel hubs. A process flowchart is created to carefully define the complete sequence of processing steps: raw material handling, straightening, cutting, and finish polish (Figure C5.1.3). Creating a process flowchart has helped all members of the team to better understand what is happening during the manufacture of the hub.

At each step along the way, your team discusses all the factors that could be contributing to the variation in the final product. To aid and guide the discussion, the group creates a cause-and-effect diagram, which helps keep the group discussions focused and allows the team to discuss all the possible sources of variation. There are several of these, including the raw materials (their properties and preparation), the methods (procedures for setup and machine operation at each of the three operations), the machine conditions (operating settings, maintenance conditions), and the operator (training, supervision, techniques). The diagram created is shown in Figure C5.1.4.

The team originally focuses on the inherent equipment capability as the key problem. This approach leads too quickly to the conclusion that new machines should be purchased. This approach does not enable team members to learn to use the equipment, processes, and people already available to their fullest potential.

FLOW PROCESS CHART

Part Charted: __Whisk wheel hub__   Chart No. __92-05__
Drawing No. __D-92-05__   Chart of Method __Present__
Chart Begins __Raw material storage__   Charted by: _____
Chart Ends __Hub assembly bin__   Date __01/27/92__   __1__ of __1__

Distance, ft	Unit Time, min	Symbols	Process Description
		$\triangledown$	In stock storage
40	0.14	$\Rightarrow$	Hand cart to straightener
	0.35	$\bigcirc$	Straighten stock
	0.02	$\bigcirc$	Load to cart
7	0.10	$\Rightarrow$	Cart to cutoff
	0.92	$\bigcirc$	Cut stock to six pc. 3.750
2	0.12	$\bigcirc$	Finish ends
1	0.02	$\bigcirc$	Load on conveyer
20	1.12	$\Rightarrow$	Conveyer to hub assembly bin
			02/92

Figure C5.1.3   Process Flowchart

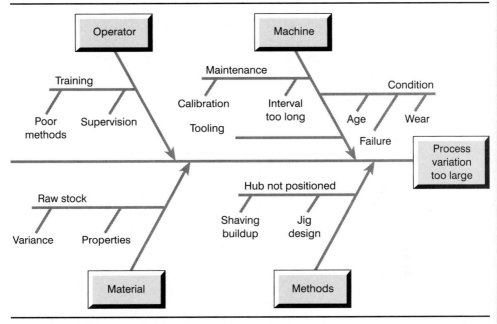

Figure C5.1.4   Cause-and-Effect Diagram

After studying and discussing the complete process flow, the team decides that they do not know enough about the process to suggest solutions. They assign team members to more fully investigate the four areas (raw materials, straightening, cutting, and finishing). Close contact among the team members will ensure that the discoveries in one area are quickly shared with other related areas. After all, in this process of making a wheel hub, no one area can function without the others.

You and your partner have been assigned to the cutting area. To discover the source of variation, the two of you decide to run $\overline{X}$ and R charts on the data from the preceding day as well as the data from this day (an additional 24 subgroups of sample size six).

 Assignment

Add the new data (Figure C5.1.5) for today to your previous file. Create an $\overline{X}$ and R chart containing both days' data and discuss what the charts look like. Use all the information available to create a histogram. Use the value for estimated sigma and the Z tables to calculate the percentage of parts produced above and below the specification limits.

DEPT.	Machine		PART NAME	Whisk Wheel	
PART NO.	01-92		MACHINE	Cutoff	
GROUP	Quality Control		VARIABLE		

Subgroup	1	2	3	4	5
Time	07:00:00	07:18:00	07:36:00	07:54:00	08:12:00
Date	01/31/96	01/31/96	01/31/96	01/31/96	01/31/96
1	3.744	3.741	3.749	3.745	3.751
2	3.753	3.744	3.747	3.750	3.737
3	3.757	3.745	3.747	3.749	3.755
4	3.749	3.754	3.757	3.745	3.751
5	3.757	3.745	3.750	3.749	3.751
6	3.749	3.747	3.755	3.741	3.739

Subgroup	6	7	8	9	10
Time	08:30:00	08:48:00	09:06:00	09:24:00	09:42:00
Date	01/31/96	01/31/96	01/31/96	01/31/96	01/31/96
1	3.751	3.747	3.749	3.751	3.747
2	3.755	3.753	3.755	3.743	3.757
3	3.749	3.737	3.743	3.753	3.747
4	3.753	3.745	3.749	3.757	3.745
5	3.755	3.749	3.752	3.749	3.751
6	3.751	3.744	3.749	3.744	3.756

Subgroup	11	12	13	14	15
Time	10:00:00	10:18:00	10:36:00	10:54:00	11:12:00
Date	01/31/96	01/31/96	01/31/96	01/31/96	01/31/96
1	3.747	3.755	3.747	3.754	3.741
2	3.741	3.742	3.749	3.747	3.739
3	3.751	3.749	3.755	3.749	3.751
4	3.750	3.755	3.749	3.751	3.753
5	3.747	3.745	3.754	3.756	3.749
6	3.740	3.745	3.746	3.754	3.743

Subgroup	16	17	18	19	20
Time	11:30:00	11:48:00	12:06:00	01:06:00	01:24:00
Date	01/31/96	01/31/96	01/31/96	01/31/96	01/31/96
1	3.751	3.758	3.745	3.755	3.747
2	3.745	3.748	3.744	3.753	3.754
3	3.757	3.743	3.752	3.750	3.741
4	3.747	3.751	3.743	3.753	3.745
5	3.749	3.748	3.750	3.751	3.759
6	3.745	3.759	3.746	3.752	3.747

Figure C5.1.5   Data for Day 2   (continued)

Subgroup	21	22	23	24
Time	01:42:00	02:00:00	02:18:00	02:36:00
Date	01/31/96	01/31/96	01/31/96	01/31/96
1	3.753	3.755	3.747	3.751
2	3.755	3.749	3.749	3.753
3	3.747	3.752	3.752	3.753
4	3.747	3.750	3.745	3.752
5	3.751	3.753	3.750	3.757
6	3.747	3.755	3.743	3.751

Figure C5.1.5   (*continued*)

PART 3

In order to determine the root causes of variation, you and your partner spend the remainder of day 2 studying the cutting operation and the operator. You randomly select a machine and an operator to watch as he performs the operation and measures the parts. You note several actions taken by the operator that could be sources of variation.

Investigation reveals that the operator runs the process in the following manner. Every 18 minutes, he measures the length of six hubs with a micrometer. The length values for the six consecutively produced hubs are averaged, and the average is plotted on a piece of charting paper. Periodically, the operator reviews the evolving data and makes a decision as to whether or not the process mean (the hub length) needs to be adjusted. These adjustments can be accomplished by stopping the machine, loosening some clamps, and jogging the cutting device back or forth depending on the adjustment the operator feels is necessary. This process takes about five minutes and appears to occur fairly often.

Based on what you have learned about process control in SQC class, it is obvious to you that the operator is adding variation to the process! He appears to be overcontrolling (overadjusting) the process because he cannot distinguish between common cause variation and special cause variation. The operator has been reacting to patterns in the data that may be inherent (common) to the process. The consequences of this mistake are devastating to a control chart. Each time an adjustment is made when it is not necessary, variation is introduced to the process that would not be there otherwise. Not only is quality essentially decreased (made more variable) with each adjustment, but production time is unnecessarily lost.

A glance at the histogram created the first day shows that overadjustment is indeed occurring, resulting in the bimodal distribution. Control charts can be used to help distinguish between the presence of common and special causes of variation. Removing this source of variation will allow the process to operate more consistently. Removing this obstacle can also help uncover the root cause of the variation.

The data from day 3 have been gathered and reflect the suggested change. The operator has been told not to adjust the process at all during the day. If the process goes beyond the previous day's limits and out of control, the operator is to contact you.

Assignment

Create an $\overline{X}$ and R chart for *only the new data from day 3* (Figure C5.1.6). Compare the new chart with the charts from the two previous days. Draw the previous day's limits on the new chart for day 3 by hand. Using only the data from day 3, create a histogram. Use the value for estimated sigma and the Z tables to calculate the percentage of parts produced above and below the specification limits.

The new chart should allow you to better distinguish between the presence of common and special causes of variation. Compare all of your mathematical and graphical results. What conclusions can you and your partner draw?

DEPT.	Machine		PART NAME	Whisk Wheel	
PART NO.	01-92		MACHINE	Cutoff	
GROUP	Quality Control		VARIABLE		

Sample	1	2	3	4	5
Time	07:00:00	07:18:00	07:36:00	07:54:00	08:12:00
Date	02/06/96	02/06/96	02/06/96	02/06/96	02/06/96
1	3.749	3.751	3.747	3.753	3.755
2	3.752	3.742	3.749	3.750	3.754
3	3.751	3.745	3.755	3.744	3.751
4	3.746	3.739	3.753	3.745	3.753
5	3.745	3.751	3.752	3.741	3.749
6	3.749	3.751	3.740	3.748	3.752

Subgroup	6	7	8	9	10
Time	08:30:00	08:48:00	09:06:00	09:24:00	09:42:00
Date	02/06/96	02/06/96	02/06/96	02/06/96	02/06/96
1	3.752	3.746	3.749	3.750	3.745
2	3.752	3.750	3.753	3.746	3.747
3	3.750	3.749	3.752	3.750	3.745
4	3.748	3.747	3.757	3.754	3.754
5	3.751	3.753	3.747	3.753	3.748
6	3.748	3.751	3.747	3.749	3.743

Subgroup	11	12	13	14	15
Time	10:00:00	10:18:00	10:36:00	10:54:00	11:12:00
Date	02/06/96	02/06/96	02/06/96	02/06/96	02/06/96
1	3.751	3.751	3.749	3.746	3.741
2	3.751	3.753	3.753	3.751	3.748
3	3.748	3.753	3.755	3.747	3.744
4	3.748	3.747	3.749	3.749	3.749
5	3.755	3.741	3.745	3.755	3.751
6	3.750	3.741	3.759	3.747	3.744

Figure C5.1.6   Data for Day 3   *(continued)*

Subgroup	16	17	18	19	20
Time	11:30:00	11:48:00	12:06:00	01:06:00	01:24:00
Date	02/06/96	02/06/96	02/06/96	02/06/96	02/06/96
1	3.749	3.745	3.743	3.744	3.743
2	3.749	3.746	3.749	3.748	3.745
3	3.745	3.753	3.745	3.754	3.749
4	3.745	3.753	3.747	3.753	3.749
5	3.749	3.751	3.755	3.755	3.749
6	3.745	3.751	3.753	3.749	3.748

Subgroup	21	22	23	24
Time	01:42:00	02:00:00	02:18:00	02:36:00
Date	02/06/96	02/06/96	02/06/96	02/06/96
1	3.748	3.747	3.752	3.747
2	3.752	3.750	3.751	3.745
3	3.752	3.748	3.753	3.751
4	3.755	3.751	3.749	3.749
5	3.750	3.755	3.751	3.753
6	3.753	3.753	3.755	3.740

Figure C5.1.6   *(continued)*

PART 4

With one source of variation identified and removed, quality and productivity on the line have improved. The process has been stabilized because no unnecessary adjustments have been made. The method of overcontrol has proven costly from both a quality (inconsistent product) and a productivity (machine downtime, higher scrap) point of view. The search continues for other sources of variation.

During day 3, you and your partner watched the methods the operator used to measure the hub. Neither of you feel that this technique is very good. Today you replace the old method and tool with a new measuring tool, and the operator is carefully trained to use the new tool.

 Assignment

Continue day 3's control chart to record the data for day 4 (Figure C5.1.7). How do the data look overall? Are there any trends or patterns? Comment on the tighter control limits as compared with days 1 and 2. Create a histogram with the data from only days 3 and 4 combined. Discuss how the overall spread of the process looks using the Z table calculations. What conclusions can be drawn?

DEPT.	Machine		PART NAME	Whisk Wheel	
PART NO.	01-92		MACHINE	Cutoff	
GROUP	Quality Control		VARIABLE		

Subgroup	1	2	3	4	5
Time	07:00:00	07:18:00	07:36:00	07:54:00	08:12:00
Date	02/10/96	02/10/96	02/10/96	02/10/96	02/10/96
1	3.745	3.753	3.751	3.747	3.749
2	3.745	3.756	3.755	3.753	3.753
3	3.751	3.750	3.750	3.744	3.749
4	3.749	3.751	3.749	3.748	3.748
5	3.753	3.749	3.751	3.750	3.745
6	3.740	3.749	3.752	3.747	3.750

Subgroup	6	7	8	9	10
Time	08:30:00	08:48:00	09:06:00	09:24:00	09:42:00
Date	02/10/96	02/10/96	02/10/96	02/10/96	02/10/96
1	3.752	3.755	3.751	3.751	3.755
2	3.749	3.749	3.750	3.750	3.750
3	3.753	3.753	3.749	3.749	3.750
4	3.749	3.752	3.749	3.751	3.751
5	3.750	3.749	3.749	3.750	3.751
6	3.751	3.753	3.751	3.752	3.752

Subgroup	11	12	13	14	15
Time	10:00:00	10:18:00	10:36:00	10:54:00	11:12:00
Date	02/10/96	02/10/96	02/10/96	02/10/96	02/10/96
1	3.749	3.750	3.752	3.751	3.747
2	3.748	3.749	3.750	3.752	3.751
3	3.752	3.749	3.751	3.751	3.748
4	3.749	3.751	3.752	3.746	3.746
5	3.749	3.750	3.751	3.749	3.749
6	3.746	3.750	3.751	3.750	3.753

Subgroup	16	17	18	19	20
Time	11:30:00	11:48:00	01:10:00	01:28:00	01:46:00
Date	02/10/96	02/10/96	02/10/96	02/10/96	02/10/96
1	3.753	3.751	3.747	3.750	3.751
2	3.747	3.750	3.745	3.749	3.750
3	3.754	3.749	3.749	3.748	3.753
4	3.754	3.748	3.748	3.749	3.750
5	3.749	3.749	3.750	3.750	3.749
6	3.750	3.750	3.750	3.749	3.754

Figure C.5.1.7   Data for Day 4   (*continued*)

Subgroup	21	22	23	24
Time	02:04:00	02:22:00	02:40:00	02:58:00
Date	02/10/96	02/10/96	02/10/96	02/10/96
1	3.750	3.749	3.753	3.755
2	3.755	3.751	3.749	3.748
3	3.746	3.755	3.745	3.749
4	3.750	3.751	3.748	3.748
5	3.751	3.752	3.749	3.748
6	3.750	3.751	3.749	3.750

Figure C5.1.7   (*continued*)

PART 5

Now that two unusual causes of variation have been removed from the process, you and your partner are able to spend the fourth day studying the resulting stable process. You are able to determine that the design of the jig used by the operation is causing a buildup of chips. Each time a part is cut, a small amount of chips builds up in the back of the jig. Unless the operator clears these chips away before inserting the new stock into the jig, they build up. The presence or absence of chips is causing variation in the length of the hub.

To correct this, during the night-maintenance shift, a slot is placed in the back of the jig, allowing the chips to drop out of the jig. Additionally, a solvent flush system is added to the fixture to wash the chips clear of the jig.

 Assignment

Create an $\overline{X}$ and R chart for just day 5's data (Figure C5.1.8). Compare the new chart with the charts from days 3 and 4. Have the control limits changed? How? How is the process doing now? Compare the percent out-of-specification found using the Z table calculations for all the days. Overall, how would you view the process?

DEPT.	Cutting		PART NAME	Whisk Wheel	
PART NO.	01-92		MACHINE	Cutoff	
GROUP	Quality Control		VARIABLE		

Subgroup	1	2	3	4	5
Time	07:00:00	07:18:00	07:36:00	07:54:00	08:12:00
Date	02/12/96	02/12/96	02/12/96	02/12/96	02/12/96
1	3.750	3.752	3.752	3.750	3.751
2	3.749	3.750	3.751	3.751	3.752
3	3.750	3.749	3.750	3.750	3.752
4	3.750	3.750	3.749	3.751	3.750
5	3.750	3.751	3.750	3.749	3.750
6	3.751	3.752	3.750	3.750	3.750

Figure C5.1.8   Data for Day 5   (*continued*)

Subgroup	6	7	8	9	10
Time	08:30:00	08:48:00	09:06:00	09:24:00	09:42:00
Date	02/12/96	02/12/96	02/12/96	02/12/96	02/12/96
1	3.749	3.750	3.750	3.751	3.751
2	3.750	3.752	3.750	3.750	3.752
3	3.750	3.750	3.750	3.750	3.751
4	3.750	3.750	3.750	3.751	3.750
5	3.751	3.750	3.751	3.752	3.749
6	3.750	3.751	3.750	3.750	3.750
Subgroup	11	12	13	14	15
Time	10:00:00	10:18:00	10:36:00	10:54:00	11:12:00
Date	02/12/96	02/12/96	02/12/96	02/12/96	02/12/96
1	3.751	3.750	3.750	3.751	3.749
2	3.750	3.751	3.751	3.750	3.750
3	3.750	3.750	3.751	3.751	3.751
4	3.749	3.749	3.750	3.751	3.750
5	3.751	3.750	3.750	3.750	3.750
6	3.750	3.750	3.750	3.750	3.752
Subgroup	16	17	18	19	20
Time	11:30:00	11:48:00	12:06:00	12:24:00	12:42:00
Date	02/12/96	02/12/96	02/12/96	02/12/96	02/12/96
1	3.750	3.750	3.750	3.751	3.752
2	3.750	3.750	3.752	3.750	3.750
3	3.751	3.749	3.750	3.751	3.751
4	3.750	3.750	3.751	3.752	3.750
5	3.749	3.751	3.749	3.750	3.749
6	3.750	3.750	3.750	3.751	3.750
Subgroup	21	22	23	24	
Time	13:00:00	13:18:00	13:36:00	13:54:00	
Date	02/12/96	02/12/96	02/12/96	02/12/96	
1	3.750	3.750	3.750	3.751	
2	3.750	3.752	3.751	3.751	
3	3.749	3.751	3.749	3.750	
4	3.749	3.750	3.751	3.750	
5	3.751	3.750	3.750	3.750	
6	3.751	3.749	3.750	3.750	

Figure C5.1.8   **(continued)**

PART 6

 Assignment

Revisit the charts you created in Part 5. How is the process behaving now that the improvements have been made? What will you recommend to management that they tell the customer? How will you support your recommendation?

CASE STUDY 5.2
Process Improvement

This case is the third in a four-part series of cases involving process improvement. The other cases are found at the end of Chapters 3, 4, and 6. Data and calculations for this case establish the foundation for the future cases; however, it is not necessary to complete this case in order to complete and understand the cases in Chapters 3, 4, and 6. Completing this case will provide insight into the use of $\overline{X}$ and R charts in process improvement. The case can be worked by hand or with the software provided.

PART 1

Figure C5.2.1 provides the details of a bracket assembly to hold a strut on an automobile in place. Welded to the auto body frame, the bracket cups the strut and secures it to the frame via a single bolt with a lock washer. Proper alignment is necessary for both smooth installation during assembly and future performance. For mounting purposes the left-side hole, A, must be aligned on center with the right-side hole, B. If the holes are centered directly opposite each other in perfect alignment, then the angle between hole centers will measure 0°. As the flowchart in Figure C5.2.2 shows, the bracket is created by passing coils of flat steel through a series of progressive dies. As

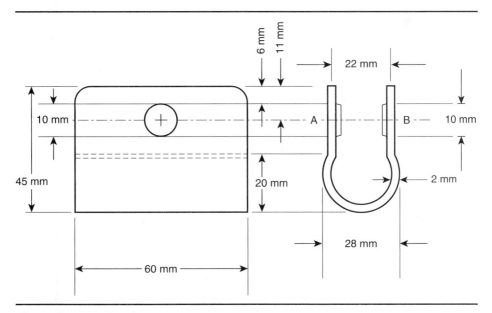

Figure C5.2.1   Bracket

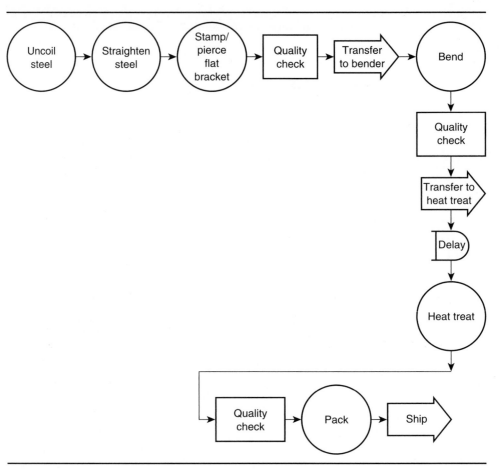

Figure C5.2.2   Flowchart of Bracket Fabrication Process

the steel moves through the press, the bracket is stamped, pierced, and finally bent into the appropriate shape.

Recently customers have been complaining about having difficulty securing the bracket closed with the bolt and lock washer. The bolts have been difficult to slide through the holes and then tighten. Assemblers complain of stripped bolts and snug fittings. Unsure of where the problem is, WP Inc.'s management assembles a team consisting of representatives from process engineering, materials engineering, product design, and manufacturing.

Through the use of several cause-and-effect diagrams, the team determines that the most likely cause of the problems experienced by the customer is the alignment of the holes. At some stage in the formation process, the holes end up off center. To confirm their suspicions, during the next production run, the bending press operator takes 20 subgroups of size 5 and measures the angle between the centers of the holes for each sample (Figure C5.2.3). The specification for the angle between insert hole A and

Subgroup / Sample	1	2	3	4	5	6	7	8	9	10	11	12	13	14	15
1	0.31	0.27	0.30	0.30	0.25	0.18	0.26	0.15	0.30	0.31	0.18	0.22	0.19	0.14	0.29
2	0.29	0.23	0.30	0.20	0.20	0.26	0.27	0.21	0.24	0.25	0.16	0.30	0.28	0.27	0.23
3	0.30	0.31	0.28	0.21	0.19	0.18	0.12	0.24	0.26	0.25	0.21	0.21	0.26	0.25	0.27
4	0.28	0.23	0.24	0.23	0.26	0.24	0.20	0.27	0.27	0.28	0.29	0.24	0.29	0.28	0.24
5	0.23	0.29	0.32	0.25	0.25	0.17	0.23	0.30	0.26	0.25	0.27	0.26	0.24	0.16	0.23

Subgroup / Sample	16	17	18	19	20
1	0.22	0.32	0.33	0.20	0.24
2	0.24	0.27	0.30	0.17	0.28
3	0.22	0.28	0.22	0.26	0.15
4	0.30	0.19	0.26	0.31	0.27
5	0.30	0.31	0.26	0.24	0.19

Figure C5.2.3   Hole A, B Alignment; Amount Above (+) or Below (−) Nominal

insert hole B is 0.00° with a tolerance of ±0.30°. The values recorded in Figure C5.2.3 represent the amount above (or when a minus sign is present, below) the nominal value of 0.00°.

Assignment

Follow the steps outlined in the chapter and utilize the data to create a set of $\overline{X}$ and R charts. You will need to calculate the mean and range for each subgroup. Describe the performance of the process.

PART 2

Having $\overline{X}$ and R charts and the accompanying statistical information tells the team a lot about the hole-alignment characteristics. Using the problem-solving method described in Chapter 3 (and followed in Case Study 3.2), the team has determined that the fixture that holds the flat bracket in place during the bending operation needs to be replaced. One of the measures of performance that they created during step 4 of their problem-solving process is the percentage of the parts out of specification. Now that the fixture has been replaced with a better one, the team would like to determine whether or not changing the fixture improved the process by removing a root cause of hole misalignment.

Assignment

Utilize the data in Figure C5.2.4 to create another set of $\overline{X}$ and R charts. Has their change to the fixtures resulted in a process improvement? How do you know? How are they doing when you compare their measure of performance, percentage of the parts out of specification, both before and after the fixture is changed?

Subgroup / Sample	1	2	3	4	5	6	7	8	9	10	11	12	13	14	15
1	0.03	0.06	0.06	0.03	−0.04	−0.02	−0.05	0.06	0.00	−0.02	−0.02	0.06	0.07	0.10	0.02
2	0.08	0.08	0.08	0.00	−0.07	0.06	−0.07	0.03	0.06	−0.01	0.06	0.02	−0.04	0.05	−0.05
3	−0.03	−0.01	0.05	0.05	0.00	0.02	0.11	0.04	0.02	0.00	−0.02	−0.01	0.08	0.03	0.04
4	0.07	0.08	−0.03	−0.01	−0.01	0.12	−0.03	0.03	−0.02	−0.10	0.02	−0.02	0.01	0.04	0.05
5	−0.02	0.02	0.03	0.07	−0.01	−0.07	0.03	0.01	0.00	−0.04	0.09	0.03	−0.04	0.06	−0.05

Subgroup / Sample	16	17	18	19	20
1	−0.05	−0.06	−0.04	−0.06	−0.01
2	0.00	−0.02	−0.02	0.00	0.02
3	0.06	0.04	−0.01	0.00	0.05
4	−0.02	0.07	0.03	0.03	0.04
5	−0.01	−0.04	−0.02	0.04	0.03

Figure C5.2.4 Hole A, B Alignment Following Process Improvement; Amount Above (+) or Below (−) Nominal

CASE STUDY 5.3
Sample-Size Considerations

PART 1

WT Corporation manufactures crankshafts for 2-L automotive engines. In order to attach a crankshaft to a flywheel, six holes are drilled in the flange end of the crankshaft. These holes are to be drilled 0.3750 ($\frac{3}{8}$) inch in diameter. The holes are not threaded and go all the way through the flange.

All six holes are drilled simultaneously. Every hour, the operator inspects four cranks resulting from four consecutive cycles of the drill press. All six holes on each of four crankshafts are measured and the values are recorded. The values are provided in Figure C5.3.1.

HOUR 1

Hole	Crank			
	1	2	3	4
1	3751	3752	3750	3750
2	3752	3751	3750	3752
3	3747	3752	3752	3749
4	3745	3745	3741	3745
5	3752	3751	3750	3752
6	3753	3750	3752	3750
X̄-bar	3750	3750	3749	3750
Range	8	7	11	7

HOUR 2

Hole	Crank			
	1	2	3	4
1	3750	3751	3752	3753
2	3749	3752	3754	3752
3	3748	3748	3753	3751
4	3745	3744	3745	3746
5	3750	3754	3753	3750
6	3751	3750	3752	3753
	3749	3750	3752	3751
	6	10	9	7

HOUR 3

Hole	Crank			
	1	2	3	4
1	3751	3749	3752	3753
2	3748	3752	3751	3753
3	3749	3749	3753	3752
4	3745	3744	3744	3743
5	3750	3751	3752	3750
6	3752	3749	3750	3753

HOUR 4

Hole	Crank			
	1	2	3	4
1	3751	3753	3752	3750
2	3750	3751	3751	3751
3	3749	3750	3751	3752
4	3741	3745	3744	3745
5	3752	3755	3751	3750
6	3753	3752	3754	3753

Figure C5.3.1   Crankshaft Measurements

(continued)

HOUR 5		Crank		
Hole	1	2	3	4
1	3751	3752	3754	3753
2	3754	3750	3751	3752
3	3752	3753	3752	3751
4	3745	3746	3747	3746
5	3751	3751	3753	3754
6	3750	3752	3753	3751

HOUR 6		Crank		
Hole	1	2	3	4
1	3752	3750	3751	3750
2	3751	3750	3752	3750
3	3753	3750	3753	3750
4	3744	3745	3746	3744
5	3751	3750	3751	3751
6	3750	3751	3750	3750

HOUR 7		Crank		
Hole	1	2	3	4
1	3751	3749	3751	3750
2	3752	3750	3754	3751
3	3753	3750	3752	3750
4	3744	3742	3754	3745
5	3750	3750	3750	3750
6	3751	3749	3751	3750

HOUR 8		Crank		
Hole	1	2	3	4
1	3752	3751	3753	3750
2	3751	3752	3753	3750
3	3753	3753	3750	3751
4	3744	3746	3745	3744
5	3751	3751	3752	3750
6	3750	3750	3752	3750

HOUR 9		Crank		
Hole	1	2	3	4
1	3750	3752	3751	3750
2	3751	3750	3751	3750
3	3752	3750	3750	3749
4	3741	3742	3740	3742
5	3751	3752	3750	3750
6	3752	3754	3750	3754

HOUR 10		Crank		
Hole	1	2	3	4
1	3750	3752	3751	3750
2	3750	3751	3752	3750
3	3750	3752	3751	3750
4	3745	3744	3746	3745
5	3750	3752	3752	3751
6	3750	3751	3752	3751

HOUR 11		Crank		
Hole	1	2	3	4
1	3750	3750	3751	3750
2	3750	3749	3751	3750
3	3751	3752	3750	3751
4	3742	3744	3743	3744
5	3750	3750	3751	3752
6	3750	3749	3750	3751

HOUR 12		Crank		
Hole	1	2	3	4
1	3750	3750	3749	3750
2	3750	3751	3750	3749
3	3750	3750	3751	3751
4	3741	3746	3745	3744
5	3751	3750	3749	3750
6	3750	3750	3751	3750

Figure C5.3.1 (continued)

 Assignment

Following the example set with the first two subgroups, use the data in Figure C5.3.1 to calculate $\overline{X}$ and R values based on the crank. Make $\overline{X}$ and R charts using the data. Interpret the control charts.

PART 2

Based on the $\overline{X}$ and R charts, the process appears to be performing smoothly. Two-thirds of the points are near the centerline, and there are no patterns or points out of control.

After shipping this group of crankshafts, you receive a call from your customer. They are very disturbed. Apparently the crankshafts are not of the quality expected. The customer feels that the hole diameters on each crank are not consistent. You point out that the process is under control, as verified by the control charts. In response, your customer suggests that you take another look at the data.

 Assignment

Referring to the sections in Chapter 5 discussing variation and choosing a rational subgroup size to be sampled, what information is being provided by the control charts? How were the averages arrived at? What data were combined? What information is the R chart providing?

PART 3

After taking a close look at how the data are organized, you should have discovered that the average is based on summing up the diameters for all six holes on the crank. The average is the average value of the diameter of all the holes on one particular crank. The cycle-to-cycle or crank-to-crank differences can be monitored by comparing one $\overline{X}$ value with another. If the data are separated into the hours in which they were produced, then the hour-to-hour differences can be seen. Both measurements are between-subgroup measurements.

To study within-subgroup measurements, the range chart is used. The range chart displays the variation present between the different hole diameters for a single crank. Reexamine the charts. Discuss the range chart in light of this information. What does the range tell you about the variation present in the average values?

 Assignment

Since the study of the data from this point of view has not yielded an answer to the customer's concerns, perhaps it would be beneficial to determine: What question are we trying to answer? What aspect of product performance is important to the customer?

PART 4

In an earlier discussion, the customer mentioned that the hole diameters on each crank are not consistent. Although the range chart reveals that significant within-crank variation is present, the charts you created do not clearly show the variation caused by each individual drill. The data combine information from six holes, which are drilled simultaneously. The subgroups in Figure C5.3.1 have been arranged to study the variation present in each crank, not the variation present in each individual drill. To study crank-to-crank and hole-to-hole differences between subgroups, the hole-size data must be reorganized.

 Assignment

Using Figure C5.3.2 and the first hour's calculations as a guide, re-create the control charts. Interpret the between-subgroup and within-subgroup variation present.

HOUR 1

Hole	1	2	3	4	AVE	R
1	3751	3752	3750	3750	3751	2
2	3752	3751	3750	3752	3751	2
3	3747	3752	3752	3749	3750	5
4	3745	3745	3741	3745	3744	4
5	3752	3751	3750	3752	3751	2
6	3753	3750	3752	3750	3751	3

(Crank columns: 1, 2, 3, 4)

HOUR 2

Hole	1	2	3	4
1	3750	3751	3752	3753
2	3749	3752	3754	3752
3	3748	3748	3753	3751
4	3745	3744	3745	3746
5	3750	3754	3753	3750
6	3751	3750	3752	3753

(Crank columns: 1, 2, 3, 4)

HOUR 3

Hole	1	2	3	4
1	3751	3749	3752	3753
2	3748	3752	3751	3753
3	3749	3749	3753	3752
4	3745	3744	3744	3743
5	3750	3751	3752	3750
6	3752	3749	3750	3753

(Crank columns: 1, 2, 3, 4)

HOUR 4

Hole	1	2	3	4
1	3751	3753	3752	3750
2	3750	3751	3751	3751
3	3749	3750	3751	3752
4	3741	3745	3744	3745
5	3752	3755	3751	3750
6	3753	3752	3754	3753

(Crank columns: 1, 2, 3, 4)

HOUR 5

Hole	1	2	3	4
1	3751	3752	3754	3753
2	3754	3750	3751	3752
3	3752	3753	3752	3751
4	3745	3746	3747	3746
5	3751	3751	3753	3754
6	3750	3752	3753	3751

(Crank columns: 1, 2, 3, 4)

HOUR 6

Hole	1	2	3	4
1	3752	3750	3751	3750
2	3751	3750	3752	3750
3	3753	3750	3753	3750
4	3744	3745	3746	3744
5	3751	3750	3751	3751
6	3750	3751	3750	3750

(Crank columns: 1, 2, 3, 4)

Figure C5.3.2   Crankshaft Measurements, by Crank   (continued)

HOUR 7

	Crank			
Hole	1	2	3	4
1	3751	3749	3751	3750
2	3752	3750	3754	3751
3	3753	3750	3752	3750
4	3744	3742	3745	3745
5	3750	3750	3750	3750
6	3751	3749	3751	3750

HOUR 8

	Crank			
Hole	1	2	3	4
1	3752	3751	3753	3750
2	3751	3752	3753	3750
3	3753	3753	3750	3751
4	3744	3746	3745	3744
5	3751	3751	3752	3750
6	3750	3750	3752	3750

HOUR 9

	Crank			
Hole	1	2	3	4
1	3750	3752	3751	3750
2	3751	3750	3751	3750
3	3752	3750	3750	3749
4	3741	3742	3740	3742
5	3751	3752	3750	3750
6	3752	3754	3750	3754

HOUR 10

	Crank			
Hole	1	2	3	4
1	3750	3752	3751	3750
2	3750	3751	3752	3750
3	3750	3752	3751	3750
4	3745	3744	3746	3745
5	3750	3752	3752	3751
6	3750	3751	3752	3751

HOUR 11

	Crank			
Hole	1	2	3	4
1	3750	3750	3751	3750
2	3750	3749	3751	3750
3	3751	3752	3750	3751
4	3742	3744	3743	3744
5	3750	3750	3751	3752
6	3750	3749	3750	3751

HOUR 12

	Crank			
Hole	1	2	3	4
1	3750	3750	3749	3750
2	3750	3751	3750	3749
3	3750	3750	3751	3751
4	3741	3746	3745	3744
5	3751	3750	3749	3750
6	3750	3750	3751	3750

Figure C5.3.2   *(continued)*

PART 5

An investigation of the new $\overline{X}$ and R charts reveals that there are significant differences between the sizes of holes being drilled on the crank. Unlike the first charts created with the same data, these charts display a definite pattern. The differences between drill bits can now easily be seen. Hole 4 is consistently being drilled undersize, creating a very noticeable pattern on the $\overline{X}$ chart. It should also be noted that based on a nominal dimension of 0.3750, the other holes are being drilled slightly oversized.

Rearranging the data has clarified the between-subgroup differences that can now be seen in the $\overline{X}$ chart. By focusing on the aspect of the product critical to the customer, the control chart more clearly answers the customer's questions. In this case, the customer is interested in whether or not systematic differences exist between the holes drilled. Investigated from this point of view, we can now understand why the customer is upset. The inconsistent hole sizes cause assembly problems, making it difficult to assemble the cranks and flywheels. Oversize and undersize holes lead to fit problems. To improve the process, each of the drills will need to be adjusted to bring the averages closer to the nominal dimension of 0.3750 inch.

The customer is also interested in whether or not there are cycle-to-cycle differences. In other words, are each of the six individual drills drilling holes of consistent size from cycle to cycle? These within-subgroup differences can be seen on the R chart. The variation present in the hole sizes is relatively consistent. Further reductions in the variation present in the process will decrease assembly difficulties later.

Assignment

Creating control charts separating data for each drill bit will enhance understanding of the process by increasing the sensitivity of the charts. When the data are separated into six charts, the users of the charts will be able to determine quickly how each drill is operating. Placing data for all six drill bits on different charts unclutters the data and more clearly shows the process centering and variation present for each drill.

Reuse your calculations of $\overline{X}$ and R from Figure C5.3.2 to create and interpret six separate control charts. Using the same values, separate them according to which drill they are from. Describe the process centering and spread present for each drill.

6

Process Capability

▪ *Learning Opportunities:*

1. To gain an understanding of the relationship between individual values and their averages
2. To understand the difference between specification limits and control limits
3. To learn to calculate and interpret the process capability indices: C_p, C_r, and C_{pk} ▪

Crystal Ball

*I*t certainly would be interesting to have some insight into the future. We would know which questions were to be on a test, whether a traffic jam existed on the road we wished to take, which investments would make us the greatest return on our money. When manufacturing a product or providing a service, decision makers would like to know if the product or service provided in the future is capable of meeting specifications. Control charts and their calculations, while they can't replace a crystal ball, can give those who use them insight into the capability of a process and what future production might be like.

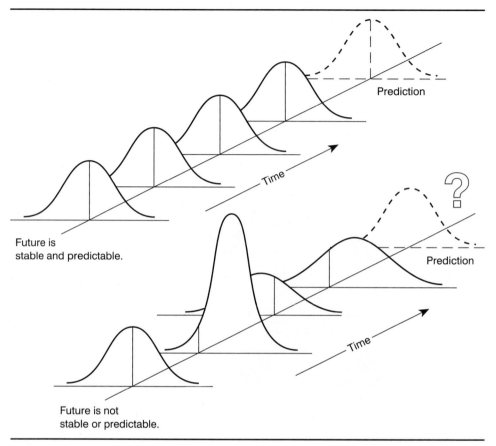

Figure 6.1   Future Predictions

Process capability refers to the ability of a process to produce products or provide services capable of meeting the specifications set by the customer or designer. As discussed in the last chapter, variation affects a process and may prevent the process from producing products or services that meet customer specifications. Reducing process variability and creating consistent quality increase the viability of predictions of future process performance (Figure 6.1). Knowing process capability gives insight into whether or not the process will be able to meet future demands placed on it.

We have all encountered limitations in process capability. Consider what happens when a student is given several major assignments from different classes that are all due on the same date. Since there are only so many hours in the day, the capability of the process (the student) will be severely affected by the overload of assignments. The student may choose to complete each of the assignments as best he can, resulting in a group of assignments of average work. Or the student may choose to perform superior work on one project and mediocre work on the remainder. Or the student may decide to turn some of the projects in late. Any number of combinations exist; however, completion of all of the assignments on the due date with perfect quality probably won't happen. The process is incapable of meeting the demands placed on it.

In industry, the concept is similar. A customer may ask for part tolerances so fine that the machines are not capable of producing to that level of exactness. In assembly, it is difficult to assemble products that vary from the high side of the specification limits to the low side of the specifications. An undersized part A may not mate correctly with an oversized part B.

Determining the process capability aids industry in meeting their customer demands. Manufacturers of products and providers of services can use process capability concepts to assist in decisions concerning product or process specifications, appropriate production methods, equipment to be used, and time commitments.

 REAL TOOLS FOR REAL LIFE

Process Capability

At RQM Inc., the manufacturing engineers are seeking the root cause of a problem involving the Model M automobile. Customers describe a banging noise when shifting gears. The sound occurs primarily when the transmission is shifted from reverse to drive. This problem is a nuisance problem for RQM's customers, affecting their perception of vehicle quality.

Through much investigation and experimentation, the engineers were able to isolate the sound as coming from the exhaust system hitting the heat shield underneath the car when shifting occurs. They evaluated whether or not the exhaust pipe clearance specifications were being met. Their investigation revealed that the clearance distance specifications of 31.0 $\pm$ 10 mm are being held; however, a significant portion of the vehicles measured had a distance of 21–22 mm, on the low side of the specification. They also noted that significant variation exists in the measurements (Figure 6.2) Because of their understanding of process capability and the relationship between samples and populations, the engineers realized that further study into the capability of this process is necessary.

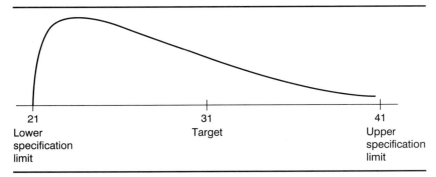

Figure 6.2   Real Tools for Real Life: Process Capability

INDIVIDUAL VALUES COMPARED WITH AVERAGES

Process capability is based on the performance of individual products or services against specifications. In quality assurance, samples are taken to study the process. Analysts use information from the samples to determine the behavior of individuals in

Table 6.1   Clutch Plate Thickness: Sums and Averages

						ΣX_i	$\overline{X}$	$\overline{R}$
Subgroup 1	0.0625	0.0626	0.0624	0.0625	0.0627	0.3127	0.0625	0.0003
Subgroup 2	0.0624	0.0623	0.0624	0.0626	0.0625	0.3122	0.0624	0.0003
Subgroup 3	0.0622	0.0625	0.0623	0.0625	0.0626	0.3121	0.0624	0.0004
Subgroup 4	0.0624	0.0623	0.0620	0.0623	0.0624	0.3114	0.0623	0.0004
Subgroup 5	0.0621	0.0621	0.0622	0.0625	0.0624	0.3113	0.0623	0.0004
Subgroup 6	0.0628	0.0626	0.0625	0.0626	0.0627	0.3132	0.0626	0.0003
Subgroup 7	0.0624	0.0627	0.0625	0.0624	0.0626	0.3126	0.0625	0.0003
Subgroup 8	0.0624	0.0625	0.0625	0.0626	0.0626	0.3126	0.0625	0.0002
Subgroup 9	0.0627	0.0628	0.0626	0.0625	0.0627	0.3133	0.0627	0.0003
Subgroup 10	0.0625	0.0626	0.0628	0.0626	0.0627	0.3132	0.0626	0.0003
Subgroup 11	0.0625	0.0624	0.0626	0.0626	0.0626	0.3127	0.0625	0.0002
Subgroup 12	0.0630	0.0628	0.0627	0.0625	0.0627	0.3134	0.0627	0.0005
Subgroup 13	0.0627	0.0626	0.0628	0.0627	0.0626	0.3137	0.0627	0.0002
Subgroup 14	0.0626	0.0626	0.0625	0.0626	0.0627	0.3130	0.0626	0.0002
Subgroup 15	0.0628	0.0627	0.0626	0.0625	0.0626	0.3132	0.0626	0.0003
Subgroup 16	0.0625	0.0626	0.0625	0.0628	0.0627	0.3131	0.0626	0.0003
Subgroup 17	0.0624	0.0626	0.0624	0.0625	0.0627	0.3126	0.0625	0.0003
Subgroup 18	0.0628	0.0627	0.0628	0.0626	0.0630	0.3139	0.0627	0.0004
Subgroup 19	0.0627	0.0626	0.0628	0.0625	0.0627	0.3133	0.0627	0.0003
Subgroup 20	0.0626	0.0625	0.0626	0.0625	0.0627	0.3129	0.0626	0.0002
Subgroup 21	0.0627	0.0626	0.0628	0.0625	0.0627	0.3133	0.0627	0.0003
Subgroup 22	0.0625	0.0626	0.0628	0.0625	0.0627	0.3131	0.0626	0.0003
Subgroup 23	0.0628	0.0626	0.0627	0.0630	0.0627	0.3138	0.0628	0.0004
Subgroup 24	0.0625	0.0631	0.0630	0.0628	0.0627	0.3141	0.0628	0.0006
Subgroup 25	0.0627	0.0630	0.0631	0.0628	0.0627	0.3143	0.0629	0.0004
Subgroup 26	0.0630	0.0628	0.0629	0.0628	0.0627	0.3142	0.0628	0.0003
Subgroup 27	0.0630	0.0628	0.0631	0.0628	0.0627	0.3144	0.0629	0.0004
Subgroup 28	0.0632	0.0632	0.0628	0.0631	0.0630	0.3153	0.0631	0.0004
Subgroup 29	0.0630	0.0628	0.0631	0.0632	0.0631	0.3152	0.0630	0.0004
Subgroup 30	0.0632	0.0631	0.0630	0.0628	0.0628	0.3149	0.0630	0.0004
						9.3981		

a process. To do this, the analyst needs an understanding of the relationship between individual values and their averages.

Subgroup sample averages are composed of individual values. Table 6.1 repeats the tally of individual and average values of clutch plate thickness data from Table 5.1. With this actual production line data, two frequency diagrams have been created in Figure 6.3. One frequency diagram is constructed of individual values; the other is made up of subgroup averages. Both distributions are approximately normal. The important difference to note is that individual values spread much more widely than their averages. When the two diagrams are compared, the averages are grouped closer to the center value than are the individual values, as described by the central limit theorem. Average values smooth out the highs and lows associated with individuals. This comparison will be important to keep in mind when comparing the behavior of averages and control limits with that of individual values and specification limits (Figure 6.4).

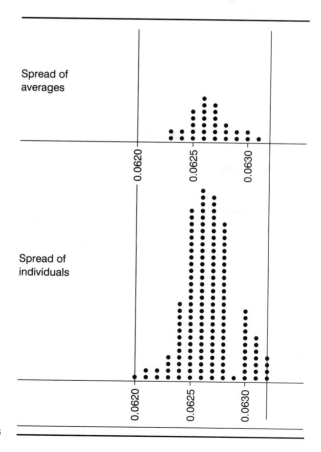

**Figure 6.3   Normal Curves
for Individuals and Averages**

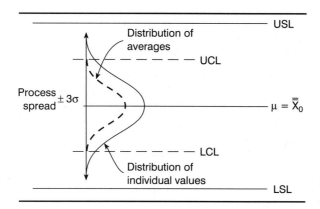

Figure 6.4   Comparison of the Spread of Individual Values with Averages

ESTIMATION OF POPULATION SIGMA FROM SAMPLE DATA

Sample values and their averages provide insight into the behavior of an entire population. The larger the sample size, n, the more representative the sample average, $\overline{X}$, is of the mean of the population, μ. In other words, $\overline{X}$ becomes a more reliable estimate of μ as the sample size is increased. The ability of $\overline{X}$ to approximate μ is measured by the expression $\sigma/\sqrt{n}$, the standard error of the mean. It is possible to estimate the spread of the population of individuals using the sample data. This formula shows the relationship between the population standard deviation (σ) and the standard deviation of the subgroup averages ($\sigma_{\overline{X}}$):

$$\sigma_{\overline{X}} = \frac{\sigma}{\sqrt{n}}$$

where

$\sigma_{\overline{X}}$ = standard deviation of subgroup averages
σ = population standard deviation
n = number of observations in each subgroup

The population standard deviation, σ, is determined by measuring the individuals. This necessitates measuring every value. To avoid complicated calculations, if the process can be assumed to be normal, the population standard deviation can be estimated from either the standard deviation associated with the sample standard deviation (s) or the range (R):

$$\hat{\sigma} = \frac{\overline{s}}{c_4} \quad \text{or} \quad \hat{\sigma} = \frac{\overline{R}}{d_2}$$

where

$\hat{\sigma}$ = estimate of population standard devation
$\overline{s}$ = sample standard deviation calculated from subgroup samples

$\overline{R}$ = average range of subgroups
c_4 as found in Appendix 2
d_2 as found in Appendix 2

Because of the estimators (c_4 and d_2), these two formulas will yield similar but not identical values for $\hat{\sigma}$. Dr. Shewhart confirmed that the standard deviation of subgroup sample means is the standard deviation of individual samples divided by the square root of the subgroup size. He did this by drawing, at random from a large bowl, numbered, metal lined, disk-shaped tags. He used this information to determine the estimators c_4 and d_2.

CONTROL LIMITS VERSUS SPECIFICATION LIMITS

A process is in control only when its process centering and the amount of variation present in the process remains constant over time. If both are constant, then the behavior of the process will be predictable. As discussed in Chapter 5, a process under control exhibits the following characteristics:

1. Two-thirds of the points are near the center value.
2. A few of the points are close to the center value.
3. The points float back and forth across the centerline.
4. The points are balanced (in roughly equal numbers) on both sides of the centerline.
5. There are no points beyond the control limits.
6. There are no patterns or trends on the chart.

It is important to note that a process in statistical control will not necessarily meet specifications as established by the customer. There is a difference between a process conforming to specifications and a process performing within statistical control. Control limits and specification limits are two separate concepts, which may, at first, seem difficult to separate. The importance of understanding the difference between the two cannot be overestimated.

Established during the design process or from customer requests, specifications communicate what the customers expect, want, or need from the process. Specifications can be considered the voice of the customer.

Control limits are the voice of the process. The centerline on the $\overline{X}$ chart represents process centering. The R and s chart limits represent the amount of variation present in the process. Control limits are a prediction of the variation that the process will exhibit in the near future. The difference between specifications and control limits is that specifications relay wishes and control limits tell of reality.

Occasionally, creators of control charts inappropriately place specification limits on control charts. Processes are unaware of specifications, they perform to the best of their capabilities. Unfortunately, specification limits on control charts encourage users to adjust the process on the basis of them instead of on the true limits of the process, the control limits. The resulting miscued changes can potentially disrupt the process and increase process variation.

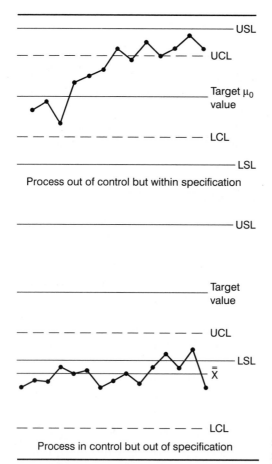

Figure 6.5   For Explanation Purposes Only, These Charts Show Control Limits versus Specification Limits

For explanatory purposes, both control limits and specification limits appear on the charts in Figure 6.5, a practice not to be followed in industry. The variation in Figure 6.5, top chart, exceeds control limits marking the expected process variation but not the specification limits. While the process is out of control, for the time being the customer's needs are being met. The process in Figure 6.5, bottom chart is under control and within the control limits, but the specification limits do not correspond with the control limits. This situation reveals that the process is performing to the best of its abilities, but not well enough to meet the specifications set by the customer or designer. In this case (Figure 6.5, bottom chart), it may be possible to shift the process centering to meet the specifications.

As we learned in Chapter 4 during the discussion of the central limit theorem and in Figure 6.3, the spread of individual values is wider than the spread of the averages. For this reason, control limits cannot be compared directly with specification limits. An $\overline{X}$ chart does not reflect how widely the individual values composing the plotted averages spread. This is one reason why an R or s chart is always used in conjunction with the $\overline{X}$ chart. The spread of the individual data can be seen only by observing

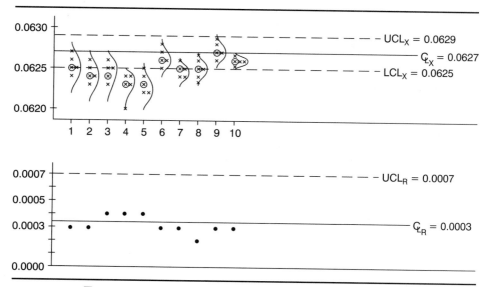

Figure 6.6   X̄ and R Chart Showing Averages and Individuals

what is happening on the R or s chart. If the values on the R or s chart are large, then the variation associated with the average is large. Figure 6.6 shows a control chart created using the concepts from Chapter 5 and the values in Table 6.1. The X̄'s are circled. Individual values shown as X's are also plotted on this chart. Note where the individual values fall in relation to the control limits established for the process. The individuals spread more widely than the averages and follow the pattern established by the R chart. Studying the R chart in conjunction with the X̄ chart can significantly increase the understanding of how the process is performing.

EXAMPLE 6.1   Using the X̄ and R Charts to Assess the Process

Engineers in a materials testing lab have been studying the results of a tensile strength test. To better understand the process performance and the spread of the individual values that compose the averages, they have overlaid the R chart pattern on the X̄ chart. To do this easily, they divided the X̄ chart into three sections (Figure 6.7) chosen on the basis of how the data on the X̄ chart appear to have grouped. X̄ values in section A are centered at the mean and are very similar. In section B, the X̄ values are above the mean and more spread out. Section C values have a slight downward trend.

Studying the sections on the R chart reveals that the spread of the data is changing (Figure 6.7). The values in section A have an average amount of variation, denoted by the normal curve corresponding to section A. Variation increases in section B, resulting in a much broader spread on the normal curve (B). The significant decrease in variation in section C is shown by the narrow, peaked distribution. The R chart describes the spread of the individuals on the X̄ chart. **Q**

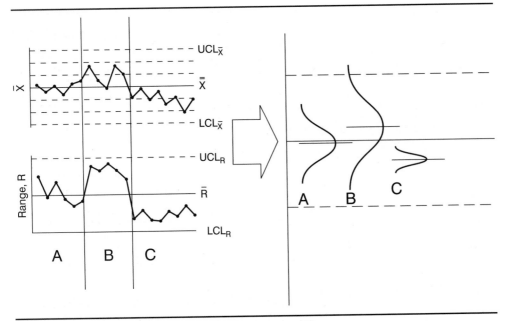

Figure 6.7   Overlaying the R Chart Pattern on the X̄ Chart

THE 6σ SPREAD VERSUS SPECIFICATION LIMITS

The spread of the individuals in a process, 6σ, is the measure used to compare the realities of production with the desires of the customers. The process standard deviation is based on either s or R from control chart data:

$$\hat{\sigma} = \frac{\bar{s}}{c_4} \quad \text{or} \quad \hat{\sigma} = \frac{\bar{R}}{d_2}$$

where

> $\hat{\sigma}$ = estimate of population standard deviation
> $\bar{s}$ = sample standard deviation calculated from process
> $\bar{R}$ = average range of subgroups calculated from process
> c_4 as found in Appendix 2
> d_2 as found in Appendix 2

Remember, because of the estimators (c_4 and d_2), these two formulas will yield similar but not identical values for $\hat{\sigma}$.

Specification limits, the allowable spread of the individuals, are compared with the 6σ spread of the process to determine how capable the process is of meeting the specifications. Three different situations can exist when specifications and 6σ are compared: (1) the 6σ process spread can be less than the spread of the specification limits; (2) the 6σ process spread can be equal to the spread of the specification limits; (3) the 6σ process spread can be greater than the spread of the specification limits.

Case I: $6\sigma <$ USL − LSL   This is the most desirable case. Figure 6.8 illustrates this relationship. The control limits have been placed on the diagram, as well as the spread

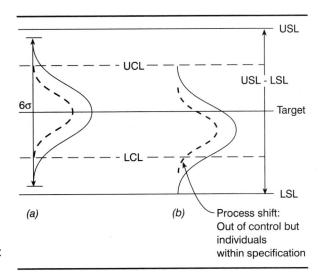

**Figure 6.8   Case I: 6σ <
USL − LSL**

of the process averages (dotted line). The 6σ spread of the process individuals is shown by the solid line. As expected, the spread of the individual values is greater than the spread of the averages; however, the values are still within the specification limits. The 6σ spread of the individuals is less than the spread of the specifications. This allows for more room for process shifts while staying within the specifications. Notice that even if the process drifts out of control (Figure 6.8b), the change must be dramatic before the parts are considered out of specification.

Case II: 6σ = USL − LSL In this situation, 6σ is equal to the tolerance (Figure 6.9a). As long as the process remains in control and centered, with no change in

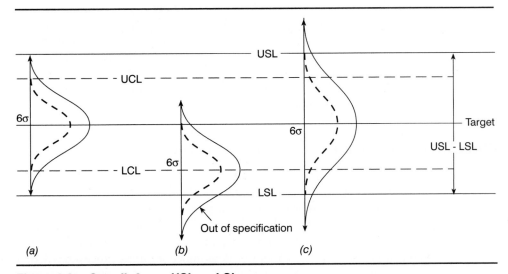

Figure 6.9   Case II: 6σ = USL − LSL

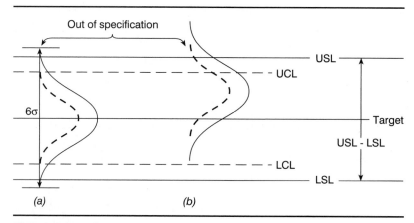

Figure 6.10   Case III: 6σ > USL − LSL

process variation, the parts produced will be within specification. However, a shift in the process mean (Figure 6.9*b*) will result in the production of parts that are out of specification. An increase in the variation present in the process also creates an out-of-specification situation (Figure 6.9*c*).

Case III: 6σ > USL − LSL   Any time that the 6σ spread is greater than the tolerance spread, an undesirable situation exists (Figure 6.10*a*). Even though the process is exhibiting only natural patterns of variation, it is incapable of meeting the specifications set by the customer. To correct this problem, management intervention will be necessary in order to change the process to decrease the variation or to recenter the process if necessary. The capability of the process cannot be improved without changing the existing process. To achieve a substantial reduction in the standard deviation or spread of the data, management will have to authorize the utilization of different materials, the overhaul of the machine, the purchase of a new machine, the retraining of the operator, or other significant changes to the process. Other, less desirable approaches to dealing with this problem are to perform 100 percent inspection on the product, increase the specification limits, or shift the process average so that all of the nonconforming products occur at one end of the distribution (Figure 6.10*b*). In certain cases, shifting the process average can eliminate scrap and increase the amount of rework, thus saving scrap costs by increasing rework costs.

CALCULATING PROCESS CAPABILITY INDICES

Process capability indices are mathematical ratios that quantify the ability of a process to produce products within the specifications. The capability indices compare the spread of the individuals created by the process with the specification limits set by the customer or designer. The 6σ spread of the individuals can be calculated for a new process that has not produced a significant number of parts or for a process currently in operation. In either case, a true 6σ value cannot be determined until the process has achieved stability, as described by the $\overline{X}$ and R charts or $\overline{X}$ and s charts. If the process is not stable, the calculated values may or may not be representative of the true process capability.

Calculating $6\hat{\sigma}$

Assuming the process is under statistical control, we use the following method to calculate $6\hat{\sigma}$ of a new process:

1. Take at least 20 subgroups of sample size 4 for a total of 80 measurements.
2. Calculate the sample standard deviation, s_i, for each subgroup.
3. Calculate the average sample standard deviation, $\bar{s}$:

$$\bar{s} = \frac{\sum_{i=1}^{m} s_i}{m}$$

where

$$s_i = \text{standard deviation for each subgroup}$$
$$m = \text{number of subgroups}$$

4. Calculate the estimate of the population standard deviation:

$$\hat{\sigma} = \frac{\bar{s}}{c_4}$$

where c_4 is obtained from Appendix 2.
5. Multiply the population standard deviation by 6.

EXAMPLE 6.2 Printer Assembly: Calculating $6\hat{\sigma}$

The individuals monitoring the process making roller shafts for printers wish to calculate $6\hat{\sigma}$. They intend to use the data gathered during a recent production run (Table 6.2). They have 21 subgroups of sample size 5 for a total of 105 measurements, more than the 80 recommended.

They calculate the sample standard deviation, s_i, for each subgroup (Table 6.2). From these values they calculate the average sample standard deviation, $\bar{s}$:

$$\bar{s} = \frac{\sum_{i=1}^{m} s_i}{m} = \frac{0.031 + 0.029 + \cdots + 0.015}{21}$$

$$= \frac{0.414}{21} = 0.02$$

The next step involves calculating the estimate of the population standard deviation:

$$\hat{\sigma} = \frac{\bar{s}}{c_4} = \frac{0.02}{0.9400} = 0.021$$

The value of c_4 is obtained from Appendix 2 and is based on a sample size of 5.

Table 6.2 $\overline{X}$ and s Values of Roller Shafts

Subgroup Number	X_1					$\overline{X}$	s
1	11.950	12.000	12.030	11.980	12.010	11.994	0.031
2	12.030	12.020	11.960	12.000	11.980	11.998	0.029
3	12.010	12.000	11.970	11.980	12.000	11.992	0.016
4	11.970	11.980	12.000	12.030	11.990	11.994	0.023
5	12.000	12.010	12.020	12.030	12.020	12.016	0.011
6	11.980	11.980	12.000	12.010	11.990	11.992	0.013
7	12.000	12.010	12.030	12.000	11.980	12.004	0.018
8	12.000	12.010	12.040	12.000	12.020	12.014	0.017
9	12.000	12.020	11.960	12.000	11.980	11.992	0.023
10	12.020	12.000	11.970	12.050	12.000	12.008	0.030
11	11.980	11.970	11.960	11.950	12.000	11.972	0.019
12	11.920	11.950	11.920	11.940	11.960	11.938	0.018
13	11.980	11.930	11.940	11.950	11.960	11.952	0.019
14	11.990	11.930	11.940	11.950	11.960	11.954	0.023
15	12.000	11.980	11.990	11.950	11.930	11.970	0.029
16	12.000	11.980	11.970	11.960	11.990	11.980	0.016
17	12.020	11.980	11.970	11.980	11.990	11.988	0.019
18	12.000	12.010	12.020	12.010	11.990	12.006	0.011
19	11.970	12.030	12.000	12.010	11.990	12.000	0.022
20	11.990	12.010	12.020	12.000	12.010	12.006	0.011
21	12.000	11.980	11.990	11.990	12.020	11.996	0.015

As the final step they multiply the population standard deviation by 6:

$$6\hat{\sigma} = 6(0.021) = 0.126$$

This value can be compared with the spread of the specifications to determine how the individual products produced by the process compare with the specifications set by the designer.

A second method of calculating $6\hat{\sigma}$ is to use the data from a control chart. Once again, it is assumed that the process is under statistical control, with no unusual patterns of variation.

1. Take the past 20 subgroups, sample size of 4 or more.
2. Calculate the range, R, for each subgroup.
3. Calculate the average range, $\overline{R}$:

$$\overline{R} = \frac{\sum\limits_{i=1}^{m} R_i}{m}$$

where

$$R_i = \text{individual range values for the subgroups}$$
$$m = \text{number of subgroups}$$

4. Calculate the estimate of the population standard deviation, $\hat{\sigma}$:

$$\hat{\sigma} = \frac{\overline{R}}{d_2}$$

where d_2 is obtained from Appendix 2.

5. Multiply the population standard deviation by 6.

Using more than 20 subgroups will improve the accuracy of the calculations.

EXAMPLE 6.3   Clutch Plate: Calculating 6σ

The engineers use the data in Table 6.1 to calculate $6\hat{\sigma}$ for the clutch plate. Thirty subgroups of sample size 5 and their ranges are used to calculate the average range, $\overline{R}$:

$$\overline{R} = \frac{\sum\limits_{i=1}^{m} R_i}{m} = \frac{0.0003 + 0.0003 + \cdots + 0.0004}{21}$$

$$\overline{R} = 0.0003$$

Next, the engineers calculate the estimate of the population standard deviation, $\hat{\sigma}$:

$$\hat{\sigma} = \frac{\overline{R}}{d_2} = \frac{0.0003}{2.326} = 0.0001$$

Using a sample size of 5, they take the value for d_2 from Appendix 2.
To determine $6\hat{\sigma}$, they multiply the population standard deviation by 6:

$$6\hat{\sigma} = 6(0.0001) = 0.0006$$

They now compare this value with the specification limits to determine how well the process is performing.

The Capability Index

Once calculated, the σ values can be used to determine several indices related to process capability. The **capability index** C_p is the ratio of tolerance (USL − LSL) and $6\hat{\sigma}$:

$$C_p = \frac{\text{USL} - \text{LSL}}{6\hat{\sigma}}$$

where

$$C_p = \text{capability index}$$
$$\text{USL} - \text{LSL} = \text{upper specification limit} - \text{lower specification limit, or tolerance}$$

The capability index is interpreted as follows: If the capability index is larger than 1.00, a Case I situation exists (Figure 6.8*a*). This is desirable. The greater this value, the better. If the capability index is equal to 1.00, then a Case II situation exists (Figure 6.9*a*). This is not optimal, but it is feasible. If the capability index is less than 1.00, then a Case III situation exists (Figure 6.10*a*). Values of less than 1 are undesirable and reflect the process's inability to meet the specifications.

EXAMPLE 6.4   Clutch Plate: Finding the Capability Index

The engineers working with the clutch plate in Example 6.3 are working with specification limits of 0.0625 ± 0.0003. The upper specification limit is 0.0628 and the lower specification limit is 0.0622. They now calculate C_p:

$$C_p = \frac{USL - LSL}{6\hat{\sigma}} = \frac{0.0628 - 0.0622}{0.0006}$$

$$= 1.0$$

A value of 1.0 means that the process is just capable of meeting the demands placed on it by the customer's specifications. To be on the safe side, changes will need to occur to improve the process performance.   **Q**

EXAMPLE 6.5   Printer Assembly: Finding the Capability Index

Those monitoring the roller shaft process in Example 6.2 want to calculate its C_p. They use specification limits of USL = 12.05, LSL = 11.95:

$$C_p = \frac{USL - LSL}{6\hat{\sigma}} = \frac{12.05 - 11.95}{0.126}$$

$$= 0.794$$

This process is not capable of meeting the demands placed on it. Improvements will need to take place to meet the customer's expectations.   **Q**

The Capability Ratio

Another indicator of process capability is called the ***capability ratio.*** This ratio is similar to the capability index, though it reverses the numerator and the denominator. It is defined as

$$C_r = \frac{6\hat{\sigma}}{USL - LSL}$$

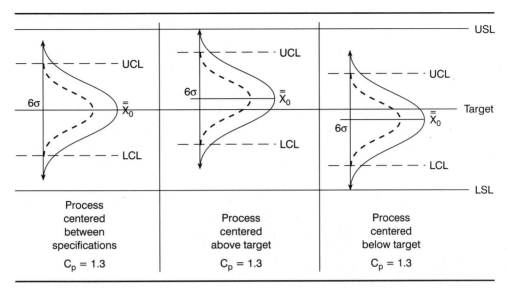

Figure 6.11   Shifts in Process Centering

A capability ratio less than 1 is the most desirable situation. The larger the ratio, the less capable the process is of meeting specifications. Be aware that it is easy to confuse the two indices. The most commonly used index is the capability index.

C_{pk}

The centering of the process is shown by C_{pk}. As shown by the Taguchi loss function described in Chapter 2, a process operating in the center of the specifications set by the designer is usually more desirable than one that is consistently producing parts to the high or low side of the specification limits. In Figure 6.11, all three distributions have the same C_p index value of 1.3. Though each of these processes has the same capability index, they represent three different scenarios. In the first situation the process is centered as well as capable. In the second, a further upward shift in the process would result in an out-of-specification situation. The reverse holds true in the third situation. C_p and C_r do not take into account the centering of the process. *The ratio that reflects how the process is performing in terms of a nominal, center, or target value is C_{pk}.* C_{pk} can be calculated using the following formula:

$$C_{pk} = \frac{Z(\min)}{3}$$

where Z(min) is the smaller of

$$Z(USL) = \frac{USL - \overline{X}}{\hat{\sigma}}$$

$$\text{or } Z(LSL) = \frac{\overline{X} - LSL}{\hat{\sigma}}$$

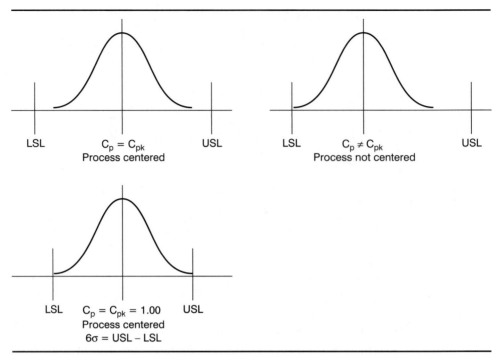

Figure 6.12   Process Centering: C_p versus C_{pk}

When $C_{pk} = C_p$ the process is centered. Figure 6.12 illustrates C_p and C_{pk} values for a process that is centered and one that is off center. The relationships between C_p and C_{pk} are as follows:

1. When C_p has a value of 1.0 or greater, the process is producing product capable of meeting specifications.
2. The C_p value does not reflect process centering.
3. When the process is centered, $C_p = C_{pk}$.
4. C_{pk} is always less than or equal to C_p.
5. When C_p is greater than or equal to 1.0 and C_{pk} has a value of 1.00 or more, it indicates the process is producing product that conforms to specifications.
6. When C_{pk} has a value less than 1.00, it indicates the process is producing product that does not conform to specifications.
7. A C_p value of less than 1.00 indicates that the process is not capable.
8. A C_{pk} value of zero indicates the process average is equal to one of the specification limits.
9. A negative C_{pk} value indicates that the average is outside the specification limits.

EXAMPLE 6.6   Printer Assembly: Finding C_{pk}

Determine the C_{pk} for the roller shaft values in Example 6.2. The average, $\overline{X}$, is equal to 11.990.

$$C_{pk} = \frac{Z(min)}{3}$$

where

$$Z(min) = \text{smaller of } \frac{(USL - \overline{X})}{\hat{\sigma}} \text{ or } \frac{(\overline{X} - LSL)}{\hat{\sigma}}$$

$$Z(USL) = \frac{(12.050 - 11.990)}{0.021} = 2.857$$

$$Z(LSL) = \frac{(11.990 - 11.950)}{0.021} = 1.905$$

$$C_{pk} = \frac{1.905}{3} = 0.635$$

A C_{pk} value of less than 1 means that the process is not capable. Because the C_p value (0.794, from Example 6.6) and the C_{pk} value (0.635) are not equal, the process is not centered between the specification limits.

EXAMPLE 6.7   Clutch Plate: Finding C_{pk}

To determine the C_{pk} for the clutch plate:

$$C_{pk} = \frac{Z(min)}{3} = \frac{1}{3} = 0.3333$$

where

$$Z(USL) = \frac{0.0628 - 0.0627}{0.0001} = 1$$

$$Z(LSL) = \frac{0.0627 - 0.0622}{0.0001} = 5$$

The C_{pk} value of 0.3333 is less than 1 and not equal to $C_p = 1$ from Example 6.4. The process is not centered between the specification limits.

REAL TOOLS FOR REAL LIFE

Is the Process Capable?

The production of integrated circuits by etching them onto silicon wafers requires silicon wafers of consistent thickness. Recall from the Real Tools for Real Life feature from Chapter 5: Monitoring Silicon Wafer Thickness, that recent quality

					$\overline{X}$	R
Subgroup 1	0.2500	0.2510	0.2490	0.2500	0.2500	0.002
Subgroup 2	0.2510	0.2490	0.2490	0.2520	0.2503	0.003
Subgroup 3	0.2510	0.2490	0.2510	0.2480	0.2498	0.003
Subgroup 4	0.2490	0.2470	0.2520	0.2480	0.2490	0.005
Subgroup 5	0.2500	0.2470	0.2500	0.2520	0.2498	0.005
Subgroup 6	0.2510	0.2520	0.2490	0.2510	0.2508	0.003
Subgroup 7	0.2510	0.2480	0.2500	0.2500	0.2498	0.003
Subgroup 8	0.2500	0.2490	0.2490	0.2520	0.2500	0.003
Subgroup 9	0.2500	0.2470	0.2500	0.2510	0.2495	0.004
Subgroup 10	0.2480	0.2480	0.2510	0.2530	0.2500	0.005
Subgroup 11	0.2500	0.2500	0.2500	0.2530	0.2508	0.003
Subgroup 12	0.2510	0.2490	0.2510	0.2540	0.2513	0.005
Subgroup 13	0.2500	0.2470	0.2500	0.2510	0.2495	0.004
Subgroup 14	0.2500	0.2500	0.2490	0.2520	0.2503	0.003
Subgroup 15	0.2500	0.2470	0.2500	0.2510	0.2495	0.004

Figure 6.13   Silicon Wafer Thickness

problems in Whisks' silicon wafer line B necessitated creating an $\overline{X}$ and R chart with the data in Figure 6.13. Though Whisks' control charts (Figures 6.14, 6.15) exhibit good control, Whisks' customer has raised questions about whether or not the process is capable of producing wafers within their specifications of 0.250 mm $\pm$ 0.005.

Using the information provided in the charts, Whisks' process engineers calculate the process capability indicators C_p and C_{pk}.

Using the values:

$$\overline{\overline{X}} = 0.250$$
$$\overline{R} = 0.004$$
$$USL_{\overline{x}} = 0.255$$
$$LSL_{\overline{x}} = 0.245$$
$$n = 4$$

To calculate C_p:

$$C_p = \frac{USL - LSL}{6\sigma}$$

$$C_p = \frac{0.255 - 0.245}{0.012}$$

$$C_p = 0.833$$

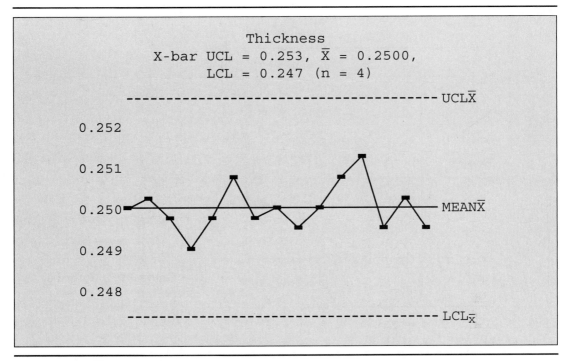

Figure 6.14 X̄ Chart for Silicon Wafer Thickness

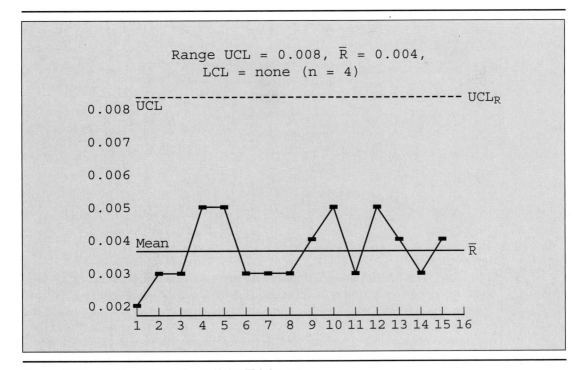

Figure 6.15 R Chart for Silicon Wafer Thickness

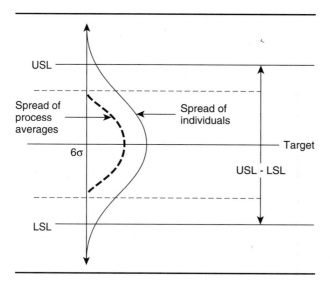

Figure 6.16   Spread of Averages, 6σ versus Specifications

To calculate C_{pk}:

$$C_{pk} = \frac{Z(min)}{3}$$

$$Z(USL) = \frac{(USL - \overline{\overline{X}})}{\sigma}$$

$$Z(USL) = \frac{(0.255 - 0.250)}{0.002} = \frac{0.005}{0.002} = 2.5$$

$$Z(LSL) = \frac{(\overline{\overline{X}} - LSL)}{\sigma}$$

$$Z(LSL) = \frac{(0.250 - 0.245)}{0.002} = 2.5$$

Therefore,

$$C_{pk} = \frac{2.5}{3}$$

$$C_{pk} = 0.833$$

Interpretation

The $\overline{X}$ and R charts in Figures 6.14 and 6.15 are within statistical control according to the guidelines discussed in this chapter. If we study process centering, the $\overline{X}$ chart (Figure 6.14) shows that the wafer thickness is centered around the target value of 0.250 mm. Studying process variation, the R chart (Figure 6.15) reveals that some variation is present in the process; not all the wafers are uniform in their thickness.

As we noted earlier in the chapter, a process within statistical control is not necessarily capable of meeting the specifications set by the customer. The control charts do not tell the entire story. Whisks' process capability index, C_p, reveals that the process is currently producing wafers that do not meet the specifications. The C_{pk} value is equal to the C_p value; the process is centered within the specifications. Essentially, the process is producing product as shown in Figure 6.16. As we suspected from earlier examination of the R chart, the C_p and C_{pk} values confirm that too much variation is present in the process.

 REAL TOOLS FOR REAL LIFE

Steering Wheel Assembly Process Capability

Most people are not aware that a single nut holds the steering wheel on a car or a tractor. Manufacturers of motorized vehicles pay careful attention to the amount of torque applied to the nut when attaching it to the steering wheel. If the torque is too high or too low, the steering wheel may fall off. Having a steering wheel come off into your hands in the last thing a driver would like to have happen.

At Friendly Farmer, Inc., the steering wheel, as a safety sensitive assembly, has its process capability monitored closely. The amount of torque applied is carefully checked both during the assembly and in a later inspection of a sample of 4 tractors per shift. The target specifications for this application are 450 kg/cm^2 with a range of 350–550 kg/cm^2.

Process control sheets describe the process of assembling the steering wheels to the tractor frame, the type of torque wrench to be used to perform the job, the torque range and target, the item being inspected, who is to perform the inspection, how often the inspection is performed, how often the wrenches are calibrated, where the results should be recorded, and who records these results.

When the inspector checks the torque with the wrench, he/she listens for one "click" when turning the wrench. This "click" signifies that the wrench dial can be read. If the number read from the dial is out of range, if there is no click, or if there is more than one click, the tractor is not released for further assembly.

The average torque of the eight inspected tractors are recorded daily on an $\overline{X}$ and R chart. The $\overline{X}$ and R charts are monitored for patterns and out-of-control situations. Based on the current $\overline{X}$ and R chart (Figure 6.17a), the process has a process capability, C_p, of 1.2. Its C_{pk} value is 1.0, showing that the process is not centered. Further investigation has revealed that the process is off center to the low side of the specifications.

Since this is a critical-to-safety feature on the tractor, the company would like to increase its process capability. A project team has investigated the causes of improper torque using a cause and effect diagram (Figure 6.18). Using the diagram as a guide, the team determined that two problems existed. The production line manufactures several different types of tractors on the same system. Due to workstation design limitations, it was easy to select the incorrect torque gun for a particular tractor. Part commonalities, one nut looking very similar to another, also caused operator error. These two errors required some workstation redesign to

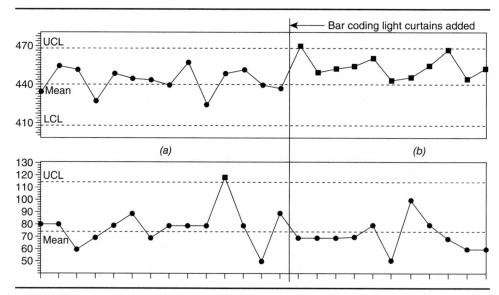

Figure 6.17   Steering Wheel Bolt Torque

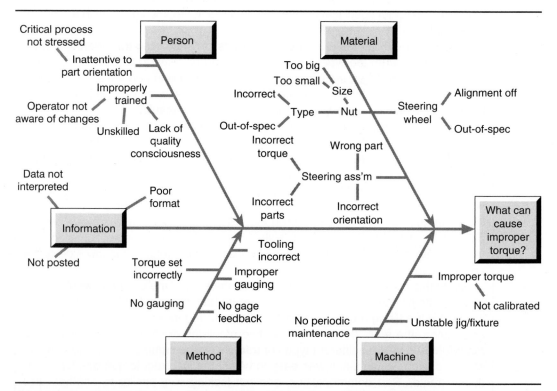

Figure 6.18   Tractor Steering Wheel Nut Torque Cause and Effect Diagram

make the operation mistake proof. Bar codes and light curtains work together to provide access to appropriate nuts and guns as a particular tractor model enters the workstation.

The new process capability, based on the results of the $\overline{X}$ and R chart values is C_p = 1.9 (Figure 6.17*b*). Even better is the fact that the C_{pk} value has improved to 1.87. The process is nearly centered and very capable.   Q

SUMMARY

Manufacturing a product or providing a service is more than meeting specifications. As reducing the variation associated with a process has become a greater concern, the use of process capability indices has increased. Used to judge how consistently the process is performing, these indices provide a great deal of information concerning process centering and the ability of the process to meet specifications. Process capability indices can guide the improvement process toward uniformity about a target value.

■ *Lessons Learned*

1. Process capability refers to the ability of a process to meet the specifications set by the customer or designer.
2. Individuals in a process spread more widely around a center value than do the averages.
3. Specification limits are set by the designer or customer. Control limits are determined by the current process.
4. $6\hat{\sigma}$ is the spread of the process or process capability.
5. C_p, the capability index, is the ratio of the tolerance (USL − LSL) and the process capability ($6\hat{\sigma}$).
6. C_r, the capability ratio, is the ratio of the process capability (6σ) and the tolerance (USL − LSL).
7. C_{pk} is the ratio that reflects how the process is performing in relation to a nominal, center, or target value. ■

■ *Formulas*

$$\hat{\sigma} = \frac{\overline{s}}{c_4}$$

$$\hat{\sigma} = \frac{\overline{R}}{d_2}$$

Capability Indices

$$C_p = \frac{USL - LSL}{6\hat{\sigma}}$$

$$C_r = \frac{6\hat{\sigma}}{USL - LSL}$$

$$C_{pk} = \frac{Z(min)}{3}$$

where $Z(min)$ is the smaller of $Z(USL) = (USL - \overline{X})/\hat{\sigma}$ or $Z(LSL) = (\overline{X} - LSL)/\hat{\sigma}$.

Chapter Problems

1. What do control limits represent? What do specification limits represent? Describe the three cases that compare specification limits to control limits.

2. Describe the relationship between averages and individuals in terms of specification limits and control limits.

3. Why can a process be in control but not be capable of meeting specifications?

4. A hospital is using $\overline{X}$ and R charts to record the time it takes to process patient account information. A sample of five applications is taken each day. The first four weeks' (20 days') data give the following values:

$$\overline{\overline{X}} = 16 \text{ min} \qquad \overline{R} = 7 \text{ min}$$

If the upper and lower specifications are 21 minutes and 13 minutes, respectively, calculate $6\hat{\sigma}$, C_p, and C_{pk}. Interpret the indices.

5. Two television manufacturers operate plants with differing quality philosophies. One plant works to target and the other works to specification limit. Describe the difference between these two philosophies.

6. For the data in Problem 4 of Chapter 5, calculate $6\hat{\sigma}$, C_p, and C_{pk}. Interpret the indices. The specification limits are 50 ± 0.5.

7. For the data in Problem 5 of Chapter 5, calculate $6\hat{\sigma}$, C_p, and C_{pk}. Interpret the indices. The specification limits are 0.50350 ± 0.00020 mm.

8. Stress tests are used to study the heart muscle after a person has had a heart attack. Timely information from these stress tests can help doctors prevent future heart attacks. The team investigating the turnaround time of stress tests has managed to reduce the amount of time it takes for a doctor to receive the results of a stress test from 68 to 32 hours on average. The team had a goal of reducing test turnaround times to between 30 and 36 hours. Given that the new average test turnaround time is 32 hours, with a standard deviation of 1, and n = 9, calculate and interpret C_p and C_{pk}.

9. Hotels use statistical information and control charts to track their performance on a variety of indicators. Recently a hotel manager has been asked whether or not his team is capable of maintaining scores between 8 and 10 (on a scale of 1 to 10) for "overall cleanliness of room." The most recent data has a mean of 8.624, a standard deviation of 1.446, and n = 10. Calculate and interpret C_p and C_{pk}.

10. The Tasty Morsels Chocolate Company tracks the amount of chocolate found in its chocolate bars. The target is 26 grams and the upper and lower specifications are 29 and 23 grams, respectively. If their most recent $\overline{X}$ has a centerline of 25 and the R chart has a centerline of 2, and n = 4, is the process capable? Calculate and interpret C_p and C_{pk}.

11. From the information in Problem 11 of Chapter 5, calculate $6\hat{\sigma}$, C_p, and C_{pk}. Interpret the indices. The specification limits are 3 ± 0.05.

12. For the data in Problem 14 of Chapter 5, use $\overline{R}/d_2$ to calculate $6\hat{\sigma}$, C_p, and C_{pk}. Interpret the indices. The specification limits are 0.0028 ± 0.0005.

13. For the data in Problem 19 of Chapter 5, use $\overline{s}/c_4$ to calculate $6\hat{\sigma}$, C_p, and C_{pk}. Interpret the indices. Specifications: 400 ± 150 particulates per million.

14. A quality analyst is checking the process capability associated with the production of struts, specifically the amount of torque used to tighten a fastener. Twenty-five samples of size 4 have been taken. These were used to create $\overline{X}$ and R charts. The values for these charts are as follows. The upper and lower control limits for the $\overline{X}$ chart are 74.80 Nm and 72.37 Nm, respectively. $\overline{\overline{X}}$ is 73.58 Nm. $\overline{R}$ is 1.66. The specification limits are 80 Nm ± 10. Calculate $6\hat{\sigma}$, C_p, and C_{pk}. Interpret the values.

15. Complete the following table by calculating $6\hat{\sigma}$, C_p, and C_{pk} for the data from Case 5.1, parts 1–5. Specifications: 3.750 ± 0.005 inch. When interpreting the completed table, be sure to compare and contrast the values to each other as well as comment about their changes over the five days. Note that you do not have to complete the cases to answer this question.

Day	1	2	3	4	5
$\overline{\overline{X}}$	3.4794	3.7493	3.7492	3.7496	3.7503
$\hat{\sigma}$	0.0048	0.0046	0.0036	0.0029	0.0008
$6\hat{\sigma}$	0.0288	0.0276			
C_p	0.3471	0.3623			
C_{pk}	0.3056	0.3116			

CASE STUDY 6.1
Process Capability

PART 1

Hop Scotch Drive-In Restaurant is considering a new marketing idea. At Hop Scotch, diners have the choice of dining inside or staying in their cars to eat. To serve those dining in their cars, carhops take the orders at the car and bring the food to the car when it's ready. Many people want fast service when they pull into the drive-in restaurant, but they also want more than a drive-through restaurant can offer. To try to meet their customers' expectations, Hop Scotch Drive-In is proposing to promise to have a server at your car in two minutes or less after your arrival at their drive-in. Before making this promise, the owners of Hop Scotch want to see how long it takes their servers to reach the cars now. They have gathered the information seen in Table C6.1.1.

 Assignment

Calculate the range for each of the subgroups containing five server times. Since the owners of Hop Scotch Drive-In are interested in the combined performance of their servers and not the performance of any particular server, the subgroups contain times from each server. Use these calculated values to determine the process capability and the C_p and C_{pk} values. How well is the process performing when compared with the specifications of 2.0 min $+0.0/-1.0$?

PART 2

Judging by the time measurements, it now takes longer to reach the cars than the proposed two minutes. Hop Scotch probably won't be able to keep up with their advertisement of two minutes or less without some changes in the process. The process capability index is too low. The C_{pk} shows that the process is not centered around the center of the specification. In fact, the C_{pk} value tells us that the average for this distribution is outside the specifications.

Management has decided to explain the proposed advertisement to their servers. They hope that by doing this, the servers will put more effort into getting to the cars in two minutes or less. Management carefully explains how moving faster to get to the cars will have a positive effect on increasing business because the customers will be happier with faster service. At first skeptical, the servers decide it might be possible to increase business by serving the customers faster. They agree to do their best to get to

336

Table C6.1.1   Server-to-Car Times in Minutes

Subgroup Number	Server 1	Server 2	Server 3	Server 4	Server 5	Range
1	2.5	2.4	2.3	2.5	2.1	0.4
2	2.5	2.2	2.4	2.3	2.8	0.6
3	2.4	2.5	2.7	2.5	2.5	0.3
4	2.3	2.4	2.5	2.9	2.9	0.6
5	2.3	2.6	2.4	2.7	2.2	
6	2.6	2.4	2.6	2.5	2.5	
7	2.7	2.6	2.4	2.4	2.5	
8	2.4	2.3	2.5	2.6	2.4	
9	2.5	2.2	2.3	2.4	2.7	
10	2.4	2.4	2.3	2.7	2.4	
11	2.5	2.4	2.5	2.5	2.3	
12	2.4	2.3	2.4	2.2	2.1	
13	2.5	2.5	2.4	2.5	2.7	
14	2.5	2.4	2.3	2.3	2.6	
15	2.4	2.3	2.3	2.4	2.8	
16	2.6	2.7	2.4	2.6	2.9	
17	2.0	2.3	2.2	2.7	2.5	
18	2.2	2.4	2.1	2.9	2.6	
19	2.3	2.5	2.6	2.4	2.3	
20	2.3	2.5	2.6	2.6	2.5	

the cars as quickly as possible. The time measurements seen in Table C6.1.2 were made after the meeting with the servers.

 Assignment

Use the new data in Table C6.1.2 to calculate the process capability, C_p, and C_{pk}. How is the process performing now?

PART 3

Based on what they learned from the previous day's study, the owners of Hop Scotch have decided to supply their servers with roller skates. The servers are obviously working very hard but are still unable to reach the cars quickly. Management hopes that after the servers become comfortable with their skates, they will be able to move faster around the restaurant parking lot. Table C6.1.3 shows the results of adding roller skates.

Table C6.1.2   Server-to-Car Times in Minutes

Subgroup Number	Server 1	Server 2	Server 3	Server 4	Server 5
1	2.3	2.2	2.0	2.4	2.2
2	2.2	2.1	2.0	2.2	2.3
3	2.2	2.1	2.0	2.3	2.0
4	2.0	2.3	2.3	2.2	2.1
5	2.0	2.3	2.3	2.1	1.9
6	2.2	2.5	2.2	2.3	2.1
7	2.2	2.2	2.3	2.4	2.0
8	2.4	2.6	2.4	2.5	2.2
9	2.5	2.2	2.4	1.9	2.2
10	2.2	2.0	2.2	2.5	2.0
11	2.0	2.3	2.1	2.2	2.1
12	2.3	2.2	2.1	2.3	2.2
13	2.1	2.2	2.1	2.1	2.0
14	2.1	2.3	2.2	2.4	2.0
15	2.2	2.1	2.1	2.3	2.0
16	2.0	2.1	2.2	2.3	2.1
17	2.1	2.0	2.3	2.4	1.9
18	2.0	2.0	2.2	1.9	2.2
19	2.3	2.1	2.4	2.3	2.3
20	2.0	2.3	2.1	1.9	2.0

 Assignment

Calculate the process capability, C_p, and C_{pk}. Are the roller skates a big help?

PART 4

Without doubt, the roller skates have improved the overall performance of the servers dramatically. As an added bonus, the drive-in has become more popular because the customers really like seeing the servers skate. For some of them, it reminds them of cruising drive-ins in the fifties; for others, they like to see the special skating skills of some of the servers. The servers seem very happy with the new skates. Several have said that their job is more fun now.

To make further improvements, the owners of Hop Scotch have decided to change how the servers serve customers. In the past, each server was assigned a section of the

Table C6.1.3   Server-to-Car Times in Minutes

Subgroup Number	Server 1	Server 2	Server 3	Server 4	Server 5
1	1.9	1.9	2.0	2.0	1.9
2	1.9	2.0	2.0	2.0	1.9
3	1.9	2.0	1.9	1.9	2.0
4	1.9	2.0	1.8	1.8	2.0
5	2.0	2.1	2.1	2.0	2.0
6	2.0	2.0	2.1	2.1	2.1
7	2.0	1.8	1.9	2.0	2.0
8	2.0	2.0	2.0	2.0	1.9
9	2.0	2.0	1.9	1.8	1.9
10	1.9	1.8	1.9	1.8	1.7
11	1.8	1.8	1.8	1.7	1.6
12	1.9	1.7	1.7	1.8	1.7
13	1.7	1.7	1.7	1.6	1.6
14	1.8	1.6	1.6	1.6	1.6
15	1.9	1.9	1.8	1.9	1.8
16	1.8	1.8	2.0	2.0	1.9
17	1.5	1.6	1.6	1.6	1.9
18	1.6	1.5	1.6	1.8	1.7
19	1.4	1.6	1.7	1.8	1.8
20	1.8	1.8	1.9	1.7	1.7

parking lot. But now, observing the activities in the restaurant parking lot, the owners see that the lot does not fill up evenly; some sections fill up first, especially when a group comes in to be served all at once. This unevenness often overwhelms a particular server while another server has very few cars to wait on. Under the new program, servers will handle any area of the parking lot, serving cars on a first-come, first-served basis.

 Assignment

Use the data in Table C6.1.4 to calculate the process capability, C_p, and C_{pk}. Do the new rules help?

Table C6.1.4   Server-to-Car Times in Minutes

Subgroup Number	Server 1	Server 2	Server 3	Server 4	Server 5
1	1.1	1.1	1.0	1.1	1.1
2	0.9	1.0	1.0	1.1	1.1
3	1.0	1.0	1.0	1.0	1.2
4	1.1	1.1	1.0	1.1	1.0
5	0.7	0.9	0.8	0.9	0.8
6	0.8	0.8	0.8	1.1	1.0
7	0.9	1.0	1.0	1.0	0.8
8	1.0	1.1	1.1	1.0	1.2
9	0.8	0.9	0.8	0.8	0.9
10	0.8	0.7	0.8	0.7	0.7
11	0.8	0.8	0.8	0.9	1.0
12	0.8	0.9	0.8	0.8	0.9
13	0.7	0.7	0.7	0.7	0.7
14	0.7	0.7	0.7	0.8	0.9
15	0.9	0.9	0.9	1.0	0.9
16	0.9	0.9	0.8	1.0	1.0
17	0.9	0.9	0.9	0.9	0.9
18	0.7	0.8	0.7	0.8	0.7
19	0.5	0.6	0.5	0.7	0.6
20	0.6	0.7	0.6	0.7	0.6

CASE STUDY 6.2
Process Improvement

This case is the fourth in a four-part series of cases involving process improvement. The other cases are found at the end of Chapters 3, 4, and 5. Data and calculations for this case establish the foundation for the future cases; however, it is not necessary to have completed the cases in Chapters 3, 4, and 5 in order to complete and understand this case. Portions of the case in Chapter 5 are repeated here and must be completed in order to calculate process capability. Completing this case will provide insight into process capability and process improvement. The case can be worked by hand or with the software provided.

PART 1

Figure C6.2.1 provides the details of a bracket assembly to hold a strut on an automobile in place. Welded to the auto body frame, the bracket cups the strut and secures it to the frame via a single bolt with a lock washer. Proper alignment is necessary for both smooth installation during assembly and future performance. For mounting purposes the left-side hole, A, must be aligned on center with the right-side hole, B. If the holes are centered directly opposite each other, in perfect alignment, then the angle between hole centers will measure 0°. As the flowchart in Figure C6.2.2 shows, the bracket is created by passing

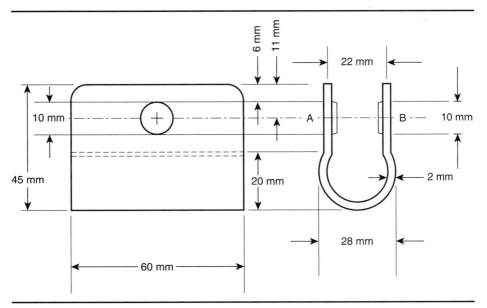

Figure C6.2.1   Bracket

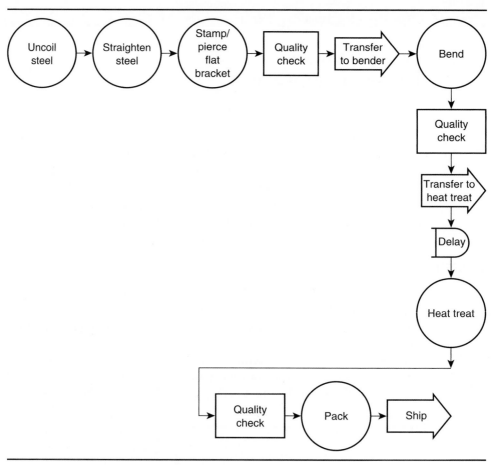

Figure C6.2.2   Flowchart of Bracket Fabrication Process

coils of flat steel through a series of progressive dies. As the steel moves through the press, the bracket is stamped, pierced, and finally bent into the appropriate shape.

Recently customers have been complaining about having difficulty securing the bracket closed with the bolt and lock washer. The bolts have been difficult to slide through the holes and then tighten. Assemblers complain of stripped bolts and snug fittings. Unsure of where the problem is, WP Inc.'s management assembled a team consisting of representatives from process engineering, materials engineering, product design, and manufacturing.

Through the use of several cause-and-effect diagrams, the team determines that the most likely cause of the problems experienced by the customer is the alignment of the holes. At some stage in the formation process, the holes end up off center. To confirm their suspicions, during the next production run, the bending press operator takes 20 subgroups of size 5 and measures the angle between the centers of the holes for each sample (Figure C6.2.3). The specification for the angle between insert hole A and

Subgroup Sample	1	2	3	4	5	6	7	8	9	10	11	12	13	14	15
1	0.31	0.27	0.30	0.30	0.25	0.18	0.26	0.15	0.30	0.31	0.18	0.22	0.19	0.14	0.29
2	0.29	0.23	0.30	0.20	0.20	0.26	0.27	0.21	0.24	0.25	0.16	0.30	0.28	0.27	0.23
3	0.30	0.31	0.28	0.21	0.19	0.18	0.12	0.24	0.26	0.25	0.21	0.21	0.26	0.25	0.27
4	0.28	0.23	0.24	0.23	0.26	0.24	0.20	0.27	0.27	0.28	0.29	0.24	0.29	0.28	0.24
5	0.23	0.29	0.32	0.25	0.25	0.17	0.23	0.30	0.26	0.25	0.27	0.26	0.24	0.16	0.23

Subgroup Sample	16	17	18	19	20
1	0.22	0.32	0.33	0.20	0.24
2	0.24	0.27	0.30	0.17	0.28
3	0.22	0.28	0.22	0.26	0.15
4	0.30	0.19	0.26	0.31	0.27
5	0.30	0.31	0.26	0.24	0.19

Figure C6.2.3   Hole A, B Alignment; Angle Above (+) or Below (−) Nominal

insert hole B is 0.00° with a tolerance of ±0.30°. The values recorded in Figure C6.2.3 represent the distance above (or when a minus sign is present, below) the nominal value of 0.00°.

 Assignment

Follow the steps outlined in Chapter 5 and utilize the data to create a set of $\overline{X}$ and R charts. You will need to calculate the mean and range for each subgroup. Describe the performance of the process. Using $\sigma = \overline{R}/d_2$, calculate $6\hat{\sigma}$, C_p, and C_{pk}. Interpret the charts and these values. Do they tell you the same thing? Is the process capable of meeting specifications?

PART 2

Having $\overline{X}$ and R charts and the accompanying statistical information tells the team a lot about the hole alignment characteristics. Using the problem-solving method described in Chapter 3 (and followed in Case Study 3.2), the team has determined that the fixture that holds the flat bracket in place during the bending operation needs to be replaced. One of the measures of performance that they created during Step 4 of their problem-solving process is percentage of the parts out of specification. Now that the fixture has been replaced with a better one, the team would like to determine whether or not changing the fixture improved the process by removing a root cause of hole misalignment.

 Assignment

Utilize the data in Figure C6.2.4 to create another set of $\overline{X}$ and R charts. Has their change to the fixtures resulted in a process improvement? Using $\sigma = \overline{R}/d_2$, calculate 6σ, C_p, and C_{pk}. Interpret the charts and these values. Do they tell you the same thing? Is the process capable of meeting specifications? How do you know? Compare the calculations from part 1 of this case with part 2. Describe the changes. How are they doing when you compare their measure of performance, percentage of the parts out of specification, both before and after the fixture is changed?

Subgroup Sample	1	2	3	4	5	6	7	8	9	10	11	12	13	14	15
1	0.03	0.06	0.06	0.03	-0.04	-0.02	-0.05	0.06	0.00	-0.02	-0.02	0.06	0.07	0.10	0.02
2	0.08	0.08	0.08	0.00	-0.07	0.06	-0.07	0.03	0.06	-0.01	0.06	0.02	-0.04	0.05	-0.05
3	-0.03	-0.01	0.05	0.05	0.00	0.02	0.11	0.04	0.02	0.00	-0.02	-0.01	0.08	0.03	0.04
4	0.07	0.08	-0.03	-0.01	-0.01	0.12	-0.03	0.03	-0.02	-0.10	0.02	-0.02	0.01	0.04	0.05
5	-0.02	0.02	0.03	0.07	-0.01	-0.07	0.03	0.01	0.00	-0.04	0.09	0.03	-0.04	0.06	-0.05

Subgroup Sample	16	17	18	19	20
1	-0.05	-0.06	-0.04	-0.06	-0.01
2	0.00	-0.02	-0.02	0.00	0.02
3	0.06	0.04	-0.01	0.00	0.05
4	-0.02	0.07	0.03	0.03	0.04
5	-0.01	-0.04	-0.02	0.04	0.03

Figure C6.2.4 Hole A, B Alignment Following Process Improvement; Angle Above (+) or Below (−) Nominal

7

Other Variable Control Charts

Individual and Moving-Range Charts
Moving-Average and Moving-Range Charts
A Chart Plotting All Individual Values
Median and Range Charts
Run Charts
A Chart for Variable Subgroup Size
Precontrol Charts
Short-Run Charts
Summary
Lessons Learned
Formulas
Chapter Problems
Case Study 7.1   Precontrol
Case Study 7.2   Run Charts

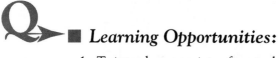

■ *Learning Opportunities:*

1. To introduce a variety of control charts: charts for individuals, median charts, moving-average/moving-range charts, and run charts
2. To introduce the concept of precontrol
3. To familiarize the student with short-run production charts ■

346

What About the Short Run?

$\overline{\mathrm{X}}$ and R or s charts track the performance of processes that have long production runs or repeated services. What happens when there is an insufficient number of sample measurements to create a traditional $\overline{\mathrm{X}}$ and R chart? How do statistical control ideas apply to new processes or short production runs? Can processes be tracked with other methods? What happens when only one sample is taken from a process? This chapter covers the variety of different statistical charts that deal with situations where traditional $\overline{\mathrm{X}}$ and R or s charts cannot be applied.

INDIVIDUAL AND MOVING-RANGE CHARTS

Charts for individuals with their accompanying moving-range charts are often used when the data collection occurs either once a day or on a week-to-week or month-to-month basis. As their title suggests, *charts for individuals and moving range are created when the measurements are single values or when the number of products produced is too small to form traditional $\overline{X}$ and R charts.*

To construct an individual values ($\overline{X}_i$) and moving-range chart, the individual X_i measurements are taken and plotted on the $\overline{X}_i$ chart. To find the centerline of the chart, the individual X_i values are summed and divided by the total number of X_i readings:

$$\overline{X}_i = \frac{\Sigma X_i}{m}$$

Moving ranges are calculated by measuring the value-to-value difference of the individual data. Two consecutive individual data-point values are compared and the magnitude or absolute value of their difference is recorded on the moving-range chart. This reading is usually placed on the chart between the space on the R chart designated for a value and its preceding value. This shows the reader of the chart that the two individual values were compared to determine the range value. An alternative method of plotting R is to place the first R value in the space designated for the second reading, leaving the first space blank (Figure 7.1).

$\overline{R}$, the centerline, is equal to the summation of the individual R values divided by the total number of R's calculated. The total number of R's calculated will be 1 less than the total number of individual $\overline{X}_i$ values:

$$\overline{R} = \frac{\Sigma R_i}{m - 1}$$

Once $\overline{R}$ has been determined, control limits for both charts are calculated by adding $\pm 3\sigma$ to the centerline:

$$UCL_{Xi} = \overline{X}_i + 3\sigma$$
$$LCL_{Xi} = \overline{X}_i - 3\sigma$$

where

$$\sigma = \frac{\overline{R}}{d_2}$$

To approximate $\pm 3\sigma$, divide 3 by the d_2 value for n = 2 found in the table in Appendix 2. The formulas become

$$UCL_X = \overline{X}_i + 2.66(\overline{R})$$
$$LCL_X = \overline{X}_i - 2.66(\overline{R})$$

The upper control limit for the R chart is found by multiplying D_4 by $\overline{R}$. From Appendix 2, $D_4 = 3.27$ when n = 2. The lower control limit for the R chart is equal to zero:

$$UCL_R = D_4 \times \overline{R}$$
$$= 3.27 \times \overline{R}$$

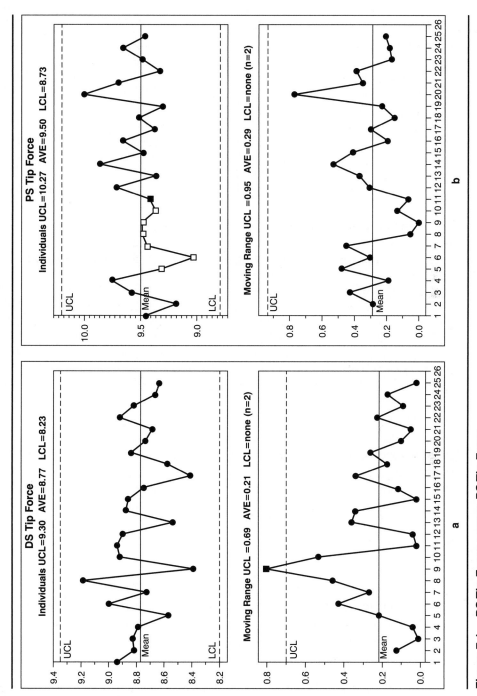

Figure 7.1   DS Tip Force versus PS Tip Force

Interpreting individual and moving-range charts is similar to the interpretation of $\overline{X}$ and R charts, as presented in previous chapters. When studying the charts, look for trends, shifts, or changes in level that indicate patterns in the process. Study the range chart to determine the amount of variation present in the process. Look for cycles or patterns in the data. On both charts, the data should randomly flow back and forth across the centerline. Data should not be concentrated at either control limit, which would indicate a skewed distribution. (See Chapter 5 for a complete review of control chart interpretation. Once the process is considered in control, process capability can be determined using the methods discussed in Chapter 6.) As with traditional variables control charts, a large number of subgroups of sample size n = 1 ensures that the distribution is approximately normal. Individual and moving-range charts are more reliable when the number of subgroups taken exceeds 80.

EXAMPLE 7.1   Creating and Interpreting Individual and Moving-Range Charts

The 05W is a windshield wiper system produced for use on automobiles. Recently, engineers have been studying this wiper system to determine if significant variation exists in the wiper arms from the driver's side (DS) to the passenger's side (PS). One critical characteristic for good wiper blade performance is arm tip force, or the amount of force that the arm exerts on the blade to hold it to the windshield. This force is measured in Newtons with specifications of 9.17 ± 2 N. For the following information, create, interpret, and compare charts for individuals and the moving range for each wiper arm.

For the Driver's Side

Step 1. Measure and Record Individual Values.   To construct individual ($\overline{X}_i$) and moving-range charts, first measure the individual values ($\overline{X}_i$) and record them (Table 7.1).

Step 2. Determine Centerline.   To find the centerline for the process charts, sum the individual X_i values and divide by the total number of X_i readings:

$$\overline{X}_i = \frac{\Sigma X_i}{m} = \frac{8.94 + 8.81 + 8.81 + \cdots + 8.62}{25}$$
$$= 8.77$$

Scale the chart and place the centerline on it (Figure 7.1).

Step 3. Plot Individuals.   Plot the individual X_i values on the chart (Figure 7.1).

Step 4. Determine Range Values.   Calculate the range values for the data, comparing each measurement with the one preceding it (Table 7.1).

Step 5. Determine Average Range.   Calculate the average of the range values using the following formula:

$$\overline{R} = \frac{\Sigma R_i}{m-1} = \frac{0.13 + 0.0 + 0.01 + 0.22 + \cdots + 0.01}{24}$$
$$= 0.21$$

Table 7.1   Recorded Values in Newtons

Driver's Side Wiper Arm Tip Force Individual Measures (N)	Range	Passenger's Side Wiper Arm Tip Force Individual Measures (N)	Range
8.94		9.45	
	0.13		0.30
8.81		9.15	
	0.0		0.44
8.81		9.59	
	0.01		0.21
8.80		9.80	
	0.22		0.50
8.58		9.30	
	0.42		0.30
9.00		9.0	
	0.26		0.46
8.74		9.46	
	0.45		0.04
9.19		9.50	
	0.79		0.00
8.40		9.50	
	0.50		0.14
8.90		9.36	
	0.01		0.04
8.91		9.40	
	0.02		0.30
8.89		9.70	
	0.37		0.35
8.52		9.35	
	0.36		0.54
8.88		9.89	
	0.01		0.40
8.87		9.49	
	0.11		0.21
8.76		9.70	
	0.34		0.30
8.42		9.40	
	0.16		0.10
8.58		9.50	
	0.24		0.24
8.82		9.26	
	0.08		0.79
8.74		10.05	
	0.05		0.34
8.69		9.71	
	0.22		0.38
8.91		9.33	
	0.09		0.16
8.82		9.49	
	0.19		0.20
8.63		9.69	
	0.01		0.22
8.62		9.47	

Note that $\overline{R}$ is calculated using $m - 1$, unlike the $\overline{X}$ calculation which uses m. $\overline{R}$ is the centerline of the R chart.

Step 6. Determine Control Limits for $\overline{X}$ Chart.   The control limits for the $\overline{X}_i$ chart for a sample size of two is calculated using the following formulas:

$$UCL_X = \overline{X}_i + 2.66(\overline{R})$$
$$= 8.77 + 2.66(0.21) = 9.30$$

$$LCL_X = \overline{X}_i - 2.66(\overline{R})$$
$$= 8.77 - 2.66(0.21) = 8.23$$

Record the control limits on the individual chart (Figure 7.1).

Step 7. Determine Control Limits for R Chart.   Find the upper and lower control limits for the R chart using the following formulas:

$$UCL_R = 3.27 \times \overline{R} = 3.27 \times 0.21$$
$$= 0.69$$

$$LCL_R = 0$$

Step 8. Create Chart.   Record the centerline, control limits, and range values on the moving-range chart (Figure 7.1).

For the Passenger's Side

Repeating the same steps as taken for the driver's side information,

$$\overline{X}_i = \frac{\Sigma X_i}{m} = \frac{9.45 + 9.15 + 9.59 + \cdots + 9.47}{25}$$
$$= 9.5$$

$$\overline{R} = \frac{\Sigma R_i}{m - 1} = \frac{0.30 + 0.44 + 0.21 + 0.50 + \cdots + 0.22}{24}$$
$$= 0.29$$

$$UCL_X = \overline{X}_i + 2.66(\overline{R})$$
$$= 9.5 + 2.66(0.29) = 10.27$$

$$LCL_X = \overline{X}_i - 2.66(\overline{R})$$
$$= 9.5 - 2.66(0.29) = 8.73$$

$$UCL_R = 3.27 \times \overline{R} = 3.27 \times 0.29$$
$$= 0.95$$

$$LCL_R = 0$$

Step 9. Interpret the Charts.   For the driver's side tip force, the average is 8.77, which is low given the target value of 9.17. The average range is 0.21. The R chart shows very little consistency at first, including an out-of-control point. Midway through production, the range decreases and becomes more steady. There are no patterns on the chart for individuals.

For the passenger's side tip force, the average is 9.50, which is high given the target value of 9.17. The average range is 0.29. The passenger's side measurements do not exhibit any patterns on the range chart. The individuals chart for the passenger's side tip force displays a run of 7 points early in the chart at or below the centerline. Then the process centers around the mean until near the end of the chart.

When the engineers examined the individual data, they noted that a majority of the driver's side measurements are between the target value and the lower specification limit. For the passenger's side measurements, the opposite is true. The majority of the parts are between the target and the upper specification limit. This interesting information will help those designing the wiper systems to improve process performance.

REAL TOOLS FOR REAL LIFE

Air Quality Monitoring Using Control Charts for Individuals

At the county waste processing facility, a specially designed L-shaped building is used as a central receiving location for waste from the entire county. On the public side, homeowners and small business customers drive through and drop off yard waste, remodeling debris, and harmful products for disposal. On the much larger commercial side, municipal garbage trucks drive in and dump (tip) their loads to the concrete floor. Workers on front-end loaders push the garbage to three rectangular holes in the floor, under which tractor trailers are positioned in sub-floor tunnels. Next to the holes, tamping cranes equipped with heavy suspended weights compact the garbage in the trailers to maximize their capacity. Full trailers are driven to a landfill while the garbage trucks are freed to resume their neighborhood routes. The public side refuse is disposed of in a similar fashion but on a much smaller scale.

In the elbow of the L, a separate building houses the Recycling Center (RC). The RC contains an educational facility and offices of the recycling effort for the county. The buildings, though essentially separate, share a common wall with two large plate glass windows. In the classroom, these windows allow children to watch activities at the tipping station. Originally designed to be constructed out of concrete, financial pressures necessitated the construction of a metal building. Unfortunately, this metal structure doesn't maintain positive pressure and allows ingress of smells, dust, and diesel fumes from the waste processing facility.

Though the access doors for trucks are left open year-round, since the entire operation takes place under roof in a confined space, workers at the facility are concerned about diesel exhaust exposure. The exhaust comes from multiple sources including the garbage and tractor trailer trucks, private vehicles, loaders and tamping cranes. The workers voiced their concerns to management who hired an Industrial Hygienist (IH) to test air quality and evaluate workers' exposures.

In order to determine the extent of the diesel exhaust exposure, the IH collected personal exposure samples for a variety of jobs. Employees were grouped into categories based on the locations of the jobs they performed. As a baseline, outdoor air quality samples, Category Two, were taken.

Category One: Operations

> Loaders
> Crane operators
> Traffic control: commercial (waste trucks)
> Traffic control: public
> Traffic control: tunnel

Category Two: Outdoor Air Quality Baseline

> Roof (0.0025)
> Entrance (0.0028)
> Fence line near freeway (0.0064)
> Walkway (0.0036)

As of 2004, no official OSHA Permissible Exposure Limit (PEL) for diesel fumes exposure exists. Often, OSHA will adopt the recommended exposure limit of other recognized organizations. In this case, there are two limits to consider for diesel exhaust particulates. The Mine Safety and Health Administration has set a limit of 0.16 mg/m^3, enforceable in 2006. The second standard comes from the American Conference of Governmental Industrial Hygienists (ACGIH) Threshold Limit Value (TLV) for selected air particulates. In 2002, the ACGIH proposed a limit of 0.15 mg/m^3 for diesel exhaust particulates. Proposed changes are debated by practitioners nationwide for a period of two years, and then are either accepted or rejected by the board. Interestingly enough, after only one year of debate, the diesel exhaust particulate standard was retracted. Testing information showed that the proposed TLV of 0.15 mg/m^3 would not be sufficiently protective. The standard will be resubmitted when it has been rewritten.

Samples were collected at seven different times, 21 days apart: January 12, 2003, February 2, 2003, February 23, 2003, March 15, 2003, April 5, 2003, April 26, 2003, and May 17, 2003 (Figure 7.2). A control chart for individuals was constructed (Figure 7.3*a*).

Category One: Operators		
2003	**Particulate**	**Moving Range**
12-Jan	0.16	
2-Feb	0.16	0
23-Feb	0.18	0.02
15-Mar	0.17	0.01
5-Apr	0.18	0.01
26-Apr	0.16	0.02
17-May	0.15	0.01
2004		
06-Jun	0.05	0.1
28-Jun	0.04	0.01
19-Jul	0.04	0.01
9-Aug	0.09	0.05

Figure 7.2   Air Quality Data Values

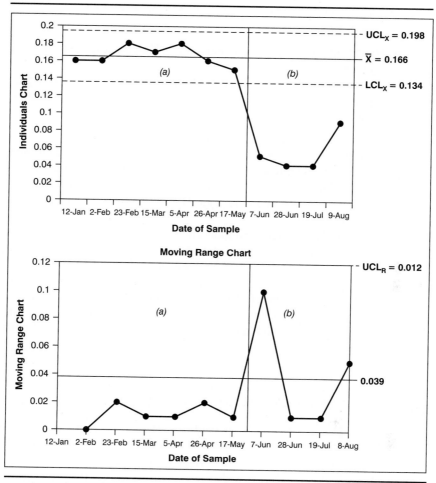

Figure 7.3   Individual and Moving Range Charts for Air Quality

To calculate the limits:

$$\overline{X} = \frac{\sum X_i}{M} = \frac{1.16}{7} = 0.166$$

$$\overline{R} = \frac{\sum R_i}{M - 1} = \frac{0.07}{6} = 0.012$$

$$UCL_X = 0.166 + 2.66(0.012) = 0.198$$

$$LCL_X = 0.166 - 2.66(0.012) = 0.134$$

$$UCL_R = 3.27(0.012) = 0.039$$

The individuals and moving range chart shows that all of the indoor readings were much higher than those taken outdoors. After a study of the data and the site, recommendations were made to management concerning how to reduce the amount of diesel fumes in the air. Management implemented two recommendations:

- Add ceiling fans, running continuously, to increase exhaust capability in ceiling to dilute the fumes.
- Add ceramic filters to the exhaust train in loaders and tamping cranes to capture particulate matter and oxidize it to form carbon dioxide at high temperatures.

The changes were made in late 2003.

Six months later, on June 7, 2004, June 28, 2004, July 19, 2004, and August 9, 2004, the IH revisited the sight to take samples in order to answer the question: Did the improvements made decrease the amount of diesel particulates in the air? These values were placed on the original control charts for individuals and moving ranges (Figures 7.3b).

As the control charts for individuals show, the investments made were worthwhile and workers at the facility benefited through significantly improved air quality. The particulate level in the air dropped dramatically. It is also interesting to note that in August 2004, unknown to management, the individual who maintained the front-end loaders removed the ceramic filters. The magnitude of the August 2004 reading alerted management that something had changed. They were quick to refit the filters on the equipment because the charts clearly show the effectiveness of the ceramic filters.   **Q**

MOVING-AVERAGE AND MOVING-RANGE CHARTS

Rather than plot each individual reading, we can use *moving-average and moving-range charts to combine* n *number of individual values to create an average.* When a new individual reading is taken, the oldest value forming the previous average is discarded. The new reading is combined with the remaining values from the previous average and the newest value to form a new average, thus the term "moving average." This average is plotted on the chart and the limits are calculated using the formulas for the $\overline{X}$ and R charts presented in Chapter 5. Capability indices can also be calculated using the methods presented in Chapter 6. The number of individual values grouped together to form a subgroup will be the size of n used to select the A_2, D_4, and D_3 values.

By combining individual values produced over time, moving averages smooth out short term variation and allow users to study the underlying trends in the data. For this reason, moving-average charts are frequently used for seasonal products. Moving averages, because of the nature of their construction, will always lag behind changes in the process, making them less sensitive to such changes. The larger the size of the moving subgroup, the less sensitivity to change. To quickly detect process changes, use the individuals and moving-range combination of charts. Moving-average charts are best used when the process changes slowly.

EXAMPLE 7.2   Creating Moving-Average and Moving-Range Charts

A manufacturer of skis is interested in making moving-average and moving-range charts of the sales figures for the past year (Table 7.2). Because of the seasonal nature of the business, they have decided to combine the individual sales values for three months. This is the average to be plotted on the chart.

Their first step is to combine the values from January, February, and March to obtain the first moving average. These values are compared and the lowest value is subtracted from the highest value to generate the range associated with the three points.

Combining these values, they find

January	75,000
February	71,000
March	68,000

$$\text{Moving average 1} = \frac{75,000 + 71,000 + 68,000}{3} = 71,333$$

$$\text{Moving range 1} = 75,000 - 68,000 = 7,000$$

These values are plotted on the chart. Subsequent values are found by dropping off the oldest measurement and replacing it with the next consecutive value. A new average and range are then calculated and plotted. Adding the month of April's figures, they find

April 59,800

$$\text{Moving average 2} = \frac{71,000 + 68,000 + 59,800}{3} = 66,267$$

$$\text{Moving range 2} = 71,000 - 59,800 = 11,200$$

Year 1	
January	75,000
February	71,000
March	68,000
April	59,800
May	55,100
June	54,000
July	50,750
August	50,200
September	55,000
October	67,000
November	76,700
December	84,000

Table 7.2   Ski Sales for the Past Year

Then May:

May 55,100

$$\text{Moving average 3} = \frac{68,000 + 59,800 + 55,100}{3} = 60,967$$

$$\text{Moving range 3} = 68,000 - 55,100 = 12,900$$

and so on.

To calculate the limits associated with a moving-average and moving-range chart combination, they use the traditional $\overline{X}$ and R chart formulas:

$$\text{Centerline } \overline{\overline{X}} = \frac{\Sigma \overline{X}_i}{m} = \frac{71,333 + 66,267 + \cdots + 75,900}{10}$$
$$= 61,132$$

$$\overline{R} = \frac{\Sigma R_i}{m} = \frac{7,000 + 11,200 + 12,900 + \cdots + 17,000}{10}$$
$$= 10,535$$

$$\text{UCL}_{\overline{X}} = \overline{\overline{X}} + A_2\overline{R}$$
$$= 61,132 + 1.023(10,535) = 71,909$$

$$\text{LCL}_{\overline{X}} = \overline{\overline{X}} - A_2\overline{R}$$
$$= 61,132 - 1.023(10,535) = 50,355$$

$$\text{UCL}_R = D_4\overline{R}$$
$$= 2.574(10,535) = 27,117$$

$$\text{LCL}_R = D_3\overline{R}$$
$$= 0$$

Figure 7.4 shows the completed chart. An investigation of the chart reveals that the sales of skis decreases dramatically from the winter months to the summer. Sales are fairly constant during the summer months, where the R chart exhibits very little variation. When sales begin to increase, there is a good deal of variation from month to month. Company sales appear to be strong, with sales later in the year increasing much more dramatically than they decreased in the earlier season. $Q\!\!\rightarrow$

A CHART PLOTTING ALL INDIVIDUAL VALUES

Control charts that plot each individual value found in a subgroup (Figure 7.5), while cluttered looking, are useful when explaining the concept of variation. As discussed in Chapters 5 and 6, the points plotted on an $\overline{X}$ chart are averages made up of individual values. The range chart accompanying the $\overline{X}$ chart gives the user an understanding of the spread of the data. Sometimes, however, a picture is worth a thousand words, or in this case, all the values read during a subgroup present a more representative picture than does a single point on the R chart.

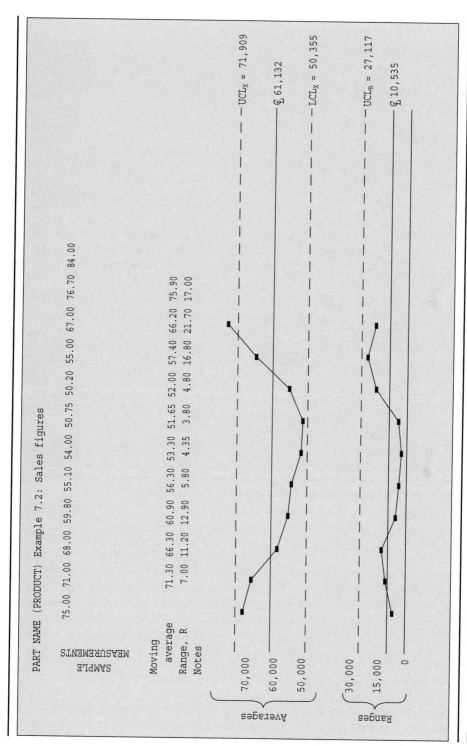

Figure 7.4   Control Chart for Moving Average with Moving Range

359

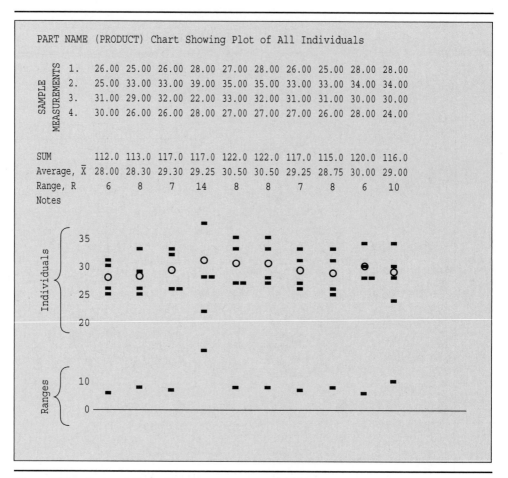

PART NAME (PRODUCT) Chart Showing Plot of All Individuals

SAMPLE MEASUREMENTS											
1.	26.00	25.00	26.00	28.00	27.00	28.00	26.00	25.00	28.00	28.00
2.	25.00	33.00	33.00	39.00	35.00	35.00	33.00	33.00	34.00	34.00
3.	31.00	29.00	32.00	22.00	33.00	32.00	31.00	31.00	30.00	30.00
4.	30.00	26.00	26.00	28.00	27.00	27.00	27.00	26.00	28.00	24.00

SUM	112.0	113.0	117.0	117.0	122.0	122.0	117.0	115.0	120.0	116.0
Average, $\bar{X}$	28.00	28.30	29.30	29.25	30.50	30.50	29.25	28.75	30.00	29.00
Range, R	6	8	7	14	8	8	7	8	6	10
Notes										

Figure 7.5   Control Chart Plotting All Individual Values

On an individual values chart, the individual values from the subgroup are represented by a small mark. The average of those values is represented by a circle. If an individual value and the average are the same, the mark is placed inside the circle. By looking at a control chart that plots all of the individual readings from a subgroup, those using the chart can gain a clearer understanding of how the data are spreading with respect to the average value (Figure 7.5). In most circumstances, because of its cluttered appearance, this chart is reserved for training people on interpreting the values of R or s charts.

MEDIAN AND RANGE CHARTS

*When a **median chart** is used, the median of the data is calculated and charted rather than the value for the average.* Just like variables control charts, median charts can be used to study the variation of process, although ease of calculation is a trade-off with some loss

n	A_6
2	1.88
3	1.19
4	0.80
5	0.69
6	0.55
7	0.51

Table 7.3   Values of A_6 Used in Median Charts Constructed with Averages of Subgroup Medians

of sensitivity. Constructed and interpreted in a manner similar to $\overline{X}$ and R charts, median and range charts are created through the following steps:

1. Calculate and record the sample measurements.
2. Arrange the sample measurements in each subgroup in order from highest to lowest.
3. Calculate the median and the range for each subgroup.
4. To find the centerline of the median chart, calculate the average of the subgroup medians.
5. To find the centerline of the range chart, calculate the average of the subgroup ranges.
6. The control limits of the median and range charts are determined by the following formulas and the values shown in Table 7.3 and Appendix 2:

$$UCL_{Md} = \overline{X}_{Md} + A_6\overline{R}_{Md}$$
$$LCL_{Md} = \overline{X}_{Md} - A_6\overline{R}_{Md}$$
$$UCL_R = D_4\overline{R}_{Md}$$
$$LCL_R = D_3\overline{R}_{Md}$$

7. Record the median and range values on their appropriate charts.
8. Interpret the chart using the information presented in Chapters 5 and 6. Patterns, trends, shifts, or points beyond the control limits should be investigated. The R chart will reveal the spread of the variation in the process, and the median chart will show the average median of the process.

EXAMPLE 7.3   Creating a Median Chart I

WP Corporation produces surgical instruments. After one particular instrument is stamped, a channel is machined into the part. Because of this channel, part thickness plays an important role in the quality of the finished product. Since die roll can effectively reduce part thickness, it is a key quality characteristic to monitor after the stamping operation. ("Die roll" is a by-product of the stamping process and refers to the feathered edge created by the downward force used to shear the metal.) In order to monitor the amount of die roll on the stamped part, WP has decided to use a median chart.

Step 1. Calculate and Record Measurements.   Using a sample size of three, the sample measurements are taken and recorded (Table 7.4).

Subgroups

1	2	3	4	5	6
0.0059	0.0054	0.0052	0.0054	0.0059	0.0060
0.0059	0.0060	0.0058	0.0054	0.0058	0.0055
0.0052	0.0057	0.0057	0.0054	0.0057	0.0056

7	8	9	10	11	12
0.0052	0.0057	0.0058	0.0056	0.0058	0.0059
0.0051	0.0055	0.0059	0.0055	0.0057	0.0057
0.0046	0.0054	0.0060	0.0054	0.0057	0.0058

Table 7.4   Recorded Values: Die Roll Measurements in Inches

Step 2. Arrange Measurements.   To create the median chart, the sample measurements for each subgroup are arranged in order from highest to lowest (Table 7.5).

Step 3. Calculate Median and Range Values.   The median and range for each subgroup are calculated (Table 7.5).

Step 4. Determine Subgroup Median Averages.   The average of the subgroup medians is calculated to find the centerline of the median chart. This value is placed on the chart (Figure 7.6).

Medians of the subgroups

$$\overline{X}_{Md} = \frac{0.0059 + 0.0057 + 0.0057 + \cdots + 0.0058}{12}$$

$$\overline{X}_{Md} = 0.0056$$

Step 5. Determine Subgroup Range Averages.   To find the centerline of the range chart, WP calculates the average of the subgroup ranges and places this value on the chart (Figure 7.6):

Table 7.5   Recorded Values Arranged in Order: Die Roll Measurements in Inches

Subgroups

	1	2	3	4	5	6
	0.0059	0.0060	0.0058	0.0054	0.0059	0.0060
Median	0.0059	0.0057	0.0057	0.0054	0.0058	0.0056
	0.0052	0.0054	0.0052	0.0054	0.0057	0.0055
Range	0.0007	0.0006	0.0006	0.0000	0.0002	0.0004
	7	8	9	10	11	12
	0.0052	0.0057	0.0058	0.0056	0.0058	0.0059
Median	0.0051	0.0055	0.0059	0.0055	0.0057	0.0058
	0.0046	0.0054	0.0060	0.0054	0.0057	0.0057
Range	0.0006	0.0003	0.0002	0.0002	0.0001	0.0002

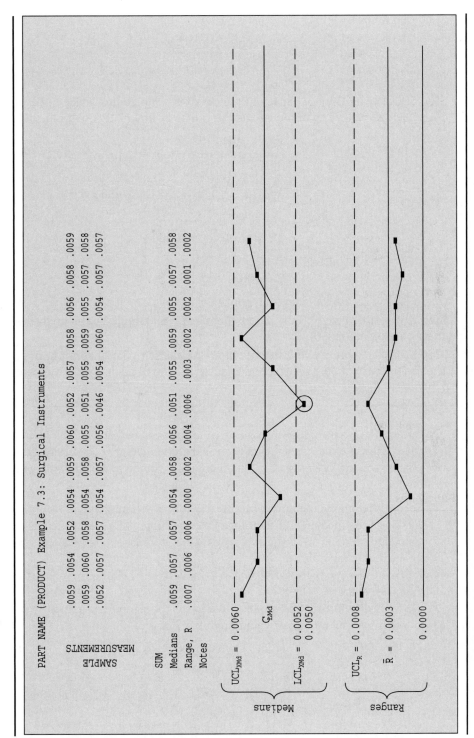

Figure 7.6   Median and Range Charts: Method I

Subgroup ranges

$$\overline{R}_{Md} = \frac{0.0007 + 0.0006 + 0.0006 + \cdots + 0.0002}{12}$$

$$\overline{R}_{Md} = 0.0003$$

Step 6. Calculate Control Limits. They determine the control limits of the median chart using the following formulas and the values in Table 7.3 and Appendix 2:

$$UCL_{Md} = \overline{X}_{Md} + A_6\overline{R}_{Md}$$
$$= 0.0056 + 1.19(0.0003) = 0.0060$$

$$LCL_{Md} = \overline{X}_{Md} - A_6\overline{R}_{Md}$$
$$= 0.0056 - 1.19(0.0003) = 0.0052$$

$$UCL_R = D_4\overline{R}_{Md}$$
$$= 2.574(0.0003) = 0.0008$$

$$LCL_R = D_3\overline{R}_{Md}$$
$$= 0(0.0003) = 0$$

where D_3 and D_4 are found in Appendix 2 using $n = 3$.

Step 7. Record Values. They record the median and range values on their appropriate charts (Figure 7.6).

Step 8. In this example, the median chart contains a point that is out of control. The R chart also should be watched to see if the run of points below the centerline continues. Q

An alternative to using the average of the subgroup medians for the centerline of the median chart is to use the median of the subgroup medians. The centerline for the range chart is the median range. The chart creation process and formulas are modified as follows:

1. Record the sample measurements on the control-chart form.
2. Calculate the median and the range for each subgroup.
3. Calculate the median of the subgroup medians. This will be the centerline of the median chart.
4. Calculate the median of the subgroup ranges. This will be the centerline of the range chart.
5. The control limits of the median and range charts are determined from the following formulas and the values in Table 7.6:

$$UCL_{Md} = Md_{Md} + A_5R_{Md}$$
$$LCL_{Md} = Md_{Md} - A_5R_{Md}$$
$$UCL_R = D_6R_{Md}$$
$$LCL_R = D_5R_{Md}$$

6. Record the median and range values on their appropriate charts.
7. Interpret the chart using the information presented in Chapters 5 and 6.

Subgroup Size	A_5	D_5	D_6	d_3
2	2.224	0	3.865	0.954
3	1.265	0	2.745	1.588
4	0.829	0	2.375	1.978
5	0.712	0	2.179	2.257
6	0.562	0	2.055	2.472
7	0.520	0.078	1.967	2.645

Table 7.6   Median Chart Values A_5, D_5, D_6, and d_3 Used in Median-Chart Construction with Median of Medians

EXAMPLE 7.4   Creating a Median Chart II

Rework Example 7.3 for WP Corporation's surgical instruments using the second method for creating median charts.

1. With a sample size of three, the sample measurements are taken and recorded (Table 7.4).
2. To create the median chart for each subgroup, the sample measurements are arranged in order from highest to lowest (Table 7.5).
3. To find the centerline of the median chart, the median of the subgroup medians is calculated and this value is placed on the chart (Figure 7.7).

Medians of the subgroups:

0.0059   0.0057   0.0057   0.0054   0.0058   0.0056
0.0051   0.0055   0.0059   0.0055   0.0057   0.0058

Arranged in order from highest to lowest:

0.0059   0.0059   0.0058   0.0058   0.0057   0.0057
0.0057   0.0056   0.0055   0.0055   0.0054   0.0051

$$Md_{Md} = 0.0057$$

4. To find the centerline of the range chart, the median of the subgroup ranges is calculated and this value is placed on the chart (Figure 7.7):

Subgroup ranges in order from highest to lowest:

0.0007   0.0006   0.0006   0.0006   0.0004   0.0003
0.0002   0.0002   0.0002   0.0002   0.0001   0.0000

$$R_{Md} = 0.00025$$

5. The control limits of the median chart are determined using the following formulas and the values in Table 7.6:

$$UCL_{Md} = Md_{Md} + A_5 R_{Md}$$
$$= 0.0057 + 1.265(0.00025) = 0.0060$$
$$LCL_{Md} = Md_{Md} - A_5 R_{Md}$$
$$= 0.0057 - 1.265(0.00025) = 0.0054$$

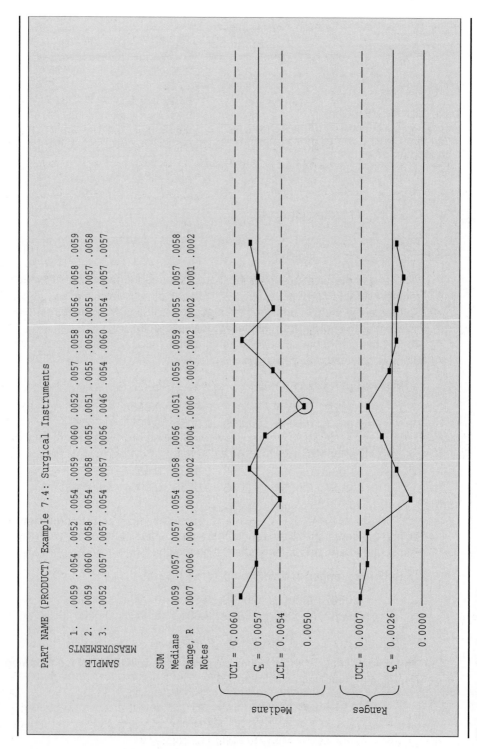

Figure 7.7 Median and Range Charts: Method II

$$UCL_R = D_6R_{Md}$$
$$= 2.745(0.00025) = 0.0007$$
$$LCL_R = D_5R_{Md}$$
$$= 0(0.00025) = 0$$

6. The median and range values are recorded on their appropriate charts (Figure 7.7).
7. The chart is interpreted using the information presented in Chapters 5 and 6. The median chart contains a single point below the lower control limit. The range chart displays a slight upward trend in the center of the chart. Both charts will be watched to see if anything of interest develops. Q→

RUN CHARTS

Run charts can be used to monitor process changes associated with a particular characteristic over time. Run charts are versatile and can be constructed with data consisting of either variables or attributes. These data can be gathered in many forms, including individual measurements, counts, or subgroup averages. Time is displayed on the x axis of the chart; the value of the variable or attribute being investigated is recorded on the y axis. Cycles, trends, runs, and other patterns are easily spotted on a run chart. As Figure 7.8 shows, financial performance over time is often displayed in the form of a run chart.

A run chart is created in five steps:

1. Determine the time increments necessary to properly study the process. These may be based on the rate at which the product is produced, on how often an event occurs, or according to any other time frame associated with the process under study. Mark these time increments on the x axis of the chart.
2. Scale the y axis to reflect the values that the measurements or attributes data will take.
3. Collect the data.
4. Record the data on the chart as they occur.
5. Interpret the chart. Since there are no control limits, the interpretation of a run chart is limited to looking for patterns in the data. A point that appears to be high or low cannot be judged as a special cause without control limits. It may be the worst data point in a series of points but that does not equate with being out of control.

EXAMPLE 7.5   Using Run Charts in Decision Making

A U.S. state highway route through a small town has had an increase in traffic accidents in recent years. The city manager has decided to do a traffic study to support the reduction of the speed limit, in hopes of reducing the number of traffic accidents. The study will cost approximately $2,000. Upon completion, the study will be turned over to the state's Department of Transportation. Factors that weigh into studying the speed limit include accident history, traffic volume, average speed of motorists, access points, and the width of the shoulder and roadway.

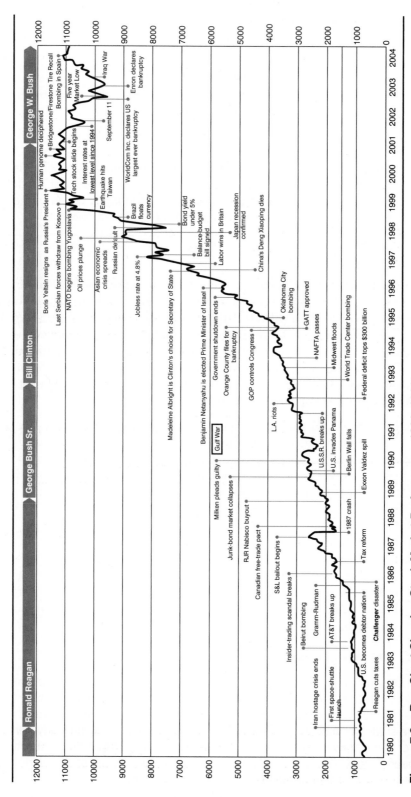

Figure 7.8   Run Chart Showing Stock Market Performance, 1980–1999
SOURCE: Stock charts.com/charts/historical

January 2000	10
May 2000	15
December 2000	10
January 2001	23
May 2001	26
December 2001	22
January 2002	30
May 2002	25
December 2002	30
January 2003	35
May 2003	38
December 2003	36

**Figure 7.9   Accident History
by Reported Month and Year**

Part of the study includes creating and studying run charts of the accident history:

1. Determine the time increments necessary to study the process properly. Under their current system, the city combines and reports accident information in January, May, and December. Information is available for the past 4 years. Time increments based on these months were marked on the x axis of the chart.
2. The y axis is scaled to reflect the number of accidents occurring each month.
3. The data were collected (Figure 7.9).
4. The data were recorded on the chart (Figure 7.10).
5. The chart, when interpreted, showed that accidents have definitely been increasing over the past four years. This will be very useful information when the state tries to determine whether or not to lower the speed limit.

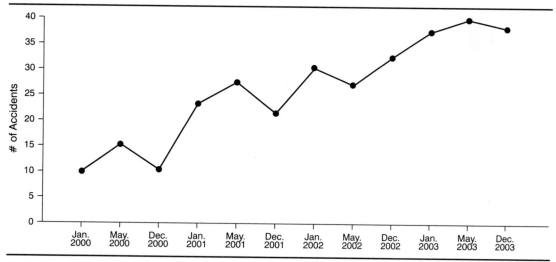

Figure 7.10   Run Chart—Accident History

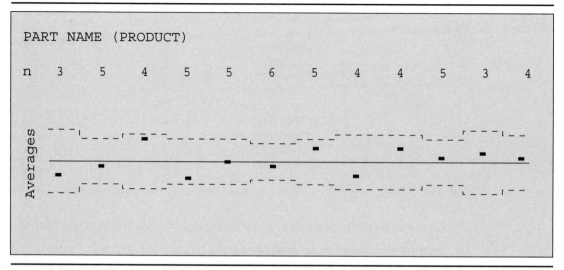

Figure 7.11   Variables Control Chart for Variable Subgroup Size

A CHART FOR VARIABLE SUBGROUP SIZE

Traditional variables control charts are created using a constant subgroup sample size. There are rare occurrences when, in the process of gathering data, the subgroup size varies. When this occurs it is necessary to recalculate the control limits to reflect the change in the A_2, D_4, and D_3 values caused by the different number of samples taken. For example, for a subgroup size n = 5, the A_2 value is 0.577; if n were to equal 3, then the A_2 value would be 1.023. Each subgroup with a different sample size will have its own control limits plotted on the chart, as shown in Figure 7.11. As discussed in previous chapters, as the subgroup size increases, the control limits will come closer to the centerline. The numerous calculations required with changing subgroup sizes limit the usefulness of this chart.

PRECONTROL CHARTS

Precontrol concepts were first introduced by Frank Satherwaite at Rath and Strong, a consulting firm, in the 1950s. *Precontrol charts study and compare product produced with tolerance limits.* The underlying assumption associated with applying precontrol concepts to a process is that the process is capable of meeting the specifications. Precontrol charts do not use control limits calculated from the data gathered from the process; the limits are created using specifications. This reliance on specifications or tolerances can result in charts that generate more false alarms or missed signals than a control chart does. Still, precontrol charts are simple to set up and run. They can be used with either variables or attribute data. They are particularly useful during setup operations and can help determine if the process setup is producing product centered within the tolerances. Precontrol charts can also be used to monitor very short production runs. Like control charts, precontrol charts can identify if the process center has shifted; they can also indicate an increase in the spread of the process. Precontrol charts are not as powerful as traditional control charts. They reveal little about the actual process performance. Unlike control charts, they cannot be used for problem-solving, nor can they be used for calculating process capability.

Keeping in mind the differences between the spread of the individuals versus the spread of the averages, some users of precontrol charts recommend using only a portion of the tolerance spread to ensure that the product produced will be within specification. How much of the tolerance to use depends on the process capability desired. If the process capability index is expected to be 1.2, then 100 percent divided by 120 percent, or 83 percent, of the tolerance should be used. Similarly, if the process capability index is expected to be 1.15, then 0.85 should be multiplied by the tolerance spread. A process capability index of 1.10 requires that 90 percent of the tolerance be used.

Creating a precontrol chart is a three-step process:

1. *Create the zones.*
   a. Place the upper and lower specification limits on the chart.
   b. Determine the center of the specification; this becomes the centerline on the chart.
   c. Create the zones by finding the center of area between the specification limits and the center of the tolerance. To do this, subtract the centerline from the upper specification limit, divide this value in half, and add the result to the centerline.
   d. To divide the lower half of the precontrol chart, subtract the lower specification limit from the centerline, divide this value in half, and subtract the result from the centerline.

These steps create four equal zones, as shown in Figure 7.12. The center two zones, one above and one below the centerline, are combined to create the green, or "go," section of the chart. The green zone centers on the process average and is the most

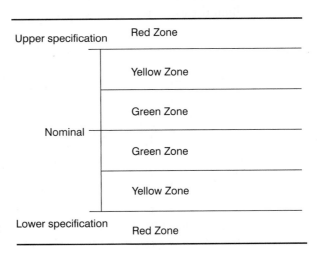

Figure 7.12   Precontrol Chart Showing Zones

Behavior of Chart	Action to Be Taken
Point in Green Zone	Continue
Point in Yellow Zone	Check Another Piece
Two Points in a Row in Same Yellow Zone	Adjust the Process Average
Two Points in a Row in Opposite Yellow Zones	Stop and Adjust Process to Remove Variation
Point in Red Zone	Stop and Adjust Process to Remove Variation

Table 7.7   Summary of Precontrol Setup Rules

desirable location for the measurements. The two sections nearest the upper or lower specification limit are colored yellow for caution. Part measurements in this area are farther away from the target value and approach the specification limits and are thus less desirable. The areas above and below the upper and lower specification limits, respectively, are colored in red. Points falling in these zones are undesirable. If the measurement falls in the red zones, the process should be stopped and adjusted.

2. *Take measurements and apply setup rules.*   Once the zones are established, measurements are plotted on the precontrol chart without further calculations. Set up the job and, beginning with the first piece, measure each piece as it is produced. Record the consecutive measurements on the chart. Use the setup rules described below and shown in Table 7.7 to monitor and adjust the process as necessary.
   a. If the measured pieces are in the green zone, continue running.
   b. If one piece is inside the specification limits, but outside the green limits, check the next piece.
   c. If the second piece is also outside the green limits, but still inside the specification limits, reset the process.
   d. If a piece is found to be outside the specification limits, stop, make corrections, and reset the process.
   e. If two successive pieces fall outside the green zone, one on the high side and one on the low side, those operating the process must immediately take steps to reduce the variation in the process.
   f. Whenever a process or machine is reset, five successive pieces inside the green zone must occur before the operator implements any type of sampling plan.
3. *Apply the precontrol sampling plan.*   When five pieces in a row fall in the green zone, it is OK to begin running the job. Use the run rules (Table 7.8), randomly sampling *two* pieces at intervals, to monitor the process. The two consecutive pieces must be selected randomly, yet with enough frequency to be representative of the process. Sampling may be based on time intervals— for instance, sampling two parts every 15 minutes. Some users of precontrol charts suggest sampling a minimum of 25 pairs between setups.

If the machine is reset for any reason, the precontrol setup rules should again be used to set up the process.

Behavior of Chart	Action to Be Taken
Both Points in Green Zone	Continue
One Point in Yellow Zone and One in Green Zone	Continue
Two Points in Same Yellow Zone	Adjust the Process Average
Two Points in Opposite Yellow Zones	Stop and Adjust Process to Remove Variation
Point in Red Zone	Stop and Adjust Process to Remove Variation; Begin Again at Precontrol Setup Rules

Table 7.8   Summary of Precontrol Run Rules

EXAMPLE 7.6   Creating a Precontrol Chart

At WP Corporation, which manufactures surgical instruments, parts are stamped from steel that arrives at the plant in coils, which are straightened before being stamped. During the setup of the straightening machine, the setup operator uses a precontrol chart to ensure that the setup operation has been performed properly. The designer has set the specifications as 0.0000 to 0.0150 inch in every 4 inches of uncoiled steel. The operator uses the following steps.

Step 1. Create the Zones.   The upper and lower specification limits to be placed on the chart are 0.0000 and 0.0150. From this the operator is able to determine the center of the specification, 0.0075, which is the centerline of the chart. After placing the specifications and centerline on the chart (Figure 7.13), the operator creates the

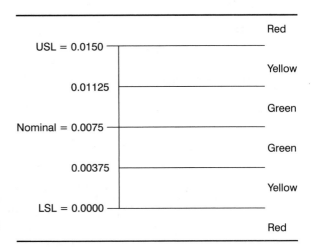

Figure 7.13   Precontrol Chart Showing Zones

zones by finding the center of the area between the specification limits and the centerline. He divides the upper half of the precontrol chart:

$$0.0150 - 0.0075 = 0.0075$$
$$0.0075 \div 2 = 0.00375$$
$$0.0075 + 0.00375 = 0.01125$$

He then divides the lower half of the precontrol chart:

$$0.0075 - 0.0000 = 0.0075$$
$$0.0075 \div 2 = 0.00375$$
$$0.0000 + 0.00375 = 0.00375$$

He thus creates four equal zones and labels them as shown in Figure 7.15.

Step 2. Take Measurements and Apply the Setup Rules.   Next the operator sets up the job, measures the coil as it is straightened, and records the measurements (Figure 7.14). As the first pieces are straightened, the operator uses the setup rules (Table 7.7) to monitor and adjust the machine as necessary.

For this example, as the consecutive measurements are placed on the precontrol chart (Figure 7.15), the following scenario unfolds. The first measurement of flatness is 0.0110, which is inside the green, or "run," zone of the precontrol chart. The second measurement is 0.0141, which is in the yellow zone. According to the rules, the next measurement must be taken: 0.0132. Since this measurement and the last one are both in the yellow zone, the process must be adjusted.

Setup Measurements

    0.0110
    0.0141
    0.0132
    0.0210
    0.0111
    0.0090
    0.0083
    0.0065
    0.0071

Run Measurements (2 taken every 10 min)

    0.0082
    0.0064

    0.0080
    0.0073

    0.0075
    0.0068

    0.0124
    0.0110

    0.0131
    0.0140

Figure 7.14   Recorded Values: Flatness

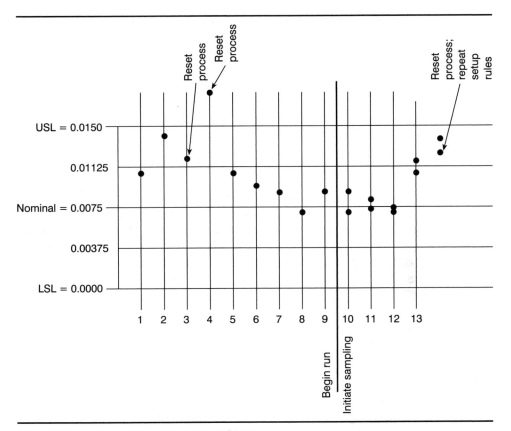

Figure 7.15   Completed Precontrol Chart

After making the adjustment, the operator takes another measurement: 0.0210. This value is in the red zone and unacceptable. The adjustment the operator made to the straightener has not worked out. Once again he must adjust the machine. The next reading is 0.0111, which is in the green zone so no further adjustments are needed. The next four pieces—0.0090, 0.0083, 0.0065, 0.0071—are also in the green zone. Since five measurements in a row are in the green zone, the machine is now ready to run, and sampling can begin.

Step 3. Apply the Precontrol Sampling Plan.   Having completed the setup and produced five pieces in a row in the green zone, the operator begins running the job. Using the run decision rules (Table 7.8), he randomly samples two pieces at intervals to monitor the process. The sampling plan for this process calls for taking two measurements every 10 minutes.

If the sets of measurements are in the green zone, the straightener should continue to run. In this instance, the first three sets of data—0.0082, 0.0064; 0.0080, 0.0073; 0.0075, 0.0068—are all within the green zone (Figure 7.15). Trouble begins to occur in the fourth subgroup—0.0124, 0.0110. The first measurement is in the yellow zone, signaling a change in the process; the second measurement is in the green zone, so no adjustment is made at this time. The next set of readings—0.0131,

0.0140—confirms that the process has shifted. Both of these measurements are in the yellow zone. At this point the operator must adjust the process. After any changes are made to the process, monitoring must begin again with the precontrol setup rules.

SHORT-RUN CHARTS

Traditional variables control charts used in statistical process control work most effectively with long, continuous production runs. But in today's competitive environment, manufacturers find it more economical to switch from one product to another as needed. As the production runs get shorter and the number of products produced during each run decreases, applying traditional variables control charts becomes more difficult. Short-run charts have been developed to support statistical process control in this new production environment.

Several different methods have been developed to monitor shorter production runs. One possibility, studying the first and last pieces of the run, does not tell the investigator anything about the parts produced in between. Another method, 100 percent inspection, is costly and time-consuming and can be inaccurate. Traditional variables control charts, with separate charts for each part number and each different run of each part number, can be used. This creates an abundance of charts, yet very little information. Usually there is not enough information from a single run to calculate the control limits. The separate charts do not allow investigators to see time-related changes in the process associated with the equipment.

Unlike traditional control charts, which only have one part number per chart, short-run charts include multiple part numbers on the same chart. Because they display multiple part numbers, short-run control charts enable users to view the impact of variation on both the process and the part numbers. This focus on the process actually aids improvement efforts because the effects of changes can be seen as they relate to different part numbers.

Nominal $\overline{X}$ and R Charts

When creating a short-run control chart, the data are coded so that all the data, regardless of the part number, are scaled to a common denominator. This creates a common distribution and set of control limits. The **nominal $\overline{X}$ and R charts** *use coded measurements based on the nominal print dimension*. For example, if the print dimension is 3.750 ± 0.005, then the nominal dimension used for coding purposes is 3.750. Coding the measurements allows all part numbers produced by a given process to be plotted on the same chart. Because all products produced on a single machine are plotted on the same chart, the nominal $\overline{X}$ and R chart combination shows process centering and process spread. A critical assumption associated with this chart is that the process variation, as seen on the range chart, is similar for each of the part numbers being graphed on the charts. To ensure this, the chart should be constructed using parts from the same operator, machine, material, methods, and measurement techniques. If the process variation of a particular part number is more than 1.3 times greater than the total $\overline{R}$ calculated, then it must be charted on a separate control chart.

Use the following steps to create a nominal $\overline{X}$ and R chart:

1. Determine which parts will be monitored with the same control chart. Pay careful attention to select parts made by the same operator using the same machine, methods, materials, and measurement techniques.
2. Determine the nominal specification for each part number.
3. Begin the chart by collecting the data. The subgroup sample size should be the same for all part numbers.
4. Once the measurements have been taken, subtract the nominal value for the appropriate part number from the measurements. $\overline{X}$ is then calculated for each subgroup.
5. Plot the coded average measurements, $\overline{X}$'s, from step 4 on the chart. The coded values will show the difference between the nominal dimension, represented by a zero on the control chart, and the average measurement.
6. Continue to calculate, code, and plot measurements for the entire run of this particular part number.
7. When another part number is to be run, repeat the above steps and plot the points on the chart.
8. When 20 subgroups have been plotted from any combination of parts, the control limits can be calculated with a modified version of the traditional variables control chart formulas:

Nominal $\overline{X}$ chart

$$\text{Centerline} = \frac{\Sigma \text{ coded } \overline{X}}{m}$$

$$UCL_X = \text{centerline} + A_2\overline{R}$$
$$LCL_X = \text{centerline} - A_2\overline{R}$$

Nominal range chart

$$\overline{R} = \frac{\Sigma R_i}{m}$$

$$UCL_R = D_4\overline{R}$$
$$LCL_R = D_3\overline{R}$$

9. Draw the centerlines and control limits on the chart.
10. Interpret the chart.

EXAMPLE 7.7   Creating a Nominal $\overline{X}$ and R Chart

The Special Garden Tools Corporation has created a variety of garden tools designed using ergonomic (human factors) concepts. One of their product lines, pruning shears, offers three different sizes. A user will choose the size according to the operation the shears will perform. The smallest tool is used for light pruning; the largest tool is used for larger jobs, such as pruning tree limbs. All the pruners are handheld and are designed so as not to place undue force requirements on the user's hands. To ensure this, the shears undergo a clasping force test before being shipped to retail outlets for sale to customers. This inspection tests the amount of force it takes to close the tool during typical operations. Since this is a just-in-time operation, the production runs tend to be small. Management wants to create a nominal $\overline{X}$ and R chart that contains information from three different runs of pruning shears.

1. Those monitoring the process have determined that measurements from three parts will be recorded on the same chart. Careful attention has been paid to ensure that the parts have been made using the same machine, methods, materials, and measurement techniques.

2. They determine the nominal specification for each part number:

   ■ Hand pruners, the smallest shears, have a force specification of 300 ± 20 N.
   ■ Pruning shears, the midsized shears, have a force specification of 400 ± 30 N.
   ■ Lopping shears, the heavy-duty shears, have a force specification of 500 ± 40 N.

3. They now collect the data. The sample size n is 3. Table 7.9 contains the data for the hand pruner samples.

	Part	Nominal	Difference	$\overline{X}_i$
	304	300	4	
1	299	300	−1	0.33
	298	300	−2	
	306	300	6	
2	308	300	8	6.33
	305	300	5	
	300	300	0	
3	298	300	−2	0.33
	303	300	3	
	306	300	6	
4	300	300	0	4.33
	307	300	7	
	305	300	5	
5	301	300	1	0.33
	295	300	−5	
	298	300	−2	
6	306	300	6	2.00
	302	300	2	
	304	300	4	
7	301	300	1	0.67
	297	300	−3	

Table 7.9   Recorded Values and Differences: Hand Pruners

4. They subtract the nominal value for the appropriate part number from the measurements (Table 7.9). $\overline{X}_1$ is calculated by adding 4, −1, and −2, and dividing by 3.

$$\overline{X}_1 = \frac{4 + (-1) + (-2)}{3} = 0.33$$

5. They plot the coded average measurements from step 4 on the chart (Figure 7.16).
6. They then continue to calculate, code, and plot measurements for the entire run of the hand pruner shears.
7. Repeating the above steps, they add lopping shears (Table 7.10) and pruning shears (Table 7.11) to the chart.

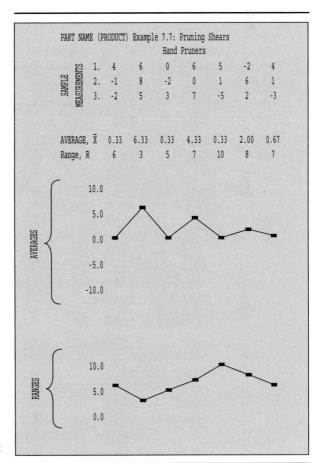

Figure 7.16   Short-Run Chart: Hand Pruners

Table 7.10   Recorded Values: Lopping Shears with a Force Specification of 500 ± 40 N

	Part	Nominal	Difference	$\overline{X}_i$
	510	500	10	
1	512	500	12	10.0
	508	500	8	
	507	500	7	
2	509	500	9	7.0
	505	500	5	
	509	500	9	
3	510	500	10	10.33
	512	500	12	
	507	500	7	
4	510	500	10	9.67
	512	500	12	
	507	500	7	
5	509	500	9	9.00
	511	500	11	
	512	500	12	
6	508	500	8	9.67
	509	500	9	
	507	500	7	
7	505	500	5	6.00
	506	500	6	
	506	500	6	
8	510	500	10	6.67
	504	500	4	

Table 7.11   Recorded Values: Pruning Shears with a Force Specification of 400 ± 30 N

	Part	Nominal	Difference	$\overline{X}_i$
	406	400	6	
1	401	400	1	2.00
	399	400	−1	
	404	400	4	
2	399	400	−1	1.67
	402	400	2	
	400	400	0	
3	402	400	2	0.00
	398	400	−2	
	395	400	−5	
4	400	400	0	−1.33
	401	400	1	
	400	400	0	
5	408	400	8	1.67
	397	400	−3	

8. Now that 20 subgroups have been plotted for the three types of pruners, they calculate the control limits with the modified version of the traditional $\overline{X}$ and R chart formulas:

Nominal $\overline{X}$ chart

$$\text{Centerline} = \frac{\Sigma \text{ coded } \overline{X}}{m} = \frac{0.33 + 6.33 + \cdots + 10 + 7 + \cdots + 1.67}{20}$$

$$= \frac{86.67}{20} = 4.33$$

$$\text{UCL}_X = \text{centerline} + A_2\overline{R}$$
$$= 4.33 + 1.023(5.55) = 10$$

$$\text{LCL}_X = \text{centerline} - A_2\overline{R}$$
$$= 4.33 - 1.023(5.55) = -1.35$$

where

$$\overline{R} = \frac{\sum R_i}{m} = \frac{111}{20} = 5.55$$

Nominal range chart

$$UCL_R = D_4\overline{R}$$
$$= 2.574(5.55) = 14.29$$
$$LCL_R = D_3R = 0$$

9. They draw the centerlines and control limits on the chart (Figure 7.17).
10. And finally they interpret the chart, which reveals that the hand pruner shears require lower forces than the target value to operate. For the lopping shears, there is less variation between shears; however, they all consistently need above average force to operate. As seen on the R chart, the pruning shears exhibit an increasing amount of variation in the force required. In general, the pruning shears require less force than the target amount to operate.

Nominal $\overline{X}$ and R charts are the most useful when the subgroup size (n) sampled is the same for all part numbers. This type of chart is best used when the nominal or center of the specifications is the most appropriate target value for all part numbers.

SUMMARY

Different control charts are applicable to different situations. With such a wide variety of charts available, creators of charts to monitor processes should determine what aspects of the process they wish to study and which chart will meet their needs.

The control chart selection flowchart in Figure 7.18 can help you select an appropriate chart.

■ *Lessons Learned*

1. Individuals and moving-range charts are used to monitor processes that do not produce enough data to construct traditional variables control charts.
2. Moving-average and moving-range charts are also used when individual readings are taken. Once a subgroup size is chosen, the oldest measurement is removed from calculations as each successive measurement is taken. These charts are less sensitive to changes in the process.
3. Charts that plot all the individual subgroup values are useful when explaining the concept of variation within a subgroup.
4. Median and range charts, though less sensitive than variables control charts, can be used to study the variation of a process. Two different methods exist to create median and range charts.
5. Run charts can be constructed using either attribute or variables data. These charts show the performance of a particular characteristic over time.

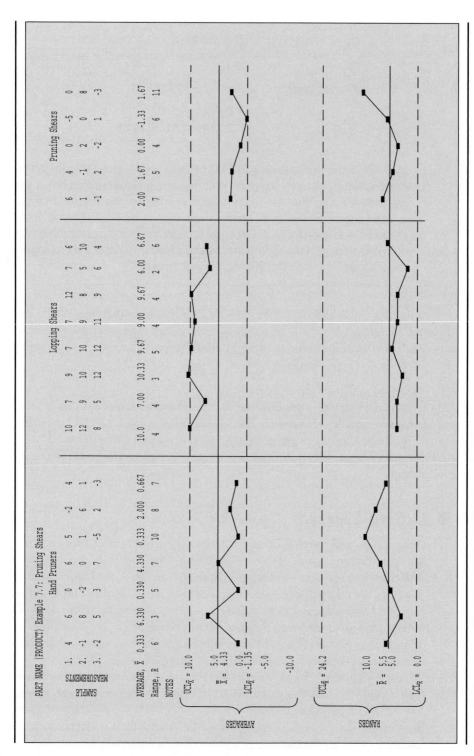

Figure 7.17 Completed Short-Run Chart, Example 7.7

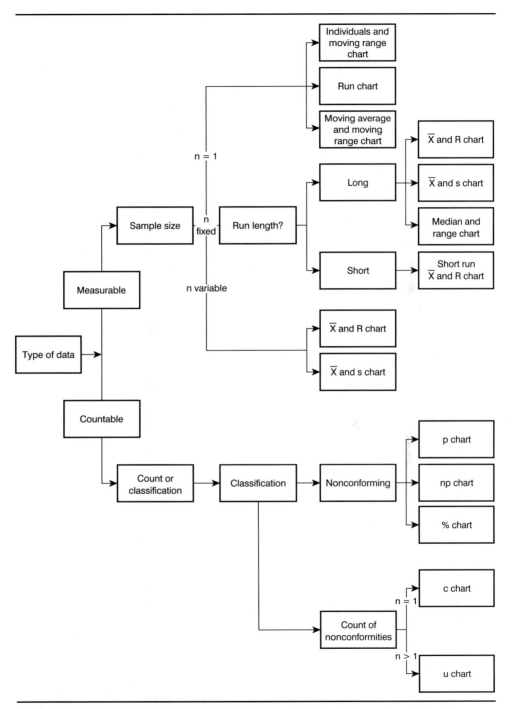

Figure 7.18   Control Chart Selection Flowchart

6. Charts for variable subgroup size require a greater number of calculations because the values of A_2, D_4, and D_3 in the formulas for the control limits change according to the subgroup sample size.
7. Precontrol charts compare the item being produced with specification limits. Precontrol charts are useful during machine setups and short production runs to check process centering.
8. The nominal $\overline{X}$ and R chart uses coded measurements to monitor process centering and spread on short production runs. ■

■ *Formulas*

Chart for Individuals with Moving-Range Chart

$$\overline{X}_i = \frac{\Sigma X_i}{m}$$

$$\overline{R} = \frac{\Sigma R_i}{m - 1}$$

$$UCL_X = \overline{X}_i + 2.66\overline{R}$$
$$LCL_X = \overline{X}_i - 2.66\overline{R}$$
$$UCL_R = 3.27\overline{R}$$

Charts for Moving Average and Moving Range

$$\text{Centerline } \overline{\overline{X}} = \frac{\Sigma X_i}{m}$$

$$\overline{R} = \frac{\Sigma R_i}{m}$$

$$UCL_{\overline{x}} = \overline{\overline{X}} + A_2\overline{R}$$
$$LCL_{\overline{x}} = \overline{\overline{X}} - A_2\overline{R}$$
$$UCL_R = D_4\overline{R}$$
$$LCL_R = D_3\overline{R}$$

Median and Range Charts

$$UCL_{Md} = \overline{X}_{Md} + A_6\overline{R}_{Md}$$
$$LCL_{Md} = \overline{X}_{Md} - A_6\overline{R}_{Md}$$
$$UCL_R = D_4\overline{R}_{Md}$$
$$LCL_R = D_3\overline{R}_{Md}$$

or

$$UCL_{Md} = Md_{Md} + A_5R_{Md}$$
$$LCL_{Md} = Md_{Md} - A_5R_{Md}$$
$$UCL_R = D_6R_{Md}$$
$$LCL_R = D_5R_{Md}$$

Short-Run Charts: Nominal $\overline{X}$ and R

$$\text{Centerline} = \frac{\Sigma \text{ coded } \overline{X}}{m}$$

$$\text{UCL}_X = \text{centerline} + A_2\overline{R}$$
$$\text{LCL}_X = \text{centerline} - A_2\overline{R}$$

$$\overline{R} = \frac{\Sigma R_i}{m}$$

$$\text{UCL}_R = D_4\overline{R}$$
$$\text{LCL}_R = D_3\overline{R}$$

Chapter Problems

Individuals Chart with Moving Range

1. Create a chart for individuals with a moving range for the measurements given below. (Values are coded 21 for 0.0021 mm.) After determining the limits, plotting the values, and interpreting the chart, calculate σ using $\overline{R}/d_2$. Is the process capable of meeting the specifications of 0.0025 $\pm$ 0.0005 mm?

   21 22 22 23 23 24 25 24 26 26 27 27 25
   26 23 23 25 25 26 23 24 24 22 23 25

2. Create a chart for individuals with a moving range from the Dow Jones Industrial Average month end data given below:

Sept.	6500	Sept.	9000
Oct.	5500	Oct.	9000
Nov.	7000	Nov.	8000
Dec.	7500	Dec.	7000
Jan.	9000	Jan.	9000
Feb.	9000	Feb.	9500
Mar.	8500	Mar.	9000
Apr.	6500		
May	6500		
June	7750		
July	7000		
Aug.	7750		

   How is the market performing?

3. Brakes are created by joining brake linings to mounting plates. Fine-blanked mounting plates are deburred before a single part is chosen randomly, and the depths of its two identical keyways are measured on the co-ordinate measuring machine and verified for accuracy and precision. For the 10 most recent samples, the depths of the keyways (in mm) have been recorded below. Create and interpret an individuals and moving range chart for each keyway. Compare the results between the keyways.

Subgroup	1	2	3	4	5	6	7	8	9	10
Keyway 1	2.0	2.1	2.0	1.9	1.9	2.0	2.0	1.9	2.0	2.0
Keyway 2	2.8	2.5	2.6	2.4	2.9	2.7	2.9	2.9	2.5	2.6

4. In a test lab, two different Rockwell hardness (R_C) testers are operated. One Rockwell hardness tester has a dial indicator; the other has a digital indicator. Both of the hardness testers are calibrated on a daily basis. For the data, shown in Table P7.1, from the C scale calibration results for the first 10 days of February, create and interpret charts for individuals and moving ranges for each of the Rockwell hardness testers.

Dial		Digital	
Individual R_c Measures	Range	Individual R_c Measures	Range
46.1		46.1	
	0.2		0.1
45.9		46.0	
	0.1		0.1
46.0		45.9	
	0.0		0.6
46.0		46.5	
	0.0		0.5
46.0		46.0	
	0.3		0.1
45.7		46.1	
	0.1		0.0
45.8		46.1	
	0.3		0.1
46.1		46.2	
	0.3		0.8
45.8		45.4	
	0.1		0.8
45.9		46.2	

Table P7.1   Recorded Values

Moving-Average with Moving-Range Charts

5. Use the following miles-per-gallon (mpg) data to create the centerline and control limits for a moving-average and a moving-range chart (n = 3). Comment on the chart.

	mpg		mpg
1	36	9	28
2	35	10	27
3	37	11	35
4	38	12	36
5	32	13	35
6	35	14	34
7	36	15	37
8	35		

6. Eighteen successive heats of a steel alloy are tested for R_C hardness. The resulting data are shown below. Set up control limits for the moving-average and moving-range chart for a sample size of n = 4.

Heat	Hardness
1	0.806
2	0.814
3	0.810
4	0.820
5	0.819
6	0.815
7	0.817
8	0.810
9	0.811
10	0.809
11	0.808
12	0.810
13	0.812
14	0.810
15	0.809
16	0.807
17	0.807
18	0.800

7. Create a moving-average and moving-range chart (n = 3) using the following NASDAQ information. How is the market performing?

Sept.	3650	Sept.	3900
Oct.	3550	Oct.	3900
Nov.	3700	Nov.	3800
Dec.	3750	Dec.	3700
Jan.	3900	Jan.	3900
Feb.	3900	Feb.	3950
Mar.	3850	Mar.	4000
Apr.	3650		
May	3650		
June	3775		
July	3700		
Aug.	3775		

Individual Chart

8. "Score depth" is the depth of a partial cut on a piece of metal. Pop-top lids
with pull tabs are scored to make it easy for the customer to remove the lid
but still keep the container closed during shipment and storage. Plot the
following score depth values on a chart plotting all individuals. The unit of
measure is coded for 0.0001 inch. Create the limits using the traditional $\overline{X}$
and R chart formulas presented in Chapter 5. Discuss how the spread of
the individuals is reflected in the R chart (n = 4).

Subgroup No.	1	2	3	4	5	6	7	8	9	10	11	12	13	14	15
	27	28	28	27	31	28	26	26	25	26	29	27	28	26	25
	33	32	29	33	34	34	34	33	32	32	36	34	35	33	33
	32	31	33	32	30	33	33	33	31	33	32	32	33	32	31
	26	27	33	28	28	29	27	27	28	28	29	27	31	28	25

Median and Range Chart

9. Create a median chart and a range chart with the following information.
Be sure to plot the points, limits, and centerlines (n = 3).

Subgroup No.	1	2	3	4	5	6
	6	10	7	8	9	12
	9	4	8	9	10	11
	5	11	5	13	13	10

10. "Expand curl height" refers to the curled lip on lids and tops. Curled edges of lids are crimped down to seal the top of the can. Using the following information on curl height, create median and range charts to study the process. The data are coded 74 for 0.0074 (n = 3). How is this process performing?

Sample	1	2	3	4	5	6	7	8	9	10	11	12	13	14	15	16	17	18	19
1	74	75	72	73	72	74	73	73	73	74	74	74	73	73	71	75	74	72	75
2	72	73	72	72	73	73	76	74	72	74	74	73	74	72	73	72	74	74	75
3	75	74	74	74	73	73	74	75	73	73	73	73	72	75	75	73	74	74	72

Run Charts

11. Create a run chart using the following information about the bond market. How is the market performing?

Sept.	5650	Sept.	5000
Oct.	5800	Oct.	5050
Nov.	5500	Nov.	4900
Dec.	5580	Dec.	5100
Jan.	5600	Jan.	5200
Feb.	5500	Feb.	5300
Mar.	5300	Mar.	5400
Apr.	5200		
May	5000		
June	5200		
July	5000		
Aug.	5100		

12. At a large vegetable processing plant, completed cans of product are placed in boxes containing 24 cans. These boxes are then placed on skids. When a skid is filled, the entire skid is shrink-wrapped in preparation for shipping. Concerns have been raised about the amount of shrink-wrap used in this process. A run chart was suggested as a way to keep track of material usage. Create a run chart with the following information. How does it look?

4
6
5
8
10
9
4
3
5
4
8
9
5
4
4
3
6
4

Recorded Values: Shrink-Wrap Usage

13. Create a run chart for the following torque measurements. (Values recorded left to right.)

Car Strut Nut Torque									
74.6	73.1	73.1	73.7	74.5	72.5	72.9	72.8	72.7	74.7
75.4	73.2	74.2	73.4	73.8	73.8	73.1	74.5	73.0	73.2
74.4	74.8	73.9	74.8	72.7	72.2				

14. Create a run chart for the following safety statistics from the security office of a major apartment building. The chart should track the total number of violations from 1989 to 1999. What does the chart tell you about their safety record and their efforts to combat crime?

	1989	1990	1991	1992	1993	1994	1995	1996	1997	1998	1999
Homicide	0	0	0	0	0	0	0	0	0	1	0
Aggravated Assault	2	1	0	1	3	4	5	5	6	4	3
Burglary	80	19	18	25	40	26	23	29	30	21	20
Grand Theft Auto	2	2	6	15	3	0	2	10	5	2	3
Theft	67	110	86	125	142	91	120	79	83	78	63
Petty Theft	37	42	115	140	136	112	110	98	76	52	80
Grand Theft	31	19	16	5	4	8	4	6	2	4	3
Alcohol Violations	20	17	16	16	11	8	27	15	10	12	9
Drug Violations	3	4	2	0	0	0	0	2	3	2	1
Firearms Violations	0	0	0	0	0	1	0	0	1	0	0

Precontrol

15. Describe the concept of precontrol. When is it used? How are the zones established?

16. NB Manufacturing has ordered a new machine. During today's runoff the following data were gathered concerning the runout for the diameter of the shaft machined by this piece of equipment. A precontrol chart was used to set up the machines. Recreate the precontrol chart from the following data. The tolerance associated with this part is a maximum runout value of 0.002 (upper specification). The optimal value is 0.000 (no runout), the lower specification limit.

Runout			
0.0021	0.0004	0.0009	0.0025
0.0013	0.0003	0.0020	0.0010
0.0018	0.0010	0.0012	
0.0007	0.0015	0.0021	
0.0002	0.0011	0.0022	
0.0030	0.0023	0.0004	
0.0024	0.0025	0.0027	
0.0006	0.0022	0.0020	
0.0002	0.0025	0.0011	
0.0006	0.0004	0.0018	

17. RY Inc. is in the business of producing medical and hospital products. Some of the products that they produce include surgical tables, stretchers, sterilizers, and examination tables. Surgical tables require spacer holes that are

drilled into the tables. When a drill bit becomes dull, the size of the hole being drilled becomes larger than the specification of 0.250 ± 0.010 cm. In the past, the operator would decide when to change the drill bits. RY Inc.'s quality engineer recently approved the use of precontrol charts to monitor the process. When parts enter the yellow zone, the operator knows that drill bit changing time is approaching. As soon as a part enters the red zone, the operator changes the bit. Using this information, create and interpret a precontrol chart for the following information.

0.250
0.250
0.251
0.250
0.252
0.253
0.252
0.255
0.259
0.261
0.249
0.250
0.250
0.250
0.252
0.251
0.253
0.254
0.254
0.256
0.259
0.259
0.260
0.261
0.248
0.248

Short-Run Charts

18. In an automatic transmission, a part called a parking pawl is used to hold the vehicle in park. The size of the pawl depends on the model of vehicle. Max Manufacturing Inc. makes two different thicknesses of pawls—a thin pawl, which has a nominal dimension of 0.2950 inch, and a thick pawl, which has a nominal dimension of 0.6850 inch. Both parts are stamped on the stamp machine. Max Manufacturing runs a just-in-time operation and

uses short-run control charts to monitor critical part dimensions. Pawl thickness for both parts is measured and recorded on the same short-run control chart. Create and interpret a short-run control chart for the following data:

0.2946	0.2947	0.6850	0.6853
0.2951	0.2951	0.6851	0.6849
0.2957	0.2949	0.6852	0.6852
0.2951	0.2947	0.6847	0.6848
0.2945	0.2950	0.6851	
0.2951	0.2951	0.6852	
0.2950	0.2952	0.6853	
0.2952	0.2949	0.6850	
0.2952	0.2944	0.6848	
0.2950	0.2951	0.6849	
0.2947	0.2948	0.6847	
0.2945	0.2954	0.6849	

19. A series of pinion gears for a van seat recliner are fine-blanked on the same press. The nominal part diameters are small (50.8 mm), medium (60.2 mm), and large (70.0 mm). Create a short-run control chart for the following data:

60.1	70.0	50.8
60.2	70.1	50.9
60.4	70.1	50.8
60.2	70.2	51.0
60.3	70.0	51.0
60.2	69.9	50.9
60.1	69.8	50.9
60.2	70.0	50.7
60.1	69.9	51.0
60.4		50.9
60.2		50.9
60.2		50.8

CASE STUDY 7.1
Precontrol

TIKI Inc. produces and distributes natural all fruit drinks. They sell several sizes of bottles: 10-, 16-, and 32-oz. Each bottle filling machine is capable of filling any of the three sizes of bottles. Each machine can also fill any of the seven different flavors of drinks offered by TIKI Inc. The versatility of the machines helps keep costs low.

Machine setup is required whenever the product line is changed. A change may be related to the size of bottle being filled or to the type of drink being placed in the bottle. For instance, often production scheduling will call for back-to-back runs of grape drink in all three sizes. While the mechanisms providing the grape drink are not altered, the machines must be set up to accommodate the three different bottle sizes. In order to ensure that the appropriate amount of product is placed in each bottle, careful attention is given to the setup process. TIKI Inc. uses precontrol to monitor the setup process and to prevent the operator from "tweaking" the machine unnecessarily.

Today's changeover requires a switch from the larger 32-oz family-size bottle of apple juice product to the smaller 10-oz lunch-size bottle. Since bottles that contain less than 10 oz of juice would result in fines from the Bureau of Weights and Measures, the specification limits associated with the 10-oz bottle are 10.2 ± 0.2 oz. The operator set up the chart. She created zones by dividing the width of the tolerance limits (upper specification limit minus lower specification limit) in half:

$$10.4 - 10.0 = 0.4 \text{ tolerance width}$$
$$0.4 \div 2 = 0.2$$

or 0.2 above the nominal dimension and 0.2 below the nominal. Additional zones were created by dividing the distance between each specification limit and the nominal in half:

$$10.4 - 10.2 = 0.2$$
$$0.2 \div 2 = 0.1$$
$$10.2 - 10.0 = 0.2$$
$$0.2 \div 2 = 0.1$$

As shown in Figure C7.1.1, the chart now has four sections: 10.4 to 10.3, 10.3 to 10.2, 10.2 to 10.1, and 10.1 to 10.0. The center two sections, one above and one below the centerline, are combined to create the green, or "go," section of the chart: 10.1 to 10.3. The two sections nearest the upper or lower specification limit, the yellow, or "caution," sections, include 10.3 to 10.4 and 10.0 to 10.1. The areas above and

PRECONTROL SHEET

MACHINE _____ OPERATION _____ PART NUMBER _____

DEPARTMENT _____ SHIFT _____ DATE _____ SHEET NO. _____

Specification/Dimension _____

DATE																		
TIME																		
MAX. TOL. 10.4																		
½ MAX. TOL. 10.3																		
NOMINAL 10.2																		
½ MIN. TOL. 10.1																		
MIN. TOL. 10.0																		

Specification/Dimension _____

DATE																		
TIME																		
MAX. TOL.																		
½ MAX. TOL.																		
NOMINAL																		
½ MIN. TOL.																		
MIN. TOL.																		

Figure C7.1.1   Precontrol Sheet for Case Study 7.1.

below the upper and lower specification limits—10.4 and 10.0, respectively—are colored in red.

Having created her chart, the operator set up and ran the 10-oz apple juice job. During the setup process the machine can be operated by hand to allow the operator to produce one bottle, stop the machine, check the fill level, and then start the machine to produce another bottle.

 Assignment

Using the following data, begin with the first column and create a precontrol chart. Be sure to apply both the setup rules and the run rules where applicable. When necessary, include a brief statement on the chart reflecting the decision rule that has been applied. Read the data in column format.

Sample Data		
10.35	10.20	10.25
10.41	10.18	10.12
10.33	10.21	10.22
10.31	10.25	10.27
10.22	10.26	10.28
10.20	10.31	10.26
10.19	10.28	10.26
10.20	10.25	10.22
10.23	10.21	10.20
10.21	10.17	10.15
10.20	10.09	10.11
10.22	10.08	10.09

CASE STUDY 7.2
Run Charts

MYRY Inc. designs and manufactures equipment used for making books. Their equipment includes binderies, printers, control systems, and material-handling devices. Until recently, they have been having difficulty during the final assembly process. Far too often, during the final assembly of a machine, a needed part would not be present. There has been no correlation between the missing parts and the type of machine being assembled. If a part is not available, an assembly person writes up an unplanned issue request. Once the assembly person receives a signature from the line supervisor, he or she can go to the stockroom and receive the part immediately. Unplanned issue parts are undesirable for two reasons. First, when a part is needed, work stops on the line. This time lost during assembly idles workers and equipment, costs money, and could cause delays in shipping. Second, the unplanned issued part must be taken from inventory, which means it may not be available when it is needed for the next machine.

The project engineers in charge of isolating the root cause of this problem and correcting it have used cause-and-effect diagrams to isolate the problem. Their investigation has shown that the computerized parts scheduling and tracking system is not up to the task. The data from their investigation convinced management to purchase and install a new parts scheduling and tracking system. The new system is a highly disciplined system, where all parts needed for constructing a piece of equipment are tracked from the moment the order is placed until construction is complete. In order for a part to be on the assembly floor, a requirement must exist in the system. The computer system turned out to be much more than a means of installing a counting system. Not only does the system track parts availability more accurately, when implementing the new system, MYRY had to improve their ordering and manufacturing processes. The new system enables all areas of the company to work together and communicate more efficiently. For example, purchasing can relay information directly to their vendors and track incoming part quality, eliminating stockouts due to late deliveries or quality problems. Bills of material from the engineering department can be transferred immediately to the factory floor or purchasing, wherever the information is needed. Manufacturing process changes have enabled them to route the equipment under construction through the factory more efficiently, avoiding lost parts and decreasing assembly time.

 Assignment

Create a run chart to track the performance of the parts scheduling and tracking system both before and after the change. Can you pick out where the change occurs? How do you know? Does the new system make a significant difference?

How do you know? Can you see the period of time where MYRY was getting used to the new system? What was the average number of unplanned issues before the change? During? After? What do you think the new level of total unplanned issues per week will average out to?

Total Unplanned Issues per Week

Week 1	164
Week 2	160
Week 3	152
Week 4	156
Week 5	153
Week 6	155
Week 7	150
Week 8	140
Week 9	145
Week 10	148
Week 11	138
Week 12	150
Week 13	147
Week 14	152
Week 15	168
Week 16	159
Week 17	151
Week 18	149
Week 19	154
Week 20	160
Week 21	108
Week 22	105
Week 24	92
Week 25	85
Week 26	60
Week 27	42
Week 28	31
Week 29	15
Week 30	6
Week 31	5
Week 32	6
Week 33	4
Week 34	5

III

Control Charts
for Attributes

8

Probability

 Learning Opportunities:

1. To become familiar with seven probability theorems
2. To become familiar with the discrete probability distributions: hypergeometric, binomial, and Poisson
3. To review the normal continuous probability distribution
4. To become familiar with the binomial approximation to the hypergeometric, the Poisson approximation to the binomial, and other approximations ■

Thirty People at a Party

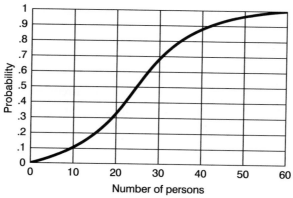

The Likelihood of Sharing a Birthday

Often we are surprised at a party or in a class to discover that someone has the same birthday as we do. It seems like such an unusual coincidence. In fact, as seen in the chart above, as the number of people gathered together increases, the chance of two people in the group having the same birthday increases dramatically. Try verifying this phenomenon in your class.

Probability is the chance that an event will occur. When an event has a certain probability, that doesn't mean the event will definitely happen; probabilities specify the chance of an event happening. This chapter discusses probability and its application to quality.

Probability affects all aspects of our lives. Intuitively we understand things like the chance it will rain, the probability of there being a traffic jam on the commute to school or to work, or the chance that a particular concert will sell out on the first day that tickets go on sale. **Probability** *is the chance that something will happen.* Probabilities *quantify* the chance that an event will occur. However, having a probability attached to an event does not mean that the event will definitely happen.

A person's first exposure to probability theory usually occurs early in life in the form of the coin toss. A fair coin is tossed and the winner is the person who correctly predicts whether the coin will land face up or face down. After observing the way the coin lands a number of times, we see a pattern emerge: approximately half of the tosses land face up, half face down. In future coin tosses, whenever a pattern inconsistent with this 50-50 split emerges, we wonder if the coin is "fair."

Probability plays a role in the quality of products being produced or services being provided. There is the chance that a tool will break, that a line will clog, that a person will be late for an appointment, or that a service will not be performed on time.

PROBABILITY THEOREMS

The probability of an occurrence is written as $P(A)$ *and is equal to*

$$P(A) = \frac{\text{number of occurrences}}{\text{total number of possibilities}} = \frac{s}{n}$$

EXAMPLE 8.1   Determining Probabilities

$$P(\text{opening a 309-page book to page 97}) = \frac{1}{309}$$

There is only one successful case possible, only one page 97, out of the total cases of 309.
   Or

$$P(\text{heads}) = \frac{\text{coin lands head side up}}{\text{two sides of a coin}} = \frac{1}{2}$$

Or during a production run, two test parts are mixed in with a box of 25 good parts. During an inspection, the probability of randomly selecting one of the test parts is

$$P(\text{selecting a test part}) = \frac{2}{27}$$

Or a 104-key computer keyboard has been disassembled and the keys have been placed in a paper sack. If all of the keys, including the function keys, number keys, and command keys, are in the bag, what is the probability that one of the 12 function keys will be drawn randomly from the bag?

$$P(\text{selecting one of the 12 function keys}) = \frac{12}{104}$$

Theorem 1: Probability Is Expressed as a Number Between 0 and 1:

$$0 \leq P(A) \leq 1$$

If an event has a probability value of 1, then it is a certainty that it will happen; in other words, there is a 100 percent chance the event will occur. At the other end of the spectrum, if an event will not occur, then it will have a probability value of 0. In between the certainty that an event will definitely occur or not occur exist probabilities defined by their ratios of desired occurrences to the total number of occurrences, as seen in Example 8.1.

Theorem 2: The Sum of the Probabilities of the Events in a Situation Is Equal to 1.00:

$$\sum P_i = P(A) + P(B) + \cdots + P(N) = 1.00$$

EXAMPLE 8.2   The Sum of the Probabilities

A manufacturer of piston rings receives raw materials from three different suppliers. In the stockroom there are currently 20 steel rolls from supplier A, 30 rolls of steel from supplier B, and another 50 rolls from supplier C. From these 100 rolls of steel in the stockroom, a machinist will encounter the following probabilities in selecting steel for the next job:

$$P(\text{steel from supplier A}) = 20/100 = 0.20 \text{ or } 20\%$$
$$P(\text{steel from supplier B}) = 30/100 = 0.30 \text{ or } 30\%$$
$$P(\text{steel from supplier C}) = 50/100 = 0.50 \text{ or } 50\%$$

And from Theorem 2:

$$P(\text{steel from A}) + P(\text{steel from B}) + P(\text{steel from C}) = 0.20 + 0.30 + 0.50 = 1.00$$

Theorem 3: If P(A) Is the Probability That an Event A Will Occur, Then the Probability That A Will Not Occur Is

$$P(A') = 1.00 - P(A)$$

EXAMPLE 8.3   Determining the Probability that an Event Will Not Occur

Currently, the stockroom contains steel rolls from only suppliers A and B. There are 20 rolls from supplier A and 30 rolls from supplier B. If the roll selected was from supplier A, what is the probability that a roll from supplier B was not selected?

$$P(A') = 1.00 - P(A)$$

where

$$P(A) = P(\text{selecting a roll from supplier A}) = \frac{20}{50} = 0.40$$

Then

$$P(A') = P(\text{selecting a roll from supplier B}) = 1.00 - 0.40 = 0.60$$

Events are considered **mutually exclusive** if they cannot occur simultaneously. Mutually exclusive events can happen only one at a time. When one event occurs it prevents the other from happening. Rolling a die and getting a 6 is an event mutually exclusive of getting any other value on that roll of the die.

Theorem 4: For Mutually Exclusive Events, the Probability That Either Event A or Event B Will Occur Is the Sum of Their Respective Probabilities:

$$P(A \text{ or } B) = P(A) + P(B)$$

Theorem 4 is called "the additive law of probability." Notice that the "or" in the probability statement is represented by a "+" sign.

EXAMPLE 8.4   Probability in Mutually Exclusive Events I

At a party you and another partygoer are tied in a competition for the door prize. Those hosting the party have decided that each of you should select two values on a single die. When the die is rolled, if one of your values comes up, then you will be the winner. You select 2 and 4 as your lucky numbers. What is the probability that either a 2 or a 4 will appear on the die when it is rolled?

$$P(\text{rolling a 2 or a 4 on a die}) = P(2) + P(4)$$
$$P(2) = 1/6 \qquad P(4) = 1/6$$
$$P(\text{rolling a 2 or a 4 on a die}) = 1/6 + 1/6 = 1/3$$

EXAMPLE 8.5   Probability in Mutually Exclusive Events II

At the piston ring factory in Example 8.2, a machine operator visits the raw materials holding area. If 20 percent of the steel comes from supplier A, 30 percent from supplier B, and 50 percent from supplier C, what is the probability that the machinist will randomly select steel from either supplier A or supplier C?

$$P(\text{steel from supplier A}) = 0.20$$
$$P(\text{steel from supplier B}) = 0.30$$
$$P(\text{steel from supplier C}) = 0.50$$

Since the choice of steel from supplier A precludes choosing either supplier B or C, and vice versa, these events are mutually exclusive. Applying theorem 4, we have

$$P(\text{steel from A or steel from C}) = P(A) + P(C)$$
$$= 0.20 + 0.50$$
$$= 0.70$$

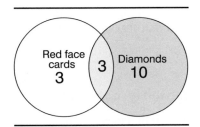

Figure 8.1   Venn Diagram

*Events are considered **nonmutually exclusive events** when they may occur simultane-ously.* If both can happen, then Theorem 4 must be modified to take into account the overlapping area where both events can occur simultaneously. For instance, in a deck of cards the King, Queen, and Jack of diamonds are both diamonds and red face cards (Figure 8.1).

> **Theorem 5: When Events A and B Are Not Mutually Exclusive Events, the Probability That Either Event A or Event B or Both Will Occur Is**

$$P(A \text{ or } B \text{ or both}) = P(A) + P(B) - P(both)$$

EXAMPLE 8.6   Probability in Nonmutually Exclusive Events I

A quality-assurance class at the local university consists of 32 students, 12 female and 20 male. The professor recently asked, "How many of you are out-of-state stu-dents?" Eight of the women and five of the men identified themselves as out-of-state students (Figure 8.2). Apply Theorem 5 and determine the probability that a student selected at random will be female, out-of-state, or both:

$$P(\text{female or out-of-state or both}) = P(F) + P(O) - P(both)$$

Counting the number of occurrences, we find

$$P(\text{female}) = 12/32$$
$$P(\text{out-of-state}) = 13/32$$
$$P(\text{both}) = 8/32$$
$$P(\text{female or out-of-state or both}) = 12/32 + 13/32 - 8/32$$
$$= 17/32$$

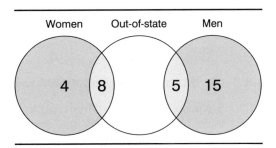

Figure 8.2   A Venn Diagram for Example 8.6

If the overlap of eight students who are both female and out-of-state had not been subtracted out, then, as shown by Figure 8.2, the total (25/32) would have been incorrect.

EXAMPLE 8.7   Probability in Nonmutually Exclusive Events II

The manager of a local job shop is trying to determine what routings parts make the most often through the plant. Knowing this information will help the manager plan machine usage. The manager has uncovered the following information:

$$P(\text{part requires plating}) = 0.12$$
$$P(\text{part requires heat-treating}) = 0.29$$

Parts that need plating may also need heat-treating. Therefore these events are not mutually exclusive, and

$$P(\text{part requires both plating and heat-treating}) = 0.07$$

The manager would like to know the probability that the part will require either plating or heat-treating. Applying Theorem 5:

$P(\text{part requires plating or heat-treating})$

$= P(\text{part requires plating}) + P(\text{part requires heat-treating})$
$\quad - P(\text{part requires both plating and heat-treating})$

$= 0.29 + 0.12 - 0.07$

$= 0.34$

It is not unusual for one outcome or event to affect the outcome of another event. *When the occurrence of one event alters the probabilities associated with another event, these events are considered* **dependent.**

Theorem 6: If A and B Are Dependent Events, the Probability That Both A and B Will Occur Is

$$P(A \, and \, B) = P(A) \times P(B|A)$$

In this theorem, the occurrence of B is dependent on the outcome of A. This relationship between A and B is represented by $P(A|B)$. The vertical bar ($|$) is translated as "given that." The probability that both A and B will occur is the probability that A will occur multiplied by the probability that B will occur, given that A has already occurred.

EXAMPLE 8.8   Probability in Dependent Events I

Suppose that a student from Example 8.6 has been chosen at random from the 32 in the class. If the student selected is female, what is the probability that she will be from out of state?

This is a conditional probability: the answer is conditioned on the selection of a female student. The formula in Theorem 6 will need to be rearranged to determine the answer:

$$P(B|A) = \frac{P(A \text{ and } B)}{P(A)}$$

$$P(\text{out-of-state}|\text{female}) = \frac{P(\text{female and out-of-state})}{P(\text{female})}$$

The probability of selecting one of the 12 females in the class is equal to P(female = 12/32. Since being female and being from out of state are dependent events, the probability of being both female and out-of-state [P(female and out-of-state)] = 8/32. These values can be verified by looking at Figure 8.2.

Completing the calculation, we find

$$P(\text{out-of-state}|\text{female}) = \frac{8/32}{12/32} = 2/3$$

Given that the student selected is female, the probability that she will be from out of state is 2/3.

EXAMPLE 8.9   Probability in Dependent Events II

In order to attend a business meeting in Los Angeles, a business traveler based in Cincinnati must first fly to Chicago and board a connecting flight. Because of the nature of the flights, the traveler has very little time to change planes in Chicago. On his way to the airport, he ponders the possibilities. On the basis of past traveling experience, he knows that there is a 70 percent chance that his plane will be on time in Chicago [P(Chicago on time) = 0.70]. This leaves a 30 percent chance that his Cincinnati-based plane will arrive late in Chicago. Knowing that if he arrives late, he may not be able to make the connecting flight to Los Angeles, he decides that the probability that he will be late in Chicago and on time in Los Angeles is 20 percent [P(Chicago late and Los Angeles on time) = 0.20]. Suppose that the traveler arrives late in Chicago. Given that he arrived late in Chicago, what is the probability that he will reach Los Angeles on time?

$$P(\text{L.A. on time}|\text{Chicago late}) = \frac{P(\text{Chicago late and L.A. on time})}{P(\text{Chicago late})}$$

From reading the problem, we know

$$P(\text{Chicago on time}) = 0.70$$

$$P(\text{Chicago late}) = 1 - 0.70 = 0.30$$

$$P(\text{Chicago late and L.A. on time}) = 0.20$$

$$P(\text{L.A. on time}|\text{Chicago late}) = \frac{0.20}{0.30} = 0.07$$

When events are **independent,** *one event does not influence the occurrence of another.* The result of one outcome or event is unaffected by the outcome of another event. Mathematically, events are considered independent if the following are true:

$$P(A|B) = P(A) \quad \text{and} \quad P(B|A) = P(B) \quad \text{and} \quad P(A \text{ and } B) = P(A) \times P(B)$$

EXAMPLE 8.10   Probability in Independent Events

A local mail order catalog business employs 200 people in the packaging and shipping departments. The personnel department maintains the records shown in Table 8.1. Questions have arisen concerning whether there has been a tendency to place female workers in the packaging department instead of in the shipping department. Management feels that there is no relationship between being female and working in the packaging department. In other words, they feel that these two events are independent. A quick probability calculation can enable the firm to determine whether this is true.

If an employee is selected at random from the 200 total employees, what is the probability that the employee works for the packaging department?

$$P(\text{Packaging}) = 80/200 = 0.4$$

If the employee selected is female, what is the probability that the employee works in the packaging department?

$$P(\text{packaging}|\text{female}) = \frac{P(\text{female and packaging})}{P(\text{female})} = \frac{32/200}{80/200} = 0.4$$

Independence can be established if the following are true:

$$P(\text{packaging}|\text{female}) = P(\text{packaging})$$
$$0.4 = 0.4$$

and

$$P(\text{female}|\text{packaging}) = P(\text{female})$$
$$\frac{32/200}{80/200} = 0.4$$

and from Table 8.1, it can be seen that

$$P(\text{female and packaging}) = P(\text{female}) \times P(\text{packaging})$$
$$32/200 = 80/200 \times 80/200$$
$$0.16 = 0.16$$

Since the three probability comparisons are equal, they are independent.

Theorem 7: If A and B Are Independent Events, Then the Probability That Both A and B Will Occur Is

$$P(A \text{ and } B) = P(A) \times P(B)$$

Sex	Department		
	Packaging	Shipping	Total
Female	32	48	80
Male	48	72	120
Total	80	120	200

Table 8.1   Employee Records

This is often referred to as a *joint probability*, meaning that both A and B can occur at the same time.

EXAMPLE 8.11   Joint Probability I

A company purchases fluorescent lightbulbs from two different suppliers. Sixty percent of the fluorescent bulbs come from WT Corporation, 40 percent from NB Corporation. Both suppliers are having quality problems. Ninety-five percent of the bulbs coming from WT Corporation perform as expected. Only 80 percent of the bulbs from NB Corporation perform.

What is the probability that a bulb selected at random will be from WT Corporation and that it will perform as expected?

Since the lightbulbs from supplier WT are separate and independent of the lightbulbs from supplier NB, Theorem 7 may be used to answer this question:

$$P(WT \text{ and perform}) = P(WT) \times P(\text{perform})$$
$$= (0.60) \times (0.95) = 0.57$$

Similarly, the probability that a bulb selected at random will be from NB Corporation and perform is

$$P(NB \text{ and perform}) = P(NB) \times P(\text{perform})$$
$$= (0.40) \times (0.80) = 0.32$$

The probabilities associated with the bulbs not performing can be calculated in a similar fashion:

$$P(NB \text{ and not performing}) = (0.40) \times (0.20) = 0.08$$
$$P(WT \text{ and not performing}) = (0.60) \times (0.05) = 0.03$$

EXAMPLE 8.12   Joint Probability II

The company is interested in determining the probability that any one bulb selected at random, regardless of the supplier, will not perform. This value can be found by remembering Theorem 2: The sum of the probabilities of the events of a situation is equal to 1.00:

$$P(A) + P(B) + \cdots + P(N) = 1.00$$

and Theorem 3: If P(A) is the probability that event A will occur, then the probability that A will not occur is

$$P(A) = 1.00 - P(A)$$

In this instance, four events can take place:

> The bulb tested is from WT Corporation and it performs.
> The bulb tested is from WT Corporation and it does not perform.
> The bulb tested is from NB Corporation and it performs.
> The bulb tested is from NB Corporation and it does not perform.

If the probabilities from these four events are summed, they will equal 1.00 (Theorem 2).

We already know the probabilities associated with the bulb performing:

$$P(WT \text{ and perform}) = (0.60) \times (0.95) = 0.57$$
$$P(NB \text{ and perform}) = (0.40) \times (0.80) = 0.32$$

Therefore, using Theorem 1, the probability that any one bulb selected at random, regardless of the supplier, will not perform is

$$P(\text{bulb not performing}) = 1.00 - P(WT \text{ and perform}) - P(NB \text{ and perform})$$
$$= 1.00 - 0.57 - 0.32$$
$$= 0.11$$

PERMUTATIONS AND COMBINATIONS

As the number of ways that a particular outcome may occur increases, so does the complexity of determining all possible outcomes. For instance, if a part must go through four different machining operations and for each operation there are several machines available, then the scheduler will have a number of choices about how the part can be scheduled through the process. Permutations and combinations are used to increase the efficiency of calculating the number of different outcomes possible.

 REAL TOOLS FOR REAL LIFE

Permutations and Combinations at RQM Inc.

The quality specialist at RQM Inc., an automotive manufacturer, received the following information in a report written by a field specialist, whose job it is to let the plant know about warranty complaints, issues, and claims.

Condition/Symptom   Customers have been requesting warranty service for inoperative and incorrectly read fuel gages for recently purchased Automobile Models R and Q.

Probable Cause   Incorrect fuel gages or incorrect fuel pumps installed at factory.

Immediate Corrective Action   Replace fuel units (pump and gages) with correct part depending on model.

Market Impact   To date there have been 39 warranty claims associated with fuel systems on Models R and Q. Each claim costs $2,000 in parts and labor.

The quality specialist visited the Fuel System Creation workstation to study its layout and its process flow map (Figures 8.3 and 8.4). She was able to determine that the creation of the fuel system requires that the operator visually identify the handwritten designation of the fuel tank type and install the correct fuel system (pump and gage combination). Visiting the related work stations, she determined that the labeling of the tank is currently done by hand at the station where the part is unloaded from the paint rack. The part sequence, date, shift, and model type are written in a location visible to the person at the Fuel System Installation workstation, but not easily read by the operator at the Fuel System Creation workstation. The pumps and gages are not labeled, but arrive at the workstation on separate conveyors. At the

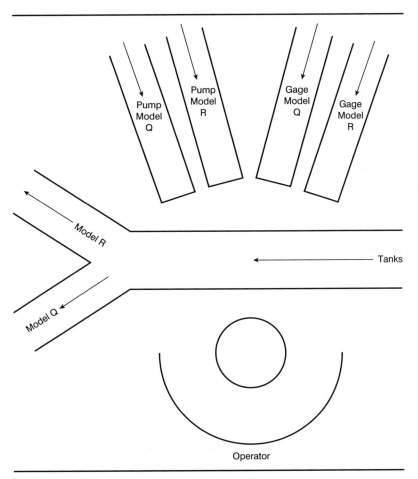

Figure 8.3   Workstation Layout for Fuel Systems

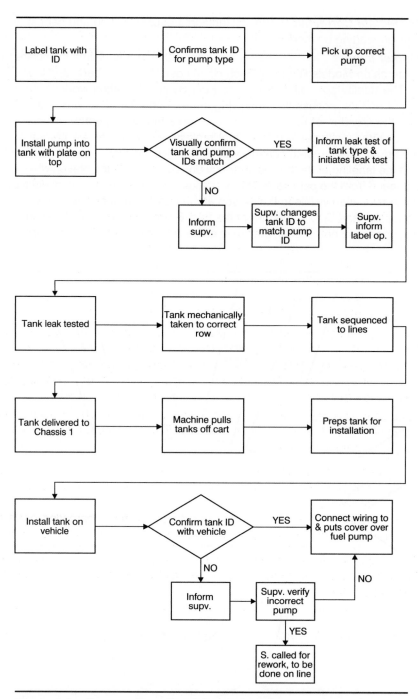

Figure 8.4   Process Flow Map for Fuel Systems

following station, the unit is checked for leaks. This operator is responsible for designating the tank type and sequencing the tank into the correct production line for either Model R or Model Q. The unit then proceeds to the final assembly line.

Models R and Q are produced on the same final assembly line. Similar in size, they require fuel pumps, gages, and tanks which on the outside look remarkably similar. Contemplating this problem, the quality specialist can see that a variety of permutations may exist.

> An R pump and gage combination may be correctly installed in a Model R.
> A Q pump and gage combination may be correctly installed in a Model Q.
> An R pump and gage combination may be installed in a Model Q.
> A Q pump and gage combination may be installed in a Model R.
> An R pump with a Q gage may be installed in a Model Q.
> An R pump with a Q gage may be installed in a Model R.
> A Q pump with an R gage may be installed in a Model Q.
> A Q pump with an R gage may be installed in a Model R.
> The pump may be inoperable or substandard.
> > Repeating the same permutations above.
> The gage may be inoperable or substandard.
> > Repeating the same permutations above.

It is enough to make a person's head spin and it certainly could become confusing for an operator who has 55 seconds to select and assemble a pump, a gage, and a tank. The possible errors an operator might make include: misreading the handwritten identification of the fuel tank, selecting the wrong pump, selecting the wrong gage, and placing the completed tank on the wrong assembly line.

Countermeasures   Having realized the large number of permutations and combinations that can result in errors for this process, the quality specialist proposes the following countermeasures:

- Label all components (tank, gage, pump) with a barcode.
- Install barcode readers on the conveyors feeding the fuel system creation workstation.
- Utilize computer software that compares the three barcoded parts selected and alerts the operator by sounding a bell if the components don't match.

This simple automated system should help simplify the selection process and eliminate sources of error in the process caused by the large number of permutations and combinations.

A ***permutation*** *is the number of arrangements that* n *objects can have when* r *of them are used:*

$$P_r^n = \frac{n!}{(n - r)!}$$

The order of the arrangement of a set of objects is important when calculating a permutation.

EXAMPLE 8.13   Calculating a Permutation I

While waiting in an airport, you strike up a conversation with a fellow traveler. She is trying to decide whether or not to phone a friend. Unfortunately she can remember only the first four digits (555-1???) of the friend's phone number, and she knows that the last three digits are not the same. How many different permutations are there when determining the last three digits?

To solve this equation, it is important to remember that the order is important. For instance, if the three needed numbers are a 1, a 2, and a 3, are the last three digits in the phone number 123 or 321 or 312 or 213 or 132 or 231? For each missing number there are 10 choices (0–9). Since no one number is repeated, those 10 choices must be taken three at a time:

$$P_r^n = \frac{n!}{(n-r)!} = \frac{10!}{(10-3)!} = 720$$

Should she try to discover her friend's phone number?

EXAMPLE 8.14   Calculating a Permutation II

At a local manufacturing facility, a scheduler is facing a dilemma. A part must go through the following three different machining operations in order, and for each of these operations there are several machines available. The scheduler's boss has asked him to list all the different ways that the part can be scheduled. The scheduler is reluctant to begin the list because there are so many different permutations. Using the following information, he calculates the number of permutations possible:

> Grinding (4 machines): The part must go to two different grinding machines, each set up with different tools.
> Heat-treating (3 units): Heat-treating the part takes only one heat treatment unit.
> Milling (5 machines): The part must go through three different milling machines, each set up with different tools.

The scheduler knows that order is important, and so the number of permutations for each work center must be calculated. These values will then be multiplied together to determine the total number of schedules possible.

Grinding (four machines selected two at a time):

$$P_r^n = \frac{n!}{(n-r)!} = \frac{4!}{(4-2)!} = 12$$

This can also be found by writing down all the different ways that the two machines can be selected. Remember, order is important:

$$12 \quad 13 \quad 14 \quad 23 \quad 24 \quad 21 \quad 34 \quad 32 \quad 31 \quad 43 \quad 42 \quad 41$$

Heat-treating (three machines selected one at a time):

$$P_r^n = \frac{n!}{(n-r)!} = \frac{3!}{(3-1)!} = 3$$

Milling (five machines selected three at a time):

$$P_r^n = \frac{n!}{(n - r)!} = \frac{5!}{(5 - 3)!} = 60$$

Since there are 12 different permutations to schedule the grinding machines, 3 for the heat treatment units, and 20 for the milling machines, the total number of permutations that the scheduler will have to list is 12 × 3 × 60 = 2160!   **Q**

When the order in which the items are used is not important, the number of possibilities can be calculated by using the formula for a **combination.** The calculation for a combination uses only the number of elements, with no regard to any arrangement:

$$C_r^n = \frac{n!}{r!(n - r)!}$$

EXAMPLE 8.15   Calculating a Combination

A problem-solving task force is being created to deal with a situation at a local chemical company. Two different departments are involved, chemical process engineering and the laboratory. There are seven members of the chemical process engineering group and three of them must be on the committee. The number of different combinations of members from the chemical process engineering group is

$$C_r^n = \frac{n!}{r!(n - r)!} = \frac{7!}{3!(7 - 3)!} = 35$$

There are five members of the laboratory group and two of them must be on the committee. The number of different combinations of members from the laboratory group is

$$C_r^n = \frac{n!}{r!(n - r)!} = \frac{5!}{2!(5 - 2)!} = 10$$

For the total number of different arrangements on the committee, multiply the number of combinations from the chemical process engineering group by the number of combinations from the laboratory group:

$$\text{Total} = C_3^7 \times C_2^5 = 35 \times 10 = 350 \qquad \textbf{Q}$$

DISCRETE PROBABILITY DISTRIBUTIONS

For a probability distribution to exist, a process must be defined by a random variable for which all the possible outcomes and their probabilities have been enumerated. Discrete probability distributions count attribute data, the occurrence of nonconforming activities or items, or nonconformities on an item.

Hypergeometric Probability Distribution

When a random sample is taken from a small lot size, the hypergeometric probability distribution will determine the probability that a particular event will occur. The hypergeometric is most effective when the sample size is greater than 10 percent of the size of the population (n/N > 0.1) and the total number of nonconforming items is known. To use the hypergeometric probability distribution, the population must be finite and samples must be taken randomly, without replacement. The following formula is used to calculate the probability an event will occur:

$$P(d) = \frac{C_d^D \, C_{n-d}^{N-D}}{C_n^N}$$

$$P(d) = \frac{\dfrac{D!}{d!(D-d)!}\left[\dfrac{(N-D)!}{(n-d)![(N-D)-(n-d)]!}\right]}{\dfrac{N!}{n!(N-n)!}}$$

where

D = number of nonconforming or defective units in lot
d = number of nonconforming or defective units in sample
N = lot size
n = sample size
$N - D$ = number of conforming units in lot
$n - d$ = number of conforming units in sample

The hypergeometric distribution is an exact distribution; the P(d) translates to the probability of exactly d nonconformities. In the numerator, the first combination is the combination of all nonconforming items in the population and in the sample. The second combination is for all of the conforming items in the population and the sample. The denominator is the combination of the total population and the total number sampled.

EXAMPLE 8.16   Forgery Detection Using the Hypergeometric Probability Distribution

To help train their agents in forgery detection, officials have hidden four counterfeit stock certificates with 11 authentic certificates. What is the probability that the trainees will select one counterfeit certificate in a random sample (without replacement) of three?

D = number of counterfeits in lot = 4
d = seeking the probability that one counterfeit will be found = 1
N = lot size = 15
n = sample size = 3
$N - D$ = number of authentic certificates in lot = 11
$n - d$ = number of authentic certificates in sample = 2

$$P(1) = \frac{C_1^4 C_2^{11}}{C_3^{15}}$$

$$= \frac{\left[\dfrac{4!}{1!(4-1)!}\right]\left[\dfrac{11!}{2!(11-2)!}\right]}{\dfrac{15!}{3!(15-3)!}} = 0.48$$

If the officials were interested in determining the probability of selecting two or fewer of the counterfeit certificates, the result would be

$$P(2\text{ or fewer}) = P(0) + P(1) + P(2)$$

$$P(0) = \frac{C_0^4 C_{3-0}^{15-4}}{C_3^{15}}$$

$$= \frac{\left[\dfrac{4!}{0!(4-0)!}\right]\left[\dfrac{11!}{3!(11-3)!}\right]}{\dfrac{15!}{3!(15-3)!}} = 0.36$$

$$P(1) = 0.48$$

$$P(2) = \frac{C_2^4 C_{3-2}^{15-4}}{C_3^{15}}$$

$$= \frac{\left[\dfrac{4!}{2!(4-2)!}\right]\left[\dfrac{11!}{1!(11-1)!}\right]}{\dfrac{15!}{3!(15-3)!}} = 0.15$$

The probability of selecting two or fewer counterfeit certificates is

$$P(2\text{ or fewer}) = P(0) + P(1) + P(2) = 0.48 + 0.36 + 0.15 = 0.99$$

The above probability can also be found by using Theorem 2 and calculating

$$P(2\text{ or fewer}) = 1 - P(3)$$

What is the probability selecting all four counterfeits? This can't be calculated because the sample size is only three. ℚ⟶

Binomial Probability Distribution

The **binomial probability distribution** was developed by Sir Issac Newton *to categorize the results of a number of repeated trials and the outcomes of those trials.* The "bi" in binomial refers to two conditions: The outcome is either a success or a failure. In terms of a product being produced, the outcome is either conforming or nonconforming. The distribution was developed to reduce the number of calculations associated with a large number of trials containing only two possible outcomes: success (s) or failure (f). Table 8.2 shows how complicated the calculations become as the number of trials held increases.

Number of Trials	Possible Outcomes*
1	s f
2	ss ff sf fs
3	sss fff ssf sff sfs fss ffs fsf
4	ssss ffff sfff ssff sffs sssf fsss ffss fffs fssf sfsf fsfs ssfs sfss ffsf fsff
5	sssss fffff sffff sfffs sffss sfsss fssss fsssf fssff fsfff sfsfs fsfsf ssfff ssffs ssfss ffsss ffssf ffsff ssssf sssff fffss ffffs sfsff fsfss sffsf fssfs sfssf fsffs ssfsf ffsfs fffsf sssfs

*Success = s; failure = f.

Table 8.2   Binomial Distribution: Outcomes Associated with Repeated Trials

The binomial probability distribution can be used if two conditions are met:

1. There is a nearly infinite number of items or a steady stream of items being produced.
2. The outcome is seen as either a success or a failure. Or in terms of a product, it is either conforming or nonconforming. The binomial formula for calculating the probability an event will occur is

$$P(d) = \frac{n!}{d!(n-d)!}p^d q^{n-d}$$

where

d = number of nonconforming units, defectives, or failures sought
n = sample size
p = proportion of nonconforming units, defectives, or failures in population
q = (1 − p) = proportion of good or conforming units or successes in population

This distribution is an exact distribution, meaning that the P(d) translates to the probability of exactly d nonconforming units or failures occurring. The mean of the binomial distribution is μ = np. The standard deviation of the binomial distribution is $\sigma = \sqrt{np(1-p)}$. The binomial distribution tables are found in Appendix 3.

EXAMPLE 8.17   Using the Binomial Probability Distribution in the Billing Department

The billing department of a local department store sends monthly statements to the store's customers. In order for those statements to reach the customer in a timely fashion, the addresses on the envelopes must be correct. Occasionally errors are made with the addresses. The billing department estimates that errors are made two percent of the time. For this continuous process, in which an error in the address is considered a nonconforming unit, what is the probability that in a sample of size eight, one address will be incorrect?

$$P(d) = \frac{n!}{d!(n-d)!}p^d q^{n-d}$$

where

d = number of nonconforming units sought = 1
n = sample size = 8
p = proportion of population nonconforming = 0.02
q = $(1 - p)$ = proportion of conforming units = $1 - 0.02$

$$P(1) = \frac{8!}{1!(8-1)!}0.02^1 0.98^{8-1} = 0.14$$

Cumulative binomial distribution tables are included in Appendix 4. To utilize the appendix, match the sample size (n) with the number of nonconforming/defective units sought (d) and the proportion of nonconforming units/defectives in the population (p). Since this table is cumulative and we are seeking the probability of exactly 1 (P(1)), we must subtract the probability of exactly 0 (P(0)). For this example,

From Appendix 4:

$$P(1) = Cum\ P(1) - Cum\ P(0)$$
$$= 0.9897 - 0.8508$$
$$= 0.1389 \quad \text{or } 0.14 \text{ when rounded}$$

d = 1					↓		$\widehat{n = 8}$		
p = 0.02	**p** **d**	*0.01*	*0.02*	*0.03*	*0.04*	*0.05*	*0.06*	*0.07*	
	0	0.9227	0.8508	0.7837	0.7214	0.6634	0.6096	0.5596	
	→ 1	0.9973	0.9897	0.9777	0.9619	0.9428	0.9208	0.8965	
n = 8	2	0.9999	0.9996	0.9987	0.9969	0.9942	0.9904	0.9853	

EXAMPLE 8.18   Using the Binomial Probability Distribution with Ceramic Tile

From experience, a manufacturer of ceramic floor tiles knows that 4 percent of the tiles made will be damaged during shipping. Any chipped, scratched, or broken tile is considered a nonconforming unit. If a random sample of 14 tiles is taken from a current shipment, what is the probability that two or fewer tiles will be damaged?

The binomial distribution can be applied because a steady stream of tiles is being manufactured and a tile can be judged either conforming or nonconforming. In order to calculate the probability of finding two or fewer, Theorems 2 and 3 must be applied:

$$P(2 \text{ or fewer}) = P(0) + P(1) + P(2)$$

$$P(d) = \frac{n!}{d!(n-d)!} p^d q^{n-d}$$

where

d = number of nonconforming units sought
n = sample size
p = proportion of population that is nonconforming
$q = (1 - p)$ = proportion of conforming units

$$P(0) = \frac{14!}{0!(14-0)!} 0.04^0 0.96^{14-0} = 0.57$$

$$P(1) = \frac{14!}{1!(14-1)!} 0.04^1 0.96^{14-1} = 0.33$$

$$P(2) = \frac{14!}{2!(14-2)!} 0.04^2 0.96^{14-2} = 0.09$$

Summing these values,

$$P(2 \text{ or fewer}) = P(0) + P(1) + P(2)$$
$$= 0.57 + 0.33 + 0.09 = 0.99$$

The binomial distribution tables from Appendix 4 may also be used in this example. This time, however, the probability being sought, P(2 or fewer), is cumulative. To utilize the appendix, match the sample size (n) with the number of nonconforming/defective units sought (d) and the proportion of nonconforming units/defectives in the population (p). For this example,

From Appendix 4:

$$P(2 \text{ or fewer}) = 0.9833$$

The differences here are from rounding.

d = 2 or fewer

p = 0.04

n = 14

↓　　(n = 14)

d \ p	0.01	0.02	0.03	0.04	0.05	0.06	0.07
0	0.8687	0.7536	0.6528	0.5647	0.4877	0.4205	0.3620
1	0.9916	0.9690	0.9355	0.8941	0.8470	0.7963	0.7436
→ 2	0.9997	0.9975	0.9923	0.9833	0.9699	0.9522	0.9302
3	1.0000	0.9999	0.9994	0.9981	0.9958	0.9920	0.9864
4	1.0000	1.0000	1.0000	0.9998	0.9996	0.9990	0.9980

REAL TOOLS FOR REAL LIFE

Drinking Water Quality

The Environmental Protection Agency (EPA) requires municipalities to regularly sample the water they provide in order to ensure safe drinking water. Contaminants are measured in units of parts per million (ppm) and parts per billion (ppb). Hortonville recently sampled for lead, copper, nitrate, and arsenic. Following sand filtration (Figure 8.5), samples were collected at 20 different times during the past month.

Lead and copper, from sources such as corrosion of household plumbing systems and erosion of natural deposits, have permissible levels of 15 ppb and 1.3 ppm, respectively. Nitrate can enter water sources through runoff from fertilizer use, leaching from septic tanks, sewage, and erosion of natural deposits. The nitrate permissible level is set at 10 ppm. Arsenic, from erosion of natural deposits, runoff from orchards, or glass and electronics production wastes, has a limit of 50 ppb.

The EPA requires testing only once per year for these contaminants because their concentration levels do not change frequently. Since water testing occurs relatively infrequently, the officials of Hortonville want to understand the probabilities associated with the contaminants. The binomial probability distribution is appropriate because the water is a steady stream and the outcome is seen as either a success or failure, either the contaminants are over the limit or they are not. First they set out to determine the probability that two or more samples will be found to have lead levels in excess of the limit of 15 ppb.

$$P(2 \text{ or more}) = 1.00 - P(1 \text{ or fewer}) = 1.00 - P(1) - P(0)$$

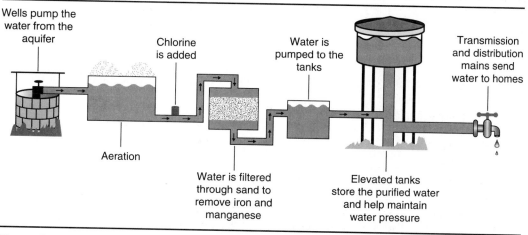

Figure 8.5 Water Distribution Chart

where

        d = number of nonconforming tests = 0, 1

        n = sample size = 20

        p = proportion of nonconforming tests = 0.05 from previous testing

        q = proportion of good tests = 0.95

$$P(1) = \frac{20!}{1!(20-1)!}(0.05)^1(0.95)^{19} = 0.38$$

$$P(0) = \frac{20!}{0!(20-0)!}(0.05)^0(0.95)^{20} = 0.36$$

$$P(2 \text{ or more}) = 1.00 - P(1 \text{ or fewer}) = 1.00 - 0.38 - 0.36 = 0.26$$

There is a 26% chance that the lead contaminant level in two or more of the next samples taken will be higher than the permissible limit of 15 ppb.

    For copper, nitrate, and arsenic, the same type of calculations were made.

    For copper:

where

        d = number of nonconforming tests = 0, 1

        n = sample size = 20

        p = proportion of nonconforming tests = 0.01 from previous testing

        q = proportion of good tests = 0.99.

$$P(2 \text{ or more}) = 1.00 - P(1 \text{ or fewer}) = 1.00 - P(1) - P(0) = 0.01$$

There is a 1% chance that 2 or more tests will contain concentrations of copper above the limit of 1.3 ppm.

    For nitrate:

where

        d = number of nonconforming tests = 0, 1

        n = sample size = 20

        p = proportion of nonconforming tests = 0.04 from previous testing

        q = proportion of good tests = 0.96.

$$P(2 \text{ or more}) = 1.00 - P(1 \text{ or fewer}) = 1.00 - P(1) - P(0) = 0.19$$

There is a 19% chance that 2 or more tests will contain concentrations of nitrate above the limit of 10 ppm.

    For arsenic:

where

        d = number of nonconforming tests = 0, 1

        n = sample size = 20

        p = proportion of nonconforming tests = 0.02 from previous testing

        q = proportion of good tests = 0.98.

$$P(2 \text{ or more}) = 1.00 - P(1 \text{ or fewer}) = 1.00 - P(1) - P(0) = 0.05$$

There is a 5% chance that 2 or more tests will contain concentrations of arsenic above the limit of 50 ppb.

These probabilities have given the officials a much better understanding of the possibilities that their constituents are drinking safe water. Due to the high probabilities associated with finding lead and nitrate in unacceptable concentrations in the drinking water, officials have begun work on a plan to improve the filtration system at the existing water treatment plant.

Poisson Probability Distribution

First described by Simeon Poisson in 1837, the **Poisson probability distribution** *quantifies the count of discrete events*. To use the Poisson distribution successfully, it is important to identify a well-defined, finite region known as the *area of opportunity* in which the discrete, independent events may take place. This finite region, or area of opportunity, may be defined as a particular space, time, or product. The Poisson distribution is often used when calculating the probability that an event will occur when there is a large area of opportunity, such as in the case of rivets on an airplane wing. The Poisson distribution is also used when studying arrival-rate probabilities. The formula for the Poisson distribution is

$$P(c) = \frac{(np)^c}{c!} e^{-np}$$

where

np = average count or number of events in sample
c = count or number of events in sample
$e \approx 2.718281$

EXAMPLE 8.19   Using the Poisson Probability Distribution

Each week the manager of a local bank determines the schedule of working hours for the tellers. On average the bank expects to have two customers arrive every minute. What is the probability that three customers will arrive at any given minute?

$$P(3) = \frac{2^3}{3!} e^{-2} = 0.18$$

where

np = average number of customers in sample = 2
c = number of customers in sample = 3
$e \approx 2.718281$

While calculating probabilities associated with the Poisson distribution is simpler mathematically than using either the hypergeometric or the binomial distribution, these calculations can be further simplified by using a Poisson table (Appendix 4). To establish the probability of finding an expected number of nonconformities (c) by using the table, np and c must be known.

EXAMPLE 8.20   Using a Poisson Table

The local branch office of a bank is interested in improving staff scheduling during peak hours. For this reason the manager would like to determine the probability that three or more customers will arrive at the bank in any given minute. The average number of customers arriving at the bank in any given minute is two.

P(3 or more customers arriving in any given minute)
$$= P(3) + P(4) + P(5) + P(6) + \cdots$$

Since it is impossible to solve the problem in this fashion, Theorems 2 and 3 must be applied:

P(3 or more customers arriving in any given minute)
$$= 1 - P(2 \text{ or fewer}) = 1 - [P(2) + P(1) + P(0)]$$

From the table in Appendix 5, np = 2, c = (2 or less) . Using the column for cumulative values,

$$1 - 0.677 = 0.323$$

or by calculation:

$$1 - \left[\frac{(2)^2}{2!} e^{-2} + \frac{(2)^1}{1!} e^{-2} + \frac{(2)^0}{0!} e^{-2} \right]$$

where

$$np = \text{average number of customers in sample} = 2$$
$$c = \text{number of customers in sample} = 0, 1, 2$$
$$e \approx 2.718281$$

The Poisson probability distribution is also an exact distribution. P(c) is the probability of exactly c nonconformities. The mean of the Poisson distribution is $\mu = np$. The standard deviation of the Poisson distribution is $\sigma = \sqrt{np}$.

REAL TOOLS FOR REAL LIFE

Injury and Cost Predictions Based on Probabilities

Treat and Plate Corporation, a second-tier automotive supplier, heat-treats and plates vehicle body components. Over time, their incident, accident, and injury rates have been steadily climbing. To reverse this trend, they have contacted the Bureau of Worker's Compensation (BWC) and asked for a site evaluation. Site evaluations involve visits from the three service branches of the BWC: ergonomics, safety, and industrial hygiene. BWC representatives visited Treat and Plate Corporation and studied plant operations.

Using Treat and Plate's claims history and nature of injury data, they created a Pareto diagram of the number of injuries within type categories. Figure 8.6 shows

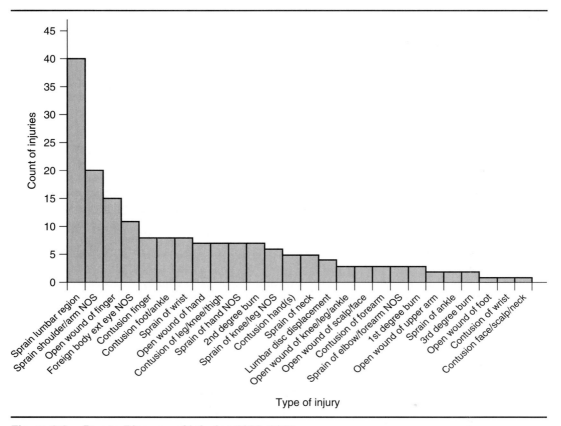

Figure 8.6   Pareto Diagram of Injuries 1998–2003

Sprain Lumbar Region as the most frequently occurring injury and Sprain of Shoulder and Arm as the second. Past experience with other companies statewide has shown that Sprain Lumbar Region and Sprain of Shoulder and Arm are rarely seen at the top of a list. Usually, Foreign Body in Eye or Open Wound of Finger lead the list.

Further investigation into the source of the sprains revealed that plant employees engage in a large amount of overhead work, including putting or pulling vehicle parts in and out of heat-treating units or plating vats. Workers frequently lift large parts, like hoods of cars, over waist height and sometimes up to face height. No lift assist devices exist anywhere in the plant. In this type of environment, Sprain of Shoulder and Arm and Sprain Lumbar Region injuries are bound to happen and when they do, they are expensive injuries to treat.

Though Treat and Plate could clearly see that these two types of sprains were prevalent in their plant, unfortunately, like many employers, they see insurance costs to cover injuries as part of the cost of doing business. The BWC representatives know that money talks and they used their knowledge of probability in order to show Treat and Plate that with their current injury occurrence rate, they have a high probability of incurring these two types of injuries in the next twelve months. High incident rates equal higher insurance rates.

Year	Sprain Lumbar Region	Sprain Shoulder/Arm
2003	3	2
2002	4	2
2001	7	5
2000	6	3
1999	9	6
1998	11	2
Totals	40	20
np =	6.67	3.3

Table 8.3   Sprains of Lumbar Region and Shoulder/Arm Occurrences

The BWC reps chose the Poisson distribution to use in their probability calculations because the Poisson distribution quantifies counts of discrete events, like injuries. The plant, with its 170 full-time and 75 part-time employees, it is a well defined finite region in which these discrete independent events take place, making the Poisson distribution applicable.

To calculate the probabilities associated with Sprain of Lumbar Region, the BWC reps first created a table showing the number of occurrences during each of the past six years (Table 8.3). From this data, they calculated np, the average number of Sprain of Lumbar Region occurrences during the past six years. Using this np value and the Poisson distribution, they created the Poisson probability distributions shown in Tables 8.4 and 8.5 and graphed in Figures 8.7 and 8.8.

For instance, to calculate P(5), the probability that five Sprain of Lumbar Region injuries, will occur is:

$$P(5) = \frac{(np)^c}{c!} e^{-np} = \frac{(6.7)^5}{5!} e^{-6.7} = 0.138$$

c	np	P(c)	Cum P(c)
0	6.7	0.001231	0.001231
1	6.7	0.008247	0.009478
2	6.7	0.027628	0.037106
3	6.7	0.061702	0.098808
4	6.7	0.103351	0.202159
5	6.7	0.13849	0.340649
6	6.7	0.154648	0.495297
7	6.7	0.14802	0.643317
8	6.7	0.123967	0.767284
9	6.7	0.092286	0.85957
10	6.7	0.061832	0.921402
11	6.7	0.037661	0.959063
12	6.7	0.021027	0.98009

Table 8.4   Sprain Lumbar Region Probabilities of Occurrence

c	np	P(c)	Cum P(c)
0	3.3	0.036883	0.036883
1	3.3	0.121714	0.158598
2	3.3	0.200829	0.359426
3	3.3	0.220912	0.580338
4	3.3	0.182252	0.76259
5	3.3	0.120286	0.882877
6	3.3	0.066158	0.949034
7	3.3	0.031189	0.980223
8	3.3	0.012865	0.993088
9	3.3	0.004717	0.997805
10	3.3	0.001557	0.999362
11	3.3	0.000467	0.999829
12	3.3	0.000128	0.999958

Table 8.5   Sprain Shoulder/ Arm Probabilities of Occurrence

In other words, there is a 13.8% chance that five Sprain of Lumbar Region injuries will occur in 2004. Table 8.4 shows calculations up to a dozen injuries, while Figure 8.7 shows both the probabilities and their cumulative sums. The probability of having 4, 5, or 6 Sprain of Lumbar Region injuries is relatively high, summing to:

$$P(4 \text{ or } 5 \text{ or } 6) = P(4) + P(5) + P(6) = 0.103 + 0.138 + 0.155 = 0.396$$

There is nearly a 40% chance of having 4, 5, or 6 Sprain of Lumbar Region injuries in 2004.

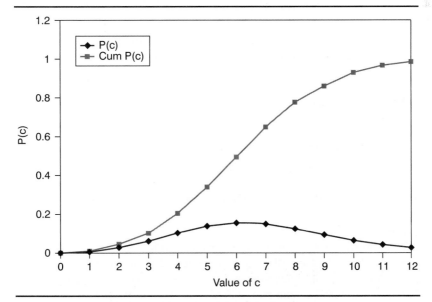

Figure 8.7   Probability of Sprain of Lumbar Region

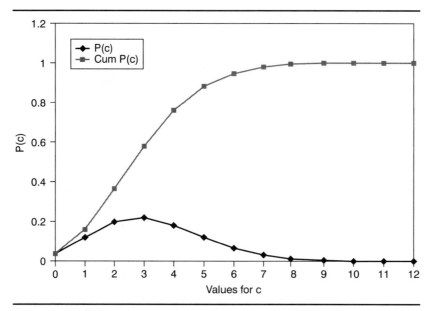

Figure 8.8   Probability of Sprain of Shoulder and Arm

They repeated this process for Sprain of Shoulder and Arm (Table 8.5 and Figure 8.8). For instance, the probability of having exactly three Sprain of Shoulder and Arm injuries in the next year would be calculated as:

$$P(3) = \frac{(np)^c}{c!} \, e^{-np} = \frac{(3.3)^3}{3!} \, e^{-3.3} = 0.221$$

Studying the data reveals that there is a 60.4% chance of having 2, 3, or 4 Sprain of Shoulder and an Arm injuries happen in 2004.

$$P(2 \text{ or } 3 \text{ or } 4) = P(2) + P(3) + P(4) = 0.201 + 0.221 + 0.182 = 0.604$$

Now that the probabilities are known, the BWC reps calculated the average costs associated with these types of injuries;

Sprain of Shoulder and Arm $8,850 per injury
Sprain of Lumbar Region $10,350 per injury

They also noted that the range associated with these values varied as much as $300 to $75,000 for Sprain of Shoulder and Arm and $200 to nearly $200,000 for Sprain of Lumbar Region.

Based on the high probabilities associated with these injuries and the high costs associated with treatment, Treat and Plate is engaging in job redesign to eliminate excessive lifting. Lift assists will also be added to many workstations. After all, the average cost of a lift assist device for their operations is $3000, significantly less than their expected losses due to injury.

CONTINUOUS PROBABILITY DISTRIBUTION

Normal Distribution

In situations where the data can take on a continuous range of values, a discrete distribution, such as the binomial, cannot be used to calculate the probability that an event will occur. For these situations, the normal distribution, a continuous probability distribution, should be used. Covered in Chapter 4, this distribution is solved by finding the value of Z and using the Z tables in Appendix 1 to determine the probability an event will occur:

$$Z = \frac{X_i - \overline{X}}{s}$$

where

$$Z = \text{standard normal value}$$
$$X_i = \text{value of interest}$$
$$\overline{X} = \text{average}$$
$$s = \text{standard deviation}$$

The values in the Z table can be interpreted either as frequencies or as probability values. The mean of the normal is np. The standard deviation of the normal is $\sqrt{npq}$.

EXAMPLE 8.21   Using the Normal Distribution to Choose Tool Resharpening Times

A tool on a stamping press is expected to complete a large number of strokes before it is removed and reworked. As a tool wears, the dimensions of the stamped part change. Eventually, the parts are unable to meet specifications. As a tool wears, it is removed from the press and resharpened. For this particular example, a combination of $\overline{X}$ and R charts is being used to monitor part dimensions. The $\overline{X}$ chart tracks the dimension of the part. After it reaches a certain point, the tool is pulled and reground. Those tracking the process have determined that the average number of strokes or parts the tool can complete is 60,000, with a standard deviation of 3,000. Determine the percentage of tools that will require regrinding before 55,000 strokes.

Figure 8.9 shows the normal probability distribution associated with this example. The area in question is shaded.

$$Z = \frac{55,000 - 60,000}{3,000} = -1.67$$

From the table in Appendix 1, the area to the left of 55,000 is equal to 0.0475. Only 4.75 percent of the tools will last for fewer than 55,000 strokes.

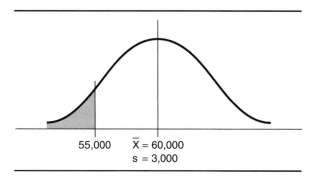

55,000 $\bar{X}$ = 60,000
          s = 3,000

Figure 8.9   Normal Probability Distribution for Example 8.21

EXAMPLE 8.22   Using Normal Distribution

If the normal operating life of a car is considered to be 150,000 miles, with a standard deviation of 20,000 miles, what is the probability that a car will last 200,000 miles? Assume a normal distribution exists.

Figure 8.10 shows the normal probability distribution associated with this example. The area in question is shaded:

$$Z = \frac{200{,}000 - 150{,}000}{20{,}000} = 2.5$$

From the table in Appendix 1, the area to the left of 200,000 is equal to 0.9938. To find the area in question,

$$1 - 0.9938 = 0.0062$$

There is a probability of 0.62 percent that the car will last for more than 200,000 miles.

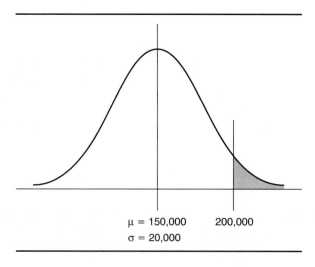

μ = 150,000   200,000
σ = 20,000

Figure 8.10   Normal Probability Distribution for Example 8.22

DISTRIBUTION INTERRELATIONSHIPS AND APPROXIMATIONS

Under certain situations the binomial, Poisson, and normal probability distributions can be used to approximate another distribution. Calculations associated with the hypergeometric distribution can be simplified under certain circumstances by using the binomial as an approximation. This substitution works best if the sample size n is less than ten percent of the population lot size ($n/N \leq 0.10$). The hypergeometric can also be approximated by the Poisson, provided the following is true: $n/N \leq 0.10$, $p \leq 0.10$, and $np \leq 5$.

The Poisson distribution can be used to approximate the binomial distribution if three conditions can be met: The population of the lot can be assumed to be infinite, the average fraction nonconforming (p) is less than 0.10 ($p \leq 0.10$), and the value of $np \leq 5$.

EXAMPLE 8.23   Using the Poisson Approximation to the Binomial

In Example 8.17, the binomial distribution was used to determine the probability that in a sample of size eight, one billing address will be incorrect. Use the Poisson approximation to the binomial to make the same calculation. Assume that the population of bills is nearly infinite.

Since the billing department estimates that errors are made two percent of the time, $p \leq 0.10$. With a sample size of eight, $np = (8 \times 0.02) = 0.16$; therefore, $np \leq 5$.

$$P(1) = \frac{0.16^1}{1!}e^{-0.16} = 0.14$$

where

$$np = \text{average number of customers in sample} = 0.16$$
$$c = \text{number of customers in sample} = 1$$
$$e \approx 2.718281$$

From Example 8.18,

$$P(1) = \frac{8!}{1!(8-1)!}0.02^1 0.98^{8-1} = 0.14$$

In this case, the Poisson is an excellent approximation to the binomial.

When p nears 0.5 and $n \geq 10$, the normal distribution can be used to approximate the binomial. Since the binomial distribution is discrete and the normal distribution is continuous, adjustments must be made to the normal distribution calculations when using the normal distribution to approximate the binomial. In Figure 8.11, a frequency diagram has been constructed using binomial data. The shaded cells in the figure are read as P(exactly 0) = 0.0282, P(exactly 1) = 0.1211, etc. A normal curve has been overlaid on the histogram. To use the normal distribution to approximate the probability of two nonconforming [P(2)], the area of a rectangle centered at 2 must be determined. Since the normal distribution is a continuous distribution, to capture this information, the area between 1.5 and 2.5 must be calculated. Instead of determining P(2), we must find the $P(1.5 \leq 2 \leq 2.5)$. In summary, to use the normal distribution to approximate the binomial, 0.5 must be added to and/or subtracted from the desired value according to the situation.

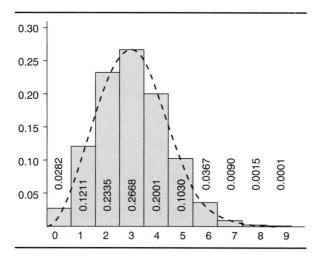

Figure 8.11   Binomial Distribution with Normal Distribution Overlay

EXAMPLE 8.24   Using the Normal Approximation to the Binomial

On average, 30 percent of the customers visiting a theme park take a ride on the train. Assume that visitors compose a steady stream and that they either ride on the train or they don't. Use the binomial distribution to determine the probability that 2 out of 10 randomly chosen visitors to the park will ride on the train:

$$P(2) = \frac{10!}{2!(10 - 2)!}0.30^2 0.70^{10-2} = 0.23$$

There is a 23 percent chance that two visitors from a sample of 10 will ride the train.

Refer to Figure 8.11 and use the normal approximation to the binomial to calculate the same probability. To determine P(2), $P(1.5 \le 2 \le 2.5)$ must be calculated. Using the normal distribution Z formula,

$$Z = \frac{X_i - \overline{X}}{s}$$

where

$$\overline{X} = np = 10(0.3) = 3$$
$$s = \sqrt{np(1 - p)} = \sqrt{10(0.3)(1 - 0.3)} = 1.45$$
$$P(1.5 \le 2 \le 2.5) = \frac{1.5 - 3}{1.45} \le Z \le \frac{2.5 - 3}{1.45}$$
$$-1.03 \le Z \le -0.34$$

Using the Z tables in Appendix 1,

$$P(1.5 \le 2 \le 2.5) = 0.22$$

This is a fairly close approximation to the binomial.

Use the normal approximation to the binomial to determine the probability that 2 or fewer visitors in a sample of 10 will ride on the train:

$$P(2 \text{ or fewer}) = P(0) + P(1) + P(2)$$

$$P(0 \le 2 \text{ or fewer} \le 2.5) = \frac{0 - 3}{1.45} \le Z \le \frac{2.5 - 3}{1.45}$$

Using the Z tables in Appendix 1,

$$-2.07 \le Z \le -0.34$$

$$0.3669 - 0.0192 = 0.3477, \text{ rounded to } 0.35$$

The same calculation performed using the binomial distribution will equal

$$P(2 \text{ or fewer}) = 0.38$$

In this situation, the normal approximation is a fairly close approximation to the binomial. Had the normal approximation not been adjusted, the approximation would not be close to the true probability value:

$$P(0 \le 2) = \frac{0 - 3}{1.45} \le Z \le \frac{2 - 3}{1.45}$$

$$-0.69 \le Z \le -2.07$$

$$0.2451 - 0.0192 = 0.23$$

SUMMARY

Probability, its theorems and distributions, plays an important role in understanding situations that arise in quality. Probability concepts also support the creation of control charts for attributes, which will be covered in the next chapter. The binomial distribution serves as the foundation for control charts for nonconforming units or activities. Control charts for nonconformities have the Poisson distribution as their basis.

■ *Lessons Learned*

1. Seven theorems exist to explain probability.
2. Discrete and continuous probability distributions exist to describe the probability that an event will occur.
3. The hypergeometric, binomial, and Poisson distributions are all discrete probability distributions.
4. The normal distribution is a continuous probability distribution.
5. The binomial and Poisson distributions can be used to approximate the hypergeometric distribution.
6. The Poisson and normal distributions can be used to approximate the binomial distribution. ■

 ■ *Formulas*

$$P(A) = \frac{\text{number of occurrences}}{\text{total number of possibilities}} = \frac{s}{n}$$

Theorem 1: Probability Is Expressed as a Number Between 0 and 1:

$$0 \leq P(A) \leq 1$$

Theorem 2: The Sum of the Probabilities of the Events in a Situation Is Equal to 1.00:

$$\Sigma P_i = P(A) + P(B) + \cdots + P(N) = 1.00$$

Theorem 3: If P(A) Is the Probability That an Event A Will Occur, Then the Probability That A Will Not Occur Is

$$P(A') = 1.00 - P(A)$$

Theorem 4: For Mutually Exclusive Events, the Probability That Either Event A or Event B Will Occur Is the Sum of Their Respective Probabilities:

$$P(A \, or \, B) = P(A) + P(B)$$

Theorem 5: When Events A and B Are Not Mutually Exclusive Events, the Probability That Either Event A or Event B or Both Will Occur Is

$$P(A \, or \, B \, or \, both) = P(A) + P(B) - P(both)$$

Theorem 6: If A and B Are Dependent Events, the Probability That Both A and B Will Occur Is

$$P(A \, and \, B) = P(A) \times P(B|A)$$

Theorem 7: If A and B Are Independent Events, Then the Probability That Both A and B Will Occur Is

$$P(A \, and \, B) = P(A) \times P(B)$$

Permutations

$$P_r^n = \frac{n!}{(n - r)!}$$

Combinations

$$C_r^n = \frac{n!}{r!(n - r)!}$$

Hypergeometric Probability Distribution

$$P(d) = \frac{C_d^D C_{n-d}^{N-D}}{C_n^N}$$

where

$$
\begin{aligned}
D &= \text{number of nonconforming or defective units in lot} \\
d &= \text{number of nonconforming or defective units in sample} \\
N &= \text{lot size} \\
n &= \text{sample size} \\
N - D &= \text{number of conforming units in lot} \\
n - d &= \text{number of conforming units in sample}
\end{aligned}
$$

Binomial Probability Distribution

$$
P(d) = \frac{n!}{d!(n-d)!}p^d q^{n-d}
$$

where

d = number of nonconforming units, defectives, or failures sought
n = sample size
p = proportion of nonconforming units, defectives, or failures in population
$q = (1 - p)$ = proportion of good or conforming units, or successes, in population

Poisson Probability Distribution

$$
P(c) = \frac{(np)^c}{c!}e^{-np}
$$

where

$$
\begin{aligned}
np &= \text{average count or number of events in sample} \\
c &= \text{count or number of events in sample} \\
e &\approx 2.718281
\end{aligned}
$$

Normal Distribution

$$
Z = \frac{X_i - \overline{X}}{s}
$$

using the Z table in Appendix 1.

Approximations

Hypergeometric distribution can be approximated by the binomial when $n/N \le 0.10$.

Hypergeometric distribution can be approximated by the Poisson when $n/N \le 0.10$, $p \le 0.10$, and $np \le 5$.

Binomial distribution can be approximated by the Poisson when the population of the lot is assumed to be infinite, $p \le 0.10$, and $np \le 5$.

Binomial distribution can be approximated by the normal when p nears 0.5 and $n \ge 10$.

Chapter Problems

Probability Theorems

1. The probability of drawing a pink chip from a bowl of different-colored chips is 0.35, the probability of drawing a blue chip is 0.46, the probability of drawing a green chip is 0.15, and the probability of drawing a purple chip is 0.04. What is the probability that a blue or a purple chip will be drawn?

2. At a local county fair, the officials would like to give a prize to 100 people selected at random from those attending the fair. As of the closing day, 12,500 people have attended the fair and completed the entry form for the prize. What is the probability that an individual who attended the fair and completed the entry form will win a prize?

3. At the county fair, the duck pond contains eight yellow ducks numbered 1 to 8, six orange ducks numbered 1 to 6, and ten gray ducks numbered 1 to 10. What is the probability of obtaining an orange duck numbered with a 5? Of obtaining an orange duck? Of obtaining a duck labeled with a 5?

4. If there are five different parts to be stocked but only three bins available, what is the number of permutations possible for five parts taken three at a time?

5. If a manufacturer is trying to put together a sample collection of her product and order is not important, how many combinations can be created with 15 items that will be placed in packages containing five items? If order is important, how many permutations can be created?

6. An assembly plant receives its voltage regulators from two different suppliers: 75 percent come from Hayes Voltage Co. and 25 percent come from Romig Voltage Co. The percentage of voltage regulators from Hayes that perform according to specification is 95 percent. The voltage regulators from Romig perform according to specification only 80 percent of the time. What is the probability that any one voltage regulator received by the plant performs according to spec?

7. If one of the voltage regulators from Problem 6 performed according to spec, what is the probability that it came from Hayes?

8. A large apartment complex may house as many as 500 tenants. Maintenance of the units is a full-time job. Most tenants treat their apartments with care, but some do not. In order to schedule maintenance workloads, one apartment complex tracks the probability of damage to their units. For their 300 tenant complex, 150 tenants are undergraduate students, 75 are graduate students, and 75 are working people. Five percent of undergraduate student tenants may damage their apartments, while only one percent of each of the other two categories of tenants will damage theirs. What is the probability that when inspecting an apartment, that particular apartment will have been damaged?

9. Suppose a firm makes couches in four different styles and three different fabrics. Use the table to calculate the probability that a couch picked at random will be made from fabric 1. If the couch is style 1, what is the probability that it will be made from fabric 2? What is the probability that a couch of style 4 will be selected at random? If a couch is made from fabric 3, what is the probability that it is a style 3 couch?

		Fabric		
Style	*F1*	*F2*	*F3*	*Total*
S1	150	55	100	305
S2	120	25	70	215
S3	80	60	85	225
S4	110	35	110	255
Total	460	175	365	1000

10. Use the information from Example 8.10 to calculate the following probabilities:

   a. If the employee selected at random is male, what is the probability that he works for the shipping department?

   b. If the employee selected at random is male, what is the probability that he works for the packing department?

   c. Is the probability of being male independent?

Hypergeometric Probability Distribution

11. The owner of a local office supply store has just received a shipment of copy machine paper. As the 15 cases are being unloaded off the truck, the owner is informed that one of the cases contains blue paper instead of white. Before the owner can isolate the case, it is mixed in with the other cases. There is no way to distinguish from the outside of the case which case contains blue paper. Since the cases sell for a different price than individual packages of paper, if the owner opens the case, it cannot be replaced (sold as a case). What is the probability that the manager will find the case that contains blue paper in one of the first three randomly chosen cases?

12. A robot is used to prepare cases of peanut butter for shipment. As the 12 cases are being loaded, two of the cases are dropped. Before the operator can isolate the cases, they are mixed in with the other cases. (This is the end of the production run, so there are no replacement cases.) What is the probability that the operator will find the two broken cases in the first four randomly chosen cases?

13. A rather harried father is trying to find a very popular doll for his daughter for Christmas. He has a choice of ten stores to go to. From a radio

announcement, he learned that the doll can definitely be found at four of the ten stores. Unfortunately, he did not hear which four stores! If the store he stops at does not have the doll, he will leave without buying anything; in other words, there is no replacement. He has time to go to only three stores. What is the probability that he will find the doll in two or fewer stops?

14. A lot of ten bottles of medicine has four nonconforming units. What is the probability of drawing two nonconforming units in a random sample of five? What is the probability that one or fewer nonconforming units will be chosen in a sample of five?

15. A group of 15 stock certificates contains 4 money making stocks and 11 stocks whose performance is not good. If two of these stocks are selected at random and given to an investor (without replacement), what is the probability that the investor received one money making stock?

16. Twenty water balloons are presented for inspection; four are suspected to have leaks. If two of these water balloons are selected at random without replacement, what is the probability that one balloon of the two selected has a hole in it?

17. A collection of 12 jewels contains 3 counterfeits. If two of these jewels are selected at random (without replacement) to be sold, what is the probability that neither jewel is counterfeit?

18. The local building inspector is planning to inspect ten of the most recently built houses for code violations. The inspector feels that four of the ten will have violations. Those that fail the inspection will be judged not suitable for occupation (without replacement). In a sample of three, what is the probability that two of the houses will fail inspection?

19. Coating chocolate with a hard shell began with M&M's during World War II. Coated candies were easier to transport because the coating prevented them from melting. Candy makers are very concerned about obtaining just the right mix of candies in each bag. They are also concerned about the appearance of their candies. Defective candies are those that are not completely color coated, those that are cracked or chipped, those whose colors do not meet standards, and misshapen candies. Tasty Morsels, Inc. is testing a new process that coats the chocolate centers with a gentler rotating motion. They are hoping that this new method will enable them to have fewer candies that are misshapen or damaged. During the runoff of the machine, the engineers are planning a small run of just enough candies to fill 12 bags. If they were to take a sample of just 3 bags, what is the probability that one nonconforming bag (a bag with defective candy) will be found?

Binomial Probability Distribution

20. A steady stream of bolts is sampled at a rate of 6 per hour. The fraction nonconforming in the lot is 0.034. What is the probability that 1 or fewer of the 6 parts will be found nonconforming?

21. An environmental engineer places monitors in a large number of streams to measure the amount of pollutants in the water. If the amount of pollutants exceeds a certain level, the water is considered nonconforming. In the past, the proportion nonconforming has been 0.04. What is the probability that one of the fifteen samples taken per day will contain an excessive amount of pollutants?

22. A steady stream of product has a fraction defective of 0.03. What is the probability of obtaining 2 nonconforming in a sample of 20?

23. Returning to Example 8.18, what is the probability that more than four tiles will be damaged in a shipment?

24. A steady stream of newspapers is sampled at a rate of 6 per hour. The inspector checks the newspaper for printing legibility. If the first page of the paper is not clearly printed, the paper is recycled. Currently, the fraction nonconforming in the lot is 0.030. What is the probability that 2 of the 6 papers checked will be nonconforming?

25. An assembly line runs and produces a large number of units. At the end of the line an inspector checks the product, labeling it as either conforming or nonconforming. The average fraction of nonconforming is 0.10. When a sample of size 10 is taken, what is the probability that 5 nonconforming units will occur?

26. An insurance company processes claim forms on a continuous basis. These forms, when checked by adjusters, are either filed as written or, if there is an error, returned to sender. Current error rates are running at 10 percent. In a sample of 6, what is the probability that more than two claims will be rejected because of errors?

27. A random sample of 3 bottles is selected from the running conveyor system. When the bottles are inspected, they are either properly labeled or they are not. Rejected bottles are scrapped. The proportion nonconforming is 0.25. What is the probability of there being 1 or fewer nonconforming units in the sample?

28. Plastic milk containers are produced by a machine that runs continuously. If five percent of the containers produced are nonconforming, determine the probability that out of four containers chosen at random, less than two are nonconforming.

Poisson Probability Distribution

29. A receptionist receives an average of 0.9 calls per minute. Find the probability that in any given minute there will be at least one incoming call.

30. If on the average 0.3 customers arrive per minute at a cafeteria, what is the probability that exactly three customers will arrive during a five minute span?

31. A computer software company's emergency call service receives an average of 0.90 calls per minute. Find the probability that in any given minute there will be more than one incoming call.

32. A local bank is interested in the number of customers who will visit the bank in a particular time period. What is the probability that more than two customers will visit the bank in the next 10 minutes if the average arrival rate of customers is three every 10 minutes?

33. The Tasty Morsel company wants to study the candy bag inspector's testing rate. Sample bags are opened and the contents checked. Inspectors can get very busy when production increases shortly before any holiday. From past experience, the inspectors have their workstations set up to handle two new bags arriving every minute on average. Find the probability that in any given minute, the inspectors will have to deal with five bags arriving to be inspected.

Normal Probability Distribution

34. The mean weight of a company's racing bicycles is 9.07 kg, with a standard deviation of 0.40 kg. If the distribution is approximately normal, determine (a) the percentage of bicycles weighing less than 8.30 kg and (b) the percentage of bicycles weighing between 8.00 and 10.10 kg.

35. Multicar accidents often result in fatalities. Across the nation, records are kept of the total number of accidents involving 10 or more vehicles. Over the past 25 years, the average number of accidents involving 10 or more cars is 7 per year. The standard deviation is 4. Assume that the distribution is approximately normal and determine (a) the percentage of years accumulating fewer than 4 multicar accidents and (b) the percentage of years having more than 12 multicar accidents.

Approximations

36. Use the Poisson approximation to the binomial to calculate the answer to Problem 26. Is this a good approximation?

37. Use the Poisson approximation to the binomial to calculate the answer to Problem 27. Is this a good approximation?

38. Use the Poisson approximation to the binomial to calculate the answer to Problem 21. Is this a good approximation?

39. Use the normal approximation to the binomial to calculate the answer to Problem 25. How good is the approximation?

40. Use the normal approximation to the binomial to calculate the answer to Problem 27. How good is the approximation?

CASE STUDY 8.1
Probability

PART 1

The registrar's office at a nearby university handles thousands of student class registrations every term. To take care of each student's needs efficiently and correctly, the registrar sees to it that a significant amount of time is spent in training the staff. Each staff member receives one of two types of training: A refresher course is given for current employees, and a general training course is given for new hires.

At the end of each of the training courses, a short exam tests the staff member's ability to locate errors on a registration form. A group of 15 registration forms contains 5 forms with errors. During the test, the staff member is asked to randomly select four forms and check them for errors. The sampling is to be done without replacement.

A major concern of those administering the test is that the forms with errors will not be selected by the staff member who is randomly selecting four forms.

 Assignment

Find the probability that in a lot of 15 forms, a sample of 4 forms will have no errors.

PART 2

The registrar receives a steady stream of registration forms for the three weeks prior to each term. While the office tries to provide easy-to-comprehend forms with complete instructions, a few forms are completed that are incorrect. Forms are considered incorrectly filled out if any key information is missing. Key information includes the student's local or permanent address, a course number or title, program or area of study, etc. When incorrect forms are received by the registrar's office they are sent back to the student for correction. This process delays the student's registration. While methods, forms, and instructions have been improving, the registrar feels that five percent of the forms are filled out incorrectly. To help continue improving the forms and instructions, he has 10 forms sampled each day to determine the types of errors being made. This information is shared with a quality improvement team whose members are currently working on improving the existing forms.

Assignment

Given that the process has a fraction nonconforming (p) of 5 percent (p = 0.05), what is the probability that in a sample of 10 forms, 3 or fewer will be found with errors?

PART 3

For the three weeks prior to the beginning of every term and for the first two weeks of the term, the registrar's office is very busy. To help determine staffing needs, the registrar decides to study the number of students and/or parents utilizing the office's services during any given minute. From past experience he knows that on average three new customers arrive every minute.

 Assignment

Find the probability that in any given minute, five new customers will arrive. What is the probability that more than seven new customers will arrive in a given minute?

CASE STUDY 8.2
Normal Probability Distribution

This case is the first of three related cases found in Chapters 8, 9, and 12. These cases seek to link information from the three chapters in order to resolve quality issues. Although they are related, it is not necessary to complete the case in this chapter in order to understand or complete the cases in the following chapters.

PART 1

Max's B-B-Q Inc. manufactures top-of-the-line barbeque tools. The tools include forks, spatulas, knives, spoons, and shish-kebab skewers. Max's fabricates both the metal parts of the tools and the resin handles. These are then riveted together to create the tools (Figure C8.2.1). Recently, Max's hired you as a process engineer. Your first assignment is to study routine tool wear on the company's stamping machine. In particular, you will be studying tool-wear patterns for the tools used to create knife blades.

In the stamping process, the tooling wears slightly during each stroke of the press as the punch shears through the material. As the tool wears, the part features become smaller. The knife has specifications of 10 mm ± 0.025 mm; undersized parts must be scrapped. The tool can be resharpened to bring the parts produced back into specification. To reduce manufacturing costs and simplify machine scheduling, it is critical to pull the tool and perform maintenance only when absolutely necessary. It is very important for scheduling, costing, and quality purposes that the average number of

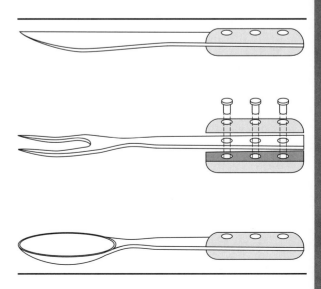

Figure C8.2.1   Barbeque Tools

strokes, or tool run length, be determined. Knowing the average number of strokes that can be performed by a tool enables routine maintenance to be scheduled.

It is the plant manager's philosophy that tool maintenance be scheduled proactively. When a tool is pulled unexpectedly, the tool maintenance area may not have time to work on it immediately. Presses without tools don't run, and if they are not running, they are not making money. As the process engineer studying tool wear, you must develop a prediction for when the tool should be pulled and resharpened.

The following information is available from the tool maintenance department.

- The average number of strokes for a tool is 45,000.
- The standard deviation is 2,500 strokes.
- A punch has a total of 25 mm that can be ground off before it is no longer useful.
- Each regrind to sharpen a punch removes 1 mm of punch life.
- The cost to regrind is

    2 hours of press downtime to remove and reinsert tool, at $300 per hour
    5 hours of tool maintenance time, at $65 per hour
    5 hours of downtime while press is not being used, at $300 per hour

- The average wait time for unplanned tool regrind is 15 hours at $300 per hour.
- Because of the large number of strokes per tool regrind, this is considered to be a continuous distribution. The normal curve probability distribution is applicable.

 Assignment

One percent of the tools wear out very early in their expected productive life. Early tool wearout—and, thus, an unplanned tool pull—can be caused by a variety of factors, including changes in the hardness of the material being punched, lack of lubrication, the hardness of the tool steel, and the width of the gap between the punch and the die. Key part dimensions are monitored using $\overline{X}$ and R charts. These charts reveal when the tool needs to be reground in order to preserve part quality. Use the normal probability distribution and the information provided to calculate the number of strokes that would result in an early wearout percentage of 1 percent or fewer. If the plant manager wants the tool to be pulled for a regrind at 40,000 strokes, what is the chance that there will be an early tool wearout failure before the tool reaches 40,000 strokes?

PART 2

Now that you have been at Max's B-B-Q Inc. for a while, the plant manager asks you to assist the production scheduling department with pricing data on a high volume job requiring knife blades for the company's best customer. As you know, it is the plant manager's philosophy to be proactive when scheduling tool maintenance (regrinds) rather than have to unexpectedly pull the tool. However, pricing will be a very important factor in selling this job to the customer. Essentially, the plant manager wants no unplanned tool pulls, but sales needs pricing cost reductions. The production scheduler would like a tool regrind schedule that results in minimal inventory.

 Assignment

You will soon be meeting with the plant manager and the managers from sales and production scheduling. They are expecting you to have an answer to the question: given the need to balance maximizing tool use, minimizing inventory, minimizing production disruption, and minimizing cost, how many strokes should you recommend to run this tool before pulling for a regrind?

Create a graph that shows the number of unplanned pulls versus the number of strokes. The graph should comprise at least six data points. Next, complete the spreadsheet in Figure C8.2.2. showing the costs of each individual's plan. Using the graph and the spreadsheet, prepare a response for the question, How many strokes should the tool be run before pulling it for a regrind? Your analysis should include answers to the following questions: How will this number balance tool use, cost, inventory, and production disruption? What are the economics of this situation?

	Plant Manager	Production Scheduler	Sales Manager	You
Strokes Before Pull	40,000	42,000	43,000	
Number of Pulls	25	25	25	
Production Over Life of Tool	1,000,000	1,050,000	1,075,000	
Cost of Each Pull	$2,425	$2,425	$2,425	$2,425
Additional Cost of an Unplanned Pull	$4,500	$4,500	$4,500	$4,500
Chance of Unplanned Pulls				
Total Additional Cost Due to Unplanned Pulls				
Total Cost				

Figure C8.2.2   Spreadsheet of Individual Plan Costs

Quality Control Charts for Attributes

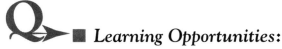

■ *Learning Opportunities:*

1. To learn how to construct fraction nonconforming (p) charts for both constant and variable sample sizes
2. To learn how to construct number nonconforming (np) charts
3. To learn how to construct percent nonconforming charts
4. To learn how to construct charts for counts of nonconformities (c charts)
5. To learn how to construct charts for nonconformities per unit (u charts) for both constant and variable sample sizes
6. To understand how to interpret p, np, c, and u charts ■

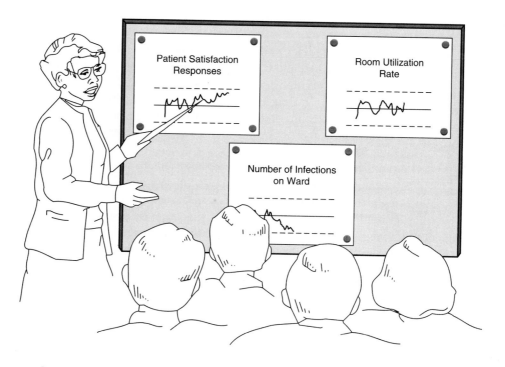

Service providers strive to give their customers what they want. How does a hotel or other service industry keep track of the quality of the services they are providing? What is the best way for a company to study the number of complaints or returns? How does a firm assess the nonconforming product being produced? Attribute charts, discussed in this chapter, can assist in monitoring processes providing goods or services. These charts can be used whenever counts or percentages of nonconformities can be obtained. Attribute charts enable users to track performance, monitor process stability, and discover where improvements can be made.

ATTRIBUTES

Attributes are characteristics associated with a product or service. These characteristics either do or do not exist, and they can be counted. Examples of attributes include the number of leaking containers, of scratches on a surface, of on-time deliveries, or of errors on an invoice. Attribute charts are used to study the stability of processes over time, provided that a count of nonconformities can be made. Attribute charts are used when measurements may not be possible or when measurements are not made because of time or cost issues.

Attribute data are relatively easy and inexpensive to collect. The product, when studied, either conforms to specifications or it does not. The most difficult part about collecting attribute data lies in the need to develop precise operational definitions of what is conforming and what is not. For instance, at first glance, creating specifications to judge the surface finish of a television screen appears straightforward. The surface should be free from flaws and imperfections. Simple enough, until questions arise concerning how will an imperfection be identified.

There are some disadvantages to using attribute charts. Attribute charts do not give any indication about why the nonconformity occurred, nor do the charts provide much detail. The charts do not provide information to answer questions like: Do several nonconformities exist on the same product? Is the product still usable? Can it be reworked? What is the severity or degree of nonconformance? The charts measure the increases and decreases in the level of quality of the process but provide little information about why the process changes.

Types of Charts

When nonconformities are investigated, two conditions may occur. The product or service may have a single nonconformity or several that prevent it from being used. These conditions are called "nonconforming." In other situations, the nonconforming aspect may reduce the desirability of the product but not prevent its use; consider, for example, a dented washing machine that still functions as expected. These are called "nonconformities." *When the interest is in studying the proportion of products rendered unusable by their nonconformities, a fraction nonconforming (p) chart, a number nonconforming (np) chart, or a percent nonconforming chart should be used. When the situation calls for tracking the count of nonconformities, a number of nonconformities (c) chart or a number of nonconformities per unit (u) chart is appropriate.*

CHARTS FOR NONCONFORMING UNITS
Fraction Nonconforming (p) Charts: Constant Sample Size

The *fraction nonconforming chart is based on the binomial distribution and is used to study the proportion of nonconforming products or services being provided.* This chart is also known as a fraction defective chart or p chart. A nonconforming or defective product or service is considered unacceptable because of some deviation from an expected level of performance. For a p chart, nonconformities render the product or service unusable and therefore nonconforming. Sometimes called "charts for defective or discrepant items," these charts are used to study situations where the product or service can be judged to be either good or bad, correct or incorrect, working or not working. For example, a container is either leaking or it is not, an engine starts or it does not, and an order delivered to a restaurant patron is either correct or incorrect.

Because of the structure of their formulas, p charts can be constructed using either a constant or variable sample size. A p chart for constant sample size is constructed using the following steps:

1. *Gather the data.* In constructing any attribute chart, careful consideration must be given to the process and what characteristics should be studied. The choice of the attributes to monitor should center on the customer's needs and expectations as well as on current and potential problem areas. Once the characteristics have been identified, time must be spent to define the acceptance criteria. When gathering the data concerning the attributes under study, identify nonconforming units by comparing the inspected product with the specifications. The number nonconforming (np) is tracked. Since a p chart studies the proportion or fraction of a process that is nonconforming, acceptance specifications should clearly state the expectations concerning conformance. In some cases, go/no-go gauges are used; in others, pictures of typical conforming and nonconforming products are helpful. In the service industry, details of incorrect bills, faulty customer service, or other performance criteria should be clearly established.

Once the characteristics have been designated for study and a clear understanding has been reached about what constitutes a conforming product or service, there are two aspects to gathering the data that must be dealt with: the sample size n and the frequency of sampling. The sample sizes for attribute charts tend to be quite large (for example, n = 250). Large sample sizes are required to maintain sensitivity to detect process performance changes. The sample size should be large enough to include nonconforming items in each subgroup. When process quality is very good, large sample sizes are needed to capture information about the process. When selected, samples must be random and representative of the process.

2. *Calculate p, the fraction nonconforming.* The fraction nonconforming (p) is plotted on a fraction nonconforming chart. As the products or services are inspected, each subgroup will yield a number nonconforming (np). The fraction nonconforming (p), plotted on the p chart, is calculated using n, the number of inspected items, and np, the number of nonconforming items found:

$$p = \frac{np}{n}$$

3. *Plot the fraction nonconforming (p) on the control chart.* Once calculated, the values of p for each subgroup are plotted on the chart. The scale for the p chart should reflect the magnitude of the data.

4. *Calculate the centerline and control limits.* The centerline of the control chart is the average of the subgroup fraction nonconforming. The number nonconforming values are added up and then divided by the total number of samples:

$$\text{Centerline } \bar{p} = \frac{\displaystyle\sum_{i=1}^{n} np}{\displaystyle\sum_{i=1}^{n} n}$$

The control limits for a p chart are found using the following formulas:

$$\text{UCL}_p = \bar{p} + 3\frac{\sqrt{\bar{p}(1 - \bar{p})}}{\sqrt{n}}$$

$$\text{LCL}_p = \bar{p} - 3\frac{\sqrt{\bar{p}(1 - \bar{p})}}{\sqrt{n}}$$

On occasion, the lower control limit of a p chart may have a negative value. When this occurs, the result of the LCL_p calculation should be rounded up to zero.

5. *Draw the centerline and control limits on the chart.* Using a solid line to denote the centerline and dashed lines for the control limits, draw the centerline and control limits on the chart.

6. *Interpret the chart.* The interpretation of a fraction nonconforming chart is similar in many aspects to the interpretation of a variables control chart. As with variables charts, in interpreting attribute charts emphasis is placed on determining if the process is operating within its control limits and exhibiting random variation. As with a variables control chart, the data points on a p chart should flow smoothly back and forth across the centerline. The number of points on each side of the centerline should be balanced, with the majority of the points near the centerline. There should be no patterns in the data, such as trends, runs, cycles, or sudden shifts in level. All of the points should fall between the upper and lower control limits. Points beyond the control limits are immediately obvious and indicate an instability in the process. One difference between the interpretation of a variables control chart and a p chart is the desirability in the p chart of having points that approach the lower control limits. This makes sense because quality improvement efforts reflected on a fraction nonconforming chart should show that the fraction nonconforming is being reduced, the ultimate goal of improving a process. This favorable occurrence should be investigated to determine what was done right and whether or not there are changes or improvements that should be incorporated into the process on a permanent basis. Similarly, a trend toward zero nonconforming or shift in level that lowers the fraction of nonconforming should be investigated.

The process capability is the $\bar{p}$, the centerline of the control chart.

EXAMPLE 9.1   Special Plastics: Making a p Chart with Constant Sample Size

Special Plastics, Inc., has been making the blanks for credit cards for a number of years. They use p charts to keep track of the number of nonconforming cards that are created each time a batch of blank cards is run. Use the data in Table 9.1 to create a fraction nonconforming (p) chart.

Step 1. Gather the Data.   The characteristics that have been designated for study include blemishes on the card's front and back surfaces, color inconsistencies, white spots or bumps caused by dirt, scratches, chips, indentations, or other flaws. Several photographs are maintained at each operator's workstation to provide a clear understanding of what constitutes a nonconforming product.

Batches of 15,000 blank cards are run each day. Samples of size 500 are randomly selected and inspected. The number of nonconforming units (np) is recorded on data sheets (Table 9.1).

Step 2. Calculate p, the Fraction Nonconforming.   After each sample is taken and the inspections are complete, the fraction nonconforming (p) is calculated using n = 500, and np, the number of nonconforming items. (Here we work p to three

Subgroup Number	n	np	p
1	500	20	0.040
2	500	21	0.042
3	500	19	0.038
4	500	15	0.030
5	500	18	0.036
6	500	20	0.040
7	500	19	0.038
8	500	28	0.056
9	500	17	0.034
10	500	20	0.040
11	500	19	0.038
12	500	18	0.036
13	500	10	0.020
14	500	11	0.022
15	500	10	0.020
16	500	9	0.018
17	500	10	0.020
18	500	11	0.022
19	500	9	0.018
20	500	8	0.016
	10,000	312	

Table 9.1   Data Sheet: Credit Cards

decimal places.) For example, for the first value,

$$p = \frac{np}{n} = \frac{20}{500} = 0.040$$

The remaining calculated p values are shown in Table 9.1.

Step 3. Plot the Fraction Nonconforming on the Control Chart.   As they are calculated, the values of p for each subgroup are plotted on the chart. The p chart in Figure 9.1 has been scaled to reflect the magnitude of the data.

Step 4. Calculate the Centerline and Control Limits.   The centerline of the control chart is the average of the subgroup fraction nonconforming. The number of nonconforming values from Table 9.1 are added up and then divided by the total number of samples:

$$\text{Centerline } \bar{p} = \frac{\sum\limits_{i=1}^{n} np}{\sum\limits_{i=1}^{n} n} = \frac{312}{20(500)} = 0.031$$

The control limits for a p chart are found using the following formulas:

$$UCL_p = \bar{p} + 3\frac{\sqrt{\bar{p}(1 - \bar{p})}}{\sqrt{n}}$$

$$= 0.031 + 0.023 = 0.054$$

$$LCL_p = \bar{p} - 3\frac{\sqrt{\bar{p}(1 - \bar{p})}}{\sqrt{n}}$$

$$= 0.031 - 0.023 = 0.008$$

Step 5. Draw the Centerline and Control Limits on the Chart.   The centerline and control limits are then drawn on the chart (Figure 9.1), with a solid line denoting the centerline and dashed lines the control limits.

Step 6. Interpret the Chart.   The process capability for this chart is $\bar{p}$, 0.031, the centerline of the control chart. Point 8 in Figure 9.1 is above the upper control limit and should be investigated to determine if an assignable cause exists. If one is found, steps should be taken to prevent future occurrences. When the control chart is studied for any nonrandom conditions, such as runs, trends, cycles, or points out of control, connecting the data points can help reveal any patterns. Of great interest is the significant decrease in the fraction nonconforming after point 13. This reflects the installation of a new machine.

Revising the p Chart

Once an assignable cause has been isolated and the process has been modified to prevent its recurrence, then the centerline and control limits can be recalculated to reflect the changes. The points that have been isolated as due to an assignable cause will be removed from the calculations. To revise the centerline and control

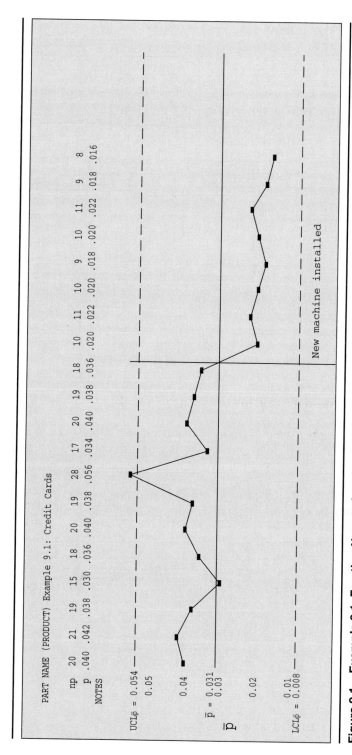

Figure 9.1   Example 9.1: Fraction Nonconforming (p) Chart

453

limits of a p chart,

$$\bar{p}_{new} = \frac{\sum\limits_{i=1}^{n} np - np_d}{\sum\limits_{i=1}^{n} n - n_d}$$

$$UCL_{p_{new}} = \bar{p}_{new} + 3\frac{\sqrt{\bar{p}_{new}(1 - \bar{p}_{new})}}{\sqrt{n}}$$

$$LCL_{p_{new}} = \bar{p}_{new} - 3\frac{\sqrt{\bar{p}_{new}(1 - \bar{p}_{new})}}{\sqrt{n}}$$

The process capability of the revised chart is the newly calculated $\bar{p}_{new}$.

There are cases in which improvements are made to the process that dramatically alter the process. Under these circumstances, it is appropriate to revise the centerline and control limits by removing all the points prior to the change and calculating a new centerline and control limits working only with the points that occurred after the changes were made.

EXAMPLE 9.2   Special Plastics: Revising the p Chart

Special Plastics, Inc., has been involved in several quality improvement efforts that have resulted in the change in level seen in Figure 9.1. Recently a new machine has been installed and is currently being used to improve the printing and color consistency. This system safeguards against dirt in the printing ink and prevents white spots from appearing on the cards. Since the new equipment has been installed, the number of nonconforming cards has decreased (Figure 9.1). Those monitoring the process want to calculate a new centerline and control limits using only the data following the process changes; that is, points 1 through 12 should be removed. Revise the control limits and determine the new process capability:

$$\bar{p}_{new} = \frac{\sum\limits_{i=1}^{n} np - np_d}{\sum\limits_{i=1}^{n} n - n_d} = \frac{312 - 20 - 21 - 19 - 15 - \cdots - 18}{10,000 - 12(500)}$$

$$= 0.020$$

$$UCL_{p_{new}} = \bar{p}_{new} + 3\frac{\sqrt{\bar{p}_{new}(1 - \bar{p}_{new})}}{\sqrt{n}}$$

$$= 0.020 + 3\frac{\sqrt{0.020(1 - 0.020)}}{\sqrt{500}}$$

$$= 0.039$$

$$LCL_{p_{new}} = \bar{p}_{new} - 3\frac{\sqrt{\bar{p}_{new}(1 - \bar{p}_{new})}}{\sqrt{n}}$$

$$= 0.020 - 3\frac{\sqrt{0.020(1 - 0.020)}}{\sqrt{500}}$$

$$= 0.001$$

The process capability of the revised chart is 0.020, the newly calculated $\bar{p}_{new}$. In the future, the process will be expected to conform to the new limits shown in Figure 9.2.

Fraction Nonconforming (p) Charts: Variable Sample Size

In a manufacturing or service industry it is not always possible to sample the same amount each time. When the amount sampled varies, fraction nonconforming charts can be easily adapted to varying sample sizes. Constructing a p chart in which the sample size varies requires that the control limits be calculated for each different sample size, changing the value for n in the control-limit calculations each time a different sample size is taken. Calculating the centerline does not change. Control charts with variable subgroup sizes are interpreted on the basis of where the point falls in relation to the centerline and each point's respective control limits.

EXAMPLE 9.3   Making a p Chart with Variable Sample Size

A local grocery has started to survey customers as they leave the store. The survey is designed to determine if the customer had a pleasant experience while shopping. A nonconforming visit is one in which the customer has a complaint such as not being able to find a particular item; receiving unfriendly service; waiting too long to be served at the deli, meat, bakery, or seafood counter; or otherwise not having their expectations met. Since the number of customers surveyed varies from day to day, a fraction nonconforming control chart for variable sample size is chosen.

Step 1. Gather the Data.   Table 9.2 shows the results of four weeks of sampling.

Step 2. Calculate p, the Fraction Nonconforming, for Each of the Samples.   For this example, the values are calculated to three decimal places. For example, for the second sample,

$$p = \frac{np}{n} = \frac{1}{100} = 0.010$$

Table 9.2 presents the calculated p values.

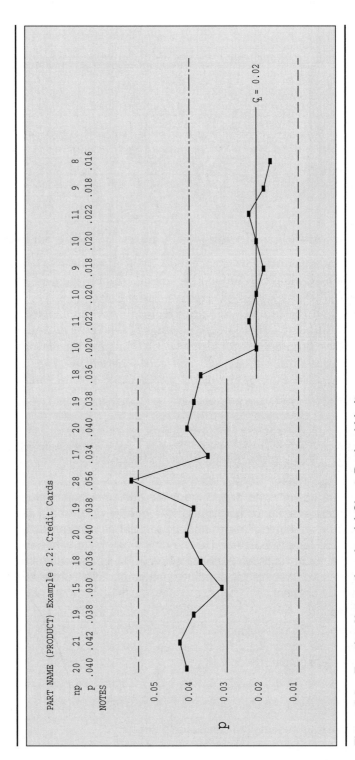

Figure 9.2   Fraction Nonconforming (p) Chart: Revised Limits

Subgroup Number	n	np	p
1	120	0	0.000
2	100	1	0.010
3	105	6	0.057
4	110	1	0.009
5	95	1	0.011
6	110	2	0.018
7	115	0	0.000
8	110	1	0.009
9	100	0	0.000
10	100	2	0.030
11	110	1	0.009
12	105	3	0.028
13	110	0	0.000
14	115	2	0.017
15	120	7	0.058
16	110	2	0.018
17	105	1	0.010
18	110	2	0.018
19	105	0	0.000
20	110	1	0.009
21	115	8	0.069
22	105	7	0.067

Table 9.2   Data Sheet: Grocery Store

Step 3. Plot the Fraction Nonconforming (p) on the Control Chart (Figure 9.3).

Step 4. Calculate the Centerline and Control Limits.

$$\text{Centerline } \bar{p} = \frac{\sum_{i=1}^{n} np}{\sum_{i=1}^{n} n} = \frac{48}{2385} = 0.020$$

At this point the control limits must be calculated for each different sample size. The control limits for this p chart are found using the following formulas and varying the sample size as needed. For example:

$$UCL_p = \bar{p} + 3\frac{\sqrt{\bar{p}(1 - \bar{p})}}{\sqrt{n}}$$

$$UCL_p = 0.020 + 3\frac{\sqrt{0.020(1 - 0.020)}}{\sqrt{120}} = 0.058$$

$$UCL_p = 0.020 + 3\frac{\sqrt{0.020(1 - 0.020)}}{\sqrt{115}} = 0.059$$

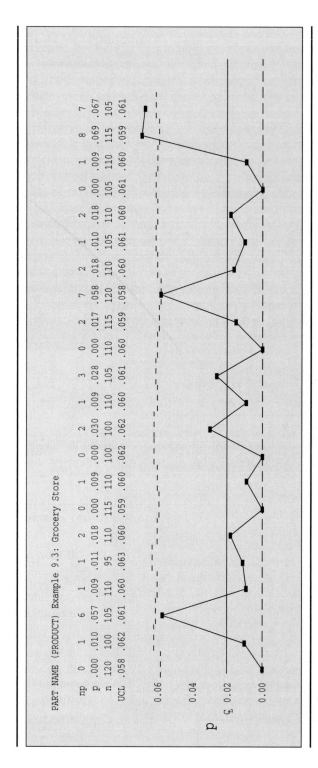

Figure 9.3   Fraction Nonconforming (p) Chart for Variable Sample Size

458

$$UCL_p = 0.020 + 3\frac{\sqrt{0.020(1 - 0.020)}}{\sqrt{105}} = 0.061$$

$$UCL_p = 0.020 + 3\frac{\sqrt{0.020(1 - 0.020)}}{\sqrt{95}} = 0.063$$

Notice that the values for the upper control limits change slightly for each different sample size. As the sample size *decreases,* the control limits get wider. As the sample size *increases,* the control limits get tighter. Larger sample sizes enable us to learn more about the process and what it produces. The tighter control limits are a reflection of this increased knowledge. This concept also applies to sample sizes for $\overline{X}$, R, or s charts.

$$LCL_p = \overline{p} - 3\frac{\sqrt{\overline{p}(1 - \overline{p})}}{\sqrt{n}}$$

$$= 0.020 - 3\frac{\sqrt{0.020(1 - 0.020)}}{\sqrt{100}} = -0.022 = 0$$

Since the lower control limits for each different sample size yield values less than zero, they will all be rounded to zero. Figure 9.3 presents calculated upper and lower control limits.

Step 5. Draw the Centerline and Control Limits on the Chart.   Draw the centerline on the chart using a solid line, just as before. The dashed lines for the control limits will increase and decrease according to the sample size.

Step 6. Interpret the Chart.   Control charts with variable subgroup sizes are interpreted on the basis of where the point falls in relation to the centerline and each point's respective control limits. Unusual patterns are interpreted as before. In this chart (Figure 9.3), there are two points out of control at the end of the chart (points 21 and 22) but no unusual patterns. Q

Calculating p Chart Control Limits Using n_{ave}

Calculating control limits for each different sample size is time consuming, especially if it must be done without the aid of a computer. To simplify the construction of a fraction nonconforming chart, n_{ave} can be used. The value n_{ave} can be found by summing the individual sample sizes and dividing by the total number of times samples were taken:

$$n_{ave} = \frac{\sum\limits_{i=1}^{m} n}{m}$$

The value n_{ave} can be used whenever the individual sample sizes vary no more than 25 percent from the calculated n_{ave}. If, in a group of samples, several of the sample sizes vary more than 25 percent from n_{ave}, then individual limits should be calculated and used to study the process.

Larger sample sizes provide more information about process quality than smaller sample sizes. With a larger number of samples, more of the production is being studied, thus providing more information. Because of this, you may have already noticed that when sample sizes are large, the control limits are tighter. This is because you know more about what is being produced. The standard deviation will also be smaller, reflecting greater confidence in the information. When sample sizes are small, we really don't get a very complete picture of the process. For this reason, the control limits are wider, allowing for a larger margin for error, a wider estimate of where the product produced in the future will fall. A small sample size also results in a larger standard deviation. This relationship holds true for both variables and attributes data.

Control limits calculated using n_{ave} are based on the average value of all of the individual sample sizes. Points lying above or near the control limits must be scrutinized to determine whether or not their individual sample size will affect the interpretation of the point's location. Those values near the upper control limits indicate a situation where the quality of the product or service has deteriorated; it is those points that should be studied in an effort to determine the causes. Points near the centerline receive less emphasis because of their proximity to the average fraction nonconforming. The interpretation of a fraction nonconforming chart created using n_{ave} can be simplified by the use of four cases.

Case I A Case I situation occurs if the point falls inside the limits, but relatively close to the upper control limit, and $n_{ind} < n_{ave}$. Here the individual limits, created using a smaller sample size, will be wider than the limits calculated for n_{ave}. Therefore, there is no need to check the specific value of the individual control limits; the point, which is under control for the average limit, will be under control for the individual limits.

Case II In Case II, the point falls inside the control limits calculated using n_{ave}, and in this case $n_{ind} > n_{ave}$. Any time a greater number of items is investigated, the limits will contract toward the centerline. A larger number of samples taken tells the user more about the process, thus enabling the process to be more discerning between good and bad quality. So in this case, the control limits associated with the individual value will be narrower than the control limits created using n_{ave}. Under these circumstances, the individual control limits should be calculated and the point checked to see if it is in control.

Case III In Case III, the point falls outside the control limits for n_{ave}, and $n_{ind} > n_{ave}$. Because n_{ave} is less than the sample size for the individual data point, the n_{ave} limits are more forgiving than are those for the individual sample size. If the point is out of control for the n_{ave} limits, then it will also be out of control for the narrower n_{ind} limits. There is no need to calculate the specific individual limits because the point will be out of control for both.

Case IV In Case IV, the point is also out of control. Here $n_{ind} < n_{ave}$. Since the individual sample size is less than that of the average sample size, the control limits for the individual sample will be wider than those for the average sample. The point should be tested to determine if it falls out of the control limits for its individual sample size.

EXAMPLE 9.4   Calculating Control Limits for a p Chart Using n_{ave}

To simplify calculations, the grocer of Example 9.3 has decided to create a control chart using n_{ave}. Using the data provided in Table 9.2, he creates a fraction nonconforming control chart using n_{ave}. He will study the chart and interpret it using the four cases.

Begin by calculating n_{ave}:

$$n_{ave} = \frac{\sum_{i=1}^{n} n}{m} = \frac{120 + 100 + 105 + 110 + \cdots + 110 + 115 + 105}{22}$$

$$= 108.4, \text{ which is rounded to 108.}$$

Verify that the values for n in Table 9.2 do not exceed 108 ± 25 percent. Calculate the centerline and control limits:

$$\text{Centerline } \bar{p} = \frac{\sum_{i=1}^{n} np}{\sum_{i=1}^{n} n} = \frac{48}{2385} = 0.020$$

$$\text{UCL}_p = 0.020 + 3\frac{\sqrt{0.020(1 - 0.020)}}{\sqrt{108}} = 0.060$$

$$\text{LCL}_p = 0.020 - 3\frac{\sqrt{0.020(1 - 0.020)}}{\sqrt{108}} = -0.020 = 0$$

After calculating the limits and placing them on the chart (Figure 9.4), check the points nearest to the upper control limit, using the four cases, to determine if they are under control. From Figure 9.4, check points 3, 15, 21, and 22 against the cases.

Case I   A Case I situation occurs if the point falls inside the limits, but relatively close to the upper control limit, and $n_{ind} < n_{ave}$. Point 3 (0.057) on the chart is close to the upper control limit of 0.060. Because the individual limits are created using a smaller sample size, the individual limits will be wider than the limits calculated for n_{ave}. There is no need to check the specific value of the individual control limits for point 3. It is under control for the average limit and will be under control for the individual limits.

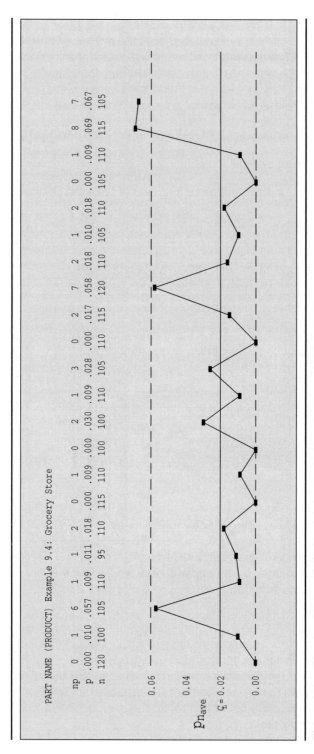

Figure 9.4   Fraction Nonconforming (p) Chart: Control Limits Calculated Using n_{ave}

Case II In Case II, the point falls inside the control limits calculated using n_{ave}, and $n_{ind} > n_{ave}$. Point 15 (0.058) fits this situation. Since a greater number of parts has been investigated (120 versus 108), the limits for point 15 will contract toward the centerline. In this case, the control limits associated with the individual value will be narrower than the control limits created using n_{ave}, and the individual control limits will need to be calculated and the point checked to see if it is in control:

$$UCL_p = 0.020 + 3\frac{\sqrt{0.020(1 - 0.020)}}{\sqrt{120}} = 0.058$$

Point 15 is on the upper control limit and should be investigated to determine the cause behind such a high level of nonconforming product.

Case III In Case III, the point falls outside the control limits for n_{ave}, and $n_{ind} > n_{ave}$. Point 21, with a value of 0.069 and a sample size of 115, fits this situation. The n_{ave} control limits will not be as tight as those for the individual sample size. Since the point is out of control for the n_{ave} limits, then it will also be out of control for the narrower n_{ind} limits. There is no need to calculate the specific individual limits.

Case IV In Case IV, the point is also out of control and $n_{ind} < n_{ave}$. Point 22 has a value of 0.067. In this case the individual sample size is less than the average sample size (105 versus 108). When calculated, the control limits for the individual sample will be wider than those of the average sample. Point 22 will need to be tested to determine if it falls out of the control limits for its individual sample size:

$$UCL_p = 0.020 + 3\frac{\sqrt{0.020(1 - 0.020)}}{\sqrt{105}} = 0.061$$

Point 22 is out of control and should be investigated.

When comparing Examples 9.3 and 9.4, note that significantly fewer calculations are necessary when using n_{ave}. To apply n_{ave} to a control chart, care must be taken to properly interpret the chart using the four cases and to check that a particular sample size does not vary more than 25 percent from n_{ave}.

Revising the p Chart

p charts with variable sample sizes are revised in a manner similar to those revised with a constant sample size. Undesired values for p are removed using the formula

$$\overline{P}_{new} = \frac{\sum_{i=1}^{n} np - np_d}{\sum_{i=1}^{n} n - n_d}$$

If a point is removed when calculating $\bar{p}_{new}$, its corresponding n_{ave} should also be removed. The new n_{ave} is used when calculating the new control limits:

$$n_{ave} = \frac{\sum\limits_{i=1}^{n} n - n_d}{m - m_d}$$

$$UCL_{p_{new}} = \bar{p}_{new} + 3\frac{\sqrt{\bar{p}_{new}(1 - \bar{p}_{new})}}{\sqrt{n_{ave}}}$$

$$LCL_{p_{new}} = \bar{p}_{new} - 3\frac{\sqrt{\bar{p}_{new}(1 - \bar{p}_{new})}}{\sqrt{n_{ave}}}$$

The process capability of the revised chart is the newly calculated $\bar{p}_{new}$.

EXAMPLE 9.5   Revising a p Chart Using n_{ave}

Assume that assignable causes for points 21 and 22 have been determined and process modifications are in place to prevent future recurrences. Remove these points from the calculations and compute the revised centerline and control limits for Example 9.4.
  Recalculating n_{ave},

$$n_{ave} = \frac{\sum\limits_{i=1}^{n} n - n_d}{m - m_d} = \frac{2385 - 115 - 105}{22 - 1 - 1} = \frac{2165}{20} = 108$$

The new centerline and control limits become

$$\bar{p}_{new} = \frac{\sum\limits_{i=1}^{n} np - np_d}{\sum\limits_{i=1}^{n} n - n_d} = \frac{48 - 8 - 7}{2385 - 115 - 105} = \frac{33}{2165} = 0.015$$

$$UCL_{p_{new}} = 0.015 + 3\frac{\sqrt{0.015(1 - 0.015)}}{\sqrt{108}} = 0.050$$

$$LCL_{p_{new}} = 0.015 - 3\frac{\sqrt{0.015(1 - 0.015)}}{\sqrt{108}} = -0.02 = 0$$

The process capability of the revised chart is 0.015, the newly calculated fraction nonconforming. $Q_{\blacktriangleright}$

Percent Nonconforming Chart

Percent nonconforming charts are another variation on the fraction nonconforming (p) chart. Under certain circumstances they are easier to understand than the traditional p chart. Constructing a *percent nonconforming chart* is very similar to the construction of a fraction nonconforming chart, but here *the p values are changed to a percentage by multiplying by a factor of 100.*

The centerline for a percent nonconforming chart is $100\bar{p}$. The control limits are

$$UCL_{100p} = 100\left[\bar{p} + \frac{3\sqrt{\bar{p}(1-\bar{p})}}{\sqrt{n}}\right]$$

$$LCL_{100p} = 100\left[\bar{p} - \frac{3\sqrt{\bar{p}(1-\bar{p})}}{\sqrt{n}}\right]$$

A percent nonconforming chart is interpreted in the same manner as is a fraction nonconforming chart. The process capability of a percent nonconforming chart is the centerline or average percent nonconforming. Percent nonconforming charts are interpreted in the same manner as fraction nonconforming charts. The points on a percent nonconforming chart should flow smoothly back and forth across the centerline with a random pattern of variation. The number of points on each side of the centerline should be balanced, with the majority of the points near the centerline. There should be no patterns in the data, such as trends, runs, cycles, points beyond the upper control limit, or sudden shifts in level. Points approaching or going beyond the lower control limits are desirable. They mark an improvement in quality and should be studied to determine their cause and to ensure that it is repeated in the future. The process capability is $100\bar{p}$, the centerline of the chart.

EXAMPLE 9.6   Making a Percent Nonconforming Chart

The managers of Special Plastics feel that a percent nonconforming chart may be more understandable for their employees. Create a percent nonconforming chart using the information presented in Example 9.1. The values to be plotted have been converted to percent and are given in Table 9.3. The centerline for a percent nonconforming chart is

$$100\bar{p} = 100(0.031) = 3.1\%$$

where:

$$\bar{p} = \frac{312}{10,000}$$

The control limits for a percent nonconforming chart are

$$UCL_{100p} = 100\left[0.031 + \frac{3\sqrt{0.031(1-0.031)}}{\sqrt{500}}\right] = 5.4\%$$

$$LCL_{100p} = 100\left[0.031 - \frac{3\sqrt{0.031(1-0.031)}}{\sqrt{500}}\right] = 0.8\%$$

Subgroup Number	n	np	p	100p
1	500	20	0.040	4.0
2	500	21	0.042	4.2
3	500	19	0.038	3.8
4	500	15	0.030	3.0
5	500	18	0.036	3.6
6	500	20	0.040	4.0
7	500	19	0.038	3.8
8	500	28	0.056	5.6
9	500	17	0.034	3.4
10	500	20	0.040	4.0
11	500	19	0.038	3.8
12	500	18	0.036	3.6
13	500	10	0.020	3.0
14	500	11	0.022	2.2
15	500	10	0.020	2.0
16	500	9	0.018	1.8
17	500	10	0.020	2.0
18	500	11	0.022	2.2
19	500	9	0.018	1.8
20	500	8	0.016	1.6
	10,000	312		

Table 9.3   Data Sheet: Credit Cards, Special Plastics

The interpretation of this chart (Figure 9.5) will be the same as that for Example 9.1. The process capability for the chart is 3.1 percent, the centerline of the control chart. Point 8 is above the upper control limit and should be investigated to determine if an assignable cause exists. A pattern exists on the chart: there is a significant decrease in the percent nonconforming after point 13, reflecting the installation of a new machine. $\mathbf{Q}$

Number Nonconforming (np) Chart

A *number nonconforming (np) chart tracks the number of nonconforming products or services produced by a process.* A number nonconforming chart eliminates the calculation of p, the fraction nonconforming.

1. *Gather the data.* We must apply the same data gathering techniques we used in creating the p chart:

- Designate the specific characteristics or attributes for study
- Clearly define nonconforming product
- Select the sample size n
- Determine the frequency of sampling
- Take random, representative samples

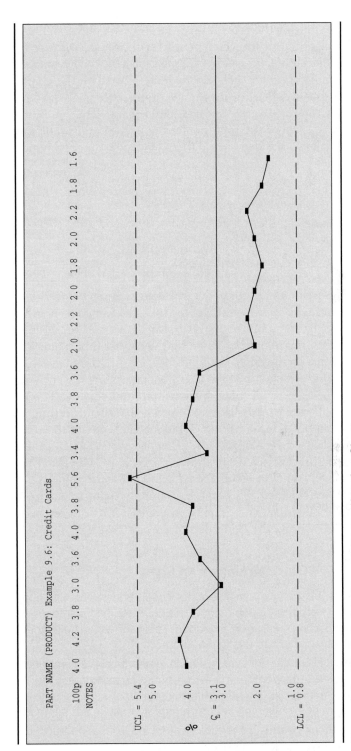

Figure 9.5 Example 9.6: Percent Nonconforming Chart

Those studying the process keep track of the number of nonconforming units (np) by comparing the inspected product with the specifications.

2. *Plot the number of nonconforming units (np) on the control chart.* Once counted, the values of np for each subgroup are plotted on the chart. The scale for the np chart should reflect the magnitude of the data.

3. *Calculate the centerline and control limits.* The centerline of the control chart is the average of the total number nonconforming. The number nonconforming (np) values are added up and then divided by the total number of samples:

$$\text{Centerline } n\bar{p} = \frac{\sum\limits_{i=1}^{n} np}{m}$$

The control limits for an np chart are found using the following formulas:

$$UCL_{np} = n\bar{p} + 3\sqrt{n\bar{p}(1 - \bar{p})}$$
$$LCL_{np} = n\bar{p} - 3\sqrt{n\bar{p}(1 - \bar{p})}$$

On occasion, the lower control limit of an np chart may have a negative value. When this occurs, the result of the LCL_{np} calculation should be rounded up to zero.

4. *Draw the centerline and control limits on the chart.* Using a solid line to denote the centerline and dashed lines for the control limits, draw the centerline and control limits on the chart.

5. *Interpret the chart.* Number nonconforming (np) charts are interpreted in the same manner as are fraction nonconforming charts. The points on an np chart should flow smoothly back and forth across the centerline with a random pattern of variation. The number of points on each side of the centerline should be balanced, with the majority of the points near the centerline. There should be no patterns in the data, such as trends, runs, cycles, points above the upper control limit, or sudden shifts in level. Points approaching or going beyond the lower control limits are desirable. They mark an improvement in quality and should be studied to determine their cause and to ensure that it is repeated in the future. The process capability is $n\bar{p}$, the centerline of the control chart.

EXAMPLE 9.7　PCC Inc.: Making an np Chart

PCC Inc. receives shipments of circuit boards from its suppliers by the truckload. They keep track of the number of damaged, incomplete, or inoperative circuit boards found when the truck is unloaded. This information helps them make decisions about which suppliers to use in the future.

Step 1. Gather the Data.　The inspectors have a clear understanding of what constitutes a nonconforming circuit board by comparing the inspected circuit boards with standards. The nonconforming units are set aside to be counted. For the purposes of this example, each shipment contains the same number of circuit boards.

Circuit boards are randomly sampled from each truckload with a sample size of $n = 50$.

Subgroup Number	n	np
1	50	4
2	50	6
3	50	5
4	50	2
5	50	3
6	50	5
7	50	4
8	50	7
9	50	2
10	50	3
11	50	1
12	50	4
13	50	3
14	50	5
15	50	2
16	50	5
17	50	6
18	50	3
19	50	1
20	50	2

Table 9.4   Data Sheet: PCC Inc.

Step 2. Plot the Number of Nonconforming Units (np) on the Control Chart.   The results for the 20 most recent trucks are shown in Table 9.4. The values of np for each subgroup are plotted on the chart in Figure 9.6, which has been scaled to reflect the magnitude of the data.

Step 3. Calculate the Centerline and Control Limits.   The average of the total number nonconforming is found by adding up the number of nonconforming values and dividing by the total number of samples. The example is worked to two decimal places:

$$\text{Centerline } n\bar{p} = \frac{\sum_{i=1}^{n} np}{m} = \frac{73}{20} = 3.65$$

The control limits for an np chart are found using the following formulas:

$$\bar{p} = \frac{\sum_{i=1}^{n} np}{\sum_{i=1}^{n} n} = \frac{73}{1000} = 0.073$$

$$\text{UCL}_{np} = n\bar{p} + 3\sqrt{n\bar{p}(1 - \bar{p})}$$
$$= 3.65 + 3\sqrt{3.65(1 - 0.073)} = 9.17$$
$$\text{LCL}_{np} = n\bar{p} - 3\sqrt{n\bar{p}(1 - \bar{p})}$$
$$= 3.65 - 3\sqrt{3.65(1 - 0.073)} = -1.87 = 0$$

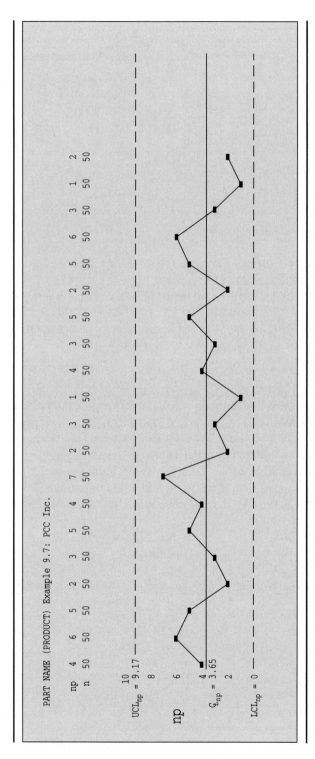

Figure 9.6 Example 9.7: Number Nonconforming (np) Chart of HVAC System Checks

Step 4. Draw the Centerline and Control Limits on the Chart.   Figure 9.6 uses a solid line to denote the centerline and dashed lines for the control limits.

Step 5. Interpret the Chart.   A study of Figure 9.6 reveals that the chart is under control. The points flow smoothly back and forth across the centerline. The number of points on each side of the centerline are balanced, with the majority of the points near the centerline. There are no trends, runs, cycles, or sudden shifts in level apparent in the data. All of the points fall between the upper and lower control limits.

 REAL TOOLS FOR REAL LIFE

Warranty Claims Investigation Using np Charts

KeepCool Inc. supplies heating/ventilating and air conditioning (HVAC) systems to the automotive industry. During the past four months, KeepCool received 24 warranty claims concerning their HVAC systems. Customers complained that when they attempted to change the HVAC airflow setting from foot to face mode, the unit did not function properly. Switching vent locations was also accompanied by a loud grating sound. At dealer repair shops, repair personnel checked the linkage of the switching mechanism and servomotors, trying to solve the problem. Often, they would find failed servomotors and replace them. Despite their efforts, the grating sound and poor operating characteristics returned.

   The number of warranty claims on this issue has been steadily increasing throughout the past year. At the assembly facility, corrective action teams got to work to determine the root cause of the problem. They employed an np chart to track the number of cars in the sample experiencing this problem (Figure 9.7). This chart enabled them to determine the full extent of the problem. On average, 4 cars exhibited the grating sound and poor operating characteristics when switching vent locations. The process, as shown by the chart, is under control; so this level of defectives can be expected in the future.

   Several HVAC units were disassembled to determine what might be causing the binding condition evidenced by the noises made during operation. The team found that the damper door and its case were out of specification for damper door clearance. This binding caused the servomotors to fail as they tried to provide enough force to move the door. Unfortunately, this meant that the HVAC system in customer vehicles had to be replaced, because simply replacing the affected servomotor would not fix the problem. Further investigation revealed that the heater case was out of specification on the low side. The small case, combined with the case mounting location also being 2 mm out of specification, resulted in the door/case binding condition customers were experiencing. Process changes were made to ensure that future vehicles would not experience this problem. Based on the large number of cars experiencing this problem, as evidenced by the np chart, KeepCool recalled this particular HVAC system and replaced the affected HVAC systems, a costly proposition.

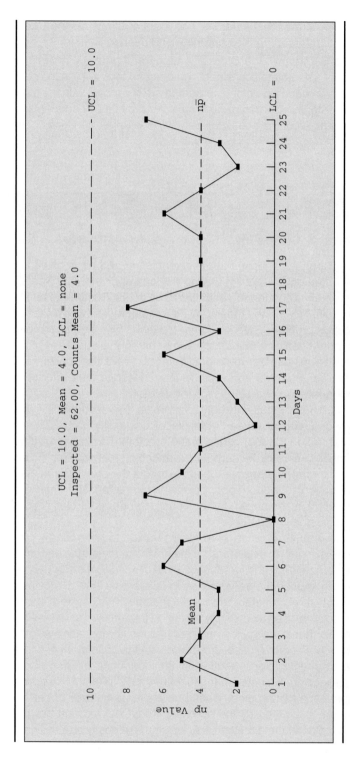

Figure 9.7   Example 9.8: Number Nonconforming (np) Chart of HVAC System Checks

CHARTS FOR COUNTS OF NONCONFORMITIES

Charts for counts of nonconformities monitor the number of nonconformities found in a sample. Nonconformities represent problems that exist with the product or service. Nonconformities may or may not render the product or service unusable. Two types of charts recording nonconformities may be used: a count of nonconformities (c) chart or a count of nonconformities per unit (u) chart. As the names suggest, one chart is for total nonconformities in the sample, and the other chart is nonconformities per unit.

Number of Nonconformities (c) Chart

The **number of nonconformities chart, or c chart,** *is used to track the count of noncon- formities observed in a single unit of product or single service experience,* n = 1. Charts counting nonconformities are used when nonconformities are scattered through a con- tinuous flow of product such as bubbles in a sheet of glass, flaws in a bolt of fabric, dis- colorations in a ream of paper, or services such as mistakes on an insurance form or er- rors on a bill. To be charted, the nonconformities must be expressed in terms of what is being inspected, such as four bubbles in a 3-square-foot pane of glass or two specks of dirt on an 8 1/2 × 11-inch sheet of paper. Count-of-nonconformities charts can com- bine the counts of a variety of nonconformities, such as the number of mishandled, dented, missing, or unidentified suitcases to reach a particular airport carousel. A con- stant sample size must be used when creating a count of nonconformities (c) chart.

1. *Gather the data.* A clear understanding of the nonconformities to be tracked is essential for successfully applying a count-of-nonconformities chart. Gathering the data requires that the area of opportunity of occurrence for each sample taken be equal, n = 1. The rate of occurrences of nonconformities within a sample or area of opportunity (area of exposure) is plotted on the c chart. For this reason, the size of the piece of paper or fabric, the length of the steel, or the number of units must be equal for each sample taken. The number of nonconformities will be de- termined by comparing the inspected product or service with a standard and counting the deviations from the standard. On a c chart, all nonconformities have the same weight, regardless of the type of nonconformity. The area of opportunity for these nonconformities should be large, with a very small chance of a particular nonconformity occurring at any one location.

2. *Count and plot c, the count of the number of nonconformities, on the control chart.* As it is inspected, each item or subgroup will yield a count of the nonconformities (c). It is this value that is plotted on the control chart. The scale for the c chart should reflect the number of nonconformities discovered.

3. *Calculate the centerline and control limits.* The centerline of the control chart is the average of the subgroup nonconformities. The number of nonconformities are added up and then divided by the total number of subgroups:

$$\text{Centerline } \bar{c} = \frac{\sum\limits_{i=1}^{n} c}{m}$$

The control limits for a c chart are found using the following formulas:

$$UCL_c = \bar{c} + 3\sqrt{\bar{c}}$$
$$LCL_c = \bar{c} - 3\sqrt{\bar{c}}$$

On occasion, the lower control limit of a c chart may have a negative value. When this occurs, the result of the LCL_c calculation should be rounded up to zero.

4. *Draw the centerline and control limits on the chart.* Using a solid line to denote the centerline and dashed lines for the control limits, draw the centerline and control limits on the chart.

5. *Interpret the chart.* Charts for counts of nonconformities are interpreted similarly to interpreting charts for the number of nonconforming occurrences. The charts are studied for changes in random patterns of variation. There should be no patterns in the data, such as trends, runs, cycles, or sudden shifts in level. All of the points should fall between the upper and lower control limits. The data points on a c chart should flow smoothly back and forth across the centerline and be balanced on either side of the centerline. The majority of the points should be near the centerline. Once again it is desirable to have the points approach the lower control limits or zero, showing a reduction in the count of nonconformities. The process capability is $\bar{c}$, the average count of nonconformities in a sample and the centerline of the control chart.

EXAMPLE 9.8   Pure and White: Making a c Chart

Pure and White, a manufacturer of paper used in copy machines, monitors their production using a c chart. Paper is produced in large rolls, 12 ft long and with a 6 ft diameter. A sample is taken from each completed roll, n = 1, and checked in the lab for nonconformities. Nonconformities have been identified as discolorations, inconsistent paper thickness, flecks of dirt in the paper, moisture content, and ability to take ink. All of these nonconformities have the same weight on the c chart. A sample may be taken from anywhere in the roll so the area of opportunity for these nonconformities is large, while the overall quality of the paper creates only a very small chance of a particular nonconformity occurring at any one location.

Step 1. Gather the Data (Table 9.5).

Step 2. Count and Plot c, the Count of the Number of Nonconformities, on the Control Chart.   As each roll is inspected, it yields a count of the nonconformities (c) that is recorded in Table 9.5. This value is then plotted on the control chart shown in Figure 9.8.

Step 3. Calculate the Centerline and Control Limits.   The centerline of the control chart is the average of the subgroup nonconformities. The number of nonconformities is added up and then divided by the total number of rolls of paper inspected:

$$\text{Centerline } \bar{c} = \frac{\sum\limits_{i=1}^{n} c}{m} = \frac{210}{20} = 10.5 \text{ rounded to } 11$$

The control limits for a c chart are found using the following formulas:

Sample Number	c
1	10
2	11
3	12
4	10
5	9
6	22
7	8
8	10
9	11
10	9
11	12
12	7
13	10
14	11
15	10
16	12
17	9
18	10
19	8
20	9
	210

Table 9.5   Data Sheet: Pure and White Paper

$$UCL_c = \bar{c} + 3\sqrt{\bar{c}}$$
$$= 11 + 3\sqrt{11} = 21$$
$$LCL_c = \bar{c} - 3\sqrt{\bar{c}}$$
$$= 11 - 3\sqrt{11} = 1$$

Step 4. Draw the Centerline and Control Limits on the Chart.   Using a solid line to denote the centerline and dashed lines for the control limits, draw the centerline and control limits on the chart (Figure 9.8).

Step 5. Interpret the Chart.   Point 6 is out of control and should be investigated to determine the cause of so many nonconformities. There are no other patterns present on the chart. Except for point 6, the chart is performing in a very steady manner. **Q**

Revising the c Chart

If improvements have been made to the process or the reasons behind special cause situations have been identified and corrected, c charts can be revised using the following formulas:

$$\text{Centerline } \bar{c}_{new} = \frac{\sum_{i=1}^{n} c - c_d}{m - m_d}$$

$$UCL_{c_{new}} = \bar{c}_{new} + 3\sqrt{\bar{c}_{new}}$$

$$LCL_{c_{new}} = \bar{c}_{new} - 3\sqrt{\bar{c}_{new}}$$

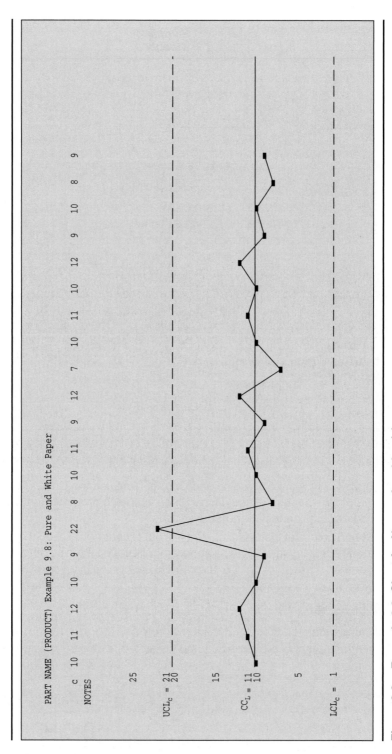

Figure 9.8   Example 9.8: Chart for Nonconformities (c)

EXAMPLE 9.9   Pure and White: Revising a c Chart

The Pure and White paper manufacturer investigated the out of control point on the count of nonconformities (c) chart in Figure 9.8 and determined that a new operator had not added sufficient bleach to the pulp mixing tank. The operator was retrained in how to mix the correct combination of chemicals to make Pure and White paper. To revise the chart and determine the process capability, Pure and White followed this procedure:

$$\text{Centerline } \bar{c}_{new} = \frac{\sum\limits_{i=1}^{n} c - c_d}{m - m_d} = \frac{210 - 22}{20 - 1} = 10$$

$$UCL_{c_{new}} = \bar{c}_{new} + 3\sqrt{\bar{c}_{new}}$$
$$= 10 + 3\sqrt{10} = 20$$

$$LCL_{c_{new}} = \bar{c}_{new} - 3\sqrt{\bar{c}_{new}}$$
$$= 10 - 3\sqrt{10} = 0.5$$

 REAL TOOLS FOR REAL LIFE

Managing Claim Filing Lag Time

Accidents and injuries come from two sources: unsafe acts committed by people; and the presence of physical or mechanical hazards. Injuries on the job are expensive. Besides the direct costs of an accident, those related to medical bills, hospital expenses, downtime, compensation, liability claims etc., there are indirect costs, such as morale, claim management time, etc. Management should assume responsibility for safety because they are in the best position to effect change in the workplace. Effective organizations manage their safety programs using methods and tools similar to quality assurance.

Experience has shown that there is a direct relationship between the cost of a medical claim and the number of days it takes to file that claim with an insurance company. Smart companies manage the filing of claims related to on-the-job injuries as carefully as they manage production. TM Corporation uses c charts to track both the lag time associated with filing a claim and medical costs associated with a claim. Each of the values in Figures 9.9 and 9.10 represent an individual case (n = 1), so a c chart is applicable.

The most noteworthy aspect of these charts is that when the lag time increased, so did the dollar amount associated with the claim. TM Corporation needs to identify what changed in the system that caused the significant increase in the lag time for filing claims which resulted in higher claims costs. What would their performance and costs have been if the lag times hadn't increased? Revise the c chart and see.

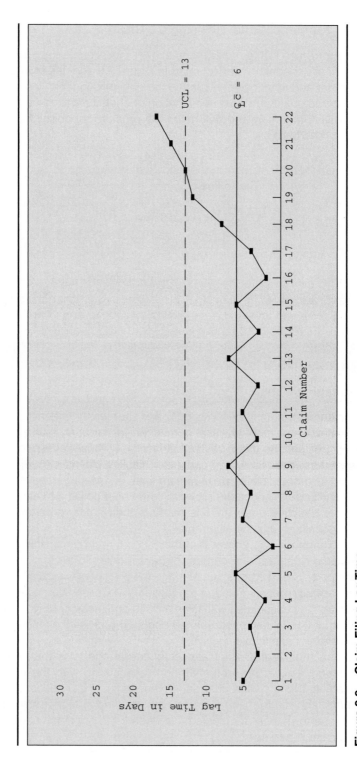

Figure 9.9   Claim Filing Lag Time

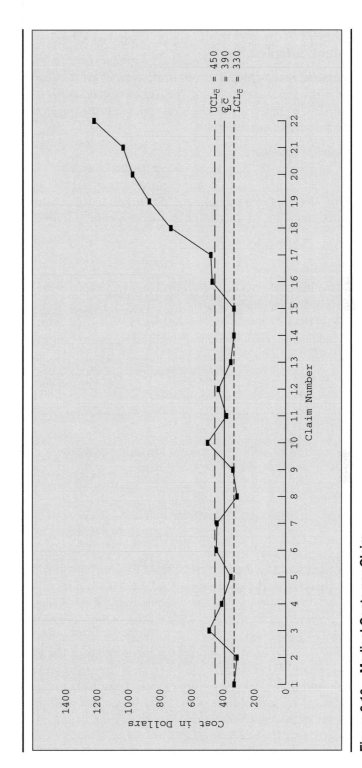

Figure 9.10   Medical Costs per Claim

Number of Nonconformities per Unit (u) Charts: Constant Sample Size

A *number of nonconformities per unit, or u, chart* is a chart that studies the number of nonconformities in a unit ($n > 1$). The u chart is very similar to the c chart; however, unlike c charts, u charts can also be used with variable sample sizes. To create a number of nonconformities per unit chart:

1. *Gather the data.*

2. *Calculate u, the number of nonconformities per unit.* As it is inspected, each sample of size n will yield a count of nonconformities (c). The number of nonconformities per unit (u), used on the u chart, is calculated using n, the number of inspected items, and c, the count of nonconformities found:

$$u = \frac{c}{n}$$

This value is plotted on the control chart.

3. *Calculate the centerline and control limits.* The centerline of the u chart is the average of the subgroup nonconformities per unit. The number of nonconformities are added up and then divided by the total number of samples:

$$\text{Centerline } \bar{u} = \frac{\sum\limits_{i=1}^{n} c}{\sum\limits_{i=1}^{n} n}$$

The control limits for the u chart are found using the following formulas:

$$UCL_u = \bar{u} + 3\frac{\sqrt{\bar{u}}}{\sqrt{n}}$$

$$LCL_u = \bar{u} - 3\frac{\sqrt{\bar{u}}}{\sqrt{n}}$$

On occasion, the lower control limit of a u chart may have a negative value. When this occurs, the result of the LCL_u calculation should be rounded to zero.

4. *Draw the centerline and control limits on the chart.* Using a solid line to denote the centerline and dashed lines for the control limits, draw the centerline and control limits on the chart.

5. *Interpret the chart.* A u chart is interpreted in the same manner as is a p, np, or c chart. The chart should be studied for any nonrandom conditions such as runs, trends, cycles, or points out of control. The data points on a u chart should flow smoothly back and forth across the centerline. The number of points on each side of the centerline should be balanced, with the majority of the points near the centerline. Quality improvement efforts are reflected on a u chart when the count of nonconformities per unit is reduced, as shown by a

trend toward the lower control limit and therefore toward zero nonconformities. When using variable sample sizes, follow the same procedure as used in creating and interpreting a p chart with variable sample sizes. Once again, when n_{ave} is used, the sample sizes must not vary more than 25 percent from n_{ave}. The process capability is $\bar{u}$, the centerline of the control chart, the average number of nonconformities per unit.

EXAMPLE 9.10   Special Plastics: Making a u Chart with Constant Sample Size

At Special Plastics, Inc., small plastic parts used to connect hoses are created on a separate production line from the credit card blanks. Special Plastics, Inc., uses u charts to collect data concerning the nonconformities per unit in the process.

Step 1. Gather the Data.   During inspection, a random sample of size 400 is taken once an hour. The hose connectors are visually inspected for a variety of noncon- formities, including flashing on inner diameters, burrs on the part exterior, incom- plete threads, flashing on the ends of the connectors, incorrect plastic compound, and discolorations.

Step 2. Calculate u, the Number of Nonconformities per Unit.   Table 9.6 shows the number of nonconformities (c) that each subgroup of sample size n = 400

Subgroup Number	n	c	u
1	400	12	0.030
2	400	7	0.018
3	400	10	0.025
4	400	11	0.028
5	400	10	0.025
6	400	12	0.030
7	400	9	0.023
8	400	10	0.025
9	400	8	0.020
10	400	9	0.023
11	400	10	0.025
12	400	11	0.028
13	400	12	0.030
14	400	10	0.025
15	400	9	0.023
16	400	22	0.055
17	400	8	0.020
18	400	10	0.025
19	400	11	0.028
20	400	9	0.023

Table 9.6   Data Sheet: Hose Connectors

yielded. The number of nonconformities per unit (u) to be plotted on the chart is calculated by dividing c, the number of nonconformities found, by n, the number of inspected items. Working the example to three decimal places, for the first sample,

$$u_1 = \frac{c}{n} = \frac{10}{400} = 0.025$$

Step 3. Calculate the Centerline and Control Limits. The centerline of the u chart is the average of the subgroup nonconformities per unit. The number of nonconformities are added up and then divided by the total number of samples:

$$\text{Centerline } \bar{u} = \frac{\displaystyle\sum_{i=1}^{n} c}{\displaystyle\sum_{i=1}^{n} n} = \frac{210}{20(400)} = 0.026$$

Find the control limits for the u chart by using the following formulas:

$$UCL_u = \bar{u} + 3\frac{\sqrt{\bar{u}}}{\sqrt{n}}$$

$$= 0.026 + 3\frac{\sqrt{0.026}}{\sqrt{400}} = 0.05$$

$$LCL_u = \bar{u} - 3\frac{\sqrt{\bar{u}}}{\sqrt{n}}$$

$$= 0.026 - 3\frac{\sqrt{0.026}}{\sqrt{400}} = 0.001$$

Step 4. Create and Draw the Centerline and Control Limits on the Chart. Using a solid line to denote the centerline and dashed lines for the control limits, draw the centerline and control limits on the chart. Values for u are plotted on the control chart (Figure 9.11).

Step 5. Interpret the Chart. Except for point 16, the chart appears to be under statistical control. There are no runs or unusual patterns. Point 16 should be investigated to determine the cause of such a large number of nonconformities per unit. Q↝

Number of Nonconformities per Unit (u) Charts: Variable Sample Size

When the sample size varies, n_{ave} is used in the formulas just as it was when creating fraction nonconforming charts for variable sample size. The sample sizes must not vary more than 25 percent from n_{ave}. If there is greater variance, then the individual control limits for the samples must be calculated.

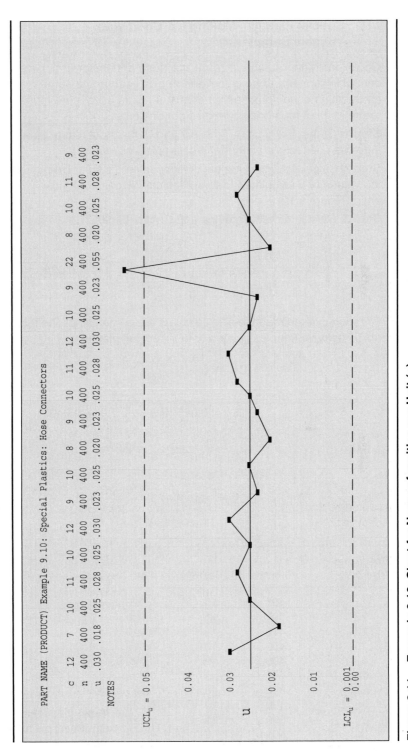

Figure 9.11 Example 9.10: Chart for Nonconformities per Unit (u)

EXAMPLE 9.11   Special Plastics: Making a u Chart with Variable Sample Size

Occasionally the sample size on the hose connector line varies. When individual control limits need to be calculated, n_{ave} is used in the same manner as described for fraction nonconformities (p) charts. If n_{ave} is used, care must be taken in the interpretation of the nonconformities per unit chart.

Step 1. Gather the Data.   Table 9.7 shows the most recent data collected concerning hose connectors. Note that the sample size varies.

Step 2. Calculate u, the Number of Nonconformities per Unit.   Table 9.7 also shows the values of u calculated to three decimal places. Plot these values on the control chart (Figure 9.12).

Step 3. Calculate the Centerline and Control Limits.

$$\text{Centerline } \bar{u} = \frac{\sum_{i=1}^{n} c}{\sum_{i=1}^{n} n} = \frac{99}{3995} = 0.025$$

For each different sample size calculate the control limits. (In this example the control limits have been calculated to four decimal places.)

$$UCL_u = \bar{u} + 3\frac{\sqrt{\bar{u}}}{\sqrt{n}}$$

$$UCL_u = 0.025 + 3\frac{\sqrt{0.025}}{\sqrt{390}} = 0.0490$$

$$UCL_u = 0.025 + 3\frac{\sqrt{0.025}}{\sqrt{400}} = 0.0487$$

$$UCL_u = 0.025 + 3\frac{\sqrt{0.025}}{\sqrt{405}} = 0.0485$$

Subgroup Number	n	c	u
21	405	10	0.025
22	390	11	0.028
23	410	12	0.029
24	400	10	0.025
25	405	9	0.022
26	400	9	0.023
27	390	8	0.021
28	400	10	0.025
29	390	11	0.028
30	405	9	0.022

Table 9.7   Data Sheet: Hose Connectors Variable Sample Size

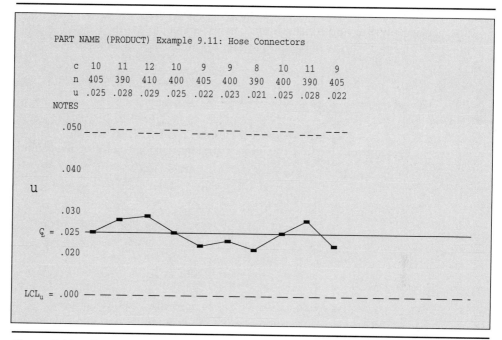

Figure 9.12   Nonconformities per Unit (u) Chart for Variable Sample Size

$$UCL_u = 0.025 + 3\frac{\sqrt{0.025}}{\sqrt{410}} = 0.0484$$

$$LCL_u = \bar{u} - 3\frac{\sqrt{\bar{u}}}{\sqrt{n}}$$

$$LCL_u = 0.025 - 3\frac{\sqrt{0.025}}{\sqrt{400}} = 0.0013$$

$$LCL_u = 0.025 - 3\frac{\sqrt{0.025}}{\sqrt{405}} = 0.0014$$

The lower control limit may be rounded to zero.

Step 4. Draw the Centerline and Control Limits on the Chart.   The centerline and control limits have been drawn in Figure 9.12.

Step 5. Interpret the Chart.   The process shown in Figure 9.12 is a stable process.

Revising the u Chart

Both the u chart for a constant sample size and a u chart for a variable sample size are revised in the same fashion as are the other attribute charts. Once the assignable causes have been determined and the process modified to prevent their recurrence, the centerline and control limits can be recalculated using the following formulas. For the u chart with variable sample size, n_{ave} must be recalculated:

$$\text{Centerline } \bar{u} = \frac{\sum\limits_{i=1}^{n} c - c_d}{\sum\limits_{i=1}^{n} n - n_d}$$

The control limits for the u chart are found using the following formulas:

$$UCL_u = \bar{u}_{new} + 3\frac{\sqrt{\bar{u}_{new}}}{\sqrt{n}}$$

$$LCL_u = \bar{u}_{new} - 3\frac{\sqrt{\bar{u}_{new}}}{\sqrt{n}}$$

$$n_{ave} = \frac{\sum\limits_{i=1}^{n} n - n_d}{m - m_d}$$

SUMMARY

You have now seen a variety of control charts. The choice of which chart to implement under what circumstances is less confusing than it first appears. To begin the selection process, care must be taken to identify the type of data to be gathered. What is the nature of the process under study? Are they variables data and therefore measurable? Or are they attribute data and therefore countable? Is there a sample size or is just one item being measured? Is there a sample size or are just the nonconformities in an area of opportunity being counted? The flowchart in Figure 9.13 can assist you in choosing a chart.

Choosing a Control Chart

I. Variables Data
   A. Use an $\overline{X}$ chart combined with an R or s chart
      1. The characteristic can be measured.
      2. The process is unable to hold tolerances.
      3. The process must be monitored for adjustments.
      4. Changes are being made to the process and those changes need to be monitored.
      5. Process stability and process capability must be monitored and demonstrated to a customer or regulating body.
      6. The process average and the process variation must be measured.

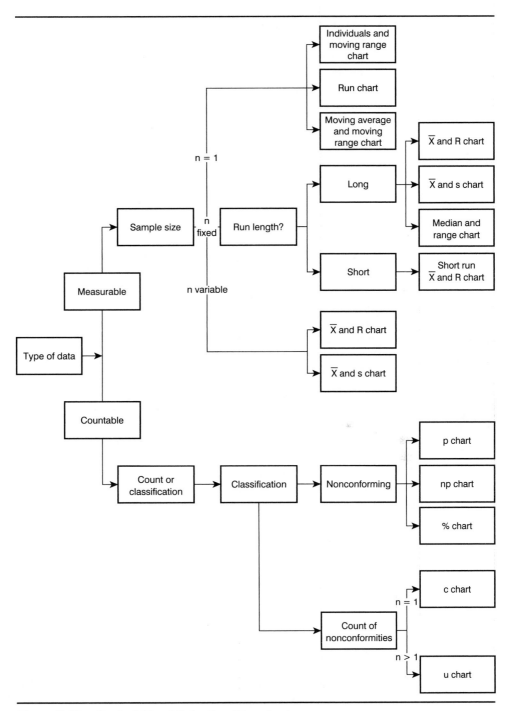

Figure 9.13   Control Chart Selection Flowchart

B. Use control charts for individuals (X_i and moving-range charts or moving-average and moving-range charts) when
   1. Destructive testing or other expensive testing procedures limit the number of products sampled.
   2. It is inconvenient or impossible to obtain more than one sample.
   3. Waiting for a large sample would not provide timely data.

II. Attribute Data
   A. Use charts for nonconforming units or fraction nonconforming charts (p, np, 100p) when
      1. There is a need to monitor the portion of the lot that is nonconforming.
      2. The characteristics under study in the process can be judged either conforming or nonconforming.
      3. The sample size varies (p chart).
      4. Process monitoring is desired but measurement data cannot be obtained because of the nature of the product or the expense.
   B. Use charts for nonconformities (c, u) when
      1. There is a need to monitor the number of nonconformities in a process (c charts for counts of nonconformities, u charts for nonconformities per unit).
      2. The characteristics under study in the process can be judged as having one or more nonconformities.
      3. Process monitoring is desired but measurement data cannot be obtained because of the nature of the product or the expense.
      4. The sample size varies (u chart).

■ *Lessons Learned*

1. Fraction nonconforming (p) charts can be constructed for both constant and variable sample sizes because the sample size can be isolated in the formula.
2. For the fraction nonconforming chart, the product or service being provided must be inspected and classed as either conforming or not conforming.
3. Number nonconforming (np) and percent nonconforming charts may be easier to interpret than fraction nonconforming (p) charts.
4. It is possible to construct either a p or a u chart for variable sample size. Individual control limits for the different sample sizes may be calculated or n_{ave} may be used. When n_{ave} is used, care must be taken to correctly interpret the points approaching or exceeding the upper control limit.
5. Charts for counts of nonconformities (c) and nonconformities per unit (u) are used when the nonconformities on the product or service being inspected can be counted. For c charts, n = 1; for u charts, n > 1.
6. Charts for nonconformities per unit (u charts) can be constructed for both constant and variable sample sizes.
7. When interpreting p, np, c, or u charts, it is important to remember that values closer to zero are desirable. ■

■ Formulas

Fraction Nonconforming (p) Chart

$$p = \frac{np}{n}$$

$$\text{Centerline } \bar{p} = \frac{\sum_{i=1}^{n} np}{\sum_{i=1}^{n} n}$$

$$\text{UCL}_p = \bar{p} + 3\frac{\sqrt{\bar{p}(1 - \bar{p})}}{\sqrt{n}}$$

$$\text{LCL}_p = \bar{p} - 3\frac{\sqrt{\bar{p}(1 - \bar{p})}}{\sqrt{n}}$$

Revising:

$$\bar{p}_{new} = \frac{\sum_{i=1}^{n} np - np_d}{\sum_{i=1}^{n} n - n_d}$$

$$\text{UCL}_{p_{new}} = \bar{p}_{new} + 3\frac{\sqrt{\bar{p}_{new}(1 - \bar{p}_{new})}}{\sqrt{n}}$$

$$\text{LCL}_{p_{new}} = \bar{p}_{new} - 3\frac{\sqrt{\bar{p}_{new}(1 - \bar{p}_{new})}}{\sqrt{n}}$$

The process capability of the revised chart is the newly calculated p_{new}:

$$n_{ave} = \frac{\sum_{i=1}^{n} n}{m}$$

Number Nonconforming (np) Chart

$$\text{Centerline } n\bar{p} = \frac{\sum_{i=1}^{n} np}{m}$$

$$\text{UCL}_{np} = n\bar{p} + 3\sqrt{n\bar{p}(1 - \bar{p})}$$

$$\text{LCL}_{np} = n\bar{p} - 3\sqrt{n\bar{p}(1 - \bar{p})}$$

Percent Nonconforming (100p) Chart

The centerline for a percent nonconforming chart is $100\bar{p}$.

$$\mathrm{UCL}_{100p} = 100\left[\bar{p} + \frac{3\sqrt{\bar{p}(1 - \bar{p})}}{\sqrt{n}}\right]$$

$$\mathrm{LCL}_{100p} = 100\left[\bar{p} - \frac{3\sqrt{\bar{p}(1 - \bar{p})}}{\sqrt{n}}\right]$$

Count of Nonconformities (c) Chart

$$n = 1$$

$$\text{Centerline } \bar{c} = \frac{\sum\limits_{i=1}^{n} c}{m}$$

$$\mathrm{UCL}_c = \bar{c} + 3\sqrt{\bar{c}}$$

$$\mathrm{LCL}_c = \bar{c} - 3\sqrt{\bar{c}}$$

Revising:

$$\text{Centerline } \bar{c}_{new} = \frac{\sum\limits_{i=1}^{n} c - c_d}{m - m_d}$$

$$\mathrm{UCL}_{c_{new}} = \bar{c}_{new} + 3\sqrt{\bar{c}_{new}}$$

$$\mathrm{LCL}_{c_{new}} = \bar{c}_{new} - 3\sqrt{\bar{c}_{new}}$$

Nonconformities per Unit (u) Chart

$$n > 1$$

$$u = \frac{c}{n}$$

$$\text{Centerline } \bar{u} = \frac{\sum\limits_{i=1}^{n} c}{\sum\limits_{i=1}^{n} n}$$

$$\mathrm{UCL}_u = \bar{u} + 3\frac{\sqrt{\bar{u}}}{\sqrt{n}}$$

$$\mathrm{LCL}_u = \bar{u} - 3\frac{\sqrt{\bar{u}}}{\sqrt{n}}$$

Chapter Problems

1. Use an example when explaining the difference between a common cause and a special cause. Is this true for all charts—p, c, u, $\overline{X}$, and R?

2. How would you determine that a process is under control? How is the interpretation of a p, u, or c chart different from that of an $\overline{X}$ and R chart?

Charts for Fraction Nonconforming

3. Given the following information about mistakes made on tax forms, make and interpret a fraction nonconforming chart.

Sample Size	Nonconforming	Sample Size	Nonconforming
20	0	20	10
20	0	20	2
20	0	20	1
20	2	20	0
20	0	20	1
20	1	20	0
20	6	20	0
20	0	20	1
20	0	20	1
20	2	20	0
20	3	20	2
20	1	20	0
20	1	20	4
20	0	20	1
20	2	20	0

4. The following table gives the number of nonconforming product found while inspecting a series of 12 consecutive lots of galvanized washers for finish defects such as exposed steel, rough galvanizing, and discoloration. A sample size of n = 200 was used for each lot. Find the centerline and control limits for a fraction nonconforming chart. If the manufacturer wishes to have a process capability of $\overline{p}$ = 0.005, is the process capable?

Sample Size	Nonconforming	Sample Size	Nonconforming
200	0	200	0
200	1	200	0
200	2	200	1
200	0	200	0
200	1	200	3
200	1	200	1

5. Thirst-Quench, Inc., has been in business for more than 50 years. Recently Thirst-Quench updated their machinery and processes, acknowledging their out-of-date style. They have decided to evaluate these changes. The engineer is to record data, evaluate those data, and implement strategy to keep quality at a maximum. The plant operates 8 hours a day, 5 days a week, and produces 25,000 bottles of Thirst-Quench each day. Problems that have arisen in the past include partially filled bottles, crooked labels, upside down labels, and no labels. Samples of size 150 are taken each hour. Create a p chart.

Subgroup Number	Number Inspected n	Number Nonconforming np	Proportion Nonconforming p
1	150	6	0.040
2	150	3	0.020
3	150	9	0.060
4	150	7	0.047
5	150	9	0.060
6	150	2	0.013
7	150	3	0.020
8	150	5	0.033
9	150	6	0.040
10	150	8	0.053
11	150	9	0.060
12	150	7	0.047
13	150	7	0.047
14	150	2	0.013
15	150	5	0.033
16	150	7	0.047
17	150	4	0.027
18	150	3	0.020

(continued)

Subgroup Number	Number Inspected n	Number Nonconforming np	Proportion Nonconforming p
19	150	9	0.060
20	150	8	0.053
21	150	8	0.053
22	150	6	0.040
23	150	2	0.013
24	150	9	0.060
25	150	7	0.047
26	150	3	0.020
27	150	4	0.027
28	150	6	0.040
29	150	5	0.033
30	150	4	0.027
Total	4500	173	

6. Nearly everyone who visits a doctor's office is covered by some form of insurance. For a doctor, the processing of forms in order to receive payment from an insurance company is a necessary part of doing business. If a form is filled out incorrectly, the form cannot be processed and is considered nonconforming (defective). Within each office, an individual is responsible for inspecting and correcting the forms before filing them with the appropriate insurance company. A local doctor's office is interested in determining whether or not errors on insurance forms are a major problem. Every week they take a sample of 20 forms to use in creating a p chart. Use the following information to create a p chart. How are they doing?

	Nonconforming
1	2
2	5
3	8
4	10
5	4
6	7
7	6
8	3
9	7
10	5
11	2

(continued)

Nonconforming	
12	3
13	17
14	5
15	2
16	4
17	5
18	2
19	3
20	2
21	6
22	4
23	5
24	1
25	2

7. For 15 years, a county has been keeping track of traffic fatalities. From the total number of fatal traffic accidents each year, a random sample is taken and the driver is tested for blood alcohol level. For the sake of creating control charts, a blood alcohol level higher than 80 mg is considered nonconforming. Given the following information, create a p chart with a sample size that varies.

   Consider the following information when interpreting the chart. In 1991, the county began a three-pronged attack against drunk driving. Mandatory seat belt legislation was enacted, advertisements on radio and TV were used to increase public awareness of the dangers of drinking and driving, and harsher sentences were enacted for drunk driving. Based on your knowledge of chart interpretations, were these programs successful? How do you know?

Year	No. of Driver Fatalities Tested	No. of Driver Fatalities Tested with a Blood Alcohol Level over 80 mg
1983	1,354	709
1984	1,501	674
1985	1,479	687
1986	1,265	648
1987	1,261	583
1988	1,209	668
1989	1,333	665
1990	1,233	641
1991	1,400	550

(continued)

Year	No. of Driver Fatalities Tested	No. of Driver Fatalities Tested with a Blood Alcohol Level over 80 mg
1992	1,181	545
1993	1,237	539
1994	1,186	535
1995	1,291	557
1996	1,356	537
1997	1,341	523
	19,627	9,061

8. Use the data from Problem 7 and create a p chart using n average. Use n_{ave} to interpret the chart.

9. The House of Bolts is one of the largest producers of industrial (Class III) bolts. The bolts are sampled daily with a sample size of 500. The bolts are inspected for thread engagement and overall design. A nonconforming bolt would display an irregular bolt size or poor thread engagement. The control chart shows the fraction of nonconforming bolts per sample size. Create a p chart with the following data. Assume assignable causes and revise the chart.

Subgroup Number	Number Inspected n	Number Nonconforming np	Fraction Nonconforming p
1	500	13	0.026
2	500	5	0.010
3	500	11	0.022
4	500	6	0.012
5	500	2	0.004
6	500	8	0.016
7	500	8	0.016
8	500	3	0.006
9	500	10	0.020
10	500	0	0.000
11	500	5	0.010
12	500	12	0.024
13	500	11	0.022
14	500	5	0.010
15	500	0	0.000

(continued)

Subgroup Number	Number Inspected n	Number Nonconforming np	Fraction Nonconforming p
16	500	0	0.000
17	500	7	0.014
18	500	9	0.018
19	500	10	0.020
20	500	6	0.012
Total	10,000	131	

10. The House of Bolts has changed their data collecting techniques. The bolts are inspected daily, but not at a constant sample size. Guidelines for nonconforming bolts have not changed. The bolts are inspected for thread engagement and overall design. As before, a nonconforming bolt would be an irregular bolt size or poor thread engagement. Create a p chart for variable subgroup size. Assume assignable causes and revise the chart. Does the control chart change significantly from the chart in Problem 9?

Subgroup Number	Number Inspected n	Number Nonconforming np	Fraction Nonconforming p
1	500	13	0.026
2	500	5	0.010
3	500	11	0.022
4	450	6	0.013
5	450	2	0.004
6	450	8	0.018
7	600	8	0.013
8	600	3	0.005
9	600	10	0.017
10	400	0	0.000
11	400	5	0.013
12	400	12	0.030
13	550	11	0.020
14	550	5	0.009
15	550	0	0.000
16	450	0	0.000
17	450	7	0.016
18	450	9	0.020
19	600	10	0.017
20	600	6	0.010
Total	10,050	131	

11. The following are data on 5-gal containers of paint. If the color mixture of the paint does not match the control color, then the entire container is considered nonconforming and is disposed of. Since the amount produced during each production run varies, use n_{ave} to calculate the centerline and control limits for this set of data. Carry calculations to four decimal places. Remember to round n_{ave} to a whole number; you can't sample part of a 5-gal pail.

Production Run	Number Inspected	Number Defective
1	2,524	30
2	2,056	84
3	2,750	76
4	3,069	108
5	3,365	54
6	3,763	29
7	2,675	20
8	2,255	25
9	2,060	48
10	2,835	10
11	2,620	86
12	2,250	25

Which points should be tested? Use the cases presented in the chapter to discuss why or why not. Show calculations if the points need to be tested.

12. Given the chart in Figure P9.1, discuss the state of control the charts are exhibiting. What percent nonconforming should the company expect in the future for process 1?

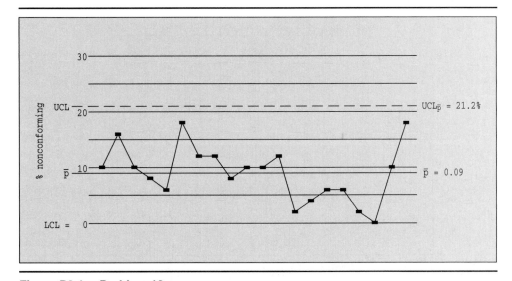

Figure P9.1   Problem 12

13. The board of directors is meeting to discuss quality on a particular product. The quality supervisor wants to create a chart that is easy to understand. What chart would you choose? Use n = 50 and p = 0.09 to calculate the control limits and centerline. Create and interpret this chart.

Subgroup No.	1	2	3	4	5	6	7	8	9	10
Nonconforming	5	4	3	2	6	18	5	8	2	2

14. Given Figure P9.2, complete the calculations for the remaining shifts and finish the chart. Assume the assignable causes have been determined and corrected. Remove those points that exhibit out of control conditions and recalculate the limits.

15. At Fruits and Such, a local frozen fruit concentrate manufacturer, frozen grape juice is packed in 12-ounce cardboard cans. These cans are formed on a machine by spinning them from preprinted cardboard stock and attaching two metal lids, one for the top and one for the bottom. After the filling operation, samples (n = 100) of the production are taken hourly. Inspectors look

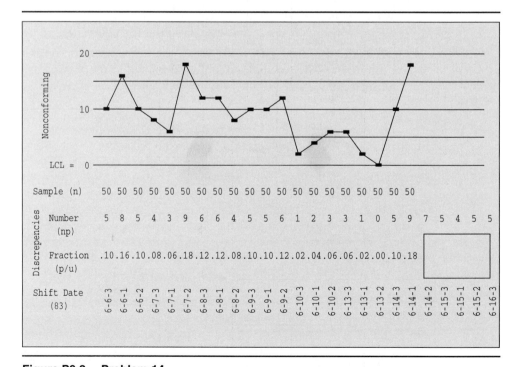

Figure P9.2   Problem 14

for several things that would make the can defective: how well the strip for opening the can operates, whether there are proper crimps holding the lids to the cardboard tube, if the lids are poorly sealed, etc. Create and interpret an np chart for the following data.

Subgroup	Defectives	Subgroup	Defectives
1	12	14	12
2	15	15	22
3	8	16	8
4	10	17	10
5	4	18	5
6	7	19	13
7	16	20	12
8	9	21	20
9	14	22	18
10	10	23	24
11	5	24	15
12	6	25	8
13	17		

16. From a lot of 1,000 soup cans, a sample size 160 (n = 160) is taken. The following data show the results of 15 such subgroups. Use the data to create a number nonconforming chart.

Lot	n	np
1	160	12
2	160	15
3	160	13
4	160	15
5	160	11
6	160	11
7	160	10
8	160	15
9	160	13
10	160	12
11	160	16
12	160	17
13	160	13
14	160	14
15	160	11

17. A manufacturer of lightbulbs is keeping track of the number of nonconforming bulbs (the number that don't light). Create the centerline and control limits for a number nonconforming chart. What is the capability of the process? Assume assignable causes and revise the chart.

	n	np		n	np
1	300	10	11	300	31
2	300	8	12	300	32
3	300	9	13	300	10
4	300	12	14	300	8
5	300	10	15	300	12
6	300	11	16	300	10
7	300	9	17	300	11
8	300	10	18	300	9
9	300	12	19	300	10
10	300	11	20	300	8

18. The Tri-State Foundry Company is a large volume producer of ball joints for various automotive producers. The ball joints are sampled four times daily. The sample size is a constant of 400 parts. The chart shows how many nonconforming parts are found in a sample size. Nonconforming quality comes from an outer diameter that is larger than 1.5 inches. The 1.5 inch limit is a strict guideline because any parts that are larger will not work with the female coupling assembly. Create an np chart with the following data. Assume assignable causes and revise the chart.

Subgroup Number	Number Inspected n	Number Nonconforming np
1	400	3
2	400	4
3	400	1
4	400	7
5	400	6
6	400	3
7	400	11
8	400	13
9	400	4
10	400	10
11	400	5
12	400	0

(continued)

Subgroup Number	Number Inspected n	Number Nonconforming np
13	400	2
14	400	2
15	400	4
16	400	8
17	400	5
18	400	3
19	400	1
20	400	12

Charts for Nonconformities

19. A line produces leather jackets. Once each hour a jacket is selected at random from those made during that hour. Small imperfections (missed stitches, zipper catch, buttons missing, loose threads) are counted. Recent data show an average of eight imperfections (nonconformities) in each sample. Using the formulas for a c chart, calculate the control limits and centerline for this situation. If management wants a process capability of four nonconformities per sample, will this line be able to meet that requirement?

20. A production line manufactures compact discs. Twice an hour, one CD is selected at random from those made during the hour. Each disc is inspected separately for imperfections (defects), such as scratches, nicks, discolorations, and dents. The resulting count of imperfections from each disc is recorded on a control chart. Use the following data to create a c chart. If the customer wants a process capability of 1, will this line be able to meet that requirement?

Hour	Imperfections	Hour	Imperfections
1	2	14	1
2	0	15	1
3	2	16	0
4	1	17	0
5	0	18	2
6	1	19	4
7	0	20	1
8	2	21	2
9	0	22	0
10	2	23	2
11	1	24	1
12	2	25	0
13	0		

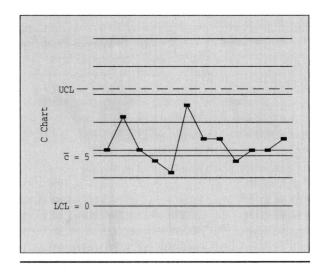

Figure P9.3   Problem 21

21. A production line produces large plastic Santas. Once each hour a Santa is selected at random from those made during that hour. Small imperfections in the plastic Santa (bubbles, discolorations, and holes) are counted. The count of nonconformities is recorded on control charts. Recent data have averaged five imperfections (nonconformities) in each sample.

    a. Calculate the control limits and centerline for this c chart.
    b. If management wants a process capability of two nonconformities per sample, will this line be able to meet that requirement? Why or why not?
    c. Given the figure of several hours of production, how does this process look? In other words, interpret the chart in Figure P9.3.

22. The Par Fore Golf Company is a producer of plastic divot fixers. They produce the fixers in bags of 30. They consider these bags a sample size of 1. The nonconformities range from overall size to individual flaws in the production of the plastic tool. These tools are inspected four times daily. Create a chart with the following data. Assume assignable causes and revise the chart.

	Serial Number	Count of Nonconformities	Comment
1	JG100	7	
2	JG101	3	
3	JG102	5	
4	JG103	4	
5	JG104	6	
6	JG105	6	
7	JG106	17	Wrong Mold Used

(*continued*)

	Serial Number	Count of Nonconformities	Comment
8	JG107	7	
9	JG108	2	
10	JG109	0	
11	JG110	3	
12	JG111	4	
13	JG112	2	
14	JG113	0	
15	JG114	21	Not Enough Time in Mold
16	JG115	3	
17	JG116	2	
18	JG117	7	
19	JG118	5	
20	JG119	9	
		113	

23. When printing full color glossy magazine advertising pages, editors do not like to see blemishes or pics (very small places where the color did not transfer to the paper). One person at the printer has the job of looking at samples of magazine pages ($n = 20$) and counting blemishes. Below are her results. The editors are interested in plotting the nonconformities per unit on a u chart. Determine the centerline and control limits. Create a chart of this process. If the editors want only two nonconformities per unit on average, how does this compare with the actual process average?

Subgroup Number	Count of Nonconformities
1	65
2	80
3	60
4	50
5	52
6	42
7	35
8	30
9	30
10	25

24. A manufacturer of holiday light strings tests 400 of the light strings each day. The light strings are plugged in and the number of unlit bulbs are counted and recorded. Unlit bulbs are considered nonconformities, and they are replaced before the light strings are shipped to customers. These data are then

used to aid process engineers in their problem-solving activities. Given the following information, create and graph the chart. How is their performance? What is the process capability?

Subgroup	Sample Size	Nonconformities
1	400	50
2	400	23
3	400	27
4	400	32
5	400	26
6	400	38
7	400	57
8	400	31
9	400	48
10	400	34
11	400	37
12	400	44
13	400	34
14	400	32
15	400	50
16	400	49
17	400	54
18	400	38
19	400	29
20	400	47
	8,000	780

25. The Davis Plastic Company produces plastic Wiffle-ball bats for a major sporting goods company. These bats are inspected daily but are not inspected at a constant number each day. The control chart shows how many bats were inspected and how many nonconformities were found per unit. Nonconformities include wrong taper on bat, incomplete handle, bad knurl on grip, or deformed bat ends. Create a u chart with the following data. Assume assignable causes and revise the chart.

Date	Number Inspected n	Count of Nonconformities c	Nonconformities per Unit u
April			
17	126	149	1.18
18	84	91	1.08
19	96	89	0.93

(*continued*)

Date	Number Inspected n	Count of Nonconformities c	Nonconformities per Unit u
20	101	97	0.96
21	100	140	1.40
24	112	112	1.00
25	79	89	1.13
26	93	119	1.28
27	88	128	1.46
28	105	117	1.11
May			
1	99	135	1.36
2	128	155	1.21
3	113	145	1.28
4	120	143	1.19
5	81	94	1.16
8	85	104	1.22
9	130	157	1.21
10	97	121	1.25
11	78	83	1.06
12	110	120	1.09
	2,025	2,388	

26. A manufacturer of aspirin monitors the potency of their product using a u chart. Samples are taken from batches of 1000 aspirin and those with incorrect potencies are recorded, only to be crushed and recycled later. Create and interpret a u chart using n_{ave}.

Subgroup Number	n	c	Subgroup Number	n	c
1	29	2	12	25	3
2	30	3	13	33	7
3	31	17	14	31	3
4	30	2	15	30	6
5	32	6	16	29	2
6	28	1	17	27	4
7	30	5	18	31	13
8	35	4	19	29	23
9	28	7	20	26	3
10	30	3	21	34	13
11	32	5	22	30	6

CASE STUDY 9.1
Attribute Control Charts: np Charts

PART 1

At Fruits and Such, a local frozen fruit concentrate manufacturer, frozen orange juice concentrate is packed in 12-ounce cardboard cans. These cans are formed on a machine by spinning them from preprinted cardboard stock and attaching two metal lids, one for the top and one for the bottom. After filling, the container is carefully inspected. The inspectors test how well the strip to open the can operates. If a strip breaks, the can is considered nonconforming and unusable. Other packaging nonconformities include improper crimps holding the lids to the cardboard tube or poorly sealed lids. Fill rates are carefully checked to ensure that the containers truly contain 12 ounces. Inspectors also check the cosmetics of the can. Incorrectly wrapped cans or crooked labels are considered nonconforming and unusable.

An np chart for tracking unusable nonconformities needs to be established to track the level of nonconformities produced on a daily basis. The first 30 subgroups of size $n = 50$ are found in Figure C9.1.1.

 Assignment

Use the total number of defectives to create the np chart. How is the process currently performing? What is the process capability?

While the np chart keeps track only of the number of nonconformities and not the type, Figure C9.1.1 reveals that the inspectors have also been keeping track of the types of nonconformities.

 Assignment

Perform a Pareto analysis and discuss which problems are most prevalent and which should be investigated first.

PART 2

An investigation of the Pareto analysis reveals that the two largest problems are the fill level of the orange juice cans and the breakage of the plastic opening strip. Since the fill level appears to be the largest problem, the investigators decide to start their problem-solving efforts there.

DEPT.: Forming			PART NAME: OJ can	
PART NO.: OJ-1			MACHINE: Spinner	
GROUP: 1			VARIABLE: Seal	

Subgroup	1	2	3	4	5
Time	07:00:00	07:16:00	07:32:00	07:48:00	08:04:00
Date	03/03/XX	03/03/XX	03/03/XX	03/03/XX	03/03/XX
Sample Size	50	50	50	50	50
Defective	12	15	8	10	4
STRIP BRK	4	5	2	4	2
CRIMP	0	2	0	1	0
WRAP	2	0	0	1	0
BASE	0	0	0	1	0
LABEL	2	2	2	1	0
FILL	4	6	4	2	2
Subgroup	6	7	8	9	10
Time	08:20:00	08:36:00	08:52:00	09:08:00	09:24:00
Date	03/03/XX	03/03/XX	03/03/XX	03/03/XX	03/03/XX
Sample Size	50	50	50	50	50
Defective	7	16	9	14	10
STRIP BRK	2	4	4	5	2
CRIMP	1	2	0	1	2
WRAP	0	2	0	1	0
BASE	0	0	0	1	1
LABEL	0	2	0	2	1
FILL	4	6	5	4	4
Subgroup	11	12	13	14	15
Time	09:30:00	09:46:00	10:02:00	10:18:00	10:34:00
Date	03/03/XX	03/03/XX	03/03/XX	03/03/XX	03/03/XX
Sample Size	50	50	50	50	50
Defective	5	6	17	12	22
STRIP BRK	2	3	8	4	8
CRIMP	0	0	2	2	0
WRAP	0	0	1	0	0
BASE	0	0	0	1	1
LABEL	1	0	0	2	2
FILL	2	3	6	3	11

Figure C9.1.1   (*continued*)

DEPT.: Forming   PART NAME: OJ can
PART NO.: OJ-1   MACHINE: Spinner
GROUP: 1   VARIABLE: Seal

Subgroup	16	17	18	19	20
Time	10:50:00	11:06:00	11:22:00	11:38:00	11:54:00
Date	03/03/XX	03/03/XX	03/03/XX	03/03/XX	03/03/XX
Sample Size	50	50	50	50	50
Defective	8	10	5	13	12
STRIP BRK	3	2	1	4	4
CRIMP	1	2	1	1	1
WRAP	0	0	0	1	2
BASE	0	0	0	1	0
LABEL	0	0	0	1	0
FILL	4	6	3	5	5

Subgroup	21	22	23	24	25
Time	12:10:00	12:26:00	12:42:00	12:58:00	13:14:00
Date	03/03/XX	03/03/XX	03/03/XX	03/03/XX	03/03/XX
Sample Size	50	50	50	50	50
Defective	20	18	24	15	9
STRIP BRK	7	7	10	6	4
CRIMP	1	1	2	1	0
WRAP	2	2	0	2	0
BASE	1	1	2	2	0
LABEL	1	1	3	0	0
FILL	8	6	7	4	5

Subgroup	26	27	28	29	30
Time	13:30:00	13:46:00	14:02:00	14:18:00	14:34:00
Date	03/03/XX	03/03/XX	03/03/XX	03/03/XX	03/03/XX
Sample Size	50	50	50	50	50
Defective	12	7	13	9	6
STRIP BRK	4	3	4	4	3
CRIMP	1	1	1	0	0
WRAP	1	0	1	0	0
BASE	1	0	2	0	0
LABEL	1	0	0	0	0
FILL	4	3	5	5	3

Figure C9.1.1   (*continued*)

Upon checking the operation, they determine that there is a serious lack of precision in filling the orange juice cans. The current method fills the can by timing the flow of the product into the can. This type of filling method does not account for the change in pressure in the level of the supply tank. With a full storage tank of orange juice there is more pressure in the lines, resulting in the overfilling of cans. As the volume in the orange juice storage tank decreases, the cans are underfilled.

Replacing the existing tanks and delivery system, retrofitting pressure meters onto the system, or installing a weight sensitive pad and fill monitor to the existing line are all suggestions for improving this process. An economic analysis reveals that the weight sensitive pad and fill monitoring equipment would be the most economical change. The can rests on the pad during the filling operation. When the can reaches a preset weight, the can is indexed to the next station. Previously, the can was indexed on the basis of time. This new method ensures that the volume in each can changes very little from can to can. The weighing device has been calibrated so that the variance in empty can weight and density will produce only a slight variation in the can fill volume.

 Assignment

The decision has been made to add the weight sensitive pad and fill monitoring equipment for a trial period. Create an np chart and perform a Pareto analysis with the information in Figure C9.1.2. How does the chart look compared with the previous 30 subgroups of size n = 50? What is the process capability? Were there any changes found by the Pareto analysis? What should be investigated next?

DEPT.: Forming			PART NAME: OJ can		
PART NO.: OJ-1			MACHINE: Spinner		
GROUP: 1			VARIABLE: Seal		
Subgroup	1	2	3	4	5
Time	07:00:00	07:16:00	07:32:00	07:48:00	08:04:00
Date	03/16/XX	03/16/XX	03/16/XX	03/16/XX	03/16/XX
Sample Size	50	50	50	50	50
Defective	6	4	6	5	7
STRIP BRK	4	2	3	2	2
CRIMP	0	0	1	0	1
WRAP	1	0	0	1	1
BASE	0	0	0	1	1
LABEL	0	1	1	1	2
FILL	1	1	1	0	0

Figure C9.1.2   (*continued*)

DEPT.: Forming			PART NAME: OJ can	
PART NO.: OJ-1			MACHINE: Spinner	
GROUP: 1			VARIABLE: Seal	

Subgroup	6	7	8	9	10
Time	08:20:00	08:36:00	08:52:00	09:08:00	09:24:00
Date	03/16/XX	03/16/XX	03/16/XX	03/16/XX	03/16/XX
Sample Size	50	50	50	50	50
Defective	6	5	3	7	6
STRIP BRK	4	1	1	5	0
CRIMP	1	0	1	1	1
WRAP	0	1	0	0	1
BASE	0	1	0	0	1
LABEL	1	1	1	1	2
FILL	0	1	0	0	1

Subgroup	11	12	13	14	15
Time	09:40:00	09:56:00	10:12:00	10:28:00	10:42:00
Date	03/16/XX	03/16/XX	03/16/XX	03/16/XX	03/16/XX
Sample Size	50	50	50	50	50
Defective	2	4	3	6	5
STRIP BRK	2	3	1	3	4
CRIMP	0	0	0	1	0
WRAP	0	0	1	1	0
BASE	0	0	0	0	0
LABEL	0	1	0	1	1
FILL	0	0	1	0	0

Subgroup	16	17	18	19	20
Time	11:00:00	11:16:00	11:32:00	11:48:00	12:30:00
Date	03/16/XX	03/16/XX	03/16/XX	03/16/XX	03/16/XX
Sample Size	50	50	50	50	50
Defective	4	5	6	7	5
STRIP BRK	2	4	2	4	1
CRIMP	0	0	0	0	1
WRAP	0	0	1	0	1
BASE	1	0	1	1	0
LABEL	1	1	1	1	1
FILL	0	0	1	1	1

Figure C9.1.2   (*continued*)

PART 3

Correction of the strip breakage problem involves some investigation into the type of plastic currently being used to make the strips. The investigators have determined that the purchasing department recently switched to a less expensive type of plastic from a new supplier. The purchasing department never checked into the impact that this switch would have in the manufacturing department.

The investigators have shown the purchasing agent the results of the Pareto analysis and control charts and the old supplier has been reinstated, effective immediately. The unused plastic from the new supplier has been taken out of use and returned.

In a separate incident, the investigators have observed that the operators are not well trained in changing the cardboard-roll stock material. A direct correlation exists between the changeover times and the situations when the label is off center on the can. The operators involved in this operation are currently undergoing retraining.

 Assignment

To verify that the changes discussed above have had an impact on process quality, create an np chart and a Pareto diagram on the newest data in Figure C9.1.3. Discuss the results. What is the process capability now compared with before the changes? What should be done now?

| DEPT.: Forming | | | PART NAME: OJ can | | |
| PART NO.: OJ-1 | | | MACHINE: Spinner | | |
GROUP: 1			VARIABLE: Seal		
Subgroup	1	2	3	4	5
Time	07:00:00	07:18:00	07:36:00	07:54:00	08:12:00
Date	03/18/XX	03/18/XX	03/18/XX	03/18/XX	03/18/XX
Sample Size	50	50	50	50	50
Defective	2	1	2	0	1
STRIP BRK	0	0	0	0	1
CRIMP	0	0	1	0	0
WRAP	0	1	0	0	0
BASE	0	0	0	0	0
LABEL	2	0	1	0	0
FILL	0	0	0	0	0

Figure C9.1.3   (*continued*)

DEPT.: Forming   PART NAME: OJ can
PART NO.: OJ-1   MACHINE: Spinner
GROUP: 1   VARIABLE: Seal

Subgroup	6	7	8	9	10
Time	08:30:00	08:48:00	09:06:00	09:24:00	09:42:00
Date	03/18/XX	03/18/XX	03/18/XX	03/18/XX	03/18/XX
Sample Size	50	50	50	50	50
Defective	0	1	0	1	2
STRIP BRK	0	0	0	0	0
CRIMP	0	0	0	0	1
WRAP	0	0	0	0	0
BASE	0	1	0	1	0
LABEL	0	0	0	0	1
FILL	0	0	0	0	0
Subgroup	11	12	13	14	15
Time	10:00:00	10:18:00	10:36:00	10:54:00	11:12:00
Date	03/18/XX	03/18/XX	03/18/XX	03/18/XX	03/18/XX
Sample Size	50	50	50	50	50
Defective	1	0	2	1	2
STRIP BRK	0	0	1	0	0
CRIMP	0	0	0	1	1
WRAP	0	0	1	0	0
BASE	1	0	0	0	1
LABEL	0	0	0	0	0
FILL	0	0	0	0	0
Subgroup	16	17	18	19	20
Time	11:30:00	11:48:00	12:06:00	12:24:00	12:42:00
Date	03/18/XX	03/18/XX	03/18/XX	03/18/XX	03/18/XX
Sample Size	50	50	50	50	50
Defective	2	0	1	1	0
STRIP BRK	0	0	0	1	0
CRIMP	0	0	0	0	0
WRAP	0	0	0	0	0
BASE	0	0	1	0	0
LABEL	2	0	0	0	0
FILL	0	0	0	0	0

Figure C9.1.3   (*continued*)

CASE STUDY 9.2
Attribute Control Charts: u Charts

This case is the second of three related cases found in Chapters 8, 9, and 12. These cases seek to link information from the three chapters in order to resolve quality issues. Although they are related, it is not necessary to complete the case in this chapter in order to understand or complete the cases in the other chapters.

Max's B-B-Q Inc. manufactures top-of-the-line barbeque tools. The tools include forks, spatulas, knives, spoons, and shish-kebab skewers. Max's fabricates both the metal parts of the tools and the resin handles. These are then riveted together to create the tools (Figure C9.2.1). Recently, Max's hired a process engineer. His first assignment is to study routine tool wear on the company's stamping machine. In particular, he will be studying tool wear patterns for the tools used to create knife blades (Figure C9.2.2 on pages 515–516).

Each quarter, Max's makes more than 10,000,000 tools. Of these, approximately 240,000 are inspected for a variety of problems, including handle rivets, fork tines, handle cracks, dents, pits, butts, scratches, handle color, blade grinds, crooked blades, and others. Any tool that has a defect is either returned to the line to be reworked or it is scrapped. Figure C9.2.2 provides information for their first quarter inspection results.

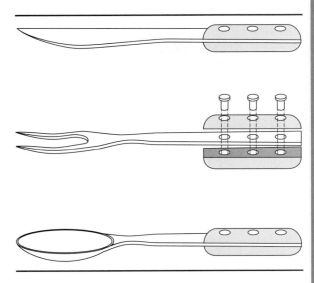

Figure 9.2.1   Barbeque Tools

Assignment

Create a Pareto chart with the information provided in Figure C9.2.2. Are any of the categories related? Can they be grouped in any way? What problems should be tackled first?

 Assignment

Create a chart for nonconformities using the data in Figure C9.2.3. How is the process performing? What is the process capability?

Subgroup #	n	c
1	1250	43
2	1250	40
3	1250	45
4	1250	39
5	1250	44
6	1250	42
7	1250	41
8	1250	40
9	1250	46
10	1250	45
11	1250	42
12	1250	43
13	1250	40
14	1250	38
15	1250	43
16	1250	42
17	1250	45
18	1250	43
19	1250	37
20	1250	39
21	1250	43
22	1250	44
23	1250	45
24	1250	41
25	1250	46
	32000	1056

Figure C9.2.3   February Summary of Daily Final Inspection Data for Table Knife Production. For Nonconformities by Type, See Figure C9.2.2.

FINAL INSPECTION
DEPARTMENT 8
FEBRUARY 1996

DEFECT	Table Knife	Steak Knife	Paring Knife	Filet Knife	Basting Spoon	Ladle Spoon	Perforated Spoon	Skewer
Bad handle rivets								
Bad steel	37						1	
Bad tines								
Bad/bent points	16							
Bent					1			
Buff concave								
Burn	146	57						
Burned handles	1							
Burrs	24	14						
Cloud on blades								
Cracked handle		32						
Cracked steel	1							
Crooked blades								
DD edge	41	2						
Dented								
Edge	31							
Etch								
Finish							1	
Grind in blade								
Haft at rivets					4		3	
Hafting marks handles	64							
Hafting marks steel								
Handle color	27	182				5		3
Heat induct	110	37					2	
High handle rivets								
High-speed buff								
Hit blades								
Hit handle	239							
Holder marks								

Figure C9.2.2

(continued)

FINAL INSPECTION
DEPARTMENT 8
FEBRUARY 1996

DEFECT	Table Knife 1759	Steak Knife 1759W	Paring Knife 1706	Filet Knife 1707	Basting Spoon 1712	Ladle Spoon 1712W	Perforated Spoon 1713	Skewer 1713W
Honing								
Narrow blades	4							
Nicked and scratched	105	10			9	2	7	
Open at rivet								
Open handles							1	
Open steel								
Pitted blades		1					1	
Pitted bolsters								
Raw backs								
Raw fronts								
Rebend								
Recolor concave	2	43						
Rehone								
Reruns								
Rivet								
Scratched blades	105	53		1	12	2	4	
Scratched rivets								
Seams/holes	11	50						
Seconds				2				
Stained blades	84	18			5	1		
Stained rivets								
Vendor rejects								
Water lines					15			
Wrap	8							
Total Inspected	32,000	28,811	5	277	3,145	1,504	2,008	1,805
Total Accepted	30,944	28,312	5	274	3,098	1,494	1,988	1,802
Total Rejected	1,056	499	0	3	47	10	20	3

Figure C9.2.2 *(continued)*

IV

Expanding the Scope of Quality

10

Reliability

 Learning Opportunities:

1. To know what to look for in a comprehensive reliability program
2. To understand the importance of system reliability
3. To understand how performance during the life of a product, process, or system is affected by its design and configuration
4. To be able to compute the reliability of systems, including systems in series, parallel, and hybrid combinations ■

Cars in a Snowstorm

Product designers and manufacturers must pay careful attention to the customer's expectations concerning a product's intended function, life, and environmental conditions for use. Customers judge a product's performance on much more than what can be seen at the moment of purchase. Consider the figure above. What are the intended function, life, and conditions for use of a passenger car? Most readers would agree that the intended function of a passenger car is to carry passengers from one location to another. Expectations concerning the life of such a vehicle may vary; a reasonable estimate may be 100,000 to 150,000 miles of use. The prescribed environmental conditions may at first appear to be easily defined: transport passengers on paved surface roads. But what about the vehicle's performance in snow, ice, or floods? Should the car start easily in temperatures significantly below zero? What temperature should it be able to endure before overheating? How deep a flood can it drive through and still run? These are just a few of the factors that define reliability. Reliability plays a key role in the consumer's perception of quality.

RELIABILITY

A car, the Internet, an automated teller machine, electricity, running water, pagers, the telephone—are these everyday items that you take for granted? Have you ever contemplated what happens if they fail? What happens if your car won't start? Do you get a ride from someone? Stay home? Take the bus or a cab? What happens if the Internet fails? Loss of access to information? Millions of missing e-mail messages? Lost Web pages? And if the telephone doesn't work? Can't call home? Can't call the hospital? What happens if the data processing centers, which tell ATMs whether or not to hand out money, have a system failure? No cash for you?

Our society depends on the high tech devices that make our lives easier. We have become so used to their presence in our lives that their sudden failure can bring about chaos. Yet, how much attention do we pay to the reliability of the devices we take for granted? Sometimes we become aware of reliability issues only when the device fails at a particularly critical time.

Reliability, or quality over the long term, is the ability of a product to perform its intended function over a period of time and under prescribed environmental conditions. The reliability of a system, subsystem, component, or part is dependent on many factors, including the quality of research performed at its conception, the original design and any subsequent design changes, the complexity of the design, the manufacturing processes, the handling received during shipping, the environment surrounding its use, the end user, and numerous other factors. The causes of unreliability are many. Improper design, less-than-specified construction materials, faulty manufacturing or assembly, inappropriate testing leading to unrealistic conclusions, and damage during shipment are all factors that may contribute to a lack of product reliability. Once the product reaches the user, improper start-ups, abuse, lack of maintenance, or misapplication can seriously affect the reliability of an item. Reliability studies are looking for the answers to such questions as: Will it work? How long will it last?

EXAMPLE 10.1   Sudden Failure

Consider the chaos caused in 1998, when a communication satellite failed, rendering digital pagers across the United States silent. Imagine the effect on a personal level. Romances on the rocks when couples unaware of the problem try unsuccessfully to page each other. (Why didn't you return my page?) Parents unable to check in with their kids, and vice versa. (Where were you?) Imagine not being able to contact doctors, nurses, or police to respond to emergencies. (My wife is having a baby . . . where is the doctor?) The satellite relayed signals for nearly 90 percent of the 45 million pagers in the United States as well as signals for dozens of broadcasters and data networks. Besides the silent pagers, gas stations couldn't take credit cards; broadcasting stations went off the air; some data information networks were inoperable; in some buildings, elevator and office Muzak was silenced; and many flights were delayed as air traffic controllers and pilots sought information on high altitude weather.

Eight of the nation's 10 biggest paging companies used this satellite because of its large area of coverage, the entire United States and the Caribbean. To regain communications, users had to switch to other satellites. For some, this involved climbing up on roofs and manually reorienting thousands of satellite dishes. Others were able to get up and running more quickly by temporarily recoding their systems to use other satellites.

All this chaos occurred because of the failure of the onboard computer that kept a five-year-old communication satellite pointed at the earth in a synchronized orbit 22,300 miles high. The $250 million, nine-foot cube with two 50-foot solar-panel wings had a projected failure rate of less than one percent. No backup systems were in place or considered necessary. Is a failure rate of less than one percent acceptable? How was system reliability determined? What can be done to improve system reliability? This chapter provides an introduction to reliability concepts.

Not worried about pagers? Remember, automatic teller machines share data processing centers, air traffic controllers share regional radar centers, and the Internet depends on a relatively small number of server computers for routing communications. . . .

"The Day the Beepers Died," *Newsweek,* June 1, 1998, p. 48.
"One Satellite Fails, and the World Goes Awry," *The Wall Street Journal,* May 21, 1998.

Recognizing that reliability, or quality over the long run, plays a key role in the consumer's perception of quality, companies understand the importance of having a sound reliability program. Reliability testing enables a company to better comprehend how their products will perform under normal usage as well as extreme or unexpected situations. Reliability programs provide information about product performance by systematically studying the product. To ensure product quality, reliability tests subject a product to a variety of conditions besides expected operational parameters. These conditions may include excessive use, vibration, damp, heat, cold, humidity, dust, corrosive materials, and other environmental or user stresses. By providing information about product performance, a sound reliability program can have a significant effect on a company's financial statements. Early product testing can prevent poorly designed products from reaching the marketplace. Later testing can improve upon products already in use.

RELIABILITY PROGRAMS

Reliability programs endeavor to incorporate reliability concepts into system design. Reliability issues surface in nearly every facet of system design, development, creation, use, and service. A well thought out reliability program will include the areas of design, testing, manufacture, raw material and component purchases, production, packaging, shipping, marketing, field service, and maintenance. A sound reliability program developed and implemented to support an entire system will consider the following aspects.

1. The entire system. What composes the system? What goals does the system meet? What are the components of the system? How are they interrelated? How do the interrelationships influence system reliability? What are the system reliability requirements set by the customer?

Critical to ensuring system reliability is a complete understanding of purpose of the product. Everyone involved in providing the system must have a complete understanding of the product. The consumer's reliability needs and expectations must be a part of product reliability. Also important is an understanding of the life of a product. How is it shipped? How is it transported and stored? What type of environment will it face during usage? Comprehensive knowledge of a product and its life is the foundation of a strong reliability program.

2. The humans in the system. What are their limitations? What are their capabilities? What knowledge do they have of the product? How will this knowledge affect their use of the product? How might they misuse the product?

Product reliability can be increased if greater emphasis is placed on proper training and education of the users of the product. Appropriate steps must also be taken to ensure that the sales department does not promise more than the product can deliver. Setting the expectations of the users is as important as showing them how to use a product.

3. Maintenance of the system. Can the components or subassemblies be maintained separately from the system? Are the system components accessible? Is the system designed for replacement components or subsystems? Are those components or subsystems available? Can those components or subsystems be misapplied or misused? Will maintenance be performed under difficult circumstances?

If and when a component or a system fails, those using the system or component will be interested in the length of time it takes to return the failed system, subsystem, or component to full operational status. Changes to product, process, or system design based on maintainability considerations are sure to include an investigation of factors such as ease of repair or replacement of components, costs, and time. Well designed policies, practices, and procedures for effective preventive maintenance before a failure occurs and timely corrective maintenance after a failure occurs increase overall system reliability.

4. Simplicity of design. Will a simple design be more effective than a complicated one? Will a reduction in the number of elements increase the system reliability? Will the addition of elements increase the system reliability?

Simple, straightforward designs will increase system reliability. Designs of this sort are less likely to break down and are more easily manufactured. In some instances, the effort to impress with the current technological wizardry decreases the product's reliability. The greater the number of components, the greater the complexity and the easier it is for some aspect of the product, process, or system to fail.

5. Redundant and fail-safe features. Can the addition of redundant components or fail-safe features prevent overall system failure? At what cost?

Incremental increases in reliability should be balanced against costs. Products can be overdesigned for their purposes. There is a diminishing return on investment for this approach to achieving a reliable product. Is it preferable to avoid specially designed parts and components for the sake of easy availability? Will interchangeability decrease maintenance complexity?

6. Manufacturing methods and purchasing requirements. Have the chosen manufacturing methods enhanced system quality and reliability? Have purchasing policies been designed to support quality and reliability?

Purchasing and manufacturing must be made aware of how critical it is to purchase and use the materials deemed appropriate for the life cycle of this product.

7. Maintenance of complete product or system performance records. Can this information be used to increase future system reliability?

System reliability information from tests or from actual experience with the product or system should be gathered in a manner that will be meaningful when used for decisions concerning product or system design changes, development of new products or systems, product or system manufacture, operation, maintenance, or support.

8. Communication. Have clear channels of communication been established among all those involved in the design, manufacture, shipment, maintenance, and use of the product or system?

While perhaps not a complete list, the above areas for consideration form the basis of a well structured reliability program. When the program provides answers to the questions, system reliability is enhanced.

EXAMPLE 10.2   Disasters That Could Have Been Averted

Sometimes it is difficult to comprehend that a complete reliability program improves overall system reliability. Consider some examples from real life events where the critical aspects we discussed above were ignored:

Aspect 1. The entire system

In 1981, a walkway at the Kansas City Hyatt Regency Hotel collapsed, resulting in the loss of 100 lives. The failure was caused by a design change that substituted two short rods in place of the original long rod. An understanding of the entire system could have averted this disaster. The use of two rods doubled the load on the washer and nut holding the assembly together, but when the design was changed, the washer and nut were not strengthened. The undersized nut and washer allowed the rod to be pulled through the box beam. The entire system, including the nut and washer, should have been considered in the new design.

Aspect 1. The entire system

In 1989, United Airlines Flight 232 crashed in Sioux City, Iowa, despite heroic efforts on the part of the flight crew. The DC-10's tail engine exploded in flight and destroyed the plane's hydraulic lines. Although the plane could fly on its two wing-mounted engines, the loss of hydraulic power rendered the plane's main control systems (flaps and gear) inoperable. A study of the plane's design revealed that, although backup hydraulic systems existed, all three hydraulic lines, including backups, went through one channel, which rested on top of the third engine in the tail. When the engine failed, debris from the engine severed all the hydraulic lines at the same time. In his March 28, 1997, *USA Today* article, "Safety Hearings End Today on Cracks in Jet Engines," Robert Davis stated, "The nation's airlines could be forced to spend more time and money using new techniques for inspecting engines." Those familiar with reliability issues know that the problems are more complicated than an airline's maintenance practices.

Aspect 1. The entire system

During the summer of 1996, power outages plagued Western states, leaving offices, businesses, and homes without lights, air conditioning, elevators, computers, cash registers, faxes, electronic keys, ventilation, and a host of other services. Traffic chaos resulted when traffic signals failed to function. During one outage, 15 states were without power. This particular power failure occurred when circuit breakers at a transmission grid were tripped. The interrupted flow of power caused generators further down the line to overload. Automatic systems, activated in the event of an overload, cut power to millions of customers. Six weeks later, a second power grid failure resulted when sagging transmission lines triggered a domino effect similar to the previous outage. This outage affected 10 states and at least 5.6 million people for nearly 24 hours. When millions of people rely upon highly complex and integrated systems such as power transmission and satellites, these systems need careful consideration from a reliability point of view.

Not much has changed since 1996. Power outages continue to be prevalent. One massive power outage on August 14, 2003, left 50 million people in the U.S. and Canada without power for days. In the summer of 2004, Athens, Greece experienced a series of power outages that threatened to disrupt the Olympics. Studies of power outages reveal the shortcomings that contribute to these massive failures. Blackouts can be caused by unreliable or faulty equipment, voluntary reliability standards, overloaded transmission lines, untrained, unprepared, or overtaxed repair personnel, and poor planning.

Aspect 2. Often we think of reliability as an equipment based system, however, reliable systems are needed in other, more human oriented systems. As reported in the *Wall Street Journal* article "It's 9 P.M., Do You Know Where You Parked Your Car?" guest services managers at all major parking lots have systems in place designed to reunite patrons with their vehicles. While some guest services managers operate handheld computers running a license plate information location program which finds cars based on license plate information scanned from parked cars, most still rely on the guest's memory.

Aspect 3. Maintenance of the system

Sinks, showers, and bathtubs are all common items found in homes. These systems are so reliable that we take them for granted—that is, until they break. In many homes, it is these items' very reliability that causes designers and builders to overlook creating access to the plumbing. When no access has been provided, maintenance of the system may require cutting holes in walls. With some forethought about system repair needs, maintenance access panels can be installed.

Aspect 3. Maintenance of the system

According to a 2004, Purdue University, study of 1300 aviation incidents and accidents, maintenance errors, such as incomplete or incorrect tasks, were the primary contributing factors in 14% of aviation incidents and 8% of accidents. These figures, compiled from 1984–2002 records, are for all types of planes, from propeller to jumbo jet. The leading cause: Failure to Follow Maintenance Procedures. Though weather, turbulence, and pilot error still contribute the largest share of accidents and incidents, these maintenance figures reveal a problem exists.

Aspect 4. Simplicity of design

The design of the rocket joints on the space shuttle Challenger was based on the highly successful Titan III rocket. The joints of the Titan contained a single O-ring. When adapting the design for the space shuttle, designers felt that adding a second O-ring would make the design even more reliable. Investigation of the design after the explosion revealed that the additional O-ring had contributed to the disaster. Designers have redesigned the rocket to include a *third* O-ring, but will it increase reliability?

Aspect 5. Redundant and fail-safe features

The interchangeability of air filters from the lunar module and the command ship became an issue for the astronauts on Apollo 13. The air filters for the command ship could not be used on the lunar module, and vice versa. There were no redundant or backup systems available when the main systems failed. Only through the ingenuity of the scientists and engineers at NASA, who managed to use available materials on both ships to create a substitute filter, was disaster prevented.

Aspect 5. Redundant and fail-safe features

In September of 1991, American Telephone and Telegraph Co. experienced its third major system breakdown. Besides disrupting long distance service for 1 million people, the system failure abruptly cut off contact between air traffic controllers and airline pilots in the Northeast. While no serious accidents occurred —fast thinking pilots communicated their positions to each other—a massive tie-up in air traffic occurred across the country. In the months prior to this disruption, the Federal Aviation Administration had lobbied unsuccessfully to gain permission from the General Services Administration to switch to a phone system with greater reliability and redundancy.

Aspect 5. Redundant and fail-safe features

On December 20, 1997, air traffic over the central United States was disrupted by a multiple level power failure. Air traffic control systems maintain three backup systems. The combined reliability of such systems is considered to be greater than 99.5 percent. On December 20, however, one system was shut down for scheduled maintenance, the commercial power failed, and a technician mistakenly pulled a circuit card from the remaining power system. With no other backups, the air traffic control information system, including computers, software, and displays, was inoperable for about five hours. The unexpected failure of the redundant and backup systems needs to be carefully considered as part of overall reliability. **Q**

PRODUCT LIFE CYCLE CURVE

The life cycle of a product is commonly broken down into three phases: early failure, chance failure, and wear-out (Figure 10.1). The early failure, or infant mortality, phase is characterized by failures occurring very quickly after the product has been produced or put into use by the consumer. The curve during this phase is exponential, with the number of failures decreasing the longer the product is in use. Failures at this stage have a variety of causes. Some early failures are due to inappropriate or inadequate materials, marginal components, incorrect installation, or poor manufacturing techniques. Incomplete testing may not have revealed design weaknesses that become apparent only as the consumer uses the system. Inadequate quality checks could have allowed substandard products to leave the manufacturing area. The manufacturing processes or tooling may not have been capable of producing to the specifications needed by the designer. The consumer also plays a role in product reliability. Once the product reaches the consumer, steps must be taken to ensure that the consumer understands the appropriate environment for product use. Consumers need to receive training on how to operate and handle the product. Using improper procedures will affect the reliability of a product.

During the chance failure portion of a product's useful life, failures occur randomly. This may be due to inadequate or insufficient design margins. Manufacturing or material problems have the potential to cause intermittent failures. At this stage the consumer can also affect product reliability. Misapplication or misuse of the product by the consumer can lead to product failure. Overstressing the product is a common cause of random failures. Because of their unfamiliarity with product capabilities, consumers may inadvertently overstress the product.

As the product ages, it approaches the final stage of its life cycle, the wear-out phase. During this phase, failures increase in number until few, if any, of the product are left. Wear-out failures are due to a variety of causes, some related to actual product function, some cosmetic. A system's reliability, useful operation, or desirability may decrease if it becomes scratched, dented, chipped, or otherwise damaged. Age and the associated wear, discolorations, and brittleness may lead to material failure. Normal wear could decrease reliability through misalignments, loose fittings, and interference between components. Combined stresses placed on the product (like the zipper or latches on a suitcase) during its lifetime of use are a source of decreased reliability. Neglect or inadequate preventive maintenance lessens product reliability and shortens product life.

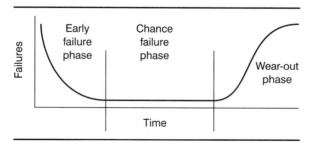

Figure 10.1   Life Cycle Curve

REAL TOOLS FOR REAL LIFE

Aircraft Landing Gear Life Cycle Management

Ever since Charles E. Taylor, the father of aviation maintenance, began working with the Wright Brothers to repair parts and components on such early models as the Wright B flier, aircraft maintenance programs have existed. Airlines recognize that the effectiveness of their organization depends on aircraft operational readiness, the overall reliability of their planes. The wisdom of participating in a preventive maintenance program is often justified by tracking reliability measures such as mean time to failure, mean time to repair, and availability rates.

Knowing that the reliability of landing gear components can materially affect aircraft operational readiness, CLP Corporation reviewed their two approaches to maintaining the reliability of their two separate fleets of aircraft. The objective of their review was to determine whether or not life cycle management of landing gear increased aircraft reliability and cost effectiveness.

In order to better manage maintenance, repair, and replacement costs, aircraft owners study their fleets, monitoring the reliability of key components. Aircraft landing gear reliability is often judged based on the number of takeoff-and-landing cycles completed. Planes, as well as their individual components, follow the life cycle curve presented in Figure 10.1. Fortunately, robust designs of key components and routine maintenance and repair often keep planes flying long after their predicted number of take off-and-landing cycles or flights has passed. In this example, the expected life of landing gear for both larger and smaller jets is eight thousand takeoff-and-landing cycles.

CLP's two jet fleets are managed as separate business entities. The smaller jets make short hops around the country, while the larger jets, with their greater fuel capacity, tend to be used for cross-country or cross-continent, longer duration flights. A study of the maintenance records revealed that CLP's smaller, 150-passenger jets experienced a greater number of landing gear reliability issues than the larger, 250-passenger jets. In short, the smaller jets are not as reliable as the larger jets.

At first glance, it may appear that the greater number of landing gear mishaps may be due to the smaller jets' greater number of landings and takeoffs. Further investigation uncovered that, as they aged, the smaller jets experienced lower landing gear reliability than the larger jets. Landing gear related mishaps accounted for nine percent of total aircraft mishaps from 1995 through 2004. Of 13 landing gear related mishaps, 11 occurred on smaller jets and two occurred on larger jets. True to the life cycle curve, as the jets have aged, failures have increased.

Although mishaps can not always be prevented through maintenance, aircraft that had a program of landing gear maintenance experienced reduced mishap rates and had greater reliability. A fully defined life cycle management process for the larger jets' landing gear from the time of acquisition through production and deployment has been in place for several years. Because the smaller jets did not have this process in place, they were less reliable, needing maintenance, repair, and replacement at a greater rate and at higher costs than the larger jets.

Table 10.1   Cost Analysis for Planned Maintenance Using Mean Time Between Failures

	MTBF with Planned Maintenance	Cost with Planned Maintenance	Aircraft Availability	MTBF w/o Planned Maintenance	Cost w/o Planned Maintenance	Aircraft Availability
Left Main Landing Gear*	8,300	$380,140	99%	3,917	$506,680	78%
Right Main Landing Gear*	8,186	$421,127	99%	3,043	$568,438	74%
Nose Landing Gear*	7,400	$407,392	98%	5,138	$473,413	68%

*Expected life: 8,000 takeoff-and-landing cycles.

The smaller jets have historically been maintained on an as-needed, on-location program rather than returning to a single maintenance facility. The larger jets, with their maintenance process, have all but emergency work taken care of at a single maintenance facility. One significant benefit of having repairs performed at a single location is the increase in worker knowledge of the aircraft of and its components. Another critical factor in reducing mean time to repair is that one location provides easy access to replacement parts. As the smaller jets aged, flight line maintenance becomes less effective, reliability levels decrease, and maintenance, repair, and replacement costs increase.

The larger jet management team maintained thorough records related to maintenance, repair, and replacement costs both before and after implementing the preventive maintenance program for the larger jets. In Table 10.1, these differences have been quantified using reliability concepts. The mean time between failure rates were calculated based on the number of failures observed by the maintenance staff and the number of takeoff-and-landing cycles the jets had completed. Aircraft availability calculations include the mean time to repair, that is, the average time it takes to return the jet to service after repairing a landing gear system component. The maintenance costs are the average total costs to repair or replace the failed landing gear.

The reliability calculations related to mean time between failure and availability show the significant difference between the costs associated with planned maintenance and unplanned maintenance, as well as the difference between availabilities of aircraft. Based on operational maintenance records, CLP Corporation recognized that reduced reliability related to landing gear, coupled with aging aircraft concerns, necessitated a change in its maintenance processes for its smaller jets. By comparison, the larger jets, with their maintenance process approach, have highly maintainable landing gear with an extended life and increased aircraft reliability. The landing gear maintenance process is only one of their many preventive maintenance programs. Overall, the larger jets' preventive maintenance program is projected to save the corporation over $100 million in a 10 year period.

Having a preventive maintenance process increases product reliability resulting in:

Increased effectiveness (availability for deployment)
Lower risk of failure
Increased component life
Reduced remote location maintenance workload
Greater maintenance knowledge at single facility
Increased ability to project life cycle costs associated with maintenance and
      component replacement
Lower risk of grounding an aircraft or an entire fleet
Fewer incidents needing crisis management
Increased morale

MEASURES OF RELIABILITY

Systems are orderly arrangements or combinations of parts, components, and sub-assemblies. These elements interact with each other and with external factors, such as humans and other systems, to perform their intended functions. Overall system reliability depends on the individual reliabilities associated with the parts, components, and subassemblies. Reliability values are sought to determine the performance of a product. Reliability studies also reveal any recurring patterns of failure and the underlying causes of those failures.

Reliability tests exist to aid in determining if distinct patterns of failure exist during the product's or system's life cycle. Reliability tests determine what failed, how it failed, and the number of hours, cycles, actuations, or stresses it was able to bear before failure. Once these data are known, decisions can be made concerning product reliability expectations, corrective action steps, maintenance procedures, and costs of repair or replacement. Several different types of tests exist to judge the reliability of a product, including failure-terminated, time-terminated, and sequential tests. The name of each of these tests says a good deal about the type of the test. *Failure-terminated tests* are ended when a predetermined number of failures occur within the sample being tested. The decision concerning whether or not the product is acceptable is based on the number of products that have failed during the test. A *time-terminated test* is concluded when an established number of hours is reached. For this test, product is accepted on the basis of how many products failed before reaching the time limit. A *sequential test* relies on the accumulated results of the tests.

Failure Rate, Mean Life, And Availability

When system performance is time dependent, such as the length of time a system is expected to operate, then reliability is measured in terms of mean life, failure rates, availability, mean time between failures, and specific mission reliability. As a system is used, data concerning failures become available. This information can be utilized to estimate the mean life and failure rate of the system. Failure rate, λ, the probability of a failure during a stated period of time, cycle, or number of impacts, can be calculated as

$$\lambda_{estimated} = \frac{\text{number of failures observed}}{\text{sum of test times or cycles}}$$

From this, θ, the average life, can be calculated:

$$\theta_{estimated} = \frac{1}{\lambda}$$

or

$$\theta_{estimated} = \frac{\text{sum of test times or cycles}}{\text{number of failures observed}}$$

The average life θ is also known as the mean time between failure or the mean time to failure. Mean time between failure (MTBF), how much time has elapsed between failures, is used when speaking of repairable systems. Mean time to failure is used for nonrepairable systems.

EXAMPLE 10.3   Calculating Failure Rate and Average Life

Twenty windshield wiper motors are being tested using a time-terminated test. The test is concluded when a total of 200 hours of continuous operation have been completed. During this test, the number of windshield wipers that fail before reaching the time limit of 200 hours is counted. If three wipers failed after 125, 152, and 189 hours, calculate the failure rate λ and the average life θ:

$$\lambda_{estimated} = \frac{\text{number of failures observed}}{\text{sum of test times of cycles}}$$

$$= \frac{3}{125 + 152 + 189 + (17)200} = 0.0008$$

From this, θ, the average life, can be calculated:

$$\theta_{estimated} = \frac{1}{\lambda} = \frac{1}{0.0008} = 1250 \text{ hours}$$

or

$$\theta_{estimated} = \frac{\text{sum of test times or cycles}}{\text{number of failures observed}}$$

$$= \frac{125 + 152 + 189 + (17)200}{3} = 1289 \text{ hours}$$

The average life of the windshield wiper motor is 1289 hours.

Here, the difference between $\theta_{estimated}$ based on $1/\lambda$ and $\theta_{estimated}$ calculated directly is due to rounding. Q

Mean times between failures (MTBF) and mean times to failure (MTTF) describe reliability as a function of time. Here the amount of time that the system is actually operating is of great concern. For example, without their radar screen, air traffic controllers are sightless and therefore out of operation. To be considered reliable, the radar must be functional for a significant amount of the expected operating time. Since many systems need preventive or corrective maintenance, a system's reliability can be judged in terms of the amount of time it is available for use:

$$\text{Availability} = \frac{\text{mean time to failure (MTTF)}}{\text{MTTF} + \text{mean time to repair}}$$

MTBF values can be used in place of MTTF.

EXAMPLE 10.4   Determining Availability

Windshield wiper motors are readily available and easy to install. Calculate the availability of the windshield wipers on a bus driven eight hours a day, if the mean time between failure or average life θ is 1250 hours. When the windshield wiper motor must be replaced, the bus is out of service for a total of 24 hours.

$$\text{Availability} = \frac{\text{mean time between failure (MTBF)}}{\text{MTBF} + \text{mean time to repair}}$$

$$= \frac{1250}{1250 + 24} = 0.98$$

The bus is available 98 percent of the time.

Calculating System Reliability

When system performance is dependent on the number of cycles completed successfully, such as the number of times a coin operated washing machine accepts the coins and begins operation, then reliability is measured in terms of the probability of successful operation. This type of reliability calculation has probability theory as its basis. **Reliability** *is the probability that a product will not fail during a particular time period*. Like probability, reliability takes on numerical values between 0.0 and 1.0. A reliability value of 0.78 is interpreted as 78 out of 100 parts will function as expected during a particular time period and 22 will not. If n is the total number of units being tested and s represents those units performing satisfactorily, then reliability R is given by

$$R = \frac{s}{n}$$

System reliability is determined by considering the reliability of the components and parts of the system. To calculate system reliabilities, the joint probabilities of

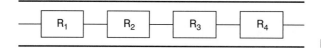

Figure 10.2   System in Series

their independent failure rates must be utilized. As systems become more complex, these calculations become increasingly more difficult. Interdependence of components in a system cannot be overlooked. In a system, the failure of one component could influence the failure of another component through load transferal, changes to the immediate environment, and many other factors.

Reliability in Series

A system in series exists if proper system functioning depends on whether all the components in the system are functioning. Failure of any one component will cause system failure. Figure 10.2 portrays an example of a system in series. In the diagram, the system will function only if all four components are functioning. If one component fails, the entire system will cease functioning. The reliability of a system in series is dependent on the individual component reliabilities. To calculate series system reliability the individual independent component reliabilities are multiplied together:

$$R_s = r_1 \cdot r_2 \cdot r_3 \cdots \cdot r_n$$

where

$$R_s = \text{reliability of series system}$$
$$r_i = \text{reliability of component}$$
$$n = \text{number of components in system}$$

EXAMPLE 10.5   Calculating Reliability in a Series System I

The reliability values for the flashlight components pictured in Figure 10.3 are listed below. If the components work in series, what is the reliability of the system?

Battery	0.75	Screw cap	0.97
Lightbulb	0.85	Body	0.99
Switch	0.98	Lens	0.99
Spring	0.99		

$$\begin{aligned} R_s &= r_1 \cdot r_2 \cdot r_3 \cdots \cdot r_n \\ &= 0.75 \cdot 0.98 \cdot 0.85 \cdot 0.99 \cdot 0.97 \cdot 0.99 \cdot 0.99 \\ &= 0.59 \end{aligned}$$

This flashlight has a reliability of only 0.59. Perhaps the owner of this flashlight ought to keep two on hand!   Q

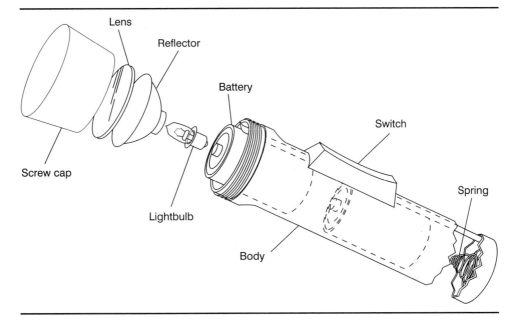

Figure 10.3   Flashlight

EXAMPLE 10.6   Calculating Reliability in a Series System II

Figure 10.4 displays a block diagram representing three clean water supply systems, each system increasing in complexity. The first filter filters out leaves and dirt that may clog the pump. Following the pump, a charcoal filter cleans microorganisms out of the water before it is chlorinated. Calculate the reliability of each of the systems.

$$
\begin{aligned}
R_{s1} &= r_1 \cdot r_2 \cdot r_3 \cdot \cdots \cdot r_n \\
&= 0.95 \cdot 0.98 \cdot 0.90 \cdot 0.99 = 0.83 \\
R_{s2} &= r_1 \cdot r_2 \cdot r_3 \cdot \cdots \cdot r_n \\
&= 0.95 \cdot 0.98 \cdot 0.98 \cdot 0.90 \cdot 0.99 = 0.81 \\
R_{s3} &= r_1 \cdot r_2 \cdot r_3 \cdot \cdots \cdot r_n \\
&= 0.95 \cdot 0.98 \cdot 0.98 \cdot 0.90 \cdot 0.99 \cdot 0.98 = 0.80
\end{aligned}
$$

Even though the reliability of the additional components is high, as the system increases in complexity, the overall system reliability decreases. $\mathbf{Q}$

Notice from this example that the reliability of a system decreases as more components are added in series. This means that the series system reliability will never be greater than the reliability of the least reliable component. Sustained performance over the life of a product or process can be enhanced in several ways. Parallel systems and redundant or standby component configurations can be used to increase the overall system reliability.

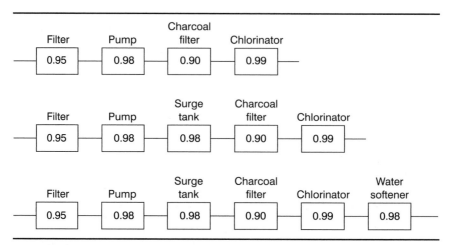

Figure 10.4   Clean Water Supply Systems

Reliability in Parallel

*A **parallel system** is a system that is able to function if at least one of its components is functioning.* Figure 10.5 displays a system in parallel. The system will function provided at least one component has not failed. In a parallel system, all of the components that are in parallel with each other must fail in order to have a system failure. This is the opposite of a series system in which, if one component fails, the entire system fails. Since the duplicated or paralleled component takes over functioning for the failed part, the reliability of this type of system is calculated on the basis of the sum of the probabilities of the favorable outcomes: the probability that no components fail and the combinations of the successful operation of one component but not the other(s). The reliability of a parallel system is given by

$$R_p = 1 - (1 - r_1)(1 - r_2)(1 - r_3) \cdots (1 - r_n)$$

where

$$R_p = \text{reliability of parallel system}$$
$$r_i = \text{reliability of component}$$
$$n = \text{number of components in system}$$

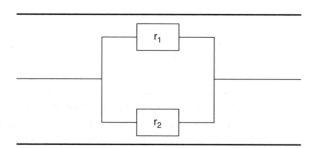

Figure 10.5   Parallel System

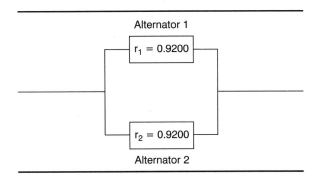

Figure 10.6   Systems in Parallel: Alternators

EXAMPLE 10.7   Determining Reliability in a Parallel System I

On a twin engine aircraft, two alternators support a single electric system. If one were to fail, the other would allow the electrical system to continue to function. As shown in Figure 10.6, these alternators each have a reliability of 0.9200. Calculate their parallel reliability:

$$R_p = 1 - (1 - r_1)(1 - r_2)$$
$$= 1 - (1 - 0.9200)(1 - 0.9200) = 0.9936$$

Even though the alternators' relability values individually are 0.9200, when combined they have a system reliability of 0.9936.

EXAMPLE 10.8   Determining Reliability in a Parallel System II

In the 1920s, an airplane called a Ford Tri-motor was built. As the name suggests, this plane had three motors to increase its reliability. Today, triple engine type aircraft include DC-10s and L-1011s. Since the duplicated or paralleled motor takes over functioning for the failed motor, the reliability of this type of system is calculated on the basis of the sum of the probabilities of the favorable outcomes: the probability that no components fail and the combinations of the successful operation of one component but not the other(s). If each of the motors on this aircraft has a reliability of 0.9500, what is the overall reliability?

$$R_p = 1 - (1 - r_1)(1 - r_2)(1 - r_3)$$
$$= 1 - (1 - 0.9500)(1 - 0.9500)(1 - 0.9500) = 0.9999$$

The overall reliability of the Ford Tri-motor is 0.9999.

System reliability increases as components are added to a parallel system. Reliability in a parallel system will be no less than the reliability of the most reliable component. Parallel redundancy is often used to increase the reliability of a critical system; however, at some point there is a diminishing rate of return where the added costs outweigh the increased reliability. Parallel components are just one type of redundancy used to increase system reliability.

Reliability in Redundant Systems and Backup Components

Backup or spare components, used only if a primary component fails, increase overall system reliability. The likelihood of needing to access the spare or backup component in relation to the reliability of the primary component is shown mathematically as

$$R_b = r_1 + r_b(1 - r_1)$$

where

$$R_b = \text{reliability of backup system}$$
$$r_1 = \text{reliability of primary component}$$
$$r_b = \text{reliability of backup component}$$
$$1 - r_1 = \text{chance of having to use backup}$$

EXAMPLE 10.9   Calculating Reliability in a Redundant System

A local hospital uses a generator to provide backup power in case of a complete electrical power failure. This generator is used to fuel the equipment in key areas of the hospital such as the operating rooms and intensive care units. In the past few years, the power supply system has been very reliable (0.9800). There has been only one incident where the hospital lost power. The generator is tested frequently to ensure that it is capable of operating at a moment's notice. It too is very reliable (0.9600). Calculate the reliability of this system:

$$R_b = r_1 + r_b(1 - r_1)$$
$$= 0.9800 + 0.9600(1 - 0.9800) = 0.9992$$

The overall reliability of this redundant system is 0.9992.

From a design point of view, redundancy is achieved through the use of design margins. These factors of safety are added to design calculations to provide coverage for the variability that exists in manufacturing, material strengths, potential misuse, and other stresses.

Invariably, redundancy increases the costs associated with a system. Whether these are initial costs or costs incurred in maintaining the system, there are trade-offs to be made between reliability, costs, and safety.

Reliability in Systems

From a cost point of view, utilizing parallel systems for every situation is ineffective. Imagine equipping every car with two sets of headlights, two sets of taillights, two or four more doors, two engines, two batteries, and so on. Designers often use the advantages of parallel systems on critical components of an overall system. These systems, containing parallel components and components in series, are called combination systems. As the next example shows, calculating the reliability of such a system involves breaking down the overall system into groups of series and parallel components.

EXAMPLE 10.10   Calculating the Reliability of a Combination System

In an endeavor to discourage thievery, a local firm has installed the alarm system shown in Figure 10.7. This system contains series, parallel, and backup components. Calculate the reliability of the system.

To calculate the overall system reliability, begin by determining the overall reliability of the components in parallel. The combined reliability of the five sensors is

$$
\begin{aligned}
R_p &= 1 - (1 - r_1)(1 - r_2)(1 - r_3) \cdots (1 - r_n) \\
&= 1 - (1 - 0.99)(1 - 0.99)(1 - 0.99)(1 - 0.99)(1 - 0.99) \\
&= 1.0
\end{aligned}
$$

The combined reliability of the power source and battery is

$$
\begin{aligned}
R_b &= r_1 + r_b(1 - r_1) \\
&= 0.92 + 0.88(1 - 0.92) \\
&= 0.99
\end{aligned}
$$

The overall reliability of the system is

$$
\begin{aligned}
R_s &= r_p \cdot r_{cpu} \cdot r_{keypad} \cdot r_{siren} \cdot r_b \\
&= 1.0 \cdot 0.99 \cdot 0.90 \cdot 0.95 \cdot 0.99 \\
&= 0.84
\end{aligned}
$$

The overall reliability of the system is 0.84.

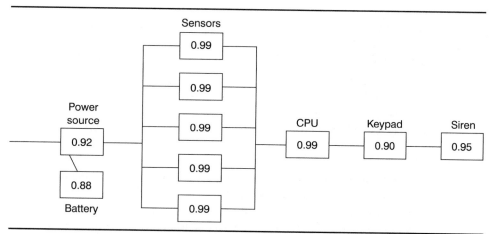

Figure 10.7   Reliability Diagram: Alarm System

RELIABILITY ENGINEERS

Reliability engineers are challenged to meet customer demands through enhanced product and process performance. Reliability engineers work to design reliability into products by defining product and process configurations, specifying materials and applications, and determining optimal operating methods and environments. During production, reliability engineers test and demonstrate the reliability of systems and their components. In circumstances where limited information is available, they attempt to predict the reliability of components and systems on the basis of information from available tests. Reliability engineers attempt to quantify the optimal maintenance schedule to reduce time between failures and increase the safe use of a product.

During the course of work, a reliability engineer may participate in design reviews; plan and conduct reliability tests; analyze the test data; and use the information gained from the tests to assist production, design engineering, quality assurance, sales, and purchasing. The information from the tests may be used to identify causes of reliability degradation. Reliability engineers may estimate the reliability of a system and try to determine the life cycle of a product. They may write specifications for purchased items or for the items being manufactured.

SUMMARY

The objective of the study of product or system reliability is to attempt to predict its useful life. Reliability tests are conducted to determine if the predicted reliability has been achieved. Reliability programs are designed to improve product or system reliability through improved product design, manufacturing processes, maintenance, and servicing. Reliability engineers work to incorporate the aspects of reliability into products and services from their conception to useful life.

 ■ *Lessons Learned*

1. Reliability refers to quality over the long term. The system's intended function, expected life, and environmental conditions all play a role in determining system reliability.
2. The three phases of a product's life cycle are early failure, chance failure, and wear-out.
3. Reliability tests aid in determining if distinct patterns of failure exist.
4. Failure rates can be determined by dividing the number of failures observed by the sum of their test times.
5. θ, or the average life, is the inverse of the failure rate.
6. A system's availability can be calculated by determining the mean time to failure and dividing that value by the total of the mean time to failure plus the mean time to repair.

7. Reliability is the probability that failure will not occur during a particular time period.
8. For a system in series, failure of any one component will cause system failure. The reliability of a series system will never be greater than that of its least reliable component.
9. For a system in parallel, all of the components in parallel must fail to have system failure. The reliability in a parallel system will be no less than the reliability of the most reliable component.
10. Overall system reliability can be increased through the use of parallel, backup, or redundant components.
11. Reliability programs are enacted to incorporate reliability concepts into system designs. A well thought out reliability program will include the eight considerations presented in this chapter. ■

■ Formulas

$$\lambda_{\text{estimated}} = \frac{\text{number of failures observed}}{\text{sum of test times or cycles}}$$

$$\theta_{\text{estimated}} = \frac{1}{\lambda}$$

or

$$\theta_{\text{estimated}} = \frac{\text{sum of test times or cycles}}{\text{number of failures observed}}$$

$$\text{Availability} = \frac{\text{mean time to failure (MTTF)}}{\text{MTTF} + \text{mean time to repair}}$$

(MTBF values can be used in place of MTTF.)

$$R = \frac{s}{n}$$
$$R_s = r_1 \cdot r_2 \cdot r_3 \cdot \cdots \cdot r_n$$
$$R_p = 1 - (1 - r_1)(1 - r_2)(1 - r_3) \cdots (1 - r_n)$$
$$R_b = r_1 + r_b(1 - r_1)$$

Chapter Problems

1. Define reliability in your own words. Describe the key elements and why they are important.
2. Study your house. What do you consider key convenience items to be? How reliable do you consider them to be? What would you do if they failed? How can you make them more reliable?

3. Describe the three phases of the life history curve. Draw the curve and label it in detail (the axes, phases, type of product failure, etc.).

4. Find examples to represent each of the different aspects of a reliability program.

Failure Rate, Mean Life, and Availability

5. Determine the failure rate λ for the following: You have tested circuit boards for failures during a 500-hour continuous use test. Four of the 25 boards failed. The first board failed in 80 hours, the second failed in 150 hours, the third failed in 350 hours, the fourth in 465 hours. The other boards completed the 500-hour test satisfactorily. What is the mean life of the product?

6. Determine the failure rate for a 90-hour test of 12 items where 2 items fail at 45 and 72 hours, respectively. What is the mean life of the product?

7. A power station has installed ten new generators to provide electricity for a local metropolitan area. In the past year (8,776 hours), two of those generators have failed, one at 2,460 hours and one at 5,962 hours. It took five days, working 24 hours a day, to repair *each* generator. Using one year as the test period, what is the mean time between failure for these generators? Given the repair information, what is the availability of all ten generators?

8. Since nothing discourages return visits more than long lines, ski resorts have to move people up the mountain quickly. The lift systems they use need to be reliable. This past summer, one resort tested the reliability of their 20 different lifts by using a time-terminated test. The text ran for 100 hours of continuous operation. During the test, four lifts broke down, at 40, 65, 80, and 89 hours. Calculate the mean life for the lifts. If it takes an average of 12 hours to repair a lift, calculate the availability of the lifts.

System Reliability

9. Why is a parallel system more reliable than a system in series?

10. Given the system in Figure P10.1, what is the system reliability?

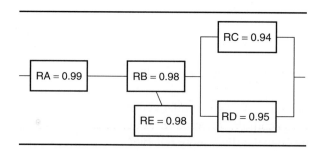

Figure P10.1   Problem 10

11. Given the diagram of the system in Figure P10.2, what is the system reliability?

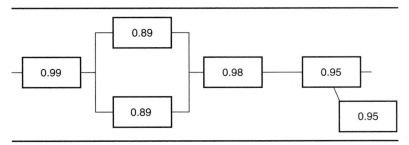

Figure P10.2   Problem 11

12. What is the reliability of the system in Figure P10.3?

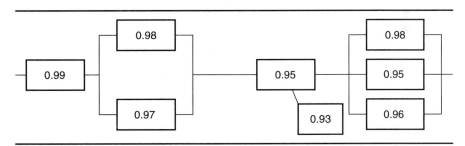

Figure P10.3   Problem 12

13. A paranoid citizen has installed the home alert system shown in Figure P10.4. What is the overall system reliability?

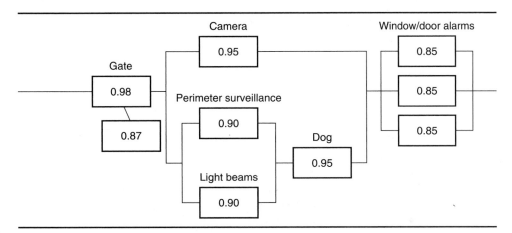

Figure P10.4   Problem 13

14. Pilots prefer to land airplanes with the wheels down and locked into position. A "wheels-down" landing is significantly more comfortable than a "belly slide"; it also gives the passenger a much more positive impression of the pilot's capabilities. In order to ensure a wheels-down landing, several systems work in series and parallel. A landing-gear-down light signals when the gear are in a down-and-locked position. Often pilots carry backup lightbulbs because the reliability of each bulb is only 0.75. The hydraulic system contains two parallel hydraulic pumps with a reliability of 0.98 each. The hydraulic system operates when signaled by an electric impulse from the gear-down switch. This switch is in series with the rest of the system and has a reliability of 0.96. What is the reliability of the entire system?

15. Pilots also have the option of bypassing the entire system described in Problem 12 with a hand crank. This hand crank serves as the final backup when the entire electric and hydraulic system fails. The hand crank operates with a reliability of 0.95. Recalculate the reliability of the system, including the hand-crank backup.

16. The next door neighbors are currently installing a new cistern that will provide water for their household. The different components for the system and their reliability are described in the diagram in Figure P10.5. Determine the reliability of the system.

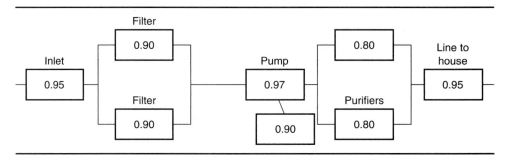

Figure P10.5   Problem 16

17. Airbags are concealed in the center of the steering wheel and in dashboards. When the front end of the vehicle strikes another object, the airbag inflates. The airbag will fully inflate upon impact in one-tenth of a second, providing a barrier to protect the driver. More advanced airbag systems have smart sensors which sense key elements related to the accident and determine the amount of force the detonator needs to emit. The diagram in Figure P10.6 shows the key elements that must operate in order for the airbag to inflate. Calculate the reliability of the system.

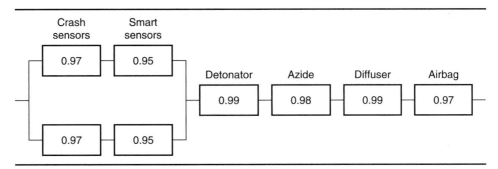

Figure P10.6   Problem 17

18. Often we think of reliability as an equipment based system, however, reliable systems are needed in other, more human oriented systems. As reported in the *Wall Street Journal* article "It's 9 P.M., Do You Know Where You Parked Your Car?" guest services managers at all major parking lots have systems in place designed to reunite patrons with their vehicles. The reliability of these systems is dependent on the reliability of the components, the location finding aids. In many major parking lots, two methods are used at once: the guest's memory as well as a license plate information location computer program. First, though, guest services needs to recognize that a guest is lost. Find the reliability of the car locating system shown in Figure P10.7.

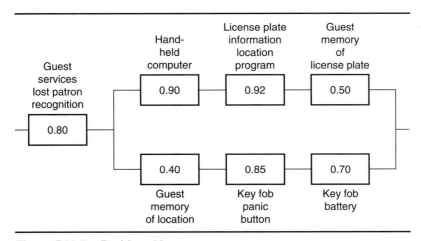

Figure P10.7   Problem 18

CASE STUDY 10.1
Reliability: The Entire System

In February of 1965, Boeing began to produce the 737 twin-engine jet. This jet, a shorter version of the 707/727 with a more radically swept-back wing, filled a market need for a more fuel-efficient, no-frills aircraft. The smaller size of the 737 enables the jet to fly cost-effectively to smaller airports and more remote locations. In 1964, the original specifications called for a plane with a capacity of between 60 and 85 passengers with an operating range of between 100 and 1000 miles. Most importantly, the plane had to be able to break even economically with a 35% load factor. Today's 737s carry 100 passengers with the range and load factors remaining the same. Three decades and a few design and fuel-efficiency modifications later, the 737 continues to be manufactured. Over the years, it has become the best-selling aircraft ever built. At any one point in time, there are about 1,200 737s in the air. That means that a 737 takes off somewhere in the world every 5.3 seconds. The 737 fleet has flown about 124 million hours in service, traveling 49 billion nautical miles or 90 billion kilometers.

Of the three thousand 737s created, most are still flying, which means that many have lasted over a quarter of a century. When the 737 was originally conceived, engineers at Boeing predicted a life expectancy of 75,000 flights, or takeoff-and-landing cycles. Based on the behavior of the current planes still flying long after the predicted 75,000 flights, a Boeing 737 may last as long as 195,000 cycles (flights).

Besides longevity, the 737 jets have the advantage of cockpit design and systems commonality with other Boeing jets. The Boeing 737 has wing mounted engines that provide less interference drag, a better center of gravity position, and more usable cabin space at the rear. From a reliability point of view, the wing mounted engines allow better access to engines for maintenance and require less pipework for fuel. The weight of the engines also provides bending relief from the lift of the wings. The marked similarity in cockpit design has simplified pilot training. Cockpit similarities allow pilots to transfer easily from cockpit to cockpit, and cockpit familiarity increases flight safety since in emergency situations pilots are not confused by control-surface differences.

Cockpit and systems commonality provides the benefits of interchangeable parts, components, subassemblies, and subsystems. Maintenance is easier since repair people familiar with one plane can transfer that knowledge to another. Parts availability, and therefore aircraft availability, increase with interchangeable parts.

The designers of the 737 kept reliability and cost in mind during the design phase. Much of the 727 design, particularly the fuselage cross section, is replicated in the 737. This gives cost savings in tooling commonality while providing 6 abreast seating in the cabin. The 737 and 727 share 60% of their parts, including doors, leading edge devices, nacelles, cockpit layout, avionics, components, and other fittings.

Redundant and fail-safe systems are also a part of the Boeing 737. The plane has two engines but is able to fly with only one. The two engines support two electrical systems. Two fuel systems exist on the 737. If a loss of pressurization occurs on an aircraft, an emergency backup oxygen system exists. During its life, the 737 rudder has been redesigned to include three hydraulic rudder control devices instead of the original two. The added system provides better rudder control in the event that one of the devices fails.

All aircraft, whether private or commercial, maintain aircraft logs. In these logs, pilots record all flights and information pertaining to the length of flight, weather conditions, system failures, or repairs needed. The logs provide a record of routine maintenance, as well as information about loss of pressurization, turbine failure, engine overheat, false alarms with the warning lights, and other such failures. Extensive tests at Boeing and field-tested information from the 3,000 aircrafts' actual logs of flight experiences have been used to make system design changes, improve manufacturing methods, modify quality checks, and select the most reliable components.

In an industry where 10 to 15 percent of the operating costs are devoted to maintenance, these aircraft are maintained in such a manner that they will last indefinitely. Planes are systematically inspected, cleaned, repaired, reinforced, rebolted, and resealed. This type of maintenance exceeds original factory standards and protects the planes from deterioration due to wear and tear and corrosion. However, as the planes age, the maintenance cost per flight hour increases significantly. The airline industry rule of thumb says that at the 25-year mark, a plane's maintenance will cost approximately double the maintenance costs associated with a new plane.

The mean life of a jet engine is approximately 15,000 hours. Jet engines can be rebuilt, overhauled, or replaced to prolong the life of the entire jet. With the Boeing 737, pilots and mechanics have discovered that engine wear can be reduced by decreasing the amount of engine thrust by 4 to 5 percent, enabling the engine to run 30 to 40 degrees cooler. Communication of this sort has resulted in significantly reduced engine wear and prolonged engine life.

 Assignment

Reliability programs have been used to prolong the lives of Boeing 737 airplanes. Using this chapter as a guide, describe the elements of Boeing's reliability program. How did Boeing use information about overall system reliability, communication, maintenance, simplicity of design, humans in the system, redundant/fail-safe features, manufacturing methods, and maintenance records, etc., to improve the reliability of the 737? Then discuss the 737 in terms of the definition of reliability. Be sure to discuss the plane's intended function and environmental conditions.

CASE STUDY 10.2
Reliability

Following indications that the explosion of TWA Flight 800 was caused by electrical arcing, in May of 1998, the Federal Aviation Administration (FAA) ordered the inspection of hundreds of Boeing 737s for potential wiring hazards. This order grounded 15 percent (297 planes) of the 737s flown in the United States. The planes in question were 737-100s and 737-200s with more than 50,000 hours, as well as later models (737-300, 400, and 500) with between 40,000 and 50,000 hours. Inspections were expected to cost $1,600 per plane.

A Boeing 737 has two fuel tanks, one in each wing. Two fuel pumps move fuel out of each tank. Inspection of aircraft wire has shown that when wear through the insulation exists, small arcs can carbonize the insulation, leading to larger arcs and a greater potential for fire. Even though the wires are encased in conduit (Figure C10.2.1), vibrations prevalent during flights cause the wires to chafe against each other and wear away the

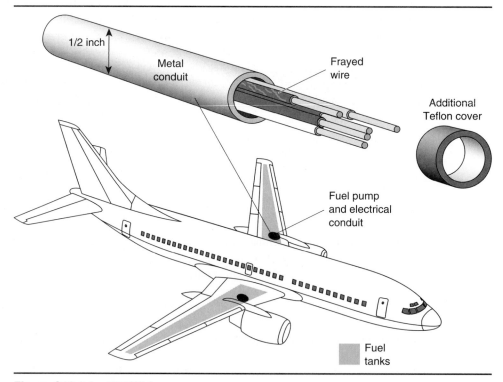

Figure C10.2.1   737 Wiring

protective insulation. Foreign bodies such as sharp drill shavings can wear away the insulation. Certain types of insulation can be degraded by the fluids they come in contact with.

Affected planes were not to be returned to service until a complete inspection had been made of their wiring and, when needed, repairs made. Mechanics searched for wear on the insulation of the fuel pump wires and the wires themselves. Worn wires were to be replaced and an additional Teflon cover was to be put in place to add protection. On average, this inspection and repair took 15 hours to complete.

This FAA action was prompted when a routine inspection found a wiring bundle that showed clear signs of arcing in one area and bare wires in another. These problems were found on a 737 with 60,000 hours of flying time. A similar situation was found on another 737 with 74,000 hours of flying time. In this instance, mechanics found fuel leaking out of two pin-sized holes in a tube that houses wires running through one of the plane's wing fuel tanks. The combination of fuel, electricity, and air could ignite a fuel tank. After this finding, FAA and Boeing officials concluded that two pin-sized holes in a pipe carrying electrical wires through a fuel tank on the wing of the 737 caused the arcing that caused the explosion of TWA Flight 800.

The inspection of the 737s continued. In the total sample of 26 planes, 13 of the 26 main pump lines inspected showed signs of wear on the wire insulation. These wiring problems are related to the aging of the aircraft. Nearly all the more than 3,000 737s built are still flying. Many of them are more than a quarter of a century old. The 737, a highly respected workhorse of a plane, was expected to have a life expectancy of 75,000 flights (takeoff-and-landing cycles). Based on its current performance, this relatively trouble-free aircraft may last as long as 195,000 cycles. Longevity has its complications though, as this wiring example shows.

 Assignment

Investigate this 1998 incident with the Boeing 737 aircraft. If we consider the long life of the 737 aircraft, what reliability considerations might have been overlooked during the design, construction, or use of the 737s? In other words, what could have been done differently to improve the 737 aircraft reliability?

 Assignment

Calculate the mean life and availability associated with the 26 airplanes sampled. Use the information provided as well as the following assumptions:

- A failure is considered to be any sign of worn wiring or insulation.
- Of the 13 failures, one occurred at 60,000 hours, the second at 74,000 hours, and the remainder at 50,000 hours.
- The remaining planes showed no signs of failure when the test was terminated at 75,000 hours.
- The average time to inspect and/or repair any of the planes was 15 hours.

CASE STUDY BIBLIOGRAPHY

Adcock, S. "FAA Orders Fix on Older 737s." *Newsday*, May 8, 1998.

Field, D. "FAA Grounds Oldest 737's." *USA Today*, May 11, 1998.

Field, D. "Order Causes Little Turbulence." *USA Today*, May 11, 1998.

"Improving Airliner Reliability." SWE, November/December 1995.

McMarthy, M. "No. 19603 Still Flies After 27 Years' Service to a Number of Airlines." *Wall Street Journal*, August 9, 1995.

"Redesign Ordered for 737 Rudders." *USA Today*, September 14, 2000.

"U.S. FAA: FAA Orders Immediate Inspection for High-time Boeing 737s, Extends Inspection Order, M2." *PressWIRE*, May 11, 1998.

11

Advanced Topics in Quality

 Learning Opportunities:

1. To understand the basics associated with creating a quality function deployment matrix
2. To create an understanding of the basic concepts associated with designing industrial experiments ▪

House of Quality

$\mathbf{A}$s this figure shows, children learn to build a house of quality through nursery rhymes. World-class companies, seeking to build their own house of quality, continually seek new methods to improve processes. Before investing significant funds in any changes, a company needs to know whether or not the changes and their associated investment will provide the desired improvements to the process. This chapter explores Quality Function Deployment and Design of Experiments; both are methods associated with determining what needs to be changed and how the resulting change might affect the system or process under study.

QUALITY FUNCTION DEPLOYMENT

Quality Function Deployment (QFD) *seeks to bring the voice of the customer into the process of designing and developing a product or service.* Quality Function Deployment (QFD) is a technique that seeks to bring the voice of the customer into the process of designing and developing a product or service. Using this information, effective organizations align their processes to meet their customers' needs the first time and every time. Companies use the voice of the customer information obtained by QFD to drive changes to the way they do business. Information taken directly from the customer is used to modify processes, products, and services to better conform to the needs identified by the customer.

Developed in Japan in the 1970s by Dr. Akao, QFD was first used in the United States in the 1980s. Essentially, *QFD is a planning process for guiding the design or redesign of a product or service. The principal objective of a QFD is to enable a company to organize and analyze pertinent information associated with its product or service.* A QFD can point out areas of strengths as well as weaknesses in both existing and new products.

Utilizing a matrix, information from the customer is organized and integrated into the product or process specifications. QFD allows for preventive action rather than a reactive action to customer demands. When a company uses the QFD format when designing a product or service, they stop developing products and services based solely on their own interpretation of what the customer wants. Instead, they utilize actual customer information in the design and development process. Two of the main benefits of QFD are the reduced number of engineering changes and fewer production problems. QFD provides key action items for improving customer satisfaction. A QFD can enable the launch of a new product or service to go more smoothly because customer issues and expectations have been dealt with in advance. Gathering and utilizing the voice of the customer is critical to the success of world class companies.

A QFD has two principal parts. The *horizontal component records information related to the customer.* The *vertical component records the technical information that responds to the customer inputs.* Essentially, a QFD matrix clearly shows what the customer wants and how the organization is going to achieve those wants. The essential steps to a QFD are shown in Figures 11.1 and 11.2.

QFD begins with the customer. Surveys and focus groups are used to gather information from the customers about their wants, needs, and expectations. Several key areas that should be investigated include performance, features, reliability, conformance, durability, serviceability, aesthetics, and perceived quality. To guide the surveys and focus groups, researchers can gain preliminary customer information from field reports, comment cards, complaint systems, warranty analysis, after-order followups, customer hospitality days, focus groups, and undercover customers. Often, customer information, specifically, the way they say it, must be translated into actionable wording for the organization. When a customer says "I can never find parking" this needs to be interpreted as "close, convenient parking readily available." In the first

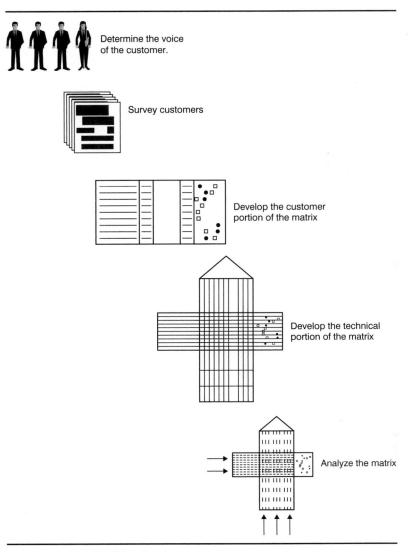

Figure 11.1   The QFD Process

statement, the customer is expressing a need. The second statement turns that need into something the organization can act on.

Once this information is organized into a matrix, the customers are contacted to rate the importance of each of the identified wants and needs. Information is also gathered about how customers rate the company's product or service against the competition. Following this input from the customers, technical requirements are developed. These technical aspects define how the customer needs, wants, and expectations will be met. Once the matrix is constructed, the areas that need to be emphasized in the design of the product or service will be apparent.

The following example shows the steps associated with building a QFD matrix.

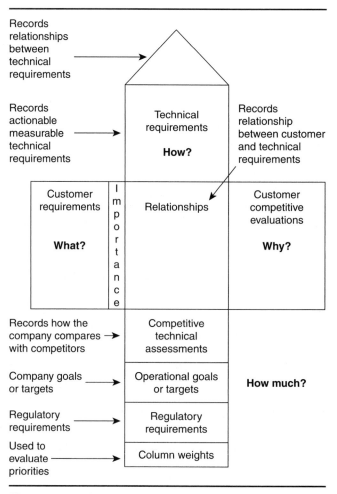

Figure 11.2   Summary of a QFD Matrix

EXAMPLE 11.1   Creating a QFD

AM Corporation sells sports drinks to the general public. They have always been very in tune to the health and nutritional needs of their customers. Recently their focus has turned to another aspect of their business: the drink containers. They have decided to utilize a QFD when redesigning their sports drink bottles.

1. *Determine the voice of the customer: What does the customer want?* The first step in creating the QFD involves a survey of the customer expectations, needs, and requirements associated with their sports drink bottles. AM Corp. met with several focus groups of their customers to capture the information. Following these meetings, they organized and recorded the wants of the customers in the column located on the left side of the matrix (Figure 11.3).

2. *Have the customer rank the relative importance of his or her wants.* After AM Corp. organized the data, they reconvened the focus groups. At that

Customer Requirements

Container	Lids	Doesn't Leak	1																	
		Interchangable Lids	2																	
		Freshness	3																	
		Open/Close Easily	4																	
		Sealed When Purchased	5																	
		Resealable Lid	6																	
	Shape	Doesn't Slip Out of Hands	7																	
		Fits In Cupholder	8																	
		Doesn't Tip Over	9																	
		Attractive	10																	
		Fits In Mini-Cooler	11																	
		Doesn't Spill When You Drink	12																	
Material	Characteristics	No Dents	13																	
		Doesn't Change Shape	14																	
		Is Not Heavy (Light)	15																	
		Does Not Break When Dropped	16																	
		Clear	17																	
		Reusable	18																	
		Recyclable	19																	
		Stays Cool	20																	
		No Sharp Edges	21																	
MISC	Cost	Inexpensive	22																	

Figure 11.3   Customer Requirements

time, they gave each of the participants an imaginary $100 to spend on the recorded wants. The participants were instructed to allocate more dollars to their more important wants. They recorded their values on the matrix next to the list of recorded wants. Following the meetings, AM Corp. created the final matrix (Figure 11.4) by combining the values assigned by all the customers. When all of the values designated by the customers have been

Customer Requirements   Ranking

Container	Lids	Doesn't Leak	1	2																	
		Interchangable Lids	2	6																	
		Freshness	3	6																	
		Open/Close Easily	4	3																	
		Sealed When Purchased	5	6																	
		Resealable Lid	6	8																	
	Shape	Doesn't Slip Out of Hands	7	4																	
		Fits In Cupholder	8	1																	
		Doesn't Tip Over	9	8																	
		Attractive	10	10																	
		Fits In Mini-Cooler	11	11																	
		Doesn't Spill When You Drink	12	9																	
Material	Characteristics	No Dents	13	11																	
		Doesn't Change Shape	14	8																	
		Is Not Heavy (Light)	15	7																	
		Does Not Break When Dropped	16	6																	
		Clear	17	10																	
		Reusable	18	6																	
		Recyclable	19	11																	
		Stays Cool	20	5																	
		No Sharp Edges	21	10																	
MISC	Cost	Inexpensive	22	5																	

Figure 11.4   Rankings

added up, the wants with higher dollar values are those the customers consider more desirable. These are then ranked, a value of 1 being assigned to the want with the highest value, a value of 2 is assigned to the want with the second highest value, and so on.

3. *Have the customer evaluate your company against competitors.* At the same meeting, the customers also evaluated AM Corp.'s competitors. In this step, the participants divided $100 among AM Corp. and its competitors by awarding money to the companies that they felt provided the best product or service for their recorded wants. Following the meetings, AM Corp. created the final matrix (Figure 11.5) by combining the values assigned by all the customers. When all of the values designated by the customers have been added up, the competitor with the highest dollar value is marked. Those wants with the highest values represented where AM Corp. needed to focus their efforts to meet or exceed what is being offered by the competitors.

4. *Determine how the wants will be met: How will the company provide for the wants?* At this point, AM Corp.'s efforts focused on determining how they were going to meet the customers' wants. They spent many hours in meetings discussing the technical requirements necessary for satisfying the customers' recorded wants. These were recorded at the tops of the columns in the matrix. AM Corp. made sure that the technical requirements or hows were phrased in terms that were measurable and actionable. Several of the wants needed two or more technical requirements to make them happen (Figure 11.6).

Container		Customer Requirements	Ranking		Customer Competitive Analysis AM G C
Container	Lids	Doesn't Leak	1	2	
		Interchangable Lids	2	6	
		Freshness	3	6	
		Open/Close Easily	4	3	
		Sealed When Purchased	5	6	
		Resealable Lid	6	8	
	Shape	Doesn't Slip Out of Hands	7	4	
		Fits In Cupholder	8	1	
		Doesn't Tip Over	9	8	
		Attractive	10	10	
		Fits In Mini-Cooler	11	11	
		Doesn't Spill When You Drink	12	9	
Material	Char.	No Dents	13	11	
		Doesn't Change Shape	14	8	
		Is Not Heavy (Light)	15	7	
		Does Not Break When Dropped	16	6	
		Clear	17	10	
		Reusable	18	6	
		Recyclable	19	11	
		Stays Cool	20	5	
		No Sharp Edges	21	10	
MISC	Cost	Inexpensive	22	5	

Figure 11.5   **Customer Competitive Analysis**

Technical Requirements

Customer Requirements

Customer Competitive Analysis

Container / Material	Sub	Customer Requirements	#	Ranking
Container	Lids	Doesn't Leak	1	2
		Interchangable Lids	2	6
		Freshness	3	6
		Open/Close Easily	4	3
		Sealed When Purchased	5	6
		Resealable Lid	6	8
	Shape	Doesn't Slip Out of Hands	7	4
		Fits In Cupholder	8	1
		Doesn't Tip Over	9	8
		Attractive	10	10
		Fits In Mini-Cooler	11	11
		Doesn't Spill When You Drink	12	9
Material	Char.	No Dents	13	11
		Doesn't Change Shape	14	8
		Is Not Heavy (Light)	15	7
		Does Not Break When Dropped	16	6
		Clear	17	10
		Reusable	18	6
		Recyclable	19	11
		Stays Cool	20	5
		No Sharp Edges	21	10
MISC	Cost	Inexpensive	22	5

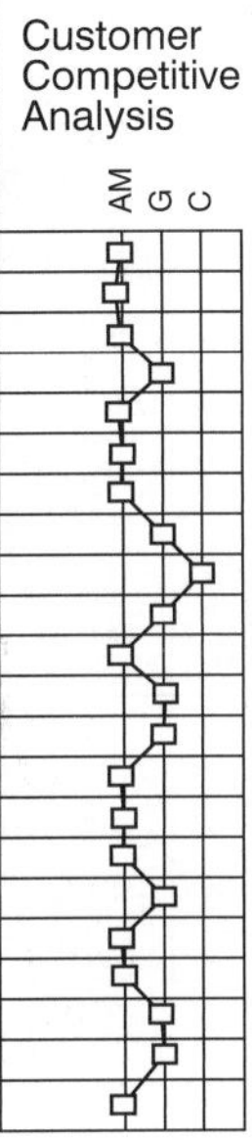

Technical Requirements columns (left to right): Fluid lost horizontal/vertical, Common lid diameter, Common thread, Volume of air-flow through seal, Torque force to open, Torque force to close, Number of nonconformities, Threaded cap, Friction force, Diameter of bottle bottom, Tip force at top, Sales data, Length of bottle, Number of spills, Diameter of orifice, Indent/force relation, Bottle wall thickness, Liquid volume, Material brittleness, Material composition, Manufacturing methods, Manufacturing cost

Customer Competitive Analysis columns: AM, G, C

Figure 11.6   Technical Requirements

5. *Determine the direction of improvement for the technical requirements.* During the meetings discussing technical requirements, those involved also discussed the appropriate specifications for the technical requirements. They were able to identify how those technical requirements could be improved. For instance, for the comment "Fluid lost horizontal/vertical," the appropriate direction of improvement for this is "less," denoted by the downward arrow (Figure 11.7).

6. *Determine the operational goals for the technical requirements.* AM Corp. identified the operational goals that will enable them to meet the technical requirements (Figure 11.8).

7. *Determine the relationship between each of the customer wants and the technical requirements: How does action (change) on a technical requirement affect customer satisfaction with the recorded want?* The team members at AM Corp. studied the relationship between the customer wants and the technical requirements (Figure 11.9). They used the following notations:

A strong positive correlation is denoted by the value 9 or a filled-in circle.
A positive correlation is denoted by the value 3 or an open circle.
A weak correlation is denoted by the value 1 or a triangle.

Figure 11.7   Direction of Improvement

Container	Category	Customer Requirements	Ranking	
Container	Lids	Doesn't Leak	1	2
Container	Lids	Interchangable Lids	2	6
Container	Lids	Freshness	3	6
Container	Lids	Open/Close Easily	4	3
Container	Lids	Sealed When Purchased	5	6
Container	Lids	Resealable Lid	6	8
Container	Shape	Doesn't Slip Out of Hands	7	4
Container	Shape	Fits In Cupholder	8	1
Container	Shape	Doesn't Tip Over	9	8
Container	Shape	Attractive	10	10
Container	Shape	Fits In Mini-Cooler	11	11
Container	Shape	Doesn't Spill When You Drink	12	9
Material	Char.	No Dents	13	11
Material	Char.	Doesn't Change Shape	14	8
Material	Char.	Is Not Heavy (Light)	15	7
Material	Char.	Does Not Break When Dropped	16	6
Material	Char.	Clear	17	10
Material	Char.	Reusable	18	6
Material	Char.	Recyclable	19	11
Material	Char.	Stays Cool	20	5
Material	Char.	No Sharp Edges	21	10
MISC	Cost	Inexpensive	22	5

Technical Requirements columns: Fluid lost horizontal/vertical; Common lid diameter; Common thread; Volume of air–flow through seal; Torque force to open; Torque force to close; Number of nonconformities; Threaded cap; Friction force; Diameter of bottle bottom; Tip force at top; Sales data; Length of bottle; Number of spills; Diameter of orifice; Indent/force relation; Bottle wall thickness; Liquid volume; Material brittleness; Material composition; Manufacturing methods; Manufacturing cost. A Customer Competitive Analysis (AM, G, C) appears to the right.

If no correlation exists, then the box remains empty.
If there is a negative correlation, the box is marked with a minus sign.

8. *Determine the correlation between the technical requirements.* The team members recorded the correlation between the different technical requirements in the roof of the QFD house. This triangular table shows the relationship between each of the technical requirements (Figure 11.10). Once again, they used the same notations:

A strong positive correlation is denoted by the value 9 or a filled-in circle.
A positive correlation is denoted by the value 3 or an open circle.
A weak correlation is denoted by the value 1 or a triangle.
If no correlation exists, then the box remains empty.
If there is a negative correlation, the box is marked with a minus sign.

9. *Compare the technical performance with that of competitors.* At this point, AM Corp. compared their abilities to generate the technical requirements with the abilities of their competitors. On the matrix, this information is shown in the technical competitive assessment (Figure 11.11).

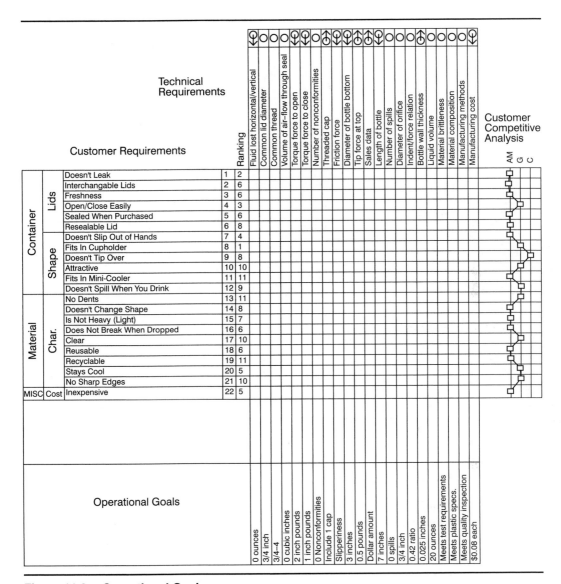

Figure 11.8   Operational Goals

10. *Determine the column weights.* At this point, the matrix is nearly finished. In order to analyze the information presented, the correlation values for the wants and hows are multiplied by the values from the ranking of the $100 test.

   For example, for the first column, a ranking of 2 for "doesn't leak" is multiplied by a value of 9 for "strong correlation," making the total 18. To this value, the ranking of 6 for "sealed when purchased" is multiplied by a value of 1 for "weak correlation." The grand total for the column is 24 (Figure 11.12).

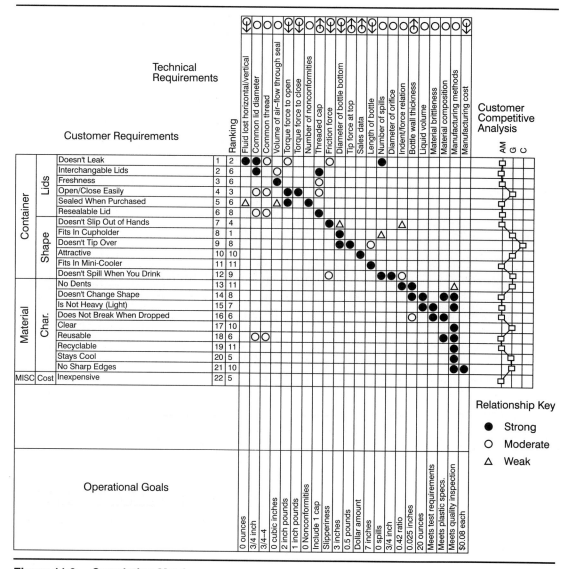

Figure 11.9   Correlation Matrix

11. *Add regulatory and/or internal requirements if necessary.* Here, any rules, regulations, or requirements not set forth by the customer but by some other agency or government were identified and recorded (Figure 11.12).

12. *Analyze the QFD matrix.* What did the customer want? How is this supported by customer rankings and competitive comparisons? How well is the competition doing? How does our company compare? Where will our company's emphasis need to be?

AM Corp. studied the matrix they created and came to the following conclusions. In order to satisfy their customers and maintain a competitive

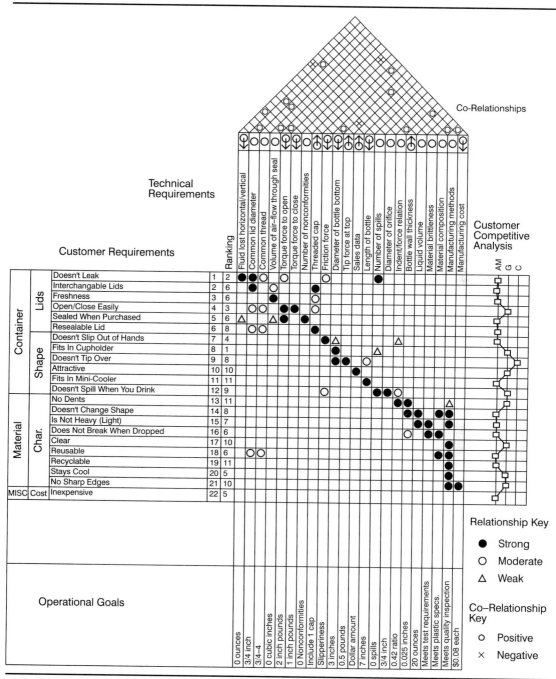

Figure 11.10   Co-relationships

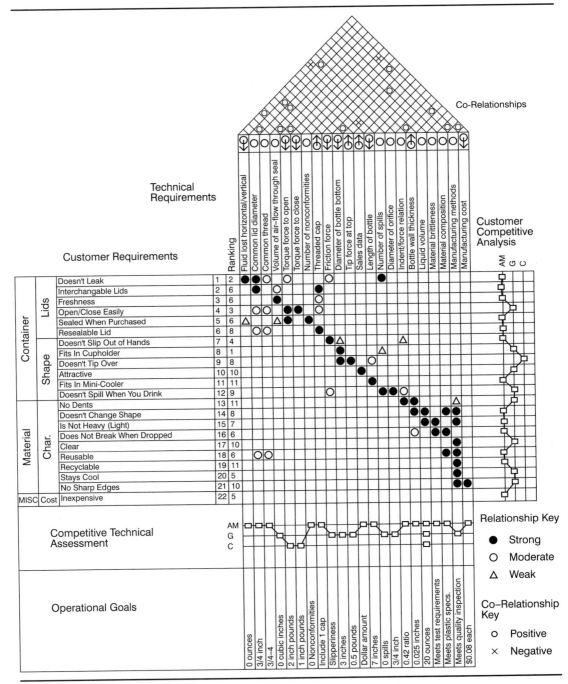

Figure 11.11   Competitive Technical Assessment

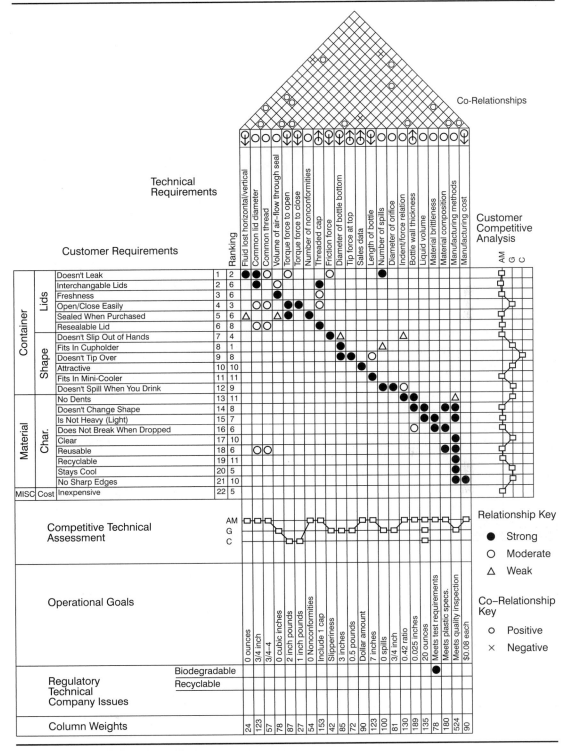

Figure 11.12   Column Weights and Regulatory Issues

advantage, they will have to focus their efforts on designing a sports drink bottle that:

Fits into a standard cup holder in a vehicle, i.e., the base must not exceed 3 inches.

Does not leak at any time in any position. The technical requirements associated with this requirement include a lid diameter no larger than ¾ in., 4 threads per cap, and a cap that must be reapplied at 1 in.-lb of force.

Is easy to open and close, requiring no more than 2 in.-lb to open and 1 in.-lb of force to close.

Does not slip out of the drinker's hand easily. For this reason, the bottle diameter should be no smaller than 3 in. The type of plastic utilized must have the appropriate coefficient of friction.   **Q**⤳

Asking customers what they want, need, and require is a time-consuming process. As was seen in the quality function deployment exercise, translating customers' wants into an organization's hows is paramount to the success of any organization seeking to align their products, services and the processes that provide them with what the customer wants. Organizations that ignore the relationship between what a customer wants and how the organization is going to provide that want can never be truly effective.

DESIGN OF EXPERIMENTS

Design of experiments (DOE) *is a method of experimenting with the complex interactions among parameters in a process or product with the objective of optimizing the process or product.* To design an experiment means creating a situation in which an organized investigation into all the different factors that can affect process or product parameters occurs. The design of the experiment provides a layout of the different factors and the values at which those factors are to be tested. Experimentation is a tool of the problem-solving process discussed in Chapter 3, not an end unto itself.

A complete study of designing experiments is beyond the scope of this text. The following information is meant to serve as an introduction to design of experiments. The coverage of experiment design in this text is designed to provide the reader with a basic understanding of the terminology, concepts, and setups associated with experiment design. Readers interested in an in-depth study of experiment design should seek one of the many excellent texts in the area.

Trial and Error Experiments

A trial and error experiment involves making an educated guess about what should be done to effect change in a process or system. Trial and error experiments lack direction and focus. They are hindered by the effectiveness of the guesswork of those designing the experiments. In other words, a good solution to the problem may be found by using this method, but in all likelihood this hit or miss approach will yield nothing useful.

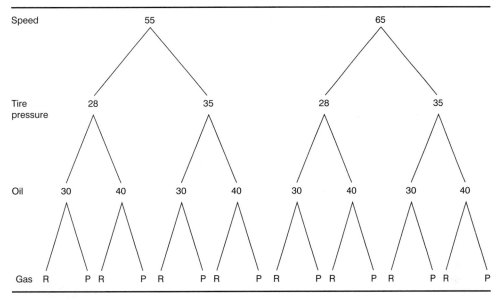

Figure 11.13   Experiment on Gas Mileage

EXAMPLE 11.2   A Trial and Error Experiment

Researchers are studying the effects of tire pressure, vehicle speed, oil type, and gas type on gas mileage.

Speed	55 mph, 65 mph
Tire Pressure	28 psi, 35 psi
Oil	30 weight, 40 weight
Gas	Regular, Premium

As seen in Figure 11.13, many different permutations of the variables exist. As more variables are factored into an experiment, the complexity increases dramatically. If an experimenter were to randomly select speed, tire pressure, oil, and gas settings, he or she may have a difficult time determining which settings provide the best gas mileage. Since random selection is not an organized approach, it is not the best use of time and materials. Essentially, it is guesswork. Design of experiments is a method to arrive at the optimum settings more effectively.

A properly designed experiment seeks to determine:

which factors significantly affect the system under study
how the magnitude of the factors affect the system
the optimal level for each of the selected factors
how to manipulate the factors to control the response

The experiment design must determine:

the number of factors to include in the experiment
the levels at which each factor will be tested
the response variable
the number of trials to be conducted at each level for each factor
the conditions (settings) for each trial

Definitions

In order to better explain the concepts, an understanding of the vocabulary is very helpful. The following terms are commonly used in the design of experiments.

Factor: A factor is the variable the experimenter will vary in order to determine its effect on a response variable. A factor is the variable that is set at different levels during an experiment, and results of those changes are observed. It may be time, temperature, an operator, or any other aspect of the system that can be controlled.

Level: A level is the value chosen for the experiment and assigned to change the factor. For instance: Temperature; Level 1: 110°F; Level 2: 150°F.

Controllable Factor: When a factor is controllable it is possible to establish and maintain the particular level throughout the experiment.

Effect: The effect is the result or outcome of the experiment. It is the value of the change in the response variable produced by a change in the factor level(s). The effect is the change exhibited by the response variable when the factor level is changed.

Response Variable: The variable(s) of interest used to describe the reaction of a process to variations in control variables (factors). It is the quality characteristic under study, the variable we want to have an effect on.

Degrees of Freedom: At its simplest level, the degrees of freedom in an experiment can be determined by examining the number of levels. For a factor with three levels, L_1 data can be compared with L_2 and L_3 data, but not with itself. Thus a factor with three levels has two degrees of freedom. Extending this to an experiment, the degrees of freedom can be calculated by multiplying the number of treatments by the number of repetitions of each trial and subtracting one ($f = n \times r - 1$).

Interaction: Two or more factors that together produce a result different than what the result of their separate effects would be. Well designed experiments allow two or more factor interactions to be tested, where other trial and error models only allow the factors to be independently evaluated.

Noise Factor: A noise factor is an uncontrollable, but measurable, source of variation in the functional characteristics of a product or process. This error term is used to evaluate the significance of changes in the factor levels.

Treatment: The specific combination of levels for each factor used for a particular run. The number of treatments is based on the number of factors and the levels associated with each factor. For example, if two factors (1, 2) exist and each can be at two levels (A, B), then four treatments are possible. The treatments are factor 1 at level A, factor 1 at level B, factor 2 at level A, factor 2 at level B. A treatment table will show all the levels of each factor for each run.

Run: A run is an experimental trial, the application of one treatment.

Replicate: When an experiment is replicated, it refers to a repeat of the treatment condition. The treatment is begun again from scratch.

Repetition: Repetitions are multiple runs of a particular treatment condition. Repeated measurements are taken from the same setup.

Significance: Significance is a statistical test used to indicate whether a factor or factor combination caused a significant change in the response variable. It shows the importance of a change in a factor in either a statistical sense or in a practical sense.

EXAMPLE 11.3   An Experiment Defined

A new product development team at MAR Manufacturing has been investigating the parameters surrounding their new part (Figure 11.14). The customer has specified that the part meet very tight tolerances for pierce height. A variety of factors are involved in holding this tolerance. The team would like to determine which of three proposed material suppliers to use. Though all three meet MAR's specifications for material yield and tensile strength and for material thickness, there are minute differences in material properties. Because of the interactions with the material, the experiment will also need to determine which machine setting is optimal. For this 35 ton press, the experimenters

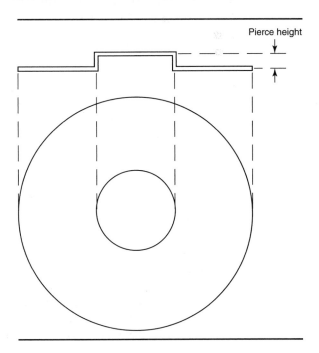

Pierce height

Figure 11.14   MAR Part

would like to determine which setting—20, 25, or 30 tons—is appropriate. Several members of the team have worked together to design an appropriate experiment to test their assumptions. To better describe the experiment to other members of their group, they have created the following explanation based on DOE definitions.

Factor: Since factors are variables that are changed during an experiment, two factors in this experiment exist: Material Supplier and Press Tonnage. Team members believe that changes to these two factors will affect the response variable, pierce height.

Level: A level is the value assigned to change the factor. In this case, each factor has three levels: Supplier (A, B, C) and Press Tonnage (20, 25, 30).

Supplier	Press Tonnage
A	20
B	25
C	30

Controllable Factor: When a factor is controllable it is possible to establish and maintain the particular level throughout the experiment. In this experiment, investigators are able to set the levels for both the material supplier and press tonnage factors.

Effect: The effect is the result or outcome of the experiment. Here the experimenters are interested in consistent pierce height, which is measured as shown in Figure 11.14.

Response Variable: The variable used to describe the reaction of a process to variations in the factors. In this example, the response variable is the pierce height.

Treatment: Since the number of treatments is based on the number of factors and the levels associated with each factor, and both factors have three levels, Supplier (A, B, C) and Press Tonnage (20, 25, 30), the result is $3 \times 3 = 9$ treatments:

Supplier	Press Tonnage
A	20
A	25
A	30
B	20
B	25
B	30
C	20
C	25
C	30

Degrees of Freedom: The degree of freedom in an experiment is the total number of levels for all factors minus 1. Here we have three levels for each factor ($3 \times 3 = 9$), so our degrees of freedom is $9 - 1$ or 8.

Interaction: Since the two factors, supplier and press tonnage, will together produce a result different than what would result if only one or the other was changed, there is an interaction between the two that must be considered in the experiment.

Noise Factor: A noise factor is an uncontrollable but measurable source of variation. For this experiment, noise factors may be material thickness, material properties, and press operating temperatures.

Run: A run is an experimental trial, the application of one treatment to one experimental unit. The Supplier A, Press Tonnage 25 combination is one run.

Replicate: When an experiment is replicated, it refers to a repeat of the treatment condition, a complete redo of the design.

Repetition: Repetitions are multiple results of a treatment condition; for example, the experimenters ran the Supplier B, Press Tonnage 20 combination multiple times.

Significance: The determination of whether or not the changes to the factor levels had a significant effect on the response variable. In other words, did changing suppliers or press tonnage significantly affect pierce height?

Conducting an Experiment: Steps in Planned Experimentation

First and foremost, *plan your experiment!* Successful experiments depend on how well they are planned. Before creating the design of an experiment, those involved must gain a thorough understanding of the process being studied. Achieving a deep understanding of the process will allow those designing the experiment to identify the factors in the process or product that influence the outcome. While planning an experiment, answer the following questions:

What are you investigating?
What is the objective of your experiment?
What are you hoping to learn more about?
What are the critical factors?
Which of the factors can be controlled?
What resources will be used?

The following are typical steps in conducting an experiment:

1. *Establish the purpose by defining the problem.* Before beginning an experiment design, the experimenters should determine the purpose of the experiment. Knowing the objectives and goals of an experiment can help the experimenters select the most appropriate experiment design as well as analysis methods.

2. *Identify the components of the experiment.* When setting up your experiment, be sure to include the following critical information:

The number of factors the design will consider.
The number of levels (options) for each factor.
The settings for each level.

The response factor.

The number of trials to be conducted.

3. *Design the experiment.* Determine the appropriate structure of the experiment. Having determined the factors involved in your experiment, select a study template for your experiment. The types of templates will be covered later in this chapter.

4. *Perform the experiment.* Run your experiment and collect data about the results. Complete the runs as specified by the template at the levels and settings selected.

5. *Analyze the data.* Perform and analyze the resulting response variables in the experiment. Determine which factors were significant in determining the outcome of the response variables. At this point, rather than performing the calculations by hand, it is easier to enter the results into an analysis program, such as DOEpack from PQ Systems. Such software makes it easier to analyze your experiment. Using statistical tools to analyze your data will enable you to determine the optimal levels for each factor. Statistical analysis methods include: Analysis of Variance, Analysis of Means, Regression Analysis, Pairwise Comparison, Response Plots, and Effects Plots.

6. *Act on the results.* Once you have analyzed the information, apply the knowledge you gained from your experiment to the situation under study. Use the information determined about the significant factors to make changes to the process or product.

 REAL TOOLS FOR REAL LIFE

Process Improvements Based on Design of Experiments

A process improvement team at KS Manufacturing studied an assembly process that welded two stamped steel parts together as the foundation of a component. The welds often failed in assembly. The goal of the team was to make the process more robust by eliminating weld failures. Team members consisted of representatives from manufacturing, engineering, setup, production, and quality.

The team turned to design of experiments when it became evident that studying the process using other quality tools and techniques hadn't provided the needed breakthrough to improve the process. An experiment based on the welds was designed and conducted. Careful analysis of the results of the runs is critical to gaining knowledge of the process. As they analyzed the results of the experiment, they realized that they were not capturing all of the main process variables. Something outside of the original design created a strong signal. Some unidentified factor that they didn't include in the original experiment was affecting the process.

This situation can sometimes occur with experimental design. Those closest to the process think they know the process inside and out and thus run the risk of overlooking something. Armed with this information, they conducted a second "screening" experiment. The structure of a screening experiment helps identify the true key variables in the process under study. The levels of these key variables can then be optimized in a follow-up experiment. Since they screen out key variables, screening experiments, which fully load the experiment design with variables, are usually the first type of experiment to be run. Is this case, the investigators would have been wiser to begin with such an experiment.

Analysis of the screening experiment enabled them to determine that some parts were cleaner than others. Here, cleaner means that some parts had less lubricant from the stamping process than others. This lubricant on the parts is what generated the noise, the unidentified signal, in the first experiment.

A third experiment was run in which the lubricant from the stamping operation was included as one of the variables. From this experiment, they were able to determine that the lubricant interfered with the ability of the weld to take hold. Excessive lubricant weakened the weld, resulting in the weld failures seen in assembly.

As a result of these experiments, the team decided to eliminate the lubricant variable altogether by changing to a lower viscosity water based lubricant. The end result is a welding process that is very consistent, eliminating the weld failures in assembly.   **Q**

Experiment Designs

Characteristics of a Good Experiment Design

There are many characteristics associated with good experiment design. An experiment should be as simple as possible to set up and carry out. It should also be straightforward to analyze and interpret, as well as easy to communicate and explain to others. A good experiment design will include all the factors for which changes are possible. A well designed experiment should provide unbiased estimates of process variables and treatment effects (factors at different levels). This means that a well designed experiment will quickly screen out the factors that do not have a pronounced effect upon the response variable while also identifying the best levels for the factors that do have a pronounced effect upon the response variable. The experiment should plan for the analysis of the results, generating results that are free from ambiguity of interpretation. When analyzed, the experiment should provide the precision necessary to enable the experimenter to detect important differences between significant and insignificant variables. The analysis of the experiment must produce understandable results in a form which can be easily communicated to others interested in the information. The analysis should reliably be able to detect any signals that are present in the data. The experiment should point the experimenter in the direction of improvement.

Single Factor Experiments

A single factor experiment allows for the manipulation of only one factor during an experiment. Designers of these experiments select one factor and vary it while holding the other factors constant. The experiment is run for each variation of each factor, and the results are recorded. The objective in a single factor experiment is to isolate the changes in the response variable as they relate to a single factor. Single factor experiments are simple to analyze because only one thing changes at a time and the experimenter can see what effect that change has on the system or process. Unfortunately, single factor experiments are time consuming due to the need to change only one thing at a time, which results in dozens of repeated experiments. Another drawback of these types of experiments is that interactions between factors are not detectable. These experiments rarely arrive at an optimum setup because a change in one factor frequently requires adjustments to one or more of the other factors in order to achieve the best results. In life, single factor changes rarely occur that are not interrelated to other factors.

EXAMPLE 11.4   Single Factor Experiment Treatment Table

Researchers are studying the effects of tire pressure, gas type, oil type, and vehicle speed on gas mileage. Problem: What combination of factors provide the best gas mileage?

Factor	Level 1	Level 2
Tire Pressure	28 psi	35 psi
Speed	55 mph	65 mph
Oil	30 weight	40 weight
Gas	Regular	Premium

Response Variable: Gas mileage

Tire	Speed	Oil	Gas
28	55	30	R
35	55	30	R
28	65	30	R
28	55	40	R
28	55	30	P
35	65	40	P
28	65	40	P
35	55	40	P
35	65	30	P
35	65	40	P

In each of these treatments, only one factor is changing at a time. The others are reverting to their original settings (Level 1 or Level 2). Either the remaining three will all be at Level 1 or all at Level 2. Note the complexity this creates when trying to study all the different changes in levels. Realize also that this type of experimentation does not allow experimenters to study the interactions that occur when more than one factor is changed at a time within a treatment. In order to study all the interactions, a full factorial experiment must be conducted.

Full Factorial Experiments

A **full factorial design** *consists of all possible combinations of all selected levels of the factors to be investigated.* This type of experiment examines every possible combination of all factors at all levels. To determine the number of possible combinations or runs, multiply the number of levels for each factor by the number of factors. For example, in an experiment involving six factors at two levels, the total number of combinations will be 2^6 or 64. If the experiment had four factors, two with two levels and two with three levels, a full factorial will have: 2 levels $\times$ 2 levels $\times$ 3 levels $\times$ 3 levels or 36 treatments. A full factorial design allows the most complete analysis because it can determine the:

> main effects of the factors manipulated on response variables
> effects of factor interactions on response variables

A full factorial design can estimate levels at which to set factors for the best results. This type of experiment design is used when adequate time and resources exist to complete all of the runs necessary. A full factorial experiment design is useful when it is important to study all the possible interactions that may exist. Unfortunately, a full factorial experiment design is time consuming and expensive due to the need for numerous runs. Example 11.5 shows an example of a full factorial experiment layout.

EXAMPLE 11.5   Full Factorial Experiment Treatment Table

Researchers are studying the effects of tire pressure, gas type, oil type, and vehicle speed on gas mileage. Problem: What combination of factors provide the best gas mileage?

Factor	Level 1	Level 2
Tire Pressure	28 psi	35 psi
Speed	55 mph	65 mph
Oil	30 weight	40 weight
Gas	Regular	Premium

Response variable: gas mileage

Tire	Speed	Oil	Gas
28	55	30	R
35	55	30	R
28	55	30	P
35	55	30	P
28	65	30	R
35	65	30	R
28	65	30	P
35	65	30	P
28	55	40	R
35	55	40	R
28	55	40	P
35	55	40	P
28	65	40	R
35	65	40	R
28	65	40	P
35	65	40	P

The complexity of this type of experimentation can be seen in Figure 11.13. Each path that is followed represents one treatment.

Q

Fractional Factorial Experiments

To reduce the total number of experiments that have to be conducted to a practical level, a limited number of the possibilities shown by a full factorial experiment may be chosen. A fractional factorial experiment studies only a fraction or subset of all the possible combinations. A selected and controlled multiple number of factors are adjusted simultaneously. By using this method, the total number of experiments is reduced. Designed correctly, fractional factorial experiments still reveal the complex interactions between the factors, including which factors are more important than others. One must be careful when selecting the fractional or partial group of experiments to be run to ensure that the critical factors and their interactions are studied. Many different experiment designs exist, including Plackett-Burman Screening designs and Taguchi designs, as shown in Examples 11.6 and 11.7. When utilizing experiments in industry, reference texts and software programs can provide a wide variety of experiment designs from which an appropriate experiment design can be selected.

Plackett-Burman Screening Designs

Plackett-Burman screening designs are a subset of fractional factorial experiment designs. They provide an effective way to consider a large number of factors with a minimum number of runs. Users select the most appropriate design for their experiment needs. These screening designs are most effectively used when a large number of factors must be studied and time and resources are limited. Screening designs can be selected from pre-prepared tables from sources such as *Tables of Screening Designs* by Donald Wheeler. Figures 11.15 to 11.18 show several Plackett-Burman designs. The + and − signs show the levels of the factors [Level 1 (−), Level 2 (+)]. A, B, C, etc., represent the factors. Treatments are labeled 1 to 8.

Treatment \ Factors	A	B	C	D	E	F	G
1	−	−	−	−	−	−	−
2	−	−	−	+	+	+	+
3	−	+	+	+	+	−	−
4	−	+	+	−	−	+	+
5	+	+	−	−	+	+	−
6	+	+	−	+	−	−	+
7	+	−	+	+	−	+	−
8	+	−	+	−	+	−	+

Figure 11.15   The Basic Eight Run Plackett-Burman Design

Treatment \ Factors	A	B	C	D	E	F	G	H	I	J	K
1	−	−	−	−	−	−	−	−	−	−	−
2	−	−	−	+	+	+	−	−	+	+	+
3	−	−	+	−	+	+	+	+	−	−	+
4	−	+	+	−	+	−	−	+	+	+	−
5	−	+	+	+	−	−	+	−	+	−	+
6	−	+	−	+	−	+	+	+	−	+	−
7	+	+	−	+	+	−	−	+	−	−	+
8	+	+	−	−	+	+	+	−	+	−	−
9	+	+	+	−	−	+	−	−	−	+	+
10	+	−	+	+	−	+	−	+	+	−	−
11	+	−	+	+	+	−	+	−	−	+	−
12	+	−	−	−	−	−	+	+	+	+	+

Figure 11.16   The Basic 12 Run Plackett-Burman Design

Treatment \ Factors	A	B	C	D	E	F	G	H	I	J	K	L	M	N	O
1	−	−	−	−	−	−	−	−	−	−	−	−	−	−	−
2	−	−	−	−	−	−	−	+	+	+	+	+	+	+	+
3	−	−	−	+	+	+	+	+	+	+	+	−	−	−	−
4	−	−	−	+	+	+	+	−	−	−	−	+	+	+	+
5	−	+	+	+	+	−	−	−	−	+	+	+	+	−	−
6	−	+	+	+	+	−	−	+	+	−	−	−	−	+	+
7	−	+	+	−	−	+	+	+	+	−	−	+	+	−	−
8	−	+	+	−	−	+	+	−	−	+	+	−	−	+	+
9	+	+	−	−	+	+	−	−	+	+	−	−	+	+	−
10	+	+	−	−	+	+	−	+	−	−	+	+	−	−	+
11	+	+	−	+	−	−	+	+	−	−	+	−	+	+	−
12	+	+	−	+	−	−	+	−	+	+	−	+	−	−	+
13	+	−	+	+	−	+	−	−	+	−	+	+	−	+	−
14	+	−	+	+	−	+	−	+	−	+	−	−	+	−	+
15	+	−	+	−	+	−	+	+	−	+	−	+	−	+	−
16	+	−	+	−	+	−	+	−	+	−	+	−	+	−	+

Figure 11.17   The Basic 16 Run Plackett-Burman Design

Factors / Treatment	A	B	C	D
1	+	+	+	+
2	+	+	−	−
3	+	−	−	+
4	+	−	+	−
5	−	−	+	+
6	−	−	−	−
7	−	+	−	+
8	−	+	+	−

Figure 11.18   The Eight Run Reflected Plackett-Burman Design

EXAMPLE 11.6   Plackett-Burman Screening Designs Experiment Treatment Table

Researchers are studying the effects of tire pressure, gas type, oil type, and vehicle speed on gas mileage. Problem: What combination of factors provides the best gas mileage?

Factor	Level 1	Level 2
Tire Pressure	28 psi	35 psi
Speed	55 mph	65 mph
Oil	30 weight	40 weight
Gas	Regular	Premium

Response variable: gas mileage
Design: Plackett-Burman Eight Run Reflected (Figure 11.18)

Tire A	Speed B	Oil C	Gas D
35	65	40	P
35	65	30	R
35	55	30	P
35	55	40	R
28	55	40	P
28	55	30	R
28	65	30	P
28	65	40	R

Taguchi Designs

Taguchi designs use orthogonal arrays to determine the factors and their levels for the experiments to be conducted. Essentially, Taguchi uses orthogonal arrays that select only a few of the combinations found in a traditional factorial design. This method has the advantage of being very efficient; however, these experiments work best when there is minimal interaction among the factors. Taguchi designs are most effective when

Table 11.1   Comparison of Factorial Design and Taguchi Design

		Total Number of Experiments	
Factors	Level	Factorial Design	Taguchi
2	2	4 (2^2)	4
3	2	8 (2^3)	4
4	2	16 (2^4)	8
7	2	128 (2^7)	8
4	3	81 (3^4)	9

the experimenter already has a general feel for the interactions that may be present among the factors. A comparison of the total number of experiments needed using *factorial designs* versus *Taguchi designs* is shown in Table 11.1. Figure 11.19 shows the structure of a traditional factorial experiment and then the reduced Taguchi orthogonal array. The treatments chosen by Taguchi are labeled in the full factorial experiment as T-1, T-2, etc.

EXAMPLE 11.7   Taguchi Design Experiment Treatment Table

Researchers are studying the effects of tire pressure, gas type, oil type, and vehicle speed on gas mileage. Problem: What combination of factors provides the best gas mileage?

Factor	Level 1	Level 2
Tire Pressure	28 psi	35 psi
Speed	55 mph	65 mph
Oil	30 weight	40 weight
Gas	Regular	Premium

Response variable: gas mileage
Design: L_4 (2^3) Taguchi array (Figure 11.20)

Tire	Speed	Oil	Gas
28	55	30	R
28	55	30	P
28	65	40	R
28	65	40	P
35	55	40	R
35	55	40	P
35	65	30	R
35	65	30	P

Note that a full factorial experiment would have required 16 treatments, while a Taguchi experiment required only 8.

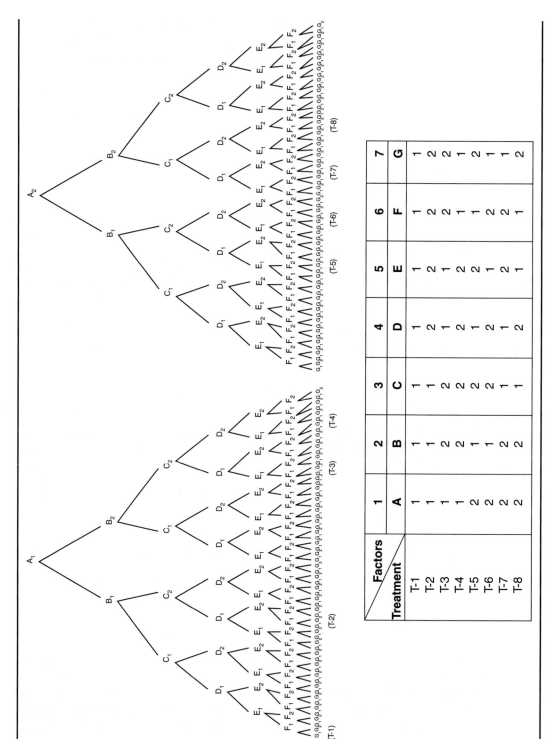

Factors	1	2	3	4	5	6	7
Treatment	A	B	C	D	E	F	G
T-1	1	1	1	1	1	1	1
T-2	1	1	1	2	2	2	2
T-3	1	2	2	1	1	2	2
T-4	1	2	2	2	2	1	1
T-5	2	1	2	1	2	1	2
T-6	2	1	2	2	1	2	1
T-7	2	2	1	1	2	2	1
T-8	2	2	1	2	1	1	2

Figure 11.19   Comparing a Full Factorial Experiment with a Taguchi Design

Factor No.	1	2	3	4	5	6	7
1	1	1	1	1	1	1	1
2	1	1	1	2	2	2	2
3	1	2	2	1	1	2	2
4	1	2	2	2	2	1	1
5	2	1	2	1	2	1	2
6	2	1	2	2	1	2	1
7	2	2	1	1	2	2	1
8	2	2	1	2	1	1	2

Figure 11.20 $L_4(2^3)$ Orthogonal Array

Hypotheses and Experiment Errors

Experimenters approach each experiment with a hypothesis about how changes in various factors will affect the response variable. Often this hypothesis is expressed as:

H_0: the change in the factor will have no effect on the response variable.
H_1: the change in the factor will have an effect on the response variable.

EXAMPLE 11.8   Hypotheses

When a metal is selected for a part that will undergo a metal forming process such as stamping, often the metal is tested to determine its bending failure point. An experiment being conducted at MAR Inc. is testing the bending failure of a particular metal that has been provided by two different suppliers. In this experiment, a sample of the metal is bent back and forth until the metal separates at the fold. The experimenters are testing the following hypotheses:

H_0: there is no difference in the bending failure point (the response variable) with respect to the following factors: suppliers (A and B), or plating (none or plated).
H_1: there is a difference in the bending failure point with respect to supplier or plating.

Experiments are designed to test hypotheses, yet the experiments themselves are not infallible. This is why the significance of the factors affecting the response variables is studied. Experimenters are also cautious to determine if errors exist in the experiment. Errors exist in experiments for a variety of reasons, including a lack of uniformity of the material and inherent variability in the experimental technique.

Table 11.2

Conclusion from Sample	H_0 True	H_0 False
H_0 True	Correct Conclusion	Type II Error β
H_0 False	Type I Error α	Correct Conclusion

Two types of errors exist:

1. Type I Error: The hypothesis is *rejected* when it is *true*. For instance, a Type I error would occur if the experimenter drew the conclusion that a factor does not produce a significant effect on a response variable when, in fact, its effect is meaningful. A Type I error is designated with the symbol alpha (α).

2. Type II Error: The hypothesis is *accepted* when it is *false*. For instance, a Type II error would occur if the experimenter drew the conclusion that a factor produces a significant effect on a response variable when, in fact, its effect is negligible (a false alarm). A Type II error is designated with the symbol beta (β).

Table 11.2 shows the relationship of these types of errors.

Experimental Analysis Methods

An **analysis of means (ANOM)** *essentially compares subgroup averages and separates those that represent signals from those that do not.* An ANOM takes the form of a control chart that identifies subgroup averages that are detectably different from the grand average. In this chart, each treatment (experiment) is compared with the grand average. An ANOM is used whenever the experimenter wants to study the differences between the subgroup averages from different treatments of the factors in the experiment. To use an ANOM, you must have more than one observation per subgroup.

An **Analysis of Variance (ANOVA)** *is a measure of the confidence that can be placed on the results of the experiment.* This method is used to determine whether or not changes in factor levels have produced significant effects upon a response variable. An ANOVA analyzes the variability of the data. In this analysis, the variance of the controllable and noise factors is examined. By understanding the source and magnitude of the variance, the best operating conditions can be determined.

When conducting an ANOVA, the variance is estimated using two different methods. An ANOVA estimates the variance of the factors in the experiment by using information such as the degrees of freedom present, the sums of squares, and mean squares. If the estimates are similar, then detectable differences between the subgroup averages are unlikely. If the differences are large, then there is a difference between the subgroup averages that is not attributable to background noise alone. An ANOVA compares the ratio of the Between Subgroup Variance Estimate with that of the Within Subgroup Variance Estimate. The Between Subgroup Variation Estimate is sensitive to differences between the subgroup averages. The Within Subgroup Variation Estimate is not sensitive to this difference.

 REAL TOOLS FOR REAL LIFE

Optimizing Order Pick, Pack, and Ship Using Design of Experiments

Order picking, packing, and shipping from a warehouse can be quite complex. Orders are submitted by customers and consist of multiple product types in various quantities. The products on these orders must be picked from the correct storage locations, packaged for safe shipment, and labeled with the appropriate destination. This would be simple if the organization carried only a few items in inventory to be shipped to a few customers. The complexity increases exponentially as the number of items and customers increase.

Doing the job right at every step is critical, not only because the customer wants to receive the correct item, but because shipping costs are based on the cube of space the package uses up, whether in a truck or the cargo hold of a plane.

At CH Shipping, an automated distribution center, pickers, packers, and shippers handle orders that may contain as many as 50 unique products, numbering up to 5000 of each unique product. CH Shipping uses "wave" processing, also known as batch picking. This method consolidates orders from several customers into one optimal inventory picking cycle (Figure 11.21). Optimal picking cycles consolidate what has been ordered, the amount ordered, and where the items are stored in the warehouse. As shown in Figure 11.22, once the pick is complete, the wave continues to the packing department, where the orders are automatically sorted using barcodes by the individual customer order and packed. Once packed, the orders proceed to a shipping station to be labeled and staged for shipment via truck or plane. Buffer staging lanes exist between each area. Downtime in a particular area results if orders are not in the system or are held up at an upstream area.

Wave processing is different from "discrete" processing. Discrete processing involves picking one order at a time, packing it, and then readying it for shipment. To

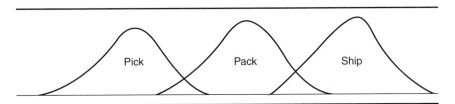

Figure 11.21   Department Workload Using Wave Order Processing

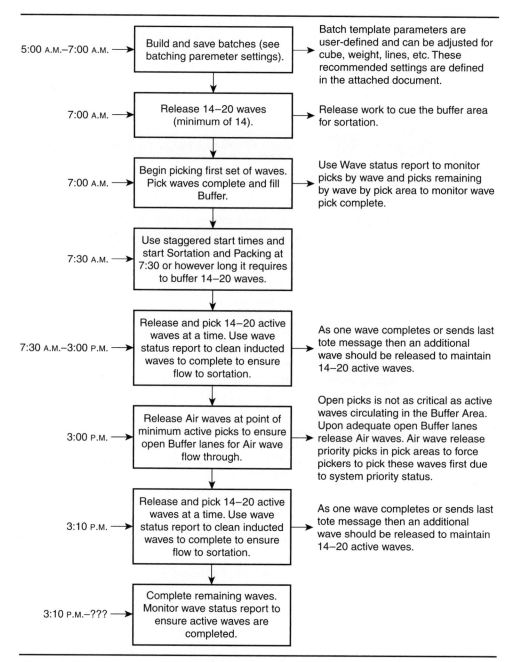

Figure 11.22   Flowchart for Order Pick, Pack, and Ship

manage the wave, order characteristics that optimize flow include: how may times the picker visits a particular location in the warehouse, how many items are picked each time, and how much space is taken up by the items picked?

The key departments involved are: Pick, Pack, and Ship. Members of the workforce in these departments work together to ensure customers receive what they need, when they need it. In order to minimize costs, maximize flexibility, and enhance customer success, the Express Logistics Center Manager has asked the industrial engineers at CH Shipping to optimize order picking, packing, and shipping. In other words, they want to maximize the peaks and valleys in Figure 11.22 through the use of design of experiments. In order to do so, the team proposed the following experiment design:

Factors

Quantity (Qty): Total number of pieces picked within a given wave
Lines: The different items (products) on the order needing to be picked
Cube: The space needed for the quantity of lines for a particular order (largest outbound parcel box cube or tote cube; a tote is a box without a top)
Weight: The weight of the quantity of lines for a particular order

Level

Max Qty	Max Lines	Max Cube	Max Weight
5000 (+)	50 (+)	Parcel (+)	150 (+)
100 (−)	10 (−)	Tote (−)	25 (−)

Controllable Factors   When a factor is controllable it is possible to establish and maintain the particular level throughout the experiment. In this experiment, investigators are able to set the levels for the quantity, lines, cube, and weight.

Response Variables   These variables are used to describe the reaction of a process to variations in the chosen factors. The response variable for this experiment is Order Per Hour.

Effect   The effect is the result or outcome of the experiment. The investigators are interested in determining the optimal wave parameters. A wave is a batch of customer orders consolidated to optimize warehouse picking activities. Instead of picking one order at a time, many orders are picked.

Treatment   The number of treatments is based on the number of factors and the levels associated with each factor. Based on the number of waves processed per day and the ease of wave building, a Full Factorial Design was chosen (Figure 11.23).

Degrees of Freedom   The degree of freedom in an experiment is the total number of levels for all factors minus 1. Here there are two levels for each factor ($4 \times 2 = 8$), so the degrees of freedom equals $8 - 1 = 7$

Interaction   Since the four factors will work together to produce a result different from what would result if each were only used singly, interactions exist between the four that must be considered in the experiment.

Test Wave	Max Qty	Max Lines	Max Cube	Max Weight
1	5000	50	Parcel	150
2	100	50	Parcel	150
3	5000	10	Parcel	150
4	100	10	Parcel	150
5	5000	50	Tote	150
6	100	50	Tote	150
7	5000	10	Tote	150
8	100	10	Tote	150
9	5000	50	Parcel	25
10	100	50	Parcel	25
11	5000	10	Parcel	25
12	100	10	Parcel	25
13	5000	50	Tote	25
14	100	50	Tote	25
15	5000	10	Tote	25
16	100	10	Tote	25

Figure 11.23   Experiment Design for Optimizing Order Pick, Pack, and Ship

Noise Factor   A noise factor is an uncontrollable but measurable source of variation. For this experiment the noise factors are buffer downtime, pick downtime, and shipping downtime.

Run   A run is an experimental trial, the application of one treatment to one experimental unit. A quantity of 100, with 10 lines, using a tote, and weighing 25 pounds is one run.

Replicate   When an experiment is replicated, it refers to a repeat of the treatment condition, a complete rerunning of the design.

Repetition   Repetitions are multiple results of a treatment condition.

Significance   The determination of whether or not the changes to the factor levels had a significant effect on the response variable. In other words, did changing the quantity, lines, cube, or weight affect the result?

To conduct the experiment, the investigators set up controlled runs based each of the 16 runs denoted by the Full Factorial Design (Figure 11.23). These runs, from actual customer orders, took place on a Saturday, outside of the normal workweek.

Following the experiment, the investigators analyzed the results (Figure 11.24) to identify the optimum wave settings to maximize flow through Pick, Pack, and Ship. They began their analysis with the most simple of methods: ANOG or Analysis of Good. This very simple but effective technique ranks the results of the experiment by the most desirable outcome: high orders per hour (Figure 11.25). Run 9, with a quantity of 5000 and 50 lines allows 8.3 orders to be picked per hour.

Test Wave	Max Qty	Max Lines	Max Cube	Max Weight	Order/ Hour
1	5000	50	Parcel	150	8.2
2	100	50	Parcel	150	8.1
3	5000	10	Parcel	150	6.1
4	100	10	Parcel	150	6.3
5	5000	50	Tote	150	7.9
6	100	50	Tote	150	8.2
7	5000	10	Tote	150	4.5
8	100	10	Tote	150	5.1
9	5000	50	Parcel	25	8.3
10	100	50	Parcel	25	8
11	5000	10	Parcel	25	5.9
12	100	10	Parcel	25	6.2
13	5000	50	Tote	25	7.8
14	100	50	Tote	25	8.1
15	5000	10	Tote	25	5.1
16	100	10	Tote	25	4.9

Figure 11.24   Experiment Results for Optimizing Pick, Pack, and Ship

ANOG Test Wave	Max Qty	Analysis of Good Max Lines	Max Cube	Max Weight	Order/ Hour
9	5000	50	Parcel	25	8.3
1	5000	50	Parcel	150	8.2
6	100	50	Tote	150	8.2
2	100	50	Parcel	150	8.1
14	100	50	Tote	25	8.1
10	100	50	Parcel	25	8
5	5000	50	Tote	150	7.9
13	5000	50	Tote	25	7.8
4	100	10	Parcel	150	6.3
12	100	10	Parcel	25	6.2
3	5000	10	Parcel	150	6.1
11	5000	10	Parcel	25	5.9
8	100	10	Tote	150	5.1
15	5000	10	Tote	25	5.1
16	100	10	Tote	25	4.9
7	5000	10	Tote	150	4.5

Figure 11.25   Analysis of Good for Optimizing Order Pick, Pack, and Ship

Further statistical analysis using ANOVA and ANOM revealed that the factor having the most significant impact on Number of Orders Per Hour was Lines Per Wave, the number of products with a unique part number and their quantity. By comparison, the weight and cube size were insignificant. The experiment determined that the combination of unique part numbers that maximizes quantities results in the optimal picking sequence. Now, the company batches its orders based on the combination of unique part numbers that provides the greatest quantity. For instance, 25 unique part numbers whose order quantity totals to 4925 or 3 unique part numbers whose order quantity totals 4976 or 1 unique part number whose order quantity totals 5000. The goal is to have a high number of items in the pick.

SUMMARY

This chapter has provided only a basic introduction to the interesting and valuable techniques of quality function deployment and design of experiments. Both quality function deployment and design of experiments enable users to understand more about the products or processes they are studying. Both methods are assets to any problem solving adventure because they provide in-depth information about the complexities of the products and processes. Since both methods are complex and time consuming, they should be used judiciously.

■ Lessons Learned

1. Quality Function Deployment is a method that allows users to integrate the voice of the customer into the design or redesign of a product, service, or process.
2. Quality Function Deployment first captures information from the customer and then determines the technical requirements necessary to fulfill the customer requirements.
3. An experimental design is the plan or layout of an experiment. It shows the treatments to be included and the replication of the treatments.
4. Experimenters can study all the combinations of factors by utilizing a full factorial design.
5. Experimenters can study partial combinations of the factors by using fractional factorial experiment designs like Plackett-Burman or Taguchi.
6. Design of Experiments seeks to investigate the interactions of factors and their effects on the response variable. ■

Chapter Problems

1. Describe the principle parts of a quality function deployment matrix.
2. How is each of the principle parts of a QFD created? What does each part hope to provide the users?

3. Why would a company choose to use a QFD?

4. When a metal is selected for a part that will undergo a metal forming process such as stamping, often the metal is tested to determine its bending failure point. An experiment being conducted at MAR Inc. is testing the bending failure of a particular metal. In this experiment, a sample of the metal is bent back and forth until the metal separates at the fold. Metal from two different suppliers is currently being studied. Plated metal from each supplier is being compared with non-plated metal. For each piece of metal from each supplier, the metal samples being tested are in two sizes, a 2 in. wide piece and a 3 in. wide piece. If all of the factors are to be tested at each of their levels, create a table showing the factors and their levels for the two sizes, two suppliers, and two surface finishes.

5. For the information given in the previous problem, follow Example 11.3 and define the components of this experiment.

6. For the metal bending failure experiment, create a matrix showing all the different treatments a full factorial experiment would have run.

7. In plastic injection molding, temperature, time in mold, and injection pressure each play an important role in determining the strength of the part. At MAR Inc., experimenters are studying the effects on part strength when the temperature is set at either 250°, 275°, or 300°F; the time in mold is either 5, 7, or 9 seconds; and the injection pressure is either 200, 250, or 300 psi. Create a table showing the factors and their levels for this information.

8. For the information in the above plastic injection molding problem, follow Example 11.3 and define the components for this experiment.

9. For the above plastic injection molding problem, how many tests would be necessary to test every possible treatment (a full factorial experiment)? Create a tree similar to those shown in Figure 11.13 showing all possible treatments.

10. Researchers are studying the effects of tire pressure and vehicle speed on gas mileage. Create a hypothesis for the following information:

Factors	Levels
Tire Pressure	28 psi, 35 psi
Speed	55 mph, 65 mph

11. Describe the difference between the two types of errors that can occur with experiments.

12. A team is currently working to redesign a compressor assembly cell. The team has several design changes that they want to test using design of

experiments. The ultimate objective of the experiment is to decrease the cell's assembly and packing throughput time. Currently, it takes 45 minutes to assemble and pack a compressor. The team is considering three changes:

Reduce current 36 inch conveyor width to either 18 inch or 24 inch
Install new parts presentation shelving, either flat surfaced or angled
Line form: either straight or curved.

Create a table showing all the factors and their levels that will need to be tested. What is the response variable being investigated?

CASE STUDY 11.1
Quality Function Deployment

Form a team, select an existing product or service, and perform a Quality Function Deployment. Some potential ideas include: cell phones, an amusement park ride, website screens, a shopping cart, a voice mail system, a light rail system connecting two major cities and surrounding suburbs, a power tool, a lawnmower, an information storage device like a Palm Pilot, or a refrigerator.

Follow the steps shown in the text. Remember, capturing the voice of the customer is the most important aspect of a quality function deployment. Begin by creating a plan of action that includes the following information:

- How will you identify your customers?
- How will you contact your customers?
- How will you interview your customers?
- How will you identify the competitors?
- How will you gather information about those competitors?
- What questions will you ask?
- How will you get at the ideas a customer has but is not expressing?
- How will you organize the data from these customers?
- How will you determine realistic cost data?
- What will the technical requirements be in order to meet the requirements set by the customer?
- What are the competitors' strengths and weaknesses?
- How does the customer view the competitors?
- Are there any government regulations that must be met?

Use this information to create and complete a QFD diagram. When completed, analyze the QFD diagram.

CASE STUDY 11.2
Design of Experiments: Airplane Experiment

In this experiment you will determine which paper airplane design stays aloft the longest. Use the following instructions to set up your experiment and use the DOE software included with this text for analysis.

People Needed:

> Timers (2)
> Thrower(s)
> Data collection person

Equipment Needed:

> Stopwatches (2)
> Measuring tape (to measure shoulder height of the thrower chosen to throw the airplanes)
> Rulers (to measure fold sizes)
> Paper (identical size)
> Instructions for making planes (see Figures C11.2.1, C11.2.2, and C11.2.3 for suggested designs)
> Stapler (if studying advanced balance)

Factors and Their Levels (any, all, or a combination):

> Plane design factors
> Nose style—The type of nose style will affect how the plane flies; for instance, levels may be blunt or pointed.
> Balance—Where the most significant amount of weight is on the plane will affect how it flies. A paper clip or staple can also be added (as levels) to change the balance of the plane.
> Wing size—The size of the paper affects weight and wing size, so be consistent in the size of paper chosen.
> Weight—The size of the paper affects weight and wing size, so be consistent in the size of paper chosen.
> Folds—Creases and folds affect the aerodynamics of the plane. Be sure to crease the folds well.
> Length of nose—The distance between tip of nose and wing leading edge; for instance, levels may be short or long.
> Wing size—The construction of plane for different wing sizes; for instance, levels may be wide or narrow.

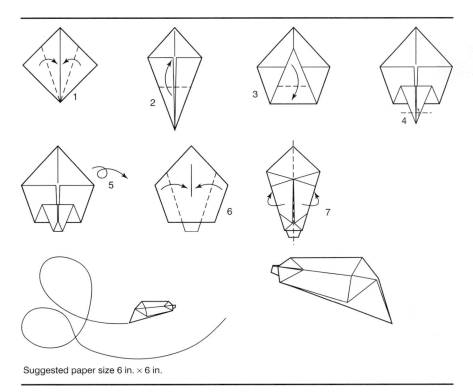

Suggested paper size 6 in. × 6 in.

Figure C11.2.1   Possible Airplane Design

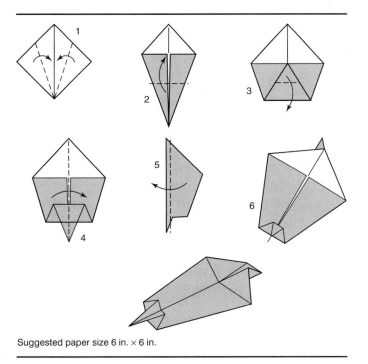

Suggested paper size 6 in. × 6 in.

Figure C11.2.2   Possible Airplane Design

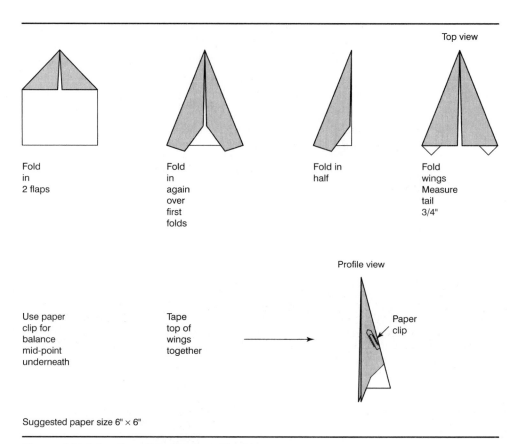

Figure C11.2.3   Possible Airplane Design

Thrower—The thrower could be the same individual throughout the experiment.

Shoulder height—If other throwers are involved, they become a factor in the experiment, and the shoulder height of the thrower must be taken into account. Shoulder height will affect time aloft if two or more throwers are chosen, especially if they are significantly different in height (so they could be levels).

Thrust—Thrust refers to the toss. The toss should be slow and steady to avoid stalls. If a stall occurs, the toss should be repeated.

Response Variable Time—Time from when the plane leaves the hand of the thrower to landing on floor.

To Run the Experiment:

Divide the participants into appropriate roles—Thrower, airplane maker, data collector, and timer

Select or create airplane designs—For instance, blunt-nosed and wide-winged versus needle-nosed and narrow-winged

Lay out the experiment design—Select the factors that will be varied in the experiment. Refer to Example 11.3 for a discussion of experiment design. Select a format for the factors: full factorial, Plackett-Burnam, Taguchi, etc.

Create the planes—Have the airplane makers create the different types of planes needed in order to fulfill the different experiment treatments. Label the planes as to which is appropriate for which treatment.

Fly the planes—Have the thrower(s) toss the airplanes.

Time the flights—Have the timers time the flights and record their response variable values.

Analyze the information using DOEpack software.

Quality Costs

Learning Opportunities:

1. To familiarize the reader with the concept of quality costs
2. To create an understanding of the interrelationships between and among the different types of quality costs
3. To gain an understanding of how quality costs can be used in decision making ■

Ship Meets Iceberg

$\mathbf{O}$*n an April night in 1912, the Titanic struck an iceberg. The ship thought to be unsinkable sank in a little over four hours. In today's business environment, a provider of goods or services must carefully navigate around icebergs that threaten to sink a company. Quality costs are similar to icebergs in that the majority of the costs associated with poor-quality products or services are hidden from view. This chapter defines the cost of failing to provide a quality product or service.*

WHAT ARE QUALITY COSTS?

What drives a company to improve? Increased customer satisfaction? Greater market share? Enhanced profitability? There are many reasons why companies seek to improve the way that they do business and one of the most important is the cost of quality. Quality costs are the costs that would disappear if every activity was performed without defects every time.

EXAMPLE 12.1   Costs of Quality

Remember the lost luggage example in the beginning of Chapter 1? Over an 11-year period, airlines have been trying to reduce the number of lost bags (Figure 12.1). As of the year 2001, the average number of lost bags per 1,000 passengers was 3.79. This means that 99.62 percent of the passengers and their luggage arrived at the same airport at the same time. Why would an airline company be interested in improving operations from 99.62 percent? Why isn't this good enough? What are the costs of quality in this situation?

In the case of lost luggage, the types of quality costs are numerous. For instance, if a passenger is reunited with his or her luggage after it arrives on the next flight, the

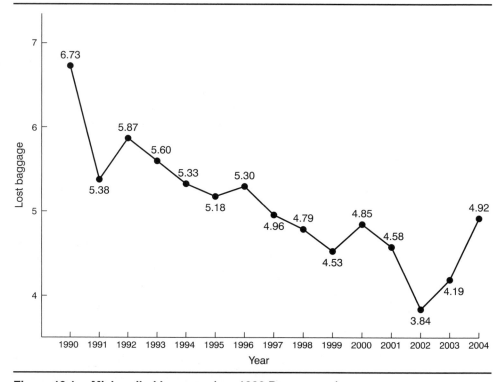

Figure 12.1   Mishandled Luggage (per 1000 Passengers)
SOURCE: K. Choquetter, "Claim Increase for Lost Baggage Still Up in the Air," *USA Today,* March 17, 1998, and www.dot.gov/airconsumer.

costs of quality include passenger inconvenience, loss of customer goodwill, and perhaps the cost of gesture of goodwill on the part of the airline in the form of vouchers for meals or flight ticket upgrades. As the scenario becomes more complex, a wider array of quality costs exists. For example, if an airline must reunite 100 bags with their owners per day at a hub airport such as Atlanta or New York, the costs can be enormous. The expenses associated with having airline employees track, locate, and reroute lost bags might run as high as 40 person-hours per day at $20/hour, for a cost of $800/day. Once located, the luggage must be delivered to the owners, necessitating baggage handling and delivery charges. If a delivery service were to charge $1/mile for the round trip, in larger cities, the average cost of delivering that bag to a customer might be $50. One hundred deliveries per day at $50 per delivery equals $5,000. Just these two costs total $5,800/day or $2,117,000/year! This doesn't include the cost of reimbursing customers for incidental expenses while they wait for their bags, the costs of handling extra paperwork to settle lost bag claims, loss of customer goodwill, and negative publicity. Add to this figure the costs associated with bags that are truly lost ($1250 for domestic flights and $9.07 per pound of checked luggage for international travelers), and the total climbs even higher. And these figures are merely the estimated cost at a single airport for a single airline!

Consider the more intangible effects of being a victim of lost luggage. If customers view airline baggage handling systems as a black hole where bags get sucked in only to resurface sometime later, somewhere else, if at all, then consumers will be hesitant to check bags. If the ever increasing amount of carry-on luggage with which people board the plane is any indication, lost luggage fears exist. Carry-on baggage presents its own problems, from dramatically slowing the process of loading and unloading of the plane, to shifting in-flight and falling on an unsuspecting passenger when the overhead bins are opened during or after the flight, to blocking exits from the airplane in an emergency. These costs, such as fees for delayed departure from the gate or liability costs, can be quantified and calculated into a company's performance and profit picture.

Is it any wonder that airlines have been working throughout the past decade to reduce the number of lost bags?

Products featuring what the customer wants at a competitive price will result in increased market share and therefore higher revenue for a company. But this is only part of the equation. Companies whose products and processes are defect-free enjoy the benefits of faster cycle times, decreased production costs, lower warranty costs, less wasted material and reduced scrap and rework costs. These lead to a lower total cost for the product or service, which leads to more competitive pricing, which results in higher revenue for the company. Companies that manage their processes improve the bottom lines on their income statements. Companies providing products with high defect rates often must lower their prices to attract customers. When customers know there is a high probability of purchasing a defective product, they often will shop elsewhere.

Two factions often find themselves at odds with each other when discussing quality. There are those who believe that no "economics" of quality exists, that it is never economical to ignore quality. There are others who feel it is uneconomical to have 100 percent perfect quality all of the time. Cries of "Good enough is not good enough" will be heard from some, while others will say that achieving perfect quality will bankrupt a company. Should decisions about the level of quality of a product or service be weighed against other factors such as meeting schedules and cost? To answer this question, an informed manager needs to understand the concepts surrounding the costs of quality. Investigating the costs associated with quality provides managers with an effective method to judge the economics and viability of a quality-improvement system. Quality costs serve as a baseline and a benchmark for selecting improvement projects and for later evaluating their success.

DEFINING QUALITY COSTS

Cost of quality, poor-quality cost, and cost of poor quality are all terms used to describe the costs associated with providing a quality product or service. A **quality cost** is *considered to be any cost that a company incurs in order to ensure that the quality of the product or service is perfect. Quality costs are the portion of the operating costs brought about by providing a product or service that does not conform to performance standards. Quality costs are also the costs associated with the prevention of poor quality.* The most commonly listed costs of quality include scrap, rework, and warranty costs. As Figure 12.2 shows, these easily identified quality costs are merely the tip of the iceberg.

Quality costs can originate from anywhere within a company. No single department has the corner of the market on making mistakes that might affect the quality of a product or service. Even departments far removed from the day-to-day operations of a firm can affect the quality of a product or service. The receptionist, often the first person the customer has contact with, can affect a customer's perceptions of the firm. The cleaning people provide an atmosphere conducive to work. Any time a process is performed incorrectly, quality costs are incurred. Salespeople must clearly define the customer's needs as well as the capabilities of the company. Figure 12.3 provides a few more examples of quality costs. Note how many re words, as in re-do, are in this list. Every department within a company should identify, collect, and monitor quality costs within their control.

Quality, in both the service and manufacturing industries, is a significant factor in allowing a company to maintain and increase its customer base. As a faulty product or service finds its way to the customer, the costs associated with the error increase. Preventing the nonconformity before it is manufactured or prepared to serve the customer is the least costly approach to providing a quality product or service. Potential problems should be identified and dealt with during the design and planning stage. An error at this phase of product development will require effort to solve, but in most cases the changes can be made before costly investments in equipment or customer service are made.

If the nonconformity with the product or service is located during the manufacturing cycle, or behind the scenes at a service industry, then the nonconformity can be corrected internally. The cost is greater here than at the design phase because the product or service is in some stage of completion. Product may need to be scrapped or, at a minimum, reworked to meet the customer's quality expectations.

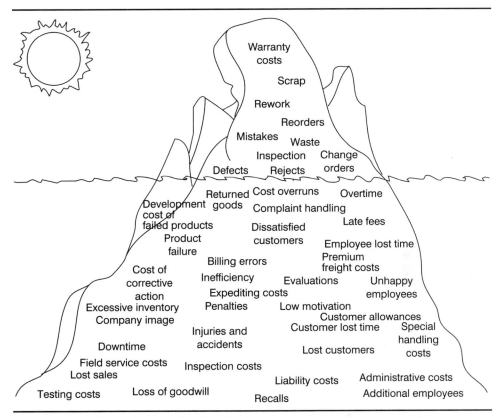

Figure 12.2   The Iceberg of Quality Costs

Rewriting an insurance policy to match customer expectations
Redesigning a faulty component that never worked right
Reworking a shock absorber after it was completely manufactured
Retesting a computer chip that was tested incorrectly
Rebuilding a tool that was not built to specifications
Repurchasing because of nonconforming materials
Responding to a customer's complaint
Refiguring a customer's bill when an error was found
Replacing a shirt the dry cleaner lost
Returning a meal to the kitchen because the meat was overcooked
Retrieving lost baggage
Replacing or repairing damaged or lost goods
Correcting billing errors
Expediting late shipments by purchasing a more expensive means of trans-
    portation
Providing on-site assistance to customers experiencing problems in the field
Providing credits and allowances

Figure 12.3   Examples of Quality Costs

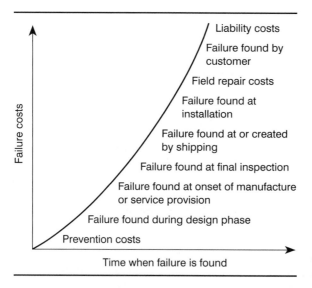

Figure 12.4   Increases in Quality Costs as Faulty Product Reaches Consumer

If the nonconforming product or service reaches the customer, the company providing it incurs the greatest costs. Customers who locate this nonconformity will experience a variety of feelings, the least of which will be dissatisfaction. Even if the customers are later satisfied by providing them with a new product, repairing their existing product, or repeating the service, the damage has already been done to the company's reputation. Disgruntled customers rarely fail to tell others about their experience. Mistakes that reach the customer result in the loss of goodwill between the present customer, future customers, and the provider. Failure cost increases as a function of the failure's detection point in the procss (Figure 12.4).

EXAMPLE 12.2   The Cost of Poor Quality

Jim and Sue Homeowners recently purchased a home on a large lot. Using their small push mower to cut the lawn proved to be a tedious, time-consuming job, so over the winter, they saved to purchase a riding lawn mower. Early in spring, they checked a variety of lawn mower sales and finally settled on Brand X. Unknown to them, this particular mower had a design flaw that had gone unnoticed by the manufacturer. The mower deck, which covers the blades, is held onto the mower through the use of bolts. Because there is too little clearance between the mower-deck fastener bolts and the blade, under certain circumstances the blades come in contact with the bolts, shearing them off and releasing the mower deck. When this happens, the damage to the blades is irreparable.

This design error was not apparent in the store lot where the Homeowners tried the mower. The lot was smooth, and the problem only becomes obvious when the mower is used on uneven ground. The Homeowners went home to try out their new lawn mower and within minutes the mower was moving along uneven terrain. A loud shearing sound was heard, and the mower deck fell off, mangling the blades in the process.

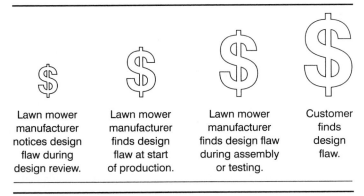

Figure 12.5   **Increasing Costs Associated with Faulty Lawn Mower**

The Homeowners immediately called the salesperson, who, understanding the importance of happy customers, quickly sent a repair person to investigate.

The repair person identified the problem, returned to the store with the mower, and replaced the first mower with a second. Even though the repair person knew what had caused the failure, he had no way of informing the manufacturer. Previous attempts to contact the manufacturer to give them information about other problems had not been successful. The manufacturer thus lost a valuable bit of information that could have improved the design.

Although they had used most of a Saturday getting the problem resolved, the Homeowners felt satisfied with the service they had received . . . until they tried the new mower. The new mower experienced the same problem on a different patch of grass. This time, the store was unable to replace the mower until the next weekend. The Homeowners resorted to their push mower.

The next Saturday was not a good day. Another mower was promptly delivered and tried out in the presence of the salesperson and the repair person. Same problem. The Homeowners returned the mower and resolved to purchase no other yard-care products—no weed whips, wagons, push mowers, or edging tools—from this company. At a barbecue that weekend, they told their neighbors about their troubles with Brand X products. Over the next few weeks, the Homeowners investigated the types of lawn mowers used by yard-service firms and golf courses. Even though it was a bit more expensive, they bought Brand Y because of its proven track record and quality reputation.

In this situation, an unsuitable product reached a consumer. Quality service from the store could not compensate for the original design flaw. As Figure 12.5 shows, failure to spot the design flaw during the design review, or during production and assembly, or during testing dramatically increased costs. The quality costs associated with providing a poorly designed lawn mower included here not only the three damaged lawn mowers but also sales of related equipment to the original customers and future sales to their friends.

TYPES OF QUALITY COSTS

The costs associated with preventing nonconformities, with appraising products or services as they are being produced or provided, and with failure can be defined. With an understanding of these costs, a manager can make decisions concerning the implementation of improvement projects. Using quality costs, a manager can determine the usefulness of investing in a process, changing a standard operating procedure, or revising a product or service design.

Prevention Costs

Prevention costs are those costs that occur when a company is performing activities designed to prevent poor quality in products or services. Prevention costs are often seen as front-end costs designed to ensure that the product or service is created to meet the customer requirements. Examples of such costs are design reviews, education and training, supplier selection and capability reviews, process capability reviews, and process improvement projects. Prevention activities must be reviewed to determine if they truly bring about improvement in the most cost-effective manner.

Unfortunately, many organizations focus on corrective actions, fixing problems, reporting savings. An emphasis on the prevention of defects is much more cost-effective, as no money is lost making mistakes in the first place. Prevention efforts try to determine the root causes of problems and eliminate them at the source so reoccurrences do not happen. Preventing poor quality stops companies from incurring the cost of doing it over again. Essentially, if they had done it right the first time, they would not have to repeat their efforts. In his book *Quality Is Free,* Philip Crosby emphasizes the need to invest in preventing problems in order to reap the benefits of reduced appraisal and failure costs.* The initial investment in improving processes is more than compensated by the resulting cost savings, so, in essence, quality is free.

Appraisal Costs

Appraisal costs are the costs associated with measuring, evaluating, or auditing products or services to make sure that they conform to specifications or requirements. Appraisal costs are the costs of evaluating the product or service during the production of the product or the providing of the service to determine if, in its unfinished or finished state, it is capable of meeting the requirements set by the customer. Appraisal activities are necessary in an environment where product, process, or service problems are found. Appraisal costs can be associated with raw materials inspection, work-in-process (activities-in-process for the service industries) evaluation, or finished product reviews. Examples of appraisal costs include incoming inspection, work-in-process inspection, final inspection or testing, material reviews, and calibration of measuring or

---

*Philip Crosby, *Quality Is Free*. New York: McGraw-Hill, 1979.

testing equipment. When the quality of the product or service reaches high levels, then appraisal costs can be reduced.

Failure Costs

Failure costs occur when the completed product or service does not conform to customer requirements. Two types exist: internal and external. *Internal failure costs are those costs associated with product nonconformities or service failures found before the product is shipped or the service is provided to the customer.* Internal failure costs are the costs of correcting the situation. This failure cost may take the form of scrap, rework, remaking, reinspection, or retesting. *External failure costs are the costs that occur when a nonconforming product or service reaches the customer.* External failure costs include the costs associated with customer returns and complaints, warranty claims, product recalls, or product liability claims. Since external failure costs have the greatest impact on the corporate pocketbook, they must be reduced to zero. Because they are highly visible, external costs often receive the most attention. Unfortunately, internal failure costs may be seen as necessary evils in the process of providing good-quality products to the consumer. Nothing could be more false. Doing the work twice, through rework or scrap, is not a successful strategy for operating in today's economic environment.

Intangible Costs

How a customer views a company and its performance will have a definite impact on long-term profitability. *Intangible costs, the hidden costs associated with providing a nonconforming product or service to a customer, involve the company's image.* Intangible costs of poor quality, because they are difficult to identify and quantify, are often left out of quality-cost determinations. They must not be overlooked, or disregarded. Is it possible to quantify the cost of missing an important deadline? What will be the impact of quality problems or schedule delays on the company's image? Intangible costs of quality can be three or four times as great as the tangible costs of quality. Even if these costs can only be named, and no quantifiable value can be placed on them, it is important for decision makers to be aware of their existence.

The four types of quality costs are interrelated. In summary, *total quality costs are considered to be the sum of prevention costs, appraisal costs, failure costs, and intangible costs.* Figure 12.6 shows some of the quality costs from Figure 12.2 in their respective categories. Investments made to prevent poor quality will reduce internal and external failure costs. Consistently high quality reduces the need for many appraisal activities. Suppliers with strong quality systems in place can reduce incoming inspection costs. High appraisal costs combined with high internal failure costs signal that poor-quality products or services are being produced. Efforts made to reduce external failure costs will involve changes to efforts being made to prevent poor quality. Internal failure costs are a portion of the total production costs, just as external failure costs reduce overall profitability. A trade-off to be aware of when dealing with

Prevention Costs	Internal Failure Costs

Prevention Costs

    Quality planning
    Quality program administration
    Supplier-rating program adminis-
      tration
    Customer requirements/expecta-
      tions market research
    Product design/development re-
      views
    Quality education programs
    Equipment and preventive mainte-
      nance

Internal Failure Costs

    Rework
    Scrap
    Repair
    Material-failure reviews
    Design changes to meet customer
      expectations
    Corrective actions
    Making up lost time
    Rewriting a proposal
    Stocking extra parts
    Engineering change notices

Appraisal Costs

    In-process inspection
    Incoming inspection
    Testing/inspection equipment
    Audits
    Product evaluations

External Failure Costs

    Returned goods
    Corrective actions
    Warranty costs
    Customer complaints
    Liability costs
    Penalties
    Replacement parts
    Investigating complaints

Intangible Costs

    Customer dissatisfaction
    Company image
    Lost sales
    Loss of customer goodwill
    Customer time loss
    Offsetting customer dissatisfaction

Figure 12.6   Categories of Quality Costs

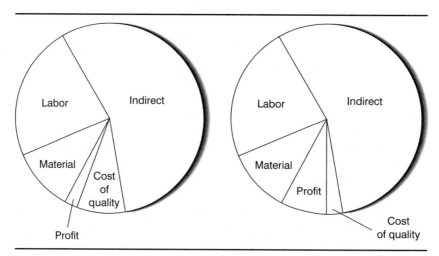

Figure 12.7   Cost of Quality Versus Profit

quality costs is the need to ensure that appraisal costs are well spent. Companies with a strong appraisal system need to balance two points of view: Is the company spending too much on appraisal for its given level of quality performance or is the company risking excessive failure costs by underfunding an appraisal program? In all three areas—prevention, appraisal, and failure costs—the activities undertaken must be evaluated to ensure that the efforts are gaining further improvement in a cost-effective manner. Figure 12.7 reveals that as quality costs are reduced or—in the case of prevention quality costs—invested wisely, overall company profits will increase. The savings associated with doing it right the first time show up in the company's bottom line.

 REAL TOOLS FOR REAL LIFE

Uncovering Quality Costs

A sheet metal stamping firm recently bid $75,000 as the price of providing an order of aluminum trays. After stamping a large number of these trays, the company investigated their costs and determined that if production continued, the cost of providing the order would be $130,000! This was nearly double what they had bid.

They immediately set out to figure out what was causing such a dramatic increase in their costs. They investigated their product design and found it to be satisfactory. Prevention costs associated with product design and development were negligible. The customer had not returned any of the completed trays. There were no customer complaints and therefore no corrective-action costs. Their investigation showed that external failure costs were zero. Appraisal costs were normal for a product of this type. Incoming material and in-process inspection costs were similar to the amount projected. The product had not required any testing upon completion.

It was only when they investigated the internal failure costs that the problem became apparent. At first, they felt that internal failure costs were also negligible since there was almost no scrap. It wasn't until a bright individual observed the operators feeding the trays through the stamping operation twice that they were able to locate the problem. When questioned, operators told the investigators that they knew that due to inappropriate die force, the product was not stamped to the correct depth on the first pass. Since the operators knew that the trays would not pass inspection, they decided among themselves to rework the product immediately, before sending it to inspection. The near doubling of the manufacturing costs turned out to be the internal failure costs associated with reworking the product.

Essentially, the company incurred a cost of quality equal to the standard labor and processing costs of the operation. To meet specifications, a significant number of trays were being handled and processed twice. Only by preventing the need for double processing can the costs of quality be reduced.

> This type of internal failure cost actually began as a prevention cost. If the manufacturer had investigated the capability of the stamping operation more closely, they would have determined that maintenance work was necessary to improve the machine's performance and therefore improve product quality. **Q**

QUALITY-COST MEASUREMENT SYSTEM

In the struggle to meet the three conflicting goals of quality, cost, and delivery, identifying and quantifying quality costs help ensure that quality does not suffer. When quality costs are discussed as a vague entity, their importance in relation to cost and delivery is not understood. By quantifying quality costs, all individuals producing a product or providing a service understand what it will cost if quality suffers. True cost reduction occurs when the root causes of nonconformities are recognized and eliminated.

A quality-cost measurement system should be designed to keep track of the different types of quality costs. Being able to define and quantify quality costs enables quality to be managed more effectively. Once quantified, these costs can be used to determine which projects will allow for the greatest return on investment and which projects have been most effective at improving processes, lowering failure rates, and reducing appraisal costs. A quality-cost measurement system should use quality costs as a tool to help justify improvement actions.

Quantifying quality costs will help to zero in on which problems, if solved, will provide the greatest return on investment. A quality-cost measurement system should try to capture and reduce significant quality costs. Effective cost reduction occurs when the processes providing products or services and their related support processes are managed correctly. Measures, as discussed in Chapter 3, are key to ensuring that the processes are performing to the best of their capability. After all, what is measured can be managed. Once cost of quality data has been measured and tabulated, this data can be used to select quality improvement projects as well as identify the most costly aspects of a specific problem. Failure costs are prevalent in all aspects of providing goods and services, from design and development to production and distribution. Support processes, such as marketing and human resources, can also be the source of quality costs. When justifying improvement projects, look for rework, waste, returns, scrap, complaints, repairs, expediting, adjustments, refunds, penalties, wait times, and excess inventory. Cost-improvement efforts should be focused on locating the largest cost contributors to the improvement. Try not to be tempted to spend time chasing insignificant, incremental measures of quality costs. Use a Pareto analysis to identify the projects with the greatest return on investment; those should be tackled first.

Those establishing a quality-cost measurement system need to keep in mind that the success of such a system is based on using quality-cost information to guide improvement. Each cost has a root cause that can be identified and prevented in the future. Remember that preventing problems in the first place is always cheaper. Those implementing a quality-cost measurement system need to establish a basic method of identifying correctable problems, correcting the problems, and achieving a new level of performance.

 REAL TOOLS FOR REAL LIFE

Costs of Quality Reduced by Problem-Solving Process

Farmer Friendly Inc. manufactures and sells farm and lawn equipment. As part of their quality-cost measurement system, Farmer Friendly monitors the costs associated with prevention of defects, product appraisal, internal and external failure costs, and, to a certain extent, the intangible costs. By monitoring these cost of quality values on a regular basis, they are able to spot issues before they become a serious problem. Recent charts have shown that despite their best prevention and appraisal efforts, external failure costs, as reflected by the number and costs of warranty claims have risen slightly on their mid-sized farm tractor (Figure 12.8). External failure costs like these are expensive when you take into account the cost of complaint investigation, complaint handling, repair, and corrective action efforts. Because the customer has found the problem, there are also intangible costs, lost sales, loss of customer goodwill and customer dissatisfaction, to be considered.

Warranty claims show that customers are complaining that the steering wheel pulls to the right while the tractor is in motion. No in-depth investigation occurred at the dealership, most repair personnel opted to merely realign the front wheels. This would satisfy the customer briefly. However, most problems reoccurred. Several customers have brought their tractor in for alignment issues as many as three times. One tractor, deemed irreparable, was bought back by the company for the original

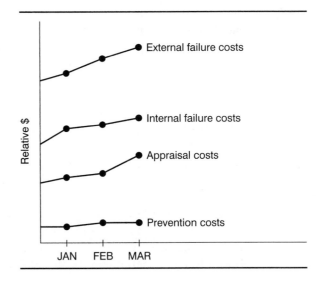

Figure 12.8   Quality Costs Chart

Returned goods (Buy back)	$31,000
Warranty costs	$600/tractor + $60/hr × 4 hr labor
Customer complaint processing	$200/complaint
Replacement parts/alignment	$500
Corrective actions (team)	$8,000 (5 people × 80 hrs × salary)
Complaint investigation	$1,200 to date

Figure 12.9   External Failure Costs: Tractor Steering Pull

purchase price. Current external failure costs associated with this problem are shown in Figure 12.9.

Recognizing the potential liability costs associated with steering problems, though the number of warranty claims is still low, Farmer Friendly immediately assigned a process improvement team to look into the situation.

Following a problem-solving approach similar to that outlined in Chapter 3, the team began by studying the warranty information provided from the field. To aid them in their search for a root cause, they created a cause and effect diagram of the reasons why *steering pull* may happen (Figure 12.10). The discussions surrounding the cause and effect diagram, combined with additional information on key product

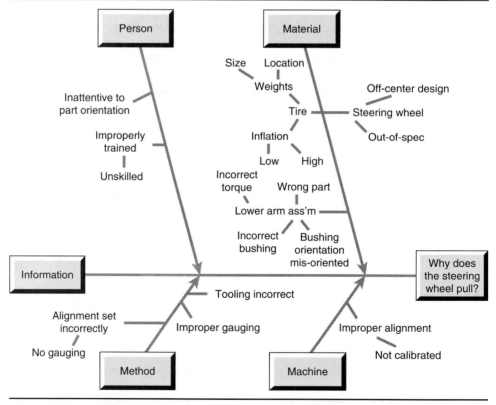

Figure 12.10   Tractor Steering Wheel Pull Cause and Effect Diagram

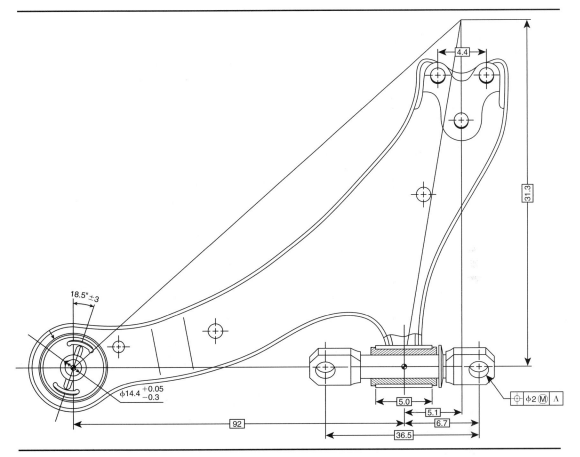

Figure 12.11   Suspension Control Arm Bushing

dimensions, pointed to suspension control arm bushing angularity discrepancies (Figure 12.11). The parts saved from the repaired tractors were studied and this bushing angularity discrepancy was verified.

Having found the problem and in order to determine how this problem could occur, the team created a WHY-WHY diagram (Figure 12.12) and mapped the process (Figure 12.13). These documents pointed to a loose work-holding device which worked intermittently. Without the support of the work-holding device, the control arm bushing could not be correctly mounted, thus affecting the angularity of the part. The team reported their findings by completing the Warranty Investigation Report shown in Figure 12.14.

Countermeasures were implemented to repair the work-holding device. The operator was also alerted to the important role the device plays in making the part to specification. To drive home its importance, information concerning the costs of quality were also shared. Careful tracking of cost of quality data alerted Farmer Friendly to a problem that had the potential to become quite costly.

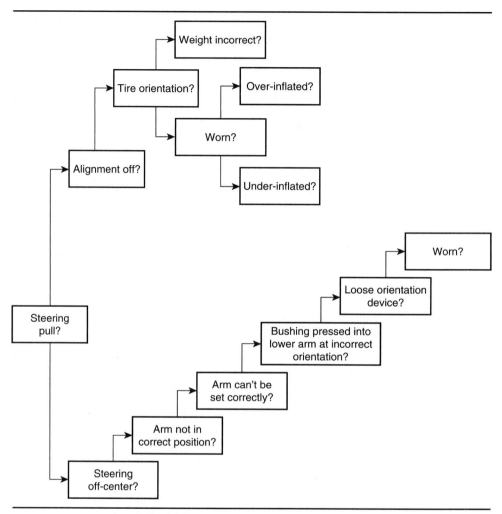

Figure 12.12   WHY-WHY Diagram for Lower Arm Bushing

UTILIZING QUALITY COSTS FOR DECISION MAKING

All initiatives undertaken by an organization must contribute to the financial success of the organization. Remember Dr. Juran's advice from Chapter 2 about becoming bilingual? Better communication with management happens when you translate quality data into business and financial terms. Quality goals and objectives should be included in an organization's business plan, but they must be stated in financial terms. Quality costs can be used as a justification for actions taken to improve the product or service. Typically, investments in new equipment, materials, or facilities require the project sponsor to determine which projects will provide the greatest return on investment. These calculations traditionally include information on labor savings,

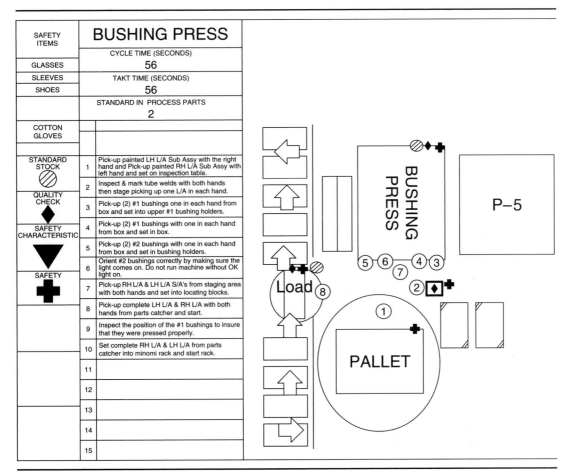

Figure 12.13   Bushing Press Process Map

production time savings, and ability to produce a greater variety of products with better quality. The "better quality" aspect of these calculations can be quantified by investigating the costs of quality, particularly the failure costs. It is important to determine the costs of in-process and incoming material inspection, sorting, repair, and scrap as well as the intangible costs associated with having a nonconforming product or service reach the customer. Making a decision with more complete quality information, such as product appraisal costs, can help determine the true profitability of a product or service.

Once quality costs are identified, those reviewing the project can determine if the money for the project is being well spent to prolong the growth of the company. Identifying and quantifying quality costs has a twofold benefit. Cost savings are identified and quality is improved. By improving the quality performance of a company, the company also improves its quality costs.

Warranty Investigation Report

Subject: **Steering wheel pull**   Responsibility: Team 12

Model Name: Mid-size Tractor

Products: Steering Assembly   Part Numbers: 1, 2, 3, 5, 8, 11, 19

Problem: Customers requesting tractor service for steering wheel pull to right.

Problem Identified: 10/21/05   Solution Due Date: 12/1/05

Observation in field:

Mechanics report that when driven, the tractors pull slightly to the right, causing the tractor to steer off-center. No abnormal sounds noticed. No vibrations either. Visual inspection of steering components revealed no immediately visible cause.

Temporary countermeasure/containment:

Steering column/component replacement in affected tractors. Check tractor production records to determine if this is an isolated problem or one affecting a series of tractors produced at the same time.

Investigation:

See attached charts and report

Cause:

Suspension control arm bushing angularity discrepancy due to working holding device slippage. Improperly oriented raw part.

Permanent countermeasure/containment:

Process changes to ensure that the work-holding device orients part correctly.

Dealer alert sent requesting that dealers conduct a bushing angularity check if tractor steering pull is not corrected after completing other troubleshooting steps. Report findings to Family Friendly, Team 12.

Sign-offs:

General Manger:

Team Leader:

Date:

Figure 12.14   Warranty Investigation Report for Tractor Steering Wheel Pull

REAL TOOLS FOR REAL LIFE

Using Process Maps to Locate Non-Value-Added Activities and Reduce Costs of Quality

The chocolate candy manufacturing line at Tasty Morsels Chocolates is a fully-automated line, requiring little human intervention. Because of this, many people at Tasty Morsels thought it odd that the production engineer insisted waste existed in the process. She based her conclusions on cost of quality information related to production cost overruns. Cost overruns can be caused by excessive scrap rates, rework amounts, inspection costs, and overtime. To tackle the cost overruns, she wanted to isolate and remove waste from the process, thus preventing defectives by removing the sources of variation. In order to enable them to better understand the production line activities, the production engineer mapped the process (Figure 12.15).

The process map revealed several non-value-added activities. Chocolate is mixed until it reaches the right consistency, then it is poured into mold trays. As the chocolates leave the cooling chamber, two workers reorganize the chocolate mold trays on the conveyor belt. This prompted the production engineer to ask: why are the trays bunching up on the conveyor in the first place? This non-value-added, inspection-type activity essentially wastes the time of two workers. It also could result in damaged chocolates if the trays were to flip over or off of the conveyor.

Tasty Morsels Chocolates prides itself on their quality product. To maintain their high standards, before packaging, the process map reveals that 4 workers inspect nearly each piece of chocolate as it emerges from the wrapping machine. A full 25% of the chocolate production is thrown out in a large garbage can. Though this type of inspection prevents defective chocolates from reaching the consumer, this is a very high internal failure cost of quality.

This huge waste of material, manpower, and production time prompted the production engineer to ask: why are the chocolates being thrown away? The simple answer was that the chocolates didn't meet standards. The production engineer persevered and discovered that the rejected chocolates were improperly wrapped. Despite the large amount of chocolate being thrown away, no one had suggested that the wrapper machine should be repaired.

If the production engineer hadn't studied the process carefully using a process map, these two enormous sources of waste and the costs associated with poor quality would have gone unnoticed:

Appraisal Costs   in-process inspection

Internal Failure Costs   scrap, rework, production cost overruns, overtime, inefficient and ineffective production, employee lost time, low employee morale

External Failure Costs   customer warranty and order issues, late, order fees, returned goods, replacement goods, corrective action costs

Intangible Costs   customer dissatisfaction, lost sales, offsetting customer dissatisfaction.

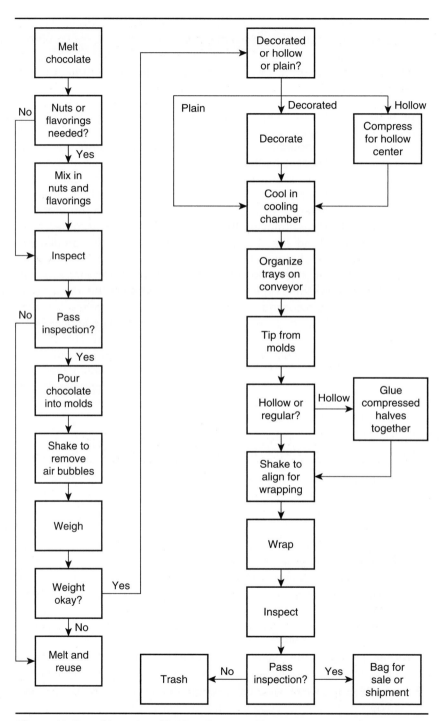

Figure 12.15   Chocolate Making Process Map

Up until this study, Tasty Morsels considered these costs part of doing business. Based on the production engineer's discoveries, investigations were undertaken to correct the production flow through the cooling chamber. Adjustments were also made to the wrapping machine to correct a fixture misalignment. By taking steps to prevent poor quality, these modifications resulted in a manpower savings of five people, who were transferred to other areas of the plant. Rejected chocolates went from 25% to 0.05%! The savings that resulted from the changes paid for the modifications 10 times over.

SUMMARY

With any quality-measurement or improvement system, the information and improvements realized need to be applied to any future activities. Deming's plan-do-study-act cycle plays a significant role. Once improvements are planned, they must be acted upon to ensure that future activities maintain the new level of quality and the decreased level of quality costs. Identifying quality costs will allow management to judge improvement investments and profit contributions. A quality program is only as valuable as its ability to contribute to customer satisfaction and, ultimately, to company profits.

■ *Lessons Learned*

1. Collecting quality costs provides a method to evaluate system effectiveness.
2. Quality costs can serve as a basis or benchmark for measuring the success of internal improvements.
3. Prevention costs are the costs associated with preventing the creation of errors or nonconformities in the first place.
4. Appraisal costs are the costs incurred when a product or service is studied to determine if it conforms to specifications.
5. Internal failure costs are the costs associated with errors found before the product or services reach the customer.
6. External failure costs are the costs associated with errors found by the customer.
7. Intangible failure costs are the costs associated with the loss of customer goodwill and respect.
8. Once quantified, quality costs enhance decision making if they are used to determine which projects will allow for the greatest return on investment and which projects are most effective at lowering failure and appraisal quality costs.
9. Quality-cost information should be used to guide improvement. ■

Chapter Problems

1. Which of the following statements about quality costs is true? Why, why not?
   a. Quality cost reduction is the responsibility of the quality control department.
   b. Quality costs provide a method of determining problem areas and action priorities.
   c. The efficiency of any business is measured in terms of the number of defective products.

2. There are four specific types of quality costs. Clearly define two of them. Give an example of each kind of quality cost you have defined.

3. What is a prevention cost? How can it be recognized? Describe where prevention costs can be found.

4. Describe the two types of failure costs. Where do they come from? How will a person recognize either type of failure cost?

5. How do the four types of quality cost vary in relation to each other?

6. Describe the relationship among prevention costs, appraisal costs, and failure costs. Where should a company's efforts be focused? Why?

7. A lamp manufacturing company has incurred the following quality costs. Analyze how this company is doing on the basis of these costs. Creating a graph of the values may help you see trends. Values given are in percentage of total cost of lamp.

	Costs			
Year	Prevention	Appraisal	Internal Failure	External Failure
1	1.2	3.6	4.7	5.7
2	1.6	3.5	4.3	4.6
3	2.2	3.8	4.0	3.8
4	2.5	2.7	3.5	2.2
5	3.0	2.0	2.8	0.9

8. How can quality costs be used for decision making?

9. Where should dollars spent on quality issues be invested in order to provide the greatest return on investment? Why?

10. Choose two industries and list specific examples of their costs of quality.

11. Why is the following statement true? The further along the process that a failure is discovered, the more expensive it is to correct.

12. What should a quality-cost program emphasize?

13. What are the benefits of having, finding, or determining quality costs?

14. On what premise is the strategy for using quality costs based?

15. For each of the following activities, identify whether the costs incurred should be allocated to the prevention, appraisal, failure (internal, external), or intangible costs category:

   a. Customer inquires about incorrect billing statement.
   b. Maintenance technician is unable to gain access to customer's premises during a service call because the service is not being performed when scheduled and no one notified the customer.
   c. Workers check/test their work before allowing it to leave their work area.
   d. Management carries out a quality systems audit.
   e. The accounts department is having difficulty obtaining monthly figures from the production department.
   f. A customer's purchase breaks because of inadequate training in the use of the item and must be replaced.
   g. Management must deal with written complaints from a customer about continuous poor service.
   h. A technician keeps an appointment after driving across town to pick up equipment from an outside supplier upon finding it out of stock in his own warehouse.
   i. An instruction manual and set of procedures are developed for maintaining a new piece of equipment.
   j. The company conducts a survey of customer requirements.

CASE STUDY 12.1
Costs of Quality

PART 1

The medicinal supplies distribution department of a large hospital provides the nursing floors and medical departments with all of the supplies needed to service the patients requiring medical attention. These items include medicines, bandages, I.V. tubing, catheters, syringes, tourniquets, strainers, scalpels, swabs, I.D. bracelets, and other items. Each floor and department has different medicinal needs, and carts carry supplies to the floor or area.

Over time, the medicinal supplies distribution department's workload has increased, while staff size has remained constant. Concerns over staffing problems, budget constraints, and maintaining the quality of service have prompted the formation of a continuous improvement task force to investigate the problems. Their mission is to provide quick, accurate service to the medical staff while continuously improving the provision process to make it more efficient, more compatible with medical staff needs, and more cost-effective.

To begin the problem-solving process, a flowchart of the process of supplying medical items is created (Figure C12.1.1). This chart details the activities involved in stocking the carts, checking inventory on the carts, reordering necessary items, and taking carts to their respective floors. Records of the items in inventory are kept by a computerized inventory-control system. When a patient uses items from the cart, nurses and other medical staff record the chargeable items on the patient's chart. These items are billed to the patient when accounts payable figures the bill. Computer inventory records are compared with a complete list of items charged to all patients' bills. When inventory records and items taken from the cart and billed don't match, a lost charge report is generated. This report is used by the medical staff to determine which patients should be charged for what items.

While patient care is first and foremost in importance, significant costs from incorrect charges are being incurred by the hospital. Other problems with medicinal supplies distribution involve items not found on carts, items out of stock on carts, incorrect inventory counts leading to incorrect reordering or product spoilage, and lengthy waits for items to be brought to the floor from inventory storage (Figure C12.1.2).

Task force members have decided to investigate this situation from a cost-of-quality point of view. At first, some of the group members are concerned about ensuring that quality patient care is not overlooked. Others think that the emphasis on quality patient care has caused costs to be ignored. Fortunately, the task force leader understands the use of quality costs in decision making. Using quality costs, a manager can determine

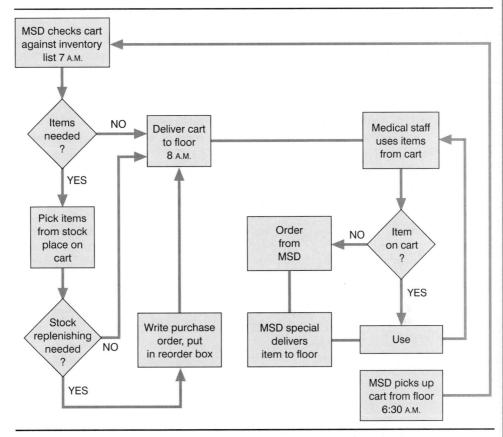

Figure C12.1.1   Flowchart: Process of Supplying Medical Items

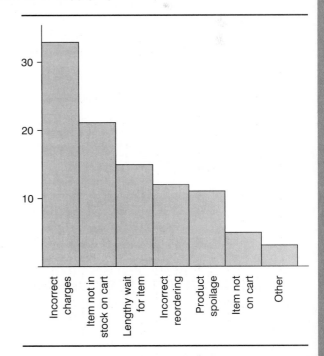

Figure C12.1.2   Pareto Analysis of One Week's Calls to the Medicinal Supplies Distribution Department

the usefulness of investing in new equipment, changing a standard operating procedure, or revising a service design. The task force intends to use quality costs to guide the changes they will make to the inventory system.

The first step is to convince group members to study this situation from a cost-of-quality point of view. The leader reminds group members that quality costs are any cost that the hospital would not have incurred if the quality of the product or service were perfect. Quality costs are the portion of the operating costs brought about by providing a medical service that does not conform to performance standards. Quality costs are also the costs associated with the prevention of poor quality. To identify quality costs, the leader encourages a brainstorming session.

 Assignment

From reading the case, and from your knowledge of hospitals, identify prevention costs, appraisal costs, failure costs, and intangible costs in this situation.

PART 2

By investigating hospital records, the task force captures the dollars associated with the quality costs identified in part 1. Their relative values are shown in Figure C12.1.3. This figure clearly shows that the appraisal and failure costs associated with this problem necessitate investigating the situation.

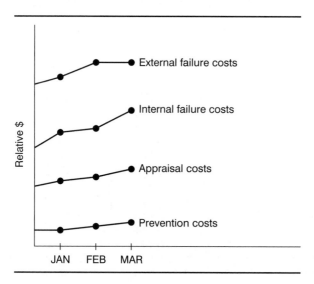

Figure C12.1.3   Quality Costs Chart

Timely patient care delivery, quality of service, and the costs of providing those services are all interrelated. By studying the process of delivering medicinal items to the patients, the task force seeks to uncover methods of meeting patient demands; increasing the quality of the services to patients, doctors, nurses, and other medical staff; and reducing the inventory cost problems currently existing at the hospital.

Inventory usage now becomes the subject of a three-month study. The study is limited to the cart supplying the second floor of the west wing in the hospital. Time studies are made of the times associated with stocking the cart, checking the cart, and obtaining items when the items are not on the cart. The number of calls for needed items is recorded with a check sheet (Figure C12.1.4).

After all the data are gathered, the times are investigated. The time to record the information on the computer is similar from person to person and dependent on computer processing time. Picking of needed items and restocking the cart involves the number of items on the cart and the number used. It is fairly obvious that the more items on the cart and the greater usage of those items, the more time it takes to restock the cart. This points to a need to understand the supplies usage. Since supplies usage is the driving force behind the stock and restock times, this becomes the area to be most closely studied.

When the material usage summaries of the three months are studied, the investigators find that there are quite a few items that are not used at all or are used very rarely. A study of the usage percentage from the usage report determines four categories of supplies usage: no use, infrequent use, some use, and frequent use. Organized in this manner, the results of the study are shared with the medical staff of the unit. Based on the study, they remove the items they feel they do not need at all and identify others that can be reduced in quantity.

Inventory Item Check Sheet Showing Number of Calls for Each Item over a Three-Month Period

Item No.	Usage	On Hand	Avg/Day	Std Dev	% Usage
1	3	0	0.033	0.181	
2	157	1350	1.744	2.256	11.6
7	7	90	0.078	0.308	7.8
12	74	180	0.822	0.894	41.1
13	70	180	0.778	0.871	38.9
22	16	450	0.178	0.646	3.6
25	5	90	0.056	0.230	5.6
31	110	0	1.222	10.582	
32	145	360	1.611	6.475	40.3
36	10	0	0.111	0.608	
38	6	0	0.067	0.292	
40	28	360	0.311	0.612	7.8
47	2	90	0.022	0.148	2.2

Figure C12.1.4   Inventory Item Check Sheet

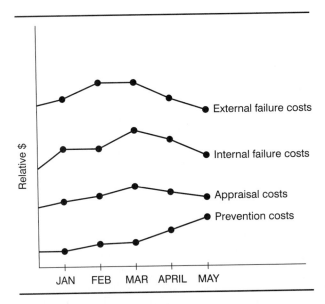

Figure C12.1.5   Quality Costs Chart

Following this, the overstocking situation is investigated. In some instances, overstocking of the cart leads to product spoilage or breach of sterilization. Overstockage rates are discussed with the staff and eventually the item amounts are decreased. Both of these decreases in inventory on the cart reduce the stocking time as well as the cost of product spoilage. Figure C12.1.5 shows the result of investing in prevention costs and allowing process changes based on continuous improvement investigations. Failure costs decrease and a small reduction in appraisal costs is noticed.

Another major change is suggested by the task force. Inventorying the carts every other day instead of every day will save on appraisal costs. As long as failure costs associated with stockouts can be prevented or limited, this change will reduce the burden on the current staff without increasing costs. A less-harried stocking staff member will be less likely to make a mistake in overlooking an expiration date or an understocked item.

Switching to an every-other-day schedule requires studying the usage summary reports for the past three months. Calculations based on these reports determine an average usage per day of each item and the standard deviation associated with the usage. From this, usage levels for a two-day period are determined. Using the standard deviation to understand the average usage reduces the number of stockouts and midday replenishing. To fail to incorporate the standard deviation in the calculations would have increased the internal failure costs (running out of stock) instead of limiting them.

After this change is approved by the staff, the amount of supplies on the cart is changed to reflect usage rates and the carts are restocked every other day. This new process is monitored to determine if costs are really reduced and if new costs of quality have not developed. The amount of usage is noted as well as the number of calls

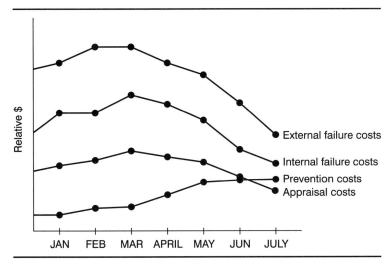

Figure C12.1.6   Quality Costs Chart

to replenish the item between cart restocking. If too many calls are made, the amount is increased on the cart. Figure C12.1.6 shows the changes in appraisal costs in relation to the other costs.

Other cost-of-quality issues are identified during this investigation. For example, the hospital does not bill patients for very low cost items (swabs, alcohol, etc.). Following the study, the limit is raised so that more items are not charged. While this means that fewer charges for minor items reach the patient, the hospital feels that these costs are recouped by eliminating the appraisal costs associated with checking for these items on patient bills and lost charges lists. Another result of the study is a noticeable reduction in the materials being wasted because of overstocking on the carts and in inventory. The preventive quality costs of studying the carts have been balanced by the savings incurred by not wasting products (a failure cost). These changes have also resulted in reductions of failure and intangible quality costs that arise when outdated materials jeopardize the quality of patient care.

 Assignment

On the basis of this reading, discuss how quality costs were used in decision making.

CASE STUDY 12.2
Quality Costs

This case is the third of three related cases found in Chapters 8, 9, and 12. These cases seek to link information from the three chapters in order to resolve quality issues. It is not necessary to have completed the cases in the other chapters in order to understand or complete this case.

PART 1

Max's B-B-Q Inc. manufactures top-of-the-line barbeque tools. The tools include forks, spatulas, knives, spoons, and shish-kebab skewers. Max's fabricates both the metal parts of the tools and the resin handles. These are then riveted together to create the tools (Figure C12.2.1).

Max's performs a final inspection before the tools are placed into kits for selling. Each quarter, Max's makes more than 1,000,000 tools. Of these, approximately 240,000 are inspected for a variety of problems, including handle rivets, fork tines, handle cranks, dents, pits, burrs, scratches, handle color, blade grinds, crooked blades, and others. Any tool that has a defect is either returned to the line to be reworked or is scrapped. Figure C12.2.2 provides information for their first-quarter inspection results.

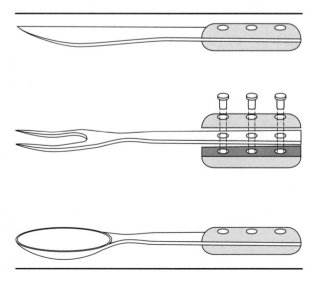

Figure C12.2.1 Barbeque Tools

FINAL INSPECTION
DEPARTMENT 8
FEBRUARY 1996

DEFECT	Table Knife	Steak Knife	Paring Knife	Filet Knife	Basting Spoon	Ladle Spoon	Perforated Spoon	Skewer
Bad handle rivets							1	
Bad steel	37				1			
Bad tines								
Bad/bent points	16							
Bent					1			
Buff concave								
Burn	146	57						
Burned handles	1							
Burrs	24	14						
Cloud on blades								
Cracked handle		32						
Cracked steel	1							
Crooked blades								
DD edge	41	2						
Dented								
Edge	31							
Finish								
Grind in blade							1	
Haft at rivets								
Hafting marks handles	64				4		3	
Hafting marks steel								
Handle color	27	182				5		3
Heat induct	110	37					2	
High handle rivets								
High-speed buff								
Hit blades								
Hit handle	239							
Holder marks								

Figure C12.2.2 Inspection Results

(continued)

FINAL INSPECTION
DEPARTMENT 8
FEBRUARY 1996

DEFECT	Table Knife	Steak Knife	Paring Knife	Filet Knife	Basting Spoon	Ladle Spoon	Perforated Spoon	Skewer
Honing								
Narrow blades	4							
Nicked and scratched	105	10			9	2	7	
Open at rivet								
Open handles							1	
Open steel								
Pitted blades		1					1	
Pitted bolsters								
Raw backs								
Raw fronts								
Rebend								
Recolor concave	2	43						
Rehone								
Reruns								
Rivet								
Scratched blades	105	53		1	12	2	4	
Scratched rivets								
Seams/holes	11	50						
Seconds				2				
Stained blades	84	18			5	1		
Stained rivets								
Vendor rejects								
Water lines					15			
Wrap	8							
Total Inspected	32,000	28,811	5	277	3,145	1,504	2,008	1,805
Total Accepted	30,944	28,312	5	274	3,098	1,494	1,988	1,802
Total Rejected	1,056	499	0	3	47	10	20	3

Figure C12.2.2 *(continued)*

Assignment

Create a Pareto chart with the information provided in Figure C12.2.2. Are any of the categories related? Can they be grouped in any way? What problems should be tackled first?

 Assignment

Given the present situation, what types of quality costs will Max's incur? Do you agree with the way they are operating? Why or why not? Where should they be making their investment? In what types of prevention costs do you feel they should be investing in order to avoid other quality costs?

PART 2

Recently, Max's hired you as a process engineer. Your first assignment is to study routine tool wear on the company's stamping machine. In particular, you will be studying tool-wear patterns for the tools used to create knife blades.

In the stamping process, the tooling wears slightly during each stroke of the press as the punch shears through the material. As the tool wears, the part features become smaller. Although the knife has specifications of 10 mm ± 0.025 mm, undersized parts must be scrapped. During their use, tools can be resharpened to enable them to produce parts within specification. To reduce manufacturing costs and simplify machine scheduling, it is critical to pull the tool and perform maintenance only when absolutely necessary. It is very important for scheduling, costing, and quality purposes that the average number of strokes, or tool run length, be determined. Knowing the average number of strokes that can be performed by a tool enables routine maintenance to be scheduled.

It is the plant manager's philosophy that tool maintenance be scheduled proactively. When a tool is pulled unexpectedly, the tool maintenance area may not have time to work on it immediately. Presses without tools don't run, and if they are not running, they are not making money. As the process engineer studying tool wear, you must develop a prediction for when the tool should be pulled and resharpened.

The following information is available from the tool maintenance department.

- The average number of strokes for a tool is 45,000.
- The standard deviation is 2,500 strokes.
- A total of 25 mm can be ground off a punch before it is no longer useful.
- Each regrind to sharpen a punch removes 1 mm of punch life (25 total regrinds per tool).

- The cost to regrind is
  - 2 hours of press downtime to remove and reinsert tool, at $300/hour
  - 5 hours of tool maintenance time, at $65/hour
  - 5 hours of downtime while press is not being used, at $300/hour
- Average wait time for unplanned tool regrind is 15 hours at $300/hour.
- Because of the large number of strokes per tool regrind, this is considered to be a continuous distribution. The normal curve probability distribution is applicable.

 Assignment

Your first assignment as process engineer is to develop a prediction routine for tool wear. As mentioned previously, the plant manager's chief concern is ensuring planned tool regrinds. Early wearout—and thus an unplanned tool pull—can be caused by a variety of factors, including changes in the hardness of the material being punched, lack of lubrication, the hardness of the tool steel, and the width of the gap between the punch and the die. Key part dimensions are monitored using $\overline{X}$ and R charts. These charts reveal when the tool needs to be reground in order to preserve part quality.

When a tool wears out earlier than expected, the tool room may not have time to work on the tool immediately. While waiting for the tool to be reground, the press and its operators will be idle. The plant manager would prefer that tools be pulled early in their wearout phase in order to avoid the chance of an unexpected tool pull. He would like to pull the tool for regrind at 40,000 strokes. What is the chance that the tool will be pulled for regrind before 40,000 strokes?

PART 3

Now that you have been at Max's B-B-Q Inc. for a while, the plant manager asks you to assist the production scheduling department with pricing data on a high-volume job requiring knife blades for the company's best customer. As you know, it is the plant manager's philosophy to be proactive when scheduling tool maintenance (regrinds) rather than to have to unexpectedly pull the tool. However, pricing will be a very important factor in selling this job to the customer. Essentially, the plant manager wants no unplanned tool pulls but sales needs pricing cost reductions. The production scheduler would like a tool-regrind schedule that results in minimal inventory.

 Assignment

You will soon be meeting with the plant manager and the managers from sales and production scheduling. They are expecting you to have an answer to the question, Given the need to balance maximizing tool use, minimizing inventory, minimizing production disruption, and minimizing cost, how many strokes should you recommend to run this tool before pulling for a regrind?

Create a graph that shows the number of unplanned pulls versus the number of strokes. The graph should comprise at least six data points. Next complete the following spreadsheet, showing the costs of each individual's plan. Using the graph and the spreadsheet, prepare a response for the question, How many strokes should the tool be run before pulling it for a regrind? Your analysis should include answers to the following questions: How will this number balance tool use, cost, inventory, and production disruption? What are the economics of this situation? What quality costs exist?

	Plant Manager	Production Scheduler	Sales Manager	You
Strokes Before Pull	40,000	42,000	43,000	
Number of Pulls	25	25	25	
Production Over Life of Tool	1,000,000	1,050,000	1,075,000	
Cost of Each Pull	$2,425	$2,425	$2,425	$2,425
Additional Cost of an Unplanned Pull	$4,500	$4,500	$4,500	$4,500
Chance of Unplanned Pulls				
Total Additional Cost due to Unplanned Pulls				
Total Cost				

13

Product Liability

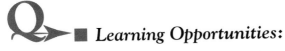

■ *Learning Opportunities:*

1. To introduce the concept of product liability
2. To broaden the reader's understanding of how designs are affected by product liability issues
3. To show how product design and development programs can help protect companies from product liability issues
4. To show how quality-assurance programs can help protect companies from product liability issues ■

- Only two of the original eighteen American firms making football helmets exist, due in part to multiple product liability suits. (*Business Week,* February 7, 1994)
- The only safe and effective antinausea drug, Bendectin, has been taken off the market because the cost of product liability insurance reached $10 million a year, over 80 percent of the annual sales. (*Nation's Business,* February 1986)
- Keen Corporation is the 18th asbestos manufacturer to declare bankruptcy due to product liability claims. (*Business Week,* February 7, 1994)
- A nationwide shortage of vaccine to protect children from diphtheria and whooping cough developed when only one company chose to continue to manufacture it, given the high liability insurance costs. (*Nation's Business,* February 1986)
- Twenty percent of a stepladder's cost goes to pay for liability insurance. (*Nation's Business,* February 1986)
- In the Washington, D.C., area, the Girl Scouts must use the profits from 87,000 boxes of cookies to cover the organization's liability insurance even though they have never been sued. (*Newsweek,* March 20, 1995)
- Due to product liability costs, production of private aircraft at Piper Aircraft Corporation fell from 17,000 planes in 1979 to only 1,535 by 1989. (*Forbes,* November 8, 1993)
- General aviation aircraft production reached a high of 17,811 planes built in 1978; by 1994 only 928 planes were produced. This decrease in planes produced resulted in the loss of over 100,000 jobs. (*AOPA,* July 2001)
- The product liability system is a $125 billion burden on the nation's economy, raising consumer prices, undercutting innovation, and depleting corporate resources that would be better spent on capital improvement, worker training, and Research and Development. (Joint Economic Committee, U.S. Congress, 2001)

Examples of the Results of Product Liability Losses

$\mathbf{A}$ *perfectly safe product is one that can do no objectionable harm at any time, under any circumstances. Relatively few such perfect products exist. Since this is the case, much must be done in the design and manufacture of a product or the provision of a service to give the consumer the safest product or service possible. In a society so highly dependent on products and services produced by others, are there ways of providing for society's needs without exposing the provider to excessive product liability costs? Product liability costs can add 15 to 30 percent to the cost of a product. This chapter provides some background in product liability as well as ideas for designing and creating safer products and services.*

THE EVOLUTION OF PRODUCT LIABILITY

The ability of an individual to recover damages after being injured by a product or service has changed considerably over time. Product liability law is case law, meaning that there are few, if any, federal mandates or legislative actions. Because it is based on common law—the decisions of judges and juries in individual cases—product liability law reflects changing social and economic conditions. Product liability laws and the outcomes of the trials vary from state to state.

A *lawsuit is a civil suit seeking money damages for injuries to either a person or property, or both.* Product liability lawsuits involve two parties: plaintiffs and defendants. **Plaintiffs** *are the injured parties who file suit in a court of law. The* **defendant** *is the person or company against whom a claim or suit is filed.* Product liability cases may be brought for many reasons, including product defects, design deficiencies, inadequate guarding, or inadequate warnings.

Negligence and Privity

Negligence *occurs when the person manufacturing the product or providing the service has been careless or unreasonable.* Negligence cases focus on the conduct of the manufacturer. In negligence cases, the injured party must prove that the defendant failed to exercise due care in the creation of the product or provision of the service. An example of failure to exercise due care would be the case where a manufacturer or service provider fails to keep current with technology. Negligence cases place the burden on the plaintiff, because it is the plaintiff's responsibility to show that the defendant's conduct was not what it should have been.

One of the earliest product liability cases based on negligence, *Winterbottom v. Wright* (1842), involved a defective mail coach. The case was settled on the basis of the concept of privity. Under **privity,** *a suit cannot be filed unless a contract (an agreement) exists between the parties of the suit.* In today's world, the concept of privity means that you would not be able to sue the maker of a toaster oven that caused a fire, unless you had bought that toaster oven directly from the manufacturer. It wasn't until 1916 that privity was no longer considered a suitable defense for negligence cases.

In the 1916 landmark case, *MacPherson v. Buick Motor Company,* the court found that an auto manufacturer had a product liability obligation to a car buyer whose car wheels were defective, even though the sales contract was between the buyer and the dealer. Presiding Judge Kellogg held that

> under the circumstances the defendant owed a duty to all purchasers of its automobiles to make a reasonable inspection and test to ascertain whether the wheels purchased and put in use by it were reasonably fit for the purposes for which it used them, and, if it fails to exercise care in that respect, that it is responsible for any defect which would have been discovered by any such reasonable inspection and test.*

Without the concept of privity, though the injured party must still prove negligence, a manufacturer's duties extend to the ultimate user of the product.

---

*MacPherson v. Buick Motor Company, 1916.

Strict Liability

In 1962, *Greenman v. Yuba* brought another change to product liability cases by introducing the concept of strict liability. Under **strict liability**, *a manufacturer who makes and sells a defective product has committed a fault. A product is considered defectively made if it has a defect that causes it to be unreasonably dangerous and the defect is the reason for an injury.* Even though there is no evidence of negligence, the manufacturer can be held strictly liable in tort. By placing the item on the market, the manufacturer has said the product is fit for use. The concept of strict liability is basically sound, although it ensures that the costs of injuries are carried by the manufacturer. It assumes that *the person was injured through no fault of his or her own; in other words, there was no* **contributory negligence.** The court's mission has changed from finding fault to determining the amount of compensation due the injured party. Some people feel that the explosion of product liability cases can be traced to the strict liability in tort doctrine.

WARRANTIES

Two kinds of warranties exist: expressed and implied. An **expressed warranty** *is part of the conditions of sale.* Expressed warranties can be written or oral, found in advertising or contracts. Expressed warranties should state the following:

- What is covered?
- What is not covered?
- When does the coverage begin?
- How long does the coverage last?
- What will the company do in the event of problems?
- How and where can the consumer get warranty service?
- Are any state laws applicable?

An **implied warranty** *is implied by law rather than by the seller.* Merchantability, the act of putting the product on the market or providing a service, implies that the product or service is fit for normal foreseeable use. The buyer purchases the product on the reasonable assumption that the product will be reliable. Merchantability also implies that the manufacturer contemplated the known risks associated with the product or service, who the intended users of the product or service were, what the necessary warnings and instructions were, and the foreseeable misuse. In 1960, the *Henninsen v. Bloomfield* breach of implied warranty case removed the concept of privity from contract cases. The judge determined that merchantability and fitness for use extends to the reasonably expected end user of the product. Several of the examples in this text, including Example 12.4, describe how warranty costs can drive continuous improvement efforts.

LIABILITY LOSS CONTROL PROGRAMS

Liability exposure exists at every phase of product development or service provision, from conception to the first preliminary design; through all design stages, development, and testing of prototypes; into the manufacturing phases, including negotiation of contracts with suppliers; through actual manufacture, testing, and assembly; into packaging, labeling, and use instructions; product service; and ultimately to the methods of promotion, marketing, and distribution, including warranty periods and service arrangements. In a product liability suit, a plaintiff must show that a defect was the cause of the injury or loss. Product or service defects can come from several sources: a flaw in the manufacturing process, a design defect, a packaging defect, or failure to warn of the dangers. Manufacturing defects may be evident in a weld that breaks under normal usage or a cracked part that causes an equipment malfunction. Design defects such as those that caused the collapse of the Kansas City hotel walkway may be due to material or weld failures, sharp edges or corners, failure to provide guarding and safety devices, a concealed danger, or just poor design, such as locating a chain saw muffler below the handle. Defective packaging may cause an accident or injury. The Tylenol poisonings are an example where proper packaging could have alerted consumers to tampering. After these poisonings, many packages have added shrink-wrapped safety seals to make tampering more visible.

Service and information industries are also vulnerable to product liability action. A city may be sued if it fails to trim roadside shrubbery and an accident occurs because of limited sight distances. A creator of software may be sued because a software glitch dropped an item from a quotation or bid. The U.S. government may be sued because a National Weather Service forecast predicted fair weather when a severe storm was developing.

In the case of a design defect, an inadvertent error may have occurred, from misplacement of a decimal or an error in reading a table. A design defect may have resulted from a conscious design choice that was considered acceptable at the time. When a manufacturing defect causes the injury or loss, the defendants have little with which to defend themselves. To protect themselves, many companies have developed liability loss control programs. These programs have two major aspects: product design and development and quality assurance. In some companies, reliability testing may also be a component of a liability loss control program.

Product Design and Development

To avoid creating a dangerous product, designers should consider the usefulness and desirability of their product. Once it has been determined that the product has value for the consumer, companies should follow several steps to minimize risks.

1. **Design to Remove Unsafe Aspects.** First and foremost, the product or service should be designed without a possible danger or hazard. This is the most important step to making a product or service safe for the consumer. All avenues of design modifications should be studied before allowing a product to be manufactured or a service to be provided if that service or product is inherently dangerous. Other, perhaps safer, products or services on the market should be studied.

Designers should consider the user and determine the likelihood of injury and the seriousness of that injury. Techniques like preliminary hazard analysis and failure modes and effects analysis (Figure 13.1) are invaluable for determining product

Preliminary Hazard Analysis (PHA). A Preliminary Hazard Analysis is an inductive technique which identifies hazards. A PHA can focus on the hazards in systems, products, components, assemblies, or subsystems. A PHA can also be used to study the hazards associated with situations and events. A PHA assesses risk by identifying accident possibilities and qualitatively evaluating the severity of a possible injury or damage associated with the accident. A complete PHA will provide proposals for safety measures and improvements.

Failure Mode and Effects Analysis (FMEA). An FMEA is an inductive method which evaluates the variety of ways (modes) a system, subsystem, or component can fail, the frequency at which it may fail, and consequences associated with failure. An FMEA assesses risk by identifying the probability of failure and the severity of that failure. A complete FMEA will provide proposals for safety measures and improvements.

Fault Tree Analysis (FTA). Unlike the PHA or FMEA, an FTA is a deductive method. It begins with the undesirable event and determines all of the elements that must be in place in order for this undesirable event to occur. Upon completion, the FTA will provide proposals for safety measures and improvements.

Figure 13.1   Hazard Analysis Techniques

hazards. While brainstorming, designers should ask questions like: What level of understanding can a reasonable and prudent user of the product or service be expected to have? How obvious is the danger? Does the public have common knowledge of the danger? And finally, if a danger exists in a product or service, can the danger be eliminated without seriously affecting the design, form, or function of the product? If the answer to this is yes, then it is the company's responsibility to do so.

Manufacturers and service providers should also investigate the area of product or service misuse. For every product or service on the market, there exists the potential for misuse by the consumer. Designers should strive to determine every foreseeable use for their product or service and design out potential hazards. Creative brainstorming sessions with future customers are often fertile grounds for discovering future misuses of the product. Designing with misuse in mind encourages designers to recheck their designs, guards, and product warnings.

2. **Guard Against Unsafe Use.** If the danger cannot be designed out of the product, or if the product is inherently dangerous, the second step a designer should take involves guarding the user against the danger. Guards prevent users from gaining access to the area that would cause them injury. When the potential exists for misuse of the product or service, guards or design features should be in place to prevent the misuse. Care must be taken to ensure that the guards are not made so inconvenient that people circumvent them, thus defeating the purpose. A list of possible hazards is provided in Figure 13.2.

3. **Provide Product Warnings and Instructions.** If the product hazards cannot be designed or guarded out of a product, then a designer's final recourse is to warn the user. In both negligence and strict liability cases, there is a duty to warn. If the

Crushing between objects
Shearing
Cutting
Entanglement
Drawing-in
Trapping
Impact
Puncture
Abrasion
Exposed electrical wiring
Thermal (heat/cold)
Noise
Exposure to gases or fumes
Fire or explosion
Unexpected start-up of equipment

Figure 13.2   Possible Hazards

manufacturer has pertinent safety information for the product, then they must pass on this knowledge to the consumer through a warning. Warnings should describe the foreseeable risk of harm that is inherent in the product or that may arise from any intended or reasonably anticipated use of the product at the time the product is marketed. In the past, the courts have found that a lack of warnings or instructions rendered the product unreasonably dangerous. Warnings and instructions are not the same. Warnings call attention to hazards or dangers, while instructions provide information for effective use of the product.

Warnings must be specific and must describe the consequences of their being ignored. Warnings should be highly visible and easily comprehensible. In today's world, warnings should be pictorial in nature or multilingual to be effective. If the warning is written, it should be clearly worded in simple language. Warnings should discuss safe installation, operation, cleaning, and repair practices. The consequences of misusing the product should be clearly stated. Warnings are a last resort, to be used when designing out or guarding against an inherent danger has proven infeasible. People tend to become accustomed to warnings and ignore them, even where there is a high probability of injury.

4. **Design to Standards.** A product should be designed to comply with industry standards. While designing to standards does not ensure a safe product, standards do tend to create safer products. Standards also encourage those providing products and services to remain current in their field. State-of-the-art knowledge enhances the design and production of a product.

5. **Conduct Design Reviews.** One of the most important aspects in a product's life cycle is a series of design reviews. During design reviews, those closest to the product or service determine whether or not it will perform as expected in a safe and reliable manner. The most common types of design review are an *introductory design* or *proposal review*, a *preliminary design review*, a *final design review*, and a *postproduction design review*. During each of these reviews, the ability to manufacture or provide the

From all points of view, is this a reasonably safe product for its intended use and intended
   end user?
How could this product fail?
Will the end user be using this product to perform a hazardous job?
Potentially, how could an end user misuse this product?
Are there any obvious dangers in this product? Any hidden?
Have any safety devices been left out in the design?
What kind of warning labels or instructions are necessary?
How does this product compare with those of our competitors?
What are the applicable government regulations?
Under what conditions will this product be used? What are the extreme conditions?
What type of product changes may occur in the foreseeable future?
How is the product to be marketed?

Figure 13.3   Design Review Questions

product or service is reviewed, as is the usability of the product or service by the customer. Reliability and liability issues are also discussed. Those involved in the design
review process should ask questions similar to those presented in Figure 13.3.

   6. **Advertise and Market Wisely.** Any advertisement should support a valid
product application and usage. Occasionally, a company creates potential product
misuse situations through its advertisements, marketing materials, and sales personnel. A manufacturer's best defense against product liability problems involves
developing advertising and warranty claims that provide completely accurate
information concerning the product's life, safety, and performance expectations.
Advertising claims about a product's life cycle, safety, material durability, environmental side effects, and usage must be truthful. Advertisements and marketing materials that show the product performing tasks it is not designed to do set the stage
for misuse of the product by the consumer. Product liability loss prevention is not
the sole responsibility of the product designer or manufacturer; misrepresentation
and exaggeration in advertisements and marketing materials may also be involved.
Proper training of distributors, dealers, and sales personnel can lower product liability costs by enabling them to give guidance and training to purchasers of the
product. Increasing a consumer's knowledge of the product and its uses can greatly
reduce the potential for harm.

EXAMPLE 13.1   Company Consciousness of Product Liability

In the past decade, the design of lawn mowers and their attachments has changed
dramatically. An inherently dangerous product, lawn mowers are commonly used
pieces of equipment in the lives of most suburban homeowners. The necessity of
mowing a lawn with something larger than an old-style human-powered lawn mower
has created a product that consumers see as useful, desirable, and valuable. In the
past decade, lawn mower manufacturers have taken the steps described in this
chapter to minimize risks.

Step 1. Design to Remove Unsafe Aspects.   Since lawn mowers are inherently dangerous, it is not possible to completely design out every possible danger or hazard. But within the lawn mower there are many changes that can be made to the design to improve the safety of the equipment. One such modification is to place the muffler in a location that makes it difficult for users to burn themselves on the hot cover. There have been lawn mowers that have been designed so that the muffler or a hot engine component is placed near the gas tank opening. Designs such as these reflect little thought to designing out hazards. The user has not been considered nor has the likelihood of burn injuries or the seriousness of those injuries. Good designers investigate all avenues of design modifications before allowing a product to be manufactured or a service to be provided that is inherently dangerous.

Step 2. Guard Against Unsafe Use.   It is in this area that lawn mowers have undergone the greatest amount of change. Since all the dangerous aspects cannot be designed out of lawn mowers, the addition of guards has changed their look. Guards on the platforms of riding lawn mowers and on the backs of push lawn mowers prevent users from gaining access to the blades. One major safety issue surrounds cleaning the duct that spews out cut grass. Here a high potential exists for misuse of the mower. People reach in to clear the duct, placing their hands or feet in close proximity to the blades. Push lawn mowers currently on the market have handles that the operator must hold in order to keep the blades spinning. It is extremely difficult for a person to reach the duct while holding the handle; thus this type of guard prevents the person from cleaning the duct while the blades are still turning.

Step 3. Provide Product Warnings.   Lawn mowers currently on the market are accompanied by a long list of warnings. Since the product hazards cannot be completely designed or guarded out, the user must be warned. Figure 13.4 shows warnings that are specific and that describe the consequences of ignoring them. The warnings are pictorial and simply and clearly worded. In the instruction booklet, the warnings discuss safe installation, operation, cleaning, and repair practices.

Step 4. Design to Standards.   Many of the design, guarding, and warning changes made to lawn mowers are a direct result of industry standards, which were created to help ensure a safer product.

Many mower manufacturers have also instituted quality-assurance programs. At the plant level, these programs link the activities of design, marketing, manufacturing, service provision, packaging, shipping, and service. New product design reviews study the basic designs of lawn mowers being offered. These reviews consider hazards, quality information, and consumer feedback to improve mower design. Information from consumer complaints, warranty claims, and product recalls is carefully investigated and the results of those investigations are used to improve the product.

Q

Product Recalls

Sometimes in the course of providing a product for consumers, it is necessary to remove that product from the marketplace. When this occurs, customers who have purchased the product must be informed of the dangers associated with it. They must also

Figure 13.4   Product Warnings

know what to do to remedy the unsafe situation related to the product. When a company considers recalling a product, they base their decision on their answers to the following questions:

- What is the utility of the product?
- What is the nature of the injury that the product might cause?

- What is society's need for the product?
- Who is exposed to the dangerous aspect of the product?
- What is the risk of injury associated with using the product?
- Are other, safer products available?
- What other information is available about the product or the customers who use it?

When a recall occurs, the primary objective of the recall is to immediately communicate accurate and understandable information about the defect, its associated hazard, and necessary corrective action to the general public. Naturally, to limit liability, the company engaged in the recall is interested in locating and removing all defective products from the distribution system and from consumers as quickly as possible. Many companies go to great efforts to design informational material to motivate retailers and the media to get the word out. In some cases, incentives are added to encourage the consumers to act quickly on the recall.

Quality-Assurance Involvement

A program to reduce the risks associated with product liability must embrace design, marketing, manufacturing, service provision, packaging, shipping, and service. To enhance their ability to deal with product liability issues, a manufacturer or service provider will want to have a strong quality assurance system in place. As more companies implement quality systems like ISO 9000, the courts uphold them as benchmarks when discussing whether or not a manufacturer or service provider has been remiss in their duties to their customers. Courts no longer solely focus on the incident surrounding the case; they are interested in the quality assurance procedures in the company. Specifically, how good is a company's system at preventing and controlling risk? Having a quality assurance system is only part of the story; being able to show proof of that system's effectiveness is also necessary. Whether or not a company utilizes a quality system like ISO 9000, their quality system should have the following components:

- Documented work method policies, procedures, and processes
- Documented production policies, procedures, and processes
- Documented testing policies, procedures, and processes
- Design review policies and procedures
- Hazard analysis procedures
- An effective reliability testing program
- Documented compliance to government standards
- An effective engineering change order program
- An effective supplier certification and selection program
- Documented inspection policies and procedures
- A documented recall program that can be implemented if needed
- Documented customer input and responses
- Education

A good quality assurance system will educate those working for a company in the necessity of good communication with customers and suppliers, both internal and external. Education will provide information about key issues to address in everything from the wording of purchase orders, warnings, and instructions, to the selection of suppliers, to holding design reviews and handling sensitive design issues, to interaction with customers, accident investigation, and product recalls. Training in techniques such as failure modes and effects analysis and preliminary hazard analysis is also needed.

In order to ensure that product liability issues are tackled before they become a major expense for a company, some companies designate a product liability expert. This individual develops a thorough technical knowledge of all of the products or services provided by the company. Normally this person also has an understanding of the legal issues surrounding product liability cases. Individuals best suited for this type of work display a high degree of professionalism and diplomacy as well as technical knowledge.

  REAL TOOLS FOR REAL LIFE

Using Quality Assurance Concepts to Reduce Product Liability Risk

In compression, concrete is unbeatable. In tension, though, concrete is fragile. In order to provide concrete with tensile strength, steel, in the form of rebar, is inserted. When two pieces of rebar need to be connected, a mechanical splice is used. Mechanical splices can play a critical role when placed in between two concrete forms. Splice failure could, unfortunately, contribute to the collapse of a structure. If this were to happen, the manufacturer of the mechanical splice could be held strictly liable. Under the concept of strict liability, a manufacturer who makes and sells a defective product, in this case, the splice, has committed a fault. A splice would be considered defectively made if it has a defect that causes it to be unreasonably dangerous and the defect is the reason for an injury.

Mechanical splice manufacturers utilize quality assurance programs in order to reduce the risks associated with product liability. These programs monitor splice production from the inception of the design, to manufacturing, packaging, and shipping, to product applications in the field. Quality assurance systems include reliability testing, compliance to standards, effective engineering change order systems, documented inspection policies and procedures, and documented, effective responses to customer issues.

Recently, a customer received 220 setting bars, rebar with a mechanical splice pre-installed on each end (Figure 13.5). Unfortunately, they were longer than the length specified. Since the bars were to be placed in between two concrete forms, the length specified by the customer is very important. Construction specifications set the walls a fixed distance apart. If the setting bar is too long, it cannot be placed between the walls. If the bar is too short, one end of the assembly cannot be nailed tight to the form, allowing concrete to get between the splice and form and preventing the splice bar from being installed in the next phase of construction. Fortunately the error was caught before any of the bars was used.

This type of external failure, the customer receiving setting bars of an incorrect length, was an expensive cost of quality issue for MM Corporation. Replacement parts were made ($1055) and shipped ($72) at MM Corporation's expense. They also had to pay to retrieve and destroy the incorrectly made setting bars at a cost of $146. The total loss amounted to $1273.

DOUBLE ENDED SETTING BARS

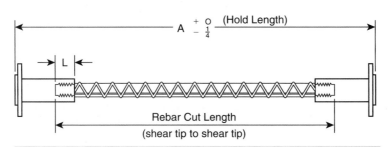

Figure 13.5   Real Tools for Real Life: Rebar with Mechanical Splice Pre-installed

An even greater concern surrounded the product liability issues. Had the setting bars actually been used and failure occurred, MM Corporation would have been held strictly liable. The splice assembly would have been considered defectively made, not made to the customer's specifications. This defect would have caused the product (the structure) to be unreasonably dangerous, and the defective splice assemblies would have been the reason behind any injuries. The product liability costs could have been high enough to bankrupt the company.

After having rectified the customer order and ensured that the incorrectly made setting bars were destroyed, a quality assurance team was created to determine the root cause behind the setting bars being made too long.

When the customer contacted MM Corporation to complain about the defective setting bars, a corrective action report was generated (Figure 13.6). The team used this corrective action report as a starting place in order to construct a WHY-WHY diagram (Figure 13.7). From this diagram, they quickly determined four things:

- The finished setting bar dimension was to be 9 inches.
- When orders are placed, the person processing the order calculates the cut length for the rebar raw stock.
- The cut length calculation is not reviewed by anyone once the calculation is completed.
- The finished pieces are not compared with the specified dimensions shown on the order.

With this information, the team realized that a system does not exist to verify either the correctness of the calculations or the correctness of the finished bar assemblies. Based on their findings, the team rectified this situation by creating:

- An easier raw rebar sizing calculation system for order processors
- A quick check section on the order document to be used to verify calculations (Figure 13.8)
- A process change to include the inspection of the first completed piece, using the customer order requirements as the specifications.

CORRECTIVE ACTION RESPONSE

Part Number: PA 32 / R		S. O. Number 204	Issue Date: July 5, 2004
Customer: TVC		Initiated By: MM	C.A.R. Number: 21
Contact Person: K. SMITH		Phone No.: 555–1212	C.A.R. Due Date: July 12, 2004
Lot Size: 160	Total Nonconforming 80 + 80 160		Customer No.: TVC 123

1. Team Members

Champion: M. MINK   Team Captain: CAROL CELIUS

Team Members: DAVID, DON, PAUL, CAROL, MIKE

2. Problem Description (Definition)

    Parts were received by the customer @ 10 1/4" long (A Dimension) and the order was for 9" (A dimension). The nonconformance was discovered on July 5 at the job site.

3. Containment Action(s):

	Completion Date: July 10, 2004
Replacement assemblies were manufactured and shipped on July 10, 2001.	Verified By: M. MINK

4. Root Cause(s):

	Verification Date:
	Verified By:

5. Interim Corrective Action(s):

	Implementation Date:
	Verified By:

6. Permanent Corrective Action(s):

	Implementation Date:
	Verified By:

7. Actions to Prevent Recurrence:

	Implementation Date:
	Verified By:

8. Closed by Initiator:

Signature:	Date Closed:

Figure 13.6   Corrective Action Response Form

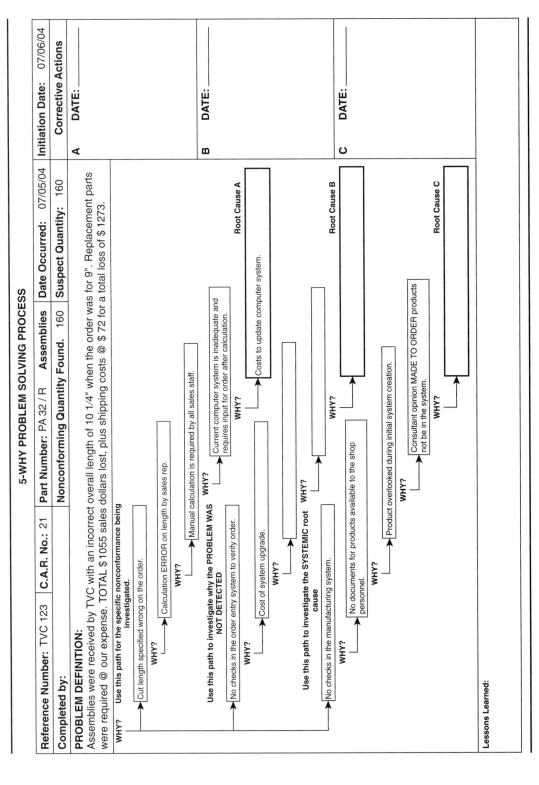

Figure 13.7 WHY-WHY Diagram

DOUBLE ENDED SETTING BARS

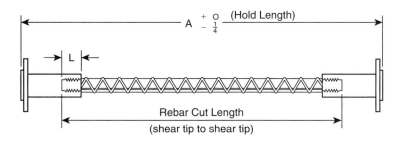

Rebar Size	Rebar Cut Length
No. 4	A – 2
No. 5	A – 2 1/4
No. 6	A – 2 3/8
No. 7	A – 2 3/4
No. 8	A – 3 3/8
No. 9	A – 4
No. 10	A – 4 5/8
No. 11	A – 5 1/8

Figure 13.8   Real Tools for Real Life: Order Document

The team recorded their results and planned changes on the corrective action report (Figure 13.9).

In this case, sound problem identification and problem-solving techniques resulted in improved ordering and manufacturing processes. Having processes in place that prevent errors from occurring can significantly reduce future product liability costs.

Product liability costs manifest themselves in many ways, including recall, replacement, and repair costs. Prevention and appraisal quality costs will also increase when a company is confronted with a product liability issue. While most people recognize the costs associated with legal defenses, awards, and liability insurance, few realize that product liability has an adverse impact in other areas. Faulty products or services create dissatisfied customers; coupled with product liability disputes, they may damage a company's reputation on a broad scale. Product liability costs may cause a company

CORRECTIVE ACTION RESPONSE

Part Number: PA 32 / R		S. O. Number 204	Issue Date: July 5, 2004
Customer: TVC		Initiated By: MM	C.A.R. Number: 21
Contact Person: K. SMITH		Phone No.: 555–1212	C.A.R. Due Date: July 12, 2004
Lot Size: 160	Total Nonconforming 80 + 80 160		Customer No.: TVC 123

1. Team Members

Champion: M. MINK   **Team Captain:** CAROL CELIUS

Team Members: DAVID, DON, PAUL, CAROL, MIKE

2. Problem Description (Definition)

    Parts were received by the customer @ 10 1/4" long (A Dimension) and the order was for 9" (A dimension). The nonconformance was discovered on July 5 at the job site.

3. Containment Action(s):

	Completion Date: July 10, 2004
Replacement assemblies were manufactured and shipped on July 10, 2001.	Verified By: M. MINK

4. Root Cause(s):

	Verification Date: July 10, 2004
The manufacturing documentation system was never in place for this product. Reference 5 WHY report attached. If there is an error on the order it may be undetected in manufacturing.	Verified By: M. MINK

5. Interim Corrective Action(s):

	Implementation Date: July 12, 2004
Trained Sales staff.	Verified By: CAROL CELIUS

6. Permanent Corrective Action(s):

	Implementation Date: July 12, 2004
Created sales quote for the product line that calculates the cut length.	Verified By: M. MINK

7. Actions to Prevent Recurrence:

	Implementation Date: July 12, 2004
Create setup order that calculates the cut length.	Verified By: M. MINK

8. Closed by Initiator:

Signature:	Date Closed:

Figure 13.9   Corrective Action Response Form

to decide against introducing new products or to discontinue existing product lines entirely. If new product introductions have decreased, then there is little encouragement to continue product research. Other companies report lost market share as a consequence of product liability issues. Lost market share can result in laid-off workers, closed production plants, or the decision to move production offshore. To remain competitive, companies must emphasize product design and quality assurance to minimize the impact of product liability.

PRODUCT LIABILITY SUITS

The Plaintiff's Actions

The plaintiff, the injured party, may file a lawsuit that alleges that the provider of a product or service is guilty of breach of warranty and negligence as well as being strictly liable. Plaintiffs are required to show that the product was defective or unreasonably dangerous, that the defect was the proximate cause of harm, and that the defect was in the product when it left the manufacturer. In strict liability cases, plaintiffs do not need to prove manufacturer's negligence. In strict liability cases, it does not matter if the injured party acted in a careless and unreasonable manner (contributory negligence). Strict liability focuses on the product. The behavior of the manufacturer and the reasonableness in which it acted is not a factor. A plaintiff who chooses to sue under warranty law needs to prove that the product was not fit for the purposes for which it was advertised.

The Defendant's Actions

In a product liability suit, the defendant must establish that the product or service provided is not defective or unreasonably dangerous. The defendant must prove that no defect existed in the product at the time of manufacture or when the service was provided. It is also important that the defendant show that the product or service was not the actual cause of the accident or injury. The defendant may do this by showing that the plaintiff exhibited bad judgment, improperly used the product, conducted improper maintenance, or changed the product after its manufacture. In essence, the manufacturer of a product or provider of a service must prove that they were and continue to be a company concerned about the products and services they provide. The defendants will need to provide documented evidence verifying that they took every reasonable step possible to ensure a safe and reliable product or service by complying with all relative specifications, codes, and standards.

The Court's Actions

When deciding a product liability case, the court examines the product or service as well as its defective aspects. It considers the usefulness and desirability of the product to the public as a whole. The availability of other suitable, safer substitutes for the product is also investigated. While making this comparison, the court determines if the manufacturer could have eliminated the unsafe nature of the product without impairing its usefulness or making it too expensive to maintain its utility. The safety of the product is examined to determine the likelihood that it will cause injury and the probable seriousness of that injury. Some products or services are inherently dangerous (for example, knives and swimming pools), so the court expects that the public had some common knowledge of the product's dangerous aspects. The court also questions the probability of an injury occurring, given reasonable care on the part of the user. The adequacy of the instructions and warnings, as well as the environment where the product is used, also plays a role. Courts have expanded their view of warranties and no longer look solely at the character of the product; they now also consider the consumer and public interest factors.

A court judges whether or not a product or service is unreasonably dangerous by considering several factors. Would a reasonable company market the product or service if they knew of this defect? Products and services are also judged on the basis of consumer expectations. Is the product or service more dangerous than a consumer could contemplate? Given the public's ordinary knowledge of the product, is the danger open and obvious? This approach raises the issue of who is a reasonable consumer with ordinary knowledge of the product or service. Can a four-year-old who uses a swimming pool understand its dangers? Can an average adult understand the consequences of using chemicals in the yard? Risk of injury versus the utility of the product is also judged. When an inherently dangerous product, such as a knife, is judged, its usefulness to society is considered.

The Expert Witness

Both defendants and plaintiffs may choose to support their arguments with the testimony of expert witnesses. Expert witnesses are chosen to inform the court about aspects of the accident, injury, product, or service. They must be technically competent in their field as evidenced by their degrees, years of experience, and professional activities. The behavior and credentials of an expert witness must be above reproach. Good expert witnesses are able to communicate in common language with the judge and the jury.

FUTURE CONSIDERATIONS

Many different interest groups have concerns about the product liability situation in the future. The following are some suggested areas for further investigation:

- Enact a statute of limitations for filing liability claims.
- Provide a release from liability for the original manufacturer if the item is modified or the safety devices have been removed or altered.
- Judge products according to state of the art at the time of manufacture or provision of service.
- Create a standard code of awards.
- Reduce or eliminate punitive damages.
- Regulate attorney's fees.
- Institute comparative negligence judgments.
- Establish standards describing types of behavior that are grounds for punitive damages.

- Establish enhanced procedures for including scientific evidence of causes of injuries.
- Create nationwide standards for awards and litigation procedures.
- Accept compliance with government standards as a valid defense in lawsuits and a guarantee against punitive damages.
- Assess the legal fees of a successful defendant against the plaintiff.

SUMMARY

Regardless of how the consumer uses the product, responsibility for the product or service goes beyond the provider's doors. Immediate responsiveness to unsatisfactory quality through product service or replacement can do a great deal to lessen the chance of a product liability suit. Companies should institute a product liability loss control program that involves designing and providing a high-quality product or service rather than simply responding as necessary to periodic crises. An inherent, built-in approach to product safety will reduce product liability risks. An old saying stresses the importance of taking care of the little things: For want of a nail, the shoe was lost; for want of a shoe, the horse was lost; for want of the horse, the goods were lost. Companies need to recognize that product liability problems can occasionally be traced to routine and relatively minor decisions made daily in nearly all areas of a company's operation and at all levels of responsibility. Just as with the nail and the horseshoe, the size and source of the error may have little relationship to the magnitude of potential loss. From this perspective, a simple decision made during the manufacturing of a product may be the cause of a product liability suit. Strong total quality assurance and loss prevention programs can prevent product liability problems from occurring.

 ■ *Lessons Learned*

1. Civil suits seek money damages for injuries to either a person or property or both. They involve two parties—the plaintiff, the injured party, and the defendant, the person or company against whom the suit is filed.
2. When a product or service has been provided in a careless or unreasonable manner, negligence occurs.
3. If a manufacturer makes and sells a defective product or provides a defective service, they can be held strictly liable if the defect renders the product or service unreasonably dangerous and the defect causes an injury.
4. Under contributory negligence, the plaintiff is found to have acted in such a way as to contribute to the injury.
5. An expressed warranty can be either written or oral, and it is part of the conditions of sale.
6. An implied warranty is implied by law.
7. An expert witness informs the court about the technical aspects of the accident, injury, or product.

8. Product liability exposure can be reduced through thoughtful design and development of products or services. Designers should design to remove unsafe aspects, guard against unsafe use, provide product warnings, design to standards, and advertise and market the product or service appropriately.

9. A program to reduce the risks associated with product liability must embrace design, marketing, manufacturing, service provision, packaging, shipping, and service. ■

Chapter Problems

Product Liability

1. Airline A uses a traditional navigation system that has been successful in the past. A new, more sophisticated and accurate system is available at a higher cost, and most other airlines have switched to the new system. During a storm, a flight of airline A hits a mountain. The follow-up investigation finds that a defective navigation system was the cause of the accident.

   a. Who is the defendant in this case?
   b. Who is the plaintiff?
   c. What could the company/individual have done to avoid liability?

2. Define negligence.

3. Describe strict liability.

4. Describe contributory negligence.

5. What is the role of the defendant in a strict liability case?

6. What is the role of the plaintiff in a strict liability case?

7. Describe the role of an expert witness during a product liability court case.

8. When deciding a product liability case, what factors does the court consider?

9. Discuss the types of changes that may be seen in future product liability laws. Why are these changes necessary? What abuses of the system might they prevent?

10. Investigate recent developments in product liability. Are there any changes or additions to the laws? Have the judges or juries adjusted their verdicts by taking into account contributory negligence? Have any statutes of limitations been enacted? If yes, for what products?

Product Liability Suits

Investigate each product liability case in Problems 11–15. Answer the following questions.

- What event or series of events occurred to cause the need for a product liability suit?
- Who are the plaintiffs?
- What are they seeking?
- What motivated them to file a product liability suit?
- What is their point of view or defense?

- What was the verdict?
- Were there punitive damages?
- Was the case appealed?
- Did the judge change the amount of the award?
- Who were the expert witnesses involved?
- What kind of loss control program would have helped the defendant?
- How could quality assurance have been involved?

11. A young couple in their twenties driving an on/off-road vehicle picked up two friends to go out for a drive. The young man went to a local off-road course. There he proceeded to drive down a very steep hill, even though course safety rules indicated that this hill was an "uphill drive only." For some reason, perhaps braking, the vehicle went down end over end, crashing upside down. Three of the people were killed instantly—two when the roll bar snapped forward, crushing them. The third individual died from head trauma. The fourth individual, a young woman, was paralyzed, having apparently been struck by the back of the vehicle.

12. After being injured in an accident in her 1991 Toyota Tercel, the plaintiff filed suit against Toyota Motor Sales U.S.A. alleging that the Tercel was poorly designed and defective because it did not have an airbag. Toyota said that the belt-restraint system provided in the Tercel met the 1966 National Traffic and Motor Vehicle Safety Act. This act, applicable to the 1991 model, does not require airbags.

13. In 1994 an elderly woman burned herself when she spilled the hot coffee she had just purchased at a McDonald's drive-through window.

14. During the 1990s, Dow Corning Inc. was forced into bankruptcy over their silicone breast implants.

15. Throughout the 1990s a variety of controversial suits were filed against cigarette manufacturers by smokers.

16. Investigate the effects of product liability law reform on small plane manufacturers. What are the positive and negative aspects of this reform? Should the same type of reform occur in other industries? Why? Why not?

17. Investigate the issues surrounding the failure of Firestone tires on Ford vehicles. What was the outcome of this product liability problem? What effects did this situation have on Firestone's income statement? On Ford's income statement?

18. Discuss the implications of the following statement from the Joint Economic Committee:

The product liability system is a $125 billion burden on the nation's economy, raising consumer prices, undercutting innovation, and depleting corporate resources that would be better spent on capital improvement, worker training, and research and development.

CASE STUDY 13.1
Product Liability: Aircraft*

XYZ Aircraft Co. prides itself on its total quality assurance efforts and excellent safety record. It has instituted preventive maintenance and training programs as part of its efforts to comply with and exceed Federal Aviation Administration (FAA) requirements.

As part of its pilot training program, XYZ Aircraft has been instructing its pilots on the use of autopilots. The training has taught the pilots to check the autopilot for malfunctions and the proper way to handle in-flight malfunctions. Although XYZ had not had an in-flight incident, it was during training and subsequent preventive maintenance checks that the company realized that uncommanded actions might occur when the plane was on autopilot. Since this discovery, XYZ has been working with the autopilot suppliers to develop corrective actions.

XYZ Aircraft is sincerely interested in the safety of its passengers and crew. This interest is the driving force behind its total quality assurance efforts. XYZ Aircraft is also very aware that from a product liability point of view, it could be held strictly liable for any incident involving its planes. In a strict liability case, it could be found to have committed a fault if its service (air transportation) is considered defective, if its aircraft had a defect that caused it to be unreasonably dangerous and the defect was the reason for an injury. XYZ would be strictly liable even if it was not negligent. For this reason, the company is diligently attempting to correct the autopilot anomalies.

Most of XYZ's aircraft are equipped with the same model autopilot. This facilitates training and ensures that pilots flying different planes from day to day are familiar with the operation of the autopilot. Nearly all autopilot systems work in the same fashion. The autopilot receives an instruction from the pilot, senses the present aircraft situation, determines the adjustments to make to align the pilot's instructions with the aircraft's attitude, and moves the controls accordingly. Essentially there are three areas that could malfunction: the sensing mechanisms that monitor the plane's position, the computation system that calculates the difference between the command and the aircraft position, and the control area that moves the aircraft controls into the appropriate position. Each of these areas has been investigated.

To avoid incurring product liability costs, XYZ Aircraft is prepared to study the design and manufacture of the autopilots and use quality-assurance information to isolate the potential cause of the problems. The most immediate step during the process is to effectively warn XYZ pilots of the incidents of uncommanded movements and

---

*This case is fictitious and is not meant to resemble any particular company or incident.

errors being made by autopilots. XYZ also continues to train pilots on recognizing and handling in-flight malfunctions.

After preliminary investigations into the three areas, attention begins to focus on the computation system of the autopilot. A manufacturer of a signaling component in the system has noted high response times in the sensor switches. Although the response times were high, the switches were within specification, and the manufacturing engineer had signed off on the product as acceptable to use. The switches were inserted into subassemblies and consequently into the autopilots. Several of these autopilots were later installed on XYZ planes.

Now that an investigation has pinpointed the switches as a potential problem source, the quality-assurance records for the switches are scrutinized. It is determined that while the parts were within response-time specifications, the times were close to the upper specification limit (Figure C13.1.1). Process capability calculations (C_p, C_{pk}) reveal that the process is capable but not centered. Causes for this are investigated and a Pareto diagram is created (Figure C13.1.2). Selecting the most frequently occurring problems to study, a production-line team has suggested improvements which have been incorporated into the process.

Although the switch could not be pinpointed as the total cause of the problem, the supplier decided to install new switches on the existing autopilots. Retrofitting is very costly: The company will have to supply the new switch and send out trained technicians, engineers, and marketing people all over the world to aircraft service centers to replace the switch. One hundred percent inspection is instituted on the parts. Reliability tests are run. During these tests, parts are put through 2,000 cycles under electrical and mechanical load to detect infant mortality.

When deciding upon a course of action, the costs of retrofitting, inspecting, and reliability testing are weighed against the costs of lawsuits and catastrophic-loss suits. Management feels that product liability suits will inevitably damage the reputation and future of the company, greatly outweighing the cost of retrofitting.

The engineers who had signed off on the original switches are now instructed in the importance of determining the causes of deviations and the potential consequences of such deviations before signing off on a change. The engineers were

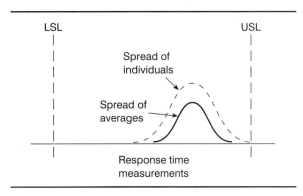

Figure C13.1.1 Histogram of Response Times

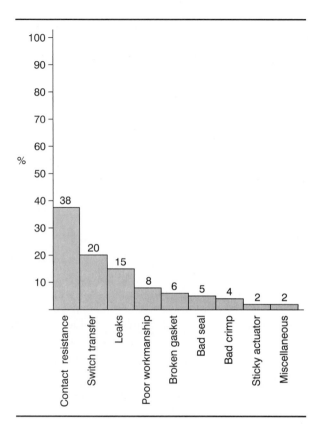

Figure C13.1.2   Pareto Diagram of Causes of Increased Response Times

unaware that quality and reliability issues were of significant importance in decisions related to the creation of a part or provision of a service. They were also unaware that any paper they sign their names to can become evidence in a liability suit. Therefore care must be taken to determine the causes of the deviations and their consequences.

For instance, if a manufacturing engineer advised by an operator that an assembly tool is not functioning properly has the tool fixed and then signs off on the tool as OK to use, that engineer can be held responsible if the tool produces parts that are used in an assembly that proves to have a quality problem. On items that may be discrepant but are found to be acceptable, engineers should be sure to look into the issue before signing off. What is the discrepancy? What are the consequences? If a problem is encountered and an investigation ensues, the engineer's name will be on the documentation and the engineer will be ultimately responsible.

Product liability issues can be reduced when proper attention is paid to the details of creating a product or providing a service.

Assignment

1. Why would XYZ Aircraft be held strictly liable if an autopilot malfunctioned during flight?
2. What activities would constitute negligent behavior on the part of XYZ Aircraft?
3. How did this particular company use quality-assurance data to help avoid a product liability problem?
4. What type of questions should an engineer ask before signing off on a product change or deviation?

CASE STUDY BIBLIOGRAPHY

"NTSB Recommends FAA Action on Faulty Autopilots." *Avionics*, December 1993, p. 46.

G. Picou. "What Autopilots Go Nuts." *IFR*, September 1994, pp. 16–19, 26.

CASE STUDY 13.2
Product Liability: Tires

As the headlines in Figure C13.2.1 show, product failure and the accompanying product liability issues can be enormously costly. The costs go beyond recalling and replacing products or the costs of settling lawsuits. The pressures of determining a root cause for the problem and a resolution for the product liability issues may create a myriad of unforeseen challenges for the companies involved. Product failures significantly impact sales and public trust. If the issues aren't resolved, the resulting slow sales will cause layoffs and plant closings. When several companies are involved, long-standing relationships between

---

Firestone Plans Sweeping Recall of 6.5 Million Tires
Sears Stops Selling Tires Involved in Probe
Firestone Warns of Nationwide Tire Shortage
Role of Ford Explorer Design Is Studied in Connection with Firestone Tire Suits
Recalled Tires Pose Disposal Problem
States Ponder Lawsuits Over Firestone Tire Recall
Congress Grills Ford, Firestone, NHTSA
Poll: Trust in Tires Falters
Deaths Continue During Firestone Recall
Deaths Linked to Tires Now at 103
Firestone's Ono May Be Replaced
Firestone Lays off 450 at Illinois Plant
New CEO Cleans House at Firestone
Tire Recall Cited as Explorer Sales Fall 16% in October
Sales of Firestone Brand Tires Plummet
Ford Says Last Year's Quality Snafus Took Big Toll—Over $1 Billion in Profit
Tire Recall Hits the Bottom Line of Japan's Bridgestone: Net Income Fell 80% in 2000
Ford Explorer Rollover Suits Total $590 Million
Firestone Sales of Tires Drop So Far in 2001
Firestone Quits as Tire Supplier to Ford
Ford Bites $3B Bullet to Replace 13M More Tires
Firestone Seeks Safety Probe of Ford SUVs
Firestone Plans to Close Troubled Decatur Factory

Figure C13.2.1
Sources for headlines in order of appearance: *Wall Street Journal,* August 9, 2000; *USA Today,* August 4, 2000; *USA Today,* August 16, 2000; *Wall Street Journal,* August 20, 2000; *USA Today,* August 31, 2000; *Wall Street Journal,* August 31, 2000; *USA Today,* September 6, 2000; *USA Today,* September 12, 2000; *Wall Street Journal,* September 14, 2000; *USA Today,* September 20, 2000; *Wall Street Journal,* October 3, 2000; *USA Today,* October 18, 2000; *Automotive News,* October 23, 2000; *USA Today,* November 2, 2000; *Wall Street Journal,* November 13, 2000; *Wall Street Journal,* January 12, 2001; *Wall Street Journal,* February 23, 2001; *Automotive News,* March 26, 2001; *Wall Street Journal,* April 6, 2001; *Wall Street Journal,* May 22, 2001; *USA Today,* May 23, 2001; *Wall Street Journal,* June 1, 2001; *Wall Street Journal,* June 28, 2001.

sellers and buyers may be severed. In some cases, the government may find it necessary to become involved. As this case shows, the ramifications of product failures are enormous.

Though it actually began much earlier, by late July of the year 2000, the world was aware that something was significantly wrong with the design and use of Firestone tires.[1,2]

1997

Firestone begins to receive numerous complaints and warranty claims about tread separation in the United States.

At this time, they also begin paying off insurance claims on accidents involving tread separation.

1998

Ford brought to Firestone's attention that the Valencia, Venezuela, factory delivered defective tires to Ford's SUVs.

1999

January, Firestone investigated tire separation and agreed to add a nylon layer to the tire to prevent separation.

Firestone begins to receive numerous complaints and warranty claims on tires in Saudi Arabia and other Middle Eastern countries.

Ford and Firestone believe that the tire problems are the result of poor maintenance and severe driving conditions, not a manufacturing defect.

2000

May, Ford begins to replace tires in South America on its Ford Explorers due to tread separation.

May, the National Highway and Traffic Safety Administration (NHTSA) begins a formal investigation of the Firestone tread separation.

July, Ford begins its own investigation into the causes of tire failure.

August, investigations by Ford and Firestone have pinpointed three tire types made at one facility as the chief source of failed tires.

August 9, Firestone recalled 6.5 million tires. The recall includes the ATX, ATX II, and Wilderness AT tires fabricated at the Decatur, Illinois, plant. The recall was for tires made between 1995 and 1997.

August, all tire manufactures boost production to meet demand for new tires.

August, congressional hearings take place and continue into September.

August, role of Ford Explorer design questioned in rollovers.

October, Firestone President Ono resigns; Lampe named as successor. Lampe plans reorganization.

October, Ford and Firestone begin to sever relationship.

October, Firestone lays off 450 at Decatur plant.

November, Firestone continues layoffs as recall affects other tire sales, resulting in lower production rates.

December, NHTSA reports fatalities involved in tread separation as 148, including 40 overseas.

---

[1]"Documents Imply Firestone Knew of Tire Trouble in 94," *USA Today*, October 4, 2000.
[2]"Drivers Complained of Tread Problems Years Before Recall," *USA Today*, November 15, 2000.

2001
January, a trial against Firestone and Ford involving a paralyzed woman begins in Texas.
January, Firestone recalls 8000 GM SUV tires.
January, the president and CEO of Bridgestone (the parent company of Firestone) resigns.
February, a trial against Firestone and Ford involving a wrongful death begins in Cook County, Illinois.
February, Ford and Firestone report huge losses for 2000 due to tire problems.
February, the total count of fatalities caused by tread separation reaches 174 according to the NHTSA (*Wall Street Journal*, February 7, 2001).
February, Firestone plans to recall the P205/55R16 tire.
May, Firestone and Ford no longer have a supplier relationship.
May, Ford decides to replace all Firestone tires on all Ford vehicles regardless of type of tire or vehicle, even though no problems have been found with other tires.
June, Firestone makes plans to close Decatur, Illinois, plant.
July, the NHTSA seeks to broaden recall of Firestone tires.
July, product liability suits are consolidated into a class action suit.
August, Firestone and Ford prepare for product liability suits.
August, Firestone and Ford have their stocks downgraded on Wall Street.

The reason this particular failure has received so much attention is because of the consequences that tread separation has on vehicle performance. For this particular situation, tread separation usually occurs when one or all of the following are true: The vehicle is travelling at a high rate of speed, the ambient temperature is high, the vehicle is fully loaded, and the tire is underinflated. There are essentially five stages to a rollover. During the first stage, the tire begins to fail, causing a vibration in the vehicle that the driver may attribute to a rough road. At some point the vibration becomes so intense that it is as if the tire has come loose or gone flat. Unfortunately, even if the driver stops and examines the tire, from the outside, the tire will appear fine. The second stage is the actual tread separation. The driver may hear a loud sound like a banging or thumping as the tread peels away from the tire. At the third stage, the wheel slows as the remnants of the tire are unable to support the vehicle. At this point, vehicle handling is severely compromised. Since the vehicle is difficult to steer, at the fourth stage, the driver must struggle to maintain vehicle control. In some cases, the fifth stage, rollover, does not occur if the driver is able to bring the vehicle to a full stop without losing control.[3,4]

PROBLEM ISOLATION

Ford and Firestone used quality assurance problem-solving techniques to isolate the potential root causes of the tire failure. Using Pareto diagrams, Ford investigated any Firestone tires that received more than 30 warranty claims. It found that the 235/75R-15

---

[3]"SUV Drivers Can Reduce Rollovers," *USA Today*, September 26, 2000.
[4]"Minimize Your Chances of Crashing," *USA Today*, August 22, 2000.

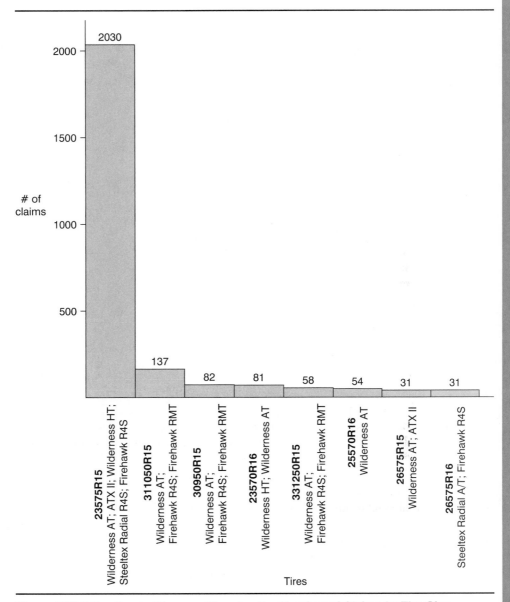

Figure C13.2.2   Pareto Diagram Showing the Number of Claims by Tire Size
SOURCE: "Ford Grows Annoyed with How Firestone Handles Tire Recall." *Wall Street Journal,* August 14, 2000.

accounted for an overwhelmingly significant number of claims (Figure C13.2.2). Of the 2,504 customer complaints reviewed at the time the investigation first took place, 81 percent involved the P235/75R-15 tires. This size includes the ATX, ATX II, and Wilderness AT.

At this point, the investigation centered on the 235/75R-15 tires. Since this tire size involved five different tires, they created another Pareto diagram showing what

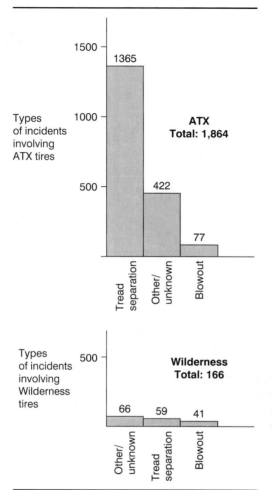

Figure C13.2.3   Pareto Diagrams Showing Tread Separation Incidents for ATX and Wilderness Tires
SOURCE: "Ford Grows Annoyed with How Firestone Handles Tire Recall." *Wall Street Journal,* August 14, 2000.

type and how many of each type of failures were recorded for each type of tire. Figure C13.2.3 shows the results for the two most significant models.

By using manufacturing records and tire numbers, the source of the failed tires was traced to the Decatur plant. The highest number of claims were made in reference to the Decatur tires produced from 1994–1997. The Wilderness AT tire failures from factories other than the Decatur plant were insignificant.[5,6,7,8,9]

Although as yet no definitive conclusion has been made, the investigation has revealed that a variety of events that occurred at the plant between 1995 and 1997

[5]"How the Tire Problem Turned into a Crisis for Firestone and Ford," *Wall Street Journal,* August 10, 2000.
[6]"Ford Steps Up Recall Without Firestone," *Wall Street Journal,* August 14, 2000.
[7]"Quality Auditor OK's Decatur Tire Plant," *USA Today,* September 8, 2000.
[8]"Lab Performs Tiresome Task," *Automotive News,* October 23, 2000.
[9]"Ford Grows Annoyed With How Firestone Handles Tire Recall," *Wall Street Journal,* August 14, 2000.

may have contributed to manufacturing problems. Other factors played a role in tire failure, including tire pressure, Explorer design, and tire design.

Manufacturing Issues.   During the 1995–1997 time period, working conditions in the plant were not optimal. Workers often worked 12-hour shifts under strong incentives to increase production. A strike during this time also contributed to the problems; replacement workers were not properly trained.[10,11,12,13,14]

Tire Pressure Concerns.   Tire pressure has been cited as a potential cause of tire failure. Ford recommended a tire pressure of 26 psi compared to Firestone's 30 psi. Ford chose the lower psi in order to give customers a smoother ride. Tire pressure is considered a crucial factor in vehicle handling safety in order to prevent loss of control, rollover, and serious injury.[15,16,17]

Explorer Design Factor.   The design of the Ford Explorer is also considered a factor in tire failure. The design of the chassis and the weight placed on the right rear tire affect the performance of that tire. Investigation revealed that the tires in question were never tested on a Ford Explorer, only on an F-150 pickup truck in 1989 when the decision was made that the tires would be standard equipment on Explorer models. The reason for this switch was that the original Explorer engine was not powerful enough to maintain the extended test speeds of 90–100 mph. Ford claims that the F-150 was rigid enough that the load on the tires was equal to an Explorer.[18,19,20,21,22,23,24]

Tire Design Questions.   The design of the tires remains controversial. Nylon caps may have prevented the failure. A nylon cap is a layer of nylon fabric that is inserted between the steel belts and the thick outer layer of rubber tread. The nylon cap acts to hold the tire together and in shape. The adhesive used to bond the layers is also considered a factor in tread separation.[25–28]

[10]"Tire Dilemma Puts Focus on Process of Manufacturing," *Wall Street Journal*, August 8, 2000.

[11]"Data Point to Firestone Tires Made at Illinois Factory," *USA Today*, August 14, 2000.

[12]"Labor Union Unrest Adds to Bridgestone/Firestone's Problems," *Automotive News*, September 4, 2000.

[13]"Firestone Admits Manufacturing Problems But Also Scrutinizes Tire-Inflation Levels," *Wall Street Journal*, December 20, 2000.

[14]"In Firestone Tire Study, Expert Finds Vehicle Weight Was Key Factor in Failure," *Wall Street Journal*, February 5, 2001.

[15]"Survey: Most Tires Inflated Wrong," *USA Today*, September 20, 2000.

[16]"Firestone Breaks With Ford Over Tire Pressure," *Wall Street Journal*, September 22, 2000.

[17]"Firestone Admits Manufacturing Problems But Also Scrutinizes Tire-Inflation Levels," *Wall Street Journal*, December 20, 2000.

[18]"Role of Ford Explorer Design Is Studied in Connection with Firestone Tire Suit," *Wall Street Journal*, August 20, 2000.

[19]"Is Explorer Part of the Problem?" *USA Today*, September 12, 2000.

[20]"Ford Investigators Focus on the Left Rear Tire," September 19, 2000.

[21]"Further Scrutiny Puts Ford in the Hot Seat," *USA Today*, September 21, 2000.

[22]"Focus Shifts to Ford," *Newsweek*, October 9, 2000.

[23]"Firestone Finds More Problems in One Line and Left Rear Tire," *Wall Street Journal*, November 7, 2000.

[24]"Firestone Seeks Safety Probe of Ford SUV's," *Wall Street Journal*, June 1, 2001.

[25]"Could $1 Worth of Nylon Have Saved People's Lives?" *USA Today*, August 9, 2000.

[26]"Nylon Caps May Have Saved Firestone Its Recall," *Wall Street Journal*, August 28, 2000.

[27]"Ford, Firestone Say Adhesive Is Linked to Bad Tires," *USA Today*, December 11, 2000.

[28]"Cost Hinders Wider Use of Nylon to Make Steel-Belted Tires Safer," *Wall Street Journal*, December 20, 2000.

Contributory Negligence.   Though motorists rank tires as the second-most important safety feature after brakes on their vehicles, only 14 percent of drivers properly check their tire inflation pressure on a regular basis. Sixty-eight percent of drivers surveyed by the AAA don't even know where to find information about the proper tire inflation pressure for their vehicle. Forty-five percent of drivers wrongly believe that a fully loaded vehicle is better off if its tires are a bit underinflated. Tires lose one pound per square inch of inflation pressure for every ten degree temperature drop. Tire pressure can also decrease suddenly if the tires run over a pothole or curb. This all adds up to one-fourth of the passenger cars on the road having at least one significantly underinflated tire. Low pressure increases tire heat and lowers the weight carrying capacity that a vehicle can carry. Underinflated tires are prone to overheating and overheating is considered one of the contributing factors of tread separation related to the crashes.[29]

Websites:

www.tiresafety.com
www.theautochannel.com
www.Goodyear.com
www.Firestone.com
www.TheWallStreetJournal.com
www.FordMotorCo.com

 Assignment

Research the events surrounding the Firestone and Ford product liability case. Answer the following questions:

1. Describe the series of events leading up to the product liability suit.
   a. How was the problem discovered?
   b. How was the tire selected for recall?
   c. Why is Ford involved?
2. What are the costs incurred by Bridgestone/Firestone and Ford? What future costs can Ford or Firestone expect to incur?
3. What kind of loss control program would have helped the defendants? How should quality assurance be involved?
4. Discuss the concepts of *negligence*, *strict liability*, and *contributory negligence* as they relate to this case. Which concept(s) is most applicable to this case?
5. Discuss the role of the plaintiffs in this case.
   a. Who are the plaintiffs?
   b. What motivated them to file a product liability suit?
   c. What will be their strategy during the prosecution of this case?
   d. What will they have to prove?

---

[29]"Regulators Push For Smarter Tires," *Wall Street Journal*, July 14, 2004.

6. Discuss the role of the defendants in this case.
   a. Who are the defendants?
   b. Why are they defendants?
   c. What will be their defense strategy during the prosecution of this case?
   d. What will they have to prove?
7. Discuss the role of the courts in this case.
   a. What will be the role of the courts in this case?
   b. What will they (the judge and jury) need to know?
   c. What should they base their decision on?
8. Act as an expert witness. Locate and summarize statistical information on tires, tire failure, tire inflation, and chassis type that you would need to be able to discuss.
9. What can be learned from the Bridgestone/Firestone and Ford product liability case?

The information in this case is current to July 14, 2004. Since that time, further developments have occurred in this ongoing product liability case. Information for this case has come from a wide variety of sources including Ford's and Firestone's websites, as well as hundreds of articles from the *Wall Street Journal*, *USA Today*, *The Detroit Free Press*, *Time*, *Newsweek*, *Time*, and *Automotive News*.

Quality Systems: ISO 9000, Supplier Certification Requirements, the Malcolm Baldrige Award, and Six Sigma

Learning Opportunities:

1. To become familiar with the requirements of ISO 9000 and ISO 14000
2. To become familiar with the requirements of QS 9000 and TS 16949
3. To become familiar with the requirements of the Malcolm Baldrige National Quality Award
4. To become familiar with the Six Sigma methodology ■

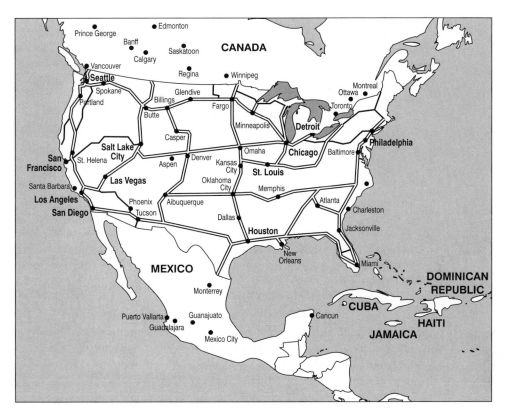

Road Map to Success

*T*hroughout this text, different ideas, concepts, and techniques have been presented. Individually, each idea, concept, and technique has merit and together they make up the supporting pieces of a total quality system. ISO 9000, supplier certification requirements, and the Malcolm Baldrige Award present more unified approaches to quality, encouraging companies to create quality systems. They provide a road map for companies to follow in their quest for quality.

QUALITY SYSTEMS

In order to best fulfill customer needs, requirements, and expectations, organizations create quality systems. *Within a **quality management system,** the necessary ingredients exist to enable the organization's employees to identify, design, develop, produce, deliver, and support products or services that the customer wants.* A quality management system is dynamic. It is able to adapt and change to meet the needs, requirements, and expectations of its customers. Managers of a quality system coordinate the efforts of those in the system to effectively provide products or services for their customers. Quality systems enable organizations to enhance their efficiency and effectiveness. Certification and registration validates compliance to a nationally recognized standard.

Management begins to develop a system by creating a vision or mission that sets the direction for the company. The vision is supported by strategies, which are in turn supported by goals and objectives. Developing and shaping visions, missions, strategies, goals, and objectives is a complicated process. Standards such as ISO 9000 and QS 9000 and awards like the Malcolm Baldrige National Quality Award provide guidance for establishing a quality management system's structure, maintaining records, and integrating the use of quality techniques. Quality systems like ISO 9000 and TS 16949 are basically asking that organizations say what they are going to do and then do what they say. These quality systems do not mandate particular policies, procedures, and actions. However, they ask organizations to document the policies and procedures they have and the actions they take.

Though ISO 9000 and QS 9000 are the best known of the quality management systems certifications, other quality management systems certifications have been developed in a variety of industries. For example, in the telecommunications industry, TL 9000 has been developed to ensure better relationships between suppliers and service providers. As the benefits from an organized quality management system become better known, an increasing number of business sectors will develop appropriate standards.

ISO 9000

Continued growth in international trade revealed the need for a set of quality standards to facilitate the relationship between suppliers and purchasers. The creation of the ISO 9000 series of international standards began in 1979 with the formation of a technical committee with participants from 20 countries. Named the International Organization for Standardization, this Geneva-based association continues to revise and update the standards. The name "ISO 9000" has its origin in the Greek word *isos*, meaning "equal." The intent of the standards is to make comparisons between companies equal. Note that ISO 9000 refers to the entire standard; when speaking of certification requirements, ISO 9001 is used.

The purpose of the ISO standards is to facilitate the multinational exchange of products and services by providing a clear set of quality system requirements. Companies competing on a global basis find it necessary to adopt and adhere to these standards. The standards provide a baseline against which an organization's quality system can be judged. This baseline has as its foundation the achievement of customer satisfaction through multidisciplinary participation in quality-improvement efforts, documentation of systems and procedures, and the basic structural elements necessary to quality systems. The generic nature of the standards allows the interested company to determine the specifics of how the standards apply to its organization. Many companies use ISO 9000 as the foundation for their continuous improvement efforts. The ISO organization estimates that 8 out of 10 cars contain parts or components designed or manufactured under the ISO 9001:2000 certification system.

ISO 9000 is applicable to nearly all organizations, including manufacturers of pieces, parts, assemblies, and finished goods; developers of software; producers of processed materials, including liquids, gases, solids, or combinations; municipalities, logistics providers (i.e., UPS, FedEx, DHL), hospitals, and service providers. Since its inception, ISO 9000 has become an internationally accepted standard for quality in business-to-business dealings. As of 2004, more than 250,000 organizations worldwide have attained certification.

In 2000, the ISO 9000 standards were revised significantly so that their structure more closely resembles the way organizations are managed. The wording of the standard was made more generic so that it is applicable to a wider variety of business sectors including manufacturing, government services, business enterprises, and service industries.

ISO 9001:2000 certification takes a process-oriented approach. The standard focuses on quality management systems and requires the identification of quality management processes as well as their sequence and interactions with key business processes. A quality management system describes the organizational structure, procedures, and resources necessary to manage quality. The ISO 9000 requirements describe *what* a company must accomplish in order to meet customer expectations. However, *how* these things are accomplished is left up to the particular company.

Eight key principles have been integrated into the ISO 9000:2000 standards. These principles are:

- Customer focused organization
- Leadership
- Involvement of people
- Process approach
- System approach to management
- Continual improvement
- Factual approach to decision-making
- Mutually beneficial supplier relationships

Nearly all quality standards, like ISO 9000, are comprised of two distinct sections: general information about the standard and how to implement it. ISO 9000 is divided into eight sections: scope, normative reference, terms and definitions, quality management system, management responsibility, resource management, production realization, and measurement, analysis, and improvement.

ISO 9000:2000 is comprised of three areas.

1. **ISO 9000:2000, Quality Management Systems: Fundamentals and Vocabulary,** provides information about the concepts and vocabulary used in the other two standards. This standard serves as a reference to support the interpretation of the ISO 9001:2000 requirements but contains no actual requirements.

2. **ISO 9001:2000, Quality Management Systems: Requirements,** provides the requirements that must be met in order to achieve certification. ISO 9001 is designed to be used by all organizations, regardless of type, size, or industry sector (Figure 14.1). ISO 9001 consists of four main sections:

Management Responsibility: This section focuses on how the analysis of data affects the performance of the organization's quality management system. Information is sought on how the organization's management establishes quality policies, makes plans, achieves objectives, and communicates customer requirements.

Resource Management: The requirements in this section call for details on resource availability and deployment. Resources include information, facilities, communication, people, and work environment. Training effectiveness is also evaluated.

Product and/or Service Realization: Product and/or service realization concentrates on how customer requirements and organizational self-assessments lead to continued improvement of processes and work methods.

Measurement, Analysis, and Improvement: This section examines the methods a company uses to measure its systems, processes, products, or services.

3. **ISO 9004:2000, Quality Management Systems: Guidelines for Performance Improvement,** provides guidelines for those companies wishing to go beyond ISO 9001:2000 and establish a quality management system that not only meets customer requirements but also focuses on improving performance: ISO 9004:2000 is not a requirement and does not lead to certification. For organizations that wish to go beyond accreditation, ISO 9004 provides a continuous improvement model.

Documentation and record keeping are important aspects of ISO 9000. ISO 9000 requires records of many plant activities, including employee training records: procedures, policies, and instructions; process control charts and capability records; purchasing records; test and reliability data; audit records; incoming and final inspection records; and equipment calibration records. Companies following the ISO 9000 system need to keep records of any information that is useful in the operation of the organization. Evidence that procedures, policies, and instructions are being followed must also accompany these records.

The advantages of a fully documented quality management system are many. Documentation describes how work must be accomplished. Structured correctly, documentation will apply to a variety of situations, not just specific products. Documents serve as guides and ensure that work is performed consistently. Sound documentation can be used to determine and correct the causes of poor quality. Documentation defines existing work methods and provides a foundation for improvement.

In ISO 9000 a great deal of emphasis is placed on the need for excellent record keeping. In most cases, since the product has left the manufacturing facility or the service has been performed, only clearly kept records can serve as evidence of product

ISO 9001:2000
Section One: Scope

1.1 General
1.2 Application

Section Two: Normative Reference

Section Three: Terms and Definitions

Section Four: Quality Management System

4.1 General Requirements
4.2 Documentation Requirements

Section Five: Management Responsibility

5.1 Management Commitment
5.2 Customer Focus
5.3 Quality Policy
5.4 Planning
5.5 Responsibility, Authority, and Communication
5.6 Management Review

Section Six: Resource Management

6.1 Provision of Resources
6.2 Human Resources
6.3 Infrastructure
6.4 Work Environment

Section Seven: Product and/or Service Realization

7.1 Planning of Product Realization
7.2 Customers Related Processes
7.3 Design and Development
7.4 Purchasing
7.5 Production and Service Provision
7.6 Control of Monitoring and Measuring Devices

Section Eight: Measurement, Analysis, and Improvement

8.1 General
8.2 Monitoring and Measurement
8.3 Control of Nonconforming Product
8.4 Analysis of Data
8.5 Improvement

Figure 14.1   ISO 9001:2000

or service quality. Sloppy or poorly maintained records give the impression of poor quality. High-quality records are easy to retrieve, legible, appropriate, accurate, and complete. Necessary records may originate internally or be produced externally. Customer or technical specifications and regulatory requirements are considered external records. Internally produced records include forms, reports, drawings, meeting minutes, problem-solving documentation, and process control charts. A high-quality documentation control system will contain records that are easily identified and used in the decision-making process.

Companies seeking registration must have their compliance with the ISO 9001 criteria judged by an independent ISO 9000 certified registrar. Figure 14.2 shows the flow of a typical registration process. Before the ISO 9000 governing body grants certification, a registrar conducts a thorough audit to verify that the company does indeed meet the requirements as set forth in ISO 9001. When the company desiring accreditation feels it is ready, it invites an auditor to observe the company's operations and determine its level of compliance with the standards. Many firms find that conducting an internal audit before the actual registrar visit is more effective than a single audit. During this preaudit, deficiencies in the company's methods can be identified and corrected prior to the registrar's official visit. Registrars seek to determine if the actions taken by an organization have been effective at meeting or exceeding the requirements established by the standard. They investigate whether or not the organization effectively operates and controls processes. Management systems are reviewed to determine their effectiveness. Once registration has been achieved, surveillance audits are conducted, often unannounced, approximately every six months. These audits are intended to ensure continued compliance. When preparing for a certification audit, a company must develop an implementation plan that identifies the people involved and defines their roles, responsibilities, deliverables, timelines, and budgets. Once created, the plan is managed through frequent review meetings to determine the progress. Once the system has been fully documented, the company will contact a registrar and plan his or her visit.

Companies wishing to implement ISO 9000 should determine management's level of commitment. Management support can be gained by pointing out the benefits of compliance. Assess the company's current situation. What are the present costs associated with poor quality as evidenced by scrap or rework or lost customers? What new markets could open up if certification were achieved? The answers to these questions will show how achieving ISO 9001 certification will benefit the bottom line.

Obtaining ISO 9001 certification provides many benefits. Companies that have achieved certification cite increased revenue as a major benefit. Since ISO 9000 is recognized globally, certification allows these companies to expand their geographic markets. They are also able to service new customers who require ISO 9000 compliance from their suppliers. Additionally, existing customers benefit from ISO 9001 certification. Companies complying with ISO 9001 requirements have been able to improve their product and service quality and pass the benefits on to their customers. Internally, companies benefit from compliance. Reduced costs are evidenced through decreased scrap and rework, fewer warranty claims, improved customer satisfaction, reduced customer support costs, and improved productivity.

Obtaining ISO 9001 certification is a time-consuming and costly process. Depending on the current state of an organization's quality system, preparation for certification may take several thousand employee-hours and cost thousands of dollars. Costs depend on the company size, the strength of the organization's existing quality system, and the number of plants within the company requesting certification.

Decide to implement ISO 9000	Establish steering committee	Conduct internal audits	Continue internal audits	Implement and document procedures	Revise, improve, update, review, take corrective action based on initial visit	Begin preassessment procedures	Conduct registration assessment	Complete registration
Form management committee	Communicate intentions to entire corporation	Organize quality system	Begin documentation:	Initial visit made	Revise quality manual	Correct deficiencies		Strive for continuous improvement
Develop strategic plan	Select and train audit teams	Select registrar	Analyze processes		Conduct management review	Document and implement practices		Conduct surveillance audits
Begin ISO 9000 training	Continue ISO 9000 training	Continue to train audit teams	Write procedures					Continue management reviews
Educate workforce	Continue education	Continue ISO 9000 training	Continue to train audit teams					
Do cost assessment	Begin implementing standards	Continue education	Continue ISO 9000 training					
Do self-assessment		Define areas for improvement	Continue education					
			Create quality manual					
			Implement new procedures					

Figure 14.2 ISO 9000 Registration Cycle

671

As with any major process improvement, the opportunity to fail exists. Attempts to incorporate ISO 9000 into the way a company does business may be hindered by a variety of forces, including insufficient management involvement in the process, inadequate resources, lack of an implementation plan, or lack of understanding about ISO 9000 and its benefits. This last force, a lack of understanding about ISO 9000, is particularly crucial. ISO 9001 certification requires significant documentation. The additional burden of paperwork, without an understanding of how this newfound information can be used in decision-making, leads to problems. It is important to realize that standardized procedures and organized information go a long way toward preventing errors that lead to poor quality products and services. Individuals who are unaware of how to access the power that procedures and information provide may miss out on improvement opportunities. It is up to management to encourage the use of this information, thus gaining the maximum benefits from ISO 9000.

The high cost of certification is counterbalanced by the benefits an organization will receive by using the requirements as a guide to improve their processes. Quality becomes more consistent, and the percentage of "done right the first time" jobs increases. Improved procedures and removal of redundant operations also dramatically improve a company's effectiveness. ISO 9000 standards facilitate international trade and dramatically improve record keeping. To learn more about ISO 9000, visit the ISO website at www.iso.org.

SUPPLIER CERTIFICATION REQUIREMENTS

Major corporations often purchase raw materials, parts, subassemblies, and assemblies from outside sources. To ensure quality products, the suppliers of these parts and materials are subjected to rigorous requirements. Purchasers establish these requirements and judge conformance to them by visiting the supplier's plant site and reviewing the supplier's quality systems. Quality management systems like ISO 9000, TL 9000, QS 9000, ISO/TS 16949, and AS 9100 document organizational policies, procedures, work instructions, and forms.

Among motor vehicle manufacturers, though purchasers developed their own requirements, strong similarities existed in quality system and documentation requirements. Redundant requirements and multiple plant visits from purchasers placed a significant burden on suppliers. Conforming to several different, yet similar, sets of requirements meant unnecessarily expended time, effort, and money. Recognizing the overlap in requirements, the major automotive manufacturers—General Motors, Ford, and Chrysler—as well as truck manufacturers, created a task force in the early 1990s to develop a quality system that has as its foundation ISO 9000. Named "Quality System Requirements QS 9000," this comprehensive requirement was intended to develop fundamental quality systems that provide for continuous improvement. QS 9000 eliminates redundant requirements while maintaining customer-specific, division-specific, and commodity-specific requirements. QS 9000 emphasizes defect prevention as well as the reduction of variation and waste. Internal and external suppliers of production and service parts, subassemblies, materials, components, or other items to the major motor vehicle manufacturers must conform to the requirements set forth by QS 9000.

QS 9000 has two major components: ISO 9001 and Customer Specific Requirements. Automotive suppliers must be ISO 9001 certified. Customer specific requirements include methods for statistical process control (SPC), Production Part Approval Process (PPAP), Failure Modes and Effects Analysis (FMEA), Measurement Systems Analysis (MSA), Advanced Product Quality Planning and Control Planning (APQP), and Quality System Assessment (QSA).

Though QS 9000 establishes customer requirements for several of the major automotive manufacturers, QS 9000 is not and never has been an international specification. To fill the need for a global automotive system, in 1999, ISO introduced ISO/TS 16949, Quality Management Systems: Automotive Suppliers—Particular Requirements for the Application of ISO 9001:2000 for Automotive Production and Relevant Service Part Organizations. Developed by the International Automotive Oversight Bureau and submitted to ISO for approval and publication, ISO/TS 16949 defines automotive industry standards worldwide. A more generic document than QS 9000, ISO/TS 16949 is based on ISO 9001:2000, AVSQ (Italian), EAQF (French), QS 9000 (U.S.), and VDA6.1 (German) systems. ISO/TS 16949 does not replace AVSQ, EAQF, QS 9000, or VDA6.1; it is a global set of standards presented as an option to these systems. As written, the document allows automotive companies to retain individual control over more of the specific requirements. Since it is based on ISO 9001, the basic format is the same as shown in Figure 14.1. Additions to the document include: terms and definitions specific to the automotive industry, requirements related to engineering specifications and records retention, process efficiency expectations, product design skills and training related to human resources management, product realization, acceptance, and change control requirements, and customer designated special characteristics. For more information concerning QS 9000 or ISO/TS 16949, contact the Automotive Industry Action Group at www.aiag.org.

While ISO 9001 is the best known of the quality systems certifications, other quality management systems certifications have been developed in a variety of industries. As the benefits of utilizing an organized quality management system become better known, an increasing number of business sectors will create appropriate standards. For example, in the telecommunications industry, TL 9000 has been developed to ensure better relationships between suppliers and service providers. In the medical devices and pharmaceutical industries, many organizations follow ISO 13485, which, in addition to product realization requirements, requires risk assessment planning be used in formulating products. The need for such a standard comes from the increasing number and variety of pharmaceutical and medicinal products, the globalization of the pharmaceutical and medical devices industries, and the changes in biotechnology and pharmaceutical sciences.

In the aerospace industry, AS9000 is used to link global corporations with their suppliers in a continuous quality chain. The International Aerospace Quality Group (IAQG) works to establish commonality of quality standards and requirements, encourage continuous improvement processes at suppliers, determine effective methods

---

4.1 Management Responsibility

4.2 Quality Systems

4.3 Contract Review

4.4 Design Control

4.5 Document and Data Control

4.6 Purchasing

4.7 Control of Customer-Supplied Product

4.8 Product Identification and Traceability

4.9 Process Control

4.10 Inspection and Testing

4.11 Control of Inspection, Measuring, and Test Equipment

4.12 Inspection and Test Status

4.13 Control of Nonconforming Product

4.14 Corrective and Preventive Action

4.15 Handling, Storage, Packing, Preservation, and Delivery

4.16 Control of Quality Records

4.17 Internal Quality Audits

4.18 Training

4.19 Servicing

4.20 Statistical Techniques

Figure 14.3   AS9100 Standards

to share results, and respond to regulatory requirements. IAQG members include Airbus, Rolls-Royce, Eurocopter, Volvo-Aero, BAE, Boeing, General Electric Aircraft Engines, Gulfstream, BF Goodrich, Bombardier, Lockheed Martin, Mitsubishi, Kawasaki, Fuji, Kera Aerospace, Hispano-Suiza, and others. AS9100 Quality Standard (Figure 14.3), proposed for the aerospace industry worldwide, is a quality standard that seeks to standardize aerospace quality expectations on a global level. AS9100 adds 83 additional and specific requirements to the 20 elements of ISO 9001, including requirements for safety, reliability, and maintainability. AS9100 emphasizes design control, process control, purchasing, inspection and testing, and control of nonconformances.

ISO 14000: ENVIRONMENTAL MANAGEMENT

The overall objective of the ISO 14000 Environmental Management Standard is to encourage environmental protection and the prevention of pollution while taking into account the economic needs of society. The standards can be followed by any organization interested in achieving and demonstrating sound environmental performance by limiting its negative impact on the environment. A company with an environmental management system like ISO 14000 is better able to meet its legal and policy requirements. Often, firms following ISO 14000 incur significant savings through better overall resource management and waste reduction. ISO 14000 provides the elements of an effective environmental management system.

ISO 14000 is divided into two main classifications, Organization/Process-Oriented Standards and Product-Oriented Standards. A company complying with these standards is monitoring its processes and products to determine their effect on the environment. Within the two classifications, six topic areas are covered: Environmental Management Systems, Environmental Performance Evaluation, Environmental Auditing, Life-Cycle Assessment, Environmental Labeling, and Environmental Aspects in Product Standards. The ISO 14000 series of standards enables a company to improve environmental management voluntarily. The standards do not establish product or performance standards, establish mandates for emissions or pollutant levels, or specify test methods. The standards do not expand upon existing government regulations. ISO 14000 serves as a guide for environmentally conscious organizations seeking to lessen their impact on the environment.

Figures 14.4 and 14.5 provide information about the general structure of the ISO 14000 series of standards. For each series, specific activities are required. For instance,

---

■ ISO 14001
   Environmental Management Systems—Specification with
   Guidance for Use

■ ISO 14004
   Environmental Management Systems—General Guidelines
   on Principles, Systems, and Supporting Techniques

■ ISO 14010
   Guidelines for Environmental Auditing—General Principles on
   Environmental Auditing

■ ISO 14011
   Guidelines for Environmental Auditing—Audit Procedures—
   Auditing of Environmental Management Systems

■ ISO 14012
   Guidelines for Environmental Auditing—Qualification Criteria
   for Environmental Auditors

■ ISO 14014
   Initial Reviews

■ ISO 14015
   Environmental Site Assessments

■ ISO 14031
   Evaluation of Environmental Performance

■ ISO 14020
   Goals and Principles of All Environmental Labeling

■ ISO 14021
   Environmental Labels and Declarations—Self-Declaration
   Environmental Claims—Terms and Definitions

**Figure 14.4   ISO 14000 Process-Oriented Document
Requirements**

- ISO 14022
  Environmental Labels and Declarations—Symbols
- ISO 14023
  Environmental Labels and Declarations—Testing and Verifications
- ISO 14024
  Environmental Labels and Declarations—Environmental Labeling
  Type 1—Guiding Principles and Procedures
- ISO 1402X
  Type III Labeling
- ISO 14040
  Life Cycle Assessment—Principles and Framework
- ISO 14041
  Life Cycle Assessment—Life Cycle Inventory Analysis
- ISO 14042
  Life Cycle Assessment—Impact Assessment
- ISO 14043
  Life Cycle Assessment—Interpretation
- ISO 14050
  Terms and Definitions—Guide on the Principles of ISO/TC 207/SC6 Terminology Work
- ISO Guide 64
  Guide for the Inclusion of Environmental Aspects of Product Standards

Figure 14.5   ISO 14000 Product-Oriented Document Requirements

within ISO 14001, Environmental Management Systems (Figure 14.6), companies must provide details concerning their environmental policy and the structure of their overall environmental management system. Section 4.2, Environmental Policy, defines the organization's environmental policy which serves as the foundation for the environmental management system. Section 4.3, Planning, provides details on the organization's program and what must be done to support the legal requirements, targets, and objectives of the organization. Section 4.4, Implementation and Operation, establishes procedures and processes that allow the system to be implemented, including training, the structure of the communication and document control systems, as well as emergency preparedness and response systems. Section 4.5, Checking and Corrective Action, monitors and measures the environmental management system. Companies seeking ISO 14000 certification are expected to have in place an internal auditing system supported by preventive and corrective action plans. Section 4.6, Management Review, ensures that the entire process is reviewed regularly so that opportunities for improvement are not overlooked.

ISO 14000
Section 1: Scope

Section 2: Normative References

Section 3: Definitions

Section 4: Environmental Management Systems Requirements

4.1 General Requirements
4.2 Environmental Policy
4.3 Planning
    4.3.1 Environmental Aspects
    4.3.2 Legal and Other Requirements
    4.3.3 Objectives and Targets
    4.3.4 Environmental Management Program(s)
4.4 Implementation and Operation
    4.4.1 Structure and Responsibility
    4.4.2 Training, Awareness, and Competence
    4.4.3 Communication
    4.4.4 Environmental Management System Documentation
    4.4.5 Document Control
    4.4.6 Operational Control
    4.4.7 Emergency Preparedness and Response
4.5 Checking and Corrective Action
    4.5.1 Monitoring and Measurement
    4.5.2 Nonconformance and Corrective and Preventive Action
    4.5.3 Records
    4.5.4 Environmental Management System Audit
4.6 Management Review

Figure 14.6   ISO 14000, Section 4: Environmental Management Systems Requirements

ISO 14001 certification becomes more popular each year. In 2003, over 60,000 companies worldwide were certified, over 13,800 in Japan, 5,000 in China, and 3,400 in the United States. As companies are becoming more environmentally conscious and more globally responsive, many are becoming ISO 14000 certified and mandating that their suppliers do so too. As with ISO 9000, this standard is reviewed and updated regularly. For more complete information, visit the ISO website at www.iso.org.

MALCOLM BALDRIGE NATIONAL QUALITY AWARD

The Malcolm Baldrige National Quality Award (MBNQA) was established in 1987 by the United States Congress. The MBNQA is named after former U.S. Secretary of State (1981–1987), Malcolm Baldrige. Due to his personal interest in quality management and improvement he was instrumental in the design and establishment of the award. Similar to Japan's Deming Prize, it sets a national standard for quality excellence. The award is open to companies in three areas: Business, Education, and Health Care. It is managed by the American Society for Quality (www.asq.org). As stated in the chapter introduction, Motorola was the first company to win the Malcolm Baldrige Award. Every year, this rigorous award attracts several dozen applicants in each category. A group of qualified examiners compares and contrasts each application with the criteria for up to 300 hours. Only a very select few reach the site-visit stage of the award process. By the completion of the on-site visits, a company may have been examined for as many as 1000 hours. Since 1988, 44 organizations have received the United States' highest award for organizational effectiveness. Organizations pursuing the MBNQA focus on their approach to doing business and the deployment of their strategic resources. These organizations have one key metric for measuring their results: the stock price. It is interesting to note that the Baldrige award winners, when their stock performance is reviewed, outperform the stocks in the Standard and Poor's 500 Index by a ratio of about 3 to 1. For more information about the Baldrige stock study, visit the following website: www.nist.gov/public_affairs/factsheet/stockstudy.htm.

The award allows companies to make comparisons with other companies. This activity is called benchmarking. **Benchmarking** *is a continuous process of measuring products, services, and practices against competitors or industry leaders*. Covered in more detail in Chapter 15, benchmarking lets an organization know where they stand compared with others in their industry. Companies also use the award guidelines to determine a baseline. **Baselining** *is measuring the current level of quality in an organization*. Baselines are used to show where a company is, so that it knows where it should concentrate its improvement efforts.

Standards to be used as baselines and benchmarks for total quality management are set in seven areas (Figure 14.7). The seven categories are leadership, information and analysis, strategic quality planning, human resource development and management, management of process quality, quality and operational results, and customer focus and satisfaction. The following descriptions are paraphrased from the Malcolm Baldrige National Quality Award criteria.

1.0 Leadership   The criteria in Section 1.0 are used to examine senior-level management's commitment to and involvement in process improvement. Company leaders are expected to develop and sustain a customer focus supported by visible actions and values on their part. This section also examines how the organization addresses its responsibilities to the public and exhibits good citizenship. Subcategories include organizational leadership and social responsibilities.

2.0 Strategic Planning   To score well in this category, a company needs to have sound strategic objectives and action plans. The examiners also investigate how the company's strategic objectives and action plans are deployed and progress measured. Subcategories are strategy development process, strategic objectives, action plan development, and deployment and performance projection.

3.0 Customer and Market Focus   The third category of the Baldrige Award criteria deals with the company's relationship with its customers. This category focuses on a company's knowledge of customer requirements, expectations, and preferences as well as marketplace competitiveness. Reviewers also determine if the

---

1.0 Leadership
   1.1 Organizational Leadership
   1.2 Social Responsibility
2.0 Strategic Planning
   2.1 Strategy Development
   2.2 Strategy Deployment
3.0 Customer and Market Focus
   3.1 Customer and Market Knowledge
   3.2 Customer Relationships and Satisfaction
4.0 Measurement, Analysis, and Knowledge Management
   4.1 Measurement and Analysis of Organizational Performance
   4.2 Information and Knowledge Management
5.0 Human Resource Focus
   5.1 Work Systems
   5.2 Employee Learning and Motivation
   5.3 Employee Well-Being and Satisfaction
6.0 Process Management
   6.1 Value Creation Processes
   6.2 Support Processes
7.0 Business Results
   7.1 Customer-Focused Results
   7.2 Product and Service Results
   7.3 Financial and Market Results
   7.4 Human Resource Results
   7.5 Organizational Effectiveness Results
   7.6 Governance and Social Responsibility Results

**Figure 14.7   Malcolm Baldrige National Quality Award Criteria
Categories, 2004 (U.S. Department of Commerce www.nist.gov)**

company has put this knowledge to work in the improvement of their products, processes, systems, and services. Success in this category leads to improved customer acquisition, satisfaction, and retention. This category clarifies a company's commitment to its customers. The subcategories are customer and market knowledge, customer relationships, and customer satisfaction determination.

4.0 Measurement Analysis, and Knowledge Management The award recognizes that information is only useful when it is put to work to identify areas for improvement. This category investigates a company's use of information and performance measurement systems to encourage excellence. Performance information must be used to improve operational competitiveness. Competitive comparisons and benchmarking are encouraged. Subcategories include measurement and analysis of organizational performance, and information and knowledge management.

5.0 Human Resource Focus Within the human resource focus section, reviewers for the Baldrige Award are interested in a company's plans and actions that enable its workforce to perform to the fullest potential in alignment with the company's overall strategic objectives. Employee involvement, education, training, and recognition are considered in this category. A company's work environment

Manufacturing

Motorola Commercial, Government & Industrial Solutions Sector
Clarke American Checks, Inc.
Dana Corporation – Spicer Driveshaft Division
ST Microelectronics, Inc. Region Americas
Boeing Airlift and Tanker Programs
Solar Turbines Incorporated
3M Dental Product Division
Solectron Corporation
ADAC Laboratories
Armstrong World Industries, Inc., Building Products Operations
AT&T Network Systems Group Transmission Systems Business Unit
Texas Instruments Incorporated Defense Systems & Electronics Group
Eastman Chemical Company
Cadillac Motor Car Company
Westinghouse Electric Corporation Commercial Nuclear Fuel Division
Xerox Corporation, Business Products Systems
IBM Rochester

Service

Caterpillar Financial Services Corporation - U.S.
Boeing Aerospace Support
Operations Management International, Inc.
Merrill Lynch Credit Corporation
Dana Commercial Credit Corporation
Verizon Information Services
AT&T Universal Card Services
The Ritz-Carlton Hotel Company
Federal Express Corporation

Small Business

Sunny Fresh Foods
Branch-Smith Printing Division
Pal's Sudden Service
Wallace Co., Inc.
Globe Metallurgical, Inc.
Granite Rock Company
Ames Rubber Corporation
Texas Nameplate Company, Inc.
Los Alamos National Bank
Trident Precision Manufacturing, Inc.

Healthcare

Baptist Hospital, Inc.
St. Luke's Hospital of Kansas City
SSM Heath Care

Education

Community Consolidated School District 15
Pearl River School District
University of Wisconsin-Stout
Chugach School District

Figure 14.8   Partial List of Malcolm Baldrige National Quality Award Winners since 1988
SOURCE: *www.quality.nist.gov/Award_Recipients.htm*

receives careful scrutiny in an effort to determine how the company has built and maintains a work environment conducive to performance excellence as well as personal and organizational growth. Subcategories include work systems, employee learning and motivation, and employee well-being and satisfaction.

6.0 Process Management   Within this category, the company is judged on its process management abilities. Companies must provide details on their key business processes as they relate to customers, products, and service delivery. Subcategories are value creation processes and support processes.

7.0 Business Results   Ultimately, the purpose of being in business is to stay in business. This category examines a company's performance and improvement in several key business areas including customer satisfaction, product and service performance, financial and marketplace performance, human resources, and operational performance. Benchmarking is encouraged to see how the company compares with its competitors. Subcategories are customer results, product and service results, financial and market results, human resources results, organizational effectiveness results, and governance and social responsibility results.

The criteria for the Malcolm Baldrige Award are updated annually. Recipients of the award are from a variety of industries, including telecommunications, banking, automotive, hospitality industry, education, hospitals, building products, and manufacturing (Figure 14.8). For more information about the award criteria, contact the U.S. Commerce Department's National Institute of Standards and Technology at www.nist.gov. For a complete list of Malcolm Baldrige National Quality Award recipients, including organization profiles and contact data, visit www.quality.nist.gov/Award_Recipients.htm.

SIX SIGMA

In the 1990s, a concept entitled Six Sigma was conceived by Bill Smith, a reliability engineer for Motorola Corporation. His research lead him to believe that the increasing complexity of systems and products used by consumers created higher than desired system failure rates. Beginning in Chapter 10, "Reliability," we learned that to increase system reliability and reduce failure rates, the components utilized in complex systems and products have to have individual failure rates approaching zero. With this in mind, Smith took a holistic view of reliability and quality and developed a strategy for improving both. Smith worked with others to develop the Six Sigma Breakthrough Strategy, which is essentially a highly focused system of problem-solving. Six Sigma's goal is to reach 3.4 defects per million opportunities over the long term. Figure 14.9 shows the impact of achieving 6σ levels of process performance. Did you know that, according to data published by ASQ, correct prescription writing, correct restaurant bill calculation and proper airline baggage handling takes place at the 4σ? Automotive expectation of quality exceed 5σ, as do safe aircraft carrier landings. Domestic airline fatality rates nearly reach 7σ.

Six Sigma is about results, enhancing profitability through improved quality and efficiency. At the strategic business level, upper management must decide to implement

99.74% Good = Three Sigma (3σ)	**99.9998% Good = Six Sigma (6σ)**
20,000 lost articles of mail per hour	Seven lost articles of mail per hour
Unsafe drinking water for almost 15 minutes each day	Unsafe drinking water one minute every seven months
5,000 incorrect surgical operations per week	1.7 incorrect surgical operations per week
Two short or long landings at most major airports each day	One short or long landing every five years
200,000 wrong drug prescriptions each year	68 wrong drug prescriptions each year
No electricity for almost seven hours each month	One hour without electricity every 34 years

Figure 14.9   Achieving 6σ Levels of Process Performance

Six Sigma. They set strategic business goals and metrics. At the operational process level, middle managers translate strategic business goals into process goals and measures. They also identify process problems and projects. At the project level, employees obtain green and black belt certifications while working on improvement projects throughout the organization.

Six Sigma seeks to reduce the variability present in processes. Improvement projects are chosen based on their ability to contribute to the bottom line on a company's income statement. Projects should be connected to the strategic objectives and goals of the corporation. Projects that do not directly tie to customer issues or financial results are often difficult to sell to management. Six Sigma projects are easy to identify. They seek out sources of waste such as overtime and warranty claims; investigate production backlogs or areas in need of more capacity; and focus on customer and environmental issues. With high volume products even small improvements can produce a significant impact on the financial statement. When choosing a Six Sigma project or any improvement project, care should be taken to avoid poorly defined objectives or metrics. Key business metrics include revenue dollars, labor rates, fixed and variable unit costs, gross margin rates, operating margin rates, inventory costs, general and administrative expenses, cash flow, warranty costs, product liability costs, and cost avoidance. The following example provides information about how to choose a project.

EXAMPLE 14.1   Justifying a Project

Queensville Manufacturing Corporation creates specialty packaging for automotive industry suppliers. The project team has been working to improve a particularly tough packaging problem involving transporting finished transmissions to the original equipment manufacturer (OEM). Company management has told the team that several key projects, including theirs, are competing for funding. In order to ensure acceptance of their project, the team wants to develop strong metrics to show how investment in their project will result in significant cost savings and improved customer satisfaction through increased quality. After brainstorming about their project, the team developed the following list of objectives and metrics for their project.

By retrofitting Packaging Machine A with a computer guidance system the following will improve:

Capacity:

      Downtime reduction from 23% to 9% daily

         (downtime cannot be completely eliminated due to product change-overs)

      Resource consumption reduction

      Twenty percent less usage of raw materials such as cardboard and shrink-wrap due to improved packing arrangement, allowing five transmissions per package instead of four previously achieved

Customer Satisfaction:

      Improved delivery performance

         Improved packaging arrangement integrates better with customer production lines saving 35% of customer start-up time

      Reduced space required for in-process inventory

         Improved packaging arrangement, allowing five transmissions per package instead of four previously achieved saving 10% of original factory floor space usage

      Reduced defect levels due to damage from shipping

         Improved packaging arrangement provides better protection during shipment saving 80% of damage costs

Revenue:

      Reduced costs $600,000 by the third quarter of the next fiscal year, given a project completion date of the fourth quarter of this fiscal year

      Reduced lost opportunity cost

         Increased customer satisfaction will result in an increased number of future orders

This project was selected as a focus for Six Sigma improvement because it could be justified by the impact it will have on overall organization performance. **Q**

Six Sigma projects have eight essential phases: recognize, define, measure, analyze, improve, control, standardize, and integrate. This cycle is sometimes expressed as DMAIC (define, measure, analyze, improve, and control). As Figure 14.10 shows, the generic steps for Six Sigma project implementation are similar to the problem-solving steps presented in Chapter 3. The tools utilized during a project include statistical process control techniques, customer input, Failure Modes and Effects Analysis, Design of Experiments, process mapping, cause-and-effect diagrams, multivariate analysis, pre-control, and design for manufacturability. Six Sigma also places a heavy reliance on graphical methods for analysis. The Six Sigma methodology is implemented in a variety of different circumstances; some companies will change these steps to suit their needs. As with any strategy, a variety of acronyms exist (Figure 14.11).

Once the project has been selected:

1. Select appropriate metrics: key process output variables (KPOVs).
2. Determine how these metrics will be tracked over time.
3. Determine current baseline performance of project/process.
4. Determine the key process input variables (KPIVs) that drive the key process output variables (KPOVs).
5. Determine what changes need to be made to the key process input variables in order to positively affect the key process output variables.
6. Make the changes.
7. Determine if the changes have positively affected the KPOVs.
8. If the changes made result in performance improvements, establish control of the KPIVs at the new levels. If the changes have not resulted in performance improvement, return to step 5 and make the appropriate changes.

Figure 14.10   Six Sigma Problem-Solving Steps

Motorola Corporation utilizes terminology from Karate as a method to designate the experience and ability levels of Six Sigma project participants. Green Belts are individuals who have completed a designated number of hours of training in the Six Sigma methodology. To achieve Green Belt status, a participant must also complete a cost-savings project of a specified size, often $10,000, within a stipulated amount of time. Black Belts are individuals with extensive training in the Six Sigma methodology. Before becoming a Black

APQP	Advanced Product Quality Planning
CTQ	Critical to quality
DFSS	Design for Six Sigma
DIAMC	Define, improve, analyze, measure, control
DPMO	Defects per million opportunities
DPU	Defect per unit
EVOP	Evolution operation
FMEA	Failure Modes and Effects Analysis
KPIV	Key process input variable
KPOV	Key process output variable
Process Owners	The individual ultimately responsible for the process and what it produces
Master Black Belts	Individuals with extensive training qualified to teach black belt training classes, who have completed a large-scale improvement project, often a Master's Degree is required
Black Belts	Individuals with extensive training in the Six Sigma methodology who have completed a number of improvement projects of significant size
Green Belts	Individuals trained in the Six Sigma methodology who have completed an improvement project of a specified size
Reliability	Measured as mean-time-to-failure
Quality	Measured as process variability and defect rates

Figure 14.11   Six Sigma Abbreviations and Terms

Responsibility	Phase
Management	Recognize
Management/Master Black Belts	Define
Black Belts/Green Belts	Measure
Black Belts/Green Belts	Analyze
Black Belts/Green Belts	Improve
Black Belts/Green Belts	Control
Management	Standardize
Management	Integrate

Figure 14.12   Six Sigma Responsibility Matrix

Belt, an individual must have completed a specified number of successful projects under the guidance and direction of Master Black Belts. Often companies expect the improvement projects overseen by a Black Belt to result in savings of $100,000 or more. Master Black Belts are individuals with extensive training who have completed a large scale improvement project, usually saving $1,000,000 or more for the company. Often before designating someone a Master Black Belt, a company will require a Master's Degree from an accredited university. Master Black Belts provide training and guide trainees during their projects. Figure 14.12 shows the responsibilities of project participants.

It is important to understand the origin of the term Six Sigma. Six Sigma is a methodology, 6σ is the value used to calculate process capability, Cp. As we learned in Chapter 6, the spread of a distribution of average process measurements can only be compared with the specifications set for the process using Cp, where

$$Cp = \frac{USL - LSL}{6\sigma}$$

When 6σ = USL − LSL, process capability Cp = 1. When this happens, the process is considered to be operating at 3σ. Three standard deviations added to the average value will equal the upper specification limit, and three standard deviations subtracted from the average value will equal the lower specification limit (Figure 14.13). When Cp = 1, the process is capable of producing products that conform to specifications provided that the variation present in the process does not increase and that the average value equals the target value. In other words, the average cannot shift. That is a lot to ask from a process, so those operating processes often reduce the amount of variation present in the process so that 6σ < USL − LSL.

Some companies choose to add a design margin of 25% to allow for process shifts, requiring that the parts produced vary 25% less than the specifications allow. A 25% margin results in a Cp = 1.33. When Cp = 1.33, the process is considered to be operating at 4σ. Four standard deviations added to the average value will equal the upper specification limit, and four standard deviations subtracted from the average value will equal the lower specification limit. This concept can be repeated for 5σ and Cp = 1.66.

When Cp = 2.00, 6σ has been achieved. Six standard deviations added to the average value will equal the upper specification limit, and six standard deviations

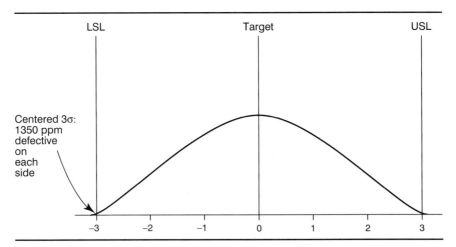

Figure 14.13   The Value of 3σ Occurs When 6σ = USL − LSL, Process Capability, Cp = 1

subtracted from the average value will equal the lower specification limit (Figure 14.14). Those who developed the Six Sigma methodology felt that a value of Cp = 2.00 provides adequate protection against the possibilities of a process mean shift or an increase in variation. Operating at a 6σ level also enables a company's production to have virtually zero defects. Long term expectations for the number of defects per million opportunities is 3.4. Compare this to a process that is operating at 3σ and centered. Such a process will have a number of defectives per million opportunities of 1,350 out of each side of the specification limits for a total of 2,700. If the process center were to shift 1.5σ, the total number of defects per million opportunities at the 3σ level would be 66,807. A process operating at 4σ will have 6,210

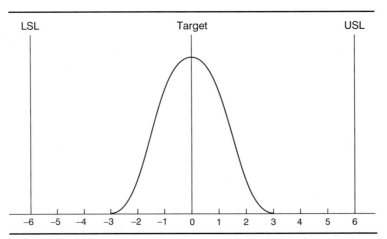

Figure 14.14   The Value of 6σ Occurs When 6σ < USL − LSL, Process Capability, Cp = 2

defects per million opportunities over the long term, while a process operating at the 5σ level will have 233 defects per million opportunities long term. The formula for long term σ is:

$$\sigma = \text{Normsinv}\ (1 - [\text{DPMO}/1{,}000{,}000]) + 1.5$$

Even if the cost to correct the defect is only $100, operating at the 3σ level while experiencing a process shift will cost a company $6,680,700 per million parts. Improving performance to 4σ reduces that amount to $621,000 per million parts produced. Six σ performance costs just $340 per million parts.

As with any process improvement methodology, there are issues that need to be examined carefully. One criticism is that Six Sigma methodology does not offer anything new. Comparisons have been made between ISO 9000 and Six Sigma, QS 9000 and Six Sigma, continuous improvement strategies and Six Sigma strategies, and significant similarities exist (Table 14.1). Comparisons have also been made between Master Black Belt qualifications and the qualifications for a Certified Quality Engineer (CQE). Once again, the similarities are striking (Table 14.2). Other certifications

Table 14.1   Comparison of ISO 9000, the Malcolm Baldrige Award Criteria, and Continuous Improvement/Quality Management

	ISO 9000	*Baldrige Award*	*CI/QM*	*Six Sigma*
Scope	Quality management system Continuous improvement	Quality of management	Quality management and corporate citizenship Continuous improvement	Systematic reduction of process variability
Basis for defining quality	Features and characteristics of product or service	Customer-driven	Customer-driven	Defects per million opportunities
Purpose	Clear quality management system requirements for international cooperation Improved record keeping	Results-driven competitiveness through total quality management	Continuous improvement of customer service	Improve profitability by reducing process variation
Assessment	Requirements-based	Performance-based	Based on total organizational commitment to quality	Defects per million opportunities
Focus	International trade Quality links between suppliers and purchasers Record keeping	Customer satisfaction Competitive comparisons	Processes needed to satisfy internal and external customers	Locating and eliminating sources of process error

Table 14.2   Body of Knowledge Comparison of CQE and Black Belt Certification

Category	ASQ Certified Quality Engineer (CQE) Certification Requirements	Black Belt Requirements
Leadership	Management and Leadership in Quality Engineering	Enterprise-Wide Deployment
Business Processes	Not covered	Business Process Management
Quality Systems	Quality Systems Development, Implementation, and Verification	Not covered
Quality Assurance	Planning, Controlling, and Assuring Product and Process Quality	Not covered
Reliability	Reliability and Risk Management	Not covered
Problem-Solving	Problem-Solving and Quality Improvement	Define-Measure-Analyze-Improve-Control
Quality Tools	Problem-Solving and Quality Improvement	DMAIC
Project Management	Not covered	Project Management
Team Concepts	Not covered	Team Leadership
Statistical Methods	Probability and Statistics Collecting and Summarizing Data	Probability and Statistics Collecting and Summarizing Data
Design of Experiments	Designing Experiments	Design of Experiments
Process Capability	Analyzing Process Capability	Analyzing Process Capability
Statistical Process Control	Statistical Process Control	Statistical Process Control
Measurement Systems (metrology/calibration)	Measurement Systems Metrology	Measurement Systems Metrology
Lean Manufacturing	Not covered	Lean Enterprise
Other Techniques	FMEA, FMECA, FTA	FMEA, QFD Multi-Variate Studies

available through ASQ (www.asq.org) include: Certified Quality Technician, Certified Quality Engineer, and Certified Quality Manager.

Another criticism is the focus on defectives per million. Can we really call them defectives? The term itself brings to mind product liability issues. How does a customer view a company that is focused on counting defectives? Should defect counts be seen as the focus or are companies really trying to focus on process improvement?

The Six Sigma methodology encourages companies to take a customer focus and improve their business processes. Using DMAIC as a guideline, companies seek opportunities to enhance their ability to do business. Process improvement of any kind leads to benefits for the company from the reduction of waste, costs, and lost opportunities. Ultimately, it is the customer who enjoys enhanced quality and reduced costs.

 REAL TOOLS FOR REAL LIFE

Becoming a Black Belt

Following graduation, Chris joined a multinational logistics organization. Early on, his manager encouraged him to further his education by becoming a Six Sigma Green Belt. Since his college program of study had included a four course series in quality assurance, Chris felt confident that he was well-prepared for this adventure. When he began his Green Belt certification process in the Fall, his classes included exposure to the quality tools listed in Figure 14.15. Since his training was really a

Quality Philosophies
Performance Measures/Metrics
Problem Solving Model
Process Mapping
Check Sheets
Pareto Analysis
Cause and Effect Diagram Analysis
Scatter Diagrams
Frequency Diagrams
Histograms
Statistics
Data Collection:
    Data types and sampling techniques
$\overline{X}$ and R charts
Process Capability Analysis
P, u, c charts
Root Cause Analysis
Variation Reduction
Six Sigma Philosophy

Green Belt Project

Figure 14.15   Training Typically Required for Green Belt Certification

Green Belt Requirements plus:

Variable Control Charts
Attributes Control Charts
Process Capability Analysis
Hypothesis Testing
Design of Experiments
Gage R&R
Reliability
ISO 9000, MBNQA
Voice of the Customer
Regression Analysis

Black Belt Project

Figure 14.16   Training Typically Required for Black Belt Certification

review of his college courses, Chris was able to quickly grasp the concepts and tools and apply them to his project. The project, selected by his Master Black Belt Mentor, involved developing a corrective action procedure to identify root causes of process failures in a package sorting line. Following an in-depth review of his training and project, the Master Black Belt, an individual accredited through the Six Sigma Academy, Chris received certification early the next spring.

That summer, Chris began Black Belt training. Over the period of a year, he attended 160 hours of training in basic statistical techniques, advanced statistics, hypothesis testing, analysis of variation, regression analysis, control charts, and design of experiments (Figure 14.16). Black Belt trainees met once a month for training and then applied what they learned for the next 3 weeks to their everyday work. At each training session, Master Black Belts reviewed what he had applied from previous training session. Training also included the study of many projects completed by other Black Belts. Trainees were given the original project plans and asked to simulate the project and analyze the results. During his last class, Chris participated in a one day project that included elements of design of experiments. For his Black Belt project, a logistics pick-pack-ship optimization project, Chris developed an experiment to study the optimal configuration for the pick-pack-ship line in his facility. He ran the experiment on Saturday, analyzed the data on Sunday, made appropriate changes to the line based on the experiment and then monitored the new setup for several weeks. Once his predicted results were confirmed, he wrote up his results, calculated financial benefits, and presented his report to management. Shortly thereafter, Chris was certified as a Six Sigma Black Belt by the Master Black Belt.

Though certification was granted by the Master Black Belt, Chris decided to formalize his certification by taking the Black Belt Certification test from the American Society for Quality. His score: 95%!   **Q**

SUMMARY

ISO 9000, supplier certification requirements, the Malcolm Baldrige Award criteria, and the Six Sigma methodology provide direction and support for companies interested in developing a total quality system. All of these require the same general approach: Establish an organizational policy, implement that policy through documented procedures, practice the procedures and policies in the work environment, and show proof that the company's day-to-day business practices support the policies. Table 14.1 summarizes how the approaches compare with one another. Perhaps the key difference among the three is the purpose of each. The Malcolm Baldrige Award is an integrated approach that uses results-based performance assessments to improve competitiveness, whereas the ISO 9000 standards focus on functional requirements and record keeping to support international cooperation. Six Sigma drives improvement focused on the bottom line. Neither of these has the clear continuous improvement mandate that characterizes a total quality system. The Baldrige Award criteria, which set standards for leadership and customer-driven quality, most closely reflect the total quality concept.

Organizational leadership must understand that quality improvement initiatives are about achieving long-term, sustained changes. These efforts take time and are not short-term fixes. Continuous improvement efforts, Six Sigma, and ISO 9000 are based on quality improvement principles that complement each other. Regardless of which approach an organization takes, all quality management systems stress eight key principles:

Customer focus: identifying customer expectations
Process improvement based on customer expectations
Fact-based decision-making: measures critical to customer expectations
Systems approach to management: tracking measures
Leadership: commitment to excellence
Involvement of people
Continuous improvement
Mutually beneficial supplier relationships

 ■ *Lessons Learned*

1. ISO 9000 is a requirements-based assessment that supports the development of a quality management system.
2. ISO 9000 standards focus on functional requirements and record keeping to support international cooperation in business-to-business dealings.
3. QS 9000 and TS 16949 combine requirements from ISO 9000 with sector- and customer-specific requirements.
4. QS 9000 and TS 16949 require that suppliers create, document, and implement a quality management system.

5. ISO 14000 is primarily focused on the efforts made by an organization to minimize any harmful impact on the environment that its business activities may cause.

6. Six Sigma is a methodology that seeks to improve profits through improved quality and efficiency.

7. Companies competing for the Malcolm Baldrige National Quality Award must perform well in the following categories: leadership, information and analysis, strategic planning, human resource focus, process management, business results, and customer and market focus.

8. The Malcolm Baldrige Award uses results-based performance assessments to improve competitiveness.

9. Neither ISO 9000 nor the Malcolm Baldrige Award has a comprehensive emphasis on continuous improvement mandated by a total quality system.

10. The Baldrige Award criteria, with their standards for leadership and customer-driven quality, most closely reflect the total quality system. ■

Chapter Problems

Quality Systems

1. What is meant by the term "quality system"?

2. Why would a quality system be critical to providing a quality product or service?

3. What attributes would you expect to be present in a company that has a sound quality system?

4. Describe the quality system that existed at your most recent place of employment. How would you rate its effectiveness? Support your rating with examples.

ISO 9000/QS 9000/ ISO 14000

5. Describe which types of companies would use ISO 9001.

6. Find an article about a company that is in the process of achieving or has achieved ISO 9000 or ISO 14000 certification. What were the steps that they had to take? What difficulties did they encounter?

7. Contact a local company that is in the process of achieving or has achieved ISO 9000 or ISO 14000 certification. What were the steps that they had to take? What difficulties did they encounter?

8. Describe the differences between the ISO 9000 series of requirements and the requirements for QS 9000 or TS 16949.

9. Find an article discussing QS 9000 or TS 16949. After reading the article, answer any or all of the following questions:
   a. Who needs to become certified?
   b. What steps does a company have to take to become certified?
   c. What are the reactions to QS 9000?

10. Describe ISO 14000 to someone who has not heard of it.

Malcolm Baldrige

11. Describe the main premise of each of the criteria for the Malcolm Baldrige Award.

12. Research a Malcolm Baldrige Award winner. What did they have to change about their quality system in order to become a winner? What did they consider the most important criterion? Why? How did they go about achieving that criterion?

13. Discuss the differences among ISO 9000, the Baldrige Award, and total quality.

Six Sigma

14. Describe the Six Sigma concept.

15. How does Six Sigma bring about a reduction of defects?

16. What tools does Six Sigma use?

17. How are Six Sigma projects selected?

18. Describe the differences among Green Belts, Black Belts, and Master Black Belts.

CASE STUDY 14.1
Malcolm Baldrige Award Criteria

Many firms have implemented comprehensive quality-improvement programs. Recent articles in trade publications as well as nationally known magazines such as *Forbes*, *Business Week*, and *Newsweek* have reported on what these companies have been doing in the area of quality.

 Assignment

Read one or more comprehensive articles from a current business or news magazine and on the basis of your reading assess the quality improvement activities of one company. Choose one of the seven areas found in the Malcolm Baldrige Award criteria and make your assessment along the same guidelines. You may wish to strengthen your assessment by contacting the company itself. Use the following questions to aid you in investigating the firm.

1. Leadership
    a. What is the attitude and involvement of top management? How is this visible? Check top management's understanding of quality, their investment of time and money in quality issues, their willingness to seek help on quality management, their support of each other and subordinates, the level of importance they place on quality, and their participation in quality process.
    b. What importance does the company management place on developing a quality culture? How is this visible? Check their understanding of quality, their investment of time and money in quality issues, their willingness to seek help on quality management, their support of each other and subordinates, the level of importance they place on quality, their participation in quality process, and their training of employees.
    c. What is your perception of importance of quality to this company? How is this visible? Is the company's position based on eliminating defects by inspection? judging cost of quality by scrap and rework? or preventing defects through design of process and product?
2. Information and Analysis
    a. What types of data and information does the company collect? Are these records on customer-related issues? on internal operations? on company performance? on cost and financial matters?
    b. How does the company ensure the reliability of the data throughout their company? Are their records consistent? standardized? timely? updated? Is there rapid access to data? What is the scope of the data?

    c. How are their information and control systems used? Do they have key methods of data collection and analysis? systematic collection on paper? systematic collection with computers? How do they use the information collected to solve problems? Can problems be traced to their source?

3. Strategic Planning

    a. What importance does the company place on quality in its strategic planning? How is this visible? Check management's understanding of quality, their investment of time and money in quality issues, how their interest is reflected in the strategic plan, the level of importance they assign the strategic plan, and whether quality control is evident throughout the plan or in just one section.

    b. How does the company develop their plans and strategies for the short term? for the long term?

    c. Which benchmarks does the company use to measure quality? Are the benchmarks relative to the market leader or to competitors in general? What are management's projections about the market?

    d. How does the company rank the following:

- Cost of manufacturing and product provision
- Volume of output
- Meeting schedules
- Quality

    e. Does the company management feel that a certain level of defects is acceptable as a cost of doing business and a way of company life?

    f. Is quality first incorporated into the process at the concept development/preliminary research level? the product development level? the production/operations level? at final inspection?

    g. Does the company define quality according to performance? aesthetic issues? serviceability? durability? features? reliability? fit and finish? conformance to specifications?

    h. Are the following measures used to evaluate overall quality?

- Zero defects
- Parts per million
- Reject or rework rate
- Cost of quality

    i. The company's quality improvement program is best described as:

- There is no formal program.
- The program emphasizes short-range solutions.
- The program emphasizes motivational projects and slogans.
- A formal improvement program creates widespread awareness and involvement.
- The quality process is an integral part of ongoing company operations and strategy.

j. Perceived barriers to a better company are

- Top-management inattention
- Perception of program costs
- Inadequate organization of quality effort
- Inadequate training
- Costs of quality not computed
- Low awareness of need for quality emphasis
- Crisis management a way of life (leaves no time)
- No formal program/process for improvement
- The management system
- The workers

k. The following steps in a quality-improvement plan have (have not) been taken:

- Obtained top-management commitment to establish a formal policy on quality
- Begun implementation of a formal companywide policy on quality
- Organized cross-functional improvement teams
- Established measures of quality (departmentally and in employee evaluation system)
- Established the cost of quality
- Established and implemented a companywide training program
- Begun identifying and correcting quality problems
- Set and begun to move toward quality goals

l. What objectives has the company set?

- Less rework
- Less scrap
- Fewer defects
- Plant utilization
- Improved yield
- Design improvements
- Fewer engineering changes (material, labor, process changes)
- Workforce training
- Improved testing
- Lower energy use
- Better material usage
- Lower labor hours per unit

4. Human Resource Focus
   a. Quality is incorporated into the human resources system through

   - Job descriptions of the president, vice president, managers, etc.
   - Performance appraisals
   - Individual rewards for quality-improvement efforts

- Hiring practices
- Education and training programs

b. How does the company encourage employees to buy in to quality?

- Through incentives
- Through stressing value to customers
- Through surveys or other forms of customer feedback
- Through the example of management

c. Has the quality message been distributed throughout the organization so that employees can use it in their day-to-day job activities? How has it been distributed?

d. If the importance of quality has been communicated throughout the corporation, how is that emphasis made visible?

- All employees are aware of the importance of quality. How is this visible?
- All employees are aware of how quality is measured. How is this visible?
- All employees are aware of the role of quality in their job. How is this visible?
- All employees are aware of how to achieve quality in their job. How is this visible?

e. Have teams been established to encourage cross-functional quality efforts?

- Yes, multifunctional teams seek continuous improvement.
- Yes, teams have been formed in nonmanufacturing and staff departments to encourage quality companywide.

f. Which of the following topics are stressed in employee participation groups? Is this stress reflected in the minutes, in attitudes, in solutions to problems?

- Product quality
- Service quality
- Quality of work life
- Productivity
- Cost
- Safety
- Energy
- Schedules
- Specifications
- Long-term versus quick-fix solutions

g. What percentage of employees have been involved in training programs in the past three years?

- On the managerial/supervisory level?
- On the nonmanagerial level?
- Among clerical and shop workers?

h. Which of the following topics are covered in the training programs? What is the depth of coverage?

- Process control
- Problem solving
- Data gathering and analysis
- Quality tools (Pareto, cause and effect charts, etc.)

5. Process Management

a. How are designs of products, services, and processes developed so that customer requirements are translated into design and quality requirements?

b. How do people handle problem solving and decision making? How is this visible?

- Crisis management prevails. Quality problems arise and are fought on an ad hoc basis.
- Individuals or teams are set up to investigate major problems.
- Problem solving is institutionalized and operationalized between departments. Attempts are frequently made to blame others.
- Problems and potential problems are identified early in development. Data and history are used for problem prevention.

c. The following quality-related costs are compiled and analyzed on a regular basis:

- Scrap
- Product liability
- Product redesign
- Repair
- Warranty claims
- Consumer contacts/concerns
- Inspection
- Specification/documentation review
- Design review
- Engineering change orders
- Service after service
- Rework
- Quality audits
- Test and acceptance
- Supplier evaluation and surveillance

d. How are costs of quality (or nonquality) calculated?

- Costs are not computed; there is little or no awareness of total costs.
- Direct costs are computed for rework, scrap, and returns, but the total cost of nonquality is not.
- Total costs are computed and are related to percentage of sales or operations.

- The costs of quality (prevention, appraisal, failure) are computed and reduced to 2–3% of actual sales.

e. Are periodic audits conducted to determine if the system is meeting the goals?

f. How are supplier relationships studied?

- Suppliers are certified by requiring evidence of statistical process control (SPC).
- Defects in shipments are identified and suppliers have to pay for them.
- A close working relationship has been established, allowing the suppliers to participate in the design/manufacture of the products.
- A just-in-time system has been established.
- Suppliers are rated with a formal system based on quality levels, capacity, production facilities, and delivery on schedule.

6. Business Results

a. How does the company track the key measures of product, service, and process quality?

b. How does the company benchmark itself against other companies?

c. How does the company justify expenditures on quality improvements?

- By traditional accounting procedures (expenditures justified only if lower than cost of product failure)
- By normal capital budgeting procedures that incorporate risk-adjusted net present value and discounted costs of capital
- By cash flow increase
- By the bottom line: return on investment, net profit percent, etc.

d. The finance and accounting system has the following roles in the quality management system:

- It calculates and tracks cost of quality.
- It measures and reports quality trends.
- It distributes quality data to appropriate persons.
- It designs performance measures.
- It compares performance to competition.
- It innovates new ways to evaluate quality investments.
- It turns the traditional cost-accounting system into a quality management system.

e. What tangible benefits has this company seen related to their quality program? How are the benefits visible? How are they measured?

- Increased sales
- Increased return on investment
- Customer satisfaction

- Lower cost
- Higher selling price
- More repeat business
- Higher market share
- Improved cash flow

7. Customer and Market Focus
   a. How does the company provide information to the customer? How easy is that information to obtain?
   b. How are service standards defined?
   c. How are customer concerns handled? What is the follow-up process?
   d. Which statement(s) describe company efforts to provide the best customer service:

   - The process has unequivocal support of top management.
   - Middle management is able to make significant changes.
   - Employees assume the major responsibility for ensuring customer satisfaction.
   - Formal training in customer satisfaction is provided to all employees.

   e. How does the company gather quality feedback from their customers?

   - Through customer surveys
   - Through a telephone hotline
   - Through customer focus groups
   - Through sales force reports
   - Through service rep reports

   f. Customer complaints are received by

   - The CEO or his/her office
   - The marketing or sales department
   - The quality-assurance staff
   - Service support departments
   - Customer complaint bureaus

15

Benchmarking and Auditing

Benchmarking
Auditing
Summary
Lessons Learned
Chapter Problems
Case Study 15.1 Benchmarking
Case Study 15.2 Auditing

 ■ *Learning Opportunities:*

1. To understand the concepts of benchmarking and auditing
2. To understand the basics of performing a benchmark assessment
3. To understand the basics of conducting an audit ■

"How Are We Doing?"

Companies have always compared their products and services with those of their competitors. Sometimes this comparison is done formally, sometimes informally. Benchmarking and auditing allow a company to judge itself against standards or competitors. Properly conducted, benchmarking against external standards or companies or auditing internal performance can provide a wealth of information about a company's competitive position.

BENCHMARKING

During a **benchmarking** *process, a company compares its performance against a set of standards or against the performance of best-in-its-class companies.* With the information provided by the comparison, a company can determine how to improve its own performance. Benchmarks serve as reference points. The measurements and information gathered are used to make conclusions about current performance and any necessary improvements. Companies may choose different aspects of their operations to benchmark. Typical areas to benchmark include procedures, operations, processes, quality-improvement efforts, and marketing and operational strategies.

Benchmarking can be done at several levels of complexity. Some companies choose to conduct a benchmarking assessment at the perception level. From a *perception benchmark assessment,* a company hopes to learn how they are currently performing. A perception assessment can focus on internal issues, seeking to answer questions related to what the people within the company think about themselves, the management, the company, or the quality-improvement process. Such an assessment reveals information about the company's current performance levels. This assessment may later serve as a baseline to compare with future benchmarking experiences.

Companies beginning the quest for ISO 9000 certification, qualified supplier certification, or a quality award may choose to perform a *compliance benchmark assessment.* This more in-depth benchmarking experience verifies a company's compliance with stated requirements and standards. The information gathered will answer questions about how a company is currently performing against the published standards. This assessment will also help a company locate where compliance to standards is weak.

A third type of benchmarking assessment investigates the effectiveness of a system a company has designed and implemented. An *effectiveness benchmark assessment* verifies that a company complies with the requirements and has effective systems in place to ensure that the requirements are being fulfilled. Complying with requirements, such as having a quality manual, does not guarantee that systems are in place to ensure the effective use of such a manual.

A fourth type of benchmarking assessment deals with continuous improvement. A *continuous improvement benchmark assessment* verifies that continuous improvement is an integral and permanent facet of an organization. It judges whether or not the company is providing lip service to process improvement issues or putting systems into place that support continual improvement on a day-to-day basis.

Perceptions, compliance, effectiveness, and continuous improvement can be verified through conducting a thorough review of the existing business practices. This review should follow an organized format. Activities can be judged on the basis of visual observations by the reviewers, interviews with those directly involved, personal knowledge, and factual documentation.

Purpose of Benchmarking

Effective organizations use benchmarking to compare their key measures of performance with those of others in order to determine where improvement opportunities exist.

Companies planning a benchmarking assessment should carefully consider the motivating factors. Specifically, why is the company planning to do this, and what do they hope to learn? Benchmarking measures an organization against recognized standards or the best-performing companies in the industry. Those beginning a benchmarking assessment program should have plans in place to use the information generated by the comparison. Benchmarking will provide targets for improved performance. A major pitfall of benchmarking is the failure to use the results of benchmarking to support a larger improvement strategy.

The reasons for benchmarking are many and varied. A company may embark on a benchmarking assessment to determine if they are able to comply with performance standards set by their customers. Benchmarking will point out areas where improvements are needed before seeking certification. Benchmarking against standards verifies whether or not a company meets the certification standards and qualifications set by a customer. On a larger scale, benchmarking can be used to determine if a company's quality systems are able to meet the requirements appropriate to meet ISO 9000 or quality award standards. Benchmarking answers such questions as: Are the company's processes properly constructed and documented? Are systems in place to allocate resources and funding appropriately? Which areas have the greatest improvement needs? What are our internal and external customer needs? The information gathered in the assessment should guide continuous improvement objectives, plans, and projects.

Benefits of Benchmarking

The primary benefit of benchmarking is the knowledge gained about where a company stands when compared against standards set by their customers, themselves, or national certification or award requirements. With this knowledge, a company can develop strategies for meeting their own continuous improvement goals. The benchmarking experience will identify assets within the company as well as opportunities for improvement. Most quality-assurance certifications involve discovering how the company is currently performing, strengthening the weaknesses, and then verifying compliance with the certification standards. Since a benchmarking assessment provides an understanding of how the company is performing, it is a valuable tool to use throughout the certification process.

Standards for Comparison

Typically, when a company chooses to perform a benchmarking assessment, one of the following is chosen for comparison: the Malcolm Baldrige National Quality Award, the International Organization for Standardization's ISO 9000, the Deming Prize, supplier certification requirements, or other companies who are the best in their field.

Malcolm Baldrige National Quality Award (MBNQA)

The Baldrige Award criteria are used by companies pursuing the United States' highest award for quality-management systems. The award criteria are also a popular and rigorous benchmarking tool for companies seeking a better understanding of their performance. Using the specific categories—leadership; strategic planning; customer and market focus; measurement, analysis, knowledge management; human resources focus; process management; and business results—companies can discover their capabilities and areas for improvement. The completeness and thoroughness of their coverage is a strong reason for using the criteria during benchmarking. The MBNQA is covered in more detail in Chapter 14.

ISO 9000

Benchmarking assessments are often employed when a company is seeking ISO 9000 certification. The ISO 9000 standard was developed to help companies effectively document the quality systems that need to be created and implemented to maintain an efficient total quality system. The standards cover areas like process management and quality assurance. The documentation serves as a guide during the benchmarking experience. Comparisons can be made between the company's existing systems and those required or suggested by ISO 9000 standards. ISO 9000 is covered in more detail in Chapter 14.

Deming Prize

The Deming Prize, its guidelines, and its criteria are overseen by the Deming Prize Committee of the Union of Japanese Scientists and Engineers. The award guidelines are rigorous and can be used to judge whether or not an organization has successfully achieved organizationwide quality.

Supplier Certification Requirements

Several larger manufacturers have supplier certification requirements, such as QS 9000 and AS 9100, that a supplier must meet in order to maintain certified or preferred supplier status. A company wishing to remain a supplier must conform to the expectations set by their customers. These guidelines are often used to help companies assess where they currently stand against the requirements and determine where improvements need to be made. Once the improvements are in place, the requirements serve as a benchmark against which company performance will be measured by the customer.

Best-in-Field Companies

Comparing one's performance against those companies judged best in their field can be a powerful tool for companies wishing to improve their position in the marketplace. By comparing their own performance with that of the market leader, companies can better understand their own assets and capabilities as well as the areas needing improvement. It is important to realize that the companies to benchmark against are companies who perform well in the area under study; they may not necessarily be competitors. For instance, a corporation interested in benchmarking its packaging

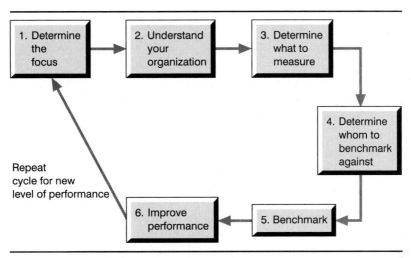

Figure 15.1   Flowchart of the Benchmarking Process

and shipping system may choose to gather information from an organization in an unrelated field that is known to possess an excellent system. Southwest Airlines benchmarked airplane turnaround time by comparing their work with the efforts of Indianapolis 500 race car pit crews. The effectiveness of comparison company benchmarking is limited by the ability to obtain performance information from the comparison company.

How to Benchmark

A variety of different plans and methods is available to aid interested companies in the benchmarking process. Certain steps and procedures will be part of every benchmarking experience. The following steps are usually facets of benchmarking (Figure 15.1).

1. *Determine the focus.* At the beginning of a benchmarking experience, those involved must determine what aspect of their company will be the focus of the study. The focus may be based on customer requirements, on standards, or on a general continuous improvement process. Information gathered during the benchmarking experience should support the organization's overall mission, goals, and objectives. Be aware that benchmarking and gathering information about processes is of greater value than focusing on metrics. The narrow focus on metrics can lead to stumbling on apples-and-oranges comparisons, while the focus on processes encourages improvement and adoption of new methods. To be of greater value, benchmarking should be a tool used to support a larger strategic objective.

2. *Understand your organization.* Critical to any process is defining and understanding all aspects of a situation. Individuals involved in the process need to

develop an understanding of the company. To create a plan and conduct the process, information concerning the external customers, internal customers, and their major inputs and outputs is vital to achieve an understanding of the system under study. Often this step receives less attention than it should. Since people working for the company are performing the benchmarking assessment, the company is a known entity. Avoid the tendency to treat this step trivially. Use flow-charts to describe the processes involved. These will greatly enhance everyone's understanding of the system to be studied during benchmarking.

3. *Determine what to measure*. Once an understanding of the systems present in a company has been gained, it is time to determine the measures of performance. These measures will allow those conducting the benchmarking assessment to judge the performance of the company. This is the time to define what is truly critical for the company to remain competitive. These critical factors for success will be supported by standards for procedures, processes, and behaviors. Benchmarking will pinpoint questions to be answered and issues to be resolved, as well as processes and procedures to be improved. It is important to identify the questions pertinent to the company's particular operations. A well-developed list of items to be benchmarked will result in more consistent assessments and comparisons.

4. *Determine whom to benchmark against*. Choices for whom to benchmark against should be made by considering the activities and operations under investigation, the size of the company, the number and types of customers, the types of transactions, even the locations of facilities. Careful attention should be paid to selecting appropriate companies. Similarities in size and types of transactions or products may be more important in some instances than selecting a competitor. For instance, the bursar's office at a university may choose to benchmark against successful banking operations, not other universities' bursar's offices. A manufacturing company studying inventory control may be interested in the inventory control activities of a mail order catalog operation. If the company is interested in ISO 9000 certification, then they might systematically select areas within its own operations to compare against the standard in order to verify compliance.

5. *Benchmark*. The areas of the company that have been chosen for the benchmarking assessment should be notified prior to beginning the process. The authorization to proceed with the process should be obtained and notification should come from the highest levels of the company to ensure cooperation. During the benchmarking process, investigators collect and analyze data pertaining to the measures established in step 3. Performance measures and standards that are critical to the success of the company are used to study the company. Investigators are charged with the duty of verifying compliance to the performance measures and standards. The ability to perform to those measures and standards is judged. Compliance can be verified on the basis of interviews of those involved and direct observation of the processes.

6. *Improve performance*. Once the data and information have been gathered, a report summarizing the significant strengths and weaknesses of the area under

study is created. In this report, the gap between the existing and the desired levels of performance is documented. A good report will focus on patterns of standards violations and elements missing from a strong system. The report should include recommendations for improving the processes. This report does not need to detail each of the observations made by the investigators. It should not be a list of all of the infractions seen.

In a successful benchmarking experience, the final report becomes a working document to aid the continuous improvement process. The information gathered in this report is used to investigate root causes, solve them, reduce process variation, and establish systems to prevent the occurrence of nonconformities. The benchmarking document is a powerful customer feedback tool and should be used accordingly.

 REAL TOOLS FOR REAL LIFE

Benchmarking at Remodeling Designs, Inc.

Remodeling Designs, Inc. began in April 1990 as a part-time job for two friends with a common hobby and a big dream. The company began as a partnership between the Eggers and the Cordonniers and was incorporated in 1991. Remodeling Designs offers full service project management for all types of remodeling jobs, specializing in residential projects such as kitchens, bathrooms, basements, and room additions. The company oversees all phases of the job from design to completion. Each year the company continues to grow steadily and now operates with several production crews. Remodeling Designs regularly uses four types of benchmarking in order to keep their operations on track and profitable for the future.

Because of their close attention to detail, both for customer jobs and for their own company performance, Remodeling Designs has received numerous awards in multiple years for remodeling. These awards include the National Remodeling Quality Gold Award for Companies Under $1 Million Volume, the Miami Valley NARI Contractor of the Year Award for Residential Bathroom $30,000–$60,000, the Miami Valley NARI Contractor of the Year Award for Residential Kitchens $30,000–$60,000, the Miami Valley NARI Contractor of the Year for Residential Interior Remodeling, the Miami Valley NARI Contractor of the Year for Residential Kitchens under $30,000, and the Better Business Bureau Eclipse Award for Customer Service—Small Company.

Step 1. Determine the Focus.   Leadership at Remodeling Designs participates in an association called the Remodelers' Executive Roundtable. This nationwide organization, comprised of the best-of-the-best remodeling companies, has provided input that has enabled Remodeling Designs to approach benchmarking wisely. Knowing that there is something to the saying "too much of a good thing," Remodeling Designs has chosen to focus on the four critical aspects that greatly affect the success of their business. These are the things that they feel they *absolutely must* *do well* in order for their business to be successful. Once they get good at benchmarking and responding to these four critical to performance values, then they can broaden their focus to include the finer details of operating their business. These four aspects will be covered in Steps 2 and 3.

Step 2. Understand your Organization.   Remodeling Designs believes that there are four keys to excellent customer relationships: communication, doing what they said they would do, doing whatever it takes to get the job done, and keeping the jobsite as clean as possible. Repeat business and referrals are essential measures of business results. Over 70% of their jobs are from repeat customers and referrals. One-third of all their new leads are generated from repeat and referral business. The average job size for Remodeling Designs is $60,000. They were recently ranked in the top 10% of remodeling businesses by the National Association of Remodeling Industries. They often find themselves in a non-competitive bid situation because customers are so pleased with their approach to remodeling and repair.

Remodeling Designs believes that their four keys to excellence of customer relations contribute significantly to their business results. Their product and service differentiators are: clients wanting excellent service, unique design skills, and high quality. Remodeling Designs has experienced very few complaints concerning the products or services they provide. They believe this is due to their judicious use of the daily logs to maintain contact with their customers during construction on the job. The most frequent negative comment is that the job took longer than expected. They are engaged in continuous improvement efforts to complete the jobs more quickly at the same level of quality.

Step 3. Determine What to Measure.   The four critical to success measures that Remodeling Designs has chosen to benchmark fall into three categories: External, Customer, and Internal.

External: To track their financial and market results, Remodeling Designs benchmarks two measures: fiscal performance and project performance.

Fiscal performance is indicated by gross profit and net profit. The benchmark for gross profit is 40%. The benchmark for net profit is 10%. Both of these benchmark values come from recommendations from the Remodelers' Executive Roundtable. This organization has been tracking profit data of their members for the past 5 years. These values represent the best-in-field performance.

Project performance is measured by benchmarking against another Remodelers' Executive Roundtable best-in-field performance value: lead generations converted to jobs. Leads-to-jobs conversion rate is 4-to-1 at best-in-field companies.

Customer: Remodeling Designs' extensive customer surveys serve as a benchmark against which to measure customer success. Figure 15.2 shows the Valued Client Feedback form they use. Upon completion of each job, the survey is benchmarked against historical performance. From this the company knows whether or not they are maintaining or improving their clients' level of satisfaction.

Internal: Remodeling Designs uses slippage as an internal benchmark. Slippage refers to the percentage by which the cost of the actual job has slipped, or not

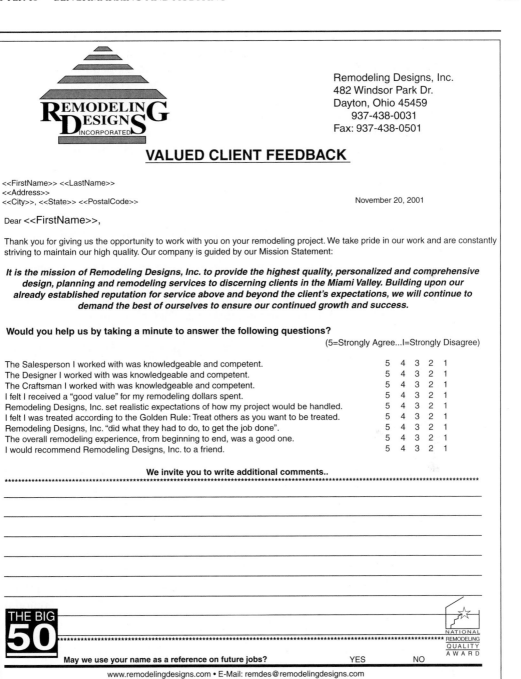

Figure 15.2   Client Feedback Form. Used with permission from Remodeling Designs.

met, the estimated cost projections. This type of internal benchmarking enables them to judge the quality of their estimations as well as their ability to keep a project on schedule and within cost. Obviously, zero slippage would be optimal, but realistically, there will be some jobs with slippage. The benchmark for this is 5%, though Remodeling Designs strives for less than 2%.

Step 4. Determine Whom to Benchmark Against.   Remodeling Designs benchmarks against best-in-field remodelers using information provided by the Remodelers' Executive Roundtable. They benchmark customer satisfaction using their own historical survey data. Historical data also serves as a foundation for their internal slippage benchmark.

Step 5. Benchmark.   Remodeling Designs benchmarks each job against the standards that they set in Step 3.

Step 6. Improve Performance.   Knowledge gained from benchmarking enables them to place themselves well in the market. Remodeling Designs has a greater focus on the customer than on their own business results. Their current focus to improve organizational effectiveness is to study their processes to determine whether they can complete their jobs in less time. They hope to identify non-value-added activities and remove them from the processes. They have set a goal of 40% gross profit on a job. Right now, they are at 37%. They are also studying their support processes to determine their effectiveness. One process under study is the advertising process. Currently they spend 4% of their total income on advertisements in home shows, television, website, mailers, etc. They are also investigating their suppliers to determine whether or not these are the best when judged from a price and timely delivery point-of-view. $\mathbf{Q}$

AUDITING

Audits are designed to appraise the activities, practices, records, or policies of an organization; they determine whether a company has the ability to meet or exceed a standard. A variety of circumstances can initiate an audit. Audit programs may be part of customer contract requirements, or government regulations may require an audit. Audits do not have to have an outside instigator; it is not unusual to see a company create internal auditing systems to verify its own performance. Internal and supplier audits allow a company the opportunity to verify conformance to specifications and procedures. Audits may also examine aspects of equipment, software, documentation, and procedures. Whatever the reason, audits provide companies with information concerning their performance, the performance of their product or service, and areas for improvement.

Audits should be a positive experience used to improve the system. When deficiencies are uncovered, they should be seen as opportunities to look for solutions, not to fix blame. Audits enable a company to answer a variety of questions. Is the company achieving its objectives? Are procedures being followed? Are new and more efficient methods of performance documented and used where applicable? Are records being properly retained and used to solve production problems? Are preventive maintenance schedules being followed? Audits of systems such as material handling can reveal poor practices that need to be improved. Supplier quality and record-keeping practices can also be checked. Since audits identify opportunities for improvement, companies may perform a product or service integrity audit to verify that the process is performing in an optimal fashion. Using audits to identify process problems reduces opportunities for nonconformities.

The frequency of audits varies according to need. Areas having a significant effect directly on product creation, service provision, and product or service safety or quality are targeted for more frequent audits. When not based on customer or government requirements, the frequency of audits is usually related to the need to balance audit effectiveness with economics. To decrease the impact and disruption caused by a major companywide audit, an organization may choose to audit one or two areas or systems at a time until all key areas have been evaluated.

An audit involves comparisons, checks of compliance, and discoveries of discrepancies. Because this news is not always positive, those conducting an audit may not be well received by the area being audited. To be successful, good auditors should be polite, objective, and professional. In some instances, a great deal of perseverance is necessary to find the information desired. Audits should be conducted in an objective and factual manner. The auditor's opinion should be unbiased, unfiltered, and undistorted. Audits are not subjective assessments against personal standards. The objectives, criteria, and measures against which an area is to be compared should be well defined before beginning the audit. Those involved in the audit should be notified as early as possible about the scope and breadth of the audit.

Types of Audits

Audits are designed to determine if deficiencies exist between actual performance and desired standards. They can cover the entire company, or a division of a company, or any portion of the processes that provide a product or service. Audits may be focused on product development and design, material procurement, or production. A customer may request an audit prior to awarding a contract to a supplier. Other types of audits include product design audits, preproduction audits, compliance audits, production audits, and supplier quality system audits.

Designing an Audit

Applying the Shewhart plan-do-study-act cycle, made popular by Dr. Deming, can help a company create an organized system for conducting an audit and using the information to make improvements. Typical auditing programs include a planning phase, the actual audit, reports recommending improvements, and follow-up action plans (Figure 15.3).

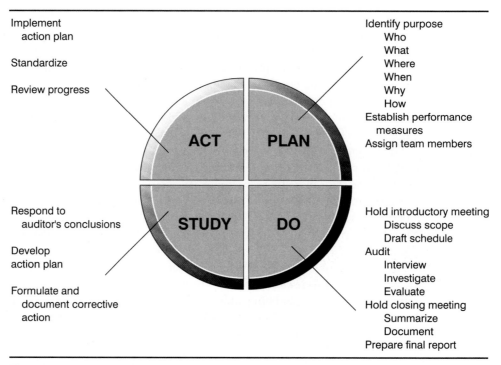

Implement
   action plan

Standardize

Review progress

Identify purpose
   Who
   What
   Where
   When
   Why
   How
Establish performance
   measures
Assign team members

ACT   PLAN

STUDY   DO

Respond to
   auditor's conclusions

Develop
action plan

Formulate and
   document corrective
   action

Hold introductory meeting
   Discuss scope
   Draft schedule
Audit
   Interview
   Investigate
   Evaluate
Hold closing meeting
   Summarize
   Document
Prepare final report

Figure 15.3   The Auditing Process

1. *Plan:* To begin, those planning the audit need to identify its purpose or objective. A statement of purpose clarifies the focus of the audit. Following this, planners will need to identify the who, what, where, when, why, and how related to the audit. Who is to be audited? Who is to perform the audit? What does this audit hope to accomplish? Is the audit to judge conformance to standards? If so, what are the critical standards? What are the performance measures? When and where the audit will be conducted must be set. Those about to be audited should be informed by an individual in a position of authority. Clear statements of the reasons behind the audit (why), the performance measures (what), and the procedures (how) should be given to those being audited. An audit is a valuable working document for improvement. It is important to determine how the results will be used and who will have access to the results before the auditing process begins.

2. *Do:* Using the information clarified in the planning phase, the audit is conducted. Often an introductory meeting is held by the participants to discuss the scope, objectives, schedule, and paperwork considerations. After the opening meeting, examiners begin the process of reviewing the process, product, or system under study. Auditors may require access to information concerning quality systems, equipment operation procedures, preventive maintenance records, inspection histories, or planning documents. Auditors may conduct interviews

Who are the customers (internal and external)?

Are the customer (internal and external) requirements known? What are they? How are they identified?

What are the key processes that support meeting customer (internal and external) requirements?

Are the process owners identified? Who are they?

What are the inputs for the process?

What are the outputs for the process?

What is the sequence and interaction of related processes?

Show us the process maps or flow charts of key processes.

Have the interfaces between processes been identified?

Are the processes documented?

What are the economic issues (cost, resource allocation, waste, etc.) associated with the process?

What are the methods in place for process improvement?

What are the resources needed for the processes?

What are the channels of communication?

How is feedback obtained?

How is process performance measured?

What is done with the information gathered from the process?

What is the corrective action process?

What is the preventive action process?

Figure 15.4   Examples of Audit Questions

with those involved in the process of providing a product or service. Any and all information related to the area under study is critical for the success of the audit. Organizations conducting audits may ask questions like those provided in Figure 15.4.

During the review process, auditors document their findings. These findings are presented in a general summary at a meeting of the participants. Within a short period of time, perhaps 10 to 20 days, the auditors will prepare a written report that documents their findings, conclusions, and recommendations.

3. *Study:* Audits provide information about the participant's strengths, weaknesses, and areas for improvement. Upon receipt, the auditor's report is read by the participants in the audit. During this phase of the audit cycle, they respond to the report and develop an action plan based on the recommendations of the auditors. This action plan should specify the steps and time frame involved in dealing with the issues raised by the audit.

4. *Act:* Once adopted, the action plan becomes the focus of the improvement activities related to the audited area. Auditors and company administrators should follow up at predetermined intervals to evaluate the status of the continuous improvement action plan. This ensures that the recommendations and conclusions reached by the auditors, and supported by an action plan, assist the company in reaching its continuous improvement goals.

EXAMPLE 15.1   Conducting an Audit

As part of checking its ability to meet the standards set by the Malcolm Baldrige National Quality Award, the WP and Me Corporation has decided to perform an internal audit on its main production line. To conduct an effective audit they followed the four steps presented in this chapter.

Step 1. Plan.   To begin, those planning the audit identified the purpose or objective of the audit as being "to judge conformance to the following standards: cleanliness/lack of contamination, nutritional quality control, and compliance with written standard operating procedures (SOPs)." Following this step, the planners made a list:

Who: Who is to be audited? The main production line
            Who is to perform the audit? W&T Consultants

What: What does this audit hope to accomplish? Assessment of conformance to the following standards: cleanliness/lack of contamination, nutritional quality control, and compliance with written SOPs
            What are the performance measures? Level of cleanliness and lack of contamination; Structure and performance of nutritional quality control system; Level of compliance with written SOPs

Where: Number 1 plant, main production line

When: February 1 through February 5
            Report from auditors due February 28
            Response from production line 1 due March 30
            Follow-up by management every 30 days to check compliance

Why: To ensure that WP and Me produces the highest-quality nutritional dog food, under the cleanest possible conditions, at an optimum performance level

How: Auditors will conduct interviews, review quality documentation, review standard operating procedures, and observe line activities to create a comparison

Main production was informed by the vice president of operations about the audit and its purpose. At this meeting, the performance measures and the procedures of conducting an audit were reviewed with those being audited. This made clear to the people on the line, as well as to their supervisors, manufacturing engineers, and others, the importance of the audit and the results generated by it. Since an audit is a valuable working document for improvement, the vice president of operations discussed how the audit results would be used to guide the improvement efforts within the department.

Step 2. Do.   Using the information clarified in the planning phase, the audit was conducted by W&T Consultants. After the introductory meeting to discuss the scope, objectives, schedule, and paperwork considerations, the examiners began reviewing the process, the quality system, equipment operation procedures, preventive maintenance records, inspection histories, and planning documents. The auditors conducted interviews with line personnel, engineers, and supervisors.

During the review process, the auditors documented their findings. While the overall cleanliness and adherence to work standards were very good, at the closing meeting the following concerns were raised:

a. In the raw material storage area, several containers of additives had been contaminated by fumes from extraction ducts that were not airtight.

b. Also in the raw material storage area, several containers had lost their labels. There are written instructions requiring the involvement of quality assurance when the labels are replaced; however, the personnel responsible for replacing the labels were unaware of the authorized procedure. The procedure they described did not match the authorized standard operating procedure.

c. On the production line, because of the lack of space, a work schedule for the cleaning crew did not list special cleaning instructions. The cleaning supervisor had been given no guidance concerning standard operating procedures.

d. While studying the procedures for ordering raw material and cleaning solutions, one of the auditors noticed that there were no purchase specifications for the critical cleaning solutions. There was also no established standard operating procedure for verifying incoming supplies.

e. The number 2 machine was not covered by a preventive maintenance program. There was no safety inspection record in the files. There was no information at all concerning the equipment's description, serial number, location, dates of inspection, condition, repairs, or standard operating procedures.

f. While the number 2 machine had almost no information available, other machines had incomplete records.

These are just a few of the findings presented in the general summary at a closing meeting of the participants. Within 20 days, the auditors prepared a written report that documented their findings, conclusions, and recommendations in detail.

Step 3. Study.   The audit provided information about the participants' strengths, weaknesses, and areas for improvement. Number 1 line spent many hours developing an action plan based on the recommendations of the auditors. The action plan listed specific steps and time frames to deal with the issues raised by the audit. For example,

a. To correct the situation with incomplete equipment documentation (concerns e and f), number 1 line members will work with the maintenance department to create files containing the following information for all machines on number 1 line: equipment description, serial number, location, standard operating procedures, safety inspection records, dates of inspection, equipment condition, and repairs. Completion date: June 1.

b. Number 1 line members will work with the maintenance department to create a preventive maintenance program suitable for all machines on number 1 line. Completion date: July 30.

c. To deal with concern c, number 1 line members will work with the cleaning department to develop standard operating procedures for all machines on number 1 line. Completion date: April 1.

d. A thorough training and review program will be established for all current and future employees on number 1 line. This will counteract situations evident in concern b. Completion date: April 30.

e. The raw material storage area will be redesigned to prevent future contamination. Completion date: August 30.

Step 4. Act.   Management at WP and Me reviewed the action plan and adopted it as the focus of the improvement activities related to line 1. The vice president of operations will follow up every 30 days to determine the progress being made and to be available to remove any obstacles preventing implementation of the plan. This will ensure that the recommendations and conclusions reached by the auditors, and supported by an action plan, will be handled in a timely fashion.

SUMMARY

Benchmarking and auditing are both processes that enable a company to learn more about itself. A company that invests time and effort in either a benchmarking assessment or an audit will be able to verify its performance and uncover areas requiring improvement. In many cases, better performance can be gained by understanding what a company is currently capable of doing versus where it needs to be performing to remain competitive.

■ Lessons Learned

1. Identification of performance measures enhances both benchmarking assessments and audits.
2. Benchmarking is the process of comparing a company's performance against a set of standards or against the performance of a best-in-its-class company.
3. Measurements and information gathered during both benchmarking and audits are used to make conclusions about current performance and any necessary improvements.
4. Audits are designed to appraise the activities, practices, records, and policies of an organization to determine the company's ability to meet or exceed a standard. ■

Chapter Problems
Benchmarking

 1. Describe the steps involved in benchmarking.
2. Why would a company be interested in benchmarking? What would they hope to gain by benchmarking?

3. Select a company, either service- or manufacturing-related, and describe the steps and activities involved in benchmarking. Be sure to indicate which type of benchmarking would be most appropriate and why, as well as whom they should benchmark against and what they should measure.

4. A local bank considers itself a full-service bank. They offer a number of products and services to individual customers, businesses, trusts, and credit card users. Recently, the bank completed an internal quality-improvement process that included determining a mission statement and resolving issues that prevented employees from performing to the best of their ability. At this time they are evaluating external customer service. Competition in the banking industry is fierce, and it is critical that the bank discover and develop policies, procedures, and practices that will lead to customer delight. The bank's mission statement is simple: "All customers, regardless of the size of their accounts or the number of their transactions, are important!" What steps should the bank managers take to benchmark? What should they benchmark?

5. The WP and Me Corporation, a pet food company, would like to determine whether or not it could perform well against the standards for the Malcolm Baldrige National Quality Award. WP and Me plans to apply for the award within the next few years. The purpose of this benchmarking experience is to see how they currently compare with the criteria and what areas they should focus on in the future. The company hopes to benefit from this type of compliance benchmarking experience before attempting to win the award. Provide details on the steps the company should take during the benchmarking process.

Auditing

6. Employees at the bank are already trained to be polite and eager to serve the customers. The bank has been able to identify several other features that are important to their customers: timeliness, accuracy, immediate service, knowledge, courtesy, convenience, and accessibility. The bank is considering benchmarking as a way to determine how they can improve. The following are some questions they must seek answers to:

   a. Which of the four types of benchmarking would be appropriate in this situation? Why?
   b. Describe the benchmarking steps that the bank should take. What should happen during each step?
   c. Describe at least three measures of performance or indicators of viability that would be appropriate for the bank to investigate. Why did you choose each of these?
   d. Against whom should the bank benchmark?
   e. After obtaining the benchmarked information, what should the bank do with it?

7. Describe the steps involved in auditing.

8. Why would a company be interested in auditing? What benefits would they hope to gain by auditing?

9. Select a company, either service- or manufacturing-related, and describe the steps and activities involved in auditing. Be sure to indicate which areas of the company would be most appropriate to audit and why, as well as who should be involved in the audit and what they should investigate.

CASE STUDY 15.1
Benchmarking

PART 1

TST, a local performing arts association, has been experiencing several years of financial prosperity. Their board of directors feels that it is time to update the formal strategic long range plan (SLRP). The purpose of the SLRP is to focus and guide the thinking and activities of the board of directors and staff of the organization. The implementation of the SLRP is the responsibility of the board as well as of the staff.

Members of the board are very enlightened about total quality management and are determined to put their knowledge to use in creating the new SLRP. They begin their revision with the creation of mission and vision statements to guide the activities of the organization.

The vision:

> Our performing arts association will advance a national reputation of excellence to ever-expanding local and touring audiences. In addition to performing, the performing arts association will embrace vigorous and respected educational and community outreach programs, which will include a school and associated preprofessional performance troupes.

The mission:

> The purpose of the performing arts association is to educate, enlighten, and entertain the widest possible audience in the city and on tour by maintaining a professional company characterized by excellence. Its purpose is also to maintain a preprofessional training company and a school. The performing arts association will develop and maintain the artistic, administrative, technical, and financial resources necessary for those endeavors.

After developing the mission and vision statements, the board has decided to determine the viability of their organization when compared with other, similar performing arts associations. They have chosen to do benchmarking for this reason.

 Assignment

1. Describe the type of benchmarking the performing arts association will be performing.
2. What benefits will the association see from benchmarking?
3. Describe the steps the association should take in the benchmarking process.

PART 2

Following the steps suggested by texts on benchmarking, the performing arts association begins its benchmarking process with a brainstorming session to determine the *focus* of the benchmarking activities. The three general areas the board feels are indications of viability are resource development, artistic excellence, and marketing effectiveness.

Resource development involves the financial aspects of the performing arts association. The association receives income from several sources, but all revenue can be classified as either unearned income—corporate and individual gifts, agency/government funding, and contributions—or earned income—ticket sales. Revenue is used to pay staff, purchase shows, employ performing artists, maintain the theater, market upcoming shows, and sponsor educational programs that are presented prior to the performance. Marketing efforts include advertising and promotional and discounted tickets. Staff members, as well as volunteers, devote a significant amount of time to efforts to solicit contributions from agencies, corporations, and individuals. These efforts are vital to the ability of the association to offer a wide variety of performances.

Artistic excellence involves such aspects as the program mix offered during the year, the performers themselves, their age and training, the number of community outreach programs, and preperformance lectures. Marketing effectiveness is based on the relationship of attendance, ticket sales, and dollars spent on marketing.

The results of the discussions are helpful in *understanding the company*, how it is viewed both internally and externally. Using their focus areas (resource development, artistic excellence, and marketing effectiveness) as a beginning, the board must *determine what to measure*.

 Assignment

For each of the three areas—resource development, artistic excellence, and marketing effectiveness—brainstorm what you consider to be appropriate measures of performance (or indicators of viability).

PART 3

To identify the appropriate measures of performance, the board holds a brainstorming session. The session reveals the following:

Indications of viability

1. Efficiency of programs
2. Marketing effectiveness
3. Educating the audience
4. Other measures of performance

Assignment

The board has listed a large number of potential measures of success or indicators of viability. To seek all of this information from the associations chosen as benchmarks would require a significant amount of time. Which would you select as the key benchmarks? Why?

PART 4

The board holds an additional session to determine the key benchmarks indicating the viability of the association. The following areas are chosen to investigate as key benchmarks:

Resource development

- Percentage of earned versus contributed income
- Percentage of contributed income from corporations, funding agencies, and individuals

Artistic excellence

- Number of performances on main stage
- Number of outreach programs
- Preperformance lecture attendance

Marketing effectiveness

- Attendance as percentage of house
- Percentage of total tickets that are complimentary or discounted tickets
- Percentage of earned income dedicated to marketing efforts

Now that the performance measures have been selected, before performing the actual benchmarking, the board needs to determine *whom to benchmark against.*

 Assignment

On what factors should the selection of whom to benchmark against be based?

PART 5

The board decides to base their selection of performing arts associations to benchmark on several factors. From this they are able to select five performing arts associations to compare themselves with.

Their next step is to begin *benchmarking.* One of the committee members is chosen to contact each of the selected associations and gather the information. At the next board meeting, this individual will share the information with the other board members. The information from their benchmarking efforts will be used to *improve performance.*

Assignment

Study Figures C15.1.1 through C15.1.8 and discuss how well the performing arts association is doing when compared with other best-in-field associations.

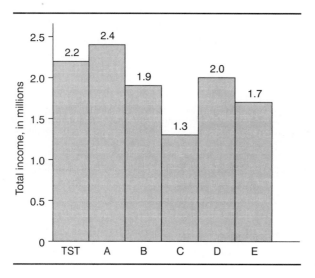

Figure C15.1.1   Total Income, in Millions

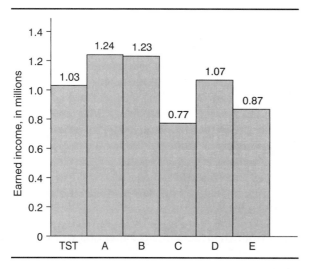

Figure C15.1.2   Earned Income, in Millions

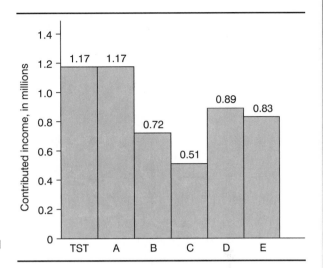

**Figure C15.1.3   Contributed
Income, in Millions**

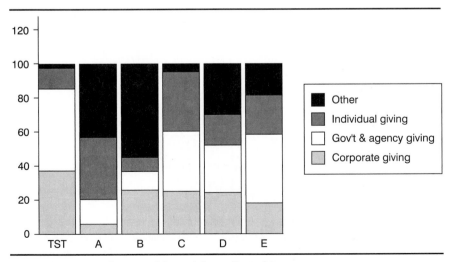

Figure C15.1.4   Composition of Contributed Income

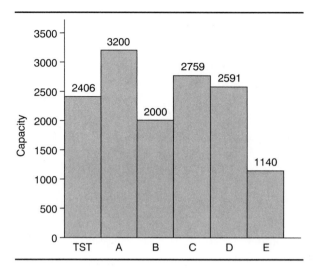

Figure C15.1.5   Performance Hall Size, Number of Seats

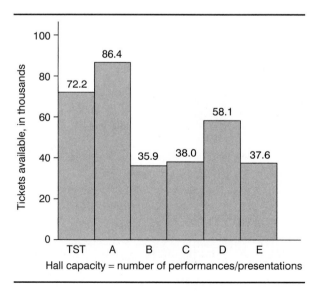

Figure C15.1.6   Total Tickets Available per Season

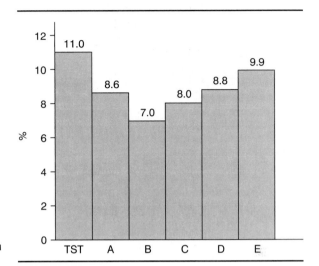

**Figure C15.1.7
Marketing Expense as a
Percent of Total Budget**

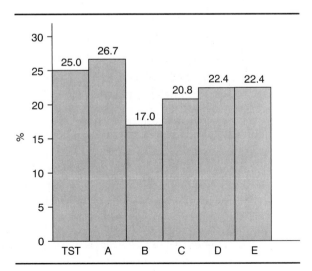

**Figure C15.1.8   Marketing
Expense a Percent of Ticket**

CASE STUDY 15.2
Auditing

This case provides information about the testing/inspection aspect of the audit. Play the role of the auditor and evaluate this company.

A supplier of oxygen valves for the oxygen system in a military aircraft has been the focus of a procedural audit. During this audit, the auditors are trying to determine if proper procedures for the design, manufacturing, and testing of the oxygen valves have been followed.

BACKGROUND

The military has contracted with PL Inc. to supply 120 oxygen valves for a military airplane. These valves are supplied in lot sizes of ten and are produced on an as-needed basis. Production and use of the valves has risen to number 96 of the 120 requested. The valves are inspected using the Approved Test Plan (ATP) developed at the awarding of the contract.

The audit was triggered by an oxygen leak in one of the valves. While troubleshooting the failure, liquid mercury was found in the valve, a dangerous occurrence for the personnel using the valves.

When first questioned during the audit about the procedure used, PL stated that they had changed the ATP to use a liquid mercury manometer to check for leaks at part serial number 096. Their records show that only four valves were tested in this manner. The mercury manometer was found to be the contamination source of mercury in the valves. PL also stated that the manometer was not used to test any other products.

The auditor asked two questions:

1. Why did they change the ATP 24 units before the end of the production run?
2. Why did they buy the mercury manometer, a special piece of testing equipment, to test just 24 remaining valves?

These questions caused PL to change their story. They now report that the ATP originally called for testing with a mercury manometer, so the ATP was never changed in the first place. What happened was that the inspector who normally tested the valves retired. Unlike the old inspector, the new inspector followed the ATP and performed the inspection with the manometer rather than air pressure gages. All units tested by the retired inspector used the air pressure gages and therefore were not contaminated by the mercury manometer.

The auditor asked three more questions:

1. Why didn't the retired inspector know how the units were to be tested according to the ATP?

2. Why didn't the supervisor ensure that the ATP was being followed?
3. Why were pressure gages used in the first place? If the ATP was not changed, then the mercury manometer should have always been used.

In response, PL stated that the old inspector took Polaroid pictures of the original setup when the first piece was inspected and used these pictures when testing the valves. The old inspector did not refer to the ATP, which would have instructed her to use the mercury manometer. All units tested through serial number 095 were tested using air pressure while the approved test plan called for the use of a liquid mercury manometer, which is a more accurate test.

The auditors asked to view the inspector performing the test. During this activity, the auditors had to remind everyone present that the inspector was to perform the test, not the supervisor (who was in the process of doing the test for the inspector). The supervisor claimed that he was helping because portions of the setups were cumbersome and could not be performed by the inspector alone. But, no, he was not always available to help. Once allowed to perform the test herself, the inspector performed the tests out-of-sequence. And when the tests called for placing the valve in an explosion proof container for a high-pressure test, the inspector merely placed the valve in a pan of water!

While discussing the ATP procedure violations, the auditors also noticed some other discrepancies as they watched the inspector test valves. Though the test was being held in a designated clean room, with everyone present attired in hair nets, smocks, and booties, upon entering the room, the auditors noticed they walked over a dirty, tacky mat. They also noticed that when they slid their hands along the front edge of the workbenches in the room, their hands turned black and gritty with dirt!

 Assignment

What are your findings as an auditor?

 Assignment

What are the potential consequences of failing the audit?

APPENDIX 1

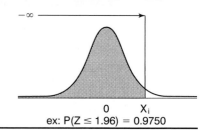

Normal Curve Areas P(Z ≤ Z$_0$)

ex: $P(Z \leq 1.96) = 0.9750$

Z	0.09	0.08	0.07	0.06	0.05	0.04	0.03	0.02	0.01	0.00
−3.8	.0001	.0001	.0001	.0001	.0001	.0001	.0001	.0001	.0001	.0001
−3.7	.0001	.0001	.0001	.0001	.0001	.0001	.0001	.0001	.0001	.0001
−3.6	.0001	.0001	.0001	.0001	.0001	.0001	.0001	.0001	.0002	.0002
−3.5	.0002	.0002	.0002	.0002	.0002	.0002	.0002	.0002	.0002	.0002
−3.4	.0002	.0003	.0003	.0003	.0003	.0003	.0003	.0003	.0003	.0003
−3.3	.0003	.0004	.0004	.0004	.0004	.0004	.0004	.0005	.0005	.0005
−3.2	.0005	.0005	.0005	.0006	.0006	.0006	.0006	.0006	.0007	.0007
−3.1	.0007	.0007	.0008	.0008	.0008	.0008	.0009	.0009	.0009	.0010
−3.0	.0010	.0010	.0011	.0011	.0011	.0012	.0012	.0013	.0013	.0013
−2.9	.0014	.0014	.0015	.0015	.0016	.0016	.0017	.0018	.0018	.0019
−2.8	.0019	.0020	.0021	.0021	.0022	.0023	.0023	.0024	.0025	.0026
−2.7	.0026	.0027	.0028	.0029	.0030	.0031	.0032	.0033	.0034	.0035
−2.6	.0036	.0037	.0038	.0039	.0040	.0041	.0043	.0044	.0045	.0047
−2.5	.0048	.0049	.0051	.0052	.0054	.0055	.0057	.0059	.0060	.0062
−2.4	.0064	.0066	.0068	.0069	.0071	.0073	.0075	.0078	.0080	.0082
−2.3	.0084	.0087	.0089	.0091	.0094	.0096	.0099	.0102	.0104	.0107
−2.2	.0110	.0113	.0116	.0119	.0122	.0125	.0129	.0132	.0136	.0139
−2.1	.0143	.0146	.0150	.0154	.0158	.0162	.0166	.0170	.0174	.0179
−2.0	.0183	.0188	.0192	.0197	.0202	.0207	.0212	.0217	.0222	.0228
−1.9	.0233	.0239	.0244	.0250	.0256	.0262	.0268	.0274	.0281	.0287
−1.8	.0294	.0301	.0307	.0314	.0322	.0329	.0336	.0344	.0351	.0359
−1.7	.0367	.0375	.0384	.0392	.0401	.0409	.0418	.0427	.0436	.0446
−1.6	.0455	.0465	.0475	.0485	.0495	.0505	.0516	.0526	.0537	.0548
−1.5	.0559	.0571	.0582	.0594	.0606	.0618	.0630	.0643	.0655	.0668
−1.4	.0681	.0694	.0708	.0721	.0735	.0749	.0764	.0778	.0793	.0808
−1.3	.0823	.0838	.0853	.0869	.0885	.0901	.0918	.0934	.0951	.0968
−1.2	.0985	.1003	.1020	.1038	.1056	.1075	.1093	.1112	.1131	.1151
−1.1	.1170	.1190	.1210	.1230	.1251	.1271	.1292	.1314	.1335	.1357
−1.0	.1379	.1401	.1423	.1446	.1469	.1492	.1515	.1539	.1562	.1587
−0.9	.1611	.1635	.1660	.1685	.1711	.1736	.1762	.1788	.1814	.1841
−0.8	.1867	.1894	.1922	.1949	.1977	.2005	.2033	.2061	.2090	.2119
−0.7	.2148	.2177	.2206	.2236	.2266	.2296	.2327	.2358	.2389	.2420
−0.6	.2451	.2483	.2514	.2546	.2578	.2611	.2643	.2676	.2709	.2743
−0.5	.2776	.2810	.2843	.2877	.2912	.2946	.2981	.3015	.3050	.3085
−0.4	.3121	.3156	.3192	.3228	.3264	.3300	.3336	.3372	.3409	.3446
−0.3	.3483	.3520	.3557	.3594	.3632	.3669	.3707	.3745	.3783	.3821
−0.2	.3859	.3897	.3936	.3974	.4013	.4052	.4090	.4129	.4168	.4207
−0.1	.4247	.4286	.4325	.4364	.4404	.4443	.4483	.4522	.4562	.4602
−0.0	.4641	.4681	.4721	.4761	.4801	.4840	.4880	.4920	.4960	.5000

Z	0.00	0.01	0.02	0.03	0.04	0.05	0.06	0.07	0.08	0.09
+0.0	.5000	.5040	.5080	.5120	.5160	.5199	.5239	.5279	.5319	.5359
+0.1	.5398	.5438	.5478	.5517	.5557	.5596	.5636	.5675	.5714	.5753
+0.2	.5793	.5832	.5871	.5910	.5948	.5987	.6026	.6064	.6103	.6141
+0.3	.6179	.6217	.6255	.6293	.6331	.6368	.6406	.6443	.6480	.6517
+0.4	.6554	.6591	.6628	.6664	.6700	.6736	.6772	.6808	.6844	.6879
+0.5	.6915	.6950	.6985	.7019	.7054	.7088	.7123	.7157	.7190	.7224
+0.6	.7257	.7291	.7324	.7357	.7389	.7422	.7454	.7486	.7517	.7549
+0.7	.7580	.7611	.7642	.7673	.7704	.7734	.7764	.7794	.7823	.7852
+0.8	.7881	.7910	.7939	.7967	.7995	.8023	.8051	.8078	.8106	.8133
+0.9	.8159	.8186	.8212	.8238	.8264	.8289	.8315	.8340	.8365	.8389
+1.0	.8413	.8438	.8461	.8485	.8508	.8531	.8554	.8577	.8599	.8621
+1.1	.8643	.8665	.8686	.8708	.8729	.8749	.8770	.8790	.8810	.8830
+1.2	.8849	.8869	.8888	.8907	.8925	.8944	.8962	.8980	.8997	.9015
+1.3	.9032	.9049	.9066	.9082	.9099	.9115	.9131	.9147	.9162	.9177
+1.4	.9192	.9207	.9222	.9236	.9251	.9265	.9279	.9292	.9306	.9319
+1.5	.9332	.9345	.9357	.9370	.9382	.9394	.9406	.9418	.9429	.9441
+1.6	.9452	.9463	.9474	.9484	.9495	.9505	.9515	.9525	.9535	.9545
+1.7	.9554	.9564	.9573	.9582	.9591	.9599	.9608	.9616	.9625	.9633
+1.8	.9641	.9649	.9656	.9664	.9671	.9678	.9686	.9693	.9699	.9706
+1.9	.9713	.9719	.9726	.9732	.9738	.9744	.9750	.9756	.9761	.9767
+2.0	.9772	.9778	.9783	.9788	.9793	.9798	.9803	.9808	.9812	.9817
+2.1	.9821	.9826	.9830	.9834	.9838	.9842	.9846	.9850	.9854	.9857
+2.2	.9861	.9864	.9868	.9871	.9875	.9878	.9881	.9884	.9887	.9890
+2.3	.9893	.9896	.9898	.9901	.9904	.9906	.9909	.9911	.9913	.9916
+2.4	.9918	.9920	.9922	.9925	.9927	.9929	.9931	.9932	.9934	.9936
+2.5	.9938	.9940	.9941	.9943	.9945	.9946	.9948	.9949	.9951	.9952
+2.6	.9953	.9955	.9956	.9957	.9959	.9960	.9961	.9962	.9963	.9964
+2.7	.9965	.9966	.9967	.9968	.9969	.9970	.9971	.9972	.9973	.9974
+2.8	.9974	.9975	.9976	.9977	.9977	.9978	.9979	.9979	.9980	.9981
+2.9	.9981	.9982	.9982	.9983	.9984	.9984	.9985	.9985	.9986	.9986
+3.0	.9987	.9987	.9987	.9988	.9988	.9989	.9989	.9989	.9990	.9990
+3.1	.9990	.9991	.9991	.9991	.9992	.9992	.9992	.9992	.9993	.9993
+3.2	.9993	.9993	.9994	.9994	.9994	.9994	.9994	.9995	.9995	.9995
+3.3	.9995	.9995	.9995	.9996	.9996	.9996	.9996	.9996	.9996	.9997
+3.4	.9997	.9997	.9997	.9997	.9997	.9997	.9997	.9997	.9997	.9998
+3.5	.9998	.9998	.9998	.9998	.9998	.9998	.9998	.9998	.9998	.9998
+3.6	.9998	.9998	.9999	.9999	.9999	.9999	.9999	.9999	.9999	.9999
+3.7	.9999	.9999	.9999	.9999	.9999	.9999	.9999	.9999	.9999	.9999
+3.8	.9999	.9999	.9999	.9999	.9999	.9999	.9999	.9999	.9999	.9999

APPENDIX 2

Factors for Computing Central Lines and 3σ Control Limits for $\bar{X}$, s, and R Charts

Observations in Sample, n	Chart for Averages			Chart for Ranges						Chart for Standard Deviations				
	Factor for Control Limits			Factor for Central Line		Factors for Control Limits				Factor for Central Line		Factors for Control Limits		
	A	A_2	A_3	d_2	d_1	D_1	D_2	D_3	D_4	c_4	B_3	B_4	B_5	B_6
2	2.121	1.880	2.659	1.128	0.853	0	3.686	0	3.267	0.7979	0	3.267	0	2.606
3	1.732	1.023	1.954	1.693	0.888	0	4.358	0	2.574	0.8862	0	2.568	0	2.276
4	1.500	0.729	1.628	2.059	0.880	0	4.698	0	2.282	0.9213	0	2.266	0	2.088
5	1.342	0.577	1.427	2.326	0.864	0	4.918	0	2.114	0.9400	0	2.089	0	1.964
6	1.225	0.483	1.287	2.534	0.848	0	5.078	0	2.004	0.9515	0.030	1.970	0.029	1.874
7	1.134	0.419	1.182	2.704	0.833	0.204	5.204	0.076	1.924	0.9594	0.118	1.882	0.113	1.806
8	1.061	0.373	1.099	2.847	0.820	0.388	5.306	0.136	1.864	0.9650	0.185	1.815	0.179	1.751
9	1.000	0.337	1.032	2.970	0.808	0.547	5.393	0.184	1.816	0.9693	0.239	1.761	0.232	1.707
10	0.949	0.308	0.975	3.078	0.797	0.687	5.469	0.223	1.777	0.9727	0.284	1.716	0.276	1.669
11	0.905	0.285	0.927	3.173	0.787	0.811	5.535	0.256	1.744	0.9754	0.321	1.679	0.313	1.637
12	0.866	0.266	0.886	3.258	0.778	0.922	5.594	0.283	1.717	0.9776	0.354	1.646	0.346	1.610
13	0.832	0.249	0.850	3.336	0.770	1.025	5.647	0.307	1.693	0.9794	0.382	1.618	0.374	1.585
14	0.802	0.235	0.817	3.407	0.763	1.118	5.696	0.328	1.672	0.9810	0.406	1.594	0.399	1.563
15	0.775	0.223	0.789	3.472	0.756	1.203	5.741	0.347	1.653	0.9823	0.428	1.572	0.421	1.544
16	0.750	0.212	0.763	3.532	0.750	1.282	5.782	0.363	1.637	0.9835	0.448	1.552	0.440	1.526
17	0.728	0.203	0.739	3.588	0.744	1.356	5.820	0.378	1.622	0.9845	0.466	1.534	0.458	1.511
18	0.707	0.194	0.718	3.640	0.739	1.424	5.856	0.391	1.608	0.9854	0.482	1.518	0.475	1.496
19	0.688	0.187	0.698	3.689	0.734	1.487	5.891	0.403	1.597	0.9862	0.497	1.503	0.490	1.483
20	0.671	0.180	0.680	3.735	0.729	1.549	5.921	0.415	1.585	0.9869	0.510	1.490	0.504	1.470

APPENDIX 3

Values of t Distribution

Values of t Distribution

df	$t_{0.10}$	$t_{0.05}$	$t_{0.025}$	$t_{0.01}$	$t_{0.005}$	df
1	3.078	6.314	12.706	31.821	63.656	1
2	1.886	2.920	4.303	6.965	9.925	2
3	1.638	2.353	3.182	4.541	5.841	3
4	1.533	2.132	2.776	3.747	4.604	4
5	1.476	2.015	2.571	3.365	4.032	5
6	1.440	1.943	2.447	3.143	3.707	6
7	1.415	1.895	2.365	2.998	3.499	7
8	1.397	1.860	2.306	2.896	3.355	8
9	1.383	1.833	2.262	2.821	3.250	9
10	1.372	1.812	2.228	2.764	3.169	10
11	1.363	1.796	2.201	2.718	3.106	11
12	1.356	1.782	2.179	2.681	3.055	12
13	1.350	1.771	2.160	2.650	3.012	13
14	1.345	1.761	2.145	2.624	2.977	14
15	1.341	1.753	2.131	2.602	2.947	15
16	1.337	1.746	2.120	2.583	2.921	16
17	1.333	1.740	2.110	2.567	2.898	17
18	1.330	1.734	2.101	2.552	2.878	18
19	1.328	1.729	2.093	2.539	2.861	19
20	1.325	1.725	2.086	2.528	2.845	20
21	1.323	1.721	2.080	2.518	2.831	21
22	1.321	1.717	2.074	2.508	2.819	22
23	1.319	1.714	2.069	2.500	2.807	23
24	1.318	1.711	2.064	2.492	2.797	24
25	1.316	1.708	2.060	2.485	2.787	25
26	1.315	1.706	2.056	2.479	2.779	26
27	1.314	1.703	2.052	2.473	2.771	27
28	1.313	1.701	2.048	2.467	2.763	28
29	1.311	1.699	2.045	2.462	2.756	29
30	1.310	1.697	2.042	2.457	2.750	30
31	1.309	1.696	2.040	2.453	2.744	31

(continued)

Values of t Distribution (*continued*)

df	$t_{0.10}$	$t_{0.05}$	$t_{0.025}$	$t_{0.01}$	$t_{0.005}$	df
32	1.309	1.694	2.037	2.449	2.738	32
33	1.308	1.692	2.035	2.445	2.733	33
34	1.307	1.691	2.032	2.441	2.728	34
35	1.306	1.690	2.030	2.438	2.724	35
40	1.303	1.684	2.021	2.423	2.704	40
45	1.301	1.679	2.014	2.412	2.690	45
50	1.299	1.676	2.009	2.403	2.678	50
55	1.297	1.673	2.004	2.396	2.668	55
60	1.296	1.671	2.000	2.390	2.660	60
70	1.294	1.667	1.994	2.381	2.648	70
80	1.292	1.664	1.990	2.374	2.639	80
90	1.291	1.662	1.987	2.368	2.632	90
100	1.290	1.660	1.984	2.364	2.626	100
200	1.286	1.653	1.972	2.345	2.601	200
400	1.284	1.649	1.966	2.336	2.588	400
600	1.283	1.647	1.964	2.333	2.584	600
800	1.283	1.647	1.963	2.331	2.582	800
999	1.282	1.646	1.962	2.330	2.581	999

APPENDIX 4

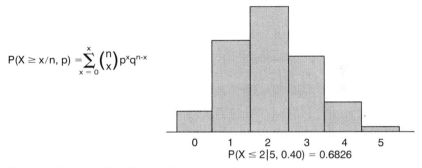

$$P(X \geq x/n, p) = \sum_{x=0}^{x} \binom{n}{x} p^x q^{n-x}$$

$P(X \leq 2|5, 0.40) = 0.6826$

Cumulative Binomial Probability Distribution

n = 5

d \ p	0.01	0.02	0.03	0.04	0.05	0.06	0.07	0.08	0.09	0.10
0	0.9510	0.9039	0.8587	0.8154	0.7738	0.7339	0.6957	0.6591	0.6240	0.5905
1	0.9990	0.9962	0.9915	0.9852	0.9774	0.9681	0.9575	0.9456	0.9326	0.9185
2	1.0000	0.9999	0.9997	0.9994	0.9998	0.9980	0.9969	0.9955	0.9937	0.9914
3	1.0000	1.0000	1.0000	1.0000	1.0000	0.9999	0.9999	0.9998	0.9997	0.9995
4	1.0000	1.0000	1.0000	1.0000	1.0000	1.0000	1.0000	1.0000	1.0000	1.0000

d \ p	0.11	0.12	0.13	0.14	0.15	0.16	0.17	0.18	0.19	0.20
0	0.5584	0.5277	0.4984	0.4704	0.4437	0.4182	0.3939	0.3707	0.3487	0.3277
1	0.9035	0.8875	0.8708	0.8533	0.8352	0.8165	0.7973	0.7776	0.7576	0.7373
2	0.9888	0.9857	0.9821	0.9780	0.9734	0.9682	0.9625	0.9563	0.9495	0.9421
3	0.9993	0.9991	0.9987	0.9983	0.9978	0.9971	0.9964	0.9955	0.9945	0.9933
4	1.0000	1.0000	1.0000	0.9999	0.9999	0.9999	0.9999	0.9998	0.9998	0.9997
5	1.0000	1.0000	1.0000	1.0000	1.0000	1.0000	1.0000	1.0000	1.0000	1.0000

d \ p	0.21	0.22	0.23	0.24	0.25	0.26	0.27	0.28	0.29	0.30
0	0.3077	0.2887	0.2707	0.2536	0.2373	0.2219	0.2073	0.1935	0.1804	0.1681
1	0.7167	0.6959	0.6749	0.6539	0.6328	0.6117	0.5907	0.5697	0.5489	0.5282
2	0.9341	0.9256	0.9164	0.9067	0.8965	0.8857	0.8743	0.8624	0.8499	0.8369
3	0.9919	0.9903	0.9886	0.9866	0.9844	0.9819	0.9792	0.9762	0.9728	0.9692
4	0.9996	0.9995	0.9994	0.9992	0.9990	0.9988	0.9986	0.9983	0.9979	0.9976
5	1.0000	1.0000	1.0000	1.0000	1.0000	1.0000	1.0000	1.0000	1.0000	1.0000

d \ p	0.31	0.32	0.33	0.34	0.35	0.36	0.37	0.38	0.39	0.40
0	0.1564	0.1454	0.1350	0.1252	0.1160	0.1074	0.0992	0.0916	0.0845	0.0778
1	0.5077	0.4875	0.4675	0.4478	0.4284	0.4094	0.3907	0.3724	0.3545	0.3370

(continued)

(continued)   n = 5

d＼p	0.31	0.32	0.33	0.34	0.35	0.36	0.37	0.38	0.39	0.40
2	0.8234	0.8095	0.7950	0.7801	0.7648	0.7491	0.7330	0.7165	0.6997	0.6826
3	0.9653	0.9610	0.9564	0.9514	0.9460	0.9402	0.9340	0.9274	0.9204	0.9130
4	0.9971	0.9966	0.9961	0.9955	0.9947	0.9940	0.9931	0.9921	0.9910	0.9898
5	1.0000	1.0000	1.0000	1.0000	1.0000	1.0000	1.0000	1.0000	1.0000	1.0000

d＼p	0.41	0.42	0.43	0.44	0.45	0.46	0.47	0.48	0.49	0.50
0	0.0715	0.0656	0.0602	0.0551	0.0503	0.0459	0.0418	0.0380	0.0345	0.0312
1	0.3199	0.3033	0.2871	0.2714	0.2562	0.2415	0.2272	0.2135	0.2002	0.1875
2	0.6651	0.6475	0.6295	0.6114	0.5931	0.5747	0.5561	0.5375	0.5187	0.5000
3	0.9051	0.8967	0.8879	0.8786	0.8688	0.8585	0.8478	0.8365	0.8247	0.8125
4	0.9884	0.9869	0.9853	0.9835	0.9815	0.9794	0.9771	0.9745	0.9718	0.9688
5	1.0000	1.0000	1.0000	1.0000	1.0000	1.0000	1.0000	1.0000	1.0000	1.0000

n = 6

d＼p	0.01	0.02	0.03	0.04	0.05	0.06	0.07	0.08	0.09	0.10
0	0.9415	0.8858	0.8330	0.7828	0.7351	0.6899	0.6470	0.6064	0.5679	0.5314
1	0.9985	0.9943	0.9875	0.9784	0.9672	0.9541	0.9392	0.9227	0.9048	0.8857
2	1.0000	0.9998	0.9995	0.9988	0.9978	0.9962	0.9942	0.9915	0.9882	0.9841
3	1.0000	1.0000	1.0000	1.0000	0.9999	0.9998	0.9997	0.9995	0.9992	0.9987
4	1.0000	1.0000	1.0000	1.0000	1.0000	1.0000	1.0000	1.0000	1.0000	0.9999
5	1.0000	1.0000	1.0000	1.0000	1.0000	1.0000	1.0000	1.0000	1.0000	1.0000

d＼p	0.11	0.12	0.13	0.14	0.15	0.16	0.17	0.18	0.19	0.20
0	0.4970	0.4644	0.4336	0.4046	0.3771	0.3513	0.3269	0.3040	0.2824	0.2621
1	0.8655	0.8444	0.8224	0.7997	0.7765	0.7528	0.7287	0.7044	0.6799	0.6554
2	0.9794	0.9739	0.9676	0.9605	0.9527	0.9440	0.9345	0.9241	0.9130	0.9011
3	0.9982	0.9975	0.9966	0.9955	0.9941	0.9925	0.9906	0.9884	0.9859	0.9830
4	0.9999	0.9999	0.9998	0.9997	0.9996	0.9995	0.9993	0.9990	0.9987	0.9984
5	1.0000	1.0000	1.0000	1.0000	1.0000	1.0000	1.0000	1.0000	1.0000	0.9999
6	1.0000	1.0000	1.0000	1.0000	1.0000	1.0000	1.0000	1.0000	1.0000	1.0000

d＼p	0.21	0.22	0.23	0.24	0.25	0.26	0.27	0.28	0.09	0.30
0	0.2431	0.2252	0.2084	0.1927	0.1780	0.1642	0.1513	0.1393	0.1281	0.1176
1	0.6308	0.6063	0.5820	0.5578	0.5339	0.5104	0.4872	0.4644	0.4420	0.4202
2	0.8885	0.8750	0.8609	0.8461	0.8306	0.8144	0.7977	0.7804	0.7626	0.7443
3	0.9798	0.9761	0.9720	0.9674	0.9624	0.9569	0.9508	0.9443	0.9372	0.9295
4	0.9980	0.9975	0.9969	0.9962	0.9954	0.9944	0.9933	0.9921	0.9907	0.9891
5	0.9999	0.9999	0.9999	0.9998	0.9998	0.9997	0.9996	0.9995	0.9994	0.9993
6	1.0000	1.0000	1.0000	1.0000	1.0000	1.0000	1.0000	1.0000	1.0000	1.0000

d＼p	0.31	0.32	0.33	0.34	0.35	0.36	0.37	0.38	0.39	0.40
0	0.1079	0.0989	0.0905	0.0827	0.0754	0.0687	0.0625	0.0568	0.0515	0.0467
1	0.3988	0.3780	0.3578	0.3381	0.3191	0.3006	0.2828	0.2657	0.2492	0.2333
2	0.7256	0.7064	0.6870	0.6672	0.6471	0.6268	0.6063	0.5857	0.5650	0.5443
3	0.9213	0.9125	0.9031	0.8931	0.8826	0.8714	0.8596	0.8473	0.8343	0.8208
4	0.9873	0.9852	0.9830	0.9805	0.9777	0.9746	0.9712	0.9675	0.9635	0.9590
5	0.9991	0.9989	0.9987	0.9985	0.9982	0.9978	0.9974	0.9970	0.9965	0.9959
6	1.0000	1.0000	1.0000	1.0000	1.0000	1.0000	1.0000	1.0000	1.0000	1.0000

d＼p	0.41	0.42	0.43	0.44	0.45	0.46	0.47	0.48	0.49	0.50
0	0.0422	0.0381	0.0343	0.0308	0.0277	0.0248	0.0222	0.0198	0.0176	0.0156
1	0.2181	0.2035	0.1895	0.1762	0.1636	0.1515	0.1401	0.1293	0.1190	0.1094

(continued)

(*continued*)   **n = 6**

d \ p	0.41	0.42	0.43	0.44	0.45	0.46	0.47	0.48	0.49	0.50
2	0.5236	0.5029	0.4823	0.4618	0.4415	0.4214	0.4015	0.3820	0.3627	0.3437
3	0.8067	0.7920	0.7768	0.7610	0.7447	0.7280	0.7107	0.6930	0.6748	0.6562
4	0.9542	0.9490	0.9434	0.9373	0.9308	0.9238	0.9163	0.9083	0.8997	0.8906
5	0.9952	0.9945	0.9937	0.9927	0.9917	0.9905	0.9892	0.9878	0.9862	0.9844
6	1.0000	1.0000	1.0000	1.0000	1.0000	1.0000	1.0000	1.0000	1.0000	1.0000

n = 7

d \ p	0.01	0.02	0.03	0.04	0.05	0.06	0.07	0.08	0.09	0.10
0	0.9321	0.8681	0.8080	0.7514	0.6983	0.6485	0.6017	0.5578	0.5168	0.4783
1	0.9980	0.9921	0.9829	0.9706	0.9556	0.9382	0.9187	0.8974	0.8745	0.8503
2	1.0000	0.9997	0.9991	0.9980	0.9962	0.9937	0.9903	0.9860	0.9807	0.9743
3	1.0000	1.0000	1.0000	0.9999	0.9998	0.9996	0.9993	0.9998	0.9982	0.9973
4	1.0000	1.0000	1.0000	1.0000	1.0000	1.0000	1.0000	0.9999	0.9999	0.9998
5	1.0000	1.0000	1.0000	1.0000	1.0000	1.0000	1.0000	1.0000	1.0000	1.0000

d \ p	0.11	0.12	0.13	0.14	0.15	0.16	0.17	0.18	0.19	0.20
0	0.4423	0.4087	0.3773	0.3479	0.3206	0.2951	0.2714	0.2493	0.2288	0.2097
1	0.8250	0.7988	0.7719	0.7444	0.7166	0.6885	0.6604	0.6323	0.6044	0.5767
2	0.9669	0.9584	0.9487	0.9380	0.9262	0.9134	0.8995	0.8846	0.8687	0.8520
3	0.9961	0.9946	0.9928	0.9906	0.9879	0.9847	0.9811	0.9769	0.9721	0.9687
4	0.9997	0.9996	0.9994	0.9991	0.9988	0.9983	0.9978	0.9971	0.9963	0.9953
5	1.0000	1.0000	1.0000	1.0000	0.9999	0.9999	0.9999	0.9998	0.9997	0.9996
6	1.0000	1.0000	1.0000	1.0000	1.0000	1.0000	1.0000	1.0000	1.0000	1.0000

d \ p	0.21	0.22	0.23	0.24	0.25	0.26	0.27	0.28	0.29	0.30
0	0.1920	0.1757	0.1605	0.1465	0.1335	0.1215	0.1105	0.1003	0.0910	0.0824
1	0.5494	0.5225	0.4960	0.4702	0.4449	0.4204	0.3965	0.3734	0.3510	0.3294
2	0.8343	0.8159	0.7967	0.7769	0.7564	0.7354	0.7139	0.6919	0.6696	0.6471
3	0.9606	0.9539	0.9464	0.9383	0.9294	0.9198	0.9095	0.8984	0.8866	0.8740
4	0.9942	0.9928	0.9912	0.9893	0.9871	0.9847	0.9819	0.9787	0.9752	0.9712
5	0.9995	0.9994	0.9992	0.9989	0.9987	0.9983	0.9979	0.9974	0.9969	0.9962
6	1.0000	1.0000	1.0000	1.0000	0.9999	0.9999	0.9999	0.9999	0.9998	0.9998
7	1.0000	1.0000	1.0000	1.0000	1.0000	1.0000	1.0000	1.0000	1.0000	1.0000

d \ p	0.31	0.32	0.33	0.34	0.35	0.36	0.37	0.38	0.39	0.40
0	0.0745	0.0672	0.0606	0.0546	0.0490	0.0440	0.0394	0.0352	0.0314	0.0280
1	0.3086	0.2887	0.2696	0.2513	0.2338	0.2172	0.2013	0.1863	0.1721	0.1586
2	0.6243	0.6013	0.5783	0.5553	0.5323	0.5094	0.4868	0.4641	0.4419	0.4199
3	0.8606	0.8466	0.8318	0.8163	0.8002	0.7833	0.7659	0.7479	0.7293	0.7102
4	0.9668	0.9620	0.9566	0.9508	0.9444	0.9375	0.9299	0.9218	0.9131	0.9037
5	0.9954	0.9945	0.9935	0.9923	0.9910	0.9895	0.9877	0.9858	0.9836	0.9812
6	0.9997	0.9997	0.9996	0.9995	0.9994	0.9992	0.9991	0.9989	0.9986	0.9984
7	1.0000	1.0000	1.0000	1.0000	1.0000	1.0000	1.0000	1.0000	1.0000	1.0000

d \ p	0.41	0.42	0.43	0.44	0.45	0.46	0.47	0.48	0.49	0.50
0	0.0249	0.0221	0.0195	0.0173	0.0152	0.0134	0.0117	0.0103	0.0090	0.0078
1	0.1459	0.1340	0.1228	0.1123	0.1024	0.0932	0.0847	0.0767	0.0693	0.0625
2	0.3983	0.3771	0.3564	0.3362	0.3164	0.2973	0.2787	0.2607	0.2433	0.2266
3	0.6906	0.6706	0.6502	0.6294	0.6083	0.5869	0.5654	0.5437	0.5219	0.5000
4	0.8937	0.8831	0.8718	0.8598	0.8471	0.8337	0.8197	0.8049	0.7895	0.7734
5	0.9784	0.9754	0.9721	0.9684	0.9643	0.9598	0.9549	0.9496	0.9438	0.9375
6	0.9981	0.9977	0.9973	0.9968	0.9963	0.9956	0.9949	0.9941	0.9932	0.9922
7	1.0000	1.0000	1.0000	1.0000	1.0000	1.0000	1.0000	1.0000	1.0000	1.0000

(*continued*)

(*continued*)   **n = 8**

d \ p	0.01	0.02	0.03	0.04	0.05	0.06	0.07	0.08	0.09	0.10
0	0.9227	0.8508	0.7837	0.7214	0.6634	0.6096	0.5596	0.5132	0.4703	0.4305
1	0.9973	0.9897	0.9777	0.9619	0.9428	0.9208	0.8965	0.8702	0.8423	0.8131
2	0.9999	0.9996	0.9987	0.9969	0.9942	0.9904	0.9853	0.9789	0.9711	0.9619
3	1.0000	1.0000	0.9999	0.9998	0.9996	0.9993	0.9987	0.9978	0.9966	0.9950
4	1.0000	1.0000	1.0000	1.0000	1.0000	1.0000	0.9999	0.9999	0.9997	0.9996
5	1.0000	1.0000	1.0000	1.0000	1.0000	1.0000	1.0000	1.0000	1.0000	1.0000

d \ p	0.11	0.12	0.13	0.14	0.15	0.16	0.17	0.18	0.19	0.20
0	0.3937	0.3596	0.3282	0.2992	0.2725	0.2479	0.2252	0.2044	0.1853	0.1678
1	0.7829	0.7520	0.7206	0.6889	0.6572	0.6256	0.5943	0.5634	0.5330	0.5033
2	0.9513	0.9392	0.9257	0.9109	0.8948	0.8774	0.8588	0.8392	0.8185	0.7969
3	0.9929	0.9903	0.9871	0.9832	0.9786	0.9733	0.9672	0.9603	0.9524	0.9437
4	0.9993	0.9990	0.9985	0.9979	0.9971	0.9962	0.9950	0.9935	0.9917	0.9896
5	1.0000	0.9999	0.9999	0.9998	0.9998	0.9997	0.9995	0.9993	0.9991	0.9988
6	1.0000	1.0000	1.0000	1.0000	1.0000	1.0000	1.0000	1.0000	0.9999	0.9999
7	1.0000	1.0000	1.0000	1.0000	1.0000	1.0000	1.0000	1.0000	1.0000	1.0000

d \ p	0.21	0.22	0.23	0.24	0.25	0.26	0.27	0.28	0.29	0.30
0	0.1517	0.1370	0.1236	0.1113	0.1001	0.8990	0.0806	0.0722	0.0646	0.0576
1	0.4743	0.4462	0.4189	0.3925	0.3671	0.3427	0.3193	0.2969	0.2756	0.2553
2	0.7745	0.7514	0.7276	0.7033	0.6785	0.6535	0.6282	0.6027	0.5772	0.5518
3	0.9341	0.9235	0.9120	0.8996	0.8862	0.8719	0.8567	0.8406	0.8237	0.8059
4	0.9871	0.9842	0.9809	0.9770	0.9727	0.9678	0.9623	0.9562	0.9495	0.9420
5	0.9984	0.9979	0.9973	0.9966	0.9958	0.9948	0.9936	0.9922	0.9906	0.9887
6	0.9999	0.9998	0.9998	0.9997	0.9996	0.9995	0.9994	0.9992	0.9990	0.9987
7	1.0000	1.0000	1.0000	1.0000	1.0000	1.0000	1.0000	1.0000	0.9999	0.9999
8	1.0000	1.0000	1.0000	1.0000	1.0000	1.0000	1.0000	1.0000	1.0000	1.0000

d \ p	0.31	0.32	0.33	0.34	0.35	0.36	0.37	0.38	0.39	0.40
0	0.0514	0.0457	0.0406	0.0360	0.0319	0.0281	0.0248	0.0218	0.0192	0.0168
1	0.2360	0.2178	0.2006	0.1844	0.1691	0.1548	0.1414	0.1289	0.1172	0.1064
2	0.5264	0.5013	0.4764	0.4519	0.4278	0.4042	0.3811	0.3585	0.3366	0.3154
3	0.7874	0.7681	0.7481	0.7276	0.7064	0.6847	0.6626	0.6401	0.6172	0.5941
4	0.9339	0.9250	0.9154	0.9051	0.8939	0.8820	0.8693	0.8557	0.8414	0.8263
5	0.9866	0.9841	0.9813	0.9782	0.9747	0.9707	0.9664	0.9615	0.9561	0.9502
6	0.9984	0.9980	0.9976	0.9970	0.9964	0.9957	0.9949	0.9939	0.9928	0.9915
7	0.9999	0.9999	0.9999	0.9998	0.9998	0.9997	0.9996	0.9996	0.9995	0.9993
8	1.0000	1.0000	1.0000	1.0000	1.0000	1.0000	1.0000	1.0000	1.0000	1.0000

d \ p	0.41	0.42	0.43	0.44	0.45	0.46	0.47	0.48	0.49	0.50
0	0.0147	0.0128	0.0111	0.0097	0.0084	0.0072	0.0062	0.0053	0.0046	0.0039
1	0.0963	0.0870	0.0784	0.0705	0.0632	0.0565	0.0504	0.0448	0.0398	0.0352
2	0.2948	0.2750	0.2560	0.2376	0.2201	0.2034	0.1875	0.1724	0.1581	0.1445
3	0.5708	0.5473	0.5238	0.5004	0.4770	0.4537	0.4306	0.4078	0.3854	0.3633
4	0.8105	0.7938	0.7765	0.7584	0.7396	0.7202	0.7001	0.6795	0.6584	0.6367
5	0.9437	0.9366	0.9289	0.9206	0.9115	0.9018	0.8914	0.8802	0.8682	0.8555
6	0.9900	0.9883	0.9864	0.9843	0.9819	0.9792	0.9761	0.9728	0.9690	0.9648
7	0.9992	0.9990	0.9988	0.9986	0.9983	0.9980	0.9976	0.9972	0.9967	0.9961
8	1.0000	1.0000	1.0000	1.0000	1.0000	1.0000	1.0000	1.0000	1.0000	1.0000

         n = 9

d \ p	0.01	0.02	0.03	0.04	0.05	0.06	0.07	0.08	0.09	0.10
0	0.9135	0.8337	0.7602	0.6925	0.6302	0.5730	0.5204	0.4722	0.4279	0.3874
1	0.9966	0.9869	0.9718	0.9522	0.9288	0.9022	0.8729	0.8417	0.8088	0.7748

(*continued*)

(*continued*)   **n = 9**

d \ p	0.01	0.02	0.03	0.04	0.05	0.06	0.07	0.08	0.09	0.10
2	0.9999	0.9994	0.9980	0.9955	0.9916	0.9862	0.9791	0.9702	0.9595	0.9470
3	1.0000	1.0000	0.9999	0.9997	0.9994	0.9987	0.9977	0.9963	0.9943	0.9917
4	1.0000	1.0000	1.0000	1.0000	1.0000	0.9999	0.9998	0.9997	0.9995	0.9991
5	1.0000	1.0000	1.0000	1.0000	1.0000	1.0000	1.0000	1.0000	1.0000	0.9999
6	1.0000	1.0000	1.0000	1.0000	1.0000	1.0000	1.0000	1.0000	1.0000	1.0000

d \ p	0.11	0.12	0.13	0.14	0.15	0.16	0.17	0.18	0.19	0.20
0	0.3504	0.3165	0.2855	0.2573	0.2316	0.2082	0.1869	0.1676	0.1501	0.1342
1	0.7401	0.7049	0.6696	0.6343	0.5995	0.5652	0.5315	0.4988	0.4670	0.4362
2	0.9327	0.9167	0.8991	0.8798	0.8591	0.8371	0.8139	0.7895	0.7643	0.7382
3	0.9883	0.9842	0.9791	0.9731	0.9661	0.9580	0.9488	0.9385	0.9270	0.9144
4	0.9986	0.9979	0.9970	0.9959	0.9944	0.9925	0.9902	0.9875	0.9842	0.9804
5	0.9999	0.9998	0.9997	0.9996	0.9994	0.9991	0.9987	0.9983	0.9977	0.9969
6	1.0000	1.0000	1.0000	1.0000	1.0000	0.9999	0.9999	0.9998	0.9998	0.9997
7	1.0000	1.0000	1.0000	1.0000	1.0000	1.0000	1.0000	1.0000	1.0000	1.0000

d \ p	0.21	0.22	0.23	0.24	0.25	0.26	0.27	0.28	0.29	0.30
0	0.1199	0.1069	0.0952	0.0846	0.0751	0.0665	0.0589	0.0520	0.0458	0.0404
1	0.4066	0.3782	0.3509	0.3250	0.3003	0.2770	0.2548	0.2340	0.2144	0.1960
2	0.7115	0.6842	0.6566	0.6287	0.6007	0.5727	0.5448	0.5171	0.4898	0.4628
3	0.9006	0.8856	0.8696	0.8525	0.8343	0.8151	0.7950	0.7740	0.7522	0.7297
4	0.9760	0.9709	0.9650	0.9584	0.9511	0.9429	0.9338	0.9238	0.9130	0.9012
5	0.9960	0.9949	0.9935	0.9919	0.9900	0.9878	0.9851	0.9821	0.9787	0.9747
6	0.9996	0.9994	0.9992	0.9990	0.9987	0.9983	0.9978	0.9972	0.9965	0.9957
7	1.0000	1.0000	0.9999	0.9999	0.9999	0.9999	0.9998	0.9997	0.9997	0.9996
8	1.0000	1.0000	1.0000	1.0000	1.0000	1.0000	1.0000	1.0000	1.0000	1.0000

d \ p	0.31	0.32	0.33	0.34	0.35	0.36	0.37	0.38	0.39	0.40
0	0.0355	1.0311	0.0272	0.0238	0.0207	0.0180	0.0156	0.0135	0.0117	0.0101
1	0.1788	0.1628	0.1478	0.1339	0.1211	0.1092	0.0983	0.0882	0.0790	0.0705
2	0.4364	0.4106	0.3854	0.3610	0.3373	0.3144	0.2924	0.2713	0.2511	0.2318
3	0.7065	0.6827	0.6585	0.6338	0.6089	0.5837	0.5584	0.5331	0.5078	0.4826
4	0.8885	0.8747	0.8602	0.8447	0.8283	0.8110	0.7928	0.7738	0.7540	0.7334
5	0.9702	0.9652	0.9596	0.9533	0.9464	0.9388	0.9304	0.9213	0.9114	0.9006
6	0.9947	0.9936	0.9922	0.9906	0.9888	0.9867	0.9843	0.9816	0.9785	0.9750
7	0.9994	0.9993	0.9991	0.9989	0.9986	0.9983	0.9979	0.9974	0.9969	0.9962
8	1.0000	1.0000	1.0000	0.9999	0.9999	0.9999	0.9999	0.9998	0.9998	0.9997
9	1.0000	1.0000	1.0000	1.0000	1.0000	1.0000	1.0000	1.0000	1.0000	1.0000

d \ p	0.41	0.42	0.43	0.44	0.45	0.46	0.47	0.48	0.49	0.50
0	0.0087	0.0074	0.0064	0.0054	0.0046	0.0039	0.0033	0.0028	0.0023	0.0020
1	0.0628	0.0558	0.0495	0.0437	0.0385	0.0338	0.0296	0.0259	0.0225	0.0195
2	0.2134	0.1961	0.1796	0.1641	0.1495	0.1358	0.1231	0.1111	0.1001	0.0898
3	0.4576	0.4330	0.4087	0.3848	0.3614	0.3386	0.3164	0.2948	0.2740	0.2539
4	0.7122	0.6903	0.6678	0.6449	0.6214	0.5976	0.5735	0.5491	0.5246	0.5000
5	0.8891	0.8767	0.8634	0.8492	0.8342	0.8183	0.8015	0.7839	0.7654	0.7461
6	0.9710	0.9666	0.9617	0.9563	0.9502	0.9436	0.9363	0.9283	0.9196	0.9102
7	0.9954	0.9945	0.9935	0.9923	0.9909	0.9893	0.9875	0.9855	0.9831	0.9805
8	0.9997	0.9996	0.9995	0.9994	0.9992	0.9991	0.9989	0.9986	0.9984	0.9980
9	1.0000	1.0000	1.0000	1.0000	1.0000	1.0000	1.0000	1.0000	1.0000	1.0000

n = 10

d \ p	0.01	0.02	0.03	0.04	0.05	0.06	0.07	0.08	0.09	0.10
0	0.9044	0.8171	0.7374	0.6648	0.5987	0.5386	0.4840	0.4344	0.3894	0.3487
1	0.9957	0.9838	0.9655	0.9418	0.9139	0.8824	0.8483	0.8121	0.7746	0.7361

(*continued*)

(*continued*)   **n = 10**

d \ p	0.01	0.02	0.03	0.04	0.05	0.06	0.07	0.08	0.09	0.10
2	0.9999	0.9991	0.9972	0.9938	0.9885	0.9812	0.9717	0.9599	0.9460	0.9298
3	1.0000	1.0000	0.9999	0.9996	0.9990	0.9980	0.9964	0.9942	0.9912	0.9872
4	1.0000	1.0000	1.0000	1.0000	0.9999	0.9998	0.9997	0.9994	0.9990	0.9984
5	1.0000	1.0000	1.0000	1.0000	1.0000	1.0000	1.0000	1.0000	0.9999	0.9999
6	1.0000	1.0000	1.0000	1.0000	1.0000	1.0000	1.0000	1.0000	1.0000	1.0000

d \ p	0.11	0.12	0.13	0.14	0.15	0.16	0.17	0.18	0.19	0.20
0	0.3118	0.2785	0.2484	0.2213	0.1969	0.1749	0.1552	0.1374	0.1216	0.1074
1	0.6972	0.6583	0.6196	0.5816	0.5443	0.5080	0.4730	0.4392	0.4068	0.3758
2	0.9116	0.8913	0.8692	0.8455	0.8202	0.7936	0.7659	0.7372	0.7078	0.6778
3	0.9822	0.9761	0.9687	0.9600	0.9500	0.9386	0.9259	0.9117	0.8961	0.8791
4	0.9975	0.9963	0.9947	0.9927	0.9901	0.9870	0.9832	0.9787	0.9734	0.9672
5	0.9997	0.9996	0.9994	0.9990	0.9986	0.9980	0.9973	0.9963	0.9951	0.9936
6	1.0000	1.0000	0.9999	0.9999	0.9999	0.9998	0.9997	0.9996	0.9994	0.9991
7	1.0000	1.0000	1.0000	1.0000	1.0000	1.0000	1.0000	1.0000	0.9999	0.9999
8	1.0000	1.0000	1.0000	1.0000	1.0000	1.0000	1.0000	1.0000	1.0000	1.0000

d \ p	0.21	0.22	0.23	0.24	0.25	0.26	0.27	0.28	0.29	0.30
0	0.0947	0.0834	0.0733	0.0643	0.0563	0.0492	0.0430	0.0374	0.0326	0.0282
1	0.3464	0.3185	0.2921	0.2673	0.2440	0.2222	0.2019	0.1830	0.1655	0.1493
2	0.6474	0.6169	0.5863	0.5558	0.5256	0.4958	0.4665	0.4378	0.4099	0.3828
3	0.8609	0.8413	0.8206	0.7988	0.7759	0.7521	0.7274	0.7021	0.6761	0.6496
4	0.9601	0.9521	0.9431	0.9330	0.9219	0.9096	0.8963	0.8819	0.8663	0.8497
5	0.9918	0.9896	0.9870	0.9839	0.9803	0.9761	0.9713	0.9658	0.9596	0.9527
6	0.9988	0.9984	0.9979	0.9973	0.9965	0.9955	0.9944	0.9930	0.9913	0.9894
7	0.9999	0.9998	0.9998	0.9997	0.9996	0.9994	0.9993	0.9990	0.9988	0.9984
8	1.0000	1.0000	1.0000	1.0000	1.0000	1.0000	0.9999	0.9999	0.9999	0.9999
9	1.0000	1.0000	1.0000	1.0000	1.0000	1.0000	1.0000	1.0000	1.0000	1.0000

d \ p	0.31	0.32	0.33	0.34	0.35	0.36	0.37	0.38	0.39	0.40
0	0.0245	0.0211	0.0182	0.0157	0.0135	0.0115	0.0098	0.0084	0.0071	0.0060
1	0.1344	0.1206	0.1080	0.0965	0.0860	0.0764	0.0677	0.0598	0.0527	0.0464
2	0.3566	0.3313	0.3070	0.2838	0.2616	0.2405	0.2206	0.2017	0.1840	0.1673
3	0.6228	0.5956	0.5684	0.5411	0.5138	0.4868	0.4600	0.4336	0.4077	0.3823
4	0.8321	0.8133	0.7936	0.7730	0.7515	0.7292	0.7061	0.6823	0.6580	0.6331
5	0.9449	0.9363	0.9268	0.9164	0.9051	0.8928	0.8795	0.8652	0.8500	0.8338
6	0.9871	0.9845	0.9815	0.9780	0.9740	0.9695	0.9644	0.9587	0.9523	0.9452
7	0.9980	0.9975	0.9968	0.9961	0.9952	0.9941	0.9929	0.9914	0.9897	0.9877
8	0.9998	0.9997	0.9997	0.9996	0.9995	0.9993	0.9991	0.9989	0.9986	0.9983
9	1.0000	1.0000	1.0000	1.0000	1.0000	1.0000	1.0000	0.9999	0.9999	0.9999
10	1.0000	1.0000	1.0000	1.0000	1.0000	1.0000	1.0000	1.0000	1.0000	1.0000

d \ p	0.41	0.42	0.43	0.44	0.45	0.46	0.47	0.48	0.49	0.50
0	0.0051	0.0043	0.0036	0.0030	0.0025	0.0021	0.0017	0.0014	0.0012	0.0010
1	0.0406	0.0355	0.0309	0.0269	0.0233	0.0201	0.0173	0.0148	0.0126	0.0107
2	0.1517	0.1372	0.1236	0.1111	0.0996	0.0889	0.0791	0.0702	0.0621	0.0547
3	0.3575	0.3335	0.3102	0.2877	0.2660	0.2453	0.2255	0.2067	0.1888	0.1719
4	0.6078	0.5822	0.5564	0.5304	0.5044	0.4784	0.4526	0.4270	0.4018	0.3770
5	0.8166	0.7984	0.7793	0.7593	0.7384	0.7168	0.6943	0.6712	0.6474	0.6230
6	0.9374	0.9288	0.9194	0.9092	0.8980	0.8859	0.8729	0.8590	0.8440	0.8281
7	0.9854	0.9828	0.9798	0.9764	0.9726	0.9683	0.9634	0.9580	0.9520	0.9453
8	0.9979	0.9975	0.9969	0.9963	0.9955	0.9946	0.9935	0.9923	0.9909	0.9893
9	0.9999	0.9998	0.9998	0.9997	0.9997	0.9996	0.9995	0.9994	0.9992	0.9990
10	1.0000	1.0000	1.0000	1.0000	1.0000	1.0000	1.0000	1.0000	1.0000	1.0000

(*continued*)

(continued) n = 11

d \ p	0.01	0.02	0.03	0.04	0.05	0.06	0.07	0.08	0.09	0.10
0	0.8953	0.8007	0.7153	0.6382	0.5688	0.5063	0.4501	0.3996	0.3544	0.3138
1	0.9948	0.9805	0.9587	0.9308	0.8981	0.8618	0.8228	0.7819	0.7399	0.6974
2	0.9998	0.9988	0.9963	0.9917	0.9848	0.9752	0.9630	0.9481	0.9305	0.9104
3	1.0000	1.0000	0.9998	0.9993	0.9984	0.9970	0.9947	0.9915	0.9871	0.9815
4	1.0000	1.0000	1.0000	1.0000	0.9999	0.9997	0.9995	0.9990	0.9983	0.9972
5	1.0000	1.0000	1.0000	1.0000	1.0000	1.0000	1.0000	0.9999	0.9998	0.9997
6	1.0000	1.0000	1.0000	1.0000	1.0000	1.0000	1.0000	1.0000	1.0000	1.0000

d \ p	0.11	0.12	0.13	0.14	0.15	0.16	0.17	0.18	0.19	0.20
0	0.2775	0.2451	0.2161	0.1903	0.1673	0.1469	0.1288	0.1127	0.0985	0.0859
1	0.6548	0.6127	0.5714	0.5311	0.4922	0.4547	0.4189	0.3849	0.3526	0.3221
2	0.8880	0.8634	0.8368	0.8085	0.7788	0.7479	0.7161	0.6836	0.6506	0.6174
3	0.9744	0.9659	0.9558	0.9440	0.9306	0.9514	0.8987	0.8803	0.8603	0.8389
4	0.9958	0.9939	0.9913	0.9881	0.9841	0.9793	0.9734	0.9666	0.9587	0.9496
5	0.9995	0.9992	0.9988	0.9982	0.9973	0.9963	0.9949	0.9932	0.9910	0.9883
6	1.0000	0.9999	0.9999	0.9998	0.9997	0.9995	0.9993	0.9990	0.9986	0.9880
7	1.0000	1.0000	1.0000	1.0000	1.0000	1.0000	0.9999	0.9999	0.9998	0.9998
8	1.0000	1.0000	1.0000	1.0000	1.0000	1.0000	1.0000	1.0000	1.0000	1.0000

d \ p	0.21	0.22	0.23	0.24	0.25	0.26	0.27	0.28	0.29	0.30
0	0.0748	0.0650	0.0564	0.0489	0.0422	0.0364	0.0314	0.0270	0.0231	0.0198
1	0.2935	0.2667	0.2418	0.2186	0.1971	0.1773	0.1590	0.1423	0.1270	0.1130
2	0.5842	0.5512	0.5186	0.4866	0.4552	0.4247	0.3951	0.3665	0.3390	0.3127
3	0.8160	0.7919	0.7667	0.7404	0.7133	0.6854	0.6570	0.6281	0.5889	0.5696
4	0.9393	0.9277	0.9149	0.9008	0.8554	0.8687	0.8507	0.8315	0.8112	0.7897
5	0.9852	0.9814	0.9769	0.9717	0.9657	0.9588	0.9510	0.9423	0.9326	0.9218
6	0.9973	0.9965	0.9954	0.9941	0.9924	0.9905	0.9881	0.9854	0.9821	0.9784
7	0.9997	0.9995	0.9993	0.9991	0.9988	0.9984	0.9979	0.9973	0.9966	0.9957
8	1.0000	1.0000	0.9999	0.9999	0.9999	0.9998	0.9998	0.9997	0.9996	0.9994
9	1.0000	1.0000	1.0000	1.0000	1.0000	1.0000	1.0000	1.0000	1.0000	1.0000

d \ p	0.31	0.32	0.33	0.34	0.35	0.36	0.37	0.38	0.39	0.40
0	0.0169	0.0144	0.0122	0.0104	0.0088	0.0074	0.0062	0.0052	0.0044	0.0036
1	0.1003	0.0888	0.0784	0.0690	0.0606	0.0530	0.0463	0.0403	0.0350	0.0302
2	0.2877	0.2639	0.2413	0.2201	0.2001	0.1814	0.1640	0.1478	0.1328	0.1189
3	0.5402	0.5110	0.4821	0.4536	0.4256	0.3981	0.3714	0.3455	0.3204	0.2963
4	0.7672	0.7437	0.7193	0.6941	0.6683	0.6419	0.6150	0.5878	0.5603	0.5328
5	0.9099	0.8969	0.8829	0.8676	0.8513	0.8339	0.8153	0.7957	0.7751	0.7535
6	0.9740	0.9691	0.9634	0.9570	0.9499	0.9419	0.9330	0.9232	0.9124	0.9006
7	0.9946	0.9933	0.9918	0.9899	0.9878	0.9852	0.9823	0.9790	0.9751	0.9707
8	0.9992	0.9990	0.9987	0.9984	0.9980	0.9974	0.9968	0.9961	0.9952	0.9941
9	0.9999	0.9999	0.9999	0.9998	0.9998	0.9997	0.9996	0.9995	0.9994	0.9993
10	1.0000	1.0000	1.0000	1.0000	1.0000	1.0000	1.0000	1.0000	1.0000	1.0000

d \ p	0.41	0.42	0.43	0.44	0.45	0.46	0.47	0.48	0.49	0.50
0	0.0030	0.0025	0.0021	0.0017	0.0014	0.0011	0.0009	0.0008	0.0006	0.0005
1	0.0261	0.0224	0.0192	0.0164	0.0139	0.0118	0.0100	0.0084	0.0070	0.0059
2	0.1062	0.0945	0.0838	0.0740	0.0652	0.0572	0.0501	0.0436	0.0378	0.0327
3	0.2731	0.2510	0.2300	0.2100	0.1911	0.1734	0.1567	0.1412	0.1267	0.1133
4	0.5052	0.4777	0.4505	0.4236	0.3971	0.3712	0.3459	0.3213	0.2974	0.2744
5	0.7310	0.7076	0.6834	0.6586	0.6331	0.6071	0.5807	0.5540	0.5271	0.5000
6	0.8879	0.8740	0.8592	0.8432	0.8262	0.8081	0.7890	0.7688	0.7477	0.7256
7	0.9657	0.9601	0.9539	0.9468	0.9390	0.9304	0.9209	0.9105	0.8991	0.8867
8	0.9928	0.9913	0.9896	0.9875	0.9852	0.9825	0.9794	0.9759	0.9718	0.9673
9	0.9991	0.9988	0.9986	0.9982	0.9978	0.9973	0.9967	0.9960	0.9951	0.9941
10	0.9999	0.9999	0.9999	0.9999	0.9998	0.9998	0.9998	0.9997	0.9996	0.9995
11	1.0000	1.0000	1.0000	1.0000	1.0000	1.0000	1.0000	1.0000	1.0000	1.0000

(continued)

(*continued*)   n = 12

d \ p	0.01	0.02	0.03	0.04	0.05	0.06	0.07	0.08	0.09	0.10
0	0.8864	0.7847	0.6938	0.6127	0.5404	0.4759	0.4186	0.3677	0.3225	0.2824
1	0.9938	0.9769	0.9514	0.9191	0.8816	0.8405	0.7967	0.7513	0.7052	0.6590
2	0.9998	0.9985	0.9952	0.9893	0.9804	0.9684	0.9532	0.9348	0.9134	0.8891
3	1.0000	0.9999	0.9997	0.9990	0.9978	0.9957	0.9925	0.9880	0.9820	0.9744
4	1.0000	1.0000	1.0000	0.9999	0.9998	0.9996	0.9991	0.9984	0.9973	0.9957
5	1.0000	1.0000	1.0000	1.0000	1.0000	1.0000	0.9999	0.9998	0.9997	0.9995
6	1.0000	1.0000	1.0000	1.0000	1.0000	1.0000	1.0000	1.0000	1.0000	0.9999
7	1.0000	1.0000	1.0000	1.0000	1.0000	1.0000	1.0000	1.0000	1.0000	1.0000

d \ p	0.11	0.12	0.13	0.14	0.15	0.16	0.17	0.18	0.19	0.20
0	0.2470	0.2157	0.1880	0.1637	0.1422	0.1234	0.1069	0.0924	0.0798	0.0687
1	0.6133	0.5686	0.5252	0.4834	0.4435	0.4055	0.3696	0.3359	0.3043	0.2749
2	0.8623	0.8333	0.8023	0.7697	0.7358	0.7010	0.6656	0.6298	0.5940	0.5583
3	0.9649	0.9536	0.9403	0.9250	0.9078	0.8886	0.8676	0.8448	0.8205	0.7946
4	0.9935	0.9905	0.9867	0.9819	0.9761	0.9690	0.9607	0.9511	0.9400	0.9274
5	0.9991	0.9986	0.9978	0.9967	0.9954	0.9935	0.9912	0.9884	0.9849	0.9806
6	0.9999	0.9998	0.9997	0.9996	0.9993	0.9990	0.9985	0.9979	0.9971	0.9961
7	1.0000	1.0000	1.0000	1.0000	0.9999	0.9999	0.9998	0.9997	0.9996	0.9994
8	1.0000	1.0000	1.0000	1.0000	1.0000	1.0000	1.0000	1.0000	1.0000	0.9999
9	1.0000	1.0000	1.0000	1.0000	1.0000	1.0000	1.0000	1.0000	1.0000	1.0000

d \ p	0.21	0.22	0.23	0.24	0.25	0.26	0.27	0.28	0.29	0.30
0	0.0591	0.0507	0.0434	0.0371	0.0317	0.0270	0.0229	0.0194	0.0164	0.0138
1	0.2476	0.2224	0.1991	0.1778	0.1584	0.1406	0.1245	0.1100	0.0968	0.0850
2	0.5232	0.4886	0.4550	0.4222	0.3907	0.3603	0.3313	0.3037	0.2775	0.2528
3	0.7674	0.7390	0.7096	0.6795	0.6488	0.6176	0.5863	0.5548	0.5235	0.4925
4	0.9134	0.8979	0.8808	0.8623	0.8424	0.8210	0.7984	0.7746	0.7496	0.7237
5	0.9755	0.9696	0.9626	0.9547	0.9456	0.9354	0.9240	0.9113	0.8974	0.8822
6	0.9948	0.9932	0.9911	0.9887	0.9857	0.9822	0.9781	0.9733	0.9678	0.9614
7	0.9992	0.9989	0.9984	0.9979	0.9972	0.9964	0.9953	0.9940	0.9924	0.9905
8	0.9999	0.9999	0.9998	0.9997	0.9996	0.9995	0.9993	0.9990	0.9987	0.9983
9	1.0000	1.0000	1.0000	1.0000	1.0000	0.9999	0.9999	0.9999	0.9998	0.9998
10	1.0000	1.0000	1.0000	1.0000	1.0000	1.0000	1.0000	1.0000	1.0000	1.0000

d \ p	0.31	0.32	0.33	0.34	0.35	0.36	0.37	0.38	0.39	0.40
0	0.0116	0.0098	0.0082	0.0068	0.0057	0.0047	0.0039	0.0032	0.0027	0.0022
1	0.0744	0.0650	0.0565	0.0491	0.0424	0.0366	0.0315	0.0270	0.0230	0.0196
2	0.2296	0.2078	0.1876	0.1687	0.1513	0.1352	0.1205	0.1069	0.0946	0.0834
3	0.4619	0.4319	0.4027	0.3742	0.3467	0.3201	0.2947	0.2704	0.2472	0.2253
4	0.6968	0.6692	0.6410	0.6124	0.5833	0.5541	0.5249	0.4957	0.4668	0.4382
5	0.8657	0.8479	0.8289	0.8087	0.7873	0.7648	0.7412	0.7167	0.6913	0.6652
6	0.9542	0.9460	0.9368	0.9266	0.9154	0.9030	0.8894	0.8747	0.8589	0.8418
7	0.9882	0.9856	0.9824	0.9787	0.9745	0.9696	0.9641	0.9578	0.9507	0.9427
8	0.9978	0.9972	0.9964	0.9955	0.9944	0.9930	0.9915	0.9896	0.9873	0.9847
9	0.9997	0.9996	0.9995	0.9993	0.9992	0.9989	0.9986	0.9982	0.9978	0.9972
10	1.0000	1.0000	1.0000	0.9999	0.9999	0.9999	0.9999	0.9998	0.9998	0.9997
11	1.0000	1.0000	1.0000	1.0000	1.0000	1.0000	1.0000	1.0000	1.0000	1.0000

d \ p	0.41	0.42	0.43	0.44	0.45	0.46	0.47	0.48	0.49	0.50
0	0.0018	0.0014	0.0012	0.0010	0.0008	0.0006	0.0005	0.0004	0.0003	0.0002
1	0.0166	0.0140	0.0118	0.0099	0.0083	0.0069	0.0057	0.0047	0.0039	0.0032
2	0.0733	0.0642	0.0560	0.0487	0.0421	0.0363	0.0312	0.0267	0.0227	0.0193
3	0.2047	0.1853	0.1671	0.1502	0.1345	0.1199	0.1066	0.0943	0.0832	0.0730
4	0.4101	0.3825	0.3557	0.3296	0.3044	0.2802	0.2570	0.2348	0.2138	0.1938
5	0.6384	0.6111	0.5833	0.5552	0.5269	0.4986	0.4703	0.4423	0.4145	0.3872
6	0.8235	0.8041	0.7836	0.7620	0.7393	0.7157	0.6911	0.6657	0.6396	0.6128
7	0.9338	0.9240	0.9131	0.9012	0.8883	0.8742	0.8589	0.8425	0.8249	0.8062

(*continued*)

(*continued*)   **n = 12**

d \ p	0.41	0.42	0.43	0.44	0.45	0.46	0.47	0.48	0.49	0.50
8	0.9817	0.9782	0.9742	0.9696	0.9644	0.9585	0.9519	0.9445	0.9362	0.9270
9	0.9965	0.9957	0.9947	0.9935	0.9921	0.9905	0.9886	0.9883	0.9837	0.9807
10	0.9996	0.9995	0.9993	0.9991	0.9989	0.9986	0.9983	0.9979	0.9974	0.9968
11	1.0000	1.0000	1.0000	0.9999	0.9999	0.9999	0.9999	0.9999	0.9998	0.9998
12	1.0000	1.0000	1.0000	1.0000	1.0000	1.0000	1.0000	1.0000	1.0000	1.0000

n = 13

d \ p	0.01	0.02	0.03	0.04	0.05	0.06	0.07	0.08	0.09	0.10
0	0.8775	0.7690	0.6730	0.5882	0.5133	0.4474	0.3893	0.3383	0.2935	0.2542
1	0.9928	0.9730	0.9436	0.9068	0.8646	0.8186	0.7702	0.7206	0.6707	0.6213
2	0.9997	0.9980	0.9938	0.9865	0.9755	0.9608	0.9422	0.9201	0.8946	0.8661
3	1.0000	0.9999	0.9995	0.9986	0.9969	0.9940	0.9897	0.9837	0.9758	0.9658
4	1.0000	1.0000	1.0000	0.9999	0.9997	0.9993	0.9987	0.9976	0.9959	0.9935
5	1.0000	1.0000	1.0000	1.0000	1.0000	0.9999	0.9999	0.9997	0.9995	0.9991
6	1.0000	1.0000	1.0000	1.0000	1.0000	1.0000	1.0000	1.0000	0.9999	0.9999
7	1.0000	1.0000	1.0000	1.0000	1.0000	1.0000	1.0000	1.0000	1.0000	1.0000

d \ p	0.11	0.12	0.13	0.14	0.15	0.16	0.17	0.18	0.19	0.20
0	0.2198	0.1898	0.1636	0.1408	0.1209	0.1037	0.0887	0.0758	0.0646	0.0550
1	0.5730	0.5262	0.4814	0.4386	0.3983	0.3604	0.3249	0.2920	0.2616	0.2336
2	0.8349	0.8015	0.7663	0.7296	0.6920	0.6537	0.6152	0.5769	0.5389	0.5017
3	0.9536	0.9391	0.9224	0.9033	0.8820	0.8586	0.8333	0.8061	0.7774	0.7473
4	0.9903	0.9861	0.9807	0.9740	0.9658	0.9562	0.9449	0.9319	0.9173	0.9009
5	0.9985	0.9976	0.9964	0.9947	0.9925	0.9896	0.9861	0.9817	0.9763	0.9700
6	0.9998	0.9997	0.9995	0.9992	0.9987	0.9981	0.9973	0.9962	0.9948	0.9930
7	1.0000	1.0000	0.9999	0.9999	0.9998	0.9997	0.9996	0.9994	0.9991	0.9988
8	1.0000	1.0000	1.0000	1.0000	1.0000	1.0000	1.0000	0.9999	0.9999	0.9998
9	1.0000	1.0000	1.0000	1.0000	1.0000	1.0000	1.0000	1.0000	1.0000	1.0000

d \ p	0.21	0.22	0.23	0.24	0.25	0.26	0.27	0.28	0.29	0.30
0	0.0467	0.0396	0.0334	0.0282	0.0238	0.0200	0.0167	0.0140	0.0117	0.0097
1	0.2080	0.1846	0.1633	0.1441	0.1267	0.1111	0.0971	0.0846	0.0735	0.0637
2	0.4653	0.4301	0.3961	0.3636	0.3326	0.3032	0.2755	0.2495	0.2251	0.2025
3	0.7161	0.6839	0.6511	0.6178	0.5843	0.5507	0.5174	0.4845	0.4522	0.4206
4	0.8827	0.8629	0.8415	0.8184	0.7940	0.7681	0.7411	0.7130	0.6840	0.6543
5	0.9625	0.9538	0.9438	0.9325	0.9198	0.9056	0.8901	0.8730	0.8545	0.8346
6	0.9907	0.9880	0.9846	0.9805	0.9757	0.9701	0.9635	0.9560	0.9473	0.9376
7	0.9983	0.9976	0.9968	0.9957	0.9944	0.9927	0.9907	0.9882	0.9853	0.9818
8	0.9998	0.9996	0.9995	0.9993	0.9990	0.9987	0.9982	0.9976	0.9969	0.9960
9	1.0000	1.0000	0.9999	0.9999	0.9999	0.9998	0.9997	0.9996	0.9995	0.9993
10	1.0000	1.0000	1.0000	1.0000	1.0000	1.0000	1.0000	1.0000	0.9999	0.9999
11	1.0000	1.0000	1.0000	1.0000	1.0000	1.0000	1.0000	1.0000	1.0000	1.0000

d \ p	0.31	0.32	0.33	0.34	0.35	0.36	0.37	0.38	0.39	0.40
0	0.0080	0.0066	0.0055	0.0045	0.0037	0.0030	0.0025	0.0020	0.0016	0.0013
1	0.0550	0.0473	0.0406	0.0347	0.0296	0.0251	0.0213	0.0179	0.0151	0.0126
2	0.1815	0.1621	0.1443	0.1280	0.1132	0.0997	0.0875	0.0765	0.0667	0.0579
3	0.3899	0.3602	0.3317	0.3043	0.2783	0.2536	0.2302	0.2083	0.1877	0.1686
4	0.6240	0.5933	0.5624	0.5314	0.5005	0.4699	0.4397	0.4101	0.3812	0.3530
5	0.8133	0.7907	0.7669	0.7419	0.7159	0.6889	0.6612	0.6327	0.6038	0.5744
6	0.9267	0.9146	0.9012	0.8865	0.8705	0.8532	0.8346	0.8147	0.7935	0.7712
7	0.9777	0.9729	0.9674	0.9610	0.9538	0.9456	0.9365	0.9262	0.9149	0.9023
8	0.9948	0.9935	0.9918	0.9898	0.9874	0.9846	0.9813	0.9775	0.9730	0.9679
9	0.9991	0.9988	0.9985	0.9980	0.9975	0.9968	0.9960	0.9949	0.9937	0.9922

(*continued*)

(*continued*)   **n = 13**

d \ p	0.31	0.32	0.33	0.34	0.35	0.36	0.37	0.38	0.39	0.40
10	0.9999	0.9999	0.9998	0.9997	0.9997	0.9995	0.9994	0.9992	0.9990	0.9987
11	1.0000	1.0000	1.0000	1.0000	1.0000	1.0000	0.9999	0.9999	0.9999	0.9999
12	1.0000	1.0000	1.0000	1.0000	1.0000	1.0000	1.0000	1.0000	1.0000	1.0000

d \ p	0.41	0.42	0.43	0.44	0.45	0.46	0.47	0.48	0.49	0.50
0	0.0010	0.0008	0.0007	0.0005	0.0004	0.0003	0.0003	0.0002	0.0002	0.0001
1	0.0105	0.0088	0.0072	0.0060	0.0049	0.0040	0.0033	0.0026	0.0021	0.0017
2	0.0501	0.0431	0.0370	0.0316	0.0269	0.0228	0.0192	0.0162	0.0135	0.0112
3	0.1508	0.1344	0.1193	0.1055	0.0929	0.0815	0.0712	0.0619	0.0536	0.0461
4	0.3258	0.2997	0.2746	0.2507	0.2279	0.2065	0.1863	0.1674	0.1498	0.1334
5	0.5448	0.5151	0.4854	0.4559	0.4268	0.3981	0.3701	0.3427	0.3162	0.2905
6	0.7476	0.7230	0.6975	0.6710	0.6437	0.6158	0.5873	0.5585	0.5293	0.5000
7	0.8886	0.8736	0.8574	0.8400	0.8212	0.8012	0.7800	0.7576	0.7341	0.7095
8	0.9621	0.9554	0.9480	0.9395	0.9302	0.9197	0.9082	0.8955	0.8817	0.8666
9	0.9904	0.9883	0.9859	0.9830	0.9797	0.9758	0.9713	0.9662	0.9604	0.9539
10	0.9983	0.9979	0.9973	0.9967	0.9959	0.9949	0.9937	0.9923	0.9907	0.9888
11	0.9998	0.9998	0.9997	0.9996	0.9995	0.9993	0.9991	0.9989	0.9986	0.9983
12	1.0000	1.0000	1.0000	1.0000	1.0000	1.0000	0.9999	0.9999	0.9999	0.9999
13	1.0000	1.0000	1.0000	1.0000	1.0000	1.0000	1.0000	1.0000	1.0000	1.0000

n = 14

d \ p	0.01	0.02	0.03	0.04	0.05	0.06	0.07	0.08	0.09	0.10
0	0.8687	0.7536	0.6528	0.5647	0.4877	0.4205	0.3620	0.3112	0.2670	0.2288
1	0.9916	0.9690	0.9355	0.8941	0.8470	0.7963	0.7436	0.6900	0.6368	0.5846
2	0.9997	0.9975	0.9923	0.9833	0.9699	0.9522	0.9302	0.9042	0.8745	0.8416
3	1.0000	0.9999	0.9994	0.9981	0.9958	0.9920	0.9864	0.9786	0.9685	0.9559
4	1.0000	1.0000	1.0000	0.9998	0.9996	0.9990	0.9980	0.9965	0.9941	0.9908
5	1.0000	1.0000	1.0000	1.0000	1.0000	0.9999	0.9998	0.9996	0.9992	0.9985
6	1.0000	1.0000	1.0000	1.0000	1.0000	1.0000	1.0000	1.0000	0.9999	0.9998
7	1.0000	1.0000	1.0000	1.0000	1.0000	1.0000	1.0000	1.0000	1.0000	1.0000

d \ p	0.11	0.12	0.13	0.14	0.15	0.16	0.17	0.18	0.19	0.20
0	0.1956	0.1670	0.1423	0.1211	0.1028	0.0871	0.0736	0.0621	0.0523	0.0440
1	0.5342	0.4859	0.4401	0.3969	0.3567	0.3193	0.2848	0.2531	0.2242	0.1979
2	0.8061	0.7685	0.7292	0.6889	0.6479	0.6068	0.5659	0.5256	0.4862	0.4481
3	0.9406	0.9226	0.9021	0.8790	0.8535	0.8258	0.7962	0.7649	0.7321	0.6982
4	0.9863	0.9804	0.9731	0.9641	0.9533	0.9406	0.9259	0.9093	0.8907	0.8702
5	0.9976	0.9962	0.9943	0.9918	0.9885	0.9843	0.9791	0.9727	0.9651	0.9561
6	0.9997	0.9994	0.9991	0.9985	0.9978	0.9968	0.9954	0.9936	0.9913	0.9884
7	1.0000	0.9999	0.9999	0.9998	0.9997	0.9995	0.9992	0.9988	0.9983	0.9976
8	1.0000	1.0000	1.0000	1.0000	1.0000	0.9999	0.9999	0.9998	0.9997	0.9996
9	1.0000	1.0000	1.0000	1.0000	1.0000	1.0000	1.0000	1.0000	1.0000	1.0000

d \ p	0.21	0.22	0.23	0.24	0.25	0.26	0.27	0.28	0.29	0.30
0	0.0369	0.0309	0.0258	0.0214	0.0178	0.0148	0.0122	0.0101	0.0083	0.0068
1	0.1741	0.1527	0.1335	0.1163	0.1010	0.0874	0.0754	0.0648	0.0556	0.0475
2	0.4113	0.3761	0.3426	0.3109	0.2811	0.2533	0.2273	0.2033	0.1812	0.1608
3	0.6634	0.6281	0.5924	0.5568	0.5213	0.4864	0.4521	0.4187	0.3863	0.3552
4	0.8477	0.8235	0.7977	0.7703	0.7415	0.7116	0.6807	0.6490	0.6188	0.5842
5	0.9457	0.9338	0.9203	0.9051	0.8883	0.8699	0.8498	0.8282	0.8051	0.7805
6	0.9848	0.9804	0.9752	0.9890	0.9617	0.9533	0.9437	0.9327	0.9204	0.9067
7	0.9967	0.9955	0.9940	0.9921	0.9897	0.9868	0.9833	0.9792	0.9743	0.9685
8	0.9994	0.9992	0.9989	0.9984	0.9978	0.9971	0.9962	0.9950	0.9935	0.9917
9	0.9999	0.9999	0.9998	0.9998	0.9997	0.9995	0.9993	0.9991	0.9988	0.9983
10	1.0000	1.0000	1.0000	1.0000	1.0000	0.9999	0.9999	0.9999	0.9998	0.9998
11	1.0000	1.0000	1.0000	1.0000	1.0000	1.0000	1.0000	1.0000	1.0000	1.0000

(*continued*)

(continued)					n = 14				

p d	0.31	0.32	0.33	0.34	0.35	0.36	0.37	0.38	0.39	0.40
0	0.0055	0.0045	0.0037	0.0030	0.0024	0.0019	0.0016	0.0012	0.0010	0.0008
1	0.0404	0.0343	0.0290	0.0244	0.0205	0.0172	0.0143	0.0119	0.0098	0.0081
2	0.1423	0.1254	0.1101	0.0963	0.0839	0.0729	0.0630	0.0543	0.0466	0.0398
3	0.3253	0.2968	0.2699	0.2444	0.2205	0.1982	0.1774	0.1582	0.1405	0.1243
4	0.5514	0.5187	0.4862	0.4542	0.4227	0.3920	0.3622	0.3334	0.3057	0.2793
5	0.7546	0.7276	0.6994	0.6703	0.6405	0.6101	0.5792	0.5481	0.5169	0.4859
6	0.8916	0.8750	0.8569	0.8374	0.8164	0.7941	0.7704	0.7455	0.7195	0.6925
7	0.9619	0.9542	0.9455	0.9357	0.9247	0.9124	0.8988	0.8838	0.8675	0.8499
8	0.9895	0.9869	0.9837	0.9800	0.9757	0.9706	0.9647	0.9580	0.9503	0.9417
9	0.9978	0.9971	0.9963	0.9952	0.9940	0.9924	0.9905	0.9883	0.9856	0.9825
10	0.9997	0.9995	0.9994	0.9992	0.9989	0.9986	0.9981	0.9976	0.9969	0.9961
11	1.0000	0.9999	0.9999	0.9999	0.9999	0.9998	0.9997	0.9997	0.9995	0.9994
12	1.0000	1.0000	1.0000	1.0000	1.0000	1.0000	1.0000	1.0000	1.0000	0.9999
13	1.0000	1.0000	1.0000	1.0000	1.0000	1.0000	1.0000	1.0000	1.0000	1.0000

p d	0.41	0.42	0.43	0.44	0.45	0.46	0.47	0.48	0.49	0.50
0	0.0006	0.0005	0.0004	0.0003	0.0002	0.0002	0.0001	0.0001	0.0001	0.0001
1	0.0066	0.0054	0.0044	0.0036	0.0029	0.0023	0.0019	0.0015	0.0012	0.0009
2	0.0339	0.0287	0.0242	0.0203	0.0170	0.0142	0.0117	0.0097	0.0079	0.0065
3	0.1095	0.0961	0.0839	0.0730	0.0632	0.0545	0.0468	0.0399	0.0339	0.0287
4	0.2541	0.2303	0.2078	0.1868	0.1672	0.1490	0.1322	0.1167	0.1026	0.0898
5	0.4550	0.4246	0.3948	0.3656	0.3373	0.3100	0.2837	0.2585	0.2346	0.2120
6	0.6645	0.6357	0.6063	0.5764	0.5461	0.5157	0.4852	0.4549	0.4249	0.3953
7	0.8308	0.8104	0.7887	0.7656	0.7414	0.7160	0.6895	0.6620	0.6337	0.6047
8	0.9320	0.9211	0.9090	0.8957	0.8811	0.8652	0.8480	0.8293	0.8094	0.7880
9	0.9788	0.9745	0.9696	0.9639	0.9574	0.9500	0.9417	0.9323	0.9218	0.9102
10	0.9551	0.9939	0.9924	0.9907	0.9886	0.9861	0.9832	0.9798	0.9759	0.9713
11	0.9992	0.9990	0.9987	0.9983	0.9978	0.9973	0.9966	0.9958	0.9947	0.9935
12	0.9999	0.9999	0.9999	0.9998	0.9997	0.9997	0.9996	0.9994	0.9993	0.9991
13	1.0000	1.0000	1.0000	1.0000	1.0000	1.0000	1.0000	1.0000	1.0000	0.9999
14	1.0000	1.0000	1.0000	1.0000	1.0000	1.0000	1.0000	1.0000	1.0000	1.0000

The Poisson Distribution

$$P(c) = \frac{(np)^c}{c!}e^{-np} \text{ (Cumulative Values Are in Parentheses)}$$

c \ np_0	0.1		0.2		0.3		0.4		0.5	
0	0.905	(0.905)	0.819	(0.819)	0.741	(0.741)	0.670	(0.670)	0.607	(0.607)
1	0.091	(0.996)	0.164	(0.983)	0.222	(0.963)	0.268	(0.938)	0.303	(0.910)
2	0.004	(1.000)	0.016	(0.999)	0.033	(0.996)	0.054	(0.992)	0.076	(0.986)
3			0.010	(1.000)	0.004	(1.000)	0.007	(0.999)	0.013	(0.999)
4							0.001	(1.000)	0.001	(1.000)

c \ np_0	0.6		0.7		0.8		0.9		1.0	
0	0.549	(0.549)	0.497	(0.497)	0.449	(0.449)	0.406	(0.406)	0.368	(0.368)
1	0.329	(0.878)	0.349	(0.845)	0.359	(0.808)	0.366	(0.772)	0.368	(0.736)
2	0.099	(0.977)	0.122	(0.967)	0.144	(0.952)	0.166	(0.938)	0.184	(0.920)
3	0.020	(0.997)	0.028	(0.995)	0.039	(0.991)	0.049	(0.987)	0.061	(0.981)
4	0.003	(1.000)	0.005	(1.000)	0.008	(0.999)	0.011	(0.998)	0.016	(0.997)
5					0.001	(1.000)	0.002	(1.000)	0.003	(1.000)

c \ np_0	1.1		1.2		1.3		1.4		1.5	
0	0.333	(0.333)	0.301	(0.301)	0.273	(0.273)	0.247	(0.247)	0.223	(0.223)
1	0.366	(0.699)	0.361	(0.662)	0.354	(0.627)	0.345	(0.592)	0.335	(0.558)
2	0.201	(0.900)	0.217	(0.879)	0.230	(0.857)	0.242	(0.834)	0.251	(0.809)
3	0.074	(0.974)	0.087	(0.966)	0.100	(0.957)	0.113	(0.947)	0.126	(0.935)
4	0.021	(0.995)	0.026	(0.992)	0.032	(0.989)	0.039	(0.986)	0.047	(0.982)
5	0.004	(0.999)	0.007	(0.999)	0.009	(0.998)	0.011	(0.997)	0.014	(0.996)
6	0.001	(1.000)	0.001	(1.000)	0.002	(1.000)	0.003	(1.000)	0.004	(1.000)

c \ np_0	1.6		1.7		1.8		1.9		2.0	
0	0.202	(0.202)	0.183	(0.183)	0.165	(0.165)	0.150	(0.150)	0.135	(0.135)
1	0.323	(0.525)	0.311	(0.494)	0.298	(0.463)	0.284	(0.434)	0.271	(0.406)
2	0.258	(0.783)	0.264	(0.758)	0.268	(0.731)	0.270	(0.704)	0.271	(0.677)
3	0.138	(0.921)	0.149	(0.907)	0.161	(0.892)	0.171	(0.875)	0.180	(0.857)
4	0.055	(0.976)	0.064	(0.971)	0.072	(0.964)	0.081	(0.956)	0.090	(0.947)
5	0.018	(0.994)	0.022	(0.993)	0.026	(0.990)	0.031	(0.987)	0.036	(0.983)
6	0.005	(0.999)	0.006	(0.999)	0.008	(0.998)	0.010	(0.997)	0.012	(0.995)
7	0.001	(1.000)	0.001	(1.000)	0.002	(1.000)	0.003	(1.000)	0.004	(0.999)
8									0.001	(1.000)

c \ np_0	2.1		2.2		2.3		2.4		2.5	
0	0.123	(0.123)	0.111	(0.111)	0.100	(0.100)	0.091	(0.091)	0.082	(0.082)
1	0.257	(0.380)	0.244	(0.355)	0.231	(0.331)	0.218	(0.309)	0.205	(0.287)
2	0.270	(0.650)	0.268	(0.623)	0.265	(0.596)	0.261	(0.570)	0.256	(0.543)
3	0.189	(0.839)	0.197	(0.820)	0.203	(0.799)	0.209	(0.779)	0.214	(0.757)
4	0.099	(0.938)	0.108	(0.928)	0.117	(0.916)	0.125	(0.904)	0.134	(0.891)
5	0.042	(0.980)	0.048	(0.976)	0.054	(0.970)	0.060	(0.964)	0.067	(0.958)
6	0.015	(0.995)	0.017	(0.993)	0.021	(0.991)	0.024	(0.988)	0.028	(0.986)
7	0.004	(0.999)	0.005	(0.998)	0.007	(0.998)	0.008	(0.996)	0.010	(0.996)
8	0.001	(1.000)	0.002	(1.000)	0.002	(1.000)	0.003	(0.999)	0.003	(0.999)
9							0.001	(1.000)	0.001	(1.000)

c \ np_0	2.6		2.7		2.8		2.9		3.0	
0	0.074	(0.074)	0.067	(0.067)	0.061	(0.061)	0.055	(0.055)	0.050	(0.050)
1	0.193	(0.267)	0.182	(0.249)	0.170	(0.231)	0.160	(0.215)	0.149	(0.199)

(continued)

(*continued*)

c \ np_0	2.6		2.7		2.8		2.9		3.0	
2	0.251	(0.518)	0.245	(0.494)	0.238	(0.469)	0.231	(0.446)	0.224	(0.423)
3	0.218	(0.736)	0.221	(0.715)	0.223	(0.692)	0.224	(0.670)	0.224	(0.647)
4	0.141	(0.877)	0.149	(0.864)	0.156	(0.848)	0.162	(0.832)	0.168	(0.815)
5	0.074	(0.951)	0.080	(0.944)	0.087	(0.935)	0.094	(0.926)	0.101	(0.916)
6	0.032	(0.983)	0.036	(0.980)	0.041	(0.976)	0.045	(0.971)	0.050	(0.966)
7	0.012	(0.995)	0.014	(0.994)	0.016	(0.992)	0.019	(0.990)	0.022	(0.988)
8	0.004	(0.999)	0.005	(0.999)	0.006	(0.998)	0.007	(0.997)	0.008	(0.996)
9	0.001	(1.000)	0.001	(1.000)	0.002	(1.000)	0.002	(0.999)	0.003	(0.999)
10							0.001	(1.000)	0.001	(1.000)

c \ np_0	3.1		3.2		3.3		3.4		3.5	
0	0.045	(0.045)	0.041	(0.041)	0.037	(0.037)	0.033	(0.033)	0.030	(0.030)
1	0.140	(0.185)	0.130	(0.171)	0.122	(0.159)	0.113	(0.146)	0.106	(0.136)
2	0.216	(0.401)	0.209	(0.380)	0.201	(0.360)	0.193	(0.339)	0.185	(0.321)
3	0.224	(0.625)	0.223	(0.603)	0.222	(0.582)	0.219	(0.558)	0.216	(0.537)
4	0.173	(0.798)	0.178	(0.781)	0.182	(0.764)	0.186	(0.744)	0.189	(0.726)
5	0.107	(0.905)	0.114	(0.895)	0.120	(0.884)	0.126	(0.870)	0.132	(0.858)
6	0.056	(0.961)	0.061	(0.956)	0.066	(0.950)	0.071	(0.941)	0.077	(0.935)
7	0.025	(0.986)	0.028	(0.984)	0.031	(0.981)	0.035	(0.976)	0.038	(0.973)
8	0.010	(0.996)	0.011	(0.995)	0.012	(0.993)	0.015	(0.991)	0.017	(0.990)
9	0.003	(0.999)	0.004	(0.999)	0.005	(0.998)	0.006	(0.997)	0.007	(0.997)
10	0.001	(1.000)	0.001	(1.000)	0.002	(1.000)	0.002	(0.999)	0.002	(0.999)
11							0.001	(1.000)	0.001	(1.000)

c \ np_0	3.6		3.7		3.8		3.9		4.0	
0	0.027	(0.027)	0.025	(0.025)	0.022	(0.022)	0.020	(0.020)	0.018	(0.018)
1	0.098	(0.125)	0.091	(0.116)	0.085	(0.107)	0.079	(0.099)	0.073	(0.091)
2	0.177	(0.302)	0.169	(0.285)	0.161	(0.268)	0.154	(0.253)	0.147	(0.238)
3	0.213	(0.515)	0.209	(0.494)	0.205	(0.473)	0.200	(0.453)	0.195	(0.433)
4	0.191	(0.706)	0.193	(0.687)	0.194	(0.667)	0.195	(0.648)	0.195	(0.628)
5	0.138	(0.844)	0.143	(0.830)	0.148	(0.815)	0.152	(0.800)	0.157	(0.785)
6	0.083	(0.927)	0.088	(0.918)	0.094	(0.909)	0.099	(0.899)	0.104	(0.889)
7	0.042	(0.969)	0.047	(0.965)	0.051	(0.960)	0.055	(0.954)	0.060	(0.949)
8	0.019	(0.988)	0.022	(0.987)	0.024	(0.984)	0.027	(0.981)	0.030	(0.979)
9	0.008	(0.996)	0.009	(0.996)	0.010	(0.994)	0.012	(0.993)	0.013	(0.992)
10	0.003	(0.999)	0.003	(0.999)	0.004	(0.998)	0.004	(0.997)	0.005	(0.997)
11	0.001	(1.000)	0.001	(1.000)	0.001	(0.999)	0.002	(0.999)	0.002	(0.999)
12						0.001	(1.000)	0.001	(1.000)	0.001	(1.000)

c \ np_0	4.1		4.2		4.3		4.4		4.5	
0	0.017	(0.017)	0.015	(0.015)	0.014	(0.014)	0.012	(0.012)	0.011	(0.011)
1	0.068	(0.085)	0.063	(0.078)	0.058	(0.072)	0.054	(0.066)	0.050	(0.061)
2	0.139	(0.224)	0.132	(0.210)	0.126	(0.198)	0.119	(0.185)	0.113	(0.174)
3	0.190	(0.414)	0.185	(0.395)	0.180	(0.378)	0.174	(0.359)	0.169	(0.343)
4	0.195	(0.609)	0.195	(0.590)	0.193	(0.571)	0.192	(0.551)	0.190	(0.533)
5	0.160	(0.769)	0.163	(0.753)	0.166	(0.737)	0.169	(0.720)	0.171	(0.704)
6	0.110	(0.879)	0.114	(0.867)	0.119	(0.856)	0.124	(0.844)	0.128	(0.832)
7	0.064	(0.943)	0.069	(0.936)	0.073	(0.929)	0.078	(0.922)	0.082	(0.914)
8	0.033	(0.976)	0.036	(0.972)	0.040	(0.969)	0.043	(0.965)	0.046	(0.960)
9	0.015	(0.991)	0.017	(0.989)	0.019	(0.988)	0.021	(0.986)	0.023	(0.983)
10	0.006	(0.997)	0.007	(0.996)	0.008	(0.996)	0.009	(0.995)	0.011	(0.994)
11	0.002	(0.999)	0.003	(0.999)	0.003	(0.999)	0.004	(0.999)	0.004	(0.998)
12	0.001	(1.000)	0.001	(1.000)	0.001	(1.000)	0.001	(1.000)	0.001	(0.999)
13									0.001	(1.000)

(*continued*)

(*continued*)

c	np₀ 4.6		4.7		4.8		4.9		5.0	
0	0.010	(0.010)	0.009	(0.009)	0.008	(0.008)	0.008	(0.008)	0.007	(0.007)
1	0.046	(0.056)	0.043	(0.052)	0.039	(0.047)	0.037	(0.045)	0.034	(0.041)
2	0.106	(0.162)	0.101	(0.153)	0.095	(0.142)	0.090	(0.135)	0.084	(0.125)
3	0.163	(0.325)	0.157	(0.310)	0.152	(0.294)	0.146	(0.281)	0.140	(0.265)
4	0.188	(0.513)	0.185	(0.495)	0.182	(0.476)	0.179	(0.460)	0.176	(0.441)
5	0.172	(0.685)	0.174	(0.669)	0.175	(0.651)	0.175	(0.635)	0.176	(0.617)
6	0.132	(0.817)	0.136	(0.805)	0.140	(0.791)	0.143	(0.778)	0.146	(0.763)
7	0.087	(0.904)	0.091	(0.896)	0.096	(0.887)	0.100	(0.878)	0.105	(0.868)
8	0.050	(0.954)	0.054	(0.950)	0.058	(0.945)	0.061	(0.939)	0.065	(0.933)
9	0.026	(0.980)	0.028	(0.978)	0.031	(0.976)	0.034	(0.973)	0.036	(0.969)
10	0.012	(0.992)	0.013	(0.991)	0.015	(0.991)	0.016	(0.989)	0.018	(0.987)
11	0.005	(0.997)	0.006	(0.997)	0.006	(0.997)	0.007	(0.996)	0.008	(0.995)
12	0.002	(0.999)	0.002	(0.999)	0.002	(0.999)	0.003	(0.999)	0.003	(0.998)
13	0.001	(1.000)	0.001	(1.000)	0.001	(1.000)	0.001	(1.000)	0.001	(0.999)
14									0.001	(1.000)

c	np₀ 6.0		7.0		8.0		9.0		10.0	
0	0.002	(0.002)	0.001	(0.001)	0.000	(0.000)	0.000	(0.000)	0.000	(0.000)
1	0.015	(0.017)	0.006	(0.007)	0.003	(0.003)	0.001	(0.001)	0.000	(0.000)
2	0.045	(0.062)	0.022	(0.029)	0.011	(0.014)	0.005	(0.006)	0.002	(0.002)
3	0.089	(0.151)	0.052	(0.081)	0.029	(0.043)	0.015	(0.021)	0.007	(0.009)
4	0.134	(0.285)	0.091	(0.172)	0.057	(0.100)	0.034	(0.055)	0.019	(0.028)
5	0.161	(0.446)	0.128	(0.300)	0.092	(0.192)	0.061	(0.116)	0.038	(0.066)
6	0.161	(0.607)	0.149	(0.449)	0.122	(0.314)	0.091	(0.091)	0.063	(0.129)
7	0.138	(0.745)	0.149	(0.598)	0.140	(0.454)	0.117	(0.324)	0.090	(0.219)
8	0.103	(0.848)	0.131	(0.729)	0.140	(0.594)	0.132	(0.456)	0.113	(0.332)
9	0.069	(0.917)	0.102	(0.831)	0.124	(0.718)	0.132	(0.588)	0.125	(0.457)
10	0.041	(0.958)	0.071	(0.902)	0.099	(0.817)	0.119	(0.707)	0.125	(0.582)
11	0.023	(0.981)	0.045	(0.947)	0.072	(0.889)	0.097	(0.804)	0.114	(0.696)
12	0.011	(0.992)	0.026	(0.973)	0.048	(0.937)	0.073	(0.877)	0.095	(0.791)
13	0.005	(0.997)	0.014	(0.987)	0.030	(0.967)	0.050	(0.927)	0.073	(0.864)
14	0.002	(0.999)	0.007	(0.994)	0.017	(0.984)	0.032	(0.959)	0.052	(0.916)
15	0.001	(1.000)	0.003	(0.997)	0.009	(0.993)	0.019	(0.978)	0.035	(0.951)
16			0.002	(0.999)	0.004	(0.997)	0.011	(0.989)	0.022	(0.973)
17			0.001	(1.000)	0.002	(0.999)	0.006	(0.995)	0.013	(0.986)
18					0.001	(1.000)	0.003	(0.998)	0.007	(0.993)
19							0.001	(0.999)	0.004	(0.997)
20							0.001	(1.000)	0.002	(0.999)
21									0.001	(1.000)

c	np₀ 11.0		12.0		13.0		14.0		15.0	
0	0.000	(0.000)	0.000	(0.000)	0.000	(0.000)	0.000	(0.000)	0.000	(0.000)
1	0.000	(0.000)	0.000	(0.000)	0.000	(0.000)	0.000	(0.000)	0.000	(0.000)
2	0.001	(0.001)	0.000	(0.000)	0.000	(0.000)	0.000	(0.000)	0.000	(0.000)
3	0.004	(0.005)	0.002	(0.002)	0.001	(0.001)	0.000	(0.000)	0.000	(0.000)
4	0.010	(0.015)	0.005	(0.007)	0.003	(0.004)	0.001	(0.001)	0.001	(0.001)
5	0.022	(0.037)	0.013	(0.020)	0.007	(0.011)	0.004	(0.005)	0.002	(0.003)
6	0.041	(0.078)	0.025	(0.045)	0.015	(0.026)	0.009	(0.014)	0.005	(0.008)
7	0.065	(0.143)	0.044	(0.089)	0.028	(0.054)	0.017	(0.031)	0.010	(0.018)
8	0.089	(0.232)	0.066	(0.155)	0.046	(0.100)	0.031	(0.062)	0.019	(0.037)
9	0.109	(0.341)	0.087	(0.242)	0.066	(0.166)	0.047	(0.109)	0.032	(0.069)
10	0.119	(0.460)	0.105	(0.347)	0.086	(0.252)	0.066	(0.175)	0.049	(0.118)
11	0.119	(0.579)	0.114	(0.461)	0.101	(0.353)	0.084	(0.259)	0.066	(0.184)
12	0.109	(0.688)	0.114	(0.575)	0.110	(0.463)	0.099	(0.358)	0.083	(0.267)
13	0.093	(0.781)	0.106	(0.681)	0.110	(0.573)	0.106	(0.464)	0.096	(0.363)
14	0.073	(0.854)	0.091	(0.772)	0.102	(0.675)	0.106	(0.570)	0.102	(0.465)

(*continued*)

(continued)

c \ np_0	11.0		12.0		13.0		14.0		15.0	
15	0.053	(0.907)	0.072	(0.844)	0.088	(0.763)	0.099	(0.669)	0.102	(0.567)
16	0.037	(0.944)	0.054	(0.898)	0.072	(0.835)	0.087	(0.756)	0.096	(0.663)
17	0.024	(0.968)	0.038	(0.936)	0.055	(0.890)	0.071	(0.827)	0.085	(0.748)
18	0.015	(0.983)	0.026	(0.962)	0.040	(0.930)	0.056	(0.883)	0.071	(0.819)
19	0.008	(0.991)	0.016	(0.978)	0.027	(0.957)	0.041	(0.924)	0.056	(0.875)
20	0.005	(0.996)	0.010	(0.988)	0.018	(0.975)	0.029	(0.953)	0.042	(0.917)
21	0.002	(0.998)	0.006	(0.994)	0.011	(0.986)	0.019	(0.972)	0.030	(0.947)
22	0.001	(0.999)	0.003	(0.997)	0.006	(0.992)	0.012	(0.984)	0.020	(0.967)
23	0.001	(1.000)	0.002	(0.999)	0.004	(0.996)	0.007	(0.991)	0.013	(0.980)
24			0.001	(1.000)	0.002	(0.998)	0.004	(0.995)	0.008	(0.988)
25					0.001	(0.999)	0.003	(0.998)	0.005	(0.993)
26					0.001	(1.000)	0.001	(0.999)	0.003	(0.996)
27							0.001	(1.000)	0.002	(0.998)
28									0.001	(0.999)
29									0.001	(1.000)

APPENDIX 6

About PQ Systems

Productivity-Quality Systems, Inc. is a full-service firm dedicated to helping customers continuously improve their organizations. They offer a comprehensive network of products and services designed to improve quality, productivity, and competitive position for all industries. The full line of improvement products and services from PQ Systems includes the following.

- **SQCpack**® combines powerful SPC techniques with flexibility and ease of use. In addition to variables, attributes, Pareto, histograms, and capability studies, *SQCpack 2000* features security, computed characteristics, SQC Quality Advisor™ filtering, and an easy import. *SQCpack 2000* is easily networked so that many users can share data.
- **CHARTrunner**® generates process performance charts and performs statistical analysis using data that is collected, stored, and managed by other applications. *CHARTrunner* eliminates the need for complex importing, time consuming exporting, and tedious data entry.
- **CHARTrunner-e**® is a web-based charting solution. It works with the desktop version of *CHARTrunner* to generate SPC and other process performance charts and performs statistical analysis using data that is collected, stored, and managed by other applications. It then makes those charts available for viewing through a standard web browser.
- **DATAjogger** assists teams working on quality improvement projects. It provides all the problem-solving and data analysis tools—such as bar graphs, fishbone diagrams, run charts, nominal group technique, affinity diagrams, and more—that are crucial to a team's progress. Teams enter the data only once, then view it in the form of many charts and diagrams to draw informed conclusions about their processes.
- **GAGEpack**® EZ is software that enables you to maintain an unlimited number of gage records containing descriptions, calibration procedures and history, and vendor information by using a database to record gage events.
- **DOEpack**® is an effective software tool for setting up and analyzing experimental designs for all stages of production to find the optimal conditions in a process.

- **SPC Workout** is an interactive multimedia training course that provides effective step-by-step instruction on how to implement and use statistical process control.
- **FMEA Investigator** is an interactive, multimedia training course that provides effective instructions on how to conduct both design and process FMEAs.
- **Gage Mentor** is a step-by-step multimedia training course that provides effective instructions on how to take successful dimensional measurements. Gage Mentor consists of two modules: Using Gages and Managing Gages. Using Gages teaches how to properly use a wide variety of dimensional gages, how to read symbols on engineering drawings, and how to avoid common measurement errors. Managing Gages teaches proper gage management and measurement system analysis.
- **Six Sigma Start-Up** is an introductory course on the principles and practices of Six Sigma. It is a computer-based interactive training system that teaches operators, engineers, supervisors, and managers the key concepts of Six Sigma so they will be better prepared to support a company's Six Sigma efforts. The program is ideal as a general introduction to Six Sigma for all employees as well as for orienting new employees to the philosophy of Six Sigma.
- **Total Quality Transformation**® offers step-by-step help in facilitating the quality transformation in organizations. Materials include *Practical Tools for Continuous Improvement, Foundations for Leaders, Team Skills, Alignment Guide, Improvement Guide, Strategic Quality Planning Guide, Improvement Tools, Total Quality Tools,* and *Total Quality Tools* for Windows. *TQT* is a part of the *Transformation of American Industry*® training project which has been used in a variety of manufacturing and service organizations since 1984.
- **Consulting and Training Services** are offered by PQ Systems for companies at all stages of their quality management programs. A staff of highly-qualified consultants brings practical experience from both industrial and academic environments. Seminars and on-site training programs are available to help companies implement successful quality management programs.

PQ Systems invites your questions and comments about its products and services Call PQ Systems at 1-937-885-2255. You can also send a fax to 937-885-2252 or an e-mail to sales@pqsystems.com. Visit PQ Systems online at http://www.pqsystems.com.

APPENDIX 7

Student Version Software

The disc that accompanies this text contains CHARTrunner, a software package that requires the creation of Excel database files in order to create the charts. The software package enables the user to create histograms, attribute and variables control charts, and Pareto diagrams. The package can also be used to perform capability analyses. Also included on the disc are other software programs offered by PQ systems.

To install the software, simply insert the disc in your computer and follow the directions. During the installation, you may select which software package, or both, that you wish to install. **Install each software package only once,** in order to avoid creating overlapping files that will prevent the software from operating. The software has a timeout function. To reactivate, contact PQ Systems. Questions concerning software installation can be directed to PQ Systems at 1-937-885-2255 or e-mail at support@ pqsystems.com.

CHARTrunner Student Version Software

The following series of figures provides information about the CHARTrunner student version software. CHARTrunner utilizes spreadsheets such as Excel as the source of input data. The following figures show how to create data files and enter data.

Begin by installing and running the software. When the software opens, select Chart Definition to begin.

Charting Data

Creating New Charts

Charts are created through the Chart definition form. This form consists of a series of seven tabs. The first three tabs, Chart name/type, Data source, and Data definition, are used to specify the chart type and to select the data for the chart. These are required for every chart definition. The remaining tabs are used for titles, control and specification limits, and chart-specific options such as x- and y-axis labels. The settings on these tabs are optional.

To create a new chart file:

1. Creating New Charts: Select Create New Chart   Right-click on Charts in the CHARTrunner Tree and select Create New Chart from the pop-up menu. The Chart definition form will open. Create New Chart is also available by clicking on the New Chart icon or by opening the File Menu and selecting New.

2. Creating New Charts: Chart Name/Type

Chart Name/Type Tab

The Chart Definition form's Chart name/type tab is displayed when you select the new or modify chart functions (Figure 1). It is used to enter the chart name and description, select the chart type and style, and set a chart refresh interval if applicable. It must be used for each new chart.

1. The Chart name/type tab will be displayed (Figure 1). Enter a name for this chart in the Chart name field. This is required.
2. Specify a chart style from the Chart style menu.

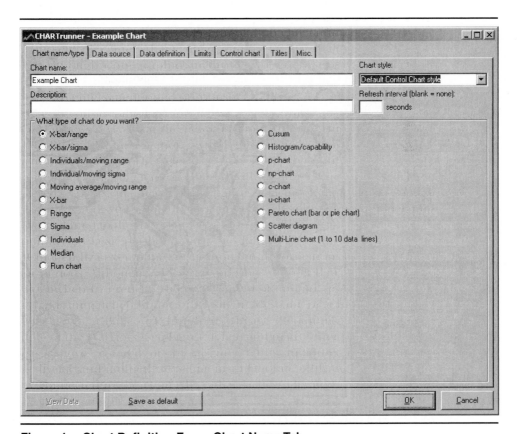

Figure 1   Chart Definition Form: Chart Name Tab

3. The description is used to provide additional information about the chart. Because a chart description can be displayed in the CHARTrunner Tree (see the topic "Preferences" in the Help file), a chart description may help users locate charts more easily. This is an optional field.

4. The refresh option will redraw the chart at the specified interval. If data is added to the source file frequently, set a Refresh interval to keep the chart current. If you want the chart to refresh, enter a number of seconds in the Refresh interval field. If you do not want the chart to refresh, leave this field blank.

Note: A refresh interval may be set for any chart. Leave this field blank if you do not want the chart to refresh. Set this to some number of seconds if you want the chart to keep refreshing while it is displayed. Each time the re-fresh interval passes, the chart will be redisplayed, reflecting any new data that may have arrived since the last refresh.

Be careful not to set a refresh interval that's too small. For example, if you add new data to the underlying database once every 30 minutes, there is re-ally no need to set the refresh interval to 10 seconds. This causes the com-puter to do unnecessary work to re-query the database and redraw the chart.

One use for the refresh interval is to monitor a chart in one location based on data that is being collected in another location. For example, in the quality lab you might set up a chart to refresh every five minutes to show data that is being collected during a manufacturing process.

5. Specify the type of chart that you want.

6. When you have finished with the Chart name/type tab, select a data source. See the next topic for more information.

3. Creating New Charts: Select a Data Source

1. Click on the Data Source tab (Figure 2). Use the Data source tab to select the type of database, spreadsheet, or text file and to specify the source file path and name (Figure 2). This tab must be filled out for each chart. For OLE and ADO sources, this form will also prompt for user name, password, and a connection string.

2. Select a data source type from the drop-down menu. Options are:

- Microsoft Excel
- Paradox
- Lotus 123 (wk3)
- ADO; OLE database provider
- Microsoft Access
- dBase
- Lotus 123 (wk4)
- Text File
- Lotus 123 (wk1)
- ODBC

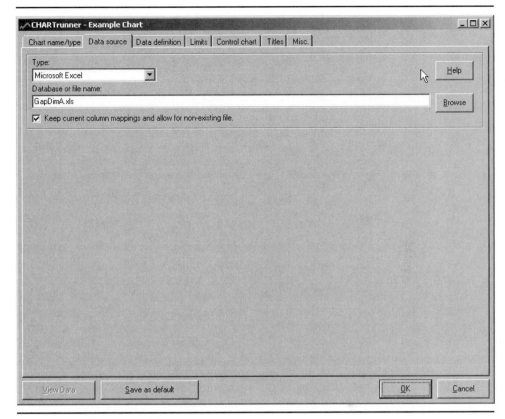

Figure 2   Data Source Tab

If your data source is a FoxPro database, select ADO.

3. Your entry in the Database or file name field depends on the data source type. For Access and Excel data source, enter the directory and data source file name in the Database or file name field or select Browse to select a file through the Select form.

4. Creating New Charts: Data Definition

1. Click on the Data definition tab. In order to create a chart, this tab must be completed. Settings in the Data definition tab tell CHARTrunner where to find and how to handle data within the source file (Figure 3). The Data definition form asks: Is the data stored in a table or a query in the database? Or do you want to create a custom query? Which columns of data should be included on the chart? Which can be ignored? Which are identifiers? Data filters and advance row selection are set through this tab as well. When the Data definition tab has been completed, the chart can be saved by selecting OK. All other tabs are optional.

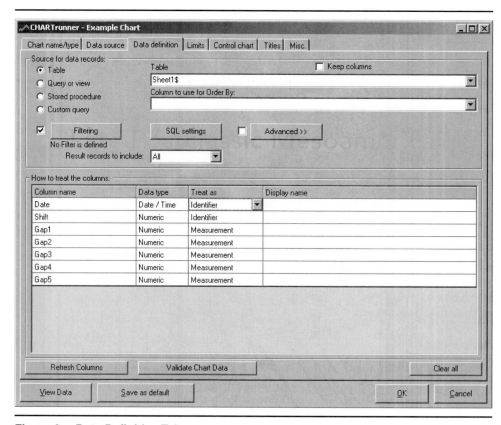

Figure 3   Data Definition Tab

2. Select a Source for data records. Options are:

- **Table:** This is the most common choice. This option tells CHARTrunner to get the records for this chart from a named table in the data source.

  If Access is your data source, all the tables found in the database will be listed in the Table dropdown menu. Select the table that contains the data for the chart you are creating.

  If Excel is your data source, this field will list all the sheets in the Excel file. Select the worksheet that contains the data for the chart you are creating.

  If your data source is not Access or Excel, this field lists the files. Select the location of the source file.

- **Query or View:** This option allows you to use queries that have already been defined in the database as a source of records for this chart. If you select this option, all the queries found in the database will be listed in the Query drop-down list box. Note that some databases call these "queries" and others call them "views." Your database may not have any predefined queries, so it is possible that the drop-down list box will be empty. These queries are created and saved using your database program.

- **Stored Procedure:** This option is similar to the Query or View option. A stored procedure may be just like a query; however, it can also be a series of database commands that do some work to come up with a new table. It is possible that your database does not support stored procedures or that none have been defined. Stored procedures are created and saved using your database program.

- **Custom Query:** If you select this option, you will see a new button called Edit Query. This allows you to enter your own SQL Select statement that will query the database. Using this option requires knowledge of both SQL and the structure of the database that you are accessing.

    Note: This is a powerful feature; care must be taken to form a correct SQL statement that does not unintentionally result in thousands of records being returned.

3. Choose the column that you want to use to establish the order of the records. Normally, a date/time column is used. This entry is not required; however, with most relational databases, it is difficult to know exactly what order the records will have if you do not make this selection.

4. After you have selected a table, procedure, or query, the grid at the bottom of the form will list information from that table. This grid consists of 3 columns: Column name, Type, and Treat As. The Treat As column provides a dropdown menu of options you can set for each data column in the source file. The options available on this list depend on the chart type. Use the Treat As column to specify how you want CHARTrunner to handle each field of data that you want to chart. The default value is Ignore.

- **Ignore (Default Value):** This tells CHARTrunner to ignore the column for this chart.

- **Identifier:** This makes the column available for use in labeling the chart or identifying each subgroup.

- **Measurement (Variables Charts Only):** This tells CHARTrunner that the column contains measurements that you are interested in charting. If you mark three columns as *Measurement*, then the subgroup size (if you are making a control chart) will be three.

- **Number Inspected (Attributes Charts Only):** This tells CHARTrunner that the column contains a *number inspected* count that is used for attributes control charts.

- **Count:** Count tells CHARTrunner that the column contains counts that can be used for attributes control charts and Pareto charts.

- **Cause:** For control chart definitions, you may define one of your columns as an assignable *cause*. This means that the column contains information explaining unusual conditions that will cause data to be excluded from the chart and from certain calculations. Note that most columns in this row will be empty.

- **Note:** This tells CHARTrunner to treat the column as a note. Notes are textual information that may explain some aspect of the data being charted.
- **Category (Pareto Charts Only):** When you are creating Pareto charts, you will normally designate some of your data columns as *categories*. Usually, this will be a text column, and all the unique entries in the column will form the categories for your Pareto chart.
- **Group By (Pareto Charts Only):** Use *Group By* to create multiple Pareto charts based on groups formed by this column.
- **Independent Variable (Scatter Diagram Only):** When doing a scatter diagram, you must define one variable of your data columns as the independent variable (x-axis).
- **Dependent Variable (Scatter Diagram Only):** When doing a scatter diagram, you must define one of your data columns as the dependent variable (y-axis).
- **Data 1 to Data 4 (Trend Chart Only):** When defining a trend chart (a run chart with up to 4 data lines) you will use these settings to describe which columns from your data source will be used for the chart.
- **Display Names:** Depending on the chart type, names entered in this field will be displayed with the data grid, legends, or axis labels.

Note: To confirm the structure of your database, click on View Data. The View Data window displays data and column headings for the current table. Click OK to close the window.

Depending on the chart type that you select, CHARTrunner expects certain columns to be defined. For example, to do an $\overline{X}$ chart, you must treat at least two columns from your data as *measurements,* unless you are using the "Advanced view selection" criteria to form subgrouped data. An individuals chart requires only one column to be treated as a *measurement.* To do a Pareto chart, you must designate at least one of your data columns as *categories.* For a scatter diagram, both a *dependent variable* and an *independent variable* column must be specified.

Limits Tab

The limits tab (Figure 4) contains information concerning the specification limits. This information is used for process capability calculations. Charts can be created with no control limits, limits computed from the data in the chart, or pre-established limits entered on this tab.

Control Chart Tab

The control chart tab (Figure 5) allows users to customize their control chart by adding additional information on the chart, including colors and data markers.

Titles Tab

The Titles tab is used to enter titles that will be displayed on the chart (Figure 6).

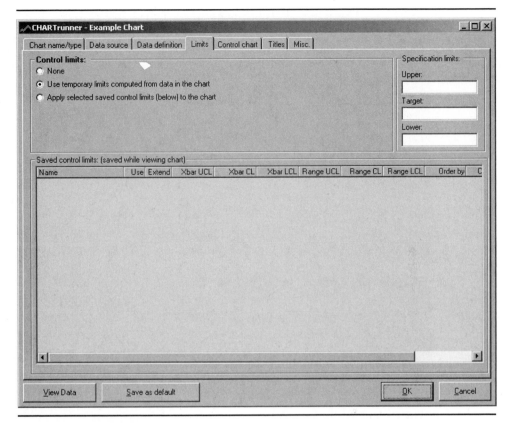

Figure 4   Limits Tab

Misc. Tab

The Misc. tab is used to set default parameters for chart image files (Figure 7). For example, most control charts should have the default print orientation set to landscape while other charts should be set to portrait.

When you have finished setting up the chart, click OK to save your settings. To display the chart, right-click on the name of the chart. Then, select Display.

Drawing Control Limits Through the Chart Display

CHARTrunner allows you to draw control limits through the chart display (Figure 8). To do this:

1. Move the mouse pointer to the first data point to be included in these control limits.
2. Click and hold the mouse button and drag the mouse pointer to the last data point to be included in these control limits. The pointer must stay within the boundaries of the chart.

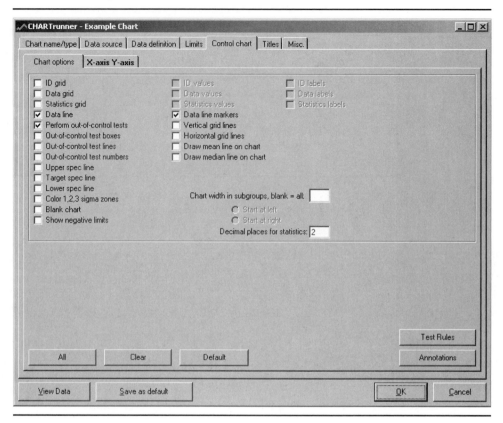

Figure 5   Control Chart Tab

3. Right-click on the selected area. From the pop-up menu, select Compute limits. The Control limits form will open (Figure 9).
4. Select a method for computing limits. Options are:

   ■ Standard (based on estimated sigma—recommended)
   ■ Based on n actual sigma where n = ___
   ■ Based on n estimated sigma where n = ___
   ■ User entered

   If you select the second or third option, you will be prompted to enter the number of sigma. If you select User entered, enter the control limits values in the fields provided at the bottom of the form.

5. The Subgroups Included field reflects the subgroups that are highlighted. You can shift the highlight by changing the subgroup range shown in these fields.

   If you entered a date column in the Order by field on the Data definition form (Figure 10), you can create control limits based on a date range. Enter the date range in the Subgroups included field.

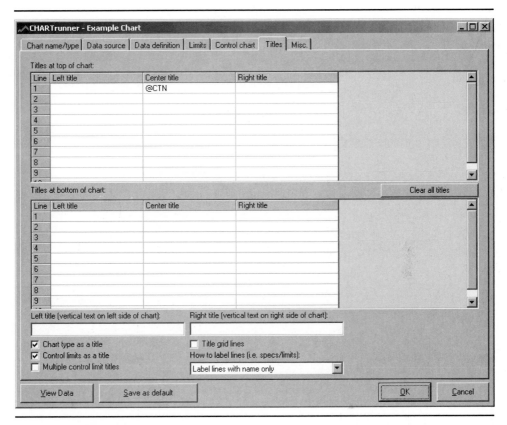

Figure 6   Titles Tab

6. If you want CHARTrunner to Extend the control limits beyond the subgroups included in the control limit calculation, select this option.

Chart Display Pop-Up Menus

There are two key pop-up menus available through the Chart display.

Data Point Pop-Up Menu

If you right-click on a data point, the menu shown in Figure 11 will appear. This menu includes the following options:

- **Edit Chart Definition:** Select to open the Chart definition form.
- **Edit Chart Style:** Select to open the Chart style form.
- **Clear Selected Subgroups:** Select to remove the highlight from the chart display.
- **View Subgroup Information:** If only one data point has been highlighted, this option will appear in the pop-up menu. If multiple data points are highlighted,

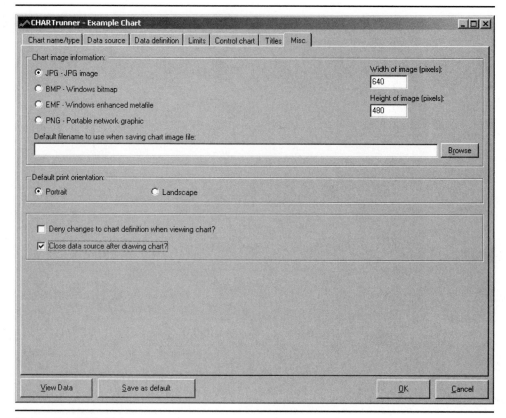

Figure 7   Misc. Tab

this option will not be available. Select this option to view the subgroup data and statistics for the highlighted data point.

- **View Data:** This option opens the View Data window. The View Data window displays data column headings for the current table. Click on OK to close the window.

Control Limit Pop-Up Menu

If you right-click on a control limit line or a control limit title, the menu shown in Figure 12 will appear.

- **Remove Limits (Set #):** To remove the selected set of control limits from the chart, select this option. This does not delete the limits from the chart definition file. If you want to restore this set of limits, open the Chart definition form and select the Limits tab. Click in the Use field for this set of limits. Note that you can enable/disable the Extend limits option through the Limits tab as well.
- **Edit Limits (Set #):** Select this option to open the Control limits form.

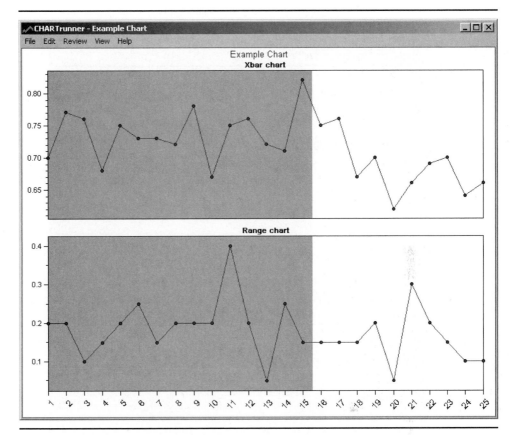

Figure 8   Example X̄ and R Chart

- **Delete Limits From the File (Set #):** To delete a set of limits from the Chart definition file completely, select this option. Control limit sets that are deleted cannot be restored. Control limits can also be deleted through the Limits tab of the Chart definition form. Highlight the set of limits that you want to delete and press the Delete key.

Databases

CHARTrunner thinks about data with a database metaphor. In a database, a table contains many rows (or records) of data. Each row will have the same fields (or columns). For example, if row 1 contains name, address, and zip code, then rows 2, 3, 4, etc., will also contain name, address, and zip code, and so on. Spreadsheets allow such flexibility in arranging data that this assumption of all rows being alike is often not valid.

CHARTrunner treats a spreadsheet like this: the spreadsheet itself (the .xls file) is seen as the database, and each worksheet within the sheet (i.e., Sheet1, Sheet2, etc.)

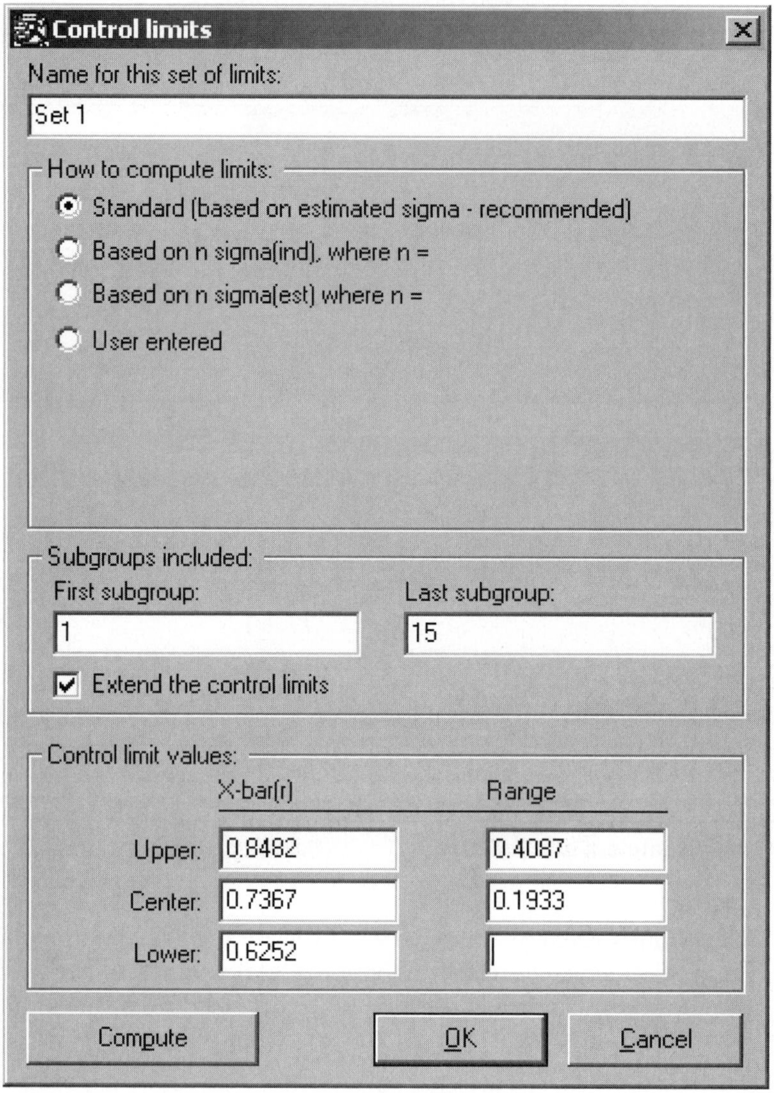

Figure 9   Control Limits Window

is seen as a table. Additionally, if you have created named regions within the spread-sheet, CHARTrunner will see these as tables.

CHARTrunner will have the easiest time with a spreadsheet formatted like the one shown in Figure 13.

Figure 14 shows how the CHARTrunner Data definition tab for the data shown in Figure 13 might look. CHARTrunner can understand this data easily. The rows are alike, there is a single row for column headings, there are no blank rows between the data, and there are no extra rows above or below.

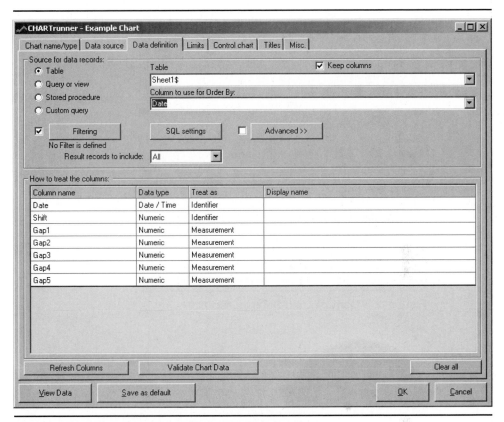

Figure 10   Entry in "Column to Use for Order By"

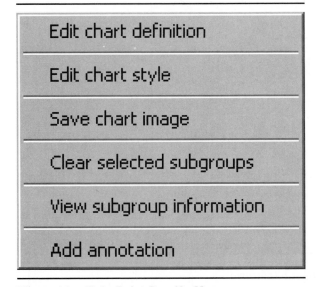

Figure 11   Data Point Pop-Up Menu

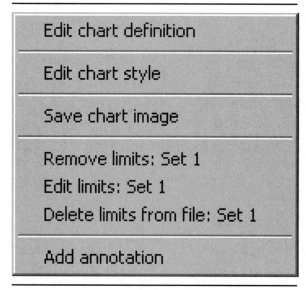

Figure 12   Control Limit Pop-Up Menu

The pop-up menu shown contains:

Edit chart definition

Edit chart style

Save chart image

Remove limits: Set 1
Edit limits: Set 1
Delete limits from file: Set 1

Add annotation

Microsoft Excel - DailyProduction.xls

File Edit View Insert Format Tools Data Window CHARTrunner Help

A1   =   Key

	A	B	C	D	E	F	G
1	Key	MfgDate	Operator	Length_1	Length_2	Length_3	Length_Cause
2	2	1/2/1999	Mary	24.12	21.14	24.56	
3	3	1/3/1998	John	25.09	20.96	23.45	Cause
4	4	1/4/1998	Sally	24.56	20.78	22.35	
5	5	1/5/1999	Tom	23.45	20.60	23.45	
6	6	1/6/1999	Sam	22.35	23.23	22.35	
7	7	1/7/1999	Tom	24.32	22.38	24.32	
8	8	1/8/1999	Sally	23.32	21.34	23.23	
9	9	1/9/1999	Jack	22.38	24.56	22.38	
10	10	1/10/1998	Susan	21.34	23.45	21.34	
11	11	1/11/1999	Sam	23.23	22.35	23.23	
12	12	1/12/1999	Mary	24.12	22.35	24.12	
13	13	1/13/1999	Mary	25.09	24.32	25.09	Cause
14	14	1/14/1999	Sally	24.56	23.23	24.56	
15	15	1/15/1999	Tom	23.45	22.38	24.56	
16	16	1/16/1999	Sam	22.35	21.34	23.45	

DailyProduction / Test /

Ready   NUM

Figure 13   Spreadsheet Example

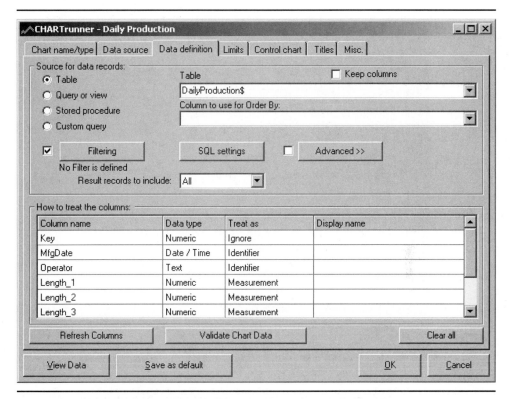

Figure 14   Data Definition Tab for Figure 13

Figure 15 shows an example sheet that may give CHARTrunner some difficulty. CHARTrunner will be able to make a chart using this data. However, since the rows summarizing Qtr 1 and Qtr 2 are different from the raw data in the other rows, the chart may not give you the results you expect. In other words, the quarterly totals will be seen as data points just like all the monthly values found in the other rows. One way to avoid this problem is to separate the quarterly totals onto a different sheet within the workbook. This way, CHARTrunner can look at the raw data using the familiar database metaphor it is based upon.

General rules for setting up Excel sheets for use with CHARTrunner include the following:

1. Separate the raw data from the summary data. If you currently have summary data in the midst of your raw data, put the raw data on one sheet within Excel and do the summarizing on a different sheet (tab) within the same workbook.
2. Have a single row for column headings and leave no blank rows between the column headings and the raw data.
3. Don't use the space above or below your raw data for other spreadsheet data. Instead, move that information off to the side of the raw data range *or* put it

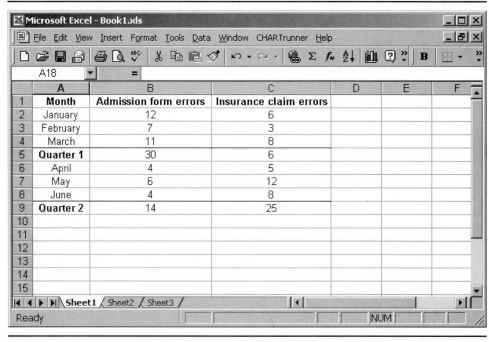

Figure 15   Example of Improperly Constructed Spreadsheet

on a different sheet within the workbook. If you must put other spreadsheet data below your raw data, then highlight your raw data and create a "Named Region" so that CHARTrunner can use only the raw data contained in this region and ignore the other spreadsheet data below your raw data.

4. Don't mix data types within the same column if it is a column you want to use in CHARTrunner. For example, don't have a cell containing text in the middle of a column where all the other values are numbers.

5. Try to keep the raw data contiguous. Avoid intervening blank rows in the midst of the raw data.

6. Arrange your data so it goes down the sheet rather than across the sheet. In other words, as you add new data, you should be adding new rows rather than adding new columns.

7. Although CHARTrunner can handle long column names, your charts and data definition forms will look better and be less confusing if you use relatively short names for your spreadsheet columns.

8. Always have column names. If you do not, the first row of your raw data will be ignored, as it will be used to provide the column names.

9. If you have data in columns A, B, and C, and you are charting data only from column A, be aware that CHARTrunner will use the number of rows that it finds in the column that contains the most rows. For example, if column A contains 25 rows of data, but column B contains 50 rows of data, when you chart column A, the chart will have 25 blank rows at the end of the data.

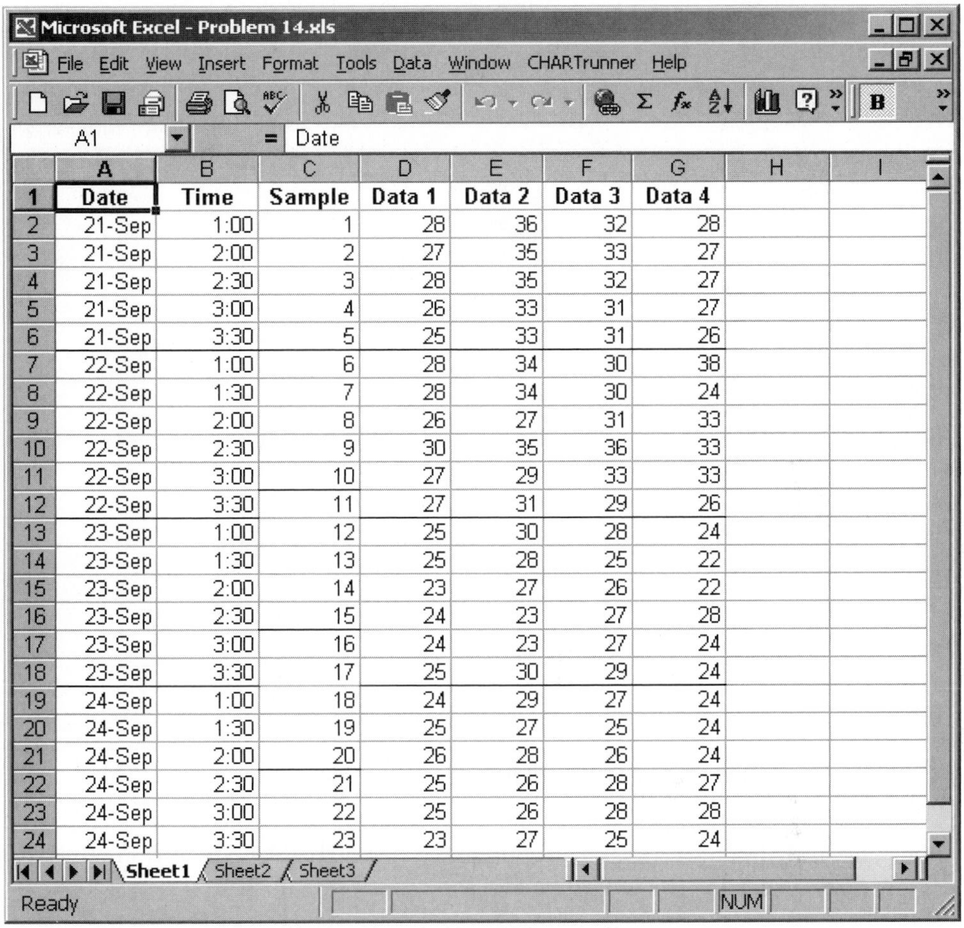

Date	Time	Sample	Data 1	Data 2	Data 3	Data 4
21-Sep	1:00	1	28	36	32	28
21-Sep	2:00	2	27	35	33	27
21-Sep	2:30	3	28	35	32	27
21-Sep	3:00	4	26	33	31	27
21-Sep	3:30	5	25	33	31	26
22-Sep	1:00	6	28	34	30	38
22-Sep	1:30	7	28	34	30	24
22-Sep	2:00	8	26	27	31	33
22-Sep	2:30	9	30	35	36	33
22-Sep	3:00	10	27	29	33	33
22-Sep	3:30	11	27	31	29	26
23-Sep	1:00	12	25	30	28	24
23-Sep	1:30	13	25	28	25	22
23-Sep	2:00	14	23	27	26	22
23-Sep	2:30	15	24	23	27	28
23-Sep	3:00	16	24	23	27	24
23-Sep	3:30	17	25	30	29	24
24-Sep	1:00	18	24	29	27	24
24-Sep	1:30	19	25	27	25	24
24-Sep	2:00	20	26	28	26	24
24-Sep	2:30	21	25	26	28	27
24-Sep	3:00	22	25	26	28	28
24-Sep	3:30	23	23	27	25	24

Figure 16 Chapter 5, Problem 14, Excel Data File

This may cause unexpected results. The way around this problem is to use named regions as described above.

Examples Utilizing CHARTrunner

The following are examples of the use of CHARTrunner.

Chapter 5, Problem 14

To create the $\overline{X}$ and sigma control chart using CHARTrunner, your screens should look similar to those shown in Figures 16 through 21.

1. Create an Excel data file (Figure 16).
2. Enter CHARTrunner and create a data file for New chart. First, identify the Chart name/type (Figure 17).
3. Define the data source (Figure 18).

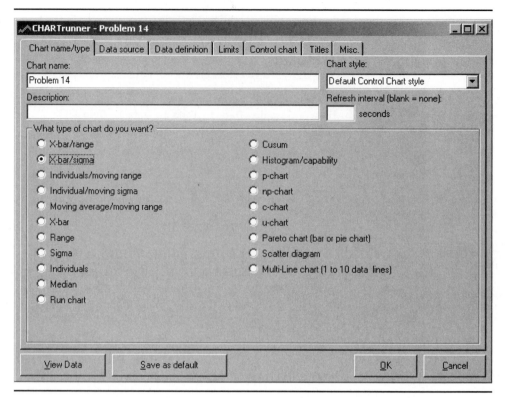

Figure 17   Chapter 5, Problem 14, Chart Name/Type Tab

4. Fill in the information required under the Data definition tab (Figure 19).
5. Define the Control chart parameters (Figure 20).
6. Select the titles for the control chart (Figure 21).
7. Create the chart.

Case Study 5.1

To define a histogram for the data in Table C5.1.1 using CHARTrunner, your screens should look similar to those in Figures 22 through 28.

1. Create an Excel data file (Figure 22).
2. Select Histogram, then define Chart name/type (Figure 23).
3. Define the Data source (Figure 24).
4. Fill in the information required under the Data definition tab (Figure 25).
5. Define the Histogram parameters (Figure 27).
6. Provide the descriptive statistics (Figure 28).
7. Create the chart.

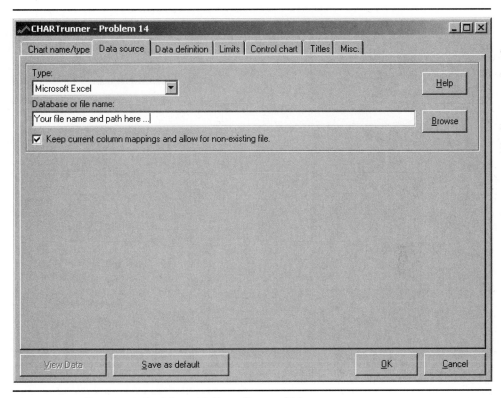

Figure 18   Chapter 5, Problem 14, Data Source Tab

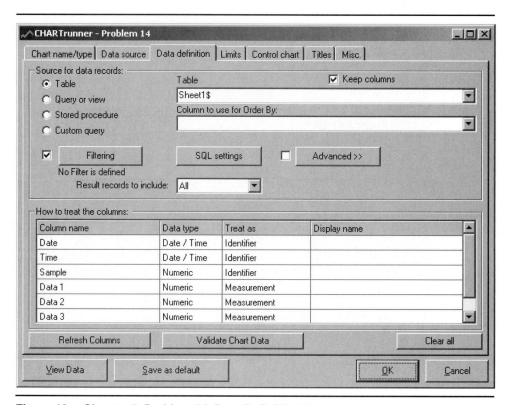

Figure 19   Chapter 5, Problem 14, Data Definition Tab

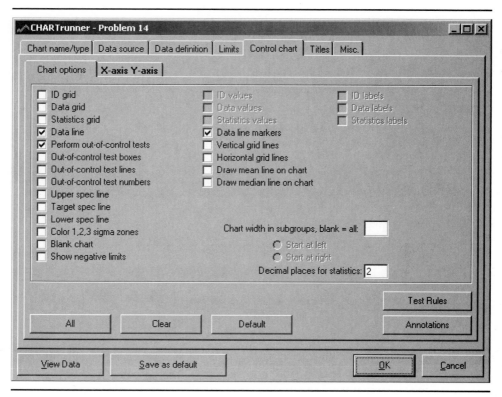

Figure 20   Chapter 5, Problem 14, Control Chart Tab

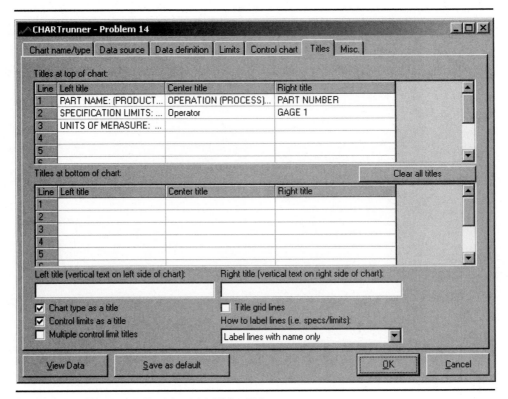

Figure 21   Chapter 5, Problem 14, Titles Tab

File Edit View Insert Format Tools Data Window CHARTrunner Help

B1 = Part Name

	Part Name	Part No.	Machine	Group	Time	Date	Subgroup	Data 1	Data 2	Data 3	Data 4
2	Whisk Wheel	01-92	Cutoff	Quality Control	7:00 AM	1/30/1996	1	3.757	3.749	3.751	3.755
3	Whisk Wheel	01-92	Cutoff	Quality Control	7:18 AM	1/30/1996	2	3.753	3.739	3.747	3.751
4	Whisk Wheel	01-92	Cutoff	Quality Control	7:36 AM	1/30/1996	3	3.744	3.745	3.74	3.741
5	Whisk Wheel	01-92	Cutoff	Quality Control	7:54 AM	1/30/1996	4	3.755	3.753	3.753	3.749
6	Whisk Wheel	01-92	Cutoff	Quality Control	8:12 AM	1/30/1996	5	3.757	3.76	3.751	3.754
7	Whisk Wheel	01-92	Cutoff	Quality Control	8:30 AM	1/30/1996	6	3.741	3.749	3.745	3.742
8	Whisk Wheel	01-92	Cutoff	Quality Control	8:48 AM	1/30/1996	7	3.746	3.743	3.753	3.751
9	Whisk Wheel	01-92	Cutoff	Quality Control	9:06 AM	1/30/1996	8	3.746	3.753	3.747	3.755
10	Whisk Wheel	01-92	Cutoff	Quality Control	9:24 AM	1/30/1996	9	3.76	3.755	3.757	3.757
11	Whisk Wheel	01-92	Cutoff	Quality Control	9:42 AM	1/30/1996	10	3.741	3.745	3.751	3.741
12	Whisk Wheel	01-92	Cutoff	Quality Control	10:00 AM	1/30/1996	11	3.749	3.751	3.757	3.754
13	Whisk Wheel	01-92	Cutoff	Quality Control	10:18 AM	1/30/1996	12	3.746	3.749	3.744	3.757
14	Whisk Wheel	01-92	Cutoff	Quality Control	10:36 AM	1/30/1996	13	3.743	3.751	3.745	3.739
15	Whisk Wheel	01-92	Cutoff	Quality Control	10:54 AM	1/30/1996	14	3.755	3.744	3.753	3.755
16	Whisk Wheel	01-92	Cutoff	Quality Control	11:12 AM	1/30/1996	15	3.745	3.751	3.747	3.751
17	Whisk Wheel	01-92	Cutoff	Quality Control	11:30 AM	1/30/1996	16	3.748	3.746	3.755	3.755
18	Whisk Wheel	01-92	Cutoff	Quality Control	11:48 AM	1/30/1996	17	3.757	3.747	3.756	3.759
19	Whisk Wheel	01-92	Cutoff	Quality Control	12:06 PM	1/30/1996	18	3.74	3.739	3.752	3.744
20	Whisk Wheel	01-92	Cutoff	Quality Control	12:24 PM	1/30/1996	19	3.756	3.757	3.749	3.755
21	Whisk Wheel	01-92	Cutoff	Quality Control	12:42 PM	1/30/1996	20	3.742	3.753	3.754	3.743
22	Whisk Wheel	01-92	Cutoff	Quality Control	1:00 PM	1/30/1996	21	3.752	3.751	3.749	3.753
23	Whisk Wheel	01-92	Cutoff	Quality Control	1:18 PM	1/30/1996	22	3.746	3.753	3.741	3.746
24	Whisk Wheel	01-93	Cutoff	Quality Control	1:36 PM	1/30/1996	23	3.745	3.762	3.753	3.75

Sheet1 / Sheet2 / Sheet3

Ready NUM

Figure 22 Case Study 5.1: Excel Data File

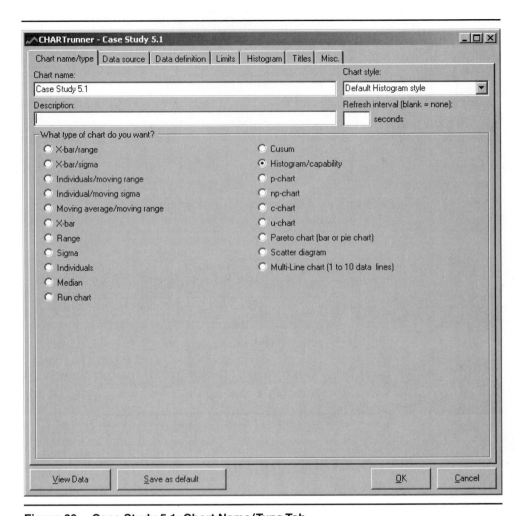

Figure 23   Case Study 5.1: Chart Name/Type Tab

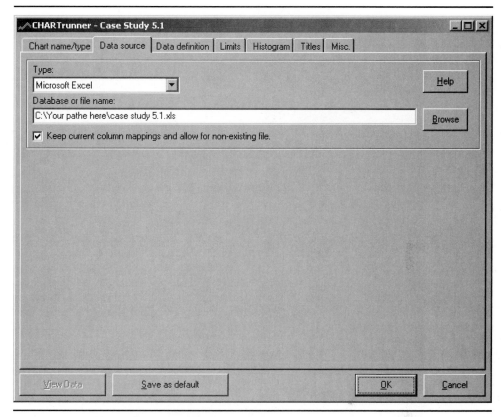

Figure 24   Case Study 5.1: Data Source Tab

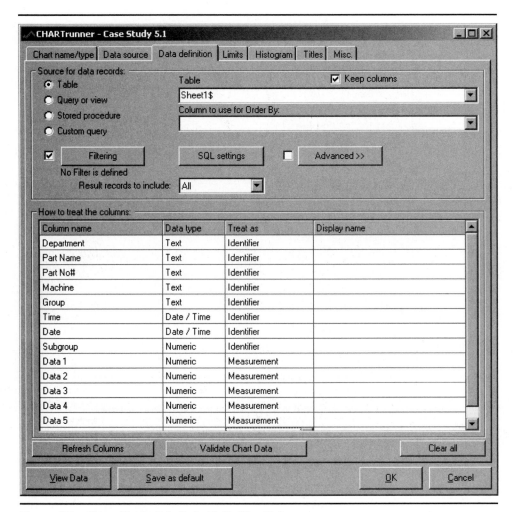

Figure 25   Case Study 5.1: Data Definition Tab

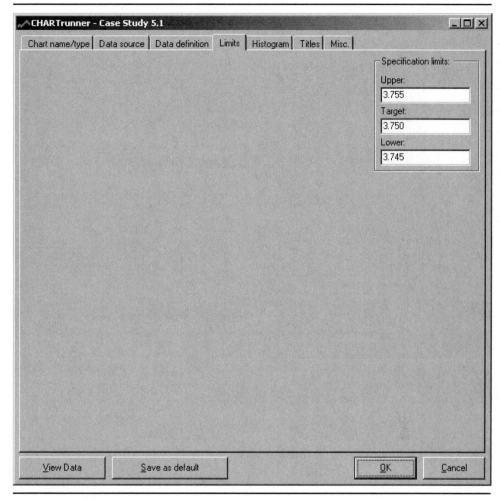

Figure 26   Case Study 5.1: Limits Tab

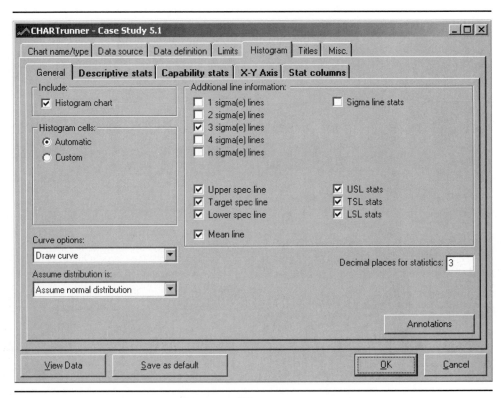

Figure 27   Case Study 5.1: Histogram Tab

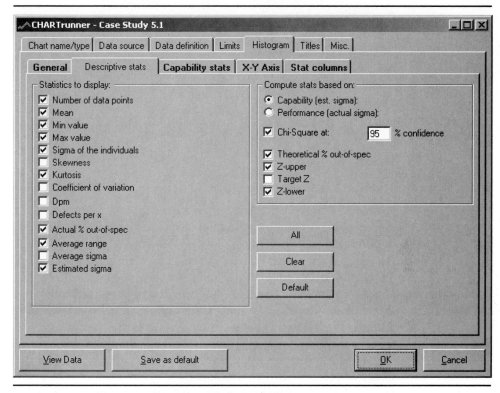

Figure 28   Case Study 5.1: Descriptive Stats Tab

Websites for Quality

American Society for Quality: www.asq.org

American Society for Quality, Statistics Division: www.asq.org/about/divisions/stats

American Society for Quality, Quality Audit Division: www.asq.org/qad

American Society for Quality, Reliability Division: www.asq-rd.org

U.S. Commerce Department's National Institute of Standards: www.nist.gov

International Organization for Standardization (ISO 9000 & 14000): www.iso.org

Automotive Industry Action Group: www.aiag.org

Quality Information: www.itl.nist.gov/div898/handbook/pmc/pmc_d.htm

Six Sigma Information: www.sixsigma.com, www.isixsigma.com

Quality in Healthcare: www.jcaho.org

Information on Quality: www.qualitydigest.com, www.quality.org, www.qualityadvisor.com

Discussion Forum: www.insidequality.com

Juran: www.juran.com

Deming: http://deming.eng.clemson.edu/pub/den/deming_map/htm

European Foundation for Quality Management: www.efqm.org

Quality Standards: http://e-standards.asq.org/perl/catalog.cgi

American Productivity and Quality Center, Benchmarking Studies: www.apqc.org

Benchmarking Exchange: www.benchnet.com

Performance Measures: www.zigonperf.com

Lean Manufacturing: www.nwlean.net

Quality Function Deployment Institute: www.nauticom.net/www.qfd

Statistical Abstract of the United States: www.census.gov

GLOSSARY

Acceptable Quality Level When a continuing series of lots is considered, a quality level that, for the purposes of sampling inspection, is the limit of a satisfactory process average.

Acceptance Sampling Inspection of a sample from a lot to decide whether to accept or not accept that lot. There are two types: attributes sampling and variables sampling. In attributes sampling, the presence or absence of a characteristic is noted in each of the units inspected. In variables sampling, the numerical magnitude of a characteristic is measured and recorded for each inspected unit; this involves reference to a continuous scale of some kind.

Acceptance Sampling Plan A specific plan that indicates the sampling sizes and the associated acceptance or non-acceptance criteria to be used. In attributes sampling, for example, there are single, double, multiple, sequential, chain, and skip-lot sampling plans. In variables sampling, there are single, double, and sequential sampling plans.

Accreditation Certification of a duly recognized body of the facilities, capability, objectivity, competence, and integrity of an agency, service or operational group or individual to provide the specific service or operation needed. For example, The Registrar Accreditation Board accredits those organizations that register companies to the ISO 9000 series standards.

*Accredited Registrars Persons who perform audits for ISO 9000 standards. They are qualified organizations certified by a national body (e.g., the Registrar Accreditation Board in the U.S.).

*Accuracy In the quality field, a term that refers to how close an observed value is to a true value.

*Alignment To create agreement between processes and activities supporting an organization's strategies, objectives, and goals.

American Society for Quality A professional, not-for-profit association that develops, promotes, and applies quality-related information and technology for the private sector, government, and academia. The Society serves more than 108,000 individual and 1,000 corporate members in the United States and 108 other countries.

---

*Definitions of asterisked terms have been provided by the author; all others are reprinted with permission from *Quality Progress*, July 2002, pp. 43–61.

*Analysis of Means (ANOM) The statistical technique used to analyze the results of experimental factors.

*Analysis of Variance (ANOVA) The statistical technique used to analyze the variation present in experimental data.

*Assessment An evaluation process that includes document reviews, audits, analysis, and report of findings.

*Assignable Cause The source or cause of variation in a process that can be identified and then isolated and removed from the process. It is not due to chance causes and is also termed *special cause*.

Attribute Data Go/no-go information. The control charts based on attribute data include percent chart, number of affected units chart, count chart, count-per-unit chart, quality score chart, and demerit chart.

*Audit A systematic appraisal procedure that examines, evaluates, and verifies that appropriate procedures, requirements, checklists, and programs are being followed effectively.

Average Chart A control chart in which the subgroup average, $\overline{X}$, is used to evaluate the stability of the process level.

Average Outgoing Quality The expected average quality level of outgoing product for a given value of incoming product quality.

Average Outgoing Quality Limit The maximum average outgoing quality over all possible levels of quality for a given acceptance sampling plan and disposal specification.

Benchmarking An improvement process in which a company measures its performance against that of best-in-class companies, determines how those companies achieved their performance levels, and uses the information to improve its own performance. The subjects that can be benchmarked include strategies, operations, processes, and procedures.

*Black Belt Designation for an improvement project team leader in a Six Sigma environment.

Blemish An imperfection that is severe enough to be noticed but should not cause any real impairment with respect to intended normal or reasonably foreseeable use. (See also Defect, Imperfection, Nonconformity.)

Brainstorming A technique that teams use to generate ideas on a particular subject. Each person in the team is asked to think creatively and write down as many ideas as possible. The ideas are not discussed or reviewed until after the brainstorming session.

c Chart or Count of Nonconformities Chart A control chart for evaluating the stability of a process in terms of the count of events of a given classification occurring in a sample of constant size.

Calibration The comparison of a measurement instrument or system of unverified accuracy to a measurement instrument or system of a known accuracy to detect any variation from the required performance specification.

*Capability The amount of variation inherent in a stable process. Capability is determined using data from control charts and histograms from stable processes. When these indicate a stable process and a normal distribution, the indices C_p and C_{pk} can be calculated.

*Cause The identified and isolated reason behind a defect or problem in a process or product.

Cause-and-Effect Diagram A tool for analyzing process dispersion. It is also referred to as the Ishikawa diagram, because Kaoru Ishikawa developed it, and the fishbone diagram, because the complete diagram resembles a fish skeleton. The diagram illustrates the main causes and subcauses leading to an effect (symptom). The cause-and-effect diagram is one of the seven tools of quality.

*Characteristic The individual elements that define a process, function, product, or service.

Checklist A tool used to ensure that all important steps or actions in an operation have been taken. Checklists contain items that are important or relevant to an issue or situation. Checklists are often confused with check sheets.

Check Sheet A simple data-recording device. The check sheet is custom-designed by the user, which allows him or her to readily interpret the results. The check sheet is one of the seven tools of quality. Check sheets are often confused with data sheets and checklists.

Common Causes Causes of variation that are inherent in a process over time. They affect every outcome of the process and everyone working in the process. (See also Special Causes.)

Company Culture A system of values, beliefs, and behaviors inherent in a company. To optimize business performance, top management must define and create the necessary culture.

*Compliance Meeting established criteria, specifications, terms, standards, or regulations.

Conformance An affirmative indication or judgment that a product or service has met the requirements of a relevant specification, contract, or regulation.

Continuous Improvement The ongoing improvement of products, services, or processes through incremental and breakthrough improvements.

Control Chart A chart with upper and lower control limits on which values of some statistical measure for a series of samples or subgroups are plotted. The chart frequently shows a central line to help detect a trend of plotted values toward either control limit.

*Control Limits Statistically calculated limits placed on a control chart. The variability of the process is compared with the limits and special and common causes of variation are identified.

Corrective Action The implementation of solutions resulting in the reduction or elimination of an identified problem.

Cost of Poor Quality The costs associated with providing poor-quality products or services. There are four categories of costs: internal failure costs (costs associated with defects found before the customer receives the product or service), external failure costs (costs associated with defects found after the customer receives the product or service), appraisal costs (costs incurred to determine the degree of conformance to quality requirements), and prevention costs (costs incurred to keep failure and appraisal costs to a minimum).

Cost of Quality A term coined by Philip Crosby referring to the cost of poor quality.

C_p A widely used process capability index. It is expressed as

$$C_p = \frac{\text{upper specification limit } - \text{ lower specification limit}}{6\sigma}$$

C_{pk} A widely used process capability index. It is expressed as

$$C_{pk} = \frac{|\mu - \text{ nearer specification limit}|}{3\sigma}$$

*Crosby, Philip Originated the zero defects concept. He has authored many books, including *Quality Is Free*, *Quality Without Tears*, *Let's Talk Quality*, and *Leading: The Art of Becoming an Executive*.

*Culture The attitudes, beliefs, values, and norms shared by a group of individuals.

Cumulative Sum Control Chart A control chart on which the plotted value is the cumulative sum of deviations of successive samples from a target value. The ordinate of each plotted point represents the algebraic sum of the previous ordinate and the most recent deviations from the target.

Customer Delight The result of delivering a product or service that exceeds customer expectations.

Customer Satisfaction The result of delivering a product or service that meets customer requirements.

Customer-Supplier Partnership A long-term relationship between a buyer and a supplier characterized by teamwork and mutual confidence. The supplier is considered an extension of the buyer's organization. The partnership is based on several commitments. The buyer provides long-term contracts and uses fewer suppliers. The supplier implements quality assurance processes so that incoming inspection can be minimized. The supplier also helps the buyer reduce costs and improve product and process designs.

*Cycle Time The time it takes from start to finish to complete a task, create a product, or provide a service.

Defect A product's or service's nonfulfillment of an intended requirement or reasonable expectation for use, including safety considerations. There are four classes of defects: Class 1, Very Serious, leads directly to severe injury or catastrophic economic loss; Class 2, Serious, leads directly to significant injury or significant economic loss; Class 3, Major, is related to major problems with respect to intended normal or reasonably foreseeable use; and Class 4, Minor, is related to minor problems with respect to intended normal or reasonably foreseeable use. (See also Blemish, Imperfection, Nonconformity.)

Deming, W. Edwards (deceased) A prominent consultant, teacher, and author on the subject of quality. After sharing his expertise in statistical quality control to help the U.S. war effort during World War II, the War Department sent Deming to Japan in 1946 to help that nation recover from its wartime losses. Deming published more than 200 works, including the well-known books *Quality, Productivity and Competitive Position*, and *Out of the Crisis*. Deming, who developed the 14 points for managing, was an ASQC Honorary member.

Deming Cycle See Plan-Do-Study-Act Cycle.

Deming Prize Award given annually to organizations that, according to the award guidelines, have successfully applied companywide quality control based on statistical quality control and will keep up with it in the future. Although the award is named in honor of W. Edwards Deming, its criteria are not specifically related to Deming's teachings. There are three separate divisions for the award: the Deming Application Prize, the Deming Prize for Individuals, and the Deming Prize for Overseas Companies. The award process is overseen by the Deming Prize Committee of the Union of Japanese Scientists and Engineers in Tokyo.

Dependability The degree to which a product is operable and capable of performing its required function at any randomly chosen time during its specified operating time, provided that the product is available at the start of that period. (Nonoperation-related influences are not included.) Dependability can be expressed by the ratio:

$$\frac{\text{Time available}}{\text{Time available} + \text{time required}}$$

Design of Experiments A branch of applied statistics dealing with planning, conducting, analyzing, and interpreting controlled tests to evaluate the factors that control the value of a parameter or group of parameters.

Diagnostic Journey and Remedial Journey A two-phase investigation used by teams to solve chronic quality problems. In the first phase—the diagnostic journey—the team journeys from the symptom of a chronic problem to its cause. In the second phase—the remedial journey—the team journeys from the cause to its remedy.

DMAIC A data-driven quality strategy for improving processes and an integral part of a Six Sigma quality initiative. DMAIC is an acronym for define, measure, analyze, improve, and control.

Dodge-Romig Sampling Plans Plans for acceptance sampling developed by Harold F. Dodge and Harry G. Romig. Four sets of tables were published in 1940: single-sampling lot tolerance tables, double-sampling lot tolerance tables, single-sampling average outgoing quality limit tables, and double-sampling average outgoing quality limit tables.

80-20 Rule A term referring to the Pareto principle, which was first defined by J. M. Juran in 1950. The principle suggests that most effects come from relatively few causes; that is, 80% of the effects come from 20% of the possible causes.

Employee Involvement A practice within an organization whereby employees regularly participate in making decisions on how their work areas operate, including making suggestions for improvement, planning, goal setting, and monitoring performance.

Empowerment A condition whereby employees have the authority to make decisions and take action in their work areas without prior approval. For example, an operator can stop a production process if he detects a problem or a customer service representative can send out a replacement product if a customer calls with a problem.

Experimental Design A formal plan that details the specifics for conducting an experiment, such as which responses, factors, levels, blocks, treatments, and tools are to be used.

External Customer A person or organization who receives a product, a service, or information but is not part of the organization supplying it. (See also Internal Customer.)

Feigenbaum, Armand V. The founder and president of General Systems Co., an international engineering company that designs and implements total quality systems. Feigenbaum originated the concept of total quality control in his book *Total Quality Control*, which was published in 1951.

Fishbone Diagram See Cause-and-Effect Diagram.

Fitness for Use A term used to indicate that a product or service fits the customer's defined purpose for that product or service.

Flowchart A graphical representation of the steps in a process. Flowcharts are drawn to better understand processes. The flowchart is one of the seven tools of quality.

Funnel Experiment An experiment that demonstrates the effects of tampering. Marbles are dropped through a funnel in an attempt to hit a flat-surfaced target below. The experiment shows that adjusting a stable process to compensate for an undesirable result or an extraordinarily good result will produce output that is worse than if the process had been left alone.

Gage Repeatability and Reproducibility The evaluation of a gaging instrument's accuracy by determining whether the measurements taken with it are repeatable (i.e., there is close agreement among a number of consecutive measurements of the output for the same value of the input under the same operating conditions) and reproducible (i.e., there is close agreement among repeated measurements of the output for the same value of input made under the same operating conditions over a period of time).

Go/No-Go State of a unit or product. The parameters are possible: go (conforms to specification) and no-go (does not conform to specification).

*Green Belt Designation for an improvement team member in a Six Sigma environment.

Histogram A graphic summary of variation in a set of data. The pictorial nature of the histogram lets people see patterns that are difficult to see in a simple table of numbers. The histogram is one of the seven tools of quality.

Imperfection A quality characteristic departure from its intended level or state without any association to conformance to specification requirements or to the usability of a product or service. (See also Blemish, Defect, Nonconformity.)

In-Control Process A process in which the statistical measure being evaluated is in a state of statistical control (i.e., the variations among the observed sampling results can be attributed to a constant system of chance causes). (See also Out-of-Control Process.)

Inspection Measuring, examining, testing, or gauging one or more characteristics of a product or service and comparing the results with specified requirements to determine whether conformity is achieved for each characteristic.

Instant Pudding A term used to illustrate an obstacle to achieving quality: the supposition that quality and productivity improvement is achieved quickly through an affirmation of faith rather than through sufficient effort and education. W. Edwards Deming used this term—which was initially coined by James Bakken of the Ford Motor Co.—in his book *Out of the Crisis*.

Internal Customer The recipient (person or department) within an organization of another person's or department's output (product, service, or information). (See also External Customer.)

*Internal Failure A process or product failure that is caught before the customer receives the product or before the customer receives the service.

Ishikawa, Kaoru (deceased) A pioneer in quality control activities in Japan. In 1943, he developed the cause-and-effect diagram. Ishikawa, an ASQC Honorary member, published many works, including *What Is Total Quality Control?*, *The Japanese Way*, *Quality Control Circles at Work*, and *Guide to Quality Control*. He was a member of the quality control research group of the Union of Japanese Scientists and Engineers while also working as an assistant professor at the University of Tokyo.

Ishikawa Diagram See Cause-and-Effect Diagram.

ISO 9000 Series Standards A set of international standards on quality management and quality assurance developed to help companies effectively document the quality system elements to be implemented to maintain an efficient quality system. The standards were developed by the International Organization for Standardization (ISO), a special international agency for standardization composed of the national standards bodies of 91 countries.

*ISO 14000 An environmental management standard that organizations use to monitor and manage how their organization's activities affect the environment around them.

*ISO/TS 16949 The international standard for quality management systems used in the manufacture of automobiles, subassemblies, components, and parts.

Juran, Joseph M. The chairman emeritus of the Juran Institute and an ASQC Honorary member. Since 1924, Juran has pursued a varied career in management as an engineer, executive, government administrator, university professor, labor arbitrator, corporate director, and consultant. Specializing in managing for quality, he has authored hundreds of papers and 12 books, including *Juran's Quality Control Handbook*, *Quality Planning and Analysis* (with F. M. Gryna), and *Juran on Leadership for Quality*.

Just-in-Time Manufacturing An optimal material requirement planning system for a manufacturing process in which there is little or no manufacturing material inventory on hand at the manufacturing site and little or no incoming inspection.

Kaizen A Japanese term that means gradual unending improvement by doing little things better and setting and achieving increasingly higher standards. The term was made famous by Masaaki Imai in his book *Kaizen: The Key to Japan's Competitive Success*.

LCL See Lower Control Limit.

Leadership An essential part of a quality improvement effort. Organization leaders must establish a vision, communicate that vision to those in the organization, and provide the tools and knowledge necessary to accomplish the vision.

*Lean Manufacturing The improvement initiatives that focus on the elimination of waste from systems and processes.

Lot A defined quantity of product accumulated under conditions that are considered uniform for sampling purposes.

Lower Control Limit Control limit for points below the central line in a control chart.

Maintainability The probability that a given maintenance action for an item under given usage conditions can be performed within a stated time interval when the maintenance is performed under stated conditions using stated procedures and resources. Maintainability has two categories: serviceability (the ease of conducting scheduled inspections and servicing) and repairability (the ease of restoring service after a failure).

Malcolm Baldrige National Quality Award An award established by Congress in 1987 to raise awareness of quality management and to recognize U.S. companies that have implemented successful quality management systems. Two awards may be given annually in each of three categories: manufacturing company, service company, and small business. The award is named after the late Secretary of Commerce Malcolm Baldrige, a proponent of quality management. The U.S. Commerce Department's National Institute of Standards and Technology manages the award and ASQ administers it.

MIL-Q-9858A A military standard that describes quality program requirements.

MIL-STD-105E A military standard that describes the sampling procedures and tables for inspection by attributes.

MIL-STD-45662A A military standard that describes the requirements for creating and maintaining a calibration system for measurement and test equipment.

*Nonconformance State that exists when a product, service, or material does not conform to the customer requirements or specifications.

*Nonconformities-per-Unit Chart A control chart used to evaluate a process in terms of the average count of occurrences per unit occurring in a sample; a defect count per unit chart.

Nonconformity The nonfulfillment of a specified requirement. (See also Blemish, Defect, Imperfection.)

Nondestructive Testing and Evaluation Testing and evaluation methods that do not damage or destroy the product being tested.

*Non-Value-Added Term describing any activity or action that does not directly affect the production of a product or the provision of a service.

*np Chart Number of nonconforming units chart.

*Number of Nonconforming Units Chart A control chart used to evaluate a process in terms of the total number of units in a sample displaying a chosen characteristic.

OC Curve Operating characteristic curve.

Operating Characteristic Curve A graph used to determine the probability of accepting lots as a function of the quality level of the lot or process when using various sampling plans. There are three types: Type A curves, which give the probability of acceptance for an individual lot coming from finite production (will not continue in the future); Type B curves, which give the probability of acceptance for lots coming from a continuous process; and Type C curves, which for a continuous sampling plan, give the long-run percentage of product accepted during the sampling phase.

Out-of-Control Process A process in which the statistical measure being evaluated is not in a state of statistical control; the variations among the observed sampling results cannot be attributed to a constant system of chance causes. (See also In-Control Process.)

Out-of-Spec A term used to indicate that a unit does not meet a given specification.

*p Chart The fraction nonconforming chart is a control chart used to monitor the proportion nonconforming in a lot of goods.

Pareto Chart A graphical tool for ranking causes from most significant to least significant. It is based on the Pareto principle, which was first defined by J. M. Juran in 1950. The principle, named after 19th century economist Vilfredo Pareto, suggests that most effects come from relatively few causes; that is, 80% of the effects come from 20% of the possible causes. The Pareto chart is one of the seven tools of quality.

*Parts per Million (PPM) Describes the performance of a process in terms of either actual or projected defective material.

*PDSA Cycle See Plan-Do-Study-Act Cycle.

Percent Chart A control chart for evaluating the stability of a process in terms of the percent of the total number of units in a sample in which an event of a given classification occurs. The percent chart is also referred to as a proportion chart.

*Plan-Do-Study-Act Cycle A four-step process for quality improvement. In the first step (Plan), a plan to effect improvement is developed. In the second step (Do), the plan is carried out, preferably on a small scale. In the third step (Study), the effects of the plan are observed. In the last step (Act), the results are studied to determine what was learned and what can be predicted. The Plan-Do-Study-Act cycle was originally called the Plan-Do-Check-Act cycle but in the early 1990s was standardized as Plan-Do-Study-Act. It is still sometimes referred to as the Shewhart cycle because Walter A. Shewhart discussed the concept in his book *Statistical Method from the Viewpoint of Quality Control* or as the Deming cycle because W. Edwards Deming introduced the concept in Japan.

*Precision The ability of a system, process, or activity to repeat its actions consistently.

*Prevention Costs The costs that occur when actions are taken to prevent nonconformities in a system, process, service, or product.

Prevention vs. Detection A term used to contrast two types of quality activities. Prevention refers to those activities designed to prevent nonconformances in products and services. Detection refers to those activities designed to detect nonconformances already in products and services. Another term used to describe this distinction is "designing in quality vs. inspecting in quality."

*Process The action of taking inputs and transforming them into outputs through the performance of value-added activities.

Process Capability A statistical measure of the inherent process variability for a given characteristic. The most widely accepted formula for process capability is 6σ.

Process Capability Index The value of the tolerance specified for the characteristic divided by the process capability. There are several types of process capability indexes, including the widely used C_{pk} and C_p.

*Process Control Using statistical process control to measure and regulate a process.

*Process Map A diagram showing the steps or activities that take place in a process.

*Process Owner The individual ultimately responsible for ensuring that the appropriate activities take place in a process.

*Production Part Approval Process (PPAP) The process of obtaining approval to produce parts.

Product or Service Liability The obligation of a company to make restitution for loss related to personal injury, property damage, or other harm caused by its product or service.

QFD See Quality Function Deployment.

QS 9000 A quality standard utilized by the automotive industry to ensure the quality of its and its supplier's components, subsystems, and finished products.

Quality A subjective term for which each person has his or her own definition. In technical usage, quality can have two meanings: (1) the characteristics of a product or service that bear on its ability to satisfy stated or implied needs and (2) a product or service free of deficiencies.

Quality Assurance/Quality Control Two terms that have many interpretations because of the multiple definitions for the words "assurance" and "control." For example, "assurance" can mean the act of giving confidence, the state of being certain, or the act of making certain; "control" can mean an evaluation to indicate needed corrective responses, the act of going, or the state of a process in which the variables are attributable to a constant system of chance causes. (For detailed discussion on the multiple definitions see ANSI/ASQC Standard A3-1987, "Definitions, Symbols, Formulas, and Tables for Control Charts.") One definition of quality assurance is: are all the planned and systematic activities implemented within the quality system that can be demonstrated to provide confidence that a product or service will fulfill requirements for quality? One definition for quality control is: the operational techniques and activities used to fulfill requirements for quality. Often, however, "quality assurance" and "quality control" are used interchangeably, referring to the actions performed to ensure the quality of a product, service, or process.

Quality Audit A systematic, independent examination and review to determine whether quality activities and related results comply with planned arrangements and whether these arrangements are implemented effectively and are suitable to achieve the objectives.

Quality Circles Quality improvement or self-improvement study groups composed of a small number of employees (10 or fewer) and their supervisor. Quality circles originated in Japan, where they are called quality control circles.

Quality Control See Quality Assurance/Quality Control.

Quality Costs See Cost of Poor Quality.

Quality Engineering The analysis of a manufacturing system at all stages to maximize the quality of the process itself and the products it produces.

Quality Function Deployment A structured method in which customer requirements are translated into appropriate technical requirements for each stage of product development and production. The QFD process is often referred to as listening to the voice of the customer.

Quality Loss Function A parabolic approximation of the quality loss that occurs when a quality characteristic deviates from its target value. The quality loss function is expressed in monetary units: the cost of deviating from the target increases quadratically the farther the quality characteristic moves from the target. The formula used to compute the quality loss function depends on the type of quality characteristic being used. The quality loss function was first introduced in this form by Genichi Taguchi.

Quality Management (QM) The application of a quality management system in managing a process to achieve maximum customer satisfaction at the lowest overall cost to the organization while continuing to improve the process.

*Quality Manual The chief document for standard operating procedures, processes, and specifications that define a quality management system. The manual serves as a permanent reference guide for the implementation and maintenance of the quality management system described by the manual.

*Quality Plan Integrates quality philosophies into an organization's environment. The plan will include specific continuous improvement strategies and actions. Plans are developed at the departmental, group, plant, division, and company level. Lower level plans should support the company's strategic objectives. A quality plan emphasizes defect prevention through continuous improvement rather than by defect detection.

*Quality Records Written verification that a company's methods, systems, and processes were performed according to the quality system documentation such as inspection or test results, internal audit results, and calibration data.

Quality Trilogy A three-pronged approach to managing for quality. The three legs are quality planning (developing the products and processes required to meet customer needs), quality control (meeting product and process goals), and quality improvement (achieving unprecedented levels of performance).

*Random Sampling Samples are chosen so that each sample under consideration has an equal chance of being selected.

Range Chart A control chart in which the subject group, R, is used to evaluate the stability of the variability within a process.

R Chart See Range Chart.

Red Bead Experiment An experiment developed by W. Edwards Deming to illustrate that it is impossible to put employees in rank order of performance for the coming year based on their performance during the past year because performance differences must be attributed to the system, not to employees. Four thousand red and white beads (20% red) in a jar and six people are needed for the experiment. The participants' goal is to produce white beads, because the customer will not accept red beads. One person begins by stirring the beads and then, blindfolded, selects a sample of 50 beads. That person hands the jar to the next person, who repeats the process, and so on. When everyone has his or her sample, the number of red beads for each is counted. The limits of variation between employees that can be attributed to the system are calculated. Everyone will fall within the calculated limits of variation that could arise from the system. The calculations will show that there is no evidence one person will be a better performer than another in the future. The experiment shows that it would be a waste of management's time to try to find out why, say, John produced four red beads and Jane produced 15; instead, management should improve the system, making it possible for everyone to produce more white beads.

Registration to Standards A process in which an accredited, independent third-party organization conducts an on-site audit of a company's operations against the requirements of the standard to which the company wants to be registered. Upon successful completion of the audit, the company receives a certificate indicating that it has met the standard requirements.

Reliability The probability of a product performing its intended function under stated conditions without failure for a given period of time.

*Repair Corrective action to a damaged product so that the product will fulfill the original specifications.

*Rework Action taken on nonconforming products or services to allow them to meet the original specifications.

s Chart See Sample Standard Deviation Chart.

Sample Standard Deviation Chart A control chart in which the subgroup standard deviation, s, is used to evaluate the stability of the variability within a process.

Scatter Diagram A graphical technique to analyze the relationship between two variables. Two sets of data are plotted on a graph, with the y-axis being used for the variable to be predicted and the x-axis being used for the variable to make the prediction. The graph will show possible relationships (although two variables might appear to be related, they might not be—those who know most about the variables must make that evaluation). The scatter diagram is one of the seven tools of quality.

Seven Tools of Quality Tools that help organizations understand their processes in order to improve them. The tools are the cause-and-effect diagram, check sheet, control chart, flowchart, histogram, Pareto chart, and scatter diagram. (See individual entries.)

Shewhart Cycle See Plan-Do-Study-Act Cycle.

Shewhart, Walter A. (deceased) Referred to as the father of statistical quality control because he brought together the disciplines of statistics, engineering, and economics. He described the basic principles of this new discipline in his book *Economic Control of Quality of Manufactured Product*. Shewhart, ASQC's first Honorary member, was best known for creating the control chart. Shewhart worked for Western Electric and AT&T Bell Telephone Laboratories in addition to lecturing and consulting on quality control.

Six Sigma Quality A term used generally to indicate that a process is well-controlled, i.e., $\pm 3\sigma$ from the centerline in a control chart. The term is usually associated with Motorola, which named one of its key operational initiatives "Six Sigma Quality."

SPC See Statistical Process Control.

Special Causes Causes of variation that arise because of special circumstances. They are not an inherent part of a process. Special causes are also referred to as assignable causes. (See also Common Causes.)

Specification A document that states the requirements to which a given product or service must conform.

SQC See Statistical Quality Control.

Standard Deviation A computed measure of variability indicating the spread of the data set around the mean.

Statistical Process Control The application of statistical techniques to control a process. Often the term "statistical quality control" is used interchangeably with "statistical process control."

Statistical Quality Control The application of statistical techniques to control quality. Often the term "statistical process control" is used interchangeably with "statistical quality control," although statistical quality control includes acceptance sampling as well as statistical process control.

*Subcontractors Persons who provide materials, parts, or services to the suppliers of original equipment manufacturers.

*Supplier Quality Assurance Confidence that a supplier's product or service will fulfill its customers' needs. This confidence is achieved by creating a relationship between the customer and supplier that ensures the product will be fit for use with minimal corrective action and inspection. According to J. M. Juran, there are nine primary activities needed: (1) define product and program quality requirements, (2) evaluate alternative suppliers, (3) select suppliers, (4) conduct joint quality planning, (5) cooperate with the supplier during the execution of the contract, (6) obtain proof of conformance to requirements, (7) certify qualified suppliers, (8) conduct quality improvement programs as required, and (9) create and use supplier quality ratings.

*Suppliers Persons who provide materials, parts, or services directly to manufacturers.

Taguchi, Genichi The executive director of the American Supplier Institute, the director of the Japan Industrial Technology Institute, and an honorary professor at Nanjing Institute of Technology in China. Taguchi is well known for developing a methodology to improve quality and reduce costs, which in the United States is referred to as the Taguchi Method. He also developed the quality loss function.

Taguchi Methods The American Supplier Institute's trademarked term for the quality engineering methodology developed by Genichi Taguchi. In this engineering approach to quality control, Taguchi calls for off-line quality control, on-line quality control, and a system of experimental design to improve quality and reduce costs.

Tampering Action taken to compensate for variation within the control limits of a stable system. Tampering increases rather than decreases variation, as evidenced by the funnel experiment.

Top-Management Commitment Participation of the highest-level officials in their organization's quality improvement efforts. Their participation includes establishing and serving on a quality committee, establishing quality policies and goals, deploying those goals to lower levels of the organization, providing the resources and training that the lower levels need to achieve the goals, participating in quality improvement teams, reviewing progress organizationwide, recognizing those who have performed well, and revising the current reward system to reflect the importance of achieving the quality goals.

Total Quality Management A term initially coined by the Naval Air Systems Command to describe its Japanese-style management approach to quality improvement. Since then, total quality management (TQM) has taken on many meanings. Simply put, TQM is a management approach to long-term success through customer satisfaction. TQM is based on the participation of all members of an organization in improving processes, products, services, and the culture they work in. TQM benefits all organization members and society. The methods for implementing this approach are found in the teachings of such quality control leaders as Philip B. Crosby, W. Edwards Deming, Armand V. Feigenbaum, Kaoru Ishikawa, and J. M. Juran.

TQM See Total Quality Management.

t-test Assesses whether the means of two groups are statistically different from each other. Use this analysis if you want to compare the means of two groups.

Type I Error An incorrect decision to reject something (such as a statistical hypothesis or a lot of products) when it is acceptable.

Type II Error An incorrect decision to accept something when it is unacceptable.

*u Chart or Nonconformities-per-Unit Chart A control chart used to evaluate a process using the average count of events per unit occurring in a sample; defect count per unit chart.

UCL See Upper Control Limit.

Upper Control Limit Control limit for points above the central line in a control chart.

*Value-Added Activities The activities in a process or system that transform raw materials, parts, or components, etc., into a usable product or service for the customer.

Value-Adding Process Activities that transform input into a customer-usable output. The customer can be internal or external to the organization.

*Value Stream The activities that take place in order to provide a product or service to a customer.

Variable Data Measurement information. Control charts based on variables data include average ($\overline{X}$) chart, range (R) chart, and sample standard deviation chart.

Variation A change in data, a characteristic, or a function that is caused by one of four factors: special causes, common causes, tampering, or structural variation.

Vision Statement: A statement which summarizes an organization's values, mission, and future direction for its employees and customers.

Vital Few, Useful Many A term used by J. M. Juran to describe his use of the Pareto principle, which he first defined in 1950. (The principle was used much earlier in economics and inventory control methodologies.) The principle suggests that most effects come from relatively few causes; that is, 80% of the effects come from 20% of the possible causes. The 20% of the possible causes are referred to as the "vital few"; the remaining causes are referred to as the "useful many." When Juran first defined this principle, he referred to the remaining causes as the "trivial many," but realizing that no problems are trivial in quality assurance, he changed it to the "useful many."

*Waste Any activity or action that fails to add value to the product or service being provided to the customer.

$\overline{X}$ **Chart** Average chart.

Zero Defects A performance standard and methodology developed by Philip B. Crosby that states, if people commit themselves to watching details and avoiding errors, they can move closer to the goal of zero defects.

ANSWERS TO SELECTED PROBLEMS

Chapter 4

4.21 Mean = 1.123
Mode = 1.122
Median = 1.123

4.22 Mean = 0.656
Mode = 0.654
Median = 0.655

4.23 Mean = 226.2
Mode = 227
Median = 227
σ = 2.36

4.24 Mean = 0.011
Mode = 0.020, 0.011
Median = 0.011
σ = 0.008
R = 0.018
73.41% of the parts will meet spec.

4.27 σ = 5.32
R = 9

4.28 σ = 0.0022
R = 0.0065

4.29 Mean = 0.656
σ = 0.0022
Median = 0.655
Mode = 0.654

4.30 Mean = 0.077
σ = 0.0032

4.31 Mean = 24
Mode = 25
Median = 25
Range = 19
σ = 5

4.35 Area = 0.8413

4.36 Area = 0.0548 or 5.48% of the parts are above 90 mm.

4.37 Area = 0.9525

4.43 Area = 0.8186

4.44 X_i = 2871.25 foot-candles

4.45 2.27% of the batteries should survive longer than 1,000 days

4.47 37.07% will be below the LSL of 11.41 inches.

Chapter 5

5.3 $\overline{\overline{X}}$ = 16, UCL_x = 20, LCL_x = 12,
R-bar = 7, UCL_R = 15, LCL_R = 0

5.4 $\overline{\overline{X}}$ = 50.2, UCL_x = 50.7, LCL_x = 49.7,
R-bar = 0.7, UCL_R = 1.6, LCL_R = 0

5.5 $\overline{\overline{X}}$ = 349, UCL_x = 357, LCL_x = 341,
R-bar = 14, UCL_R = 30, LCL_R = 0

5.10 $\overline{\overline{X}}$ = 0.0627, UCL_x = 0.0629,
LCL_x = 0.0625, R-bar = 0.0003,
UCL_R = 0.0006, LCL_R = 0

5.14 $\overline{\overline{X}}$ = 0.0028, UCL_x = 0.0032,
LCL_x = 0.0024, R-bar = 0.0006,
UCL_R = 0.0014, LCL_R = 0

5.15 $\overline{\overline{X}}$ = 0.0627, UCL_x = 0.0628,
LCL_x = 0.0626, s-bar = 0.0001,
UCL_s = 0.0002, LCL_s = 0

5.16 $\overline{\overline{X}}$ = 0.0028, UCL_x = 0.0033,
LCL_x = 0.0023, s-bar = 0.0003,
UCL_s = 0.0007, LCL_s = 0

Chapter 6

6.4 σ = 3, 6σ = 18, C_p = 0.44, C_{pk} = 0.33

6.6 σ = 0.33, 6σ = 1.98, C_p = 0.51,
C_{pk} = 0.3

6.7 σ = 0.00006, 6σ = 0.00036, C_p = 1.1,
C_{pk} = 1.1

6.11 $\sigma = 0.04, 6\sigma = 0.24, C_p = 0.42,$
      $C_{pk} = 0.27$

6.12 $\sigma = 0.0003, 6\sigma = 0.00118, C_p = 0.555,$
      $C_{pk} = 0.555$

Chapter 7

7.1 $\overline{X} = 24 \text{ mm}, UCL_x = 27, LCL_x = 21,$
      $\overline{R} = 1, UCL_r = 3.267, LCL_x = 0$

7.2 $\overline{X} = 7{,}842, UCL_x = 10{,}209,$
      $LCL_x = 5{,}475, \overline{R} = 890,$
      $UCL_r = 2{,}940, LCL_x = 0$

7.5 $\overline{X} = 34, UCL_x = 39, LCL_x = 29,$
      $\overline{R} = 5, UCL_R = 13, LCL_X = 0$

7.6 $\overline{X} = 0.812, UCL_x = 0.816,$
      $LCL_x = 0.808, \overline{R} = 0.006,$
      $UCL_r = 0.014, LCL_R = 0$

7.7 $\overline{X} = 3{,}788, UCL_x = 3{,}951,$
      $LCL_x = 3{,}625, \overline{R} = 159,$
      $UCL_r = 409, LCL_x = 0$

7.8 $\overline{X} = 30.1, UCL_x = 33, LCL_x = 28,$
      $\overline{R} = 3.5, UCL_R = 8, LCL_R = 0$

7.19 $\overline{X} = 0.036, UCL_x = 0.213,$
      $LCL_x = -0.141, \overline{R} = 0.173,$
      $UCL_R = 0.45, LCL_R = 0$

Chapter 8

8.1   0.50

8.2   0.008

8.3 $P(\text{orange } \& \ 5) = 1/24$
      $P(\text{orange}) = 6/24$
      $P(\text{five}) = 3/24$

8.4   60

8.5   Combination = 3,003
      Permutation = 360,360

8.6 $P(\text{performs}) = 0.91$

8.7 $P(H|P) = 0.78$

8.9 $P(\text{Fabric 1}) = 0.46$
      $P(\text{Fabric 2}|\text{Style 1}) = 0.18$
      $P(\text{Style 4}) = 0.255$
      $P(\text{Style 3}|\text{Fabric 3}) = 0.23$

8.10 a. 0.6
      b. 0.4
      c. independent

8.14 $P(1) + P(0) = 0.262$
      $P(1) = 0.238$
      $P(0) = 0.024$

8.15 0.419

8.17 $P(0) = 0.545$

8.18 $P(2) = 0.3$

8.20 $P(1 \text{ or less}) = 0.98$

8.22 $P(2) = 0.10$

8.23 $P(\text{more than } 4) = 1 - P(4 \text{ or less}) = 0.001$

8.24 $P(2) = 0.012$

8.25 $P(5) = 0.0015$

8.26 $P(\text{more than } 2) = 0.017$

8.27 $P(1 \text{ or less}) = 0.84$

8.28 $P(\text{less than } 2) = 0.986$

8.29 $P(\text{at least } 1) = 0.59$

8.30 $P(3 \text{ in five min}) = 0.13$

8.31 $P(\text{more than 1 call}) = 0.22$

8.32 $P(\text{more than } 2) = 0.58$

8.34 a. 2.71% of bikes will weigh below 8.3 kg
      b. Area between 8.0 kg and 10.10 kg
         $= 0.9950 - 0.00375 = 0.9913$

8.36 $P(\text{more than } 2) = 1 - 0.977 = 0.023$

8.37 $P(2) = 0.014$

Chapter 9

9.3 $\overline{p} = 0.068$
      $UCL_p = 0.237$
      $LCL_p = 0$

9.4 $\overline{p} = 0.004$
      $UCL_p = 0.0174$
      $LCL_p = 0$

9.5 $\overline{p} = 0.038$
      $UCL_p = 0.085$
      $LCL_p = 0$

9.9 $\overline{p} = 0.0131$
      $UCL_p = 0.028$
      $LCL_p = 0$

9.10 $\overline{p} = 0.0131$
      $UCL_{400} = 0.030$
      $LCL_p = 0$
      $UCL_{450} = 0.029$
      $LCL_p = 0$
      $UCL_{500} = 0.028$
      $LCL_p = 0$
      $UCL_{550} = 0.028$
      $LCL_p = 0$
      $UCL_{600} = 0.027$
      $LCL_p = 0$

9.11 $\overline{p} = 0.0185$
      $UCL_{400} = 0.0263$
      $LCL_p = 0.0107$

Check points 2, 3, 4, 9, 11
point 2, check limits, out of control
point 3, do not check limits
point 4, do not check limits
point 9, do not check limits
point 11, check limits, out of control

9.13 $n\bar{p} = 4.5$
$UCL_{np} = 11$
$LCL_{np} = 0$

9.14 $\bar{p} = 9\%$
$UCL_{\%} = 21\%$
$LCL_{\%} = 0$

9.16 $\bar{p} = 0.0825$
$n\bar{p} = 13$
$UCL_{np} = 23$
$LCL_{np} = 3$

9.17 $\bar{p} = 0.0405$
$n\bar{p} = 12$
$UCL_{np} = 22$
$LCL_{np} = 2$
process capability is np-bar $= 12$

9.18 $\bar{p} = 0.013$
$n\bar{p} = 5$
$UCL_{np} = 12$
$LCL_{np} = 0$

9.19 $\bar{c} = 8$
$UCL_c = 16$
$LCL_c = 0$

process will not meet customer's specifications

9.21 $\bar{c} = 5$
$UCL_c = 11$
$LCL_c = 0$

9.22 $\bar{c} = 6$
$UCL_c = 13$
$LCL_c = 0$

9.23 $\bar{u} = 2.345$
$UCL_u = 3$
$LCL_u = 1$

9.25 $\bar{u} = 1.18$
$n_{ave} = 101$
$UCL_u = 1.5$
$LCL_u = 0.86$

Chapter 10

10.5 $= 0.00035$ $\Theta = 2857$ hours
10.6 $= 0.00197$ $\Theta = 500$ hours
10.10 Reliability of the system $= 0.987$
10.11 Reliability of the system $= 0.9561$
10.12 Reliability of the system $= 0.9859$
10.14 Reliability of the system $= 0.8996$
10.15 Reliability of the system $= 0.9950$
10.16 Reliability of the system $= 0.855$

BIBLIOGRAPHY

Abarca, D. "Making the Most of Internal Audits." *Quality Digest*, February 1999, pp. 26–28.

Adam, P., and R. VandeWater. "Benchmarking and the Bottom Line: Translating BPR into Bottom-Line Results." *Industrial Engineering*, February 1995, pp. 24–26.

Adcock, S. "FAA Orders Fix on Older 737s." *Newsday*, May 8, 1998.

Aft, L. *Quality Improvement Using Statistical Process Control*. New York: Harcourt Brace Jovanovich, 1988.

Alsup, F., and R. Watson. *Practical Statistical Process Control*. New York: Van Nostrand Reinhold, 1993.

AMA Management Briefing. *World Class Quality*. New York: AMA Publications Division, 1990.

Amari, D., and James, D. "ISO 9001 Takes on a New Role—Crime Fighter." *Quality Progress*, May 2004, pp. 57–61.

American Society for Quality Control, P.O. Box 3005, Milwaukee, WI 53201-3005.

Azeredo, M., Silva, S., and Rekab, K. "Improve Molded Part Quality." *Quality Progress*, July 2003, pp. 72–76.

Bacus, H. "Liability: Trying Times." *Nation's Business*, February 1986, pp. 22–28.

Bamford, J. "Order in the Court." *Forbes*, January 27, 1986, pp. 46–47.

Bergamini, D. *Mathematics*. New York: Time, 1963.

Bernowski, K., and B. Stratton. "How Do People Use the Baldrige Award Criteria?" *Quality Progress*, May 1995, pp. 43–47.

Berry, Thomas. *Managing the Total Quality Transformation*. Milwaukee, WI: ASQC Quality Press, 1991.

Besterfield, D. *Quality Control*, 4th ed. Englewood Cliffs, NJ: Prentice Hall, 1994.

Biesada, A. "Strategic Benchmarking." *Financial World*, September 29, 1992, pp. 30–36.

Bishara, R., and M. Wyrick. "A Systematic Approach to Quality Assurance Auditing." *Quality Progress*, December 1994, pp. 67–69.

Block, M. "The White House Manages Green." *Quality Progress*, July 2003, pp. 90–91.

Bossert, J. "Lean and Six Sigma—Synergy Made in Heaven." *Quality Progress*, July 2003, pp. 31–32.

Bothe, D. "SPC for Short Production Runs." *Quality*, December 1988, pp. 58–59.

Bovet, S. F. "Use TQM, Benchmarking to Improve Productivity." *Public Relations Journal*, January 1994, p. 7.

Breyfogle, F., and B. Meadows. "Bottom-Line Success With Six Sigma." *Quality Progress*, May 2001, pp. 101–104.

Brocka, B., and M. Brocka. *Quality Management: Implementing the Best Ideas of the Masters.* Homewood, IL: Business One Irwin, 1992.

Brown, R. "Zero Defects the Easy Way with Target Area Control." *Modern Machine Shop*, July 1966, p. 19.

Bruder, K. "Public Benchmarking: A Practical Approach." *Public Press*, September 1994, pp. 9–14.

Brumm, E. "Managing Records for ISO 9000 Compliance." *Quality Progress*, January 1995, pp. 73–77.

Burr, I. W. *Statistical Quality Control Methods.* New York: Marcel Dekker, 1976.

Butz, H. "Strategic Planning: The Missing Link in TQM." *Quality Progress*, May 1995, pp. 105–108.

Byrnes, Daniel. "Exploring the World of ISO 9000." *Quality*, October 1992, pp. 19–31.

Campanella, J., ed. *Principles of Quality Costs.* Milwaukee, WI: ASQC Quality Press, 1990.

Camperi, J. A. "Vendor Approval and Audits in Total Quality Management." *Food Technology*, September 1994, pp. 160–162.

Carson, P. P. "Deming Versus Traditional Management Theorists on Goal Setting: Can Both Be Right?" *Business Horizons*, September 1993, pp. 79–84.

Cook, B. M. "Quality: The Pioneers Survey the Landscape." *Industry Week*, October 21, 1991, pp. 68–73.

Crosby, P. B. *Cutting the Cost of Quality: The Defect Prevention Workbook for Managers.* Boston: Industrial Education Institute, 1967.

Crosby, P. B. *The Eternally Successful Organization: The Art of Corporate Wellness.* New York: New American Library, 1988.

Crosby, P. B. *Quality Is Free.* New York: Penguin Books, 1979.

Crosby, P. B. *Quality Is Free: The Art of Making Quality Certain.* New York: McGraw-Hill, 1979.

Crosby, P. B. *Quality without Tears: The Art of Hassle-Free Management.* New York: McGraw-Hill, 1979.

Crownover, D. "Baldrige: It's Easy, Free, and It Works." *Quality Progress*, July 2003, pp. 37–41.

Crownover, D. *Take it to the Next Level.* Dallas: NextLevel Press, 1999.

Cullen, C. "Short Run SPC Re-emerges." *Quality*, April 1995, p. 44.

"Customer Satisfaction Hits Nine-Year High." *Quality Progress*, April 2004, p. 16.

Darden, W., W. Babin, M. Griffin, and R. Coulter. "Investigation of Products Liability Attitudes and Opinions: A Consumer Perspective," *Journal of Consumer Affairs*, June 22, 1994.

Davis, P. M. "New Emphasis on Product Warnings." *Design News*, August 6, 1990, p. 150.

Davis, P. M. "The Right Prescription for Product Tampering." *Design News*, January 23, 1989, p. 224.

Day, C. R. "Benchmarking's First Law: Know Thyself." *Industry Week*, February 17, 1992, p. 70.

Day, R. G. *Quality Function Deployment.* Milwaukee, WI: ASQ Quality Press, 1993.

Dean, M., and Tomovic, C. "Does Baldrige Make a Business Case for Quality?" *Quality Progress*, April 2004, pp. 40–45.

DeFoe, J. A. "The Tip of the Iceberg." *Quality Progress*, May 2001, pp. 29–37.

Deming, W. E. *The New Economics.* Cambridge, MA: MIT CAES, 1993.

Deming, W. E. *Out of the Crisis.* Cambridge, MA: MIT Press, 1986.

Dentzer, S. "The Product Liability Debate." *Newsweek*, September 10, 1984, pp. 54–57.

DeToro, I. "The Ten Pitfalls of Benchmarking." *Quality Progress*, January 1995, pp. 61–63.

DeVor, R., T. Chang, and J. Sutherland. *Statistical Quality Design and Control.* New York: Macmillan, 1992.

Dobyns, L., and C. Crawford-Mason. *Quality or Else: The Revolution in World Business.* Boston: Houghton Mifflin, 1991.

Duncan, A. *Quality Control and Industrial Statistics.* Homewood, IL: Irwin, 1974.

Eaton, B. "Cessna's Approach to Internal Quality Audits." *IIE Solutions, Industrial Engineering,* June 1995, pp. 12–16.

Eureka, W. E., and N. E. Ryan. *The Customer Driven Company.* Dearborn, MI. ASI Press, 1988.

Farahmand, K., R. Becerra, and J. Greene. "ISO 9000 Certification: Johnson Controls' Inside Story." *Industrial Engineering,* September 1994, pp. 22–23.

Feigenbaum, A. V. "Changing Concepts and Management of Quality Worldwide." *Quality Progress,* December 1997, pp. 43–47.

Feigenbaum, A. V. *Total Quality Control.* New York: McGraw-Hill, 1983.

Feigenbaum, A. V. "The Future of Quality Management." *Quality Digest,* May 1998, pp. 24–30.

Feigenbaum, A. V. "How to Manage for Quality in Today's Economy." *Quality Progress,* May 2001, pp. 26–27.

Franco, V. R. "Adopting Six Sigma." *Quality Digest,* June 2001, pp. 28–32.

Frum, D. "Crash!" *Forbes,* November 8, 1993, p. 62.

Galpin, D., R. Dooley, J. Parker, and R. Bell. "Assess Remaining Component Life with Three Level Approach." *Power,* August 1990, pp. 69–72.

Gardner, R. A. "Resolving the Process Paradox." *Quality Progress,* March 2001, pp. 51–59.

Gerling, A. "How Jury Decided How Much the Coffee Spill Was Worth." *The Wall Street Journal,* September 4, 1994.

Gest, T. "Product Paranoia." *U.S. News & World Report,* February 24, 1992, pp. 67–69.

Geyelin, M. "Product Liability Suits Fare Worse Now." *The Wall Street Journal,* July 12, 1994.

Ghattas, R. G., and S. L. McKee. *Practical Project Management.* Upper Saddle River, NJ: Prentice Hall, 2001.

Gitlow, H. S. *Planning for Quality, Productivity, and Competitive Position.* Homewood, IL: Business One Irwin, 1990.

Gitlow, H. S., and S. J. Gitlow. *The Deming Guide to Quality and Competitive Position.* Englewood Cliffs, NJ: Prentice Hall, 1987.

Goetsch, D. L. *Effective Supervision.* Upper Saddle River, NJ: Prentice Hall, 2002.

Goetsch, D. L., and S. B. Davis. *ISO 14000 Environmental Management.* Upper Saddle River, NJ: Prentice Hall, 2001.

Goetsch, D. L., and S. B. Davis. *Understanding and Implementing ISO 9000 and ISO Standards.* Upper Saddle River, NJ: Prentice Hall, 1998.

Goodden, R. "Product Reliability Considerations Empower Quality Professionals." *Quality,* April 1995, p. 108.

Goodden, R. "Reduce the Impact of Product Liability on Your Organization." *Quality Progress,* January 1995, pp. 85–88.

Gooden, R. L. "How a Good Quality Management System Can Limit Lawsuits." *Quality Progress,* June 2001, pp. 55–59.

Gooden, R. L. *Product Liability Prevention: A Strategic Guide.* Milwaukee, WI: ASQ Quality Press, 2000.

Grahn, D. "The Five Drivers of Total Quality." *Quality Progress,* January 1995, pp. 65–70.

Grant, E., and T. Lang. "Why Product-Liability and Medical Malpractice Lawsuits Are So Numerous in the United States." *Quality Progress,* December 1994, pp. 63–65.

Grant, E., and R. Leavenworth. *Statistical Quality Control.* New York: McGraw-Hill, 1988.

Grant, P. "A Great Step Backwards." *Quality,* May 1985, p. 58.

Greene, R. "The Tort Reform Quagmire." *Forbes,* August 11, 1986, pp. 76–79.

Hare, L. "SPC: From Chaos to Wiping the Floor." *Quality Progress*, July 2003, pp. 58–63.

Hare, L., R. Hoerl, J. Hromi, and R. Snee. "The Role of Statistical Thinking in Management." *Quality Progress*, February 1995, pp. 53–59.

Harry, M., and R. Schroeder. *Six Sigma: The Breakthrough Management Strategy Revolutionizing the World's Top Corporations.* New York: Doubleday, 2000.

Heldt, J. J. "Quality Pays." *Quality*, November 1988, pp. 26–27.

Heldt, J. J., and D. J. Costa. *Quality Pays.* Wheaton, IL: Hitchcock Publishing, 1988.

Himelstein, L. "Monkey See, Monkey Sue." *Business Week*, February 7, 1994, pp. 112–113.

Hockman, K., R. Grenville, and S. Jackson. "Road Map to ISO 9000 Registration." *Quality Progress*, May 1994, pp. 39–42.

Hoisington, S., and Menzer, E. "Learn to Talk Money." *Quality Progress*, May 2004, pp. 44–49.

Hoyer, R. W., and B. B. Hoyer. "What is Quality?" *Quality Progress*, July 2001, pp. 52–62.

Hutchins, G. "The State of Quality Auditing." *Quality Progress*, March 2001, pp. 25–29.

Hutchinson, E. E. "The Road to TL 9000: From the Bell Breakup to Today." *Quality Progress*, January 2001, pp. 33–37.

Hutton, D. W. *From Baldrige to the Bottom Line.* Milwaukee, WI: ASQ Quality Press, 2000.

Ireson, W., and C. Coombs. *Handbook of Reliability Engineering and Management.* New York: McGraw-Hill, 1988.

"ISO Says 8 of 10 Cars to 'Run' on ISO 9001:2000." *Quality Progress*, July 2003, p. 12.

Ishikawa, K. *Guide to Quality Control*, rev. ed. White Plains, NY: Kraus International Publications, 1982.

Ishikawa, K. *What Is Total Quality Control? The Japanese Way.* Englewood Cliffs, NJ: Prentice Hall, 1985.

Jaffrey, S. "ISO 9001 Made Easy." *Quality Progress*, May 2004, p. 104.

Johnson, K. "Print Perfect." *Quality Progress*, July 2003, pp. 48–56.

Juran, J. "A Close Shave." *Quality Progress*, May 2004, pp. 41–43.

Juran, J. M. *Juran on Leadership for Quality: An Executive Handbook.* New York: Free Press, 1989.

Juran, J. M. *Juran on Planning for Quality.* New York: Free Press, 1988.

Juran, J. M. *Juran on Quality by Design: The New Steps for Planning Quality into Goods and Services.* New York: Free Press, 1992.

Juran, J. M. "The Quality Trilogy." *Quality Progress*, August 1986, pp. 19–24.

Juran, J. M., and F. M. Gryna. *Quality Planning and Analysis: From Product Development through Usage.* New York: McGraw-Hill, 1970.

Kackar, Raghu. "Taguchi's Quality Philosophy: Analysis and Commentary." *Quality Progress*, December 1986, pp. 21–29.

Kanholm, J. "New and Improved ISO 9000:2000." *Quality Digest*, October 1999, pp. 28–32.

Kececioglu, D. *Reliability and Life Testing Handbook.* Englewood Cliffs, NJ: Prentice Hall, 1993.

Keller, C. "QOS—A Simple Method for Big or Small." *Quality Progress*, July 2003, pp. 28–31.

Ketola, J., and K. Roberts. *ISO 9001:2000 in a Nutshell*, 2d ed. Chico, CA: Paton Press, 2001.

Ketola, J., and K. Roberts. "Transition Planning for ISO 9001:2000." *Quality Digest*, March 2001, pp. 24–28.

King, R. "So What's the Law, Already?" *Forbes*, May 19, 1986, pp. 70–72.

Kolarik, W. J. *Creating Quality: Concepts, Systems, Strategies and Tools.* New York: McGraw-Hill, 1995.

Kubiak, T. "An Integrated Approach System." *Quality Progress*, July 2003, pp. 41–45.

Leibfried, K. H. *Benchmarking: A Tool for Continuous Improvement.* New York: Harper Business, 1992.

Levinson, W. A. "ISO 9000 at the Front Line." *Quality Progress*, March 2001, pp. 33–36.

Mader, D. "DFSS and Your Current Design Process." *Quality Progress*, July 2003, pp. 88–89.

Mason. R. and Young. J. "Multivariate Thinking." *Quality Progress*, April 2004, pp. 89–91.

McElroy, A., and I. Fruchtman. "Use Statistical Analysis to Predict Equipment Reliability." *Power*, October 1992, pp. 39–46.

McGuire, P. "The Impact of Product Liability," Report 908. The Conference Board, 1988.

Malcolm Baldrige National Quality Award, U.S. Department of Commerce, Technology Administration, National Institute of Standards and Technology, Gaithersburg, MD.

Marcus, A. "Limits on Personal-Injury Suits Urged." *The Wall Street Journal*, April 23, 1991.

Martin, S. "Courting Disaster: A Huge Jury Award Sends the Wrong Message." *Bicycling*, March 1994, p. 136.

Mathews, J. "The Cost of Quality." *Newsweek*, September 7, 1992, pp. 48–49.

Mauro, T. "Frivolous or Not, Lawsuits Get Attention." *USA Today*, February 23, 1995.

Meier, B. "Court Rejects Coupon Settlement in Suit Over G.M. Pickup Trucks." *New York Times*, April 18, 1995.

Milas, G. "How to Develop a Meaningful Employee Recognition Program." *Quality Progress*, May 1995, pp. 139–142.

Miller, I., and J. Freund. *Probability and Statistics for Engineers*. Englewood Cliffs, NJ: Prentice Hall, 1977.

Miller, J. R., and J. S. Morris. "Is Quality Free or Profitable?" *Quality Progress*, January 2000, pp. 50–53.

Moen, R., T. Nolan, and L. Provost. *Improving Quality through Planned Experimentation*. New York: McGraw-Hill, 1991.

Montgomery, D. *Introduction to Statistical Quality Control*. New York: John Wiley and Sons, Inc., 2001.

Moran, J. W., and P. C. La Londe. "ASQ Certification Program Gains Wider Recognition." *Quality Progress*, April 2000, pp. 29–41.

Munoz, J., and C. Nielsen. "SPC: What Data Should I Collect? What Charts Should I Use?" *Quality Progress*, January 1991, pp. 50–52.

Munro, R. A. "Linking Six Sigma with QS-9000." *Quality Progress*, May 2000, pp. 47–53.

Nakhai, B., and J. Neves. "The Deming, Baldrige, and European Quality Awards." *Quality Progress*, April 1994, pp. 33–37.

Neave, H. *The Deming Dimension*. Knoxville, TN: SPC Press, 1990.

"Needed: A Backup for Ma Bell." *U.S. News & World Report*, September 30, 1991, p. 22.

Nelsen, D. "Your Gateway to Quality Knowledge." *Quality Progress*, April 2004, pp. 26–34.

Nesbitt, T. "Flowcharting Business Processes." *Quality*, March 1993, pp. 34–38.

Neuscheler-Fritsch, D., and R. Norris. "Capturing Financial Benefits From Six Sigma." *Quality Progress*, May 2001, pp. 39–44.

Nutter, J. "Designing with Product Liability in Mind." *Machine Design*, May 24, 1984, pp. 57–60.

Okes, D. "Complexity Theory Simplifies Choices." *Quality Progress*, July 2003, pp. 35–37.

Orsini, J. "What's Up Down Under?" *Quality Progress*, January 1995, pp. 57–59.

Palmer, B. "Overcoming Resistance to Change." *Quality Progress*, April 2004, pp. 35–39.

Parsons, C. "The Big Spill: Hot Java and Life in the Fast Lane." *Gannett News Services*, October 25, 1994.

Pearson, T. A. "Measure for Six Sigma Success." *Quality Progress*, February 2001, pp. 35–40.

Petroski, H. "The Merits of Colossal Failure." *Discover*, May 1994, pp. 74–82.

Phillips-Donaldson, D. "100 Years of Juran." *Quality Progress*, May 2004, pp. 25–39.

Pittle, D. "Product Safety: There's No Substitute for Safer Design." *Trial*, October 1991, pp. 110–114.

Pond, R. *Fundamentals of Statistical Quality Control*. New York: Merrill, 1994.

PQ Systems. *Applying Design of Experiments Using DOEpack*. Dayton, OH: PQ Systems, 2001.

Press, A., G. Carroll, and S. Waldman. "Are Lawyers Burning America?" *Newsweek*, March 20, 1995, pp. 30–35.

Prevette, S. "Systems Thinking—An Uncommon Answer." *Quality Progress*, July 2003, pp. 32–35.

Pritts, B. A. "Industry-wide Shakeout." *Quality Progress*, January 2001, pp. 61–64.

"Product Liability." *Business Insurance*, October 4, 1993, p. 36.

"Product Liability: The Consumer's Stake." *Consumer Reports*, June 1984, pp. 336–339.

"Product Liability Advice: Surpass Design Expectations." *Design News*, May 17, 1993, pp. 31–35.

Pyzdek, T. *What Every Engineer Should Know about Quality Control*. New York: Marcel Dekker, 1989.

Ramberg, J. S. "Six Sigma: Fad or Fundamental." *Quality Digest*, May 2000, pp. 28–32.

Reid, R. D. "From Deming to ISO 9001:2000." *Quality Progress*, June 2001, pp. 66–70.

Reid, R. D. "Tips for Automotive Auditors." *Quality Progress*, May 2004, pp. 72–76.

Reid, R. D. "Why QS 9000 Was Developed and What's in Its Future?" *Quality Progress*, April 2000, pp. 115–117.

Rice, C. M. "How to Conduct an Internal Audit and Still Have Friends." *Quality Progress*, June 1994, pp. 39–40.

Rienzo, T. F. "Planning Deming Management for Service Organizations." *Business Horizons*, May 1993, pp. 19–29.

Robinson, C., ed. *How to Plan an Audit*. Milwaukee, WI: ASQC Press, 1987.

Rowland, F. "Liability of Product Packaging." *Design News*, February 1, 1993, p. 120.

Rowland, F. "Product Warnings Updated." *Design News*, March 9, 1992, p. 168.

Rowland, J. R. "Should Congress Ease the Product Liability Law?" *American Legion*, April 1993, p. 10.

Roy, R. *A Primer on the Taguchi Method*. New York: Van Norstrand Reinhold, 1990.

Roy, R. K. "Sixteen Steps to Improvement." *Quality Digest*, June 2001, pp. 24–27.

Russell, J. P. "Auditing ISO 9001:2000." *Quality Progress*, July 2001, pp. 147–148.

Russell, J. *Quality Management Benchmark Assessment*. Milwaukee, WI: ASQC Press, 1991.

Russell, J. "Quality Management Benchmark Assessment." *Quality Progress*, May 1995, pp. 57–61.

Savell, L. "Who's Liable When the Product Is Information?" *Editor and Publisher*, August 28, 1993, pp. 35–36.

Schonberger, R. "Make Cells Work for You." *Quality Progress*, April 2004, pp. 58–63.

Schwinn, D. R. "Six Sigma and More: On Not Losing Sight of the Big Picture." *Quality E-line*, May 2, 2001, www.pqsystems.com.

Scovronek, J. "Reliability Sample Testing, A Case History." *Quality Progress*, February 2001, pp. 43–45.

Shipley, D. "ISO 9000 Makes Integrated Systems User Friendly." *Quality Progress*, July 2003, pp. 25–28.

"Short-Run SPC Re-emerges." QEI Speaker Interview. *Quality*, April 1995, p. 44.

Smith, G. *Statistical Process Control and Quality Improvement*. New York: Merrill, 1991.

Smith, R. "The Benchmarking Boom." *Human Resources Focus*, April 1994, pp. 1–6.

Snee, R. D. "Dealing With the Achilles' Heel of Six Sigma Initiatives." *Quality Progress,* March 2001, pp. 66–72.

Spendolini, M. *The Benchmarking Book.* New York: Amcom, 1992.

Spigener, J. B., and P. A. Angelo. "What Would Deming Say?" *Quality Progress,* March 2001, pp. 61–64.

Srikanth, M., and S. Robertson. *Measurements for Effective Decision Making.* Wallingford, CT: Spectrum Publishing Co., 1995.

Stamatis, D. H. "Who Needs Six Sigma, Anyway?" *Quality Digest,* May 2000, pp. 33–38.

Stein, P. "By Their Measures Shall Ye Know Them." *Quality Progress,* May 2001, pp. 72–74.

Stevens, T. "Dr. Deming: Management Today Does Not Know What Its Job Is." *Industry Week,* January 17, 1994, pp. 20–28.

Surak, J. G. "Quality in Commercial Food Processing." *Quality Progress,* February 1999, pp. 25–29.

Taguchi, G. *Introduction to Quality Engineering.* Dearborn, MI: ASI Press, 1986.

Thorpe, J., and W. Middendorf. *What Every Engineer Should Know about Product Liability.* New York: Marcel Dekker, 1979.

Tobias, R. *Applied Reliability.* New York: Van Nostrand Reinhold, 1986.

Torok, J. "The Where and Why: A 1-2-3 Model for Project Success." *Quality Progress,* April 2004, pp. 46–50.

Travalini, M. "The Evolution of a Quality Culture." *Quality Progress,* May 2001, pp. 105–108.

Traver, R. "Nine-Step Process Solves Product Variability Problems." *Quality,* April 1995, p. 94.

Traver, R. "Pre-Control: A Good Alternative to $\overline{X}$ and R Charts." *Quality Progress,* September 1985, pp. 11–13.

Tsuda, Y., and M. Tribus. "Planning the Quality Visit." *Quality Progress,* April 1991, pp. 30–34.

"U.S. FAA: FAA Orders Immediate Inspection for High-time Boeing 737s, Extends Inspection Order." *M2 Press Wire,* May 11, 1998.

Vardeman, S. *Statistics for Engineering Problem Solving.* Boston: PWS Publishing, 1994.

Vardeman, S., and J. Jobe. *Statistical Quality Assurance Methods for Engineers.* New York: John Wiley and Sons, Inc., 1999.

Vermani, S. "Capability Analysis of Complex Parts." *Quality Progress,* July 2003, pp. 65–71.

Verseput, R. "Digging into DOE." *Quality Digest,* June 2001, pp. 33–36.

Voelkel, J. "What is 3.4 per Million?" *Quality Progress,* May 2004, pp. 63–65.

Wade. J. *Utility versus Risk: On the Nature of Strict Tort Liability for Products.* 44 Miss. L. J. 825.

Walpole, R., and R. Myers. *Probability and Statistics for Engineers and Scientists.* New York: Macmillan, 1989.

Walters, J. "The Benchmarking Craze." *Governing,* April 1994, pp. 33–37.

Walton, M. *Deming Management at Work.* New York: Pedigree Books, 1991.

Walton, M. *The Deming Management Method.* New York: Putnam, 1986.

Watson, G. "Digital Hammers and Electronic Nails—Tools of the Next Generation." *Quality Progress,* July 1998, pp. 21–26.

Watson, G. "The Legacy of Ishikawa." *Quality Progress,* April 2004, pp. 54–57.

Watson, R. "Modified Pre-control." *Quality,* October 1992, p. 61.

Weiler, G. "What Do CEOs Think About Quality?" *Quality Progress,* May 2004, pp. 52–56.

Weimer, G. A. "Benchmarking Maps the Route to Quality." *Industry Week,* July 20, 1992, pp. 54–55.

West, J. E. "Implementing ISO 9001:2000, Early Feedback Indicates Six Areas of Challenge." *Quality Progress,* May 2001, pp. 65–70.

Wheeler, D. *Advanced Topics in Statistical Process Control.* Knoxville, TN: SPC Press, 1995.

Wheeler, D. *Short Run SPC*. Knoxville, TN: SPC Press, 1991.

Wheeler, D. *Understanding Industrial Experimentation*. Knoxville, TN: SPC Press, Inc., 1990.

Wheeler, D. *Understanding Variation: The Key to Managing Chaos*. Knoxville, TN: SPC Press, 1993.

Wheeler, D., and D. Chambers. *Understanding Statistical Process Control*. Knoxville, TN: SPC Press, 1992.

Wiesendanger, B. "Benchmarking for Beginners." *Sales and Marketing Management*, November 1992, pp. 59–64.

Wilson, L. *Eight-step Process to Successful ISO 9000 Implementation*. Milwaukee, WI: ASQC Press, 1996.

Winslow, R. "Hospitals' Weak Systems Hurt Patients, Study Says." *The Wall Street Journal*, July 5, 1995.

Zaciewski, R. "Attribute Charts Are Alive and Kicking." *Quality*, March 1992, pp. 8–10.

Zollers, F. E. "Product Liability Reform: What Happened to the Crisis?" *Business Horizons*, September 1990, pp. 47–52.

Index

Acceptable quality level, 38, 783
Acceptance sampling, 783
Acceptance sampling plan, 783
Accreditation, 783
Accredited registrars, 670, 783
Accuracy, 152–55, 265, 783
Act phase, 112–22
    continuous improvement and, 113–22
    ensuring permanence in, 112–13
    root cause analysis in, 114–17
    standardizing improvements in, 113
Advanced Product Quality Planning and
    Control Planning (APQP), 673
Advertising, 637
Advocacy. See Quality advocates
Air carriers, and luggage, 6–7
Aircraft, case studies involving, 30,
    544–47, 590–93, 652–55
Airplane crashes, 523–24
Airplane experiment, 590–93
Air traffic control, 525
Akao, Dr., 552
Alignment, 783
American Society for Quality, 4, 25,
    678, 783
American Telephone and Telegraph
    Co. (AT&T), 525
Analysis of Good (ANOG), 584, 585
Analysis of means (ANOM), 580, 784
Analysis of variance (ANOVA),
    580–81, 784
Analytical data analysis, 168–85
    kurtosis, 184–85
    location, 168–73
    skewness, 182–84
    spread, 173–82
ANOG (Analysis of Good), 584, 585
ANOM (analysis of means), 580, 784
ANOVA (analysis of variance),
    580–81, 784

Appraisal costs
    decision making and, 611
    defined, 602–3
    product liability and, 645
    quality costs and, 602–3, 604, 611,
    623, 785
    total quality costs and, 603
Approximation formulas, 435
APQP (Advanced Product Quality
    Planning and Control Planning),
    673
Area of opportunity, 423
Artisans, 11–12
Assessment
    benchmark, 704, 709
    competitive technical, 558, 562
    defined, 784
    process capability, 315–18, 327–33
    Quality System Assessment, 673
Assignable causes, 223–24
    defined, 34, 223, 784, 793
    fraction nonconforming (p) charts
    and, 452
    stability and, 239–40
    variation and, 223–24, 239, 242
AT&T (American Telephone and
    Telegraph Co.), 525
Attribute(s), 448
Attribute control charts, 447–86
    case studies involving, 506–16
    for counts of nonconformities, 473–86
    disadvantages of, 448
    flowchart, 487
    fraction nonconforming (p) charts,
    448–64, 489–90
    for nonconforming units, 448–72
    number nonconforming (np) charts,
    466–72, 506–12, 790
    number of nonconformities (c)
    charts, 473–79

    number of nonconformities per unit
    (u) charts, 480–86, 513–16,
    790, 795
    percent nonconforming charts,
    464–66, 490
    types of, 448
Attribute data
    defined, 149, 784
    as discrete data, 150
    discrete probability distributions
    and, 415
    nonconforming units and, 150
    precontrol charts and, 370
    run charts and, 367
    sample size and, 460
Audits and auditing, 712–18
    case study of, 728–29
    conducting, 716–18
    defined, 712, 784
    design of, 713–18
    frequency of, 713
    ISO 9000 and, 670
    PDSA cycle and, 713–18
    quality, 792
    questions in, 715
    types of, 713
Authority, 38
Automotive Industry Action Group,
    673
Automotive manufacturers, 23–24,
    38–39, 68–70, 673
Availability
    formulas for, 539
    reliability measures and, 529–31
Average(s), 169, 170, 175
    central limit theorem and, 185–87
    grand, 231
    histograms and, 220–21
    individual values compared with,
    312–14